Lecture Notes in Artificial Intelligence   1319

Subseries of Lecture Notes in Computer Science
Edited by J. G. Carbonell and J. Siekmann

Lecture Notes in Computer Science

Edited by G. Goos, J. Hartmanis and J. van Leeuwen

Springer
Berlin
Heidelberg
New York
Barcelona
Budapest
Hong Kong
London
Milan
Paris
Santa Clara
Singapore
Tokyo

Enric Plaza   Richard Benjamins (Eds.)

Knowledge Acquisition, Modeling and Management

10th European Workshop, EKAW '97
Sant Feliu de Guixols, Catalonia, Spain
October 15-18, 1997
Proceedings

 Springer

Series Editors
Jaime G. Carbonell, Carnegie Mellon University, Pittsburgh, PA, USA
Jörg Siekmann, University of Saarland, Saarbrücken, Germany

Volume Editors

Enric Plaza
Campus Universitat Autonoma de Barcelona, IIIA/CSIC
08193 Bellaterra, Catalonia, Spain
E-mail: enric@iiia.csic.es

Richard Benjamins
Campus Universitat Autonoma de Barcelona, IIIA/CSIC
08193 Bellaterra, Catalonia, Spain
E-mail: richard@iiia.csic.es
and
University of Amsterdam, Faculty of Psychology, SWI
Roeterstraat 15, 1018 WB Amsterdam, The Netherlands

Cataloging-in-Publication Data applied for

Die Deutsche Bibliothek - CIP-Einheitsaufnahme

Knowledge acquisition, modelling and mangagement : 10th
European workshop ; proceedings / EKAW '97, Sant Feliu de
Guixols, Catalonia, Spain, October 15 - 18, 1997. Enric Plaza ;
Richard Benjaminis (ed.). - Berlin ; Heidelberg ; New York ;
Barcelona ; Budapest ; Hong Kong ; London ; Milan ; Paris ; Santa
Clara ; Singapore ; Tokyo : Springer, 1997
   (Lecture notes in computer science ; Vol. 1319 : Lecture notes in
   artificial intelligence)
   ISBN 3-540-63592-0

CR Subject Classification (1991): I.2

ISBN 3-540-63592-0 Springer-Verlag Berlin Heidelberg New York

© Springer-Verlag Berlin Heidelberg 1997
Printed in Germany

Typesetting: Camera ready by author
SPIN 10545785   06/3142 – 5 4 3 2 1 0   Printed on acid-free paper

Preface

This book contains the proceedings of the 1997 European Workshop on Knowledge Acquisition, Modeling and Management (EKAW), held at Sant Feliu de Guíxols, Catalonia (Spain), from October 15 to 18. This was the tenth EKAW and the fifth time that the proceedings have been published by Springer-Verlag.

This EKAW marks a broadening of scope and a change in name from "Knowledge Acquisition" to "Knowledge Acquisition, Modeling and Management". In fact, EKAW'97 is the first workshop to apply these changes but its sister workshops KAW (Banff) and PKAW (Pacific Rim) will follow this trend in the future. The changes reflect the fact that in recent workshops the range of topics presented in the articles, panels, and discussion groups was already broader than the name implied. Moreover, a growing interest in Knowledge Management (KM) and in the application of knowledge acquisition (KA) techniques to knowledge management motivated the creation of a common meeting place.

The work reported in this book covers several topics related to knowledge acquisition, modeling and management, some of them being mainstream KA topics, others being more innovative.

More and more enterprises are becoming aware of the potential benefits of Knowledge Management. Issues such as modeling, representing, organizing, accessing, and maintaining corporate information and know-how are now recognized as being essential factors for today's enterprises. Knowledge acquisition has traditionally been concerned with these issues in the context of building knowledge systems, but extension to other bodies of knowledge seems natural. Therefore, it is not surprising that in recent years the application of KA techniques to KM has represented a growing area of work. The papers in this book address several relevant issues in KM including corporate repositories, exploitation of existing documents, and integrating knowledge and enterprise modeling.

A related topic with potentially significant impact is knowledge acquisition from texts. Since many sources from which knowledge is extracted are still text documents, natural language processing (NLP) from written text remains an important KA topic. For this reason, NLP can have an important impact on knowledge management by studying different ways to automatically extract knowledge from existing documents, as shown by some papers in this volume.

Reuse of knowledge components represents a large body of current work on knowledge acquisition and engineering. In particular, problem-solving methods (PSMs) and ontologies have received much attention recently. It is now commonly recognized that reusable knowledge components can significantly reduce development costs and enhance quality of knowledge systems: they can be configured from existing, high-quality components, rather than being built up from scratch. Topics discussed in the papers of this volume include the development of specific ontologies and PSMs, principled approaches to constructing ontologies and PSMs, the explicit interaction between ontologies and PSMs, and reuse and adaptation of PSMs. Our expectation is that reusable knowledge components will continue to be present in future workshops, stimulated by the omni-presence of the Internet. The Web provides an excellent opportunity, and challenge, to scale up reuse and to make knowledge system technology available on a much larger scale.

Typical KA work relates to eliciting knowledge from domain experts. This can be performed using different techniques, and papers in these proceedings include work on acquiring knowledge for Bayesian networks and acquiring knowledge using ripple-down rules. On the other hand, besides experts, databases are an important source of information for knowledge acquisition. Machine learning (ML) techniques have been developed for this purpose and currently they are commercially exploited (together with statistical techniques) in data-mining applications. Papers dealing with ML cover issues like data clustering techniques and knowledge discovery in rule bases.

Knowledge acquisition research can benefit much from practical experience in specific applications. The papers in this volume discuss several applications such as the planning of an autonomous spacecraft, the design of pharmaceutical tablets, and the design of mixed hardware/software systems. Developing commercial applications with knowledge system technology is still a costly activity. For this reason, the US DARPA project "High Performance Knowledge Bases" (HPKB) is to be reckoned with. The goal of HPKB, which involves 18 different partners, is to develop the technology needed for the rapid construction of efficient and large knowledge systems. A summary of this project is presented in an invited paper by John Kingston from AIAI, the European partner in HPKB.

Acknowledgments

The editors wish to thank the members of the Program Committee who freely gave their time and dedicated attention to the review process:

- Stuart Aitken, University of Glasgow (United Kingdom)
- Hans Akkermans, University of Twente (The Netherlands)
- Nathalie Aussenac, IRIT-CNRS (France)
- Guy Boy, EURISCO (France)
- Joost Breuker, University of Amsterdam (The Netherlands)
- Dieter Fensel, University of Karlsruhe (Germany)
- Brian Gaines, University of Calgary (Canada)
- Jean-Gabriel Ganascia, LAFORIA-University Paris VI (France)
- Frank van Harmelen, Free University Amsterdam (The Netherlands)
- Gertjan van Heijst, CIBIT (The Netherlands)
- Knut Hinkelmann, DFKI (Germany)
- Robert de Hoog, University of Amsterdam (The Netherlands)
- Yves Kodratoff, LRI - University Paris Sud (France)
- Eelco Kruizinga, CIBIT (The Netherlands)
- Ramon López de Màntaras, IIIA-CSIC (Spain)
- Enrico Motta, Open University (United Kingdom)
- Pablo Noriega, LANIA (Mexico)
- Kieron O'Hara, University of Nottingham (United Kingdom)

- Nigel Shadbolt, University of Nottingham (United Kingdom)
- Franz Schmalhofer, DFKI (Germany)
- Guus Schreiber, University of Amsterdam (The Netherlands)
- Yuval Shahar, Stanford University (United States)
- Mildred Shaw, University of Calgary (Canada)
- Derek Sleeman, University of Aberdeen (United Kingdom)
- Maarten van Someren, University of Amsterdam (The Netherlands)
- Rudi Studer, University of Karlsruhe (Germany)
- Jan Treur, Free University Amsterdam (The Netherlands)
- André Valente, University of Southern California (United States)
- Hans Voss, GMD (Germany)

We would also like to thank Mària del Mar Cuñado for her excellent secretarial support and Gemma Sales for designing the EKAW'97 logo.

We gratefully acknowledge the support for EKAW'97 provided by the European Network of Excellence in Machine Learning (MLnet), the Catalan Association for Artificial Intelligence (ACIA), and the Artificial Intelligence Research Institute of the Spanish Scientific Research Council (IIIA-CSIC).

Bellaterra, Catalonia (Spain), July 1997

Enric Plaza

Richard Benjamins

Table of Contents

Long Papers

Table of Contents

Long Papers

Short Papers

Invited Paper

Index

Acquisition of Search Knowledge

Ghassan Beydoun and Achim Hoffmann
School of Computer Science and Engineering
University of New South Wales
Sydney, NSW 2052, Australia
Email: {ghassan,achim}@cse.unsw.edu.au

Abstract. The development of highly effective heuristics for search problems is a difficult and time-consuming task. We present a knowledge acquisition approach to incrementally model expert search processes. Though, experts do not normally have introspective access to that knowledge, their explanations of actual search considerations seems very valuable in constructing a knowledge level model of their search processes. The incremental method was inspired by the work on Ripple-Down Rules which allows knowledge acquisition and maintenance without analysis or a knowledge engineer. We substantially extend Ripple Down Rules to allow undefined terms in the conditions. These undefined terms in turn become defined by Ripple Down Rules. The resulting framework is called Nested Ripple Down Rules. Our system SmS1.2 (SmS for Smart Searcher), has been employed for the acquisition of expert chess knowledge for performing a highly pruned tree search. Our first experimental results in the chess domain are evidence for the validity of our approach, even though a number of the planned features are still under development.

1 Introduction

In most application areas of computer science the satisfactory treatment of search problems is of primary importance. The efficient and effective solution of these problems has a major impact on today's economy, the environment as well as on technological advances. Unfortunately, many such problems are known to be **NP**-complete or **NP**-hard, which means that no really fast algorithm for optimal solutions can be expected to be found.

Opposed to that, it is well-known that human experts are often surprisingly good in finding better solutions to a given optimisation problem then existing heuristic programs. For example in the area of circuit design, many of the combinatorial problems for finding optimised designs are too hard to be solved optimally by automatic design programs. However, it is well-known that human engineers can often improve the designs generated automatically by a program with just moderate effort. In practice, human engineers intervene into the automatic design steps performed by programs in order to optimise the overall result.

Taking the apparently low processing speed of biological neurons into account, the human way of solving such optimisation problems appears even more intriguing. The successful simulation of the human way of solving such problems would be of primary importance for significant improvements of the computer's use in most areas of today's and tomorrow's computer applications. If the way skilled humans search for solutions can be simulated on computers, then computers will probably be able to perform the search process much faster than humans.

In this paper, we describe an approach to incrementally acquire expert search control knowledge. Using our Nested Ripple Down Rules, we incrementally acquire this knowledge and represent it in a hierarchical fashion. This representation is a natural way for the expert to express his conceptualisation of the search domain. We developed a workbench which consults the expert on search problems and takes advice of what search steps should be taken in which search state. The first results we obtained are very encouraging and provide evidence that our approach may be suitable for a general framework of building high-performance problem-specific search heuristics for combinatorial problems.

The paper is organised as follows: In the next section, we discuss the nature of search control knowledge and the specific problems of acquiring it. Furthermore, we outline requirements for a knowledge acquisition tool for assisting in the acquisition of such knowledge. In section 3 we present the Nested Ripple Down Rules framework and the design of our knowledge acquisition workbench. In section 4 experimental results are presented in the domain of master-level chess play. The final section 5 presents a discussion of the achieved results and future directions of research.

2 Knowledge on Search Heuristics

Most Knowledge based systems perform a search process when applying the knowledge stored in the knowledge base to a given problem. In this paper, the effective performance of such a search process itself becomes the domain of expertise. In many activities of human intellectual endeavour, some sort of search within a set of potential solutions can be said to take place. E.g. in design processes, engineers will evaluate partial designs on their fitness for a vantage point to complete the design successfully. If a partial design seems unfit, an alternative partial design is selected etc. Capturing the expertise being employed for such skilled search processes is a difficult task. This is reflected in the great efforts being spent on building tools for semi-automatic or even automatic design for many technical problems, e.g. in circuit design [18], mechanical design [13] or architecture [14]. For example, in circuit design, usually the design produced by current design tools is optimised by human intervention. The process of such human intervention is very difficult to formalise and, thus does not usually become automated.

Formalising the employed knowledge in the human search process seems more difficult than in many other domains of human expertise, since it is rather a skill than (declarative) knowledge what is employed. And even the description of such skills seems more vague than say, the description of motor skills. Motor skills can be observed from the outside. The search for a solution of a problem, however, is a process which can - to a significant extent - only be observed by introspection. Such introspection will be limited to a certain part of the actual thoughts which produce the search process. Those thoughts the expert becomes aware of may be driven by other thoughts which are often perceived to lie at the fringe of the conscious thoughts.

Even for other types of domains of expertise it is well known that experts usually can neither explain coherently why nor under exactly which circumstances they decide as they do. Thus, it is unlikely that experts will be able to properly specify heuristic rules which could generate a search process reasonably similar to the search process the expert is adopting at the conscious level.

In fact, the expert skill used in searching for solutions seems inaccessible by introspection. Plenty of evidence can be found in philosophical considerations on human thought processes that introspectively inaccessible knowledge exists, see e.g. [11, 27], that it plays a major role in many important areas of human intelligence [3], and that it is of considerable complexity [15]. Due to its non-introspective nature and its complexity, the acquisition of such knowledge is particularly difficult.

Although there are plenty of applications of more relevance, let us consider the expert search processes in chess playing for illustration purposes. De Groot [8, 9] conducted systematic psychological studies into the thought processes involved in master chess play. A master chess player, thinking aloud, may report the following:

... Let me try to attack the pawn on f2. Ok, I can move my bishop to c5 attacking this pawn. Possibly, my opponent will move his knight to e4 defending the pawn and simultaneously attacking my bishop on c5, such that I am forced to move the bishop again. This is unpleasant - so let me see whether this problem can be fixed. Maybe, I can avoid the knight move to e4. Oh well, first I can attack the knight by moving my pawn to b4 forcing it to move to another square. If it does not move to e4, then moving my bishop to c5 is much better. ...

Obviously, such an expert search process involves more complex reasoning than just the association of move sequences which were useful in other chess positions. E.g. it involves some causal reasoning on a rather abstract level. However, it seems difficult to devise a general inference mechanism, which could accommodate such expert reasoning. This is particularly the case, since much of such reasoning will not be at a conscious level to the expert.

2.1 Acquiring Search Knowledge

Knowledge Acquisition is widely considered as a modelling activity [22, 23, 25]. What is modelled is the expertise of a domain expert. Such a model is attempted to be described at the Knowledge level [20]. Most of the Knowledge Acquisition approaches to build knowledge-based systems, e.g. [1, 22, 23, 2, 10, 24], support a problem/knowledge analysis by the expert, the knowledge engineer, general system analysts, ... or some combination of them. This may involve steps like developing a conceptual model of the knowledge being used by an expert, distinguishing different subtasks to be solved, different types of knowledge to be distinguished during reasoning processes etc. Eventually, such a knowledge engineering approach either results in a model of the expertise which is easy to turn into an operational program manually, or even an automatically generated operational program comes out of the process.

Opposed to that is our approach, which targets to skip the time-consuming process of analysing the expertise and the problem domain by a knowledge engineer, as it has been advocated, e.g. in [6]. It rather allows the experts themselves to communicate their expertise to the system. Since also experts usually need to perform a structuring of their knowledge themselves in order to articulate it, the system should allow to specify knowledge 'on the fly' and to restructure or rephrase or refine it later on. Thus, we allow the expert to develop the structure of the knowledge they want to communicate to the system during the knowledge acquisition and maintenance process.

We aim at acquiring such intractable search knowledge mainly by other than purely introspective means. We want rather (re-)construct that knowledge than to directly acquire it. We envisage a spiral process of knowledge acquisition, similar to [19] of coming stepwise closer and closer to an operationalisation of the knowledge in question. Our approach follows the work on knowledge acquisition which allows knowledge acquisition and maintenance without a knowledge engineer [5, 4, 7, 17].

We believe, that experts are usually able to explain their reasoning process on a particular problem instance in rather general terms that cover at least the given concrete next step in their search process. However, their explanation may be quite inaccurate in the sense that for other search states their explanation would not deliver the search step they would actually take. Either their explanation would not cover the step they would take or their explanation would suggest search steps they would actually not consider. Thus, we pursue an approach similar to [16], which allows to incrementally acquire complex concept definitions without demanding an operational definition from the expert. Rather, the expert is merely required to judge whether the concept applies to particular instances. This is a much more natural task for an expert than to articulate general rules on how to judge on any particular instance.

2.2 Requirements for a KA environment

As a result of our aim, a suitable knowledge acquisition tool has to support the following steps of an expert building a knowledge base of search control knowledge:

- The criteria being used to select search steps worthwhile to consider for a deepening tree search must be very flexible. I.e. the following options should be available:

- The expert can freely define concepts to characterise search states as well as search operators to be applied to the search states.
- the definition of concepts should allow the use of other expert-defined 'sub'concepts.
- The revision or modification or amendment of initially defined concepts must be possible. E.g. a vocabulary may provide terms like 'capturing move', 'attacking move', etc. Such terms are not easily defined comprehensively. As a consequence, such terms are subject to incremental refinement throughout the Knowledge Acquisition process.

  Furthermore, the side effects being introduced by an amendment of a (sub)concept must be limited or controllable in some way.

  [To address these issues we developed Nested Ripple Down Rules. They will be described in details in the next section.]
- As indicated in the example of an chess expert search process, how the search proceeds may depend on the findings of search states encountered earlier in the search. To accommodate this sort of reasoning, the system should have a search engine which logs the encountered search states along with potentially interesting findings of the encountered search states. I.e. certain characteristics of search states should be stored as well. Furthermore, the expert definable selection criteria for search operators must allow conditions which involve such findings of earlier encountered search states.

3 Nested Ripple Down Rules in SmS

In this section we first present our Nested Ripple Down Rules (NRDR) which can be seen as a set of hierarchical concept definitions. They are the central knowledge representation scheme in our system SmS1.2. We discuss their advantages and the complexity of their maintenance and demonstrate some of the graphical features of SmS1.2. The second part of this section will be a detailed discussion of SmS's architecture.

3.1 Nested Ripple Down Rules

As discussed in section 2, an essential requirement of the workbench is the ease of acquisition and maintenance of the search knowledge. For this purpose we use Ripple Down Rules as a starting point for the implementation of the knowledge base and the learning module. Ripple Down Rules (RDR) [12, 6] is a knowledge acquisition method which proved very successful for developing large knowledge bases for classification tasks. In [26], RDRs were successfully used for the acquisition of complex control knowledge. With RDR, knowledge maintenance is a simple process which can be done by the user without guidance of a knowledge engineer [6]. An RDR tree is a collection of simple rules organised in a tree structure. Every rule can have two branches to two other rules: A false and a true branch. Examples are shown in Figure 1, where every block represents a simple RDR. When a rule fires a true branch is taken, otherwise a false branch is taken.

If a 'true-branch' leads to a terminal node t and the condition of t is not fulfilled the conclusion of the rule in the parent node of t is taken. If a 'false-branch' leads to a terminal node t and the condition of t is not fulfilled the knowledge base is said to fail and requires modification. An important strength of RDRs is the fact, that they can be easily modified in order to become consistent with a new case without becoming inconsistent with previously classified cases.

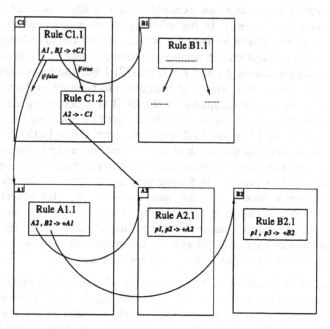

Fig. 1. A simple example of nested rules. An update in concept A2 can cause changes in the meaning of rules C1.1, C1.2, and A1.1 of the knowledge base.

In their simple form, RDRs use simple attribute-value combinations as conditions for the rules [5, 12, 6, 26]. Given a search domain, e.g. chess, the attributes used by the expert are not known a priori. The expert may use abstract attributes which he can explain using simpler attributes. The elementary level is the level of domain primitives. In our system, these primitives must be provided for every given domain by respective C-procedures [along with the instances generator]. The system allows the expert to introduce his/her vocabulary by using a Ripple Down Rule structure for allowing him/her to define a conceptual hierarchy during the KA process. For every concept definition a simple Ripple Down Rule tree is used. Conclusions of rules within a concept definition have a boolean value indicating whether the concept is satisfied by a case or not. Defined concepts can in turn be used as higher order attributes by the experts to define other concepts. Clearly, the evolving concept hierarchy depends not only on the given search domain but also on the expert and will reflect the expert's individual way of conceptualising his own search process. We call such construction of a concept hierarchy using Ripple Down Rule trees Nested Ripple Down Rule Trees (NRDR). Thus, in NRDR's the attributes used as conditions can themselves be defined in terms of lower order RDR trees. NRDR are superior to simple RDR in that they can condense the size of RDRs because the same concept defined by a lower order RDR tree can be used multiple times in higher order RDR trees. However, this hierarchical structure of the knowledge base causes problems for keeping the entire knowledge base consistent when a single concept definition needs to altered (see figure 1). In the following we show our approach in handling these problems. Given an instance which requires the knowledge base to be modified, the modification can occur in a number of places. For example, say a case x satisfies conditions A1 and B1 in rule C1.1 but the expert thinks that case x is not C1. Hence, the knowledge base needs to be modified to reflect this. A rule can be added as an exception for the RDR tree describing C1, or alternatively, the meaning of attribute A1 can be changed by updating the definition A1, or, the meaning of A2 in rule A1.1 can be changed; and so forth. The number of possibilities depends on the depth of the concept hierarchy in the knowledge base. This is where the user interface must provide assistance to the expert. A more profound update problem is dealing with inconsistencies due to localised updates in the hierarchical knowledge base. For instance, if the expert updates the meaning of A1 by changing the meaning of attribute A2 in rule A1.1, he may inadvertently cause a change in the meaning of rule C1.2 which contains A2. This inadvertent change is detected by the system after every update. The system will check the Case Data Base for inconsistencies.

Checking for inconsistencies when a concept C is modified requires access to all cases previously classified by the RDR defining C. These cases are classified again. A case x is inconsistent if the new classification is not the same as the old classification. During the discovery of x, because of the nested structure of the RDR's some lower order concept descriptions are found about x. To repair the inconsistency of the knowledge base with respect to the case, some of those concepts describing it may need to be updated. This may in turn cause more inconsistencies to occur. Hence, the process of checking inconsistencies is also recursive. However, the process is guaranteed to terminate as we don't allow recursive concept definitions nor cyclic definitions. SmS has an automatic knowledge acquisition assistant module which tracks these inconsistencies as they arise. It guides the expert towards eliminating them by highlighting the concept descriptions which may need to be changed. We are yet to give the process of eliminating inconsistencies a formal treatment.

To deal with the complexity of the knowledge representation, a visual display is important for the human expert. The interface provides a list of all available concepts. A double click on a concept will give a graphical representation of the Ripple Down Rule tree defining the concept where a horizontal link is a true branch and a vertical link is a false branch [12]. A double click on a node will give a view of the contents of the rule. A double click on a high order concept used as a condition will give a graphical view of the RDR representing this

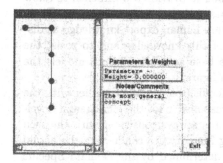 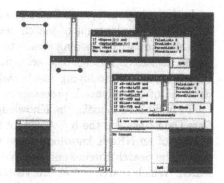

Fig. 2. Left: Graphical view of a concept definition. Right: Graphical view of the knowledge base. Concept definitions are given in separate windows.

concept (Figure 2 left). It is possible to see the full knowledge base by having a cascade of windows representing the hierarchy of the structure (Figure 2 right). For update, all points of update are available for the expert via this cascading representation.

3.2 System architecture

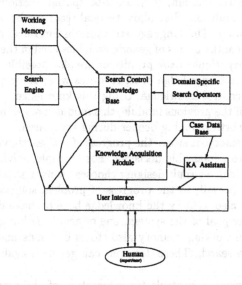

Fig. 3. SmS1.2 Architecture

In this section we first give an overview of the system's architecture. We then follow that by a detailed description of every module.

In designing our system SmS1.2, we aimed to provide a workbench to allow the efficient development of search heuristics and their easy refinement. Thus, SmS aims towards providing means to acquire human expert knowledge as discussed in section 2.2. For the acquisition of this knowledge and to assist the human expert in modifying the knowledge base as required, SmS models the structure of expert search processes as seen figure 3.

To fulfill SmS's goals, the Knowledge Acquisition Module together with the Case Data Base and the KA Assistant are responsible for the incremental development of an NRDR knowledge base which is always consistent with the seen cases. The Search Engine and the Working Memory are conducting the actual search. Which search states are visited is determined by the Domain Specific Search Operators Module and the Search Control Knowledge Base which functions as a filter on all applicable search operators. The progress of the search is stored in the working memory. This progress is often used by the expert to explain his decisions.

We now give a more detailed description of every module in the system:

- The domain specific search operators module: Given a particular search state, the module can generate all immediate next possible states. This module also allows the knowledge base to interpret any domain specific primitives used by the expert while describing his/her knowledge to the system. Note that these domain specific primitives are designed in consultation with a domain expert. They allow his/her natural description of a domain. For example, in the chess domain, they describe spatial relations between pieces and squares. In addition, they allow tactical reactions between squares and pieces to be stated. The language structure in SmS also allows existential and universal quantifications of generic variables used in the primitives. Conjunctions and negations of the primitives are also possible.
- The search control knowledge base: It stores what the expert expresses as his/her search control knowledge. Using this knowledge, given the possible next states from the previous module, this module passes through only those states seen as worth pursuing deeper during the search.
- The working memory: It stores the progress of the search which is often used by the expert to explain his decisions. For example, solving a components placement problem, a circuit designer chooses his next step based on a rough plan; this plan prevails in the progress of problem solution. Consequently, this progress is also used by the knowledge base to make decisions. That is aligned with the goal of the system, one of acquiring human search control knowledge. The working memory also stores decisions made by the search engine during a search. These decisions can get used again at a later stage of the search.
- The search engine: It controls the generation of the search tree through interactions with the knowledge base. It saves local decisions about search tree nodes in the working memory. It also examines the pruned search tree and chooses an answer according to one of several evaluation criteria set by the user.

- The knowledge acquisition module: It gets the expert input through the user interface. It maintains the knowledge base as well as the case data base.
- The case data base contains all cases classified by the expert. It allows retrieval of these cases according to their classifications time stamped. Thus, this data base contains a complete history of the interactions with the expert. Although, not all of the interactions affect the knowledge base development, they are essential for the functionality of the knowledge acquisition assistant. This is described below.
- The knowledge acquisition assistant: It provides hints to the expert to which parts of the knowledge base may need to be modified while ensuring the consistency of the knowledge base with the case data base. It relies on past interactions with the expert stored in the case data base to give these hints.
- The user interface: This module reads the expert input, displays the system answer to a search request, it also provides graphical representation of the knowledge base and graphical output of the automatic assistant to the expert.

4   Experimental results with chess as a search domain

To demonstrate our approach, we show examples of the typical knowledge acquisition cycle (or rather spiral) in the domain of chess. The objective is to develop a search knowledge base which produces a search process that resembles a human expert search process as much as possible. To do that, we defined concepts which approve moves to be considered in a minmax tree search which determines the actual move to be taken. In order to keep the searched tree small, it is important to approve only those moves which are really worthwhile considering any further. On the other hand, no dangerous move by the opponent should be excluded from the tree search in order to ensure high quality play. The knowledge acquisition process attempts to develop a concept 'good move', which applies to exactly those moves which should be considered for the tree search. Initially, no search operator in any search state will qualify, i.e. no move in any chess position will be classified as 'good move' and, hence, no tree search takes place.

4.1   Multi-point modification

Initially the Knowledge base is empty. The default rule is "If True then -Good" which means no move is considered as good. Hence, the system will consider all moves generated by the move generator as bad and none will be developed further in the search tree. So, the system develops a search tree of depth 1. It chooses a move using a simple evaluation function as used in the minmax algorithm. In figure 4 there is a pawn to be captured on e3.

The human expert plays for black Nxd5. The expert sees this as a good move because he wins a piece. Thus, on the highest level of the knowledge hierarchy he introduces a new rule "If WinPiece then Good". Subsequently, he needs to explain the meaning of the newly used attribute "WinPiece". The system creates a new Ripple Down Rule tree prompting the expert to explain the concept "WinPiece". The expert enters the root node "If WinPawn then WinPiece". Similarly, the system prompts the expert for an explanation of the attribute "WinPawn". The expert explains the concept in terms of primitives. The system settles at this point as the meaning of the primitives is clear to the system.

Fig. 4. Black to play. "Free" pawn on e3.

Assume it was white's turn, and white played Re1. Assuming the system knowledge consists of the three rules entered in the above scenario. When asked to play, the system will respond with Nxe3. To the system this is a good move because it wins a piece [it wins a piece because it wins a pawn]. The expert disagrees with this because Nxe3 is not a safe move as the black knight on e3 can be captured by the rook on e1. So he must modify the knowledge base. Note, there are three modification points for the knowledge base. At the highest level, the expert can add "If Not SafeMove then Not Good" on the true link of "If WinPiece then Good". Or, he can change the meaning of "WinPiece" by adding "If Not SafeMove then Not WinPiece"; finally, he can also change the meaning of "WinPawn" in the WinPiece Ripple Down Rule tree by adding "If Not SafeMove then Not WinPawn". Note, the choice of the point of modification is part of the knowledge acquisition process. In this particular example any of the modifications is valid.

Inserting the new rule on a higher level in the concept hierarchy can specialise the knowledge base modification more than inserting the new rule in a more specialised concept. However, modifying the more specialised concepts may cause more inconsistencies to be introduced into the knowledge base. This is since there is a greater chance for the more specialised concepts to be used as attributes. It is the responsibility of the knowledge acquisition assistant module to detect these effects and guide the expert to deal with them. It is worth mentioning that the higher the hierarchical structure of the concepts, the more condensed the knowledge base may become. In the above example, the expert chooses to modify the meaning of "WinPiece" by adding "If Not SafeMove then Not WinPiece" to the true link of Rule 1 in the "WinPiece" concept definition. Of course, the meaning of "SafeMove" needs to be explained. The expert introduces the rule "If white can reach the destination square in one move then Not SafeMove" which

Fig. 5. Pawn on e3 can or cannot be captured? Left: After 1. Re1 – Nxe3 (bad unsafe play by black). Right: Pawn on e3 is worth capturing.

is understood to the system as it is defined solely in terms of the primitives available.

4.2 Further features of the system

In figure 5(b), the pawn on e3 is protected by the rook on e1, hence, Nxe3 is not considered a good move by the system. However, capturing the protected pawn on e3 exposes the white knight on d4 to the black bishop on g7. So, the expert enters new knowledge into the system. The rule "If Expose then Good" is added on the highest level. The concept Expose(X) is explained as capturing an opponent piece Y, such that Y has been protecting the piece X for the last two positions i.e. the move exposed X to an attack. This parameter X is a variable used in the primitives explaining the concept "Expose". In position 6, white plays the bishop to b2 to protect the knight on d4. Hence, capturing the pawn on e3 no longer exposes the knight. Hence, the knowledge base needs to be altered again. In particular, inside the Ripple Down Rule tree describing the Expose concept. According to our chess expert, a black move exposes a white piece if the move removes all of the white piece's protection it had in the previous two positions.

4.3 Pruning a search tree using the knowledge base

Chess is a two players game. The search tree nodes alternate for the two players. To look ahead further than one half move, the knowledge base must be large enough to account for the responses of the opponent. In this section we develop the knowledge base further, and demonstrate the capability of the system to generate an intelligibly pruned search tree.

The expert plays for white explaining the option he takes. Thus, for figure 4(a) the expert plays Re1 to protect the pawn on e3, and for figure 5(b), he plays Bb2 to protect the knight on d4. The knowledge base is developed by the expert's input. The concept of "DefendingPiece" is introduced. As for

Fig. 6. Pawn on e3 is not worth taking anymore after White plays Bb2.

black's sake who is required to find some good moves in the absence of possible killer moves- i.e. capturing and/or exposing white's pieces, the knowledge base is extended to cover more strategic moves such as strengthen one's defence or attack. The concept of a Solid Move (increasing attack on a piece) and Safe Move (increasing defence of a piece) were introduced by the expert.

The knowledge base matured to 20 rules and 11 concepts (KB1). The hierarchy of the concepts is up to depth four. The position on the left is taken as a starting position with white to play. The table 1 shows the effectiveness of the knowledge base to prune the tree. The pruned tree was tested for intelligibility. The computer play with the pruned tree is also shown. The play was using the pruned tree of depth three. The less mature knowledge base (KB2) did not contain concepts describing strategic moves as Table 1 shows the tree pruning effect of both knowledge bases.

	Search Tree (# nodes)			Average breadth		
Depth	using KB1	using KB2	without KB	using KB1	using KB2	without KB
1	4	3	26	4	3	26
2	14	10	925	3.74	3.16	30.4
3	50	17	25880	3.68	2.57	29.6
4	110	28	757935	3.23	2.3	29.5
5	334	47	22.5 millions	3.19	2.16	29.5

Table 1. The pruning effect of two knowledge bases of different maturity. Note the deeper the tree the thinner it becomes, as more possibilities fail to be worth pursuing.

The following shows the moves of a game between SmS1.2 and an average human player starting in the position shown in figure 4.3 and ending the position of figure 4.3.

White   Black (Computer plays with the pruned heuristic tree)
1. Re1   Rd8
2. h3   Bf6
3 Nd4   Nxe3
4. Rxe3 Bxd4
5. Kf2   ..

The above play resulted in the computer gaining the upper hand against an average human player. Clearly the used knowledge base would not suffice for playing sufficiently well over an entire chess game as many more problems would occur, to which the KB has no solution yet.

Fig. 7. Average human player against our system SmS1.2. Left: The starting position. White to play against SmS1.2. Right: The resulting position. SmS 's performance (black) against an average human player (white).

However, it is clearly possible to take advantage of the human knowledge to prune the tree significantly without loosing quality of play.

5 Discussion and future work directions

In this paper, we presented a new approach to the development of effective search heuristics. We viewed the problem as a knowledge acquisition task, which resulted in a modelling of expert search knowledge at the knowledge level. This modelling process is based on expert's explanations of the expert's search process. Our experimental results, so far, suggest that it is possible for an expert to articulate introspectively inaccessible knowledge when forced to explain the outcome of the knowledge in sufficient detail. The expert was asked to explain and refine given concepts until the application of the concepts resulted in the same search steps the expert was proposing.

Our knowledge acquisition, representation and maintenance scheme, Nested Ripple-Down Rules, is more generally applicable than to the acquisition of search knowledge. Furthermore, we developed a mechanism to support keeping the knowledge base consistent with previously encountered cases as the knowledge base is updated and maintained.

In the near future, we will use a best first search algorithm for controlling the conducted search. An assessment function will be constructed as part of the knowledge acquisition process. To construct the assessment function, every introduced concept will be assigned a potential maximum gain value by the expert. When the knowledge base classifies a case, a global value will be derived using those values. In the future algorithm, the nodes within the search tree will be revisited as new information is found during the search. This will move SmS closer to simulating the skilled human search.

For further research, we also envisage the development of automatic support tools which could propose certain modifications of the knowledge base due to the independent analysis of the effectiveness search processes without a comparison to a human search.

Future work will also concern a deeper theoretical penetration of the structure and properties of Nested Ripple-Down Rules. Though, initial theoretical studies began as in [21], the properties of multiple interacting RDRs with respect to consistency maintenance and the size of the emerging knowledge base has received very little attention so far.

Acknowledgement: The work reported in this paper was supported by the Australian Research Council under Grant no. A49530412.

References

1. N. Aussenac, J. Frontin, M.-H. Riviere, and J.-L. Soubie. A mediating representation to assist knowledge acquisition with MACAO. In *Proceedings of the European Knowledge Acquisition Workshop*, pages 516–529. Springer-Verlag, 1989.

2. B. Chandrasekaran. Generic tasks in knowledge-based reasoning: High-level building blocks for expert system design. *IEEE Expert*, pages 23–30, Autumn 1986.

3. W. Clancey. Situated action: A neuropsychological interpretation. *Cognitive Science*, 17:87–116, 1993.

4. P. Compton, G. Edwards, B. Kang, L. Lazarus, R. Malor, P. Preston, and A. Srinivasan. Ripple down rules: Turning knowledge acquisition into knowledge maintenance. *Artificial Intelligence in Medicine*, 4:463–475, 1992.

5. P. Compton and R. Jansen. A philosophical basis for knowledge acquisition. *Knowledge Acquisition*, 2:241–257, 1990.

6. P. Compton, B. Kang, P. Preston, and M. Mulholland. Knowledge acquisition without knowledge analysis. In *Proceedings of the European Knowledge Acquisition Workshop*, pages 277–299. Springer-Verlag, 1993.

7. P. Compton, P. Preston, and T. Yip. Local patching produces compact knowledge bases. In *Proceedings of the European Knowledge Acquisition Workshop*, pages 104–117. Springer-Verlag, 1994.

8. A. de Groot. Thought and choice in chess. Mouton, Paris, 1965.

9. A. de Groot. Perception and memeory versus thought: some old ideas and recent findings. John Wiley and Sons, New York, 1966.

10. R. Dieng, A. Giboin, P.-A. Tourtier, and O. Corby. Knowledge acquisition for explainable, multi-expert, knowledge-based system design. In *Proceedings of the European Knowledge Acquisition Workshop*, pages 298–317. Springer-Verlag, 1992.
11. H. L. Dreyfus. *What Computers Still Can't do.* MIT Press, 1992.
12. B. Gaines. Induction and visualisation of rules with exceptions. In *Proceedings of the 6th AAAI-sponsored Banff Knowledge Acquisition for Knowledge Based Systems Workshop*, pages 7.1–7.17, 1991.
13. J. Gero and F. Sudweeks, editors. *Artificial Intelligence in Design.* Kluwer Academic Press, 1996.
14. J. Gero and E. Tyugu, editors. *Formal Design Methods for CAD.* North-Holland, 1994.
15. A. Hoffmann. Phenomenology, representations and complexity. In *Proceedings of the 10th European Conference on Artificial Intelligence*, pages 610–614, Vienna, Austria, August 1992. Wiley & Sons.
16. A. Hoffmann and S. Thakar. Acquiring knowledge by efficient query learning. In *Proceedings of the 12th International Joint Conference on Artificial Intelligence*, pages 783–788, Sydney, Australia, August 1991.
17. B. Kang, P. Compton, and P. Preston. Multiple classification ripple down rules: Evaluation and possibilities. In *Proceedings of the 9th AAAI-sponsored Banff Knowledge Acquisition for Knowledge Based Systems Workshop*, pages 17.1–17.20, 1995.
18. T. Lengauer. *Combinatorial Algorithms for Integrated Circuit Layout.* John Wiley and Sons, 1990.
19. M. Linster. Explicit and operational madels as a basis for second generation knowledge-acquisition tools. In J.-M. David, J.-P. Krivine, and R. Simmons, editors, *Second Generation Expert Systems*, pages 477–506. Springer-Verlag, 1993.
20. A. Newell. The knowledge level. *Artificial Intelligence*, 18:87–127, 1982.
21. T. Scheffer. Algebraic foundations and improved methods of induction or ripple-down rules. In *Proceedings of the 2nd Pacific Rim Knowledge Acquisition Workshop*, 1996.
22. G. Schreiber, B. Wielinga, and J. Breuker. *KADS A Principled Approach to Knowledge-Based System Development.* Academic Press, 1993.
23. T. Schreiber, B. Wielinga, J. Akkermans, W. van de Velde, and R. de Hoog. CommonKADS: A comprehensive methodology for KBS. *IEEE Expert*, 9(6):28–37, 1994.
24. N. R. Shadbolt and B. Wielinga. Knowledge-based knowledge acquisition: The next generation of support tools. In *Proceedings of the European Knowledge Acquisition Workshop*, pages 98–317. IOS Press, 1990.
25. M. L. Shaw and B. R. Gaines. Personal construct psychology foundations for knowledge acquisition and representation. In *Proceedings of the European Knowledge Acquisition Workshop*, pages 256–276. Springer-Verlag, 1993.
26. G. Shiraz and C. Sammut. Combining knowledge acquisition and machine learning to control dynamic systems. In *Proceedings of the 15th IJCAI*, page to appear, 1997.
27. T. Winograd and F. Flores. *Understanding Computers and Cognition: A new Foundation for Design.* Norwood Publisher, 1986.

A Systematic Approach to the Functionality of Problem-Solving Methods

Pascal Beys and Maarten van Someren

SWI, University of Amsterdam, Roetersstraat 15, 1018 WB Amsterdam, NL
email: {beys;maarten}@swi.psy.uva.nl

Abstract. In this paper, we define a formalization of goals based on set algebra and we show how structural properties of domain relations and goals can be used to select problem solving methods in a library indexed by methods functionality. Our work is motivated by the need to reuse model components for knowledge engineering. We show how to construct a compound method from a goal specification and an abstract description of the domain knowledge. Finally we show that by modifying the required functionality, the same domain knowledge can be used for a different goal.

1 Introduction

Knowledge-based systems are often based on the distinction between *problem solving methods* and *domain knowledge*. This distinction is useful for several reasons. Informal knowledge about a domain is often available in a descriptive form, separate from the context in which it is used. It can then be used for different tasks. For example, knowledge of the physiology and pathology of the human body is usually described outside the context of diagnosis or of the effects of medical interventions. This makes the knowledge generally applicable, for different tasks. Similarly, problem solving methods are general in the sense that they can sometimes be described independent of the domain to which they are applied. For example, solving a problem by enumerating and testing a set of possible solutions can be described independently of the solutions, the problem data and the knowledge involved in testing solutions.

Several attempts have been made to define a systematic classification of problem solving methods. The first of these attempts was given in the book *Building expert systems* [11]. Recent attempts include [3], [6], [12], [13, 14], [1], [5]. These projects demonstrate that there are three approaches to this problem that differ in emphasis. Some work emphasizes coverage of a wide range of methods that are described in the literature at the expense of operationality ([2], [5]), others are operational toolkits, without a unifying formal model and requiring substantial knowledge and skill for translating knowledge into the operational techniques ([12], [13, 14]) and the formal, unifying approaches ([1]) similarly, are not operational and tend to become rather complex in notation.

In this work we use a formalism that is relatively simple and inexpressive compared with other formal approaches ([17], [8]) but that allows operational methods to be included easily. Because the semantics are easier we expect it to be easier to use in practice. We shall demonstrate that despite the lack of expressiveness, some frequently used problem solving methods can be systematically described.

The formal approach is based on sets. Problem solving is viewed as finding one or more elements of a set of possible solutions from a set of problem data. Domain knowledge is represented as relations between sets and elements of sets. Problem solving methods correspond to algorithms (along with their implementations) that apply set relations. The *function* of a problem solving method (PSM) can now be characterized by the type of relation between problem data and solutions that a PSM computes. These relations are described in terms that only refer to structural, "topological" properties of relations and abstract from the content of the relation. In this way, PSMs are domain-independent.

This approach makes it possible to systematically describe functions of PSMs. The systematic structure is used to define "functionality-sets". A functionality-set is a description of a class of functionalities that holds several PSMs that achieve at least the functionality described in the functionality-set. Functionality-sets can be partially ordered by generality. We illustrate this with an example. Then we show how this ordering can be used to find a method for a new task. The topological properties of the domain relation, the possible problem data and solutions are used to find an appropriate method.

Throughout this paper, we illustrate our approach by describing the application of Cover&Differentiate (C&D) [7] onto a so-called *medical domain*.

Section 2 defines the terms we use in this paper. Section 3 describes the organization of a library of methods, the selection and the construction of a method. Section 4 describes the reuse process and Section 5 concludes this paper.

2 Terminology

Our framework uses some terms that may have a different meaning elsewhere. Therefore, we are going to define them precisely.

2.1 Modeling Domain Knowledge

In our framework, there are three components necessary to model domain knowledge: domain model, domain ontologies and representational ontologies. *Domain models* describe the actual knowledge of the domain. Typically, they contain ground sentences. *Domain ontologies* are explicit knowledge-level specification of a conceptualization [18]. Ontologies can be viewed as meta-models of the actual domain knowledge. They provide the vocabulary for expressing domain models and put constraints on their structure. To formulate ontologies, we make use of representational ontologies that are domain-independent meta-predicates. An example of such a representational ontology is Gruber's Frame Ontology [10].

The domain knowledge we used for our experiments describes diseases and their associated symptoms. The domain ontology (Figure 1) can be read as: a *disease* generates a set of *symptoms* by the *causes* binary-relation. Some diseases may have associated *qualifiers* that are used to qualify the truth of the presence of a disease. Figure 2 corresponds to the factual knowledge we used for our example.

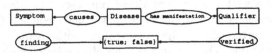

Fig. 1. Domain Ontology of the medical domain. Ovals denote binary relations, squares denote concepts.

2.2 Modeling Functionalities

Assumptions Assumptions are meta-level property that the domain knowledge has to verify [9]. They express *required functionalities*. They are described in representational ontologies terms and are formulated in domain-independent terms.

Assumption Set An assumption set is a conjunction of assumptions. An assumption set therefore constitutes an assumption itself since it represents a meta-level property of the domain knowledge.

Domain Functionality Domain functionalities are meta-level properties that the domain knowledge verifies. They are expressed like assumptions in order to ensure a mapping with them. The domain functionality of the *medical domain* (noted $\mathcal{F}_{medical\ domain}$) is:

$F_1 = \exists X : \text{set}$	$F_2 = \exists Y : \text{set}$
$F_3 = \exists Z : \text{set}$	$F_4 = \exists I : \text{set}$
$F_5 = I \subseteq X$	$F_6 = \exists R_1(X, Y) : \text{relation}$
$F_7 = \exists R_2(Y, Z) : \text{relation}$	$F_8 = \exists f_1 : X \setminus I \longrightarrow \{0, 1\} : \text{function}$
$F_9 = \exists f_2 : Z \longrightarrow \{0, 1\} : \text{function}$	

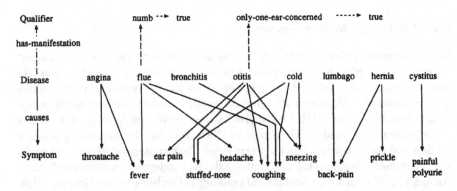

Fig. 2. Domain Model associated to the Medical Domain Ontology. Arrows denote the *causes* binary-relation.

Goal A goal g is a triple (I, O, A) where I is a set called the input set, O is a set that represents the output set and A is an assumption-set defined on I and O. In addition, a goal has a label for expressing it in natural language.

For instance, we can define the goal *sort* as being the triple (*set-to-sort*, *sorted-set*, $\exists \mathcal{R}$ total order relation defined on *set-to-sort*). Another example is a possible definition of the Cover&Differentiate goal. C&D was originally designed as a problem-solving method for diagnostic tasks. It has been formally described in [16]. We present here a different version:

Input: I: set	Assumptions Set: $A_{C\&D}$ defined as:
	• $A_a = \exists \gamma = (X, Y, \Gamma)$
	• $A_b = \exists I \subseteq X$
Output: O: set	• $A_c = O \subseteq \{y \mid (y \in Y) \wedge (\exists x, (x \in I) \wedge ((x, y) \in \Gamma))\}$
	• $A_d = \exists b : Y \longrightarrow \{0, 1\}$
	• $A_e = O = \{y \mid b(y) = 1\}$

The assumptions are to be understood as: there must exist a mapping between two sets X and Y, the output set O has to be connected to elements of the input set I. There should exist a boolean function b defined on Y and the elements of O should be made of the elements connected to I that are true according to the boolean function.

Specialization of a Goal (Subsumption Relation) We call specialization of a goal $g = (I, O, A)$ where $A = \{A_0, \cdots, A_n\}$ any triple $g' = (I, O, A')$ such that $A' \supseteq A$. The relation $\supseteq$ being defined as $(A' \supseteq A) \Leftrightarrow (\forall A_i, assumption, A_i \in A \Rightarrow A_i \in A')$. In this case, we will say that g subsumes g' (noted $g \succeq g'$). We consider the case $g' = (I', O', A')$ where I' and O' can be described from I and O as being the same case as $g = (I, O, A'')$ where A'' contains A' and assumptions about how to describe I and O from I' and O'.

For instance, we specialize the goal *sort* defined above by restricting it to the sort of different elements. We call *sort-different-elements* the goal (*set-to-sort*, *sorted-set*, ($\exists \mathcal{R}$ total order relation defined on *set-to-sort*, $\forall x, y, (x \in S) \wedge (y \in S) \Rightarrow x \neq y)$). We can then write that *sort-different-elements* $\succeq$ *sort*.

Subgoals We call subgoals of a goal $g = (X, Y, A)$ any set families $(X_i, X_{i+1}, A^i), i \in [0, n-1]$ such that $X_0 = X$, $\forall i \in [0, n-1], (X_i, X_{i+1}, A^i)$ is a goal, $\forall i, j \in [0, n], (i \neq j) \Rightarrow (X_i \neq X_j)$, and $A = \bigcup_{i \in [0, n-1]} A^i$

A goal being the description of a pair sets and an assumption-set, is reusable. Our definition of a goal differs from [9]. In their framework, a goal is included in the description of a task, and is the description of a desired final state. However their description of a task includes a description of the input set and domain knowledge requirements. Consequently, what we call a goal resembles their *task*.

The main difference between their *tasks* and our *goals* relies in the way we can relate goals to each-other by the subsumption relation and how we use goals to define our methods (see Section 2.3).

Functionality-Set The functionality-set of a goal x is the set of goals $S(x)$ subsumed by x. The way we defined the *subsumption* relation defined in 2.2 shows that $S(x)$ is partially ordered and that there exists a minimal element of $S(x)$ which is x.

Tasks A task in our framework is the reunion of a goal and a domain functionality. This definition captures the intuitive notion that a task (e.g., diagnosis) describes how the domain knowledge has to be represented and what we do with this domain. However, our tasks do not make any semantical commitment. To avoid confusion with other work, we call them *neutral tasks*.

In our example, the task (noted T) to be performed is then the following:

Input: I: set	Assumptions Set: $A_{C\&D-medical\ domain}$ defined as:
	• import $\mathcal{F}_{medical\ domain}$
Output: O: set	• import $A_{C\&D}$

2.3 Modeling Methods

Meaning of Functions in our Framework A function in our framework corresponds to the mathematical definition of a set-function: let A and B be two sets and Γ be a relation between A to B ($\Gamma \in \mathcal{P}(A \times B)$), a function f from A to B is any triple (Γ, A, B) where $\forall x \in A, \{y \mid y \in B \land (x,y) \in \Gamma\}$ is empty or contains only one element.

Methods The description of our methods is committed to the neutral task it achieves. We called these methods *task-neutral methods* (see [4]). We view a method as the explicit description of how to compute an output set from an input set. We therefore need four elements to describe a method: an input set I, an output set O, a set-function $f : I \longrightarrow O$ and assumptions that represent the meta-knowledge properties about the input set and the output set.

The description of the triple constituted by the input set, the output set and the assumptions constitute a neutral task according to our definition in Section 2.2.

The set-function f specifies how to achieve the goal and represents the explicit description of the relation between one element of the input set and its image in the output set. It can be considered as an *operational specification*.

Therefore, we view the description of a method $\mathcal{M}$ as a pair (f, g) where f represents the operational specification of $\mathcal{M}$ and t the neutral task achieved by $\mathcal{M}$. When t is subsumed (see section 2.2) by a neutral task T then t belongs to $S(T)$ the functionality-set (see Section 2.2) of T and the method $\mathcal{M}$ is said to functionally achieve T. This representation together with the subsumption relation directly shows that there is a one-to-many relation between goals and methods. A goal can be achieved by several methods.

Like we defined specializations of goals we can define specializations of methods. A method $\mathcal{M}_1 = (f_1, t_1)$ where f_1 defines the operational description of

M_1 and t_1 its neutral task, is a specialization of a method $M_2 = (f_2, t_2)$ when $t_2 \succeq t_1$.

In [9], a method M is described by three components, namely: a competence, operational specifications and requirements. In the end, the description of their components and ours can be considered as equivalent. However, in our view, the competence and the requirements are grouped in the description of the goal. This grouping comes from our use of task-neutrality: task-specific methods using different labels and roles for the type of knowledge they manipulate at the competence level *and* requirements being task-independent the need for a separation was obvious for task-dependent methods. As our methods manipulate task-neutral knowledge, there is no further need for a separation. Furthermore, our approach clearly differs in the way we relate methods to tasks and to other methods by the mean of the subsumption relation.

3 Method Selection

In this section we describe the organization of a library of methods, the selection of methods that belong to the functionality-set of the task we want to achieve and the construction of a compound method from smaller methods in order to achieve a more complex task.

3.1 Organization of the Library

We saw in Section 2.3 that a method M could be described as a pair (f, t) where f denotes the operational specification of M and t its associated neutral task. We also described in Section 2.2 how to relate goals/tasks to each-other by using the subsumption relation in order to compare their functionality.

We propose that the organization of a library should make use of this relation between tasks and to index libraries by the subsumption relation. A prototype of a library was built and its description is given in Figure 3. This library is organized as an acyclic graph and composed of nodes (functionality-sets) and leaves (methods). Each method belongs to a functionality-set and achieves the functionality described by this node. A child node includes methods that achieve a more restricted functionality (more assumptions) than the one of its parents.

Relation-Restriction Functionality-Set This node describes the generation of elements of a target set connected to an input set by a relation between the input set and the output set. It can be described as:

Input: I: set	Assumptions Set: $A_{Relation-Restriction}$ defined as
	$\bullet\ \exists X, I \subseteq X$
Output: Y': set	$\bullet\ \exists \gamma = (\Gamma, X, Y)$
	$\bullet\ Y' \subseteq \{y \mid (y \in Y) \wedge (\exists x, (x \in X) \wedge ((x, y) \in \Gamma))\}$

Set-covering Inference *Set-covering* requires the knowledge of a mapping $\gamma = (\Gamma, X, Y)$ where Γ is a relation between two sets X and Y. It takes as input a

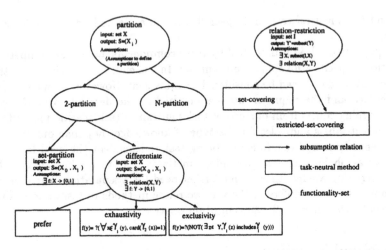

Fig. 3. Example of the organization in classes of functionality of the library

subset $\mathcal{I}$ of X and produces as an output the subset $Y' = set - covering(\mathcal{I})$ composed of the elements of Y that are connected to at least one element of $\mathcal{I}$.

$$set - covering : \mathcal{I} \to \mathcal{P}(Y)$$
$$x \mapsto set - covering(x) = \{y \mid (y \in Y) \wedge ((x, y) \in \Gamma)\}$$

Input: $\mathcal{I}$: set	Assumptions Set:
Output: $Y' = \{y \mid (y \in Y) \wedge (\exists x, x \in \mathcal{I}$	$\mathcal{A}_{set-covering}$ defined as
$\wedge ((x, y) \in \Gamma)\}$	• import $\mathcal{A}_{Relation-Restriction}$

In [15] this inference is called *cover*. It takes as input a set of observed symptoms and generates considered explanations in a diagnosis task. Although this description probably appeals more directly to a non expert user, we think that what *cover* truly achieves (which is described in our case by *set-covering*) is not bounded to the task and should be represented independently.

As a matter of fact, the application of *set-covering* can be envisioned within a *classification* task: X would then be a set of patterns that can describe an object, $\mathcal{I}$ a subset of X describing observed patterns for an object under consideration, Y the set of possible classes which an object can be related to and Γ the relation that associates a subset of patterns to a class. Applying *set-covering* would lead to the generation of a set of possibles classes associated to the object under consideration. This description of the application of *set-covering* to a *classification* task uses precisely the same task-neutral description of our inference.

We therefore believe that greater effort should be applied to the description of what the method truly achieves by abstracting from their semantical representation.

Restricted-Set-Covering Inference We define *restricted-set-covering* as being a method that takes as input a subset $\mathcal{I}$ of X and that produces as output the subset Y' of Y that contains all elements of Y that are only connected to elements of $\mathcal{I}$ by the relation Γ.

$restricted - set - covering : \mathcal{I} \rightarrow \mathcal{P}(Y)$

$$x \mapsto \{y \mid (y \in Y) \wedge (\forall x \in X, (x,y) \in \Gamma \Rightarrow (x \in \mathcal{I}))\}$$

Input: $\mathcal{I}$: set	Assumptions Set:
Output: $Y' = \{y \mid (y \in Y) \wedge (\forall x, ((x,y) \in \Gamma)$ $\Rightarrow (x \in \mathcal{I}))\}$	$A_{restricted-set-covering}$ defined as • import $A_{Relation-Restriction}$

Restricted-set-covering does not appear to be obviously useful. However we have found along our investigation on the method C&D that this inference is the core of the differentiate method and was hidden by semantical representations. Restricted-set-covering will be used in Section 3.3.

Partition Functionality-Set A partition on a set X is achieved when a set S of subsets of X is identified. These subsets are not empty, disjoint and their union is X.

Input: X: set	Assumptions Set: $A_{Partition}$ defined as:
	• $X \neq \emptyset$
	• $S \in \mathcal{P}(X)$
Output: S: set	• $\forall A, (A \in S \Rightarrow (A \neq \emptyset))$
	• $\forall A, B, (A \in S$ and $B \in S$ and $A \neq B \Rightarrow (A \cap B = \emptyset))$
	• $\bigcup_{A \in S} A = X$

The study of set-partitions in mathematics allows us to use two well-known theorems:

Theorem 1 *If one is given an equivalence relation $\mathcal{R}$ onto a non-empty set X, then the set $X_{/\mathcal{R}}$ defined by the set of equivalence classes according to $\mathcal{R}$ is a partition onto X.*

Theorem 2 *Let $f : X \longrightarrow X'$ be a function. The binary relation $\mathcal{R}$ defined on X such that: $x\mathcal{R}y \Leftrightarrow f(x) = f(y)$ is an equivalence relation.*

If we consider any method $\mathcal{M}$ under the Partition node, we can say that theorems 1 and 2 insure that the description of $\mathcal{M}$ onto a set X is equivalent to describing a function $f : X \longrightarrow X'$. This is extremely important because it points precisely at what has to be given in the assumption-set of the class Partition: a function f and a set X'. Typically f and X' are imported from the domain-knowledge. We can thus define this way as many methods $\mathcal{M}$ that achieve a partition as there are different f and X'. Consequently, we claim that focusing on the description of different methods $\mathcal{M}$ is not an issue since these methods are fully determined by domain-knowledge imports.

Here the advantage of task-neutrality clearly appears: it captures what is essential to describe a method without going into task and domain specific description that prevents the method from wide reuse.

2-Partition Functionality-Set is a child node of Partition. The specialization here consists of defining the set X' introduced in Partition: $X' = \{0,1\}$. Consequently, the function $f : X \longrightarrow \{0,1\}$ represents a boolean function. The output set is the description of two subsets constituting a partition of the input set: $X_0 = \{x \mid x \in X, f(x) = 0\}$ and $X_1 = \{x \mid x \in X, f(x) = 1\}$.

Input: X: set	Assumptions Set: $\mathcal{A}_{2-Partition}$
Output: S: set	• import $\mathcal{A}_{Partition}$
$\forall A, A \in S \Rightarrow A = \{x \mid \exists y_0 \in \{0,1\}, f(x) = y_0\}$	• $\exists f : X \longrightarrow \{0,1\}$

To relate this to our example, let us call f *finding* and X a set of *symptoms* in *diagnosis*. Then *finding* defines a partition on the set of symptoms: namely Finding(symptoms) which is constituted by all the symptoms that also verify the property *finding* and Not(Finding(symptom)) which is constituted of the rest of the symptoms.

Differentiate Functionality-Set is a child of 2-Partition. It introduces a new assumption about the boolean function f defined in 2-Partition: it should be a composition of a mapping $\gamma = (\Gamma, X, Y)$ and a boolean function b defined on Y. The output set S is composed of two subsets:
$X_0 = \{x \mid (x \in X) \wedge (\exists y \in Y((x,y) \in \Gamma) \wedge (b(y) = 0))\}$
$X_1 = \{x \mid (x \in X) \wedge (\forall y \in Y((x,y) \in \Gamma) \Rightarrow (b(y) = 1))\}$

Input: X: set	Set-Assumptions: $\mathcal{A}_{Differentiate}$ defined as:
	• import $\mathcal{A}_{2-Partition}$
Output: S: set	• $\exists b : Y \longrightarrow \{0,1\}$
	• $\exists \gamma = (\Gamma, X, Y)$
	• $\forall x, f(x) = \displaystyle\prod_{y \in \gamma(x)} b(y)$

Prefer Inference *Prefer* requires the knowledge of a mapping $\gamma = (\Gamma, X, Y)$ and a function $b : Y \longrightarrow \{0,1\}$.

$$prefer_{boolean} : X \xrightarrow{\gamma} \mathcal{P}(Y) \qquad\qquad \xrightarrow{b} \{0,1\}$$
$$x \longmapsto \gamma(x) = \{y \mid (y \in Y) \wedge (x,y) \in \Gamma\} \longmapsto b \circ \gamma(x) = \prod_{y \in \gamma(x)} b(y)$$

The function $prefer_{boolean}$ creates a partition on X. We can define $X_0 = \{x \mid (x \in X) \wedge prefer_{boolean}(x) = 0\}$ and $X_1 = \{x \mid (x \in X) \wedge prefer_{boolean}(x) = 1\} = X \setminus X_0$.
Example: We are going to apply prefer onto the subset of *Diseases* constituted of the elements: {flue, otitis, cold}. The mapping considered here is $\gamma = $ (has-manifestation, Disease, Qualifier). By *has-manifestation, flue* is connected to *numb* which has the property *true* by the relation *verified*. Similarly, *otitis* is connected to *only-one-ear-concerned* which is true. On the contrary, cold is not associated to anything and has therefore *false* as output. The subsets we defined by *prefer* are therefore: {flue, otitis} on the one hand and {cold} on the other hand.
Exhaustivity Inference Unlike *prefer*, exhaustivity only requires the knowledge of a mapping $\gamma = (\Gamma, X, Y)$. The boolean function which is required to

perform the partition is implicitly defined by the mapping γ and is $?(\forall y \in \{y \mid (y \in Y) \wedge (x,y) \in \Gamma\}, card(\gamma^{-1}(y)) = 1)$.

$$exhaustivity_{boolean} : X \longrightarrow \{0,1\}$$
$$x \longmapsto 1, if \forall y \in \gamma(x), card(\gamma^{-1}(y)) = 1$$
$$0, otherwise$$

Again, we define a partition on X. Indeed we can define two subsets of X, $X_0 = \{x \mid (x \in X) \wedge exhaustivity(x) = 0\}$ and $X_1 = \{x \mid (x \in X) \wedge exhaustivity(x) = 1\}$. Contrary to *prefer*, the boolean function necessary to achieve the partition is implicitly defined by the knowledge of γ.

The functionality of the exhaustivity inference can be read as: elements that generate elements that are not also generated by other elements are prefered.
Example: We are going to apply exhaustivity on the subset I of *Diseases* constituted by the elements: {angina, flue, hernia, cystitus}.

$$\gamma(angina) = \{throatache, fever\} \quad \gamma(flue) = \{fever, headache, coughing\}$$
$$\gamma(hernia) = \{back\text{-}pain, prickle\} \quad \gamma(cystitus) = \{painful\ polyurie\}$$

Since $\gamma^{-1}(fever) = \{angina, flue\}$ then $card(\gamma^{-1}(fever)) = 2$. Consequently, exhaustivity(angina)=0 and exhaustivity(flue)=0. However, although back-pain is connected to {lumbago, hernia}, as *lumbago* does not belong to I, then $\gamma^{-1}(back\text{-}pain) = \{hernia\}$ and exhaustivity(hernia)=1. Trivially, exhaustivity(cystitus)=1. Therefore we have defined a 2-partition on I: {hernia, cystitus} and {angina, flue}. The first subset represents the set whose image by exhaustivity is 1.

Exclusivity Inference Like *exhaustivity*, the exclusivity inference requires the knowledge of a mapping $\gamma = (\Gamma, X, Y)$ to achieve the partition on X. The boolean function it uses is : $exclusivity_{boolean}(x) = ?\neg(\exists z \in X, \gamma(x) \subseteq \gamma(z))$.

$$exclusivity_{boolean} : X \longrightarrow \{0,1\}$$
$$x \longmapsto 1, if \neg(\exists z \in X, \gamma(x) \subseteq \gamma(z))$$
$$0, otherwise$$

The functionality achieved by the exclusivity inference can be read as: elements that generate the largest sets are prefered.
Example: We apply *exclusivity* on the subset {otitis, cold}.
$\gamma(otitis) = \{ear\text{-}pain, stuffed\text{-}nose, coughing, sneezing\}$
$\gamma(cold) = \{stuffed\text{-}nose, coughing, sneezing\}$
As $\gamma(cold) \subseteq \gamma(otitis)$ then exclusivity(otitis)=1 and exclusivity(cold)=0.
Why did we not define an anticipate inference? In classical descriptions of the method C&D there exists another inference which is not described here: anticipate. The definition of this inference for a diagnosis task is the following: if a considered symptom S_1 is explained by an explanation E_1 and if this explanation also explains some other symptom S_2 then S_2 should be true (see Figure 4). Basically if we were to describe this inference within our framework, we would need the knowledge of a mapping $\gamma = (\Gamma, X, Y)$ and a boolean function $b : Y \longrightarrow \{0,1\}$. To relate this to the diagnosis task, let us call X the set

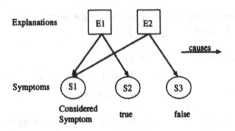

Fig. 4. Anticipate Inference in Cover & Differentiate. S_1 is the considered symptom. E_1 is anticipated because it causes both S_1 and S_2 which is true. E_2 is discarded because it causes E_3 which is false.

of *explanations*, Y the set of *symptoms*, Γ the binary relation *causes* and f the relation *finding* defined on the set of symptoms.

In our framework, the *prefer* inference achieves a partition on any set X provided the knowledge of a mapping (Γ, X, Y) and a boolean function $b : Y \longrightarrow \{0, 1\}$. This means that the application of prefer onto the set of explanations together with the knowledge of the existence of the mapping (causes, explanations, symptoms) and the boolean function *finding* defined onto the set of symptoms leads precisely to the same results as those that could be obtained by applying the anticipate inference as it has been defined above: the creation of a partition constituted on the one hand of explanations that generate observed symptoms and on the other hand explanations that generate symptoms that are not observed.

This similarity between anticipate and prefer lead us to only represent the prefer inference. However, one can argue that in [15] the main difference between anticipate and prefer is that the mapping (causes, Explanations, Symptoms) used by the anticipate inference is the same as the one used by the set-covering inference, whereas their *prefer* inference uses another mapping (has manifestation, Explanations, Symptoms). We claim that from a abstract point of view, these two inferences behave identically and that there is no need for making a distinction.

3.2 Selection of Methods Within the Library

Since our library represents a hierarchy of methods ordered by their functionality, the retrieval of a method appears to be equivalent to a matching process. When a task is constructed from a goal and a domain functionality, it points at a functionality-set in our library (Section 3.3 explains what happens when methods have to be composed from other methods to achieve a more complex functionality). This functionality-set provides a pack of methods or functionality-sets that achieve the desired task and/or that achieve a finer functionality. The final method selected may include further assumptions that have to be verified. If these assumptions cannot be verified, the method is not applicable. This allows a refinement process between the selection of the method and the construction of the domain knowledge. The domain knowledge should present some minimal functional features in order for the method to be applicable. If the domain knowledge does not directly verify these features, it can be refined. If it cannot offer these features, a new method that achieves the same task has to be considered. If there are not any method available, a new task has to be selected. A finer goal or a finer domain functionality can then be considered and the whole process can be resumed. An example of this process is given in Figure 5.

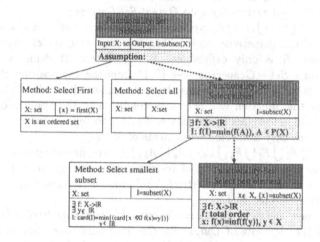

Fig. 5. Example of refinement process of the domain knowledge. P(X) denotes the power-set of X. Dashed arrows represent the specialization path. The *selection* node has been selected, then the *select-subset* node that requires that there exists a real-function defined, at the domain level, on the set on which the selection is to be performed. Finally we want to select only one element and we use the Select Best Element method that introduces the assumption that the function should define a total order on X.

In its original design, C&D was used to find possible explanations that could be generated from a set of symptoms. C&D required that the knowledge structure on which it operates should be a causal network; the nodes being the state of the system being diagnosed. C&D itself relied on a state-generation step achieved by an inference called *cover* (in order to generate potential explanation of a set of symptoms) and a differentiation step, in order to confirm or discard these explanations. This differentiation step constitutes a method itself and is achieved by four inferences: anticipate, prefer/rule-out, exhaustivity and exclusivity.

3.3 Describing Combination of Goals

We would now like to find a method that would use the inferences of our prototype library in order to solve the neutral task defined in Section 2.2 (noted $\mathcal{T}$). However, there is no such method directly available in our library. We have to construct it. Such a method would decompose $\mathcal{T}$ in subtasks corresponding to small reasoning steps achieved by inferences stocked in our library.

The problem then amounts to a design problem. Solving automatically this problem is outside the scope of this paper. However we will show how to solve it by hand. The decomposition that we found and that uses the labels A_i and F_i defined in Section 2.2 is the following:

1. $F_1 \bigcup F_2 \bigcup F_4 \bigcup F_5 \bigcup F_6 \bigcup A_a \bigcup A_b \bigcup A_c$ are necessary and sufficient conditions to apply set-covering and restricted-set-covering. We apply set-covering. The output of set-covering is called *Output-Set-Covering*.

2. $F_7 \bigcup F_9 \bigcup A_d \bigcup A_e$ are necessary and sufficient conditions to apply prefer, exhaustivity and exclusivity onto *Output-Set-Covering*.

3. However $F_6 \bigcup F_8 \bigcup A_d \bigcup A_e$ are necessary but not sufficient conditions to apply prefer, exhaustivity and exclusivity onto *Output-Set-Covering*. Indeed, since f_1 is only defined on $X \setminus I$, we cannot define a function $b : Output - Set - Ccovering \longrightarrow \{0, 1\}$ from the composition of R_1 and f_1 (*Output-Set-Covering* contains elements connected to I by R_1). The existence of this function is a necessary condition to the application of any method hold in the class Differentiate. We need to define a subset of *Output-Set-Covering* only connected to elements of $X \setminus I$.

4. Since $F_1 \bigcup F_2 \bigcup F_4 \bigcup F_5 \bigcup F_6 \bigcup A_a \bigcup A_b \bigcup A_c$ are necessary and sufficient conditions for the application of restricted-set-covering, we apply it. The output set is called *Output-Restricted-SC* which is composed of elements of Y strictly connected to I.

5. We can now define *Output-Set-Covering* \ *Output-Restricted-SC* constituted of the elements of *Output-Set-Covering* only connected to elements of $X \setminus I$. We can therefore apply prefer, exhaustivity and exclusivity onto *Output-Set-Covering* \ *Output-Restricted-SC* by using the assumptions $F_6 \bigcup F_8 \bigcup A_d \bigcup A_e$.

6. Finally we apply select-all on all the subsets created by a 2-partition and whose image by the boolean function used to create the partition is 1.

4   Reuse Process

We are now going to present how we envision the reuse process within our framework. We assume that the domain we want to reuse has been already used for some task and that some methods have been successfully applied onto this domain in order to achieve that task.

4.1   Description of the Reuse Process

We would like now to reuse as much as possible of the former system in order to achieve a different task. The questions that arise now are: how can we select new methods in order to achieve the new task, how can we determine which parts of the domain knowledge have to be kept or thrown away and finally do we have to enrich our domain knowledge?

For clarity purposes, we will call t_1 the task for which the domain was originally used, $\mathcal{M}_1$ the method that was retrieved to achieve t_1 and $\mathcal{A} = \{A_0, \cdots, A_n\}$ the set of assumptions introduced by $\mathcal{M}_1$.

But this time, once the functionality-set associated to t_2 has been identified and the pack of related methods retrieved, the selection of the method $\mathcal{M}_2$ that will achieve t_2 can be facilitated by means of the set of assumptions $A' = \{A'_0, \cdots, A'_q\}$ of $\mathcal{M}_2$. Indeed, it seems reasonable to assume that t_2 will share similarities with t_1 and that consequently the set of assumptions A' will overlap with A.

Let us call now $A^0 = \{A \cap A'\}$ the set of common assumptions between $\mathcal{M}_1$ and $\mathcal{M}_2$, $A^1 = A \setminus A^0$ the set of assumptions of $\mathcal{M}_1$ that do not appear in the description of $\mathcal{M}_2$ and $A^2 = A' \setminus A^0$ the set of assumptions of $\mathcal{M}_2$ that do not appear in the description of $\mathcal{M}_1$.

The subset A^0 constitutes assumptions that the domain knowledge already verifies and can be considered as meta-knowledge about the domain knowledge that has to be kept for achieving t_2. The subset A^1 denotes assumptions no longer useful to guarantee the achievement of the goal t_2. It constitutes meta-knowledge that can be discarded. Finally the subset A^2 describes meta-knowledge that has to be verified by the domain-knowledge. These assumptions can either be directly verified by the domain-knowledge or otherwise point precisely at which part of the domain-knowledge has to be enriched. If the enrichment of the domain-knowledge in order to fit the desired assumption leads to an inconsistency then the method should be rejected as inapplicable.

A possible application of the modification of a task is the specialization of a task and/or of a method. This time a specialization t_2 of the task t_1 points at a child of the class originally under consideration. The new set of assumptions A' contains the original set of assumptions A. The subset A^0 corresponding to the description of the knowledge that has to be kept is this time equal to A. This means that the whole domain knowledge is reused. The subset A^1 representing the knowledge that has to be discarded is empty and the subset A^2 that corresponds to the knowledge that has to be added to the domain knowledge in order to fit the new assumptions corresponds to $A' \setminus A$.

We are now going to illustrate our purposes by modifying the task of the system we used in Section 3.3. Instead of generating all possible explanations by C&D we wish to generate the *best* explanation.

4.2 Example: Application to Hill-Climbing

Let us now refine the task $\mathcal{T}$ that we defined in Section 2.2. In order to define this new task (noted $\mathcal{T}'$), we add to $\mathcal{T}$ the assumption that the output set should contain exactly one element.

Input: I: set	Assumptions Set: $A_{H\&C}$ defined as:
Output: O: element	• import $A_{C\&D-medical\ domain}$
	• $A_f = \mathrm{card}(O) = 1$

We reuse the description of the method construction that has been detailed in Section 3.3. But this time, we cannot use the *select-all* inference, because of A_f that requires that the output should be one element. The only method available is *select-one-element* (see Figure 5) that is only applicable when there exists a function f that defines a total order on the set obtained by solving $\mathcal{T}$.

4.3 Adaptation of the Domain to the New Method

We have constructed a method that can solve T'. But our domain knowledge is incomplete. We do not have any function that defines a total order on a subset of Y. However we have the knowledge of what is precisely needed in the domain knowledge in order to achieve T'. In our medical domain, we can think for instance of a function that associates a disease to a degree of priority.

5 Conclusion

Using a formalization of goals that is based on set algebra we showed how structural properties of domain relations and goals can be used to select problem solving methods that are realized as programs operating on sets. We illustrated method selection for simple tasks and compound methods construction for more complex tasks. This was illustrated by the synthesis of an operational method for Cover and Differentiate. By modifying the required functionality, the same domain knowledge can be used for a different goal (as long as the same domain relations are involved).

We expect that this approach will make it possible to systematically characterize a substantial part of the PSMs that have been formulated elsewhere in the literature although the expressiveness is currently restricted to relations between (finite) sets. The approach is based on a clear distinction between domain knowledge and methods that abstract from domain knowledge. A prototype of a system that checks assumptions of PSMs and selects a PSM for a domain and an associated goal has been constructed (based on semantic net classifiers) to support further experimentation.

We believe nevertheless that set algebra is not the easiest language to describe functionalities. Future work will focus on finding some more appealing (for an expert) way to express these descriptions and on extending the library of PSMs long with their "functionality class" descriptions and relations with other methods, elaborate the method for synthesizing compound methods and consider the possibility of modifying the domain knowledge (e.g. if no appropriate method can be found).

References

1. M. Aben. Formally specifying re-usable knowledge model components. *Knowledge Acquisition*, 5:119–141, 1993.
2. V. R. Benjamins. *Problem Solving Methods for Diagnosis*. PhD thesis, University of Amsterdam, Amsterdam, The Netherlands, June 1993.
3. V. R. Benjamins, A. Abu-Hanna, and W. N. H. Jansweijer. Suitability criteria for model based diagnostic methods. In *In Proceedings of ECAI-workshop on Model Based Reasoning*, Vienna, 1992. SKBS/A2/92-13.
4. P. Beys, R. Benjamins, and G. van Heijst. Task-neutrality: An essential factor for reuse? In The Open University, editor, *Proc. of the 7th KEML Workshop*, Milton Keynes, UK, January 1997. Knowledge Media Institute.

5. J. A. Breuker and W. Van de Velde, editors. *The CommonKADS Library for Expertise Modelling.* IOS Press, Amsterdam, The Netherlands, 1994.
6. B. Chandrasekaran. Limitations of the generic task toolkit idea. proposal for an architecture that integrates different types of problem solving. In L. Steels and J. McDermott, editors, *Expert System Foundations.* 1990.
7. L. Eshelman. MOLE: A knowledge-acquisition tool for cover-and-differentiate systems. In S. Marcus, editor, *Automating Knowledge Acquisition for Expert Systems,* pages 37–80. Kluwer, Boston, 1988.
8. D. Fensel, J. Angele, and D. Landes. Knowledge representation and acquisition language (KARL). In *Proceedings 11th International workshop on expert systems and their applications (Volume: Tools and Techniques),* pages 821–833, Avignon, France, May 1991.
9. D. Fensel, A. Schönegge, R. Groenboom, and B. Wielinga. Specification and verification of knowledge-based systems. In *Proc. Validation and Verification workshop at ECAI-96,* 1996.
10. T. R. Gruber. A translation approach to portable ontology specifications. *Knowledge Acquisition,* 5:199–220, 1993.
11. F. Hayes-Roth, D. A. Waterman, and D. B. Lenat. *Building Expert Systems.* Addison-Wesley, New York, 1983.
12. G. Klinker, C. Bhola, G. Dallemagne, D. Marques, and J. McDermott. Usable and reusable programming constructs. *Knowledge Acquisition,* 3:117–136, 1991.
13. J. McDermott. Preliminary steps towards a taxonomy of problem-solving methods. In S. Marcus, editor, *Automating Knowledge Acquisition for Expert Systems,* pages 225–255. Kluwer, Boston, 1988.
14. J. McDermott. The world would be a better place if non-programmers could program. *Machine Learning,* 4(3/4):337–338, 1989.
15. A. Th. Schreiber, B. J. Wielinga, and J. M. Akkermans. Differentiating problem solving methods. In Th. Wetter, K-D. Althoff, J. Boose, B. Gaines, M. Linster, and F. Schmalhofer, editors, *Current Developments in Knowledge Acquisition - EKAW'92,* pages 95–111, Berlin, Germany, 1992. Springer-Verlag.
16. F. van Harmelen, J. M. Akkermans, J. R. Balder, A. Th. Schreiber, and B. J. Wielinga. Formal specifications of knowledge models. ESPRIT Basic Research Action P3178 REFLECT, Deliverable R.1 RFL/ECN/I.4/1, Netherlands Energy Research Foundation ECN, August 1990. Available from: University of Amsterdam, Social Science Informatics, Roetersstraat 15, NL-1018 WB, Amsterdam, The Netherlands.
17. F. van Harmelen and J. R. Balder. (ML)^2: a formal language for KADS models of expertise. *Knowledge Acquisition,* 4(1), 1992. Special issue: 'The KADS approach to knowledge engineering', reprinted in *KADS: A Principled Approach to Knowledge-Based System Development,* 1993, Schreiber, A. Th. *et al.* (eds.).
18. G. van Heijst, S. Falasconi, A. Abu-Hanna, A. Th. Schreiber, and M. Stefanelli. A case study in ontology library construction. *Artificial Intelligence in Medicine,* 7(5):227–255, June 1995.

An Ontology Approach to Product Disassembly *

Pim Borst[1] and Hans Akkermans[1,2]

[1] University of Twente
Information Systems Department INF/IS
P.O. Box 217, NL-7500 AE Enschede
The Netherlands
Email: {borst,akkerman}@cs.utwente.nl

[2] Netherlands Energy Research Foundation ECN
P.O. Box 1, NL-1755 ZG Petten
The Netherlands
Email: akkermans@ecn.nl

Abstract. In recent years, growing ecological concern has prompted for 'design for environment'. One way to achieve this is to design products that are easy to disassemble, because this improves the ability to reuse or recycle parts of a product. This paper presents a computational theory for product modeling and reasoning about product disassembly. This theory, implemented in the PROMOD system, is based on an ontology of different connection types between product components. For the task of reasoning about disassembly, the standard topological relation that expresses that two components are connected or in contact proves to be inadequate. We therefore introduce, within a topological context, a small number of new ontological primitives concerning the rigidness of connections and the constrained degrees of freedom, which in effect are task-oriented abstractions of geometric and physical-chemical properties of products. On this basis, it is demonstrated that one can automatically generate all feasible product disassembly sequences, and in addition perform an ecological cost-benefit analysis. The latter provides a preference order over disassembly sequences, allowing to compare alternative product designs for recycling and reuse. Finally, we show how the proposed ontology for disassembly is an extension of existing ontologies dealing with physical systems, is based on the same ontology design principles and discuss how it compares to ontologies of full geometry.

1 Introduction

In recent years, growing ecological concern has prompted for 'design for environment' (Fiksel 1996). One way to achieve this is to design products that are easy to disassemble, because this improves the ability to reuse or recycle parts of a product. In analyzing

---

* This work has been carried out as part of the SUSTAIN project, with PRé Product Ecology Consultants and ECN as partners, and partially supported by the SENTER-IT Programme of the Netherlands Ministry of Economic Affairs. Helpful discussions with Mark Goedkoop (PRé) and Jan Braam (ECN) are acknowledged. We also thank Mark Goedkoop for kindly providing us with the coffee machine which we have thoroughly disassembled for the purposes of the present study.

these aspects, one needs to determine all feasible ways to disassemble a product. They can be jointly represented in an *AND/OR graph* (Fazio and Whitney 1987; Sturges Jr. and Kilani 1992), with the fully assembled product as the root, the *and-nodes* indicating a disassembly operation splitting the product into subassemblies, and the *or-nodes* representing different applicable operations that give rise to alternative ways to break up a (sub)product (see Figure1). In such an AND/OR graph, each subtree that has and-nodes as its leaves, and contains only one out of the alternative branches at each or-node it encounters, describes a distinct disassembly sequence.

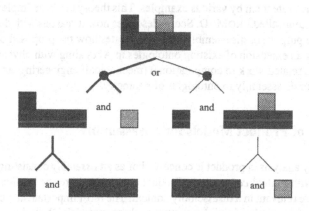

Fig. 1. Disassembly sequences of a simple product visualized in an AND/OR graph

In eco-design, an important goal is to determine the cost of disassembly as well as the environmental benefit of the subassemblies that are separated. The energy required to perform the disassembly operations might be used as a measure for the disassembly cost. All components that were separated in the disassembly process are candidates for reuse and have a positive impact on the benefits of disassembly. The degree to which the materials in a separated part of the product can be recycled is determined by the mix and the amounts of materials in that part. With such a cost-benefit analysis applied to the AND/OR graph, one can determine the disassembly sequence having the best cost-benefit ratio, as well as the impact of design decisions by comparing alternative product designs. Because it is usually only profitable to recycle or reuse a small number of parts or components of a product, a good disassembly sequence will remove only these parts from the product and leave the other parts unaffected. This is why the best *disassembly* sequence will in general be different from the reversed *assembly* sequence.

In this paper we will present a general ontology-based approach to two important tasks in product disassembly analysis:

1. automatically generating the AND/OR graph from a topological product model;
2. obtaining from the AND/OR graph the disassembly sequence having the best eco-logical cost-benefit ratio.

An ontological approach to this problem appears helpful, because it is evident in disassembly analysis that a notion of 'connectedness' plays a crucial foundational role (Clarke 1981). As we will see, the standard topological relation, that expresses that two components are connected or in contact, as incorporated in formal topological ontologies such as in (Borst, Akkermans, and Top 1997), proves to be not adequate for this purpose. Nevertheless, we show that by extending a standard topological ontology with a small number of new ontological primitives regarding the *type* of connections, we can build product models that provide the knowledge to automatically carry out the mentioned tasks.

In Sec. 2 we introduce the basic concepts needed to build product models for disassembly, and illustrate them by various examples. This theory has been implemented in a knowledge system called PROMOD. Sec. 3 describes how it reasons with these product models for the purpose of disassembly. Sec. 4 indicates how the proposed ontology for disassembly is an extension of existing ontologies in AI dealing with physical systems. Sec. 5 surveys related work in computational (mechanical) engineering, and compares our ontology of disassembly to ontologies of geometry.

2 Theory of Product Models for Disassembly

In disassembly analysis, a product is conceived of as an *assembly* consisting of *product components* with mutual *connections*. Product components are the smallest parts of a product that are relevant in a disassembly context. The most important attributes are the material(s) they are made of and the amount of these materials. With these attributes it is possible to determine to what degree the materials of a group of product components can be reused or recycled.

2.1 Component Connections

Connections specify the places of contact between product components. It is allowed that there is more than one connection between two product components. Connections have properties beyond standard topology that are important for disassembly analysis. When a component is situated between other components, the outer components are possibly in the way during disassembly. It can also be the case that the component in the middle can be removed by pulling it in another direction. But in order to do this, the product components must be connected loosely. Two properties of connections are therefore of importance: how *rigid* connections are (in the sense of physical forces) and how constrained (in a spatial or geometric sense) the *direction* of movement of components is.

Unfortunately, this implies that generally we have to deal with many, both geometric and chemical/physical concepts. This we want to avoid, practically because in the design stage of a product detailed models like 3D CAD drawings are often not yet available, and computationally because it involves strong and complex ontological commitments. However, it is possible in disassembly modeling and analysis to define task-oriented abstractions of geometric and physico-chemical connection properties that do the job. These abstractions are then brought into a topological ontology of component connection models by means of different connection types.

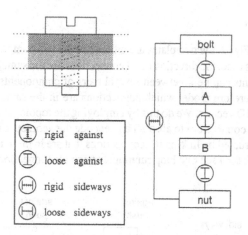

Fig. 2. The four connection types and an associated component-connection model of a bolt-and-nut system.

Distinguishing four types of connections is already sufficient to be able to perform practically useful disassembly analyses. These types are based on a dichotomy within two important orthogonal dimensions. The first discriminating dimension is the mentioned *rigidness* of a connection. A useful dichotomy here is whether a connection is rigid or loose, and relates to a distinction in engineering design known as force-based versus shape-based connections:

rigid: A physical or chemical *force* keeps the product components together, so this force must be overcome first to break the connection. (Example: components screwed or sticked together.)

loose: Product components are in contact with each other, but in a *purely spatial* sense without an additional binding force, so the connection disappears when the components are moved apart. (Example: a glass standing on a table.)

The second distinguishing dimension is the *direction* in which a connection restricts the movement of the connected components. The simplest possible conceptualization is to introduce the following dichotomy:

against: The connection restricts movement in the direction *perpendicular* to the surface of contact.

sideways: The connection restricts movement in a direction *within the plane* of the surface of contact.

This gives a two-by-two matrix, leading to four types of connections: *rigid-against, rigid-sideways, loose-against, loose-sideways*. Fig. 2 depicts graphical representations of these types, and an example how these types are used in a product model for disassembly. When the rigid connection between the bolt and nut is broken (which requires applying a physical force), the loose-against connections in the model can be simple undone by moving the connected components away from each other.

2.2 Force Loops

In the example in Fig. 2, the two plates are inbetween the two components they are connected with. In this case, the direction of all connections are the same, but generally they are not. Components can be inbetween several pairs of components in different directions. We must therefore model which connections are in the same direction, without having to specify 3D vectors. We do this by employing the topological concepts of *paths and loops* through connections to abstract and encode the geometric information. These paths can be constructed by linking the connections that are in the same direction. In the model in Fig. 2 we then see one loop running through all connections.

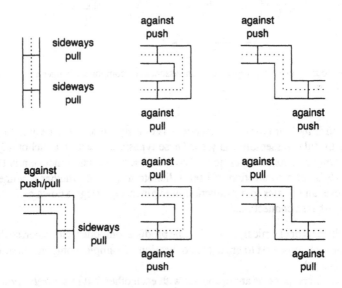

Fig. 3. The possible transitions in force loops through connected components in a disassembly model.

An easy way to determine the direction of connections and the paths that go through them is to imagine what happens when the components connected by a loose connection are pulled away from each other. For example, in Fig. 2, when the connection between A and B is pulled, this implies that plate A is pushed against the bolt, the bolt is pulled away from the nut, the nut is pushed against plate B and finally (although this may sound at first sight as a contradiction) plate B is pushed against plate A. The outcome of this sequence of forces depends on the geometry of the product and, as we will see later, turns out to be exactly the information required for disassembly analysis.

In a rigidly connected product, the geometric structure is such that the components connected by loose-against connections are pushed against each other. This will result in loops through connections, as is the case in the example. Therefore, we will speak of *force loops*. In cases where the product is not rigid, we will say that the loop is broken or not *intact*.

Because the force sequences in a force loop depend on geometry, only certain force transitions are possible when following a path, as shown in Fig. 3. When these restrictions are obeyed, the forces on connections in an intact force loop satisfy the following rules:

- Loose-against connections are always pushed.
- Rigid-against connections are pushed or pulled.
- Sideways connections are always pulled.

When two components connected by a loose connection are pushed together, we will say that the connection is *enforced*. This can only be the case when there is a loop going through the connection that is intact. A formal ontological definition of the predicate *intact* that holds for intact loops and *enforced* that holds for enforced connections reads:

$$intact(l) \leftrightarrow \neg\exists\ c\colon loops\text{-}through(l,c) \wedge (broken(c) \vee (loose(c) \wedge force(l,c,pull)))$$
$$enforced(c) \leftrightarrow rigid(c) \vee (against(c) \wedge \exists\ l\colon force(l,c,push) \wedge intact(l))$$

These definitions assume that loops are defined by the *loops-through(l,c)* predicate that relates connections *c* to the loops *l* they are in. The predicates *against(c)*, *rigid(c)* and *loose(c)* hold for against connections, rigid connections and loose connections respectively. Finally, the ternary relation *force(l,c,f)* associates a force (*push* or *pull*) to a node (connection) in a loop.

In more complex situations, there might be more than one connection in the same direction on one side of a component, like in the model in Fig. 4. This can easily be modeled by two force loops going through one connection. A situation where two connections collectively form a virtual connection is modeled in Fig. 5. Determination of the loops and forces would result in the three loops that are indicated in the figure, and the definition of *enforced* presented here must be adapted. These cases require an extension of the modelling technique that cannot be explained in this article due to lack of space.

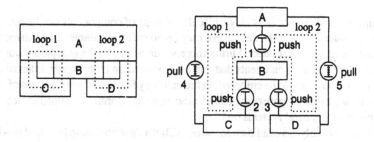

Fig. 4. Each loop individually enforces the loose connection numbered 1.

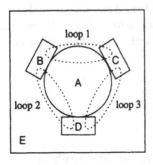 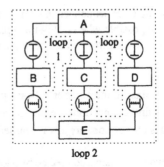

Fig. 5. Two loops collectively enforce a loose connection.

2.3 Disassembly Operations

Disassembly operations performed on a product induce changes in its disassembly model. According to the above conceptualization of connection types, two kinds of modification operators are distinguished: *loosening* operations that change a connection from being rigid to loose, and *breaking* operations that delete loose connections. The first require applying a force (energy) to undo the rigidness, while the latter refer to changing the spatial location by simply moving the components apart.

Disassembly operations like cutting, sawing and unscrewing change the types of the connections involved from rigid to loose. In the bolt-nut example, loosening the bolt is modeled by replacing the rigid-sideways connection by a loose-sideways connection. Loosening operations can cause force loops to break. As a result, some loose connections will no longer be enforced and certain parts of the product (called subassemblies) can be easily separated from the rest of the product, by breaking operations. Again, the bolt-nut example in Fig. 2 illustrates this. When the connection between the bolt and the nut has been loosened, the bolt (or the nut) can be removed from the product. This actually breaks (deletes) the connections between the bolt and the nut and the bolt and the plate.

2.4 Subassemblies

Loosening of rigid connections may cause that groups of components can be removed from the product. If this is the case, there may be no enforced connections between the group and the rest of the product. Furthermore we demand that the group does not contain smaller groups of components that can be separated. In other words, internal connections in a group have to be enforced. In the ontology for disassembly, groups of components having these properties are called *subassemblies* (formally defined in Sec. 5 as an extension of a general systems ontology).

Each subassembly is a candidate for removal, but a direction has to be found in which the subassembly can be moved away from the rest of the product. The geometric information captured in the force loops can be reused to find the desired direction.

When a subassembly has a loose external connection that is *not* linked to another external connection of the subassembly by a force loop, it means that no component blocks the subassembly in the direction of the first connection. Because other external connections of the subassembly have different directions and are not enforced, the subassembly can be removed.

When the removal of the subassembly in the direction of a connection is blocked by external components, a force loop goes through the connection and a second external connection of the subassembly. But this is only the case in situations where such a force loop leads to a connection on the opposite side of the subassembly that has not been disconnected. The geometric information in the force loop can be used to see whether this component actually blocks or not. This can be seen in Fig. 6. Situations where a force loop leads to a connection on the opposite side and the subassembly is blocked appear on the right side of the vertical line.

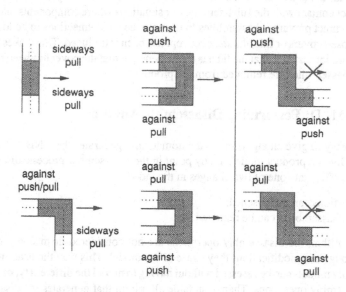

Fig. 6. Situations where a subassembly (represented by the grey shape) can be removed (left of the vertical line) or is blocked (right of the line).

It may also be the case that there are *more than one loop* going through the external connection leading to other external connections of the subassembly. Each external component connected by these other external connections may then be blocking the subassembly. Therefore, the subassembly can only be removed in the direction of an external connection when *all* force loops through the connection match a situation depicted on the left of the vertical line in Fig. 6.

A subassembly is called a *free* subassembly when it can be removed. To see whether a subassembly is free, an external connection has to be found that matches one of the three cases described above. This can be formalized as follows:

$free(a) \leftrightarrow subassembly(a) \wedge$
   $\exists\ c1: in\text{-}boundary(c1,a) \wedge \neg broken(c1) \wedge$
    $\forall\ l,c2: loops\text{-}through(l,c1) \wedge loops\text{-}through(l,c2) \wedge$
    $in\text{-}boundary(c2,sa) \wedge c1 \neq c2 \rightarrow$
     $broken(c2) \vee sideways(c1) \vee sideways(c2) \vee$
     $(against(c1) \wedge against(c2) \wedge ((force(l,c1,push) \wedge force(l,c2,pull)) \vee$
                                     $(force(l,c1,pull) \wedge force(l,c2,push))))$

In this definition we assumed that the predicate *subassembly* defines all subassemblies in a model (see also Sec. 4). The relation *in-boundary* is a systems theoretic relation that relates all connections in the system boundary of a subassembly, i.e. the external connections, to a subassembly. The predicate *broken* holds for connections that were broken earlier in the disassembly process.

Note that the above definition only takes into account blocking subassemblies that are in direct contact with the subassembly. For situations where components that are not in direct contact prevent subassemblies to be removed (or connections to be loosened), such as closed covers or lids, the *state* concept has been introduced. This makes it possible to ensure for instance that the lid has been opened or that the cover has been removed before subassemblies are removed from the product.

3 PROMOD: Performing Disassembly Analysis

It is now easy to give an algorithm that automatically generates the AND/OR tree of a product. Given a product model, at any point in the disassembly process, disassembly operations effectuate one of two changes in the model:

- connections can be loosened;
- free subassemblies can be removed.

In the algorithm, the disassembly operations are not considered themselves, but indirectly through the modifications they cause in the model. This way the usability of the disassembly models can be assessed without having to model the different types of physical disassembly operations. Then, a suitable algorithm that generates the disassembly tree (in a depth-first way) can be found in Fig. 7.

The algorithm recursively invokes itself on a model m' that is a copy of the original model m with a modification operation applied to it. In this way, the original model is available to branch off the other alternatives for disassembly of model m.

PROMOD is a prototype KBS that implements the product models for disassembly as well as the AND/OR tree generation algorithm described above. In addition, it contains a simple form of ecological cost-benefit analysis, as follows. It uses a list of product components that have to be removed from the product for recycling or reuse. Each loosening or removal operation applied to the model accounts for some given ecological cost (e.g. 5 units for loosening a connection, 1 unit for removing a subassembly). The ecological benefits depend on the degree to which the components that were marked as components to be recycled or reused have been separated from the product. For simplicity, the cost-benefit analysis does not calculate an ecological benefit, but instead a penalty (e.g. 15 units) for each unwanted component that is still attached to one of the

```
algorithm disassemble m
  do cost-benefit analysis
  foreach connection c in m do
    if c can be loosened then
      m' = m
      loosen c in m'
      disassemble m'
    endif
  end
  foreach subassembly a in m do
    if a is free then
      m' = m
      remove a from the rest in m'
      disassemble m'
    endif
  end
end
```

Fig. 7. Algorithm to Perform Disassembly Analysis.

components that should be removed. The total evaluation score of a situation in the disassembly process is then defined as $1/(cost + penalty)$.

We realize that the presented disassembly algorithm and cost-benefit calculation are too restricted for realistic disassembly analysis. The reason they are used is because they give us a way to demonstrate the usability of the disassembly models, the construction of ontologies and the practise of ontology-based application development.

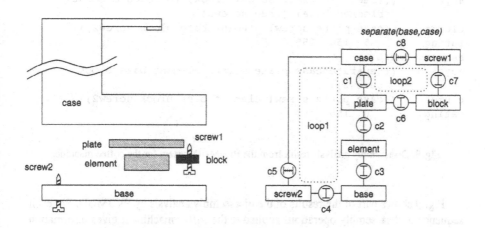

Fig. 8. Disassembly model of a coffee machine.

We will now discuss an example indicating the usability and reasoning power of the PROMOD system implementing the theory for product disassembly of this paper. Fig. 8 shows a model of a coffee machine that has been analyzed by the system. Connection *c8* can only be loosened when the base has been separated from the case (i.e. when both components are not part of a single subassembly). The component *block* has been marked as the component to be removed from the product.

```
Situations considered for 'Coffee Machine'

sequence: ((break c5) (remove screw2) (remove base)
           (break c8) (remove screw1) (remove block))
asys:      ((free case) (blocked plate) (separate screw1)
           (free element) (separate base) (separate block)
           (separate screw2))
clumps:    ((case plate element) (screw1) (base) (block)
           (screw2))
rating:       14    0    14
sequence: ((break c5) (remove screw2) (remove base)
           (break c8) (remove screw1))
asys:      ((free case) (blocked plate) (separate screw1)
           (free element) (separate base) (free block)
           (separate screw2))
clumps:    ((case plate element block) (screw1) (base)
           (screw2))
rating:       13    75    88

[many sequences removed]

sequence: ((break c5))
asys:      ((free case plate screw1 block) (blocked element)
           (blocked base) (free screw2))
clumps:    ((case plate screw1 element base block screw2))
rating:        5   150   155
sequence: NIL
asys:      ((separate case plate screw1 element base block
             screw2))
clumps:    ((case plate screw1 element base block screw2))
rating:        0   150   150
```

Fig. 9. Disassembly analysis result from the PROMOD system for the coffee machine.

Fig. 9 shows part of the results of the disassembly analysis by PROMOD. For each sequence of disassembly operations applied to the coffee machine it gives information on the subassemblies and the state of the subassemblies, on the groups of components that are separated, and on the ecological rating of the situation. The rating consists of three numbers: the ecological cost of disassembly, the total component penalty and the sum of these numbers.

4 An Ontology for Disassembly

Regarding aspects of physical systems, an extensive collection of ontologies is now available, see (Top and Akkermans 1994; Borst, Akkermans, and Top 1997; Gruber and Olsen 1994) and the KSE/Ontolingua library of ontologies. The PHYSSYS ontology (Borst, Akkermans, and Top 1997), for example, formalizes aspects of physical systems, including physical processes and related engineering mathematics, the latter by incorporating the EngMath ontology (Gruber and Olsen 1994). In order to construct large ontologies in a modular fashion, general abstract ontologies have been defined separately, such as mereology, general topology and systems theory. To define specific physical system aspects, these are imported and extended or specialized. A similar approach to enhance modularity and genericity in ontology design has been proposed in the context of a medical ontology library by (Heijst, Schreiber, and Wielinga 1997).

The same design principles hold for the construction of an ontology for disassembly. General topology defines generic properties regarding connectedness. The nature of these connections is left open. For disassembly, it is straightforward to import this general ontology, and extend it by writing axioms introducing the proposed four types of connections. In the same vein, *subassemblies* as discussed in Sec. 2.4 can be formally defined using concepts from the abstract ontology of systems theory that is part of PHYSSYS:

$$subassembly(a) \leftrightarrow subsystem\text{-}of(a,model) \land$$
$$(in\text{-}boundary(c,a) \rightarrow \neg enforced(c)) \land$$
$$(\forall \ o1,o2: part\text{-}of(o1,a) \land part\text{-}of(o2,sa) \rightarrow$$
$$connected(o1,o2)) \land$$
$$\neg \exists \ o1,o2,c: part\text{-}of(o1,sa) \land part\text{-}of(o2,sa) \land$$
$$connects(c,o1,o2) \land \neg enforced(c) \ .$$

Various abstract ontologies are reused here, including mereology (*part-of*), topology (*connects*) and systems theory (*subsystem-of, in-boundary*). Also, the formal definition given in Sec. 2.4 of a *free* subassembly reuses general systems theory. Thus, in the formal definition of the disassembly viewpoint, existing abstract ontologies theory can be reused, and modularly extended to enable reasoning about subassemblies and whether or not they are free for removal in disassembly.

Fig. 10 shows how an ontology of product disassembly can be constructed from small modules. On the left hand side can be seen that the ontologies of mereology, topology and systems theory are reused in the definition of an ontology of disassembly models. This ontology includes an additional ontology of graph theory because a graph representation of product components and enforced connections enables us to find a problem solving method (*find maximum connected subgraphs*) that defines how to compute the subassemblies in a product model.

Graph theory can also be used to define an ontology of state space. When the states in state space are related to disassembly models and edges between states to disassem-

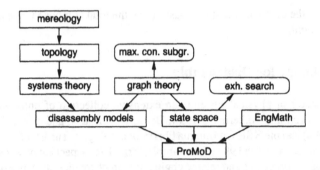

Fig. 10. Inclusion lattice of the application ontology of PROMOD. Boxes represent ontologies and arrows indicate ontology inclusion. Rounded boxes are method ontologies.

bly operations that transform one disassembly model into another, we are able to define disassembly sequences as paths through state space.

The specialization of state space in general to the state space of product disassembly is defined by the PROMOD ontology that appears at the bottom of Fig. 10. This ontology also includes the EngMath ontology of engineering mathematics to define the cost-benefit function. The cost-benefit assigns a value to a path in state space and is used by the *exhaustive search method* that finds an optimal path in state space. This method has been has been implemented as the disassembly algorithm in Sec. 3.

5 Related Work

Computational Mechanical Engineering. The problem to obtain the AND/OR graph of a product has also been considered in computational (mechanical) engineering, and several approaches are reported in the literature.

In the *reversed fishbone* approach (Ishii and Lee 1996), the designer has to come up with the preferred way to disassemble the product him/herself. This is graphically specified in a reversed fishbone diagram which can be considered as a sub-graph of the AND/OR graph. The disadvantage of this approach is that when the design of the product changes, possibly large parts of the diagram have to be changed. This makes this method less suited for comparing alternative designs.

A method to obtain the AND/OR graph automatically is to generate it from a geometric model of the product. This is done in the *degrees of freedom* (Dof) approach (Khosla and Mattikali 1989) where a 3D CAD drawing of the product is utilized. After a design modification the AND/OR graph can automatically be recomputed, but the drawback is that it needs extensive input information, which is not always available in the early stages of product design.

The third approach uses a topological *liaison diagram* (Fazio and Whitney 1987; Sturges Jr. and Kilani 1992), nodes denoting components and edges physical connections. The AND/OR graph is generated from this diagram plus additional relations specifying a partial ordering over the breaking of connections. Our theory is related to this approach. Its novel and distinguishing aspect is that by a clever choice of connection types, it can capture geometric information otherwise only available in 3D geometric models.

Ontological Engineering. In AI, much work has been done on geometric and spatial reasoning, e.g. (Joskowicz and Sacks 1991; Faltings 1992), while (Cohn, Randell, and Cui 1995) has considered related formal ontological aspects.

PROMOD's connection types and force loops are abstractions of physical and geometrical properties of connections and product structures. Although they form a sufficient basis for disassembly analysis, it would be interesting to study how they are related to ontologies of geometric and spatial reasoning. This would give us more information about the competence of the modelling technique and provides the knowledge of how to generate PROMOD models from CAD drawings in cases when these are available.

At least two approaches to formalize geometry can be found in the literature. One describes geometry in a mathematical way: mathematical equations define shapes, surfaces, lines and points in space. A system that uses a polygon representation of products to reason about mechanical assembly is described in (Wilson and Latombe 1994). The second approach extends Clarke's mereo-topology with relations to express congruence of objects (being aligned), being enclosed by an object, overlapping the convex hull of an object and so on (Borgo, Guarino, and Masolo 1996; Randell and Cohn 1992). Because these approaches avoid the introduction of points in space, the theories are called 'pointless' theories. A good example of the second approach to geometrical reasoning can be found in (Randell, Cohn, and Cui 1992).

For PROMOD's geometric abstractions, rigidness and congruence are the key aspects. Congruence is one of the basic relations in pointless approaches, so these theories are good candidates to formalize PROMOD's abstractions. It is also possible to define congruence in a mathematical way: for congruent objects it is possible to find a straight line that crosses all objects. The rigidness of connections can also be expressed in both approaches. In pointless theories they coincide with so called strong connections. In mathematical approaches, connections can be formalized with mathematical relations about the position of shapes, surfaces, lines and points. The distinction between rigid and loose connections gives rise to two interpretations of these relations. For rigid connections the relation has to be interpreted as a constraint that *must* hold, and for loose connections it is just an observation about the position of the connected objects.

Both approaches seem to be suited for formalizing the physical and geometrical abstractions used in PROMOD. Pointless approaches are well suited to gain insight on the actual meaning of the abstractions whereas mathematical approaches are closer to solid model specifications and therefore better for linking PROMOD models to CAD drawings.

6 Conclusion

In this paper, a new theory and modelling technique for disassembly of products has been presented. It is based upon an ontology that introduces unconventional but simple geometric and physical task-oriented abstractions in a topological context, by introducing connection types. Thus, advantages of several existing techniques for disassembly analysis are combined.

We have indicated how the ontology for disassembly can be neatly embedded in a broader ontology for physical systems, corroborating generic ontology construction principles proposed in the AI literature.

The proposed theory of product models has been implemented in a working prototype KBS. We have shown how the system is able to automatically generate the full disassembly graph and to carry out a simplified ecological cost-benefit analysis. How to provide a more realistic cost-benefit analysis will be investigated in the future.

References

Borgo, S., N. Guarino, and C. Masolo (1996). A pointless theory of space based on strong connection and congruence. In *Proceedings of Principles of Knowledge Representation and Reasoning (KR96)*, Boston, Massachusetts, pp. 220–229. Morgan Kaufmann.

Borst, W. N., J. M. Akkermans, and J. L. Top (1997). Engineering ontologies. *International Journal of Human-Computer Studies 46*, 365–406. Special Issue on Ontologies in KBS Development.

Clarke, B. L. (1981). A calculus of individuals based on 'connection'. *Notre Dame Journal of Formal Logic 22*(3), 204–218.

Cohn, A. G., D. A. Randell, and Z. Cui (1995). Taxonomies of logically defined qualitative spatial relations. *International Journal of Human-Computer Studies 43*, 831–846.

Faltings, B. (1992). A symbolic approach to qualitative kinematics. *Artificial Intelligence 56*, 139–170.

Fazio, T. L. D. and D. E. Whitney (1987). Simplified generation of all mechanical assembly sequences. *IEEE Journal of Robotics and Automation RA-3*(6), 640–658.

Fiksel, J. (1996). *Design For Environment: Creating Eco-Efficient Products and Processes*. New York: McGraw-Hill, Inc.

Gruber, T. R. and G. R. Olsen (1994). An ontology for engineering mathematics. In J. Doyle, P. Torasso, and E. Sandewall (Eds.), *Proceedings Fourth International Conference on Principles of Knowledge Representation and Reasoning*, San Mateo, CA, pp. 258–269. Morgan Kaufmann.

Heijst, G. V., A. T. Schreiber, and B. J. Wielinga (1997). Using explicit ontologies in KBS development. *International Journal of Human-Computer Studies 46*, 183–292. Special Issue on Ontologies in KBS Development.

Ishii, K. and B. H. Lee (1996, August). Reverse fishbone diagram: A tool in aid of design for product retirement. In *ASME Design for Manufacturability Conference*, Irvine, California. 96-DETC/DFM-1272, ASME DTC/CIE Proceedings CD, ISBN 0-7918-1232-4.

Joskowicz, L. and E. Sacks (1991). Computational kinematics. *Artificial Intelligence 51*, 381–416.

Khosla, P. K. and R. Mattikali (1989). Determining the assembly sequence from a 3-D model. *Journal of Mechanical Working Technology 20*, 153–162.

Randell, D. A. and A. G. Cohn (1992). A spatial logic based on regions and connections. In B. Nebel, C. Rich, and W. Swartout (Eds.), *Proceedings of the third National Conference on Principles of Knowledge Representation and Reasoning.*, Los Altos, pp. 165–176. Morgan Kaufmann.

Randell, D. A., A. G. Cohn, and Z. Cui (1992). Naive topology: Modeling the force pump. In B. Faltings and P. Struss (Eds.), *Recent Advances in Qualitative Physics*, pp. 177–192. Cambridge, Massachusetts: The MIT Press. ISBN 0-262-06142-2.

Sturges Jr., R. H. and M. I. Kilani (1992, February). Towards an integrated design for an assembly evaluation and reasoning system. *Computer-Aided Design 24*(2), 67–79.

Top, J. L. and J. M. Akkermans (1994, December). Tasks and ontologies in engineering modelling. *International Journal of Human-Computer Studies 41*(4), 585–617.

Wilson, R. H. and J.-C. Latombe (1994). Geometric reasoning about mechanical assembly. *Artificial Intelligence 71*, 371–396.

Knowledge Refinement for a Design System

Robin Boswell[1], Susan Craw[1] and Ray Rowe[2]

[1] School of Computer and Mathematical Sciences,
The Robert Gordon University, Aberdeen AB25 1HG
Email: rab,smc@scms.rgu.ac.uk
Tel: +44 1224 262702 Fax: +44 1224 262727
[2] ZENECA Pharmaceuticals, Hurdsfield Industrial Estate,
Macclesfield, Cheshire SK10 2NA
Tel: +44 1625 582828 Fax: +44 1625 501887

Abstract. The KRUST refinement tool has already been successfully applied to a variety of relatively simple classificatory problems, and a generic refinement framework is being developed. This paper describes the application of KRUST to a design system TFS, whose task is tablet formulation for a major pharmaceutical company. It shows how novel components can be included within KRUST's underlying knowledge model, and how KRUST's refinement mechanisms can be extended as required, by adding new operators to the existing toolsets. New mechanisms have been added whereby proofs of related examples are used to constrain and guide KRUST's refinement generation. TFS has provided valuable widening experience for attaining our eventual goal of developing a framework for a generic knowledge refinement toolkit.

Keywords:
Knowledge Refinement, Knowledge Maintenance, Design Application.

1   Introduction

Knowledge refinement is the process of correcting errors in the rulebase of a Knowledge-Based System (KBS), triggered when test cases are wrongly solved by the KBS. This paper describes how the knowledge refinement tool KRUST is being developed from a prototype, applicable to simple PROLOG rulebases, to a generic tool, applicable to industrial systems written in a variety of different shells. We demonstrate the feasibility of this approach by showing how KRUST has been applied to the Product Formulation Expert System (PFES), a shell which differs in a number of significant ways from the backward-chaining diagnostic shells which have typically been the target both of KRUST and many other refinement tools.

We first describe KRUST, and our current generic approach to the representation of knowledge and the use of refinement operators. We then introduce the expert system shell PFES, and a particular industrial application TFS, used on a regular basis by the pharmaceutical company Zeneca. We then show how the generic framework is able to handle two necessary extensions required by PFES.

First, we show how rule elements peculiar to PFES can be accommodated in KRUST's knowledge hierarchy. Secondly, we introduce new refinement operators and a new filter whereby traces of sets of related examples can be used to generate and filter refinements. These operators are the first KRUST procedures to employ induction; up to now, we have concentrated on the use of control information because of its importance for real expert system shells, but we believe induction is also essential.

We then demonstrate the effectiveness of KRUST's approach by presenting the results of applying KRUST to TFS, and showing that KRUST is able to fix actual bugs which occurred in an early version of the system. Finally, we compare KRUST with other tools, and conclude with plans for the next stage of our work on PFES.

2 Krust

The operation of any refinement system may be broken down into the following three tasks: *Blame allocation* determines which rules or parts of rules might be responsible for the erroneous behaviour; *Refinement generation* suggests rule modifications that may correct the erroneous behaviour, and *Refinement selection* picks the best of the possible refinements according to some criteria.

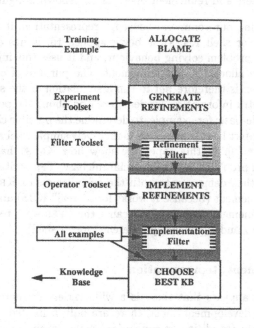

Fig. 1. The operation of KRUST

KRUST's input is a faulty KBS together with a set of examples, some of which are wrongly solved by the KBS. The refinement task consists of correcting the

KBS so that it correctly solves as many of the examples as possible. Figure 1 shows KRUST using one training example at a time to generate refinements, while the remaining examples are used to filter these refinements. More details of KRUST appear in [1].

2.1 The Development of a Generic Refinement Tool

A *generic refinement tool* [1] should satisfy three requirements:

- applicable to a variety of commercial shells;
- have a unified framework (i.e., not just a collection of separate refinement tools); and
- the framework should be extensible to apply to new shells.

The two principle features of the tool which will enable us to satisfy these requirements are:

- the ability to create an internal representation (or "knowledge skeleton") for each rulebase, using a common knowledge representation hierarchy for rule elements; and
- toolsets of filters and refinement operators, as shown in figure 1.

When discussing our common knowledge representation, it is important to note that, whatever shell KRUST is being applied to, it has direct access to the shell's actual problem solving behaviour, and it uses this information when performing blame allocation and refinement. The purpose of constructing the knowledge skeleton is therefore *not* to run a simulation of the shell, but rather to provide the extra information needed to reason about the possible effects of changes to the rule-base; for example, to determine the possible chaining of rules.

Up to now, KRUST has been applied to relatively simple rulebases in PROLOG, CLIPS, and KAPPA[9]. In this paper, we show how KRUST has recently been applied to fix real problems in a commercial rulebase, TFS, written in a different shell, PFES. We thus demonstrate both the effectiveness of KRUST's approach to knowledge refinement (because it works for a "real" KBS) and the feasibility of the generic refinement framework (because the PFES work required KRUST's extension to a new and significantly different type of shell).

2.2 Rule Element Representation

Although it first appears that there is a wide variety of representations used by various KBS development tools, there are only a limited number of roles that a rule element (condition or conclusion) plays within a rule. For example, a condition can succeed or fail, bind variables, or be involved in rule chaining. These roles are the basis of KRUST's hierarchy of rule element types.

---

[1] We have recently been awarded an EPSRC grant to extend our basic mechanism to develop such a generic refinement framework.

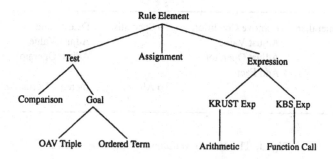

Fig. 2. KRUST's hierarchy of rule elements

A *test* is a rule condition that succeeds or fails. Tests are currently of two types: comparisons, such as inequalities, and goals. A rule element is a *goal* if and only if it can be involved in rule chaining. Two types of goal so far exist: *oav_triples* (terms of the form "Attribute of Object is Value") and *ordered_terms*, which consist of a keyword followed by arguments. Two ordered_terms unify if they have the same keyword and arity, and the corresponding arguments unify. *Assignment* has the obvious meaning. *Expressions* are rule elements that return a value. This class is divided into *KRUSTExps*, which can be evaluated within KRUST and *KBSExps*, which must be passed back to the KBS.

This hierarchy has grown during the course of the development of KRUST, and we expect that further terms will be added in the future as new KBS shells require. However, the use of a hierarchy allows us to add new rule elements within a consistent framework, and to implement procedures which take advantages of properties shared between different elements.

2.3 The Operator Toolset

To illustrate the purpose of the various toolsets shown in figure 1, we describe briefly the operator toolset, shown in more detail in figure 3. Here the labels on the left of the each column are *experiments*; that is, high-level descriptions of changes that might be made to the rule-base. Associated with each experiment are the names of the operators which actually implement these changes and create new, modified rule-bases. To add a new operator, an entry must be added in the table, and an associated Lisp function defined. For example, the new procedure described in §5.1 for learning facts from traces was implemented as an operator called *Add Fact* and associated with the experiment type *Generalise*.

3 PFES and TFS

3.1 PFES

PFES [13] is a shell whose purpose is to solve problems of design, synthesis or formulation, for which is it difficult to have access to all possible solutions in

To Generalise:	Remove Condition	To Specialise:	Delete Rule
	Adjust Value		Adjust Value
	Adjust Operator		Adjust Operator
	Add Fact		.....
	.....	To Allow:	Increase Certainty Factor
			.....

Fig. 3. The KRUST refinement operator toolset

advance, so a solution must be synthesised or generated. Its control structure is task-based, and corresponding to each task is a rule-set which is executed by forward-chaining. There is considerably less experience in building and refining such systems than for diagnostic ones. Since PFES can also be used to create traditional diagnostic systems, we believe that the application of KRUST to PFES represents a real extension to the power and applicability of refinement tools.

3.2 TFS

Drug formulation is a hard synthesis problem, and there are few formulation KBSs in regular commercial use [4]. One of these is the Tablet Formulation System (TFS) written in PFES[2], which solves the problem of selecting the inert substances, or *excipients*, which are needed to process a drug into a tablet [12]. The difficulty of the formulation task arises from the need to select a set of mutually compatible excipients, while at the same time satisfying a variety of other constraints.

The user provides a drug's name and its desired dosage. Then TFS calculates a *formulation* consisting of the most appropriate material from each excipient type, and the quantity of each required. During the initial stages of this process, TFS also calculates some intermediate results called the *specification*; these are necessary properties of the formulation which follow directly from the user's requirements. TFS input is thus drawn both from the user, and from databases containing chemical properties of drugs and excipients. TFS's output consists of the specification and formulation for the desired tablet. Figure 4 shows a typical example for KRUST, comprising requirements, specification and formulation.

3.3 How Refinement is Applied to TFS

There exist three versions of TFS: TFS-1B simply fixed a number of bugs in TFS-1A, but TFS-2, as well as fixing further bugs, represents a paradigm-shift in the approach to tablet-formulation. Our work on refining TFS is therefore divided into two phases. During the first phase, described in this paper, we applied KRUST to TFS-1A, using TFS-1B as an oracle to critique TFS-1A's output.

---

[2] We are grateful to Paul Bentley of Logica Cambridge Ltd. for his assistance with the PFES software interface.

TFS Input
  Requirement: Drug: Drug-A, Dose: 60 mg., No of fillers: 2

TFS Output
  Specification:
    full-stability: Yes
    drug-filler–concentration: 0.9
    minimum-tablet-weight: 100mg
    maximum-tablet-weight: 800mg
    target-tablet-weight: 260mg
    start-strategy: strategy-A
    filler-concentration: 66.9%
    typical-disintegrant: Maize-starch
    disintegrant-concentration: 0.05
    tablet-weight: 252.2mg

  total-concentration: 97%
  tablet-diameter: 8.73mm
  ...*various other properties*...

  Formulation:
    Tablet weight: 250mg
    Fillers: Lactose 66.7%,
           Calcium phosphate 2.4%
    Binder: Gelatin 4.1%
    Lubricant: Stearic acid 1.0%
    Disintegrant: Croscarmelose 2.1%

Fig. 4. KRUST example, made up of TFS input and output

KRUST has access to TFS-1A's rulebase, and traces of its behaviour on examples. In contrast, the oracle provides just the correct output for each example input. In the next phase, we will regard TFS-1B as the buggy system to be refined, and TFS-2 as the oracle.

4 Applying KRUST to PFES

This has required additions both to the rule element hierarchy and to the sets of operators. However, most of the existing operators were found to be applicable to PFES, and the new operators required by PFES turned out to be applicable to the other shells, so that much of the work was not PFES-specific, thereby confirming our belief in a framework approach.

4.1 Rule Element Representation

Many of PFES's rule elements (conditions and conclusions) are standard expressions found in many KBS shells. However, there is a group of rule elements that appear at first unique to PFES, and therefore potentially difficult to represent within a common framework. These *agendas* are untyped lists, where items can be read and written to the top or bottom, or directly below another given item. Agendas are used to pass data between routines that generate values and those that subsequently test or filter them.

However, TFS agendas can also be interpreted as a mechanism for storing attribute-value data. Not all agendas have the same semantics, but the number of different possibilities actually employed within TFS is fairly limited. Two of the most common types are shown in figure 5. Each example shows the contents of an agenda at some point during the running of TFS-1A, together with the

PFES rule elements that write to and read from the agenda, and the KRUST representation of these elements.

The Filler-Agenda is simply a list of excipients; their presence on the agenda indicates that they have passed a stability test.

The Property-Agenda again shows a list of excipients, but now each excipient has an associated floating-point number, representing the value of a mechanical property.

In each of these cases, the rule elements which read and write the agenda items can be represented in KRUST as ordered terms. The fact that <STABILITY> is a property of <FILLER> is implicit in the PFES statements, which write a filler to the agenda, followed by its stability. However, it is made explicit in the KRUST representation, where the **agenda-unlabelled-attribute** statement includes both the filler and its stability as arguments. One consequence of this is that PFES commands of the type **add** <ITEM> **to-bottom-of** <AGENDA> have different KRUST representations, depending on whether or not <ITEM> represents an attribute. Fortunately it is possible to determine the correct translation from the context, both in the situations described here, and in other more complex situations also arising in TFS; this enables our translator to construct the correct KRUST representation automatically.

4.2 PFES's Many-Valued Output

One consequence of PFES's formulation task is that its output is a compound answer (figure 4), in contrast to the single result typically output from a diagnostic system. TFS-1A's output typically differs from the correct values at only one or two points, but some examples have 12 points of difference. Attempting to fix all of these at once leads to a combinatorial explosion, so instead KRUST automatically determines dependencies between faults, and attempts to fix the earliest fault(s) in the dependency chain first, in the hope that this will fix the later faults as well. A *dependency chain* is a sequence of rules where each conclusion matches a condition of the next rule, and a fault lies in the chain if it matches the conclusion of a rule in the chain. This technique has been implemented and applied to those few TFS-1A examples which exhibit large numbers of errors. In these cases, it was possible to obtain a few values that are prior to all the others in terms of dependency, and so KRUST focuses its repairs on them.

5   Learning from Traces

As stated above, KRUST has direct access to the actual rule execution behaviour of a KBS. For PROLOG, CLIPS and KAPPA rulebases, it queries the KBS directly. For PFES, this is not possible, so KRUST derives equivalent information from the *trace*. This is a record of every attempt by the rule interpreter to execute a rule element, together with the result and the bindings for all the variables. It thus

---

Snapshot of FILLER-AGENDA

CELLULOSE LACTOSE CALCIUM-PHOSPHATE

PFES Read/Write Operations on FILLER-AGENDA

Conclusion: **add** <FILLER> **to-bottom-of** FILLER-AGENDA
Condition: <FILLER> **is-on** FILLER-AGENDA

Krust representation of each operation

on-agenda(FILLER-AGENDA, <FILLER>)

===

Snapshot of PROPERTY-AGENDA

CELLULOSE 46.2 LACTOSE 158.8 CALCIUM-CARBONATE 851.1

PFES Read/Write Operations on PROPERTY AGENDA

Conclusions: **add** <FILLER> **to-bottom-of** PROPERTY-AGENDA
      add <STABILITY> **to-bottom-of** PROPERTY-AGENDA
Conditions: <FILLER> **is-on** PROPERTY-AGENDA
      <STABILITY> **is-the-item-after** <FILLER> **on** PROPERTY-AGENDA

Krust representation of each of these paired operations

on-agenda(PROPERTY-AGENDA, <FILLER>)
agenda-unlabelled-attribute(PROPERTY-AGENDA, <FILLER>, <STABILITY>)

Fig. 5. Agendas and their PFES operations

provides the information needed to construct a proof-tree for the conclusions generated, which is then used for blame allocation and refinement generation.

Earlier versions of KRUST have generated refinements for a single training example at a time, subsequently using other examples for filtering and judging. We describe two recent additions to KRUST which enable it to use *sets* of traces from *related* examples to guide the refinement process at an earlier stage. The approach in both cases is as follows:

- to select as positive examples those examples and their traces that exhibit a particular fault, and as negative examples those that do not;
- to identify features distinguishing these two groups; and finally
- to use these features as inputs to refinement generation and selection.

We shall describe two techniques: using traces to learn facts, and for refinement filtering. The goal of the second technique is to reduce KRUST's search space, so we shall postpone its description until §7, after the results *without* the new filter. The remainder of this section is therefore devoted to the first technique: using traces to learn facts.

5.1 Using Traces to Learn Facts

Most of KRUST's refinements take the form of modifications to existing rule elements. However, one of the available refinement operators adds a new fact to the database. Such a refinement is generated when the new fact is required to satisfy a currently unsatisfied condition in a rule, and hence enable that rule to fire. Induction from several examples should be applied at this point, because typically the training example imposes insufficient constraints on the new fact.

We now illustrate this technique with reference to faults of type 1, in which TFS-1A incorrectly recommends the filler Calcium Phosphate. The reason is that the MAX-LEVEL of Calcium Phosphate is missing from the data-base, so that the second rule, **Remove-Excessive-Fillers**, fails to fire and hence fails to remove Calcium Phosphate from the filler agenda (figure 6). Hence Calcium Phosphate remains on the agenda to be read by **Get-Insoluble-Filler**.

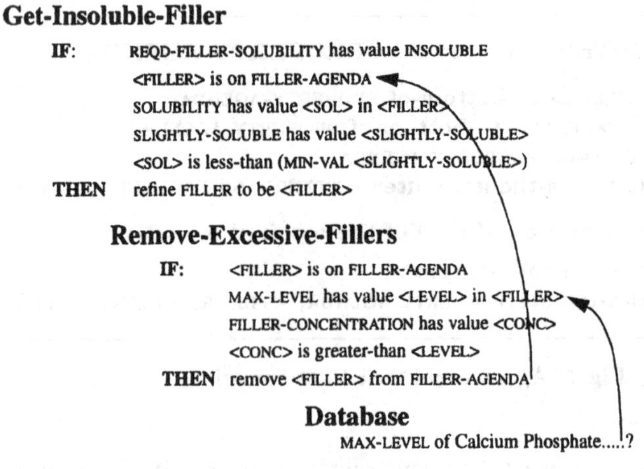

Get-Insoluble-Filler

IF: REQD-FILLER-SOLUBILITY has value INSOLUBLE
       <FILLER> is on FILLER-AGENDA
       SOLUBILITY has value <SOL> in <FILLER>
       SLIGHTLY-SOLUBLE has value <SLIGHTLY-SOLUBLE>
       <SOL> is less-than (MIN-VAL <SLIGHTLY-SOLUBLE>)
THEN   refine FILLER to be <FILLER>

Remove-Excessive-Fillers

IF: <FILLER> is on FILLER-AGENDA
       MAX-LEVEL has value <LEVEL> in <FILLER>
       FILLER-CONCENTRATION has value <CONC>
       <CONC> is greater-than <LEVEL>
THEN   remove <FILLER> from FILLER-AGENDA

Database
       MAX-LEVEL of Calcium Phosphate.....?

Fig. 6. Rule chain for wrong filler example

KRUST identifies the missing database value as one possible cause of the error by backward chaining from the erroneous conclusion: <FILLER> = **Calcium Phosphate**. One way of *preventing* the rule **Get-Insoluble-Filler** from firing for Calcium Phosphate is to *enable* the rule **Remove-Excessive-Fillers** to fire. To do so, it is necessary to enable the condition: MAX-LEVEL **has value** <LEVEL> **in** <FILLER> which can only be done by adding an entry for MAX-LEVEL of Calcium Phosphate to the database. KRUST has three sources of constraints on the value to which MAX-LEVEL should be set:

1. The current training example.
2. Other positive examples of the same fault — that is, examples for which TFS-1A wrongly recommends Calcium Phosphate.
3. Negative examples of the fault — i.e., examples in which TFS-1A correctly recommends Calcium Phosphate.

We consider first the way in which the current training example and the other positive examples are used. In the following discussion, rule R_f is the rule whose failure is being corrected, so here, R_f is **Remove-Excessive-Fillers**. For the positive examples, KRUST first checks that rule R_f failed on the same condition as for the training example, and thereafter processes the training example and the other positive examples identically. KRUST must first determine the constraints on MAX-LEVEL that must be satisfied for R_f to succeed. Here, the value of MAX-LEVEL is stored in the variable <LEVEL>, and there is only one constraint: <CONC> **is greater-than** <LEVEL>. The value of <CONC> is not available from the trace of R_f, as the rule interpreter never reached this condition; however, the rule that set the value of <CONC> will have fired, and the value of <CONC>, and hence the constraint imposed on MAX-LEVEL may be obtained from its trace. Thus the training example and the other positive examples provides a set of bounds on MAX-LEVEL. Here, these are all upper bounds, which reduce to the single constraint **58% is greater-than** MAX-LEVEL.

Negative examples are examples for which the system gives the same conclusion as in the training case (here, <FILLER> = **Calcium Phosphate**) but for which the conclusion is accepted by the expert, and for which the rule R_f failed. KRUST constrains the new fact added to the database so that it will not interfere with the proofs of these examples by causing R_f to succeed. It must therefore ensure that at least one condition of R_f will continue to *fail*. Here, the relevant condition is <CONC> **is greater-than** <LEVEL>, so that the values of <CONC> arising in the various negative examples provide a *lower* bound for MAX-LEVEL, (here, 11.5%).

These two constraints define an interval delimiting the new value, and can be used in one of two ways: they can either be shown to an expert, who can then be asked to provide the new fact or else adjudicate on any inconsistencies (e.g., caused by noise); or else KRUST can choose the value from within the constraints whose insertion constitutes the most conservative change. In our example, this will be the greatest value for MAX-LEVEL of Calcium Phosphate that lies within the bounds induced from the examples; i.e., 57%.

6   Results with TFS-1A and TFS-1B

Since our work is designed to solve problems of knowledge-base refinement rather than machine learning [2], the traditional machine learning approach involving learning graphs is inappropriate. KRUST, like MOBAL [6], is not well described by the paradigm of "learn a concept and then use this concept to classify previously unseen examples". Rather, its purpose is to refine real KBSs, with real faults, and to generate real repairs. TFS-1A was not intended to be faulty (i.e., we did not introduce artificial faults for KRUST to find), and TFS-1B contains the actual fixes for those bugs. The goal of our experiments was thus to determine whether KRUST was able to fix these faults in TFS-1A.

We first generated 208 TFS inputs, evenly distributed over the requirement space, and ran TFS-1A and TFS-1B on each of them. Any difference between the outputs of the two system for a given input constituted a fault in TFS-1A. A hierarchical clustering mechanism grouped these faults into the classes shown in figure 7. These in fact correspond to the three differences between TFS-1A and TFS-1B. We now describe a set of typical runs where we have selected one example for each of the faults.

Fault 1: Incorrect filler

Example 5 — (110 mg, DRUG-A, 1 filler)
1A *filler:* Calcium phosphate 57.3% 1B *filler:* Calcium carbonate 58.5%

Example 33 — (110 mg, DRUG-F, 1 filler)
1A *filler:* Calcium phosphate 55.5% 1B *filler:* Magnesium carbonate 56.6%

Fault 2: Incorrect quantity of binder

Example 1 — (10 mg, DRUG-A, 1 filler)
1A *binder:* Gelatin 4.1% 1B *binder:* Gelatin 2.1%

Fault 3: Multiple faults in specification produced

Example 183 — (360 mg, DRUG-A, 1 filler)
1A *target tablet weight:* 400mg 1B *target tablet weight:* 450mg
1A *drug concentration:* 9/10 1B *drug concentration:* 4/5
1A *filler concentration:* 0.0 1B *filler concentration:* 0.1
... *various other discrepancies*

Fig. 7. Contradictory formulations generated by TFS-1A and TFS-1B

6.1 Fault 1: Wrong Filler

One of the 61 refinements involved the induction module (§5.1). It returned a value of 57%, but this was overridden when the expert provided a value of 30%.

All but one of the refined knowledge bases (KBs) were rejected at the first filtering stage because they did not give the correct output for the training example. The refined KB recommended by KRUST coincided with the "correct" TFS-1B KB, and was the original TFS-1A KB, with the addition of the following database entry: MAX-LEVEL **of Calcium Phosphate is 30%**.

6.2 Fault 2: Wrong Binder Level

93 refinements were generated. Again, only one of the refined KBs passed the first filtering stage. The KB recommended by KRUST coincided with the "correct" TFS-1B KB and was the original KB, except that the conclusion to the rule **Default-Binder-Level** had been changed from **Set the value of** <BINDER> **in the** FORMULATION **to be 0.04** to **Set the value of** <BINDER> **in the**

FORMULATION **to be 0.02**. Again, this proved to be the correct fix, the refined KB coinciding with the TFS-1B KB.

The effectiveness of evaluating the refined KBs on the training example for faults 1 and 2 at first seems surprising, since for other applications it is common for many refined KBs to pass this stage, necessitating further filtering. However, TFS's output is a complex formulation, so that an incorrect perturbation of TFS-1A's KB is far less likely to lead to a correct solution for the original training example. This is one benefit of refining a design system, and contrasts with our experience with diagnostic systems, where the difficulty is to select appropriate test examples with which to filter the many refined KBs that are generated [10].

6.3 Fault 3: Multiple Faults in Specification

Since the system and oracle outputs differed on multiple fields for this fault, the technique described in section 4.2 was applied to these fields, and selected **Target-Tablet-Weight** as the independent one. It turned out that all the cases of multiple faults in the specification were in fact caused by an error in an equation in the rule **1st-Guess-Weight**. KRUST was unable to fix this error, because it currently has no operators for transforming equations.

RULE **1st-Guess-Weight**
IF   DRUG has value <DRUG> in the FORMULATION
  AND   <DRUG> has value <DOSE> in the FORMULATION
  AND   <WEIGHT> = (ROUND-TO-NEAREST 5 <DOSE> / 0.1 + (0.00221 * <DOSE>))
THEN
    Set the value of TARGET-TABLET-WEIGHT in the SPECIFICATION to be <WEIGHT>

KRUST was nonetheless able to *identify* the faulty rule, and generate 3 refinements to it, specialising each of the 3 conditions. The small number of refinements is explained by the fact that a single rule was responsible for the faulty conclusion, and no chaining was involved. KRUST also attempted to propagate the desired value of <WEIGHT> back through the equation in the third condition to give a corresponding value for <DOSE>, but this did not lead to a refinement, since the value of <DOSE> may not be altered.

The correct fix may be found in TFS-1B, where an additional rule uses a cubic equation to calculate TARGET-TABLET-WEIGHT for high values of <DOSE>. We believe functionally equivalent rules could be learned by an extension of the inductive techniques described in §5.1; this is work in progress.

7 Using Traces for Refinement Filtering

We now return to the use of traces to guide KRUST's behaviour, and introduce the second technique for the use of traces.

The refinements generated by KRUST are derived from the system's incorrect conclusion and its proof, together with the expert's conclusion. Therefore, if we also consider proofs that are similar to the faulty proof but yet lack the fault, we may obtain new information useful to the refinement process. We have used this new information to filter out refinements that are unlikely to fix the fault. Our trace comparator takes a pair of traces, and compares the firing behaviour for each of the rules for which KRUST proposes a repair. The procedure for filtering is as follows.

1. Let R be the set of rules which KRUST is refining.
2. Select sets of examples F and C, where examples F exhibit the fault (that exhibited by the current training example) and C do not.
3. Run the comparator for each rule $r_k \in R$ and for each pair of examples $(f_i, c_j) \in F \times C$. We define the comparator function $\text{diff}(r_k, f_i, c_j)$ to be 1 if the firing behaviour for rule r_k differs for examples f_i and c_j, 0 otherwise.
4. Then we say that the behaviour of rule r_k is relevant to the fault iff $\exists j$ such that $\forall i \, \text{diff}(r_k, f_i, c_j) = 1$.

Note that the appearance of a fault in one example and not in another may arise in two ways:

- it could be that a certain rule r fires in one case and not in the other, or
- it could be that r's firing behaviour is the same in both cases, but that this behaviour is faulty in the first case but correct in the second case.

The comparator will detect the difference in the first case, but not in the second. Hence we cannot choose as a criterion of relevance that the behaviour of r should differ for *all* faulty/non-faulty pairs.

7.1 Results of Refinement Filtering

The trace comparison technique was applied after KRUST had already been run without it, as described in §6, so that it was already known which of the refinements generated was the correct one. The purpose of this experiment was to determine whether the technique could be used to remove irrelevant refinements at the refinement filtering stage (figure 1), thus avoiding the necessity for KRUST to write out the refined KBs, load them into PFES, and test them.

The algorithm was applied to the runs described in §6.1 and §6.2[3]. The second column in tables 1 and 2 indicates which rules were involved in the chaining process that lead to the faulty conclusion, and the third column shows which rules the trace comparator identified as potentially relevant to the fault. The tables show that, for both faults, the technique could be used to filter out some refinements that were indeed unrelated to the faulty conclusion, while not rejecting any that *were* relevant. The apparently poor behaviour for fault 1, where the technique highlighted only one of a possible three irrelevant rules, may be explained as follows. Fault 1 is a rarely-occurring fault, and all the examples of this fault happen to share certain other attributes: viz., they use no

---

[3] For fault three, KRUST generated refinements to a single rule only, so the algorithm was not required.

surfactant, and the drugs involved are soluble. These attributes are reflected in the firing behaviour of the rules related to these attributes (**Insoluble-Drug-Rule** and **Initial-Surfactant-Level**), so that the comparison algorithm also identified these rules as potentially relevant.

Rule	Involved in faulty conclusion	Trace comparator indicates relevance
Get-Soluble-Filler		
Insoluble-Drug-Rule		√
Get-Insoluble-Filler	√	√
Remove-Excessive-Fillers	√	√
Initial-Surfactant-Level		√

Table 1. Trace Comparator applied to Fault 1: Wrong Filler

Rule	Involved in faulty conclusion	Trace comparator indicates relevance
Default-Binder-Level	√	√
Update-Formulation	√	√
High-Dose-Binder-Level		√
Try-Dose-Again		
Find-Stable-Surfactant		
Default-Surfactant		

Table 2. Trace Comparator applied to Fault 2: Wrong binder level

7.2 Further Developments

These examples have illustrated how groups of traces from related examples can be used to reduce KRUST's search. However, we believe that these techniques will acquire even greater importance when we refine TFS-1B up to TFS-2, since this task will be substantially harder that the refinement of TFS-1A to TFS-1B. The reason for this is the nature of the "paradigm shift" exemplified by TFS-2. Its principle feature is the introduction of three categories to which all excipients are assigned. Formulators now have the further constraint of being required to choose excipients from the lowest possible category. Consequently the task of refining TFS-1B so that it behaves like TFS-2 will include the problem of learning rules which implement the new formulation policy. This is harder than any of the refinements required by TFS-1A, and will demand the use of induction. However, the extension of KRUST to extract as much information as possible from multiple related examples is well-suited to this type of problem.

8 A Comparison with Related Work

The program CLIPS-R [7] refines forward-chaining production systems written in CLIPS, and so has to deal with some of the problems discussed in this paper.

CLIPS-R's approach to refinement is similar to KRUST's in that it identifies faulty rule elements by working backwards from observed faulty behaviour, but it also differs from KRUST in a number of ways.

1. It requires traces containing more information than PFES traces, such as the fact-list prior to each rule firing, and information linking facts and their sources.
2. It has been applied to diagnostic but not design systems. It is not clear how well CLIPS-R's grouping of traces sharing an initial sequence of rule firings would apply to production rules functioning in the generate and test mode found in design problems.
3. It can use, though does not require, a variety of user-supplied constraints on the correct behaviour of the KBS.

Many theory revision tools such as EITHER [8] and FORTE [11] are restricted to PROLOG programs, and SEEK [5], TEIRESIAS [3] and ODYSSEUS [14] are each applicable only to a single shell. KRUST on the other hand is currently usable with PROLOG, CLIPS, KAPPA and PFES applications. Other tools select refinements before implementing them as new KBs, so may not detect unintended side-effects. KRUST is unusual in that it generates and tests many refined knowledge bases.

Some tools can reason about a shell's control strategy (for example, ODYSSEUS makes use of meta-rules to guide the learning of new object rules) but they are often tied to a particular shell. KRUST can deal with backward and forward-chaining rules, can reason about a rule's priority under conflict resolution, and is not tied to one particular shell. This ability is due both to the explicit representation of control information, and to the fact that KRUST has direct access to the shell's actual problem solving behaviour. This contrasts with EITHER's approach, which is to treat a PROLOG program as a logical theory, ignoring the ordering of rules, and hence also the order in which solutions are generated. This approach is less suited than KRUST's to the refinement of real systems, where conflict resolution and rule ordering are usually important aspects.

Knowledge refinement tools such as KRUST also require fewer examples, although theory revision tools are more adept at adding new knowledge, based on many examples. CLIPS-R shares properties of both types of tool, and our current work on KRUST is aimed at giving it some of the desirable properties of theory revision tools, such as induction, while continuing to develop its ability to cope with real-world systems.

9 Conclusions

The experience of applying KRUST to a PFES KBS indicates that its basic refinement techniques are equally applicable to design systems. It also confirms our belief that a relatively small set of basic knowledge components are commonly used in KBSs, and also that novel ones may be fairly closely related to existing ones; i.e., the roles of knowledge components (not the knowledge itself) are fairly limited. This also suggests that our goal of a more general refinement framework is feasible. One gain of refining a design system is the relative complexity of the conclusion, which proves very helpful in isolating relevant rules and hence repairs. We also take advantage of the knowledge contained in PFES traces. Information from multiple traces guides and constrains refinement generation. Traces also allow KRUST to propose new knowledge, a feature more usually associated with theory revision systems. Both these techniques will be increasingly relevant when KRUST must learn the more complex concepts required in the most recent version, TFS-2.

References

1. Susan Craw and Paul Hutton. Protein folding: Symbolic refinement competes with neural networks. In Armand Prieditis and Stuart Russell, editors, *Machine Learning: Proceedings of the Twelfth International Conference*, pages 133–141, Tahoe City, CA, 1995. Morgan Kaufmann.
2. Susan Craw, Derek Sleeman, Robin A. Boswell, and Leonardo Carbonara. Is knowledge refinement different from theory revision? In Stefan Wrobel, editor, *Proceedings of the MLNet Familiarization Workshop on Theory Revision and Restructuring in Machine Learning (ECML-94)*, pages 32–34, Catania, ITALY, 1994. GMD Technical Report Number 842.
3. R. Davis and D.B. Lenat. *Knowledge-Based Systems in Artificial Intelligence*. McGraw-Hill, 1982.
4. Jürgen Frank, Birgit Rupprecht, and Weit Schmelmer. Knowledge-based assistance for the development of drugs. *IEEE Expert*, 12(1):40–48, 1997.
5. Allen Ginsberg, Sholom M. Weiss, and Peter G. Politakis. Seek2: A generalized approach to automatic knowledge base refinement. In *Proceedings of the Ninth IJCAI Conference*, pages 367–374, 1985.
6. Katharina Morik, Stephan Wrobel, Jörg-Uwe Kietz, and Werner Emde. *Knowledge Acquisition and Machine Learning*. Academic Press, London, 1993.
7. Patrick M. Murphy and Michael J. Pazzani. Revision of production system rulebases. In W. W. Cohen and H. Hirsh, editors, *Machine Learning: Proceedings of the Eleventh International Conference*, pages 199–207, New Brunswick, NJ, 1994. Morgan Kaufmann.
8. Dick Ourston and Raymond Mooney. Theory refinement combining analytical and empirical methods. *Artificial Intelligence*, 66:273–309, 1994.
9. Gareth Palmer. Applying KRUST to a new KBS tool: experience with Kappa. Technical Report 95/9, SCMS, Robert Gordon University, October 1995.
10. Gareth J. Palmer and Susan Craw. The selection of training cases for automated knowledge refinement. In *EUROVAV-97*, 1997.
11. Bradley L. Richards and Raymond J. Mooney. Refinement of first-order hornclause domain theories. *Machine Learning*, 19(2):95–131, 1995.
12. Ray Rowe. An expert system for the formulation of pharmaceutical tablets. *Manufacturing Intelligence*, 14:13–15, 1993.
13. John Turner. Product formulation expert system. *Manufacturing Intelligence*, (8):12 – 14, 1991.
14. David C. Wilkins. Knowledge base refinement as improving an incorrect and incomplete domain theory. In Y. Kodratoff and R. S. Michalski, editors, *Machine Learning Volume III*, pages 493–513. Morgan Kaufmann, San Mateo, CA, 1990.

Compositional Verification of Knowledge-Based Systems: A Case Study for Diagnostic Reasoning

Frank Cornelissen, Catholijn M. Jonker, Jan Treur

Vrije Universiteit Amsterdam
Department of Mathematics and Computer Science
Artificial Intelligence Group
De Boelelaan 1081a, 1081 HV Amsterdam, The Netherlands
URL: http://www.cs.vu.nl/~{frankc,jonker,treur}
Email: {frankc,jonker,treur}@cs.vu.nl

Abstract In this paper a compositional verification method for models of knowledge-based systems is introduced. Required properties of the system are formally verified by deriving them from assumptions that themselves are properties of sub-components, which in their turn may be derived from assumptions on sub-sub-components, and so on. The method is based on properties that are formalised in terms of temporal semantics; both static and dynamic properties are covered. The compositional verification method imposes structure on the verification process. By the possibility to focus at one level of abstraction (information and process hiding), compositional verification provides transparency and limits the complexity per level. Since verification proofs are structured in a compositional manner, they can be reused in case of modification of the system. The method is illustrated for a generic model for diagnostic reasoning.

Keywords Compositional verification, knowledge-based systems, diagnostic reasoning model, formal compositional modelling.

1 Introduction

When designing complex knowledge-based systems, it is often hard to guarantee that the specification of a system that has been designed actually fulfills the needs, i.e., whether it satisfies the design requirements. Especially for critical applications, for example in aerospace domains, there is a need to prove that the designed system will have certain properties under certain conditions (assumptions). While developing a proof of such properties, the assumptions that define the bounds within which the system will function properly are generated.

In this paper, in Section 3, a structured verification method for complex knowledge-based systems is introduced, called *compositional verification*. Roughly spoken, the requirements of the whole system are formally verified by deriving them from assumptions that themselves are properties of sub-components, which in their turn may be derived from assumptions on sub-sub-components, and so on. This process ends when primitive components are reached: components that are not composed, but specified by means of a knowledge base (or any other means).

The method introduced here is illustrated for a generic task model for diagnostic reasoning. For this example task model, requirements are formulated (both the required static and dynamic properties), and a compositional system specification is introduced in Section 4. The compositional specification is based on a task composition that specifies how the main task is composed of the tasks hypothesis determination and hypothesis validation, and how the sub-task hypothesis validation is composed of the tasks observation determination, observation execution and hypothesis evaluation. The compositional specification itself is expressed in the modelling framework DESIRE, briefly described in Section 2. The application of the compositional verification method to the example task model is presented in Section 5 (top level of the composition), Section 6 (lower level), and Section 7 (primitive components).

2 Compositional Modelling of Knowledge-Based Systems

The example task model described in this paper is specified within the compositional modelling framework DESIRE for knowledge-based systems and multi-agent systems (framework for DEsign and Specification of Interacting REasoning components; cf. (Brazier, Treur, Wijngaards and Willems, 1995; Brazier, Dunin-Keplicz, Jennings, Treur, 1995)). A number of generic models for agents and tasks have been developed and used for a number of applications. The architectures upon which compositional specifications are based are the result of analysis of the tasks performed. Task compositions include specifications of interaction between tasks at each level within a task composition. Models specified within DESIRE define the structure of *compositional architectures.*: Components in a compositional architecture are directly related to tasks in a task composition. The hierarchical structures of tasks, interaction and knowledge are fully preserved within compositional architectures. Below the formal compositional framework for modelling multi-agent tasks DESIRE is introduced, in which the following aspects are modelled and specified: (1) task composition, (2) information exchange, (3) sequencing of tasks, (4) task delegation, (5) knowledge structures.

The semantics of the modelling language are based on temporal logic (cf., Brazier, Treur, Wijngaards and Willems, 1996). Design is supported by graphical tools within the DESIRE software environment. Translation to an operational system is straightforward; the software environment includes implementation generators with which formal specifications can be translated into executable code. DESIRE has been successfully applied to design both single agent and multi-agent knowledge-based systems.

3 Compositional Verification

The purpose of verification is to prove that, under a certain set of assumptions, a system will adhere a certain set of properties, for example the design requirements. In our approach, this is done by a mathematical proof (i.e., a proof in the form mathematicians are accustomed to do) that the specification of the system together with the assumptions implies the properties that it needs to fulfill.

3.1 The Compositional Verification Method

A compositional system can be viewed at different levels of abstraction. Viewed from the top level, denoted by L_0, the complete system is one component D, with interfaces, whereas internal information and processes are hidden (information and process hiding). At the next lower level of abstraction, the top level component D can be viewed as a composition of sub-components, information links, and task control. The compositional verification method takes into account this compositional structure. The primitive reasoning components can be verified using more traditional verification methods such as described in (Treur and Willems, 1994; Leemans, Treur and Willems, 1993). Verification of a composed component is done using properties of the sub-components it embeds and the task control knowledge. This introduces a form of compositionality in the verification process: the proof that a certain component adheres to a set of properties depends on the (assumed) properties of its sub-components. The assumptions under which the component functions properly, are the properties to be proven for its sub-components. This implies that properties at different levels of abstraction are involved in the verification process. These properties have hierarchical logical relations in the sense that at each level a property is logically implied by (a conjunction of) the lower level properties that relate to it in the hierarchy (see Fig. 1).

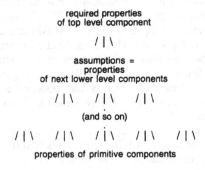

Fig. 1 Hierarchical relations between properties in compositional verification

Often these properties are not given at the start of the verification process. Actually, the process of verification has two main aims:

- to find the properties
- to prove the higher level properties from lower level properties

The verification proofs that connect one abstraction level with the other are compositional in the following manner: any proof relating level i to level i+1 can be combined with any proof relating level i-1 to level i, as long as the same properties at level i are involved. This means, for example, that the whole compositional structure beneath level i can be replaced by a completely different design as long as the same properties at level i are achieved. After such a modification the proof from level i to level i-1 can be reused; only the proof from level i+1 to level i has to be adapted. In this sense the method supports reuse of verification. The *compositional verification method* can be formulated in more detail as follows:

A. Verifying one abstraction level against the other
For each abstraction level the following top-down procedure is followed:
1. Determine which properties are of interest (for the higher level).
2. Determine assumptions (at the lower level) that guarantee these properties.
3. Prove the properties on the basis of these assumptions.

B. Verifying a primitive component
For primitive knowledge-based components a number of techniques exist in literature, see for example (Treur, Willems 1994; Leemans, Treur, Willems 1993). For primitive non-knowledge-based components, such as data bases, or neural networks, or optimization algorithms, verification techniques can be used that are especially tuned for that type of component.

C. The overall verification process
To verify the complete system
1. Determine the properties are that are desired for the whole system.
2. Apply the above procedure **A** iteratively until primitive components are reached.
   In the iteration the desired properties of abstraction level L_i are either:
   * those determined in step **A1**, if $i = 0$, or
   * the assumptions made for the higher level L_{i-1}, if $i > 0$
3. Verify the primitive components according to **B**.

The results of verification are:
* Properties and assumptions at the different abstraction levels.
* Logical relations between the properties of different abstraction levels (cf. Fig. 1).

Notes:
* Both static and dynamic properties and connections between them are covered.
* Both the determination of the properties and assumptions and the proofs of the logical relations are made by hand (in the style of mathematicians' work)
* Reuse of verification results is supported: refining an existed verified compositional model by further decomposition, leads to a verification of the refined system in which the verification structure of the original system can be reused.
* Process and information hiding limits the complexity of the verification per abstraction level.
* A requirement to apply the compositional verification method described above is the availability of an explicit specification of how the system description at an abstraction level L_i is composed from the descriptions at the lower abstraction level L_{i+1}; the compositional modelling framework DESIRE is an instance of a modelling framework that fulfills this requirement.
* In principle, a similar, bottom-up procedure, can be formulated as well.
* For any set of assumptions obtained in A., if it is required that it does not contain superfluous elements, for each assumption in the set an example may be constructed in which the assumption does not hold, whereas the other assumptions in the set hold and one or more of the properties fail. If for one of the assumptions no example is possible, then try to eliminate it.

3.2 Semantics Behind the Compositional Verification Method

In principle, verification is always relative to semantics of the system descriptions that are verified. For the Compositional Verification Method, these semantics are based on compositional information states and time steps in which transitions from one state to the other occur. In this sub-section a brief overview of these assumed semantics is given.

An *information state* M of a component D is an assignment of truth values {true, false, unknown} to the set of ground atoms that play a role within D. The compositional structure of D is reflected in the structure of the information state. A formal definition can be found in (Brazier, Treur, Wijngaards and Willems, 1996). The set of all possible information states of D is denoted by IS(D).

A *trace* $\mathcal{M}$ of a component D is a sequence of information states $(M)_{t \in N}$ in IS(D). The set of all traces is denoted by IS(D)^N, or Traces(D). Given a trace $\mathcal{M}$ of component C, state$_C(\mathcal{M}, t, input(C'))$ denotes the information state of the input interface of component C' at time point t of the component C, where C' is either C or a sub-component of C. Analogously, state$_C(\mathcal{M}, t, output(C'))$, denotes the information state of the output interface of component C' at time point t of the component C. Given a trace $\mathcal{M}$ of component C, the task control information state of component C' at time point t of the component C is denoted by state$_C(\mathcal{M}, t, tc(C'))$, where C' is either C or a sub-component of C.

To connect neighbouring levels of abstraction in a verification proof for a DESIRE specification, the following elements can be used:
- the assumptions of the sub-components specified within component D
- the interactions between the sub-components of D and / or the interfaces of D
- the input / output information states of the sub-components of D
- the task control information states of the sub-components of D
- the information states of component D
- the task control information states of component D

4 The Example Diagnostic Reasoning Model

The example model described in this section is based on the generic model for diagnostic reasoning analysed in (Treur, 1993). Diagnostic reasoning is the analysis of the cause of a disturbed situation. In most of these situations not all relevant observational facts are known in advance. The process of acquisition of additional (observation) information is an essential part of most diagnostic processes (Treur, 1993). Therefore, dynamics play an important role in diagnosis. In general diagnostic reasoning consists of a number of sub-tasks such as the determination of hypothesis, the choice of applicable tests, the performance of tests and the interpretation of the test results. Strategic information such as the suitability of a test, likeliness of a hypothesis being true and the cost and effect of a test play an important role. In this section the model of diagnosis to be verified is described. First the task hierarchy is given, and each component is described, followed by the interaction between the components.

4.1 Task Composition

The task composition of the system is given in Fig. 2. The task Hypothesis Determination generates hypotheses that are validated by the task Hypothesis Validation.

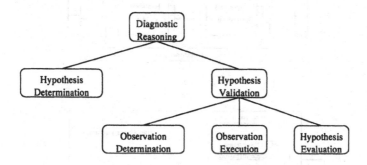

Fig. 2 Task composition of the diagnostic reasoning task

The two tasks are described in the subsequent sections. In this section HYPS stands for the set of all (possible) hypotheses and OBS for the set of all (possible) observations.

4.2 Hypothesis Determination

The task Hypothesis Determination suggests hypotheses to be validated. This is done using information on which hypothesis have been rejected so far. The input and output interfaces are defined by

input atoms	rejected(h), confirmed(h) ; h ∈ HYPS
output atoms	focus(h) ; h ∈ HYPS

Whenever an hypothesis has been rejected or confirmed, it should not be suggested as a focus. The selection of hypotheses for the focus could for example be based on the frequency at which the hypotheses occur. This component should select one or more hypotheses whenever not all hypotheses have been rejected. This task is specified as a primitive component in the example.

4.3 Hypothesis Validation

The main task of Hypothesis Validation is to determine whether the hypotheses of a given focus set are valid. In addition to that it keeps track of hypotheses that have already been validated. The interface and internal atoms for Hypothesis Validation are the following:

input atoms	focus(h) ; h ∈ HYPS
internal atoms	observed(o); o ∈ OBS
output atoms	rejected(h), confirmed(h); h ∈ HYPS

The input is obtained from Hypothesis Determination.

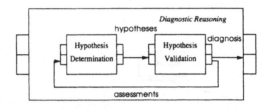

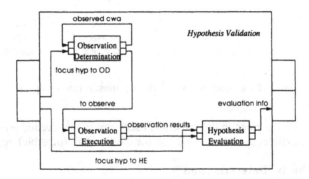

Fig. 3 Composition and Information Exchange at two levels

The task Hypothesis Validation is composed of three primitive tasks. Each of these are described shortly in the following paragraphs.

Observation Determination

To validate a hypotheses, observations have to be performed. These observations are selected by the sub-task Observation Determination . The knowledge required for this selection might include cost of doing observations, reliability, and so on. The information required by this task are the hypotheses that are in focus and observations that have already been performed. The interface of this task is

input atoms   focus(h) , observed(o); h ∈ HYPS, o ∈ OBS
output atoms   to_observe(o); o ∈ OBS

Observation Execution

The Observations are made in the sub-task Observation Execution. The information this task requires are the observations it needs to perform. The output consists of the results of those observations. The interface of this component is as follows:

input atoms   target(o) ; o ∈ OBS
output atoms   o ; o ∈ OBS

Note that these atoms o are at the object level, whereas the atoms such as to_observe(o) are at a meta-level (in which case o is a term, naming the atom o ; for convenience we use the same notation). By the information link to_observe from Observation Determination to Observation Execution, the meta-atom to_observe(o) is linked to the meta-atom target(o).

Hypothesis Evaluation

Given observation results, the task Hypothesis Evaluation derives conclusions about which hypotheses are true. This task has the same level as Observation Execution since it uses the observations made there to derive truth values of hypothesis in focus by means of anti-causal knowledge. The interface of this task is

input atoms	o ; o ∈OBS
output atoms	h ; h ∈HYPS

In Fig. 3 the interaction within the whole system S is shown. The link hypotheses transfers the hypotheses determined in Hypothesis Determination to Hypothesis Validation. The link assessments transfers the results from the evaluation in Hypothesis Evaluation to Hypothesis Determination so this component knows which hypothesis are rejected. The last link, diagnosis transfers the diagnosis determined by the system to the output interface of the main component.

5   Verification of the System S as a Whole

First the manner in which time points are attached to the reasoning process is discussed.

5.1   Time Points

For the verification of this system we need to introduce time points to reason about the dynamics of this system as explained in Section 3. For the component S time points are defined as:
- Time point 1 corresponds to the termination time of the first activation of component Hypothesis Validation
- Time point $t + 1$ is after the subsequent activations of Hypothesis Determination and Hypothesis Validation have been finished.

For the component Hypothesis Validition the time points are defined as:
- Time point 0 corresponds to no activation of the component.
- Time point $t + 1$ is after Hypothesis Evaluation has been active, or Hypothesis Validation terminates.

The time steps within both components are illustrated by a sample trace of the system in Fig. 4.

5.2   Properties for the Top Level of the System

First, it is determined which properties the system as a whole should satisfy. Considering that the system s is a diagnostic reasoning system, it is expected that s produces output of the form confirmed(h) and / or rejected(h) for some hypotheses h. A first requirement is that output generated by the system in terms of assessments of hypotheses is correct, i.e., if the system derives that a hypothesis has been confirmed, it is true in the world situation, and if the system derives it is rejected, it is false in the world situation. Let the current world state be denoted by M. The following property relates the output of the system to the current world state.

		Time within HV	Time within S
			0
Hypothesis Validation		0	
Observation Determination			
		1	
			1
Hypothesis Determination			
			1
Hypothesis Validation		1	
Observation Determination			
		1	
Observation Execution			
		1	
Hypothesis Evaluation			
		2	
Observation Determination			
		2	
Observation Execution			
		2	
Hypothesis Evaluation			
		3	
			2

Fig. 4 Trace of the diagnostic system with annotated time points

Assessment correctness of s

The system s is called *assessment correct* if:

($\forall M \in$ Traces(S) $\forall t \forall h$ state$_S$(M, t, output(S)) $\models$ confirmed(h) $\Rightarrow M \models h$) $\wedge$
($\forall M \in$ Traces(S) $\forall t \forall h$ state$_S$(M, t, output(S)) $\models$ rejected(h) $\Rightarrow M \models \neg h$)

Next, the system is required to be effective in generating assessments: during the process it should derive at least some positive assessment output, except in case all hypotheses are false; then the system should derive that all hypotheses are rejected:

Assessment effectiveness of s

The system s is called *assessment effective* if:

($\exists h$ $M \models h$ $\Rightarrow \forall M \in$ Traces(S) $\exists t \exists h'$ state$_S$(M, t, output(S)) $\models$ confirmed(h')) $\wedge$
($\forall h$ $M \models \neg h$ $\Rightarrow \forall M \in$ Traces(S) $\exists t \forall h$ state$_S$(M, t, output(S)) $\models$ rejected(h))

It is undesirable (for a static world situation) that the system changes its mind during the process. Therefore the requirement is chosen that once an assessment has been derived, this is never revised:

Assessment conservativity of s

The system s is called *assessment conservative* if:

a) $\forall M \in$ Traces(S) $\forall t \forall h$ [state$_S$(M, t, output(S)) $\models$ confirmed(h) $\Rightarrow$
   state$_S$(M, t+1, output(S)) $\models$ confirmed(h)]

b) $\forall M \in$ Traces(S) $\forall t \forall h$ [state$_S$(M, t, output(S)) $\models$ rejected(h) $\Rightarrow$
   state$_S$(M, t+1, output(S)) $\models$ rejected(h)]

Also termination of the system may be a relevant property:

Termination of s

The system s *always terminates* if: $\forall \mathcal{M} \in$ Traces(S) $\exists$ t state$_S$($\mathcal{M}$, t, tc(S)) $\models$ stop

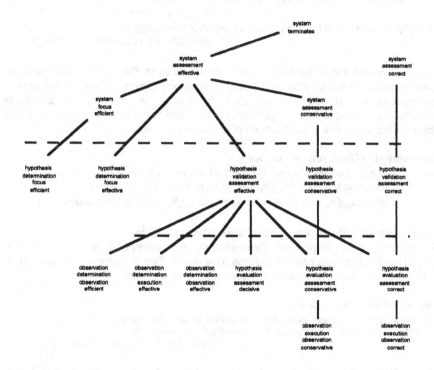

Fig. 5 Logical relations between properties at different levels for the
diagnostic reasoning model

5.3 Assumptions Needed to Prove the Properties of the Top Level

The required properties of the system have been proven from assumed properties of the
components at one level lower. During this proof process these assumptions have
been discovered.

5.3.1 Assumptions on Hypothesis Validation

Some assumptions are quite straightforward. For example, assessment correctness
simply inherits upward from Hypothesis Validation:

Assessment correctness of HV

The component hypothesis_validation is called *assessment correct* if:

a) $(\forall \mathcal{M} \in \text{Traces(HV)}\ \forall t\ \forall h\ \text{state}_{HV}(\mathcal{M}, t, \text{output(HV)}) \models \text{confirmed}(h) \Rightarrow M \models h)$

b) $(\forall \mathcal{M} \in \text{Traces(HV)}\ \forall t\ \forall h\ \text{state}_{HV}(\mathcal{M}, t, \text{output(HV)}) \models \text{rejected}(h) \Rightarrow M \models \neg h)$

Similarly, for assessment conservation:

Assessment conservativity of HV
The component hypothesis_validation is called *assessment conservative* if:

a) $\forall \mathcal{M} \in \text{Traces(HV)}\ \forall t\ \forall h \quad \text{state}_{HV}(\mathcal{M}, t, \text{output(HV)}) \models \text{rejected}(h) \Rightarrow$
$$\text{state}_{HV}(\mathcal{M}, t+1, \text{output(HV)}) \models \text{rejected}(h)$$

b) $\forall \mathcal{M} \in \text{Traces(HV)}\ \forall t\ \forall h \quad \text{state}_{HV}(\mathcal{M}, t, \text{output(HV)}) \models \text{confirmed}(h) \Rightarrow$
$$\text{state}_{HV}(\mathcal{M}, t+1, \text{output(HV)}) \models \text{confirmed}(h)$$

For effectiveness, the relationship is not one-to-one as in the case of correctness and conservativity. However, also in this case, at least one (among others) of the required assumptions on Hypothesis Validation is that it is effective in generating assessments, as long as focus hypotheses are provided to it. Here, and in the sequel the abbreviation assessed(h) is used instead of confirmed(h) ∨ rejected(h).

Assessment effectiveness of HV
The component hypothesis_validation is called *assessment effective* if:

$(\forall \mathcal{M} \in \text{Traces(HV)}\ \forall t\ [\ \exists h\ \text{state}_{HV}(\mathcal{M}, t, \text{input(HV)}) \models \text{focus}(h)\ ] \Rightarrow$
$[\ \exists h'\ \text{state}_{HV}(\mathcal{M}, t, \text{input(HV)}) \models \text{focus}(h') \wedge \text{state}_{HV}(\mathcal{M}, t, \text{output(HV)}) \models \text{assessed}(h')\ ]\ )$

5.3.2 Assumptions on Hypothesis Determination
For the component Hypothesis Determination the assumption is made that it is efficient and effective in generating focus hypotheses. Focus efficiency means that no hypotheses are chosen in focus that already have been assessed.

Focus efficiency of HD
The component hypothesis_determination is called *focus efficient* if:

$\forall \mathcal{M} \in \text{Traces(HD)}\ \forall t\ \forall h\ [\ \text{state}_{HD}(\mathcal{M}, t, \text{input(HD)}) \models \text{assessed}(h) \Rightarrow$
$$\text{state}_{HD}(\mathcal{M}, t, \text{output(HD)}) \not\models \text{focus}(h)\ ]$$

Focus effectiveness means that as long as not all hypotheses have been assessed, there will be generated focus hypotheses.

Focus effectiveness of HD
The component hypothesis_determination is called *focus effective* if:

$\forall \mathcal{M} \in \text{Traces(HD)}\ \forall t \quad [\ \exists h\ \text{state}_{HD}(\mathcal{M}, t, \text{input(HD)}) \not\models \text{assessed}(h)\ ] \Rightarrow$
$$[\ \exists h'\ \text{state}_{HD}(\mathcal{M}, t, \text{output(HD)}) \models \text{focus}(h')\ ]$$

5.3.3 Domain Assumptions
The properties at the top level also need assumptions on the (domain) ontology and knowledge to be used by the task model. These are the assumptions of the type considered in (Fensel, 1995; Fensel and Benjamins, 1996).

Finite number of hypotheses: The number of hypotheses is finite.

Static world: The world state is static during the processing of the system s.

5.4 Proofs of the Properties of the Top Level

For reasons of space limitation, the proofs have been omitted in this paper; see however the longer report version (Cornelissen, Jonker and Treur, 1997). In Fig. 5 the logical connections between the properties at different levels are depicted. An important notion used in the proofs is the notion of progression:

Definition (progression of s)
Given a trace $\mathcal{M} \in$ Traces(S) and a timepoint t, system s shows progression from time point t to time point t+1 if

$$\exists h \ [\ \text{state}_s(\mathcal{M}, t, \text{output(S)}) \not\models \text{assessed(h)} \ \wedge \ \text{state}_s(\mathcal{M}, t+1, \text{output(S)}) \models \text{assessed(h)} \ ]$$

At each step that the system shows progression, due to assessment conservativity, the set of assessed hypotheses becomes strictly larger. The proofs follow the pattern that the assumptions guarantee that as long as not all hypotheses have been assessed the system will show progression. If the number of hypotheses is finite, say N, then within at most N time steps the set of assessed hypotheses will become the set of all hypotheses, and the system terminates.

It can be noted that for a static world the property of assessment correctness implies assessment conservatism, so in the graph of Fig. 5 more logical relationships can be drawn. However, to avoid a complicated graph we did not attempt to give a complete account of all possible logical relationships in Fig. 5.

6 Assumptions to Prove the Properties of HV

The properties of Hypothesis Validation needed to prove the properties of the top level of the system were discussed in Section 5.3 (see Fig. 5). The assumed properties of the sub-components of Hypothesis Validation, needed to prove these properties can also be found in Fig. 5, at the lower level. For shortness, these properties are only explained informally; for formal definitions, see the full report.

The required properties of *Observation Determination* are:

Observation efficiency of OD: No observations are generated that already were performed.

Observation effectiveness of OD: If there exists at least one hypothesis in focus, and not all observations have been performed, then at least one observation is generated.

Execution effectiveness of OD: Every generated observation is performed

The required properties of *Observation Execution* are:

Observation conservativity of OE: Once an observation result has been obtained, it will persist.

Observation correctness of OE: Every observation result that is obtained is true in the world situation.

The required properties of *Hypothesis Evaluation* are:

Assessment conservativity of HE: Once an hypothesis assessment has been derived, it will persist.

Assessment decisiveness of HE: If for all possible observations, observation results have been input, then for every hypothesis an assessment can be derived.

Assessment correctness of HE: If a hypothesis is derived, then it is true in the world situation; if the negation of a hypothesis is derived, then the hypothesis is false in the world situation.

In addition to the *domain assumptions* mentioned in Section 5.3.3, the following are needed:

Empirically foundedness: The hypotheses can be uniquely characterised by means of observations; in other words: if two world situations satisfy exactly the same observations, then they also satisfy exactly the same hypotheses; see (Treur and Willems, 1994).

Finite number of observations: The number of observations needs to be finite because (in the worst case) the system should be able to do all (relevant) observations to assess all hypotheses.

7 Verification of Properties of Primitive Components

In Sections 5 and 6 verification of the generic model was described, based on assumed properties of the primitive components. If the model is to be used, instances are required for the primitive components (e.g., containing domain knowledge), and for these instances it has to be verified whether they satisfy the required properties.

The instances of primitive components can be verified making use of the more standard methods described in (Treur and Willems, 1994). For example, the component Hypothesis Determination should satisfy focus efficiency and focus effectiveness. Actually, these properties reduce to the following static properties of Hypothesis Determination:

For any input model M of HD it holds
$$\forall h \, [\, M \models \text{assessed}(h) \;\Rightarrow\; M \not\vdash_{HD} \text{focus}(h) \,] \,\wedge$$
$$[\, \exists h \, M \not\models \text{assessed}(h) \;\Rightarrow\; \exists h' \, M \vdash_{HD} \text{focus}(h') \,]$$

This type of static properties can be verified automatically for a given knowledge base, by tools as described in (Leemans, Treur and Willems, 1993). In a similar manner the properties observation effectiveness and observation efficiency of the component Observation determination reduce to static properties.

Correctness of Observation Execution and of Hypothesis Evaluation reduce to the (static) property of soundness defined in (Treur and Willems, 1994; Leemans, Treur and Willems, 1993). The property of assessment decisiveness of Hypothesis Evaluation reduces to the static notion decisiveness, which in its turn depends on the domain assumption of empirically foundedness (see Theorem 6.3 of (Treur and

Willems, 1994)). The property observation conservativity of the component Observation Execution depends on the static world assumption (and on correctness of observation results).

8 Discussion

The modelling framework DESIRE is based on compositionality. The compositional verification method described in this paper fits well to DESIRE, but can also be useful to any other compositional modelling approach. The advantage of a compositional approach to modelling is to be able to reuse components and task models easily; the compositional verification method extends this to the reuse of proofs for properties of components that are reused. For example, the diagnostic reasoning system described in this paper could be modified by changing the component Hypothesis Validation. If this changed component has the same properties as the current, the proof of the top level properties can be reused to show that the new system has the same properties as the original. This has high value for a library of generic task models, where the domain knowledge is not yet known. The verification of generic task models forces one to find the assumptions under which the generic task model is applicable for the considered domain, as is also discussed in (Fensel, 1995, Fensel and Benjamins, 1996). A library of reusable components and task models will be set up, consisting of both specifications of the components and models, and their design rationale. Although the precise contents of the design rationale is currently under study, at least the properties of the components and their logical relations (e.g., as represented in Fig. 5) are to be part of it.

Due to the compositional nature of the verification method, a distributed approach to verification is facilitated. This implies that several persons can work on the verification of the same system at the same time, once the properties to be verified have been determined. Since the proof of properties of a composed component depends on the properties of its sub-components, it is only necessary to know or to agree on the properties of these sub-components. The method proposed in this paper is useful for compositional knowledge-based systems as well as compositional multi-agent systems.

A main difference of the current paper in comparison to the work in (Fensel, 1995, Fensel and Benjamins, 1996; Fensel et al, 1996) is that in our approach compositionality of the verification is addressed; in the work as referred only domain assumptions are taken into account, and no hierarchical relations between properties are defined. Compared to (Fensel and Benjamins, 1996), where also properties of diagnosis are identified, in the current paper the properties are formalised in formal semantical terms (they are expressed in terms of temporal formal semantics), whereas in the paper as referred the properties are not (yet) formalised. For example, the formalisation of the assumption 'heuristic search knowledge' (see Table 3 in Section 4 in the paper as mentioned) in terms of the semantics of the behaviour of the system might turn out far from trivial. Especially the semantical formalisation of such dynamic properties and their logical relationships is a challenge. Furthermore, assumptions on the dynamics of hypothesis determination and the heuristic knowledge involved, as presented in our paper, have been left out of consideration. On the other hand, the value of the paper is that it gives an extensive account on various assumptions for model-based diagnosis; this was left out of consideration in our paper. Besides compositionality, a difference of our approach with (Harmelen and Teije,

1997) is that in the latter approach only static properties of diagnosis are considered, whereas in our approach also dynamic properties are covered, formalised in temporal semantics.

Previous work on verification of compositional knowledge-based systems, described in (Treur and Willems, 1995), was based on the formulation of a compositional verification principle described in (Abadi and Lamport, 1993), applied to knowledge-based systems. This principle lifts properties of the sub-components to the component in which these are embedded. If all sub-components satisfy a certain property, and they are connected in the right manner, then the component as a whole will satisfy that property. The properties that can be verified in this way are the properties such as 'functions properly'. However, for most real-world systems it gives more insight to explicit 'proper functioning' in the form of (task and domain) specific properties, as has been shown above. In this sense the current paper is a further development and refinement of the work described in (Treur and Willems, 1995).

A continuation of this work covers the case of multi-agent models; for some first results, see (Jonker and Treur, 1997). Moreover, in future work the development of tools for verification will be considered. At the moment tools exist for the verification of primitive components but not for the verification of composed components. To support the handwork of verification it would be useful to have tools to assist in the creation of the proofs. This could be done by formalizing the proofs of a verification process using a first order logic in which time and states are represented explicitly, and an interactive theorem prover to support the proofs. Another option to be explored is whether the tool KIV (based on dynamic logic) can be used; see (Reif, 1995). Some first, positive experiences with KIV for verification of an example model of a knowledge-based system are reported in (Fensel et al., 1996).

Acknowledgements
Dieter Fensel provided useful comments on an earlier version of this paper.

References
Abadi, M. and L. Lamport (1993). Composing Specifications, ACM Transactions on Programming Languages and Systems, Vol. 15, No. 1, 1993, pp. 73-132.

Benjamins, R., Fensel, D., Straatman, R. (1996). Assumptions of problem-solving methods and their role in knowledge engineering. In: W. Wahlster (Ed.), Proceedings of the Twelfth European Conference on Artificial Intelligence, ECAI'96, John Wiley and Sons, 1996, pp. 408-412.

Brazier, F.M.T. , Dunin-Keplicz, B., Jennings, N.R. and Treur, J. (1995). Formal Specification of Multi-Agent Systems: a Real-World Case. In: V. Lesser (Ed.), Proceedings of the First International Conference on Multi-Agent Systems, ICMAS'95, MIT Press, Cambridge, MA, pp. 25-32. Extended version in: International Journal of Cooperative Information Systems, M. Huhns, M. Singh, (Eds.), special issue on Formal Methods in Cooperative Information Systems: Multi-Agent Systems, vol. 6, 1997, pp. 67-94.

Brazier, F.M.T., Treur, J., Wijngaards, N.J.E. and Willems, M. (1995). Formal Specification of Hierarchically (De)Composed Tasks. In: B.R. Gaines, M.A. Musen (Eds.), Proceedings of the 9th Banff Knowledge Acquisition for Knowledge-based Systems workshop, KAW'95, Calgary: SRDG Publications, Department of Computer Science, University of Calgary, 1995, pp. 25/1-15/20.

Brazier, F.M.T., Treur, J., Wijngaards, N.J.E. and Willems, M. (1996). Temporal semantics of complex reasoning tasks. In: B.R. Gaines, M.A. Musen (Eds.), Proceedings of the 10th Banff Knowledge Acquisition for Knowledge-based Systems workshop, KAW'96,

Calgary: SRDG Publications, Department of Computer Science, University of Calgary, 1996, pp. 15/1-15/17. Extended version to appear in: Data and Knowledge Engineering, 1997

Cornelissen, F., Jonker, C.M. and Treur, J. (1997). Compositional Verification of Knowledge-based Systems: a Case Study for Diagnostic Reasoning. Technical Report, Vrije Universiteit Amsterdam, Department of Mathematics and Computer Science, 1997

Fensel, D. (1995). Assumptions and limitatons of a problem solving method: a case study. In: B.R. Gaines, M.A. Musen (Eds.), Proceedings of the 9th Banff Knowledge Acquisition for Knowledge-based Systems workshop, KAW'95, Calgary: SRDG Publications, Department of Computer Science, University of Calgary, 1995.

Fensel, D., Benjamins, R. (1996) Assumptions in model-based diagnosis. In: B.R. Gaines, M.A. Musen (Eds.), Proceedings of the 10th Banff Knowledge Acquisition for Knowledge-based Systems workshop, KAW'96, Calgary: SRDG Publications, Department of Computer Science, University of Calgary, 1996, pp. 5/1-5/18.

Fensel, D., Schonegge, A., Groenboom, R., Wielinga, B. (1996). Specification and verification of knowledge-based systems. In: B.R. Gaines, M.A. Musen (Eds.), Proceedings of the 10th Banff Knowledge Acquisition for Knowledge-based Systems workshop, KAW'96, Calgary: SRDG Publications, Department of Computer Science, University of Calgary, 1996, pp. 4/1-4/20.

Harmelen, F. van, Teije, A. ten (1997). Validation and verification of diagnostic systems based on their conceptual model. In: Proceedings of the Fourth European Symposium on the Validation and Verification of Knowledge-based Systems, EUROVAV'97, 1997.

Harmelen, F. van and Fensel, D. (1995). Formal Methods in Knowledge Engineering. Knowledge Engineering Review, Volume 10, Number 4, 1995.

Jonker, C.M. and Treur, J. (1998). Compositional Verification of Multi-Agent Systems: a Formal Analysis of Pro-activeness and Reactiveness. In: H. Langmaack, A. Pnueli, W.P. De Roever, A. Strassner, (eds.) Proceedings of the International Symposium on Compositionality, COMPOS'97, Springer Verlag, 1998, to appear.

Leemans, P., J. Treur, and M. Willems (1993). On the verification of knowledge-based reasoning modules, Report IR-346, Department of Mathematics & Computer Science, Artifical Intelligence Group, Vrije Universiteit Amsterdam, 1993.

Reif, W. (1995). The KIV Approach to Software Engineering. In: M. Broy, S. Jänichen (eds.), Methods, Languages, and Tools for the Construction of Correct Software, Lecture Notes in Computer Science, vol. 1009, Springer Verlag, 1995.

Treur, J. (1993). Heuristic reasoning and relative incompleteness. International Journal of Approximate Reasoning, vol. 8, 1993, pp. 51-87.

Treur, J., and M. Willems (1994). A logical foundation for verification. In: Proceedings of the Eleventh European Conference on Artificial Intelligence, ECAI'94, A.G. Cohn (Ed.), John Wiley & Sons, Ltd., 1994, pp. 745-749.

Treur, J., and M. Willems (1995). Formal notions for verification of dynamics of knowledge-based systems. In: Proceedings of the Third European Symposium on the Validation and Verification of Knowledge-based Systems, EUROVAV'95, 1995, pp. 189-199.

Treur, J. and Th. Wetter (1993). Formal Specification of Complex Reasoning Systems. Ellis Horwood, 1993.

An Enterprise Reference Scheme for Integrating Model Based Knowledge Engineering and Enterprise Modelling[1]

Stefan Decker[a], Manfred Daniel[b], Michael Erdmann[a],
and Rudi Studer[a]

[a]Institute AIFB, University of Karlsruhe (TH),
D-76128 Karlsruhe
e-mail: {decker I erdmann I studer}@aifb.uni-karlsruhe.de

[b]Fachhochschule Schmalkalden, D-98574 Schmalkalden
e-mail: daniel@informatik.fh-schmalkalden.de

Abstract

In recent years the demand on business process modelling (BPM) became apparent in many different communities. To provide a unifying framework for different needs on enterprise modelling we define an enterprise reference scheme and show how the development of knowledge based systems can be incorporated in such a framework. From this framework conclusions for tool support are drawn.

1 Introduction

In recent years the demand on business process modelling (BPM) became apparent in many different communities, e.g. information systems engineering [Sch94], requirements engineering [KiB94], software engineering and knowledge engineering (e.g. [SWH+94]). This suggests to aim at a unifying view on business process modelling in all these disciplines. To achieve the business goals some problems which obstruct these goals must be solved. This can be done either by restructuring the business process, by application of standard software, or by developing individual software components, such as knowledge based systems (KBSs). To be able to model business goals and to analyse problems occurring during the business processes these processes including organisational structures and activities have to be modelled. This is also true when building a KBS in an enterprise environment. Because the KBS is only a small part of the whole business organisation, it must be embedded into or at least linked to all relevant business processes, i.e. it should not be a stand-alone solution. For this purpose we extend the MIKE approach [AFS96] in the BMBF project WORKS (Work Oriented Design of Knowledge Systems) by offering business models for modelling relevant aspects of an enterprise. Although there are many approaches for enterprise reference schemes (e.g.[HBM+96][KiB94][RaV95][Sch94]), none of them seems completely appropriate for our purposes: most approaches dot not consider KBS as a

---

1. The work reported in this paper is partially supported by the BMBF (German Ministry of Education, Science, Research and Technology) under grant number 01HS014.

possibility for improving an enterprise's processes (for a general framework, see e.g. [DES96]) or the enterprise model is not elaborated enough. To be able to define an integrated framework including other possibilities to improve business processes (e.g. development of information systems) we determine the standard views of an enterprise and suggest a common notation for all views. This works extends the MIKE approach to cover organisational aspects. To reach this goal, we define relevant views of an enterprise and define the integration of the enterprise views with the models of MIKE. The ideas are illustrated by an example, derived from several elicitations.

1.1 The MIKE Approach

MIKE (Model-based and Incremental Knowledge Engineering) ([AFS96]) defines an engineering framework for eliciting, interpreting, formalizing, and implementing knowledge in order to build KBSs. It aims at integrating the advantages of life cycle models, prototyping, and formal specification techniques into a coherent framework for the knowledge engineering process. Subsequently, we will discuss the main principles and methods of MIKE.

In contrast to other approaches which assume that the expert creates the model himself, it is assumed that the knowledge engineer is the moderator of this modelling process. Considering knowledge engineering as a modelling activity implies that this process is *cyclic*, *faulty* and *approximative*.

Within the modelling process a large gap has to be bridged between informal descriptions of the expertise which have been gained from the expert using knowledge elicitation methods and the final realization of the KBS. Dividing this gap into smaller ones reduces the complexity of the whole modelling process because in every step different aspects may be considered independently from other aspects.

The knowledge gained from the expert in the elicitation phase is described in natural language. It mainly consists of interview protocols, protocols of verbal reports, etc. These knowledge protocols define the *elicitation model* ([Neu93]). This knowledge represented in natural language must be interpreted and structured. The result of this step is described semi-formally in the so-called *structure model* ([Neu93][Neu94]), using predefined types of nodes and links. The structure model consists of four contexts: the concept context defines the domain terminology, the activity context defines the task decomposition, the data flow context defines the data flow between the subtasks and the ordering context defines their control flow.

According to the KADS approach the knowledge-level description of the functionality of the system is given in the *model of expertise* (cf. [SWB93]). For describing the model of expertise in a formal way the formal and operational specification language KARL ([Ang93][Fen95][FAS97]) has been developed. KARL is based on first order logic and dynamic logic and offers language primitives for each of the three different layers of the model of expertise. The contexts of the structure model correspond to the domain-, task-, and inference layer of KADS' model of expertise.

The model of expertise finally includes all functional requirements of the desired system. For the realization of the final system, additional requirements have to be considered which are still independent of the final implementation of the system. These requirements are non-functional requirements such as efficiency of the problem-solving method, maintainability of the system, persistency of data etc. ([LaS95]). Capturing such decisions within the *design model* divides the gap between the model of expertise and the implementation of the final system. For the description of the design model the language KARL has been extended to the language DesignKARL [Lan94] which allows to describe data structures, algorithms and offers additional structuring primitives like clusters and modules.

2 Enterprise Modelling

2.1 Notation

It is generally accepted that for an operational description of a system three views are sufficient (see figure 1 taken from [RaV95]). These three perspectives have a more principal relationship to modelling: they are generally used to describe the kind of the modelled information (structure vs. dynamic), and therefore can not be used to identify useful views of an enter-

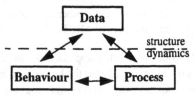

Fig. 1 . Model Perspectives

prise. For example dynamics can be identified in several parts of an enterprise and therefore also in several views (e.g. in the business processes and in the processes, that are executed in a software system). Although the level of abstraction is different in these two processes and they are probably modelled in different layers of an enterprise model, the same notation can be used for both. A notation for modelling an enterprise should fulfill the following objectives: it should be understandable and widely accepted, it should be useful for different types of software systems (e.g. information systems and knowledge based systems) and powerful enough to model all relevant aspects. At last it should bridge the gap between the user world and the developers world. OMT (Object Modelling Technique) (cf. [RBP+91]) has proved its usefulness in several areas: software system design, design of knowledge-based systems [ScW93] and enterprise modelling ([BKM94], [KKM95]). For these reasons we use OMT in our integration approach. The data constituent in figure 1 corresponds to the static object model of OMT, the behaviour constituent corresponds to the dynamic model and the process constituent corresponds to the functional model. So statecharts are used for the behaviour constituent and DFDs (dataflow diagrams) are used for the process constituent.

2.2 Views

2.2.1 Introduction to the Views

Models mostly have the objective to simplify complex realities by representing only aspects relevant for decisions or actions. Depending on the ensemble of aspects or objects of the reality which are observed, different views reflected by a model are distinguished. In the WORKS approach, nine different views are introduced. The selection and definition is on the one hand determined by the example of well-known views (e.g. in business administration) and on the other hand by the special aims and questions considered in WORKS.

For organisation modelling, the distinction between *organisation structure* and *organisation processes* is useful. In addition, for a work examination, people working in the organisation (*staff view*) and their working tools (*working tool view*) are relevant. The *data view* is a standard view of organisations, when the development of information systems is concerned. So to speak, data are working objects of information processing activities. Communication and cooperation play a special role under criteria of task design (e.g. task splitting between human and computer [Dan93]) and are therefore treated as a particular view (*communication and cooperation view*).

The *expertise view* is founded on the special focus of the WORKS approach on knowledge-based systems. It is the adoption of a standard modelling concept (MIKE or CommonKADS [SWH+94]). In connection with this, the usable knowledge sources (*source view*) are interesting for the purpose of knowledge acquisition. Transverse to the former views, so to say, the *strong points'-/deficient points' view* is located, in which valuing statements concerning organisational, technical and work engineering matters are collected ([DuV92], [DaF92]) . The last view is not further considered in this paper, because its contents is largely informal (e.g. natural text). In the next sections some of the views are introduced in more detail.

2.2.2 The Data View

The data view (figure 7 part b) is essentially a model of the static object model of OMT: Data can be grouped by relations. Special relations are specialisation, aggregation and associations. Both can be enriched by attributes. In applications a much more enriched reference scheme may be required, but it is straightforward to construct one out of these modelling primitives.

2.2.3 The Process View

The process view (see figure 7 part a) is the heart of an enterprise model: it describes the dynamic aspects of an organisation with two main constituents: "process" and "task". The overall modelling activity starts by modelling the business goals. These business goals have to be achieved by business processes [SWH+94]: a process results in a task decomposition of the original goal and the definition of the control flow and the data flow between the subtasks. The subtasks (defined by the business process) can either be business tasks or job tasks etc. We define three levels of processes, which we want to distinguish for enterprise modelling: the business level, the job level, and the job part level, but each of these levels can have an arbitrary depth (on the other hand the process view of an enterprise should not be too detailed, but focus on relevant aspects). The business level deals with processes related to several departments, the job level with rather small processes usually done in one department, and the job part level with processes done by one person to achieve a particular goal. To achieve an integrated modelling technique we use the dynamic and the functional model notation of OMT to describe the data flow and the control flow of a process, i.e. DFDs (dataflow diagrams) and statecharts. By this we adopted the approach of [BKM94]: by an unconventional use of notation the task decomposition is modelled with the object view of OMT. The modelled "subtask classes" are used as processes in the dynamic model description (the control flow).

2.2.4 Organisational Structure View

The organisational structure view is intended to capture the static organisational aspects of an enterprise. The first thing to model is the structure of the organisational units. Therefore we model a decomposition of the organisational unit class into smaller organisational units. Another relation exists between organisational units and jobs or collection of jobs. A job is also related to a

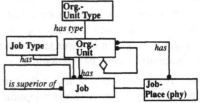

Fig. 2 . Organisational Structure View

collection of tasks, which is a connection from the organisational structure view to the process view. An organisational unit is also related to a set of tasks (modelled in the process view) which it fulfills. Further we want to differentiate between jobs and job places, because both are important to take into account for human needs (and possible problems to solve). To allow statements about larger enterprises the job type and organisation unit type class are used to allow statements about collections of objects.

2.2.5 Staff View

The staff view allows us to incorporate a human centric view into the modelling process. This covers several aspects: e.g. the engineering of human centric business processes as well as the design of ergonomic software products. For this purpose the two classes "Role" and

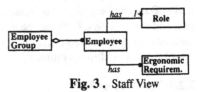

Fig. 3 . Staff View

"Ergonomic Requirements" were defined. Role objects capture the relation between employees and the jobs. In some modelling approaches the "staff view" and the "working tool view" are mixed together into a "resource view". This is not an appropriate choice: modelling should always be done with requirements of the staff in mind. Processes and information systems have to be designed explicitly to conform with human ergonomic requirements.

2.2.6 Working Tool View

The working tool view allows to model dependencies between a task and a tool that is needed to perform it. To design business processes one should know the tools used in the process to detect e.g. media breaks. Therefore we need additional attributes to characterize working tools: type can be e.g. computer (in general), knowledge

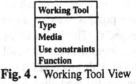

Fig. 4 . Working Tool View

based system (more specific) or a type writer. The attribute "media" says something about the media used in or with that tool, e.g. electronic documents (for a computer system). So there exists a link from the "Working Tool" to the data view. With the attribute "use constraints" restrictions of the working tool can be expressed: e.g. a computer system is not usable during system maintenance. The function attribute should give information about the role of the working tool in the business processes, e.g. give answers to the following questions: Is it essential? For which tasks is the tool usable?

2.2.7 Expertise View

The expertise view (figure 7 part c) is oriented towards the structure model of MIKE and the model of expertise in CommonKADS [SWH+94]: A task is solved by a problem solving method, which needs domain knowledge. The problem solving method defines a task decomposition ("divide and conquer") of the original task and the data - resp. the control flow of these subtasks. The expertise view is a special view: it is the only one, which contains all different model views (cf. figure 1). This is due to the fact, that it represents a complete description of a knowledge based system. So all the other views realize only the frame of the expertise view. The expertise view is of course generally much more complex - however, the integrational approach is very much the same, even in more complicated situations. More advanced techniques for modelling problem solving methods (e.g. ontology mappings [SEG+96]) are not considered in the basic approach.

2.2.8 Source View

The aim of the source view (figure 5) is to provide a possibility to model relevant sources for the knowledge elicitation process. Therefore it is one of the model constituents, that are necessary for the development of a knowledge based system. It supports the planning of the knowledge elicitation

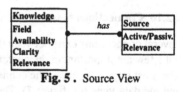

Fig. 5 . Source View

process, where e.g. different staff members have to be interviewed. Therefore, we distinguish between sources of the knowledge and the knowledge itself. Sources can be e.g. employees (which are active) but also books, which are passive. After taking the decision, what knowledge is relevant for a business process improvement, it can be determined which knowledge should be elicited and modelled and what sources are relevant for that knowledge. The knowledge can be further classified: Which field does it belong to? Is it directly available and clear (how much effort has the knowledge engineer to put into the elicitation)? The answers to these questions can be modelled using the different attributes.

2.2.9 Communication/Cooperation View

For the development of an information system as well as for a knowledge based system it is important to know, at which point in the work the employee needs additional information to perform his task. The design of the communication/cooperation view is similar to known techniques of describing human/computer interaction (interaction diagrams) [RBP+91]. The communication/cooperation

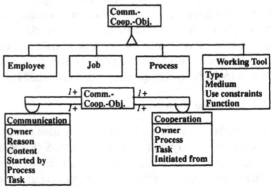

Fig. 6. Communication/Cooperation View

objects can be instances of the classes employee, job, process, working tool, i.e. these are the objects, that can communicate/cooperate with each other. This provides the possibility of several levels of detail for modelling. The lower part of the diagram defines a relation and corresponds to a simple link between two of these objects: the link is annotated with attributes, which make assertions about the owner, the contents etc. of the communication/cooperation. If two persons communicate/cooperate with each other, they do this usually within a task. To model the information flow, this task/process dependency can be noted in an attribute.

2.2.10 Connections between the Views

Several connections exist between these views: most of them are standard connections, but a few are important in the context of the development of knowledge based systems. The most important one is the connection between the process view, the expertise view and the data view (cf. figure 7). The point, where a knowledge based system can support an employee is at the job part task level. At this level an employee works on a closed task, where mainly his knowledge determines how to solve the task. This is the point, where a knowledge based system may come into the game. The tasks performed by problem solving methods are just subtasks of the task the employee perfoms.

Another important link is the connection between the data view and the domain layer in the expertise view: an employee (the expert) does his job in the context of the enterprise, especially in the context of its data. So the input-output of his problem solving behaviour consists mostly of data elements of the data view. Therefore the domain layer of the expertise view has a nonempty intersection with the data view of the enterprise. To perform the knowledge elicitation task the links between the working tool view, the staff view, and the source view are important. These deliver the information, which persons have to be interviewed.

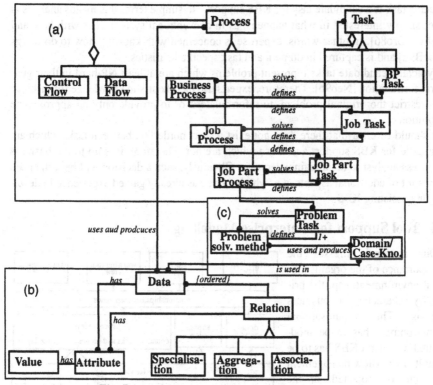

Fig. 7 . Core Relations between (a) Process View,
(b) Data View and (c) Expertise View

3 Knowledge Based Systems and Organisation Modelling

Having developed a framework for modelling business processes in general and for embedding them into an organisational environment the question arises which part of a business process could or should be handled by an assisting KBS and not for instance by an information system. Due to the nature of a KBS there does not exist a complete checklist for answering that question. Nevertheless, a few characteristics may be identified: In our framework (the process view) part of a job task is amenable to such an assistance by a KBS. I.e. we do not envision that a complete business process is supported by a KBS. Rather, a task which is handled by a single person or few cooperating persons is a candidate task.

If there exists a completely formal model for specifying the task and for computing a corresponding solution, for instance an optimization model as known from operations research, there is typically no need for a KBS approach. Instead, a KBS approach is advised "when we do not have overt domain and problem solving models" [ShG92].

If domain and task specific problem solving knowledge, which "encodes" the experience of an expert, is needed in order to be able to solve the task in an efficient manner, such a task is a candidate task for KBS support. "In simple terms this means analysis is not simply interested in what happens, as in conventional systems, but with how and why" [Bro86]. In other words, expertise is concerned with knowing how to do things [ScB96] and is captured in domain and task specific heuristics.

Typically, candidate tasks represent problems which are at least NP-hard in their general formulation [Neb96]. Therefore, experts use their heuristic knowledge for instance to restrict the original problem, to reformulate it or to provide only an approximate solution.

It should be clear that there does not exist a strict borderline between tasks which are suitable for KBS support and those which are not. Therefore, it is up to the business process analyst to make a final decision. Obviously, such a decision will be influenced by a lot of additional aspects, e.g. whether one has already gained experience in developing assisting KBS.

4 Tool Support for Enterprise Modelling

Our approach stresses the importance of the organisational environment, esp. the primary character of business goals. This organisational environment has to be modelled whether a KBS has to be built, a workflow management system is projected, or the business processes are reorganized in any other way. The construction of the above

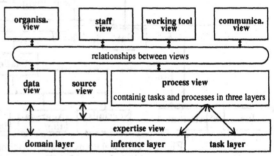

Fig. 8 . Architecture of the Views in a Tool

described views should be supported by an appropriate tool. This claim is realized for example by the ARIS-Toolset [Sch94]. The ARIS model contains slightly different views and concepts and thus the tool set as well. But in principle this tool set can be used to develop an enterprise model which serves as the base for the decision whether to build a KBS or any other means of reorganisation. ARIS is not specifically headed towards building KBSs: it does not support the modelling of the expertise view.

Therefore we extend our MIKE-Tool, which then contains mainly three different sets of views. The first view is the so called elicitation model (not contained in figure 8). The second subset consists of those views which serve to model the environment, i.e the organisational view, the staff view, the working tool view, the communication/ cooperation view, the data view, the source view, and mainly the process view. All these views are interrelated by several relationships (as outlined in figure 8). The third subset consists of the expertise view, which is decomposed into three different layer (domain layer, inference layer, and task layer). The two sets are connected mainly via the process view, the data view, and the source view. So this tool describes business processes and tasks and relates them to problem solving methods and tasks of the expertise view and the data of the enterprise as part of the domain layer of the model of expertise resp. Following MIKE's philosophy of modelling, also for the enterprise views an elicitation has to take place: the result of this elicitation consists of natural language protocols, images or sound files. The techniques, that MIKE offers for constructing the structure model, can also be used to construct the semiformal enterprise views: The informal protocols are structured and interpreted to constitute the different views. These views are linked to one another by defining relationships between related entities. Furthermore a certain kind of link (*elicitation link* [Neu94]) is established automatically between the protocols and the structured information. Thus everything that is modelled can be traced back to the protocols and thus is put into the correct context. By that inconsistencies and failures during modelling can be found and the communication between the modeller (knowledge engineer) and the information provider (expert) becomes easier.

The business modelling process was started because certain problems arose which obstructed business goals. The areas surrounding these problems and goals should be modelled in more detail than other (possibly less relevant) areas. If a relatively stable state is reached a decision must be made which states how to solve these problems. If the decision yields constructing a KBS then the second subset of views becomes relevant. Further information must be elicited to model problem solving behaviour, so further protocols are produced which complete the input for the expertise view. Now MIKE's structure model is defined. This is done by identifying entities relevant both in the expertise view and in the business views and linking them. Also all elicited protocols may contain relevant information for defining a problem solving process. Largely this process resembles the regular specification process in MIKE, i.e. informal information (from protocols) is interpreted and structured to yield a semi-formal model. The main difference lies in the fact that also semi-formally modelled information contained in "outside" models (i.e. the business views) has to be considered in the structuring process. In that way the higher level business views are closely connected with the structure model in the expertise view. The next step of modelling in MIKE consists or formalizing the semi formal structure model to constitute the formal model of expertise specified in the language KARL. This specification can be tested because KARL is an operational language so that the KBS may be evaluated (in the business setting) by prototyping.

5 An Example Model

5.1 Introduction

To illustrate the ideas we present an example model using the primitives of OMT. The example was derived during the WORKS project. The aim of the project was to build a KBS to support industrial designers concerning ergonomic questions. However, in the course of the project it turned out that "just" a KBS is not enough: large portions of knowledge can only be represented informally, knowledge is built through lessons learned and case studies, and many process steps in the design process have to be supported. Therefore we are aiming now for a knowledge management system, incorporating many techniques. For the requirements elicitation of this system the process of industrial design was modelled and analysed for support needs in some design companies. Parametric design problem solving (see [MoZ96]) was found as one possibility to support the design process. In the following we present a simplified version of these process models and show, how a specific problem solving method (modelled in the expertise view) is integrated into the whole design process. We elicitated several views, but due to the lack of space (and because the modelled companies were rather small), we only present the core views (data, process and expertise view).

5.2 The Data View

During the design process several documents are created or used (cf. figure 9), e.g. a briefing document delivered by the customer specifying initial requirements for the design object, general information about similar products or usable components in the design task, a design object description where e.g. drawings or the component architecture is defined and elaborated. Physical models of the design are created and tested against the requirements. The documents created in the design task have usually a special structure. This structure can be made explicit.

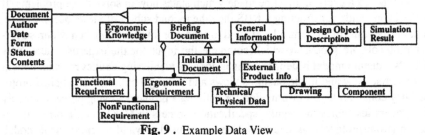

Fig. 9 . Example Data View

5.3 The Process View

The design process modelled in figure 10 is usually performed by one person, so it is located on the job part level (figure 7). The task "design process" is decomposed into seven subtasks. To elaborate the process model we have to define the control flow (by statecharts) and the dataflow between the subtasks. One subtask is viewed as a state of the overall task "design". Events in the statechart (depicted with the arrows) specify when the task performs a state transition from one state to another (see figure 10 part 2). Dataflow diagrams as used here resemble KADS' inference structures (cf. [ScW93]) and use the data view for defining the concepts of the dataflow.

5.4 The Expertise View

The simplified design process presented above shows several opportunities for computer based support, e.g. document management, organisational memory, CAD, etc. We focus now on a knowledge based system aiming at supporting the "Technical & Functional Elaboration" step of the design process. At this step of the design process most components, possible assignments for the components, constraints and requirements are known. This configuration leads directly to problem solving methods for parametric design ([MoZ96]). We integrate the first decomposition level of the problem solving method "CMR" (complete model then revise) into the design process (cf. figure 11). At this decomposition level the PSM is rather simple. However, it is useful

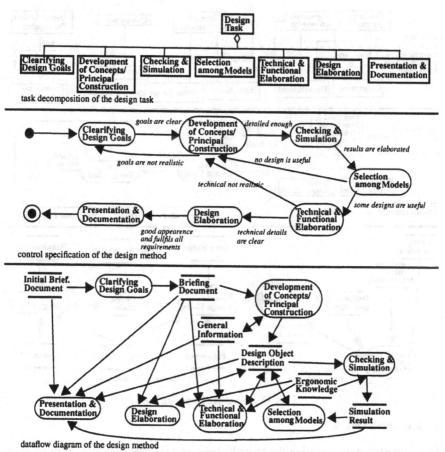

Fig. 10. Example Process View

for demonstrating the integration of PSMs into an business process and it is simple to extend this CMR version to a full fledged PSM. We first deal with the data view and the domain/case knowledge. We have chosen different concepts, so we have to introduce a mapping association between the concepts of the data view and the concepts of the domain/case knowledge. The mapping association has to perform an ontology mapping between the two different levels.

The task decomposition of the step "Technical & Functional Elaboration" is just the two steps of the PSM CMR: complete design model and revise design model. So in the statechart the two subtasks can be viewed as substates of the "Technical & Functional Elaboration" state.

In the dataflow diagram the dataflow in the expertise view is just a refinement of the dataflow in the process view. The mapping association performs the mapping of the documents of the overall task to concepts usable for the PSM: For every data store in the right dataflow diagram there has to be at least one corresponding (through a mapping association) data store in the left dataflow diagram.

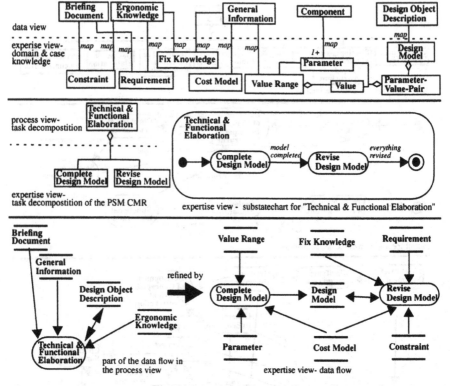

Fig. 11 . Example Expertise View

6 Related Work

The importance of capturing the characteristics of the workplace context in which a KBS should be used is stressed in [VaM94]. This approach proposes a so-called workplace ontology to describe among others the organizational embedding of the system, available resources, and expected problems. However, in contrast to our approach, there does not exist an explicit model of the workflow the KBS is embedded in. I.e. the proposal of Vanwelkenhuysen and Mizoguchi is representing static aspects of a workplace, whereas our approach also takes into account the dynamic aspects of a workplace context.

Another widespread modelling approach (including tool support) suitable for comparison is ARIS ("Architektur integrierter Informationssysteme", integrated information systems architecture [Sch94]). The architecture or basic orientation frame of MIKE and ARIS is given by two dimensions orthogonal to each other. In one dimension, both approaches distinguish distinct *views* on the object worlds to be modelled. The dimension 'degree of formalisation' in MIKE (informal, semiformal, formal) corresponds to the dimension of *levels* in ARIS (application level, data processing concept level, implementation level). Both dimensions refer to increasing formalisation or data processing orientation, respectively. However, ARIS does not consider informal models, so a reference from the semiformal models of the application level to respective primary inquiry information cannot be realised. Relevant modelling aspects for MIKE that are not supported by ARIS are for example the modelling of knowledge (expertise view), qualification profiles of employee groups (staff view), the distribution of tasks (cooperation view), and the communication (communication view) between human and computer.

The reference scheme of [RaV95] is similar to ours: they define a reference scheme with a non standard notation for business modelling and show an operationalisation with high level petri nets. We, however, focus on the standard notation OMT and especially the interface between knowledge engineering (esp. problem solving methods) and business process modelling.

In [KiB94] the notion of an Enterprise Model is introduced. Such an Enterprise Model is composed of several submodels: objectives model, activities and usage model, actors model, concept model, and information systems requirements model. In that way, the Enterprise Model aims at capturing all aspects which are relevant when developing an information system in a business context, i.e. it defines a meta-level framework which specifies the type of knowledge which has to be modelled within each of the submodels. We can interpret our approach as a concrete instance of such a meta-model, i.e. as a proposal of how to represent such submodels and their relationships.

A meta-model approach for modelling business processes is described in [JJP+96]. Jarke et al. propose the definition of a language meta model which can be used to describe different views on business processes. Their proposal for a meta language aims at modelling quality-oriented business processes and puts emphasis a.o. on supporting the negotiation process which is needed to achieve coherent views. On the other hand, their approach does not consider the development of a KBS and does not pay much attention to the persons working in an organisation.

The Brahms-Framework (cf. [CSS+96]) is oriented towards the informal modelling of scenarios in a situated way: every activity of an employee is collected and described in a so called workframe. A workframe contains a semiformal description of an activity which can be further analysed. Also Brahms' models are somewhere between cognitive models and business process models regarded to the level of detail. The main differences to our approach is that we don't focus on informal aspects of an enterprise: instead we model several views of an enterprise aiming at a smooth transition from business process models to problem solving methods using a standard graphical notation from software engineering. Also Brahms is not especially directed to the development of KBS.

The organisation model of CommonKADS [HBM+96] is oriented towards knowledge engineering. The organisation model is constructed when a project has been set up for building a KBS. This is in contrast to our approach which considers the development of a KBS just as one alternative for achieving a business goal. Furthermore CommonKADS does not support graphical modelling in a unified modelling language:

e.g. the process constituent is not very elaborated: no description method is provided to allow a modelling of business processes and to link them explicitly with the model of expertise.

It is not very surprising, that the entities and concepts dealt with in other modelling approaches are very similar to ours. It would be very surprising, if this would not be the case. However, none of the approaches has paid attention to the following: integration of the development of knowledge based systems in a business process reengineering methodology for enterprises. We achieved this by defining a common model for enterprise modelling [DES96], defining a reference scheme usable for many different problems and proposing a common modelling language for the reference scheme, which is usable in enterprise modelling, software engineering and knowledge engineering.

7 Conclusion and Future Work

We defined an enterprise meta model and showed, how it is connected to model-based knowledge engineering: as mentioned above, by using the MIKE approach to model the business views as well, the modelling of the KBS is tightly connected with business modelling. In that way relevant information can be extracted from according views. It is already structured and serves as a reference because of the links established from the model of expertise to the process and data view and to all the other business views. Thus traceability of information or requirements is highly supported by this integration of BPM and KBS development.

The generic process model of [DES96] does not state explicitly how solutions to business problems should look like. These solutions could consist of a KBS, an information system, a workflow engine or any other means of business functions. In this aspect the MIKE approach can be useful in a more generic way: although it is oriented towards building KBS, parts of it can be used as well for developing other kinds of software, i.e. MIKE could be viewed as the basis for a general requirements modelling and system specification method for knowledge management systems.

8 References

[Ang93] J. Angele: Operationalisierung des Modells der Expertise mit KARL (Operationalization of the Model of Expertise with KARL), Ph.D. Theses in Artificial Intelligence, No. 53 , infix, St. Augustin, 1993.

[AFS96] J. Angele, D. Fensel, and R. Studer: Domain and Task Modeling in MIKE. In: Proceedings of the IFIP WG 8.1/ 13.2 Joint Working Conference, Domain Knowledge for Interactive System Design, Geneva, May 1996.

[BKM94] B.M. Bauer, C. Kohl, H.C. Mayr, J. Wassermann: Enterprise Modeling using OOA Techniques,In: Proceedings Connectivity '94: Workflow Management - Challenges, Paradigms and Products. München: R. Oldenbourg-Verlag, 1994, pp. 96-111.

[Bro86] A.G. Brooking: The Analysis Phase in Development of Knowledge-Based Systems. In: A. Gale (ed.): AI and Statistics. Addison-Wesley Publ. Co., 1986.

[CSS+96] W. J. Clancey, P. Sachs, M. Sierhuis, R. van Hoff: Brahms: Simulating Practice for Work Systems Design, Proceedings of PKAW'96.

[DaF92] M. Daniel, G. Fieguth: Möglichkeiten der kontrastiven Aufgabenanalyse auf die Entwicklung wissensbasierter Systeme. Forschungsbericht, ibek GmbH, Karlsruhe 1992

[Dan93] M. Daniel: Formen der Unterstützung von Diagnosetätigkeiten, ibek GmbH, Karlsruhe 1993

[DES96] S. Decker, M. Erdmann, R. Studer: A Unifying View on Business Process Modelling and Knowledge Engineering. In: Proceedings of the 10th Knowledge Aquisition Workshop (KAW 96), Banff, Canada, November 1996.

[DuV92]   H. Dunckel et. al: Kontrastive Aufgabenanalyse. Das KABA-Verfahren. Verlag der Fachvereine, Zürich 1992.

[Fen95]   D. Fensel: The Knowledge Acquisition and Representation Language KARL, Ph. D. Thesis, University of Karlsruhe, 1993. Kluwer Academic Publisher, Boston, 1995.

[FAS97]   D. Fensel, J. Angele, R. Studer: The Knowledge Acqusition und Representation Language KARL. to appear in IEEE Trans. on Knowledge and Data Engineering, 1997

[HBM+96] R. de Hoog, B. Benus, M. Vogler, C. Metselaar: The CommonKADS Organisation Model: Content, Usage and Computer Support. In: Journal of Expert Systems with Applications, Vol.11, No. 1, pp.29-40, 1996

[JJP+96] M. Jarke, M.A. Jeusfeld, P. Peters, and K. Pohl: Coordinating Distributed Organizational Knowledge. To appear in: Data & Knowledge Engineering, 1997

[KJO+95] H. Kangassalo, H. Jaakkola, S. Ohsuga, B. Wangler (eds): Information Modelling and Knowledge Bases VI, IOS Press, 1995

[KKM95]   R. Kaschek, C. Kohl, H. C. Mayr: Cooperations - An Abstraction Concept Suitable for Business Process Re-Engineering. In: J. Györkös, M. Krisper, H.C. Mayr (eds.): ReTIS'95 - Re-Technologies for Information Systems. OCG Lecture Notes 80, Oldenbourg, 1995.

[KiB94]   M. Kirikova and J.A. Bubenko: Software Requirements Acquisition through Enterprise Modeling. In: Proc. 6th Int. Conf. on Software Engineering and Knowledge Engineering (SEKE'94), Jurmala, 1994.

[Lan94]   D. Landes: DesignKARL - A language for the design of knowledge-based systems. In: Proc. 6th International Conference on Software Engineering and Knowledge Engineering SEKE'94, Jurmala, Lettland, 1994, 78-85.

[LaS95]   D. Landes and R. Studer: The Treatment of Non-Functional Requirements in MIKE. In Wilhelm Schäfer, Pere Botella (eds.): Proceedings of the 5th European Software Engineering Conference ESEC'95 (Sitges, Spain, September 25 - 28, 1995), Berlin, Springer 1995 (Lecture Notes in Computer Science; 989).

[MoZ96]   E. Motta, Z. Zdrahal: Parametric Design Problem Solving. In: Proceedings of the 10th Knowledge Aquisition Workshop (KAW 96), Banff, Canada, November 1996.

[Neu93]   S. Neubert: Model construction in MIKE (Model-based and Incremental Knowledge Engineering). In: N. Aussenac et.al. (eds): Proceedings of the 7th European Workshop EKAW'93 (Toulouse), LNAI 723, Springer-Verlag, Berlin, 1993.

[Neu94]   S. Neubert: Modellkonstruktion in MIKE - Methoden und Werkzeuge. Ph.D. Thesis in Artificial Intelligence, No. 60, infix, St. Augustin, 1994 (in German).

[Neb96]   B. Nebel, Artificial Intelligence: A Computational Perspective. In: G. Brewka (ed.): Essentials in Knowledge Representation. Studies in Logic, Language and Information, CSLI Publications, pp. 237-266, 1996

[RaV95]   G.J. Ramackers, A.A. Verrijn-Stuart: Conceptual Model Requirements for Integrated Business and Information System Development. In:[KJO+95], pp.: 197-213

[RBP+91] J. Rumbaugh, M. Blaha, W. Premerlani, F. Eddy, W. Lorensen: Object-Oriented Modeling and Design. Prentice Hall, Englewood Cliffs 1991.

[Sch94]   A.-W. Scheer: Business Process Engineering: Reference Models for Industrial Enterprises, Springer, 2nd ed. 1994.

[ScB96]   A.Th. Schreiber and B. Birmingham (eds.): International Journal of Human-Computer Studies (IJHCS), Special Issue: The Sisyphus-VT Initiative, 1996.

[ShG92]   M.G. Shaw and B.R. Gaines: The Synthesis of Knowledge Engineering and Software Engineering. In: P. Loucopoulos (ed.): Advanced Information Systems Engineering, LNCS 593, Springer Verlag, 1992.

[SWB93]   G. Schreiber, B. Wielinga, and J. Breuker (eds.): KADS. A Principled Approach to Knowledge-Based System Development, Knowledge-Based Systems, vol 11, Academic Press, London, 1993.

[ScW93]   G. Schreiber, B. Wielinga: Model Construction. In [SWB93], pp 93-118..

[ScW93]   G. Schreiber, B.J. Wielinga: KADS and Conventional Software Engineering. In: KADS - A Principled Approach To Knowledge Based System Development, Academic Press, 1993

[SWH+94] A.Th. Schreiber, B.J. Wielinga, R. de Hoog, H. Akkermans, and W. van de Velde: CommonKADS: A Comprehensive Methodology for KBS Development. In: IEEE Expert, December 1994, 28-37.

[SEG+96] R. Studer, H. Eriksson, J. Gennari, S. Tu, D. Fensel, M. Musen: Ontologies and the Configuration of Problem-Solving Methods. In: Proceedings of the 10th Knowledge Aquisition Workshop (KAW 96), Banff, Canada, November 1996.

[VaM94]   J. Vanwelkenhuysen and R. Mizoguchi: Maintaining the Workplace Context in a Knowledge Level Analysis. In: Proc. 3rd Japanese Knowledge Acquisition for Knowledge-Based Systems Workshop(JKAW'94), Hatoyama, 1994

The Tower-of-Adapters Method for Developing and Reusing Problem-Solving Methods

Dieter Fensel

University of Karlsruhe, Institute AIFB, 76128 Karlsruhe, Germany.
fensel@aifb.uni-karlsruhe.de, http://www.aifb.uni-karlsruhe.de/WBS/dfe

Abstract. The paper provides three novel contributions to knowledge engineering. First, we provide a structured approach for the development and adaptation of problem-solving methods. We start from very generic search strategies with weak data structures and add adapters that refine the states and state transitions of the search process and that add assumptions necessary to link the competence of a method with given problem definitions and domain knowledge. Second, we show how the usability-reusability trade-off of task-specific versus task-independent problem-solving methods can easily be overcome by the *virtual* existence of specific methods. Third, we provide the concept of an integrated library combining reusable problem definitions, problem-solving methods, and adapters.

1   Introduction

Problem-solving methods (PSMs) are used by most of the current knowledge-engineering frameworks (e.g. Generic Tasks [Chandrasekaran et al., 1992]; Configurable Role-Limiting Methods [Puppe, 1993]; CommonKADS [Schreiber et al., 1994]; the Method-To-Task approach [Eriksson et al., 1995]; Components of Expertise [Steels, 1990]; GDM [Terpstra et al., 1993]; MIKE [Angele et al., 1996]). Libraries of PSMs are described in [Benjamins, 1995], [Breuker & Van de Velde, 1994], [Chandrasekaran et al., 1992], [Motta & Zdrahal, 1996], and [Puppe, 1993]. Despite the strong agreement on the usefulness of PSMs and the large body of documented PSMs there is still a lack of clear methodological support in developing PSMs and in (re-)using them. Recent work [Akkermans et al., 1993], [Fensel, 1995], [Wielinga et al., 1995], [Benjamins & Pierret-Golbreich, 1996], [Benjamins et al., 1996], [Fensel & Benjamins, 1996], [Fensel et al., 1996], [Fensel & Straatman, 1996], [Motta & Zdrahal, 1996], [Fensel & Schönegge, 1997a], [ten Teije, 1997], and [Breuker, 1997] provide in-depth analysis of the essence and main rationales of some PSMs. Some of these papers also outline general steps that have to be taken in developing PSMs. However, it still remains rather unclear how to develop PSMs, how to adapt PSMs to given problems and domain-specific circumstances and how to select PSMs from a library, i.e. how to organise such a library.

Our contribution is concerned with these three problems. We show a principled way of developing and adapting PSMs and provide a new way of organising a library of PSMs to support their reuse. This is mainly achieved by using *adapters* as a means of expressing the refinement of PSMs. Adapters were originally introduced in [Fensel & Groenboom, 1997] to allow the independent specifications of problem definitions[1],

PSMs, and domain knowledge. Building knowledge-based systems from reusable elements requires adapters that properly link these elements and adapt them to the application-specific circumstances. Because these elements should be reusable, they must abstract from application-specific circumstances and because they are specified independently from each other there is a need to introduce their mappings. Originally intended as glue that brings other elements together, we will give adapters a much more prominent role during this paper. They will play a central role in refining PSMs. Actually, a refined version of a PSMs is achieved by combining it with an adapter.

The stepwise introduction of adapters can be used to stepwise refine generic PSMs. This process can be used to *develop* and to *adapt* PSMs. More specifically, three processes are supported by our approach:

- the terminological structure of the states of a method can be refined by introducing ontological commitments;
- the refined terminological structure in describing states can be used to refine state transitions of a method; and
- assumptions can be introduced to link the competence of a method with problem definitions and domain knowledge.

This also leads to a entirely new organisation of a unified library providing problem definitions, PSMs and assumptions organised at different levels of refinement.

The technical machinery for specifying and verifying our examples is provided by the KIV approach (Karlsruhe Interactive Verifier) [Reif, 1995]. In KIV, the entire specification of a system can be split into smaller and more tractable pieces to support understandability and reuse of the different parts. Each *elementary specification* introduces a signature and a set of axioms. The semantics of such a specification is the isomorphic class of all algebras that satisfy the first-order axioms and that are generated by the operations indicated in the generation clauses (i.e., *loose* semantics is applied [Wirsing, 1990]). In addition to (elementary) specifications, KIV provides *module* to describe implementations in a Pascal-like style. A module defines a collection of procedures provided in an export specification. Internally, the module describes the algorithmic realization of these procedures. A more detailed discussions of KIV and most of the proofs our examples rely on are given in [Fensel & Schönegge, 1997b], [Fensel & Schönegge, 1997a].

The content of the paper is organised as follows. In section 2, we discuss the problem-specific refinement of methods. First, we present the specification of the incomplete search strategy hill-climbing, a common search strategy for local optima. Then we add an adapter that transforms the method into a method specialized on minimizing sets. Here, the search strategy remains the same but the ontological commitments of the methods become refined. States and state transitions are described with an enriched vocabulary. A further adapter transforms this method into a method for abductive diagnosis (by adding additional ontological requirements). Besides adding ontological

---

1. We used originally the term *task* definition. However our task definitions define only goals and requirements and not a way to achieve a goal. Therefore, the term *problem* definition is more appropriate, see [Breuker, 1997].

commitments, it is necessary to add assumptions to close the gap between a method and a problem. In section 3 it is shown how these methods that search for a local optimum can be applied to problems that define a global optimum and how this leads to a refinement of problem definitions and assumptions similar to the refinement of PSMs. We draw conclusions on how to organise a unified library of methods, problem definitions and assumptions. Finally, section 4 provides conclusions, related work and outlines possible directions of future work.

2   Refining Problem-Solving Methods

We start by describing the development process of PSMs with a very generic search schema. During the following sections this schema will become refined to more concrete control of the search process and the states it searches through. However, we do not make a commitment to this top-down like development process. The process can start at any level and can take the direction of specialization or generalization because we provide a library containing these generic schemas and their adaptations. *Specialization* is achieved by adding an adapter to an existing PSM-adapter combination and *generalization* is achieved by deleting an adapter from an existing PSM-adapter combination.

[Smith & Lowry, 1990] present a theory of search algorithms to support the transformation of problem definitions into implementations. Fig. 1 shows their hierarchy of search methods providing local search as an instance of generate&test-like approaches working on local structures. The general algorithmic structure of a

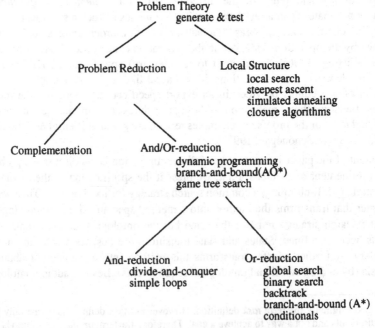

Fig. 1   Refinement hierarchy of algorithm theories.

local search strategy can be described by an initialization and a recursion (see Fig. 2). Unlike to all other PSMs that will be discussed in this paper we cannot prove termination of this general algorithmic structure. Therefore, we do not regard it is a PSMs. Instead it is a starting point for deriving PSMs via refinement.[2]

2.1 Hill Climbing

A local search strategy is necessarily incomplete because it checks only a subset of the transitive closure of the successor relationship of an initial node. Fig. 3 provides a refined specification of a local search algorithm by introducing competence, control, inferences and the knowledge requirements of hill-climbing. It can be used to find a local optimum of a set of elements. The proof that the specified algorithm terminates and has the competence as defined is given in [Fensel & Schönegge, 1997a]. The specification of hill climbing will be the backbone of all our examples during the paper. All other refined versions will be achieved by combining hill climbing with adapters.

Hill climbing refines the generic local search strategy to an algorithm (1) for which termination can be proven and (2) the competence of the method being defined in terms of a preference and a successor relation. The output is a local optimal element in the sense that it does not have a successor that is preferred. However this method is very generic and can be applied to nearly any type of task with a successor relationship (a local search structure) and a preference relation. In the next step we will specialize this method to a method for minimizing sets. We will see that the preference relation need not to be defined explicitly. It can also be provided implicitly by ontological commitments used to characterize states and state transitions of the method.

2.2 Set Minimizer

[Fensel & Schönegge, 1997b] present a method called set minimizer that can be used to find a minimal but still correct subset of a given set. The specification of this method is provided in Fig. 4. Its only requirement is that the original set is correct. It returns a correct set which is locally minimal in the sense that there is no correct subset that has

```
                        Local search
current := select-start(input); output := local search(current)
local search(X)
    begin
        successors := generate(X);
        new := select-successors(X,successors)
        if goal(X,new)
            then    output := X
            else    recursion(new)
        endif
    end
```

Fig. 2 The specification of local search.

---

2. What we can prove is that if it terminates its output fulfils its goal.

Problem-solving method Hill climbing

competence

    output ∈ input

    $\exists x$. $(x \in input \land select\text{-}criterion(x ,input) \land (x < output \lor x = output))$

    $\neg \exists x$. $(successor(output,x) \land x \in input \land output < x)$

control

    hill-climbing(input)

        begin

            current := select-start(input);

            output := recursion(current)

        end

    recursion(X)

        begin

            successors := generate(X);

            new := select-successors(X,successors)

            if *goal(X,new)*

                then *output := X*

                else *recursion(new)*

            endif

        end

inference actions

    select-start

        /* select-start must select an element of input and uses a selection criterion. */

        select-start(x) ∈ x ∧ select-start(x) ∈ select-criterion(select-start(x),x)

    generate

        /* generate selects input elements that are in successor relation with the current object.*/

        x ∈ generate(y) ↔ x ∈ input ∧ successor(y,x)

    select-a-best

        /* select-successors selects the current object if no better successors exist or a successor if a better successor exists. In the latter case the selected successor must be better than the current object and there need not to be another successor that is better than the selected successor. */

        $\neg \exists z$. $(z \in \{y\} \cup y' \land select\text{-}successors(y,y') < z)$

        $\neg \exists z$. $(z \in y' \land y < z) \rightarrow select\text{-}successors(y,y') = y$

        $\exists z$. $(z \in y' \land y < z) \rightarrow select\text{-}successors(y,y') \in y' \land y < select\text{-}successors(y,y'))$

    goal

        goal(x,y) ↔ x = y

requirements

    input requirement

        $\exists x$. $(x \in input \land x \in select\text{-}criterion)$

    knowledge requirement

        $\neg(x < x)$

        $x < y \land y < z \rightarrow x < z$

Fig. 3   The specification of hill-climbing.

one element less. This method is obviously a local search method specialized for a specific type of problems. Set minimizer refines hill climbing with the following refinements:

- A generic state of hill climbing is characterized as a set in set minimizer. That is, set minimizer adds additional ontological commitments used to characterize states of the search process.

- The successor relationship is hard-wired into set minimizer. A set is a successor of another set if it is a subset with one element less. The ontological commitment used to characterize states is used to refine the definition of state transitions.

- A preference on entities is only defined implicitly. Smaller sets are preferred if they are still correct.

Set minimizer describes only one of several possible problem-specific adaptations of hill climbing. Traditionally for each variant the specification has to be re-done, all termination and correctness proofs of the method have to be re-done, and the method has to be re-implemented. Our approach provides adapters as means to add the problem-specific refinement to hill-climbing, however keeping the adaptation separate. Therefore, the complete specifications, proofs, and implementations of hill-climbing can be reused. Only the problem-specific aspects have to be specified, proven and implemented by an adapter. Fig. 6 provides the definition of such an adapter. Its main proof obligations is to prove that the way the preference is defined fulfils the requirement on such a relation (cf. [Fensel & Schönegge, 1997b]).

By keeping the problem-specific refinement separate from the generic core of the

---

Problem-solving method Set minmizer
competence
   $output \subseteq input$,
   $correct(output)$,
   $x \in output \rightarrow \neg correct(output \setminus \{x\})$
control
   $output := set\text{-}minimizer(input)$
   $set\text{-}minimizer(X)$
      begin
         $successors := generate(X)$;
         if $\neg \exists x . (x \in successors \wedge correct(x))$
            then $output := X$
            else
               $new := select\text{-}successors(successors)$
               $set\text{-}minimizer(new)$
         endif
      end
inference actions
   generate
      /* *generate* creates subsets that contain one element less.*/
      $x \in generate(y) \leftrightarrow \exists z . (z \in y \wedge x = y \setminus \{z\})$
   select-successors
      /* A selected successor has to be correct. */
      $\exists x . (x \in y \wedge correct(x)) \rightarrow$
         $(correct(select\text{-}successors(y)) \wedge select\text{-}successors(y) \in y)$
input requirement
   $correct(input)$

Fig. 4   The specification of set minimizer.

method it is easy to overcome what was viewed as the *usability/reusability trade-off* of PSMs [Klinker et al., 1991]. The original version of hill-climbing can be reused for different problems requiring different kinds of refinement. The combination of hill-climbing and the set-minimizer adapter can be used for problems that can be expressed in terms of minimizing sets. While this combined version is less reusable, it is much more usable for cases it can be applied to. For achieving a problem-specific variant of a method it is not necessary to change the method itself. Instead, a problem-specific adapter is added. These adapters can also be piled up (stacked) to increase the problem specificity of methods. We will show this in the following section where we adapt set minimizer to abductive diagnosis.

2.3 Abductive Diagnosis

The task of abductive diagnosis receives a set of observations as input and delivers a complete and parsimonious explanation (see e.g. [Bylander et al., 1991]). An explanation is a set of hypotheses. A complete explanation must explain all input data (i.e., observations) and a parsimonious explanation must be minimal (that is, no subset of it has the same or a greater explanatory power). The goal of the task is such a complete and parsimonious explanation (see Fig. 5).

The problem-specific refinement of set-minimizer is straightforwards (Fig. 6). The set of all hypotheses is the set that must be minimized and correctness is defined in terms of completeness. However we have to introduce assumptions to ensure that the local-minimal-set found by set-minimizer is a complete and parsimonious explanation. First, we have to require that the input of the method is a complete explanation. Second, based on the adapter we can prove that our method set-minimizer finds a set that is parsimonious in the sense that each subset that contains one element less is not a complete explanation. However, we cannot guarantee that it is parsimonious in general. There may exist smaller subsets that are complete explanations. The adapter has to introduce a new requirement on domain knowledge or an assumption (in the case that it does not follow from the domain model) to guarantee that the competence of the PSM is strong enough to achieve the goal of the task. The *monotony assumption* (cf. Fig. 6) is sufficient and necessary [Fensel & Schönegge, 1997a] to prove that the (global) parsimonious of the output of the PSM follows from its local parsimoniality. It defines a natural subclass of abduction. For example [de Kleer, 1992] examine their role in model-based diagnosis. The assumption holds for applications, where no knowledge that constrains fault behaviour of devices is provided or where this knowledge respects the *limited-knowledge-of-abnormal behaviour assumption*. This is used by [de Kleer & Williams, 1987] as a *minimal diagnosis hypothesis* to reduce the average-case effort of finding all parsimonious and complete explanations with GDE.

Problem Abductive diagnosis
goal
    $goal(x) \leftrightarrow complete(x) \wedge parsimonious(x)$
    $complete(x) \leftrightarrow expl(x) = observables$
    $parsimonious(x) \leftrightarrow \neg \exists x'. (x' \subset x \wedge expl(x) \subseteq expl(x'))$

Fig. 5 The specification of abductive diagnosis.

PSM refinement adapter hill-climbing -> set-mimimizer
   /* The input set must be correct. */
     $correct(input)$
   /* select- start must select the input set. */
     $select\text{-}start(x) = \{x\}$
   /* Successors are subsets that contain one element less.*/
     $successor(x,y) \leftrightarrow \exists z . (z \in x \wedge y = x \setminus \{z\})$
   /* We prefer smaller sets if they are still correct. */
     $x < y \leftrightarrow correct(y) \wedge y \subset x$

PSM refinement adapter set-mimimizer -> abduction-method
   $correct(x) = complete(x);$
   $input = \{h \mid h \text{ is } hypothesis\};$

PSM refinement adapter abduction-method -> abductive diagnosis
   $H_1 \subseteq H_2 \rightarrow expl(H_1) \subseteq expl(H_2)$

Assumption adapter hill climbing -> global optimum
   $x \in input \rightarrow (\exists y . (y \in input \wedge successor(x,y) \wedge x < y) \vee \neg \exists z . (z \in input \wedge x < z))$

Fig. 6   The adapters.

2.4   Resume

We discussed four steps of the derivation of a refined PSM for abductive problems from a generic local search frame via adapters (cf. Fig. 6):

- hill climbing := PSM-refinement-adapter$_{\text{local search -> hill-climbing}}$(local search)
- set minimizer := PSM-refinement-adapter$_{\text{hill climbing -> set minimizer}}$(hill climbing)
- abductive method := PSM-refinement-adapter$_{\text{set minimizer -> abductive method}}$(set minimizer)
- abductive diagnosis :=
Assumption-adapter$_{\text{abductive method -> abductive diagnosis}}$(abductive method)

The first adapter[3] refines mainly the definition of state transitions and introduces knowledge requirements that allows the definition of the competence of the method in terms of finding a local optimum. The second adapter refines the notion of states (entities) to sets and refine the definition of state transition via defining a successor relationship between sets. The third adapter adds some simple terminological mappings that express the method in terms of abduction. Finally, an assumption is added to guarantee that this methods achieves the goal as given by the problem definition.

---

3. For reasons of limited space we do not provide the formal definition of this adapter in the paper.

3   An Integrated Library of Problem Definitions, Problem-Solving Methods and Adapters

So far, we have illustrated the stepwise refinement of PSMs. We started with a generic search strategy that became instantiated to hill-climbing that became later on refined to set minimizer that became later on refined to a method for abductive problems. In the same way we refined PSMs we can also refine problem definitions and assumptions necessary to link PSMs and problem definitions. In [Fensel & Schönegge, 1997a] we showed *that the monotony assumption is a problem-specific refinement of an assumption that is necessary and sufficient to prove that hill climbing finds a global optimum.* Hill climbing can solve the problem of finding a global optimum if we assume the *better neighbour assumption,* i.e. each entity that is not a global optimum has a better neighbour. Fig. 7 provides the definition of the corresponding problem and Fig. 6 of the better-neighbour assumption. Therefore, it is not only possible to refine PSMs but also problem definitions and assumptions. Fig. 8 summarizes our problem definitions, assumptions and methods. With simple extensions of the mappings of the two refinement adapters in Fig. 6 (by defining mappings for terms that were only used in problem and assumption definitions) we can use them to refine corresponding problem definitions and assumptions necessary to relate PSMs and problems as we did in section 2 for PSMs.

The dimension of this refinement is the ontological commitments made by problem definition, assumptions and PSMs. Notice that this specializations are kept separate via adapters. Therefore, it is always possible to reuse very specific or very generic entities from our library. We get an unified library of problem definitions, assumptions, and PSMs where the refinements have a *virtual* existence via adapters.

A second dimension of the library are the algorithmic schemas that are used to derive the PSMs. Instead of local search we can also choose branch and bound or A* as schemas that define the basic search algorithm of a method.

When organising such a library we have to go into the question of what are the differences between problems, assumptions, and PSMs and whether these differences have consequences in organising the library. We realized some significant properties of these elements when specifying them with KIV. KIV is designed for the specification and verification of programs. The entire specification of a system can be split into smaller and more tractable pieces. A specification defines the functionality of a program using algebraic specification techniques. In addition to specifications, KIV provides modules to describe implementations. A module defines a collection of

Problem global optimum
goal
    $global\text{-}optimum \in input$
    $\neg \exists x . (x \in input \land global\text{-}optimum < x)$
requirement
    $\neg(x < x)$
    $x < y \land y < z \rightarrow x < z$

Fig. 7   The specification of the problem finding a global optimum.

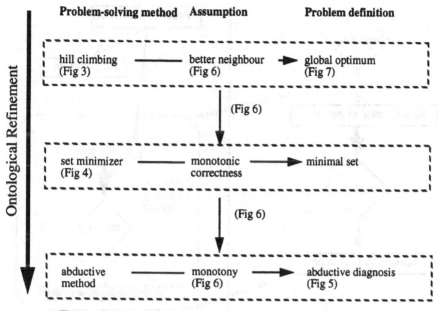

Fig. 8 Refining PSMs, assumptions, and problem definitions.

procedures provided in an export specification. It internally describes the algorithmic realization of these procedures. It uses, through an import specification, operations that are specified by other specifications (and realized by their modules). Usually a specification in KIV has the following pattern:

- A specification defines the functionality of operations that are imported by a module, i.e. by an implementation.
- A module imports some operations und uses them to implement new operations that are exported.
- A second specification defines the required functionality of the exported operations. Then a new implementation would use these operations as import.

The left side of Fig. 9 provides the structure of such a typical development graph. The single specifications are the rectangles in the graph and modules are modelled by the rhomboid units in the graph. Such a typical development graph corresponds with the specification and operationalization of a PSM (viewed at the right side of Fig. 9).

- The inference actions are defined in the import specification of the PSM. No algorithmic realization of the inference action is provided.
- The algorithmic realization of the knowledge requirements is also not part of the PSM because this aspect is assumed to be covered by the domain knowledge or by other agents of the entire problem-solving process. Therefore, its realization is beyond the scope of the specification of the PSM.
- The operationalization of a PSM corresponds to an implementation module. It describes how a specific competence can be achieved by defining control over the execution of imported operations (knowledge and inferences).

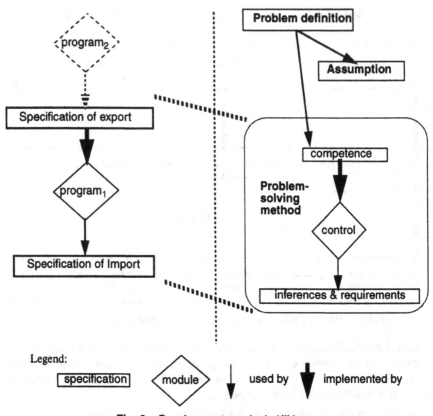

Fig. 9 Development graphs in KIV.

- Finally the competence of a PSM corresponds to the specification of the functionality of a module.

A distinction between typical development graphs in KIV and our specifications is introduced by problem definitions and assumptions. Usually in software engineering it is assumed that the problem that should be solved is identical with the functionality of the program. However most problems tackled with KBSs are inherently complex and intractable (cf. [Nebel, 1996], [Fensel & Straatman, 1996]). A PSM can only solve such problems with reasonable computational effort by introducing assumptions that restrict the complexity of the problem, or by strengthening the requirements on domain knowledge. Therefore, a specification of the problem independent from the specification of the competence as well as the specification of assumptions are introduced in our context. A method does not have the direct competence to solve the problem. Only when adding assumptions that limit the problem can this be guaranteed. The entire problem is therefore decomposed into a part that can be solved by the PSM and for which an operationalization is provided and a second part of which the solution is only assumed. This makes quite clear *how assumptions help to reduce the effort of realizing an implementation and computing an actual solution.* They define a part of the entire problem for which no implementation has to be provided. Therefore, the system can be realized more easily and in system runtime this part of the problem does not need to be computed.[4]

In general, there is no distinction between problem specification, assumption specification and the specification of the competence of a method. They are all specification units. Only their roles within the entire specification differ. That is, it is their context that creates their distinction:

- A *problem* defines a specifications that becomes "realized" by two other specification. One of these specifies the part that is actually solved (the competence of a PSM) and the other specifies the part that is assumed to be solved (an assumption specification).

- An *assumption* is a specification that has *no* realization at all. Its realization is *assumed* only.

- Finally, the *competence* of a PSM is a specification that is directly realized by a module that defines an operationalization. Again this operationalization relies on a specification defining its knowledge requirements and inferences. Their realization are either external to the specification or introduce a new level of hierarchical refinement by being formulated as new problems.

4   Conclusion, Related and Future Work

We have show how to use adapters for developing PMSs and for organizing a library of PSMs including problem definitions and assumptions. The development process of PSMs is viewed as a refinement process that:

- introduces ontological commitments used to characterize initial, intermediate and terminal states of the method;

- uses ontological commitments to specialize the state transitions of a method; and

- introduces assumption to bridge the gap between competence of a method and a problem definition.

All these refinement were achieved by adding adapters to existing elements. A number of authors [Beys et al., 1996][van Heijst and A. Anjewerden, 1996] have proposed that PSMs should be described not only in a domain-independent, but also task-independent way, so that they can become more broadly reusable. However, there is a known trade-off between usability and reusability [Klinker et al., 1991]. With our approach this dilemma disappears. PSMs can either be reused in their generic or more problem-specific variant. The latter does not modify the former but adds only an external description to it.

Existing approaches for developing PSMs either stop at the level of the competence of the methods [Akkermans et al., 1993], [Wielinga et al., 1995], [ten Teije, 1997] or view PSM development as process of hierarchically refining inference actions

---

4. See [O'Hara & Shadbolt, 1996] for a discussion of different dimensions of efficiency.

[Benjamins, 1995], [Terpstra et al., 1993]. The former deal only with a very limited aspects of the methods as a method is essentially a description of *how* to achieve some goals. The latter assume that adapting a PSM to a given problem is an activity of decomposing a problem in subproblems and defining control over the solution of the subproblems (and recursively refining the subproblems). However it was often reported in the literature that different control regimens can be applied to solve the same problem and the same control regime can be applied to very different problems [Breuker, 1997]. Therefore, we think that adapting a control regime is neither the only nor the central point in adapting a PSM to a given problem. When defining the overall control schema (i.e., local search, branch and bound, etc.) one mainly refers to properties of the domain knowledge. For example, only when a useful successor relation is provided local search can be applied and A* can only be applied if a useful heuristic estimation function is provided. Besides this, they can be applied to any type of problem that can be solved by a search process. An important distinction between [Benjamins, 1995], [Terpstra et al., 1993] and our approach is that [Benjamins, 1995], [Terpstra et al., 1993] express a PSM immediately in problem-specific terms (like symptom detection, hypothesis generation, hypothesis discrimination, etc.) whereas we describe general algorithmic schemas that become instantiated to a specific class of problem via adapters. Therefore we can discuss these algorithmic schemas of PSMs independently from specific problems reflecting the fact that the same PSM (or better the same algorithmic schema) can be applied to different problem classes.

For organizing a library of PSMs we made the following proposals:

- Extending the library by including problem definitions and assumptions necessary to relate the competence of method with the problems. By including problem definitions in the library we can use them to select appropriate PSMs as proposed by [Breuker, 1997]. We argue for inclusion of assumptions within our library because they are as important as PSMs. Assumptions define the parts of the problem that cannot be solved by the PSM but must be assumed as given (either as domain knowledge or as problem restriction [Benjamins et al., 1996]). They are the complement of the PSM relative to a selected problem. A kind of library of assumptions for a specific type of problems is described in [Fensel & Benjamins, 1996].

- Using adapters to relate units of problems, PSMs and assumptions of different specificity to get rid of the usability-reusability trade-off of [Klinker et al., 1991].

- Defining two orthogonal dimensions for organising such a unified library: (1) the specificity of problems, PSMs and assumptions (see Fig. 8) and (2) the algorithmic schema used to derive the PSM (i.e., local search, branch and bound etc., see Fig. 1).[5] Current libraries of PSMs [Benjamins, 1995], [Breuker & Van de Velde, 1994], [Chandrasekaran et al., 1992], [Motta & Zdrahal, 1996], [Puppe, 1993] interweave these two dimensions. As a consequence the literature is full of

---

5. One reviewer was wondering whether abduction should be solved by local search like we illustrate in this paper. Especially he makes the point that there are many other search and optimization techniques. Actually this circumstance is the reason for the second dimension in our framework that allows different algorithm schemas as core of PSMs.

worries that (1) methods specified for one problem type can be applied to other problems (requiring some renaming) and (2) not only the methods that are provided for a problem class in the library can be applied to it.

During the paper we used simple examples to make the paper easy to understand. The simple examples allowed us to present most of the details necessary to follow our arguments. However this does not at all imply that we designed our framework for block worlds. Currently we are applying our concept to the family of PSMs for parametric design that are developed by [Motta & Zdrahal, 1996]. It turns out that it is quite easy to scale up our approach. For example, propose & revise turns out to be a loop of two local searches applied in different contexts. One proposes extensions of design models (i.e., the propose step) and one revises design models in cases when they are incorrect. So simply put it is a loop of two instantiations of hill climbing. The different instantiations can be achieved by defining different successor relationships (one via extension and one via correction of models). A formalization of the problem definition of parametric design is already provided in [Fensel et al., 1997].

Acknowledgement. The paper conceptualizes work that was done together with Arno Schönegge on specifying and verifying problem-solving methods. Also I would like to thank Stefan Decker, Enrico Motta and Zdenek Zdrahal with whom I am currently experimenting in applying the ideas to parametric design and Rudi Studer and two anonymous reviewers for helpful comments.

References

[Akkermans et al., 1993] J. M. Akkermans, B. Wielinga, and A. TH. Schreiber: Steps in Constructing Problem-Solving Methods. In N. Aussenac et al. (eds.): *Knowledge-Acquisition for Knowledge-Based Systems*, Lecture Notes in AI, no 723, Springer-Verlag, 1993.

[Angele et al., 1996] J. Angele, D. Fensel, and R. Studer: Domain and Task Modelling in MIKE. In A. Sutcliffe et al. (eds.), *Domain Knowledge for Interactive System Design*, Chapman & Hall, 1996.

[Benjamins, 1995] R. Benjamins: Problem Solving Methods for Diagnosis And Their Role in Knowledge Acquisition, *International Journal of Expert Systems: Research and Application*, 8(2):93—120, 1995.

[Benjamins & Pierret-Golbreich, 1996] R. Benjamins and C. Pierret-Golbreich: Assumptions of Problem-Solving Method. In N. Shadbolt et al. (eds.), *Advances in Knowledge Acquisition*, Lecture Notes in Artificial Intelligence (LNAI), no 1076, Springer-Verlag, Berlin, 1996.

[Benjamins et al., 1996] R. Benjamins, D. Fensel, and R. Straatman: Assumptions of Problem-Solving Methods and Their Role in Knowledge Engineering. In *Proceedings of the 12. European Conference on Artificial Intelligence (ECAI-96)*, Budapest, August 12-16, 1996.

[Beys et al., 1996] P. Beys, R. Benjamins, and G. van Heijst: Remedying the Reusability-Usability Tradeoff for Problem-solving Methods. In *Proceedings of the 10th Banff Knowledge Acquisition for Knowledge-Based System Workshop (KAW'96)*, Banff, Canada, November 9-14, 1996.

[Breuker, 1997] J. Breuker: Problems in Indexing Problem Solving Methods. In *Proceeedings of the Workshop on Problem-Solving Methods during the IJCAI-97*, Japan, August 24, 1997.

[Breuker & Van de Velde, 1994] J. Breuker and W. Van de Velde (eds.): *The CommonKADS Library for Expertise Modelling*, IOS Press, Amsterdam, The Netherlands, 1994.

[Bylander et al., 1991] T. Bylander, D. Allemang, M. C. Tanner, and J. R. Josephson: The Computational Complexity of Abduction, *Artificial Intelligence*, 49, 1991.

[Chandrasekaran et al., 1992] B. Chandrasekaran, T.R. Johnson, and J. W. Smith: Task Structure Analysis for Knowledge Modeling, *Communications of the ACM*, 35(9): 124—137, 1992.

[David et al., 1993] J.-M. David, J.-P. Krivine, and R. Simmons (eds.): *Second Generation Expert Systems*, Springer-Verlag, Berlin, 1993.

[de Kleer & Williams, 1987] J. de Kleer and B. C. Williams: Diagnosing Multiple Faults, *Artificial Intelligence*, 32:97-130, 1987.

[de Kleer, 1992] J. de Kleer, K. Mackworth, and R. Reiter: Characterizing Diagnoses and Systems, *Artificial Intelligence*, 56, 1992.

[Eriksson et al., 1995] H. Eriksson, Y. Shahar, S. W. Tu, A. R. Puerta, and M. A. Musen: Task Modeling with Reusable Problem-Solving Methods, *Artificial Intelligence*, 79(2):293—326, 1995.

[Fensel & Benjamins, 1996]D. Fensel and R. Benjamins: Assumptions in Model-Based Diagnosis. In *Proceedings of the 10th Banff Knowledge Acquisition for Knowledge-Based System Workshop (KAW'96)*, Banff, Canada, November 9-14, 1996.

[Fensel, 1995] D. Fensel: Assumptions and Limitations of a Problem-Solving Method: A Case Study. In *Proceedings of the 9th Banff Knowledge Acquisition for Knowledge-Based System Workshop (KAW-95)*, Banff, Canada, January 26 - February 3, 1995.

[Fensel et al., 1996] D. Fensel, H. Eriksson, M. A. Musen, and R. Studer: Developing Problem-Solving by Introducing Ontological Commitments, *International Journal of Expert Systems: Research & Applications,* vol 9(4), 1996.

[Fensel & Straatman, 1996] D. Fensel and R. Straatman: The Essence of Problem-Solving Methods: Making Assumptions for Efficiency Reasons. In N. Shadbolt et al. (eds.), *Advances in Knowledge Acquisiiton, LNAI* 1076, Springer-Verlag, 1996.

[Fensel & Groenboom, 1997] D. Fensel and R. Groenboom: Specifying Knowledge-Based Systems with Reusable Components. In *Proceedings of the 9th International Conference on Software Engineering & Knowledge Engineering (SEKE-97)*, Madrid, Spain, June 18-20, 1997.

[Fensel & Schönegge, 1997a] D. Fensel and A. Schönegge: Assumption Hunting as Development Method for Knowledge-Based Systems. In *Proceeedings of the Workshop on Problem-Solving Methods for Knowledge-based Systems at the 15th International Joint Conference on AI (IJCAI-97)*, Nagoya, Japan, August 23, 1997.

[Fensel & Schönegge, 1997b] D. Fensel and A. Schönegge: Specifying and Verifying Knowledge-Based Systems with KIV. In *Proceedings of the European Symposium on the Validation and Verification of Knowledge Based Systems EUROVAV-97*, Leuven Belgium, June 26-28, 1997.

[Fensel et al., 1997] D. Fensel, E. Motta, S. Decker, Z. Zdrahal: Using Ontologies For Defining Tasks, Problem-Solving Methods and Their Mappings. To appear in *Proceedings of the European Knowledge Acquisition Workshop (EKAW-97)*, Sant Feliu de Guixols, Catalonia, Spain, October 15-18,LNAI, Springer-Verlag, 1997.

[Harel, 1984] D. Harel: Dynamic Logic. In D. Gabby et al. (eds.), *Handbook of Philosophical Logic, vol. II*, Extensions of Classical Logic, Publishing Company, Dordrecht (NL), 1984.

[Klinker et al., 1991] G. Klinker, C. Bhola, G. Dallemagne, D. Marques, and J. McDermott: Usable and Reusable Programmin Constructs, *Knowledge Acquisition*, 3:117—136, 1991.

[Marcus, 1988] S. Marcus (ed.). *Automating Knowledge Acquisition for Experts Systems*, Kluwer Academic Publisher, Boston, 1988.

[Motta & Zdrahal, 1996] E. Motta and Z. Zdrahal: Parametric Design Problem Solving. In *Proceedings of the 10th Banff Knowledge Acquisition for Knowledge-Based System Workshop (KAW'96)*, Banff, Canada, November 9-14, 1996.

[Nebel, 1996] B. Nebel: Artificial intelligence: A Computational Perspective. In G. Brewka (ed.), *Essentials in Knowledge Representation*, 1996.

[O'Hara & Shadbolt, 1996] K. O'Hara and N. Shadbolt: The Thin End of the Wedge: Efficiency and the Generalized Directive Model Methodology. In N. Shadbolt (eds.), *Advances in Knowledge Acquisition*, LNAI 1076, Springer-Verlag, Berlin, 1996.

[Puppe, 1993] F. Puppe: *Systematic Introduction to Expert Systems: Knowledge Representation and Problem-Solving Methods*, Springer-Verlag, Berlin, 1993.

[Reif, 1992] W. Reif: The KIV-System: Systematic Construction of Verified Software, *Proceedings of the 11th International Conference on Automated Deduction*, CADE-92, Lecture Notes in Computer Science (LNCS), no 607, Springer-Verlag, Berlin, 1992.

[Reif, 1995] W. Reif: The KIV Approach to Software Engineering. In M. Broy and S. Jähnichen (eds.): *Methods, Languages, and Tools for the Construction of Correct Software*, LNCS 1009, Springer-Verlag, 1995.

[Smith & Lowry, 1990] D. R. Smith and M. R. Lowry: Algorithm Theories and Design Tactics, *Science of Computer Programming*, 14:305—321, 1990.

[Schreiber et al., 1993] A. Th. Schreiber, B. J. Wielinga, and J. A. Breuker (eds.): *KADS: A Principled Approach to Knowledge-Based System Development, vol 11 of Knowledge-Based Systems Book Series*, Academic Press, London, 1993.

[Schreiber et al., 1994] A. TH. Schreiber, B. Wielinga, J. M. Akkermans, W. Van De Velde, and R. de Hoog: CommonKADS. A Comprehensive Methodology for KBS Development, *IEEE Expert*, 9(6):28—37, 1994.

[Steels, 1990] L. Steels: Components of Expertise, *AI Magazine*, 11(2), 1990.

[ten Teije, 1997] A. ten Teije: *Automated Configuration of Problem Solving Methods in Diagnosis*, PhD thesis, University of Amsterdam, Amsterdam, NL, 1997.

[Terpstra et al., 1993] P. Terpstra, G. van Heijst, B. Wielinga, and N. Shadbolt: Knowledge Acquisition Support Through Generalised Directive Models. In M. David et al. (eds.): *Second Generation Expert Systems*, Springer-Verlag, 1993.

[van Heijst and A. Anjewerden, 1996] G. van Heijst and A. Anjewerden: Four Propositions concerning the specification of Problem-Solving Methods. In *Supplementary Proceedings of the 9th European Knowledge Acquisition Workshop EKAW-96*, Nottingham, England, May 14-17, 1996.

[Wielinga et al., 1995] B. J. Wielinga, J. M. Akkermans, and A. Th. Schreiber: A Formal Analysis of Parametric Design Problem Solving. In *Proceedings of the 9th Banff Knowledge Acquisition Workshop (KAW-95)*, Banff, Canada, January 26 - Feruary 3, 1995.

[Wirsing, 1990] M. Wirsing: Algebraic Specification. In J. van Leeuwen (ed.), *Handbook of Theoretical Computer Science*, Elsevier Science Publ, 1990.

Using Ontologies for Defining Tasks, Problem-Solving Methods and Their Mappings

D. Fensel[1], E. Motta[2], S. Decker[1], and Z. Zdrahal[2]

[1] Institut AIFB, University of Karlsruhe, D-76128 Karlsruhe,
{dieter.fensel,stefan.decker}@aifb.uni-karlsruhe.de

[2] Knowledge Media Institute, The Open University, Milton Keynes MK7 6AA, United Kingdom,
{e.motta,z.zdrahal}@open.ac.uk

Abstract. In recent years two main technologies for knowledge sharing and reuse have emerged: *ontologies* and *problem solving methods* (PSMs). Ontologies specify reusable conceptualizations which can be shared by multiple reasoning components communicating during a problem solving process. PSMs describe in a domain-independent way the generic reasoning steps and knowledge types needed to perform a task. Typically PSMs are specified in a task-specific fashion, using modelling frameworks which describe their control and inference structures as well as their knowledge requirements and competence. In this paper we discuss a novel approach to PSM specification, which is based on the use of formal ontologies. In particular our specifications abstract from control, data flow and other dynamic aspects of PSMs to focus on the logical theory associated with a PSM (method ontology). This approach concentrates on the competence and knowledge requirements of a PSM, rather than internal control details, thus enabling black-box-style reuse. In the paper we also look at the nature of PSM specifications and we show that these can be characterised in a task-independent style as generic search strategies. The resulting 'modelling gap' between method-independent task specifications and task-independent method ontologies can be bridged by constructing the relevant *adapter* ontology, which reformulates the method ontology in task-specific terms. An important aspect of the ontology-centred approach described here is that, in contrast with other characterisations of task-independent PSMs, it does away with the simple, binary distinction between weak and strong methods. We argue that any method can be defined in either task-independent or task-dependent style and therefore such distinction is of limited utility in PSM reuse. The differences between PSMs which affect reuse concern the ontological commitments which they make with respect to domain knowledge and goal specifications.

1   Introduction

The concept of *generic problem-solving method* (PSM) is present in several knowledge-engineering frameworks (e.g. Generic Tasks [Chandrasekaran et al., 1992]; Configurable Role-Limiting Methods [Puppe, 1993]; CommonKADS [Schreiber et al., 1994]; the Method-To-Task approach [Eriksson et al., 1995]; Components of Expertise [Steels, 1990]; GDM [Terpstra et al., 1993]; MIKE [Angele et al., 1996]). In general a PSM describes in a domain-independent way which reasoning steps and which types of knowledge are needed to perform a task. Libraries of PSMs have been developed, e.g.

see [Benjamins, 1995], [Breuker & Van de Velde, 1994], [Chandrasekaran et al., 1992], [Motta & Zdrahal, 1996], and [Puppe, 1993], which support reuse-centred models of KBS development, thus improving the efficiency of the development process and the robustness of the target application system.

In this paper, we look at two fundamental issues associated with PSM specifications: i) the epistemology of the modelling frameworks used to characterise PSMs and ii) the nature of PSM specifications. These issues are discussed below.

Reuse-centred PSM descriptions

Describing PSMs in the style of CommonKADS [Schreiber et al., 1994] requires to specify much of the internal reasoning process of a PSM. In particular, the following descriptions need to be given:

1) the internal reasoning steps of the PSM;
2) the data flows between the reasoning steps;
3) the control that guides the dynamic execution of the internal reasoning steps;
4) the knowledge requirements of a PSM;
5) the goals that can be achieved by a PSM.

However, most of these aspects have to do with understanding how a PSM achieves its goals. To assess the applicability of a PSM one only needs knowledge about its competence and domain requirements - i.e. (4) and (5) above ([van de Velde, 1988], [Akkermans et al., 1993]). In particular, our approach to the specification of the competence of a PSM makes use of *formal ontologies*. This approach provides two main advantages:

- A formal specification adds a precise meaning and enables mechanised support. Specifications in natural language are necessarily imprecise, contain ambiguity and are difficult to verify for completeness and consistency [van Harmelen & Fensel, 1995]. Moreover, establishing the competence of a PSM in relation to some ontological assumptions may require difficult proof processes that are only realistic if some mechanised proof support can be provided [Fensel & Schönegge, 1997].

- An ontology provides "an explicit specification of a conceptualization" [Gruber, 1993], which can be shared by multiple reasoning components communicating during a problem solving process. Using ontological engineering for describing PSMs provides two important benefits with respect to reuse. The resulting PSM specification i) is grounded on a common, shared terminology and ii) its knowledge requirements are conceptualised as ontological *commitments* [Gruber, 1995].

The nature of PSM descriptions

PSMs are normally described in a task-specific way. There are two main reasons for this. Task-independent PSMs are often regarded as *weak* methods [Mc Dermott, 1988] and much KBS research of the past two decades can be seen as a reaction to the weak - i.e. task-independent - problem solving paradigms used in the sixties and early seventies [Newell & Simon, 1972]. This reaction has taken different forms and has been formulated according to different principles - see for instance the *knowledge as power principle* [Lenat & Feigenbaum, 1987] and the *knowledge interaction hypothesis*

[Bylander & Chandrasekaran, 1988]. But essentially the message here is that efficient, knowledge-based problem solving subscribes to either task- or application-specific paradigms. The other reason which explains the limited 'appeal' of task-independent PSMs is the trade-off between *usability* and *reusability* [Klinker et al., 1991]. The more reusable a PSM, the larger the distance between this PSM and an application specification, which means that more work is required to bridge the representation gap between the PSM and the application.

Nonetheless, in recent years there has been renewed interest in task-independent specifications of PSMs (cf. [Beys et al., 1996][van Heijst and A. Anjewerden, 1996]). van Heijst and Anjewerden point out that the "task specific formulation of PSMs unnecessarily limits the applicability of PSMs" [van Heijst and A. Anjewerden, 1996], and suggest that the applicability conditions of PSMs can be specified in terms of domain-independent meta-characteristics of the target domain model.

However, the trade-off between usability and reusability requires techniques which facilitate the process of configuring a task-independent PSM for a particular task and domain. We see this problem as one of *ontology mapping* and in this paper we characterise PSM configuration as a specialization process, during which ontological commitments are introduced. Specifically, our approach comprises three phases:

- The specification of method-independent ontologies which define task or problem types.
- The task-independent specification of generic search methods.
- The specification of *adapters* [Fensel & Groenboom, 1997] which map the ontology of a generic search method to task-specific terms to produce task-specific PSMs. Because adapters can be stacked on top of each other (cf. [Fensel, 1997b]) we view the task-specific refinement of generic search strategies as a stepwise process overcoming the dualistic view of weak and strong PSMs. Hence, our approach postulates a continuum between both extremes where a step into a more task-specific variant of a PSM is achieved by means of the relevant adapter.

Contents of the paper

In the following we will illustrate the approach in a formal way, by discussing a test case which involves the configuration of a task-independent specification of a PSM for a class of tasks. Specifically, we will discuss the following model components.

- Section 2 describes a specification of a method-independent ontology for *parametric design* tasks [Wielinga et al., 1995][Motta & Zdrahal, 1996].
- Section 3 specifies a *method ontology* for a propose & revise PSM [Marcus & McDermott, 1989] [Zdrahal & Motta, 1995]. This method ontology expresses the competence of propose & revise in terms of assumptions over the properties of two types of state transitions: *propose* transitions and *revise* transitions. The former enrich the completeness of a state, the latter specify a transition from an incorrect to a correct state. No further commitments are made. This method specification is highly task-independent. It can be applied to any task whose problem space can be expressed as a search process on correct, complete and preferred states.
- Section 4 describes the *adapter* which specialises the propose & revise method

ontology for parametric design. Similar adapters can be defined to adapt propose & revise to other tasks - see [Fensel, 1997a] for a description of a configuration of a propose & revise PSM for assignment tasks.

Finally, section 5 discusses the significance of the work, compares our approach to alternative proposals, and outlines directions of future research.

2   A Task Ontology for Parametric Design

In the following we present a task ontology for parametric design. First, we provide an informal description of the ontology. Then we discuss a specification using Sloppy-logic (S-logic). S-logic makes use of rich semantic modelling primitives within the framework defined by Frame-logic [Kifer et al., 1995] - see Fig. 1.

2.1   A Sketch of Parametric Design

Design can be characterised in generic terms as the process of constructing artifacts. Thus, the essential feature of design problem solving is its *constructive* nature: solutions are constructed rather than retrieved from a pre-existing set.

In order to construct an artifact one needs some *building blocks* - i.e. a *technology* [Chandrasekaran, 1990]. In addition, the design process is subjected to a number of *constraints*, which can be related either to the design technology - e.g. technological limitations impose constraints on the minimum size of supporting walls - or to external factors - e.g. most civilised countries require a minimum ceiling height in living rooms.

Design is a goal-driven process, where the goals are specified in terms of a number of functionalities which the target artifact should provide. A good way of informally characterizing the goal-oriented nature of the design process is to see it as driven by *needs* and *desires* [Wielinga et al., 1995]. Thus, the design process[1] can be characterised as a function which takes as input a set of needs, desires, constraints and a possibly incomplete set of building blocks, and produces an artifact as output.

A restricted class of design problems is *configuration design* [Mittal & Frayman, 1989], which can be defined as a design problem where all building blocks are given as input to the design process. [Mittal & Frayman, 1989] show that the complexity of the configuration task decreases significantly by assuming that "the artifacts are configured according to some known functional architectures". For instance, a computer configuration can be functionally described in terms of processor, printing, memory, data communication, etc. This assumption makes it possible to impose a structure on the space of feasible designs, thus restricting the number of possible configurations. This assumption can be characterised as postulating the existence of one or more *functional solution templates*.

A stronger assumption, which further restricts the space of possible designs is that which postulates the existence of a *parametrised solution template* for the target artifact. In this scenario design problem solving can be described as the process of assigning values to *design parameters* in accordance with the given needs, constraints, and desires. Applications for which this assumption holds are called *parametric design* applications.

---

1. This is of course an idealised description of the design process.

The VT elevator design problem [Marcus et al., 1988] [Yost & Rothenfluh, 1996] provides a well-known example of a parametric design task. Here the problem is to configure an elevator in accordance with the given requirement specification and the applicable constraints. The parametrised solution template consists of 199 design parameters which specify the various structural and functional aspects of an elevator - e.g. number of doors, speed, load, etc.

More precisely a parametric design application can be characterised as a mapping from a six-dimensional space <P, VR, C, R, Pr, cf> to a set of solution designs, { D_{sol_1} ,........, D_{sol_n} }, where

- P = Parameters = {p_1,......, p_n};
- Vr = Value ranges = {V_1,......, V_n}, where V_i = {v_{i1},......, v_{in_i}};
- C = Constraints = {c_1,......, c_m};
- R = Requirements = {r_1,......, r_k};
- Pr = Preferences = {pr_1,......, pr_j};
- cf = Cost Function.

These concepts are discussed in the next section, where we illustrate a semi-formal specification - given in S-logic - of the different entities which make up the parametric design task ontology.

2.2   A Semiformal Specification of Parametric Design with S-Logic

The basic element of parametric design is the concept of *parameter*. We model parameters by means of a class, Parameter (see Def 2.1 in Fig. 2). Each parameter has a value range, which constrains the possible values which the parameter can take in a design model. The union of all value ranges defines the set of all legal parameter values. The latter is modelled by means of class Value range. The attribute allowed values associates a range with a set of values (Def 2.2). The attribute range models the association between a parameter and a range (Def 2.1).

One could also expect that a parameter is directly associated with a value. But a parameter gets a value assigned by a design model and has not a value by itself. That is, there is no functional (i.e., attributional) dependency between parameters and values. It is a design model that introduces a mapping between parameters and values. Such a design model can therefore be modelled as a (partial) function between the parameters and values provided by their ranges (see Def 2.4.a). Incomplete design models, i.e., design models that do not assign a value to each parameter are partial functions. The class Design model models the solution space of our task.

Two further sets are used to characterize subspaces of the solution space. Requirements should be satisfied by a solution and constraints should not be violated by it. We can model a requirement as the set of design models that fulfils it and a constraint as the set of design models that violate it. Therefore, we introduce two classes, Requirement and Constraint, defined as sets of design models (see Def 2.5, Def 2.6 & Def 2.7). These definitions should not be confused with their extensional or intensional representation. The actual set of design models that fulfil a requirement can be described extensionally

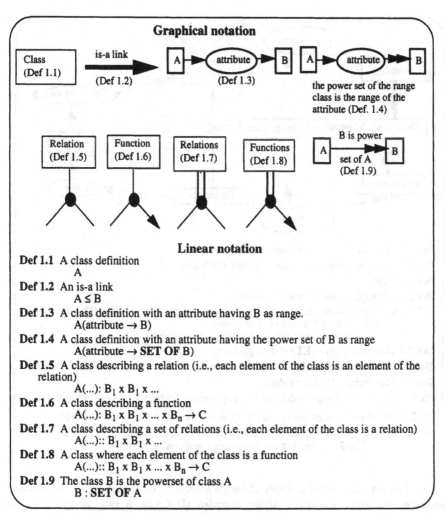

Fig. 1 Legend of S-logic.

by enumerating the design models or by providing an intensional characterisation of the sufficient and necessary conditions for fulfilling the requirement.[2]

The attributes fulfil and violate deliver for each design model the set of fulfilled requirements and violated constraints (see Def 2.4.a). The two axioms, Ax 2.1 and Ax 2.2, ensure the appropriate relationships between design models, requirements, and constraints.

---

2. The reader might find surprising that requirements and constraints are modelled as set of design models. The advantage of the approach we have chosen is that it does not require to postulate the existence of an additional domain lexicon to support the specification of constraints and requirements. For instance, the parametric design framework discussed in [Wielinga et al., 1995] introduces a domain vocabulary and the notion of domain theory. Here, we have chosen to minimise the number of concepts required to discuss the ontology and therefore we characterise requirements and constraints as subset of design models. However, the rationale for this choice is pragmatic, rather than ontological.

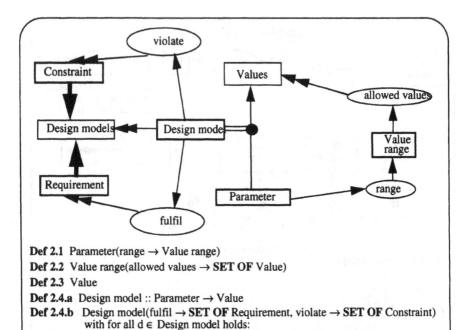

Def 2.1 Parameter(range → Value range)

Def 2.2 Value range(allowed values → **SET OF** Value)

Def 2.3 Value

Def 2.4.a Design model :: Parameter → Value

Def 2.4.b Design model(fulfil → **SET OF** Requirement, violate → **SET OF** Constraint)
with for all d ∈ Design model holds:
  d(p) ∈ allowed values(range(p)) if d is defined for p.

Def 2.5 Design models : **SET OF** Design model

Def 2.6 Requirement ≤ Design models

Def 2.7 Constraint ≤ Design models

Ax 2.1 For all d ∈ Design model and r ∈ Requirement holds: d ∈ r ↔ r ∈ fulfil(d)

Ax 2.2 For all d ∈ Design model and c ∈ Constraint holds: d ∈ c ↔ c ∈ violate(d)

Fig. 2   Entities in the parametric design task ontology.

Figure 3 shows a taxonomy of types of design models. A *solution* design is defined as a design model which is both *valid* and *complete* (Def 3.6). A valid design model is *suitable* and *consistent* (Def 3.5). A suitable design model fulfils all requirements (Def 3.2 and Ax 3.1). A consistent design model does not violate any constraint (Def 3.3 and Ax 3.2). A complete design model is one in which each parameter has a value (Def 3.4 and Ax 3.3).

Def 3.1 introduces the notion of *preferences*. Preferences describe task knowledge which, given two design models, D_1 and D_2, is used to specify which of the two - if any - is the 'better' one, in accordance with some criterion. We model each preference as a binary relation which specifies a partial order over design models. Each element of the class Preference is such a relation.

While preferences typically define local criteria to choose between alternative design models, a cost function provides a global criterion for assessing the cost of a design model. The class Cost has to be well-founded to introduce an order on costs (Def 3.7).

The ontology associates a cost with a solution design, rather than with a generic design

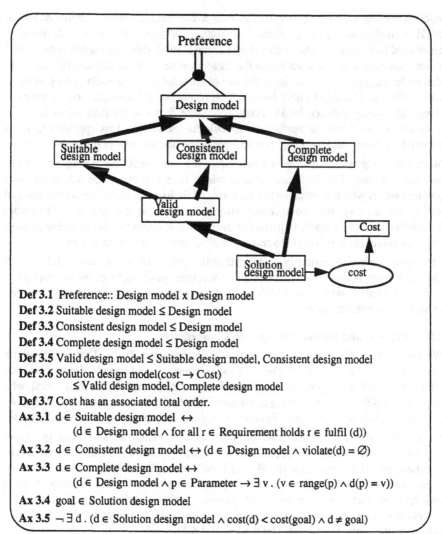

Def 3.1 Preference:: Design model x Design model
Def 3.2 Suitable design model ≤ Design model
Def 3.3 Consistent design model ≤ Design model
Def 3.4 Complete design model ≤ Design model
Def 3.5 Valid design model ≤ Suitable design model, Consistent design model
Def 3.6 Solution design model(cost → Cost)
          ≤ Valid design model, Complete design model
Def 3.7 Cost has an associated total order.
Ax 3.1 d ∈ Suitable design model ↔
          (d ∈ Design model ∧ for all r ∈ Requirement holds r ∈ fulfil (d))
Ax 3.2 d ∈ Consistent design model ↔ (d ∈ Design model ∧ violate(d) = ∅)
Ax 3.3 d ∈ Complete design model ↔
          (d ∈ Design model ∧ p ∈ Parameter → ∃ v . (v ∈ range(p) ∧ d(p) = v))
Ax 3.4 goal ∈ Solution design model
Ax 3.5 ¬ ∃ d . (d ∈ Solution design model ∧ cost(d) < cost(goal) ∧ d ≠ goal)

Fig. 3. Types of design models.

model, in order to minimise *ontological commitments* [Gruber, 1993]. However, it is feasible to envisage situations in which cost is defined also for non solution models. For instance, a design system which uses a case-based approach to design could use cost as one of a number of criteria for selecting a design model from a case library. In this scenario the selected model is not necessarily a solution model.

Finally, Ax 3.4 and Ax 3.5 define the goal of the task. It is to find the optimal solution design - i.e. the cheapest of all possible solution design models.

3 A PSM-Ontology for Propose & Revise

A well-known problem solving method which can be used for parametric design problem solving is *propose & revise* [Marcus & McDermott, 1989] [Zdrahal & Motta, 1995]. Actually, as argued in [Zdrahal & Motta, 1995] the term 'propose & revise' is better used to describe a class, rather than a specific PSM; different control regimes and revision strategies can be used within the basic propose & revise framework. The basic idea underlying propose & revise is the use of *knowledge-based backtracking* to focus search. That is, instead of either backtracking to the last chronological choice point or using dependency-directed backtracking, a propose & revise problem solver reacts to inconsistency by means of application-specific *fix knowledge*. This approach removes the need for 'blind' backtracking, thus improving the performance of the problem solver.

In the following, we define method ontologies for both 'weak' and 'strong' versions of propose & revise. The first specification, which is shown in section 3.1, describes a problem solver which is assumed to be capable of finding complete, correct and optimal states. To achieve this competence strong assumptions on available (heuristic) knowledge have to be made. In particular the method assumes that the available propose and fix knowledge is sufficient to reach complete, correct and optimal states.

This specification is obviously quite 'optimistic' and therefore in section 3.2 we will discuss a more 'realistic version of propose & revise, which replaces the assumption of global optimality with one which only assumes locally optimal transitions, thus exhibiting weaker competence.

3.1 Propose and Revise with optimal Competence

We take a state-based view to describe task-independent PSMs. That is, PSMs are described in terms of state (cf. Def 4.1) and (elementary and complex) state transition (Def 4.6). Such an approach is in accordance with [Motta & Zdrahal, 1996] who characterise KBS problem solving as a search-based process. Thus, in the following, we provide a task-independent specification of propose & revise as a search-based process.

Propose & revise distinguishes two types of state transitions and, as a result, two types of states these transitions are applied to. A Propose transition (cf. Def 4.7) extends the *completeness* of a state while the Revise transition (cf. Def 4.8) transforms an illegal state into a *correct* one. Thus, the ontological commitment here is not formulated in task-specific terms but in terms of generic notions such as completeness and correctness. In other words we assume that the problem solver is able to identify complete and correct states (cf. Def 4.3 and Def 4.5).

Def 4.2 introduces a preference on states that is used to model the assumption that propose and revise steps in our problem solver always result into optimal states (Ax 4.2, Ax 4.4, Ax 4.7). Of course this assumption formulates very strong requirements on both propose and revise knowledge. Specifically, it assumes that the search space defined by propose and revise steps is complete with respect to optimality. This assumption is much too strong, for instance it is not satisfied by the fix knowledge in the VT domain, and therefore in the next section we will substitute it with a weaker notion of optimality, which is contextualised with respect to the space of possible moves.[3]

The competence of the method is characterized by Ax 4.1 and Ax 4.2. The output is a complete, correct and optimal state. To achieve this competence the following

---

3. Not even completeness is guaranteed in the VT case.

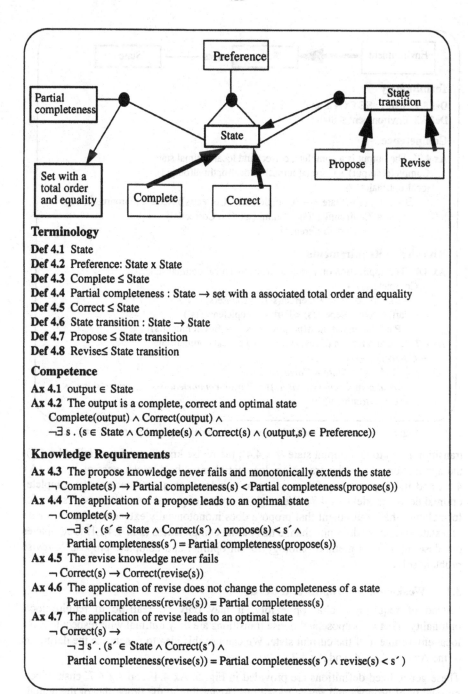

Terminology

Def 4.1 State

Def 4.2 Preference: State x State

Def 4.3 Complete ≤ State

Def 4.4 Partial completeness : State → set with a associated total order and equality

Def 4.5 Correct ≤ State

Def 4.6 State transition : State → State

Def 4.7 Propose ≤ State transition

Def 4.8 Revise≤ State transition

Competence

Ax 4.1 output ∈ State

Ax 4.2 The output is a complete, correct and optimal state

Complete(output) ∧ Correct(output) ∧

¬∃ s . (s ∈ State ∧ Complete(s) ∧ Correct(s) ∧ (output,s) ∈ Preference))

Knowledge Requirements

Ax 4.3 The propose knowledge never fails and monotonically extends the state

¬ Complete(s) → Partial completeness(s) < Partial completeness(propose(s))

Ax 4.4 The application of a propose leads to an optimal state

¬ Complete(s) →

¬∃ s′ . (s′ ∈ State ∧ Correct(s′) ∧ propose(s) < s′ ∧

Partial completeness(s′) = Partial completeness(propose(s)))

Ax 4.5 The revise knowledge never fails

¬ Correct(s) → Correct(revise(s))

Ax 4.6 The application of revise does not change the completeness of a state

Partial completeness(revise(s)) = Partial completeness(s)

Ax 4.7 The application of revise leads to an optimal state

¬ Correct(s) →

¬ ∃ s′ . (s′ ∈ State ∧ Correct(s′) ∧

Partial completeness(revise(s)) = Partial completeness(s′) ∧ revise(s) < s′)

Fig. 4. A method ontology for a globally optimal propose & revise.

requirements on propose and revise knowledge are necessary: the propose knowledge
never fails and monotonically extends the state (Ax 4.3); the application of a propose

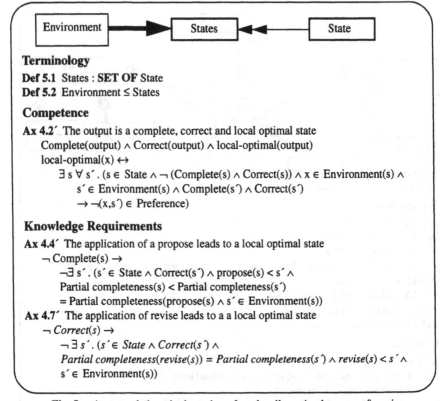

Terminology

Def 5.1 States : **SET OF** State

Def 5.2 Environment ≤ States

Competence

Ax 4.2′ The output is a complete, correct and local optimal state
  Complete(output) ∧ Correct(output) ∧ local-optimal(output)
  local-optimal(x) ↔
    ∃ s ∀ s′ . (s ∈ State ∧ ¬ (Complete(s) ∧ Correct(s)) ∧ x ∈ Environment(s) ∧
      s′ ∈ Environment(s) ∧ Complete(s′) ∧ Correct(s′)
      → ¬(x,s′) ∈ Preference)

Knowledge Requirements

Ax 4.4′ The application of a propose leads to a local optimal state
  ¬ Complete(s) →
    ¬∃ s′ . (s′ ∈ State ∧ Correct(s′) ∧ propose(s) < s′ ∧
    Partial completeness(s) < Partial completeness(s′)
    = Partial completeness(propose(s) ∧ s′ ∈ Environment(s))

Ax 4.7′ The application of revise leads to a a local optimal state
  ¬ *Correct*(s) →
    ¬∃ s′ . (s′ ∈ *State* ∧ *Correct*(s′) ∧
    Partial completeness(revise(s)) = Partial completeness(s′) ∧ revise(s) < s′ ∧
    s′ ∈ Environment(s))

Fig. 5. An extended method ontology for a locally optimal propose & revise.

transition leads to an optimal state (Ax 4.4); the revise knowledge never fails (Ax 4.5); the application of a revise transition does not change the completeness of a state (Ax 4.6); and the application of a revise transition leads to a (not necessarily complete) optimal design model (Ax 4.7). We need the notion of partial completeness of states for formulating the requirement that propose does monotonically extend the completeness of a state and revise does not change this partial completeness (Def 4.4). This completes our description of a method ontology for an optimal and complete propose & revise problem solver.

3.2 Weakening of Propose and Revise

Instead of requiring global optimality, it may only be realistic to require local optimality. That is, propose and revise transitions are only optimal with respect to same local environment of the current state. We can use this idea to generalize the definition of the Ax 4.2, Ax 4.4, and Ax 4.7.

These generalized definitions are provided in Fig. 5. Ax 4.4′ and Ax 4.7′ ensure local optimality of propose and revise transitions. According to the properties of the domain knowledge used to define such environments these axioms define relatively weaker or stronger requirements. The definitions correspond to the original axioms of section 3.1 in the case where each environment consists of the entire problem space.

A drawback of this generalized specification is the weakened notion of the competence of the method. We can guarantee optimality only in the sense that a successor state is a local optimum of the environment of a predecessor state (see Ax 4.2′).

4 Integrating Method and Task Ontologies to Produce Task-specific Versions of a PSM

In the previous sections we have specified a task ontology for parametric design and weaker and stronger versions of a task-independent propose & revise problem solver. It remains to connect both, i.e. to configure propose & revise for parametric design.

This step consists of producing the relevant *adapter* - see Fig. 6.[4] The main ontological decision is to interpret a state in terms of a design model. Specifically, the definitions in Fig. 6 identify correct states with valid design models, complete states with complete design models, and partial completeness with the set of parameters which are assigned a value by a design model. Order and equality of partial completeness are defined in terms of set inclusion and set equality of parameter sets.

The crucial axiom is Ax 6.3, which ensures that the output of the method corresponds to the goal of the task. The proof of this axiom is rather trivial. The main effort in verifying our ontological specification is to ensure the optimality of the output of propose and revise as assumed by Ax 4.2. Methodologies and tools for verifying such axioms are described in [Fensel & Schönegge, 1997].

5 Conclusions, Related and Future Work

In this paper we have defined i) an ontology for the parametric design task, which is independent of any domain and PSM; ii) an ontology for propose & revise, which is independent of any domain and task model; and finally iii) an adapter which integrates task and method specifications. The resulting model constitutes a task-specific variant of propose & revise: propose & revise for parametric design. Thus, we have provided descriptions which enable reuse of task specifications as well as reuse of task-independent and task-specific PSMs.

Def 6.1 $\text{State}_{P\&R}$: Design model$_{PD}$

Def 6.2 $\text{Complete}_{P\&R}$: Complete design model$_{PD}$

Def 6.3 Set with a total order and equality$_{P\&R}$: **SET OF** parameter$_{PD}$

Def 6.4 $<_{P\&R}$: $\subseteq_{PD}$, $=_{P\&R}$: $=_{PD}$

Def 6.5 $\text{Correct}_{P\&R}$ = Valid design model$_{PD}$

Ax 6.1 $\text{Preference}_{P\&R}(s_{P\&R}, s'_{P\&R}) \leftrightarrow \text{cost}(d_{PD}) < \text{cost}(d'_{PD}) \land s_{P\&R} = d_{PD} \land s'_{P\&R} = d'_{PD}$

Ax 6.2 $\text{Partial completeness}_{P\&R}(d_{P\&R}) = \{p_{PD} \mid (p_{PD}, v_{PD}) \in d_{PD}\}$

Ax 6.3 $\text{output}_{P\&R} = \text{goal}_{PD}$

Fig. 6. The PSM ontology of propose & revise for parametric design.

---

4. The infix-notation in is used to distinguish terms from parametric design (infix PD) and terms from propose & revise (infix P&R).

A number of authors have discussed task-independent PSM specifications. In particular [van Heijst and A. Anjewerden, 1996] formulate task-independent PSMs in terms of *acceptance criteria*. For instance, their task-independent formalization of cover & differentiate states that the 'cover' part of the method is applicable to domains where there is a relation X, which is transitive, anti-symmetric and anti-reflexive. However, this formulation does not say anything about the feasibility of applying the method to a domain. In other words it does not provide a replacement problem solving model (or paradigm) for the task-specific model provided by cover & differentiate. As a matter of fact most of the time it won't make much sense to apply the cover sub-method to a relation with the given properties. In contrast with this approach our task-independent PSMs are described as variations of search methods - i.e. they substitute a task-specific problem solving paradigm with a generic one.

The approach taken by [van Heijst and A. Anjewerden, 1996] also postulates a clear separation between task-specific and task-independent descriptions of PSMs. A similar, dualistic view is also taken by McDermott [Mc Dermott, 1988], who compares role-limiting methods to weak methods and indicates that "a weak method is more open with respect to control than a role-limiting method can be; a weak method does not put any limits on the nature or complexity of the task-specific control knowledge it uses". We believe this characterization of strong vs weak methods is too coarse-grained. For instance a weak method such as A* makes precise assumptions about the existence of heuristic knowledge, which make it possible to converge to an optimal solution. Moreover, as this paper shows, it is possible to reformulate a strong method such as propose & revise as a specialised, but task-independent search mechanism. So, is such a task-independent propose & revise a weak or a strong method? Basically it is a search algorithm - just like hill-climbing and A* - which makes strong assumptions about the availability of domain-specific knowledge to avoid backtracking when an inconsistent state is found. In a nutshell there are no strong and weak methods, there is a continuum in which one can define search strategies which make stronger and stronger assumptions about the availability of task-specific control knowledge. But there is no sharp dividing line.

In this paper we have characterised this method specialization process as one which consists of carrying out the appropriate ontology mappings. This approach clearly separates the specification of a task-independent reasoning strategy from the issue of adapting the strategy to alternative classes of tasks. Another example of this approach is given in [Fensel et al., 1996] who investigated the board game method. This method is a refinement of chronological backtracking for one-player board games. Therefore, the board game method is already a task-specific refinement of a generic search strategy. However, it can be further specialized to become applicable to assignment or parametric design tasks (cf. [Eriksson et al., 1995]).

The use of ontologies for characterising tasks and PSMs is not completely new. For example, [ten Teije, 1997] defines a task ontology for diagnostic problems and [Gennari et al., 1994] have proposed to use ontologies as a way to specify the knowledge requirements of a problem solving method. However, the latter define mainly names for knowledge types and neither approach provides a black-box-style specification of the competence of PSMs ([ten Teije, 1997] abstracts from all heuristic search knowledge that is essential in specifying PSMs). In contrast with these approaches we use formal ontologies to provide declarative, axiomatic specifications of both generic problem classes (task ontologies) and PSMs (method ontologies). Moreover, we demonstrated the use of adapters as a formal technique to integrate tasks and method ontologies.

An ontology-driven bottom-up development process is described in [Reynaud & Tort, 1997], which shows how to derive a reasoning method from an expert ontology. Therefore, their aim is orthogonal to our approach, which is concerned with the reuse of existing reasoning methods. However, it would be worthwhile to investigate whether their approach can be used to select and refine PSMs based on the ontological characterization proposed here.

[Mizoguchi et al., 1995] use ontologies to characterize tasks. A task ontology is used to decompose a task into subtasks, to identify the required knowledge types and to construct a problem solver that simulates the problem-solving behaviour of a domain expert. Again, the main distinction to our approach is that we aim for a declarative (black-box) characterization of problems and PSMs which does not refer to internal details of the problem-solving process.

In conclusion, in this paper we have shown an approach which centres on formal, axiomatic, reuse-oriented specifications of generic KBS components. Like all research on software reuse, it is the ultimate effectiveness of our approach will have to be validated empirically, by trying it out on a number of different application domains.

Acknowledgement. We thank Annette ten Teije, Frank van Harmelen, Mark Willems, and two anonymous reviewers for helpful comments on drafts of the paper.

6   References

[Akkermans et al., 1993] J. M. Akkermans, B. Wielinga, and A. TH. Schreiber: Steps in Constructing Problem-Solving Methods. In N. Aussenac et al. (eds.): *Knowledge-Acquisition for Knowledge-Based Systems*, Lecture Notes in AI, no 723, Springer-Verlag, 1993.

[Angele et al., 1996] J. Angele, D. Fensel, and R. Studer: Domain and Task Modelling in MIKE. In A. Sutcliffe et al. (eds.), *Domain Knowledge for Interactive System Design*, Chapman & Hall, 1996.

[Benjamins, 1995] R. Benjamins: Problem Solving Methods for Diagnosis And Their Role in Knowledge Acquisition, *International Journal of Expert Systems: Research and Application*, 8(2):93—120, 1995.

[Beys et al., 1996] P. Beys, R. Benjamins, and G. van Heijst: Remedying the Reusability-Usability Tradeoff for Problem-solving Methods. In *Proceedings of the 10th Banff Knowledge Acquisition for Knowledge-Based System Workshop (KAW'96)*, Banff, Canada, November 9-14, 1996.

[Breuker & Van de Velde, 1994] J. Breuker and W. Van de Velde (eds.): *The CommonKADS Library for Expertise Modelling*, IOS Press, Amsterdam, The Netherlands, 1994.

[Bylander & Chandrasekaran, 1988] T. Bylander, and B. Chandrasekaran: Generic Tasks in Knowledge-Based Reasoning: The Right Level of Abstraction for Knowledge Acquisition. In B. Gaines et al. (eds.), *Knowledge Acquisition for Knowledge-Based Systems*, vol 1, pp. 65—77. Academic Press, London, 1988.

[Chandrasekaran, 1990] B. Chandrasekaran: Design Problem Solving: A Task Analysis. *AI Magazine*, 11(4):59—71, Winter Issue, 1990.

[Chandrasekaran et al., 1992] B. Chandrasekaran, T.R. Johnson, and J. W. Smith: Task Structure Analysis for Knowledge Modeling, *Communications of the ACM*, 35(9): 124—137, 1992.

[Eriksson et al., 1995] H. Eriksson, Y. Shahar, S. W. Tu, A. R. Puerta, and M. A. Musen: Task Modeling with Reusable Problem-Solving Methods, *Artificial Intelligence*, 79(2):293—326, 1995.

[Farquhar et al., 1997] A. Farquhar, R. Fickas, and J. Rice: The Ontolingua Server: a Tool for Collaborative Ontology Construction, *International Journal of Human-Computer Studies (IJHCS)*, 46(6):707—728, 1997.

[Fensel, 1997a] D. Fensel: An Ontology-based Broker: Making Problem-Solving Method Reuse Work. In *Proceeedings of the Workshop on Problem-Solving Methods for Knowledge-based Systems (W26) during IJCAI-97*, Japan, August 23, 1997.

[Fensel, 1997b] D. Fensel: The Tower-of-Adapters Method for Developing and Reusing Problem-Solving Methods. To appear in *Proceedings of European Knowledge Acquisition Workshop (EKAW-97)*, LNAI, Springer-Verlag, 1997.

[Fensel & Groenboom, 1997] D. Fensel and R. Groenboom: Specifying Knowledge-Based Systems with Reusable Components. In *Proceedings of the 9th International Conference on Software Engineering & Knowledge Engineering (SEKE-97)*, Madrid, Spain, June 18-20, 1997.

[Fensel & Schönegge, 1997] D. Fensel and A. Schönegge: Specifying and Verifying Knowledge-Based Systems with KIV. In *Proceedings of the European Symposium on the Validation and Verification of Knowledge Based Systems EUROVAV-97*, Leuven Belgium, June 26-28, 1997.

[Fensel et al., 1996] D. Fensel, H. Eriksson, M. A. Musen, and R. Studer: Developing Problem-Solving by Introducing Ontological Commitments, *International Journal of Expert Systems: Research & Applications*, vol 9(4), 1996.

[Gennari et al., 1994] Gennari, J. H., Tu, S. W., Rothenfluh, T. E., Musen, M. A. Mapping Domains to Methods in Support of Reuse. In *Proceedings of the 8th Banff Knowledge Acquisition Workshop (KAW-94)*, Banff, Canada, 1994.

[Gruber, 1993] T. R. Gruber: A Translation Approach to Portable Ontology Specifications, *Knowledge Acquisition*, 5(2), 1993.

[Gruber, 1995] T. R. Gruber: Toward Principles for the Design of Ontologies Used for Knowledge Sharing, *International Journal of Human-Computer Studies (IJHCS)*, 43(5/6):907—928, 1995.

[Kifer et al., 1995] M. Kifer, G. Lausen, and J. Wu: Logical Foundations of Object-Oriented and Frame-Based Languages, *Journal of the ACM*, 42, 1995.

[Klinker et al., 1991] G. Klinker, C. Bhola, G. Dallemagne, D. Marques, and J. McDermott: Usable and Reusable Programmin Constructs, *Knowledge Acquisition*, 3:117—136, 1991.

[Lenat & Feigenbaum, 1987] D. B. Lenat and E. A. Feigenbaum: On the Thresholds of Knowledge. In *Proceedings of the 10th International Joint Conference on Artificial Intelligence (IJCAI-87)*, 1987.

[Marcus et al., 1988] S. Marcus, J. Stout, and J. McDermott VT: An Expert Elevator Designer That Uses Knowledge-based Backtracking, *AI Magazine*, 9(1):95—111, 1988.

[Marcus & McDermott, 1989] S. Marcus, and J. McDermott: SALT: A Knowledge Acquisition Language for Propose and Revise Systems, *Artificial Intelligence*, 39(1):1—37.

[Mc Dermott, 1988] J. Mc Dermott: Preliminary Steps Toward a Taxonomy of Problem-Solving Methods. In S. Marcus (ed.). *Automating Knowledge Acquisition for Experts Systems*, Kluwer Academic Publisher, Boston, 1988.

[Mittal & Frayman, 1989] S. Mittal and F. Frayman: Towards a Generic Model of Configuration Tasks. In *Proceedings of the 11th International Joint Conference on Artificial Intelligence - IJCAI '89*, San Mateo, CA, Morgan-Kaufman, 1989.

[Mizoguchi et al., 1995] R. Mizoguchi, J. Vanwelkenhuysen, and M. Ikeda: Task Ontologies for reuse of Problem Solving Knowledge. In N. J. I. Mars (ed.), *Towards Very Large Knowledge Bases*, IOS Press, 1995.

[Motta & Zdrahal, 1996] E. Motta and Z. Zdrahal: Parametric Design Problem Solving. In *Proceedings of the 10th Banff Knowledge Acquisition for Knowledge-Based System Workshop (KAW'96)*, Banff, Canada, November 9-14, 1996.

[Newell & Simon, 1972] A. Newell and H. A. Simon: *Human Problem Solving*, Prentice Hall, 1972.

[Puppe, 1993] F. Puppe: *Systematic Introduction to Expert Systems: Knowledge Representation and Problem-Solving Methods*, Springer-Verlag, Berlin, 1993.

[Reynaud & Tort, 1997] C. Reynaud and F. Tort: Using Explicit Ontologies to Create Problem Solving Methods, *International Journal of Human-Computer Studies (IJHCS)*, 46:339—364, 1997.

[Schreiber et al., 1994] A. TH. Schreiber, B. Wielinga, J. M. Akkermans, W. Van De Velde, and R. de Hoog: CommonKADS. A Comprehensive Methodology for KBS Development, *IEEE Expert*, 9(6):28—37, 1994.

[Steels, 1990] L. Steels: Components of Expertise, *AI Magazine*, 11(2), 1990.

[ten Teije, 1997] A. ten Teije: *Automated Configuration of Problem Solving Methods in Diagnosis*, PhD thesis, University of Amsterdam, Amsterdam, NL, 1997.

[Terpstra et al., 1993] P. Terpstra, G. van Heijst, B. Wielinga, and N. Shadbolt: Knowledge Acquisition Support Through Generalised Directive Models. In M. David et al. (eds.): *Second Generation Expert Systems*, Springer-Verlag, 1993.

[Top & Akkermans, 1994] J. Top and H. Akkermans: Tasks and Ontologies in Engineering Modeling, *International Journal of Human-Computer Studies (IJHCS)*, 41:585—617, 1994.

[van Heijst and A. Anjewerden, 1996] G. van Heijst and A. Anjewerden: Four Propositions concerning the specification of Problem-Solving Methods. In *Supplementary Proceedings of the 9th European Knowledge Acquisition Workshop EKAW-96*, Nottingham, England, May 14-17, 1996.

[van de Velde, 1988] W. van de Velde: Inference Structure as a Basis for Problem Solving. In *Proceedings of the 8th European Conference on Artificial Intelligence (ECAI-88)*, Munich, August 1-5, 1988.

[van Harmelen & Fensel, 1995] F. van Harmelen and D. Fensel: Formal Methods in Knowledge Engineering, *The Knowledge Engineering Review*, 10(4), 1995.

[van Heijst et al., 1997] G. van Heijst, A. T. Schreiber, and B. J. Wielinga: Using Explicit Ontologies in Knowledge-Based System Development, *International Journal of Human-Computer Interaction (IJHCI)*, to appear 1997.

[Wielinga et al., 1995] B. J. Wielinga, J. M. Akkermans, and A. Th. Schreiber: A Formal Analysis of Parametric Design Problem Solving. In *Proceedings of the 9th Banff Knowledge Acquisition Workshop (KAW-95)*, Banff, Canada, January 26 - Feruary 3, 1995.

[Yost & Rothenfluh, 1996] G. R. Yost and T.R. Rothenfluh: Configuring elevator systems, *International Journal of Human-Computer Studies (IJHCS)*, 44(3/4):521—568, 1996.

[Zdrahal & Motta, 1995] Z. Zdrahal and E. Motta: An In-Depth Analysis of Propose & Revise Problem Solving Methods. In *Proceedings of the 9th Banff Knowledge Acquisition Workshop (KAW-95)*, Banff, Canada, January 26 - Feruary 3, 1995.

An Empirical Evaluation
of a System for Text Knowledge Acquisition

Udo Hahn & Klemens Schnattinger

⟨ΩΓ⟩ Text Knowledge Engineering Lab, Freiburg University
Werthmannplatz 1, D-79085 Freiburg, Germany
http://www.coling.uni-freiburg.de/

Abstract. We introduce a formal model and a corresponding system architecture for the acquisition of new concepts from real-world natural language texts. Our approach is centered around the linguistic and conceptual "quality" of various forms of evidence underlying the generation and refinement of concept hypotheses. Based on a terminological (meta)reasoning platform, hypotheses are continuously annotated by a stream of linguistic and conceptual evidence, preferentially ranked and, finally, selected according to their overall credibility. We discuss the results of an empirical evaluation study, concentrating on the system's learning rate and learning accuracy.

1 Introduction

Learning new concepts as a result from reading and understanding natural language texts builds on at least two different sources of evidence. The prior knowledge of the domain the texts are about and linguistic constructions in which unknown lexical items occur. While there may be many reasonable guesses when an unknown item occurs for the very first time in a text, their number quite rapidly decreases when more and more evidence is gathered. Our model tries to make explicit the kind of qualitative reasoning that is behind this kind of plausible learning.

We here propose a *knowledge-intensive* model of concept learning from *few* natural language texts that is tightly integrated with the non-learning mode of text understanding. Both, learning and understanding, build on a given core ontology in the format of terminological assertions and, hence, make abundant use of terminological reasoning facilities. The "plain" text understanding mode can be considered the instantiation and continuous role filling with respect to *single concepts* already available in the knowledge base. Under learning conditions, however, for each unknown item a *set of alternative concept hypotheses* are managed, with each hypothesis denoting a newly created conceptual interpretation tentatively associated with the unknown item.

Two types of evidence are taken into account for continuously discriminating and refining the set of concept hypotheses — the type of linguistic construction in which an unknown lexical item occurs and conceptually motivated annotations of concept hypotheses reflecting structural patterns of consistency, mutual

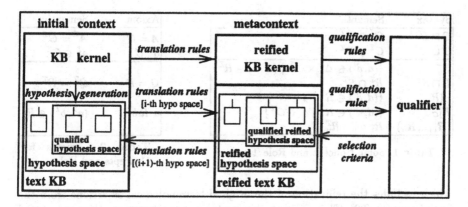

Fig. 1. System Architecture for Quality-Based Text Knowledge Acquisition

justification, analogy, etc. in the continuously updated knowledge base. These kinds of initial evidence are represented by a set of quality labels. Concept acquisition can then be viewed as a *quality-based decision task* which is decomposed into three constituent parts: the continuous generation of quality labels for single concept hypotheses (reflecting the *reasons* for their formation and their significance in the light of other hypotheses), the estimation of the overall *credibility* of single concept hypotheses (taking the available set of quality labels for each hypothesis into account), and the computation of a *preference order* for the entire set of competing hypotheses, which is based on these accumulated quality judgments.

2 System Architecture for Text Knowledge Acquisition

The methodology and corresponding system architecture for text knowledge acquisition (cf. Fig. 1) we propose serves the representation of quality-based assertions about certain propositions and the reasoning about characteristic properties and relations between these assertions. The text understanding processes use a terminological model of the underlying domain, the knowledge base *KB kernel*, on the basis of which the parser [7] generates a conceptual interpretation of the text in the *text KB*. Whenever an unknown lexical item occurs during the text understanding process, and this item is considered relevant for learning according to distributional criteria, conceptual hypotheses are generated [6]. These take linguistic criteria (mirrored by the assignment of corresponding *linguistic* quality labels) as well as conceptual conditions into account. Multiple concept hypotheses for a single lexical item are organized in terms of a corresponding hypothesis space as part of the text KB, each subspace holding different or further specialized concept hypotheses.

In order to reason about the credibility of these hypotheses a mirror image of the *initial context* which combines the KB kernel and the text KB is generated — the so-called *metacontext*. This is achieved by a truth-preserving mapping

Syntax	Semantics
$C \sqcap D$	$C^{\mathcal{I}} \cap D^{\mathcal{I}}$
$C \sqcup D$	$C^{\mathcal{I}} \cup D^{\mathcal{I}}$
R^{-1}	$\{(d, d') \in \Delta^{\mathcal{I}} \times \Delta^{\mathcal{I}} \mid (d', d) \in R^{\mathcal{I}}\}$
$R \sqcap S$	$R^{\mathcal{I}} \cap S^{\mathcal{I}}$
$c\|R$	$\{(d, d') \in R^{\mathcal{I}} \mid d \in C^{\mathcal{I}}\}$
$R\|_c$	$\{(d, d') \in R^{\mathcal{I}} \mid d' \in C^{\mathcal{I}}\}$
$(R_1, .., R_n)$	$R_1^{\mathcal{I}} \circ .. \circ R_n^{\mathcal{I}}$

Table 1. Some Concept and Role Terms

Axiom	Semantics
$A \doteq C$	$A^{\mathcal{I}} = C^{\mathcal{I}}$
$a : C$	$a^{\mathcal{I}} \in C^{\mathcal{I}}$
$Q \doteq R$	$Q^{\mathcal{I}} = R^{\mathcal{I}}$
$a \, R \, b$	$(a^{\mathcal{I}}, b^{\mathcal{I}}) \in R^{\mathcal{I}}$

Table 2. Axioms for Concepts and Roles

which includes the reification of the original terminological assertions from the initial context [22]. These reified representation structures are then submitted to conceptual *qualification rules* which determine purely conceptual indicators of credibility of the associated hypotheses and assign corresponding *conceptual* quality labels to them in the *reified hypothesis space*. A classifier extended by an evaluation metric for quality-based selection criteria, the *qualifier*, then determines the most credible concept hypotheses [21]. Only those will be remapped from their reified to the original terminological form by way of (inverse) translation rules, and thus become available again for the text understanding process. Thus, we come full circle. The entire cycle is triggered for each new evidence that becomes available for a concept to be learned as the text understanding process proceeds.

In the following, we will illustrate the working of this architecture in more detail based on processing the example phrase (1) *"The Itoh-Ci-8 has .."* as the first learning step for the unknown item *"Itoh-Ci-8"*. Other learning steps are based on continuing the processing of phrase (1) by *".. a size of .."*, and then considering the phrase (3) *"The switch of the Itoh-Ci-8 .."*.

2.1 Terminological Logics

We use a concept description language (for a survey, cf. [15]) with a standard set-theoretical semantics (the interpretation function $\mathcal{I}$). The language has several constructors combining *atomic* concepts, roles and individuals (see Table 1). By means of *terminological axioms* a symbolic name can be defined for each concept and role term; concepts and roles are associated with concrete individuals by *assertional axioms* (see Table 2). Consider the following example:

(P1) *switch*-01 : SWITCH

(P2) *Itoh-Ci*-8 HAS-SWITCH *switch*-01

(P3) HAS-SWITCH $\doteq$

   (OUTPUTDEV $\sqcup$ INPUTDEV $\sqcup$ STORAGEDEV $\sqcup$ COMPUTER)$|$HAS-PART$|$SWITCH

The assertions P1 and P2 read as: the instance *switch*-01 belongs to the concept SWITCH, and the tuple $\langle Itoh\text{-}Ci\text{-}8, switch\text{-}01 \rangle$ belongs to the binary relation HAS-SWITCH. The relation HAS-SWITCH is defined as all HAS-PART relations which have their domain restricted to the disjunction of the concepts OUT-PUTDEV, INPUTDEV, STORAGEDEVices or COMPUTER and have their range restricted to SWITCH.

2.2 Quality Labels

Linguistic quality labels reflect structural properties of phrasal patterns or discourse contexts in which unknown lexical items occur — we here assume that the type of grammatical construction exercises a particular interpretative force on the unknown item and, at the same time, yields a particular level of credibility for the hypotheses being derived. As a concrete example of a high-quality label, consider the case of APPOSITION. This label is generated for constructions such as *".. the printer @A@ .."*, with "@..@" denoting the unknown item. The apposition almost unequivocally determines "@A@" (considered as a potential noun)[1] to denote a PRINTER. This assumption is justified independent of further conceptual conditions, simply due to the nature of the linguistic construction being used. Still of good quality but already less constraining are occurrences of the unknown item in a CASEFRAME construction as illustrated by *".. @B@ has a size of .."*. In this example, case frame specifications of the verb *"has"* that relate to its AGENT role carry over to *"@B@"*. Given its final semantic interpretation, "@B@" may be anything that has a size, e.g., a physical object.

Conceptual quality labels result from comparing the conceptual representation structures of a concept hypothesis with already existing representation structures in the underlying domain knowledge base from the viewpoint of structural similarity, incompatibility, etc. The closer the match, the more credit is lent to a hypothesis. For instance, a very positive conceptual quality label such as M-DEDUCED is assigned to multiple derivations of the same concept hypothesis in different hypothesis (sub)spaces. Still positive labels are assigned to terminological expressions which share structural similarities, though they are not identical. For instance, the label C-SUPPORTED is assigned to any hypothesized relation $R1$ between two instances in case another relation, $R2$, already exists in the KB involving the same two instances, but where the role fillers occur in "inverted" order (note that $R1$ and $R2$ need not necessarily be conceptually inverse relations such as with *"buy"* and *"sell"*). This rule captures the inherent symmetry between concepts related via quasi-inverse conceptual relations.

2.3 Hypothesis Generation

Depending on the type of the syntactic construction in which the unknown lexical item occurs different hypothesis generation rules may fire. For instance, in our example *(3): "The switch of the Itoh-Ci-8 .."*, a genitive noun phrase places only few constraints on the item to be learned. In the following, let *target* be the unknown item *("Itoh-Ci-8")* and *base* be the known item *("switch")*,

---

[1] Such a part-of-speech hypothesis can directly be derived from the inventory of valence and word order specifications underlying the dependency grammar model we use [7].

the conceptual relation of which to the target is constrained by the syntactic relation in which their lexical counterparts co-occur. The main constraint for genitives says that the target concept fills (exactly) one of the n roles of the base concept (for more details, cf. [6]). Since it cannot be decided on the correct role yet, n alternative hypotheses have to be opened (unless additional constraints apply) and the target concept is assigned as a filler of the i-th role of base in the corresponding i-th hypothesis space. As a consequence, the classifier is able to derive a suitable concept hypothesis by specializing the target concept (initially TOP, by default) according to the value restriction of the base concept's i-th role. Additionally, this rule assigns a syntactic quality label to each i-th hypothesis indicating the type of syntactic construction in which target and base co-occur.

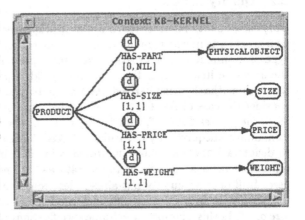

Fig. 2. Conceptual Representation of PRODUCT

Considering our example, the target *Itoh-Ci-8* is already predicted as a PRODUCT after the first two learning steps (i.e., the processing of phrase *(1)*). The conceptual representation of PRODUCT is given in Figure 2. At this level of conceptual restriction, four roles remain to be considered for relating the target ITOH-CI-8 – as a tentative PRODUCT – to the base concept SWITCH. Three of them, HAS-SIZE, HAS-PRICE, and HAS-WEIGHT, are ruled out due to the violation of a simple integrity constraint

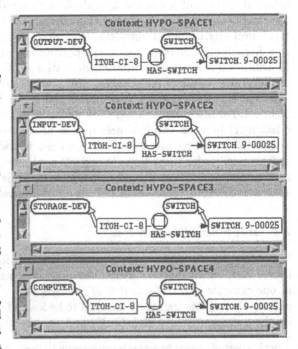

Fig. 3. Four Hypothesis Spaces

THRESH1	$\doteq$	HYPO ⊓
		MAX(APPOSITION *term*)
THRESH2	$\doteq$	THRESH1 ⊓
		MAX(CASEFRAME *term*)

CRED1	$\doteq$	THRESH2 ⊓
		MAX(M-DEDUCED *term*)
CRED2	$\doteq$	CRED1 ⊓
		MAX(C-SUPPORTED *term*)

Table 3. Threshold Levels

Table 4. Credibility Levels

(SWITCH does not denote a measure unit). Therefore, only the role HAS-PART must be considered. Due to the definition of HAS-SWITCH (cf. P3, Subsection 2.1), the instantiation of HAS-PART is specialized to HAS-SWITCH by the classifier, since the range of the HAS-PART relation is already restricted to SWITCH. As the classifier aggressively pushes hypothesizing to be maximally specific, four distinct hypotheses are immediately created due to the domain restrictions of the role HAS-SWITCH, *viz.* OUTPUTDEV, INPUTDEV, STORAGEDEV and COMPUTER, and are managed in the hypothesis spaces 1, 2, 3 and 4, respectively (cf. Fig. 3).

2.4 Conceptual Qualification

Quality annotations of the conceptual status of concept hypotheses are derived from qualification rules. For instance, one of the rules applies to the case where the same assertion is deduced in at least two different hypothesis spaces (cf. H and H' in Fig. 4). We take this quasi-confirmation as a strong support for the hypothesis under consideration. Hence, the very positive conceptual quality label M-DEDUCED is derived (for a formal specification of several qualification rules, cf. [5]).

Considering our example, for *"Itoh-Ci-8"* the concept hypotheses OUTPUTDEV, INPUTDEV and STORAGEDEV were derived independently of each other in different hypothesis spaces. Hence, DEVICE as their common superconcept has been multiply derived by the classifier in each of these spaces, too.

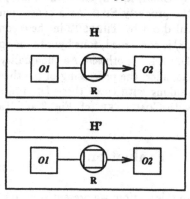

Fig. 4. A Conceptual Qualification Scenario

2.5 Quality-Based Classification

Whenever new evidence for or against a concept hypothesis is brought forth in a single learning step the entire set of concept hypotheses is reevaluated. First, a selection process eliminates weak or even untenable hypotheses from further consideration. The corresponding quality-based selection among hypothesis spaces is grounded on threshold levels as defined in Table 3 (in Section 3 this selection level will be referred to as **TH**). Their definition takes mostly linguistic evidence into account and evolved in a series of validation experiments. At the first threshold level, all hypothesis spaces HYPO with the maximum of APPOSITION labels are selected. If more than one hypothesis is left to be considered, at the second threshold level only concept hypotheses with the maximum number of CASE-FRAME assignments are approved. Those hypothesis spaces that have fulfilled these threshold criteria will then be classified relative to two different credibility levels as defined in Table 4 (in Section 3 this selection level will be referred to as **CB**). The first level of credibility contains all of the hypothesis spaces which have the maximum of M-DEDUCED labels, while at the second level (again, with more than one hypothesis left to be considered) those are chosen which are assigned the maximum of C-SUPPORTED labels. Threshold and credibility criteria make use of composed roles, a specific domain and range restriction on roles (in Tables 3 and 4 abbreviated as "X *term*"), and a new constructor MAX for the path computation. A complete terminological specification of the entire qualification calculus (including the generation of quality labels, their combination and evaluation) is given in [21].

To illustrate the use of threshold criteria, consider the first phrase: *"The Itoh-Ci-8 has a size of .."*, for which a CASEFRAME assignment is triggered in those hypothesis spaces where the unknown item is considered a PHYSICALOBJECT. The remaining hypotheses (cf. Table 6, learning step 2) cannot be annotated by CASEFRAME, since the concepts they represent cannot be associated with the property SIZE. As a consequence, the corresponding hypothesis spaces are ruled out by THRESH2 in the second learning step. As far as the sample phrase *(3)* is concerned, four hypothesis spaces are generated three of which stipulate a DEVICE hypothesis. As the quality label M-DEDUCED has been derived by the classifier, the processing of the third sample phrase already yields a preliminary ranking with these three DEVICE hypotheses preferred over the one associated with COMPUTER (cf. Fig. 3 and Table 6, learning step 3).

3 Evaluation

In this section, we present some data from an empirical evaluation of the quality-based concept acquisition system. We focus here on the issues of learning accuracy and the learning rate. Due to the given learning environment, the measures we apply deviate from those commonly used in the machine learning community. In concept learning algorithms like IBL [2] there is no hierarchy of concepts. Hence, any prediction of the class membership of a new instance is either true or false. However, as such hierarchies naturally emerge in terminological frameworks, a prediction can be more or less precise, i.e., it may approximate the goal concept at different levels of specificity. This is captured by our measure of *learning accuracy* which takes into account the conceptual distance of a hypothesis to the goal concept of an instance, rather than simply relating the number of correct and false predictions, as in IBL.

	Phrase	Semantic Interpretation
1.	The *Itoh-Ci-8 has*	(CaseFrame,possess.1,agent,Itoh-Ci-8)
2.	a *size* of ..	(CaseFrame,possess.1,patient,Size.1)
		↦ (Itoh-Ci-8,has-size,Size.1)
3.	The *switch* of the *Itoh-Ci-8* ..	(GenitiveNP,Itoh-Ci-8,has-switch,Switch.1)
4.	The *case* from the *Itoh-Ci-8* ..	(PP-Attach,Itoh-Ci-8,has-case,Case.1)
5.	*Itoh-Ci-8* with a *main memory* ..	(PP-Attach,Itoh-Ci-8,has-memory,Memory.1)
6.	*Itoh-Ci-8's LED lines* ..	(GenitiveNP,Itoh-Ci-8,has-part,LED-Line.1)
7.	*Itoh-Ci-8's toner supply* ..	(GenitiveNP,Itoh-Ci-8,has-part,TonerSupply.1)
8.	*Paper cassette* of the *Itoh-Ci-8* ..	(GenitiveNP,Itoh-Ci-8,has-part,PaperSupply.1)
9.	*Itoh-Ci-8* with a *resolution rate* ..	(PP-Attach,Itoh-Ci-8,has-rate,Resolution.1)

Table 5. Semantic Interpretation Fragments of a Text Featuring *"Itoh-Ci-8"*

In our approach, learning is achieved by the refinement of *multiple* hypotheses about the class membership of an instance. Thus, the measure of *learning rate* we propose is concerned with the reduction of hypotheses as more and more *information* becomes available about one particular new instance. In contrast, IBL-style algorithms consider only one concept hypothesis per learning cycle and their notion of *learning rate* relates to the increase of correct predictions as more and more *instances* are being processed.

We considered a total of 101 texts taken from a corpus of information technology magazines. For each of them 5 to 15 learning steps were considered. A *learning step* is operationalized here by the representation structure that results from the semantic interpretation of an utterance which contains the unknown lexical item. In order to clarify the input data available for the learning system, consider Table 5. It consists of nine single learning steps for the unknown item *"Itoh-Ci-8"* that occurred while processing an entire text. Each learning step is associated with a particular natural language phrase in which the unknown lexical item occurs[2] and the corresponding semantic interpretation in the text knowledge base.

3.1 Learning Accuracy

In a first series of experiments, we investigated the *learning accuracy* of the system, i.e., the degree to which the system correctly predicts the concept class which subsumes the target concept under consideration (the *target* being the new item to be learned). Learning accuracy (*LA*) is defined here as (*n* being the number of concept hypotheses for a single target):

$$LA := \sum_{i \in \{1...n\}} \frac{LA_i}{n} \quad \text{with} \quad LA_i := \begin{cases} \dfrac{CP_i}{SP_i} & \text{if } FP_i = 0 \\ \dfrac{CP_i}{FP_i + DP_i} & \text{else} \end{cases}$$

---

[2] Note that our text database consists of German language data. The translations we provide give only rough English correspondences.

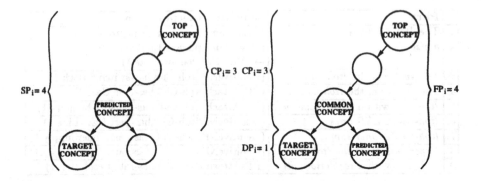

Fig. 5. LA Configuration for an Under-specified Concept Hypothesis

Fig. 6. LA Configuration for a Slightly Incorrect Concept Hypothesis

SP_i specifies the length of the *shortest path* (in terms of the number of nodes being traversed) from the TOP node of the concept hierarchy to the maximally specific concept subsuming the instance to be learned in hypothesis i; CP_i specifies the length of the path from the TOP node to that concept node in hypothesis i which is *common* both for the shortest path (as defined above) and the actual path to the predicted concept (whether correct or not); FP_i specifies the length of the path from the TOP node to the predicted (in this case *false*) concept and DP_i denotes the node *distance* between the predicted (false) node and the most specific common concept (on the path from the TOP node to the predicted false node) still correctly subsuming the target in hypothesis i. Figures 5 and 6 depict sample configurations for concrete LA values involving these parameters. Fig. 5 illustrates a correct, yet too general prediction with $LA_i = .75$, while Fig. 6 contains an incorrect concept hypothesis with $LA_i = .6$.

Given the measure for learning accuracy, Table 6 and Table 7 illustrate how the various concepts hypotheses for ITOH-CI-8 develop in accuracy from one step to the other. The numbers in brackets in the column **Concept Hypotheses** indicate for each hypothesized concept the number of concepts subsumed by it in the underlying knowledge base; **LA CB** gives the accuracy rate for the full qualification calculus including threshold and credibility criteria, **LA TH** for threshold criteria only, while **LA –** depicts the accuracy values produced by the terminological reasoning component without incorporating the qualification calculus. As can be seen from Tables 6 and 7, the full qualification calculus produces either the same or even more accurate results, the same or fewer hypothesis spaces (indicated by the number of rows), and derives the correct prediction more rapidly (in step 6) than the less knowledgeable variants (in step 9).

The data also illustrate the continuous specialization of concept hypotheses achieved by the terminological classifier, e.g., from PHYSICALOBJECT[3] in step 1 via PRODUCT in step 2 to OUTPUTDEVICE and PRINTER in step 3 and 4, respectively. The overall learning accuracy – due to the learner's aggressive specializa-

---

[3] The upper-level concepts of our ontology are taken from Nirenburg and Raskin [16].

Concept Hypotheses	LA –	LA TH	LA CB	Concept Hypotheses	LA –	LA TH	LA CB
PHYSICALOBJ(176)	0.30	0.30	0.30	PRODUCT(136)	0.50	0.50	0.50
MENTALOBJ(0)	0.16	0.16	0.16	MENTALOBJ(0)	0.16		
INFORMATOBJ(5)	0.16	0.16	0.16	INFORMATOBJ(5)	0.16		
MASSOBJ(0)	0.16	0.16	0.16	MASSOBJ(0)	0.16		
NORM(3)	0.16	0.16	0.16	NORM(3)	0.16		
TECHNOLOGY(1)	0.16	0.16	0.16	TECHNOLOGY(1)	0.16		
MODE(5)	0.16	0.16	0.16	MODE(5)	0.16		
FEATURE(0)	0.16	0.16	0.16	FEATURE(0)	0.16		
	ϕ:0.18	ϕ:0.18	ϕ:0.18		ϕ:0.21	ϕ:0.50	ϕ:0.50
Learning Step 1				**Learning Step 2**			
COMPUTER(5)	0.50	0.50		NOTEBOOK(0)	0.43	0.43	
				PORTABLE(0)	0.43	0.43	
				PC(0)	0.43	0.43	
				WORKSTATION(0)	0.43	0.43	
				DESKTOP(0)	0.43	0.43	
OUTPUTDEV(9)	0.80	0.80	0.80	PRINTER(3)	0.90	0.90	0.90
				VISUALDEV(2)	0.66	0.66	0.66
				LOUDSPEAKER(0)	0.66	0.66	0.66
				PLOTTER(0)	0.66	0.66	0.66
STORAGEDEV(5)	0.55	0.55	0.55	RW-STORE(2)	0.50	0.50	0.50
				RO-STORE(1)	0.50	0.50	0.50
INPUTDEV(2)	0.55	0.55	0.55	MOUSE(0)	0.50	0.50	
				KEYBOARD(0)	0.50	0.50	
	ϕ:0.60	ϕ:0.60	ϕ:0.63		ϕ:0.54	ϕ:0.54	ϕ:0.65
Learning Step 3				**Learning Step 4**			

Table 6. Learning Steps for a Text Featuring *"Itoh-Ci-8"*

tion strategy – may even temporarily decrease in the course of hypothesizing (e.g., from step 3 to 4 or step 5 to 6 for **LA –** and **LA TH**), but the learning accuracy value for the full qualification calculus (**LA CB**) always increases. These data for learning the ITOH-CI-8 concept are graphically re-interpreted in Fig. 7.

Generalizing from the learning behavior for a single concept like ITOH-CI-8, Fig. 8 depicts the learning accuracy curve for the entire data set (101 texts). We also have included the graph depicting the growth behavior of hypothesis spaces (Fig. 10). The corresponding graph for *Itoh-Ci-8* is given in Fig. 9. For both data sets, we distinguish again between the measurements for **LA –**, **LA TH** and **LA CB**. In Fig. 8 the evaluation starts from LA values in the interval between 48% to 54% for **LA –/LA TH** and **LA CB**, respectively, in the first learning step, whereas the number of hypothesis spaces range between 6.2 and 4.5 (Fig. 10). In the final step, LA rises up to 79%, 83% to 87% for **LA –**, **LA TH** and **LA CB**, respectively, and the **NH** values reduce to 4.4, 3.6 and 2.5 for each of the three criteria, respectively.

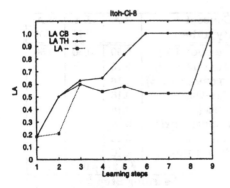

Fig. 7. Learning Accuracy (LA) for Acquiring the *Itoh-Ci-8* Concept

Fig. 8. Learning Accuracy (LA) for the Entire Data Set

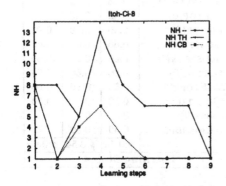

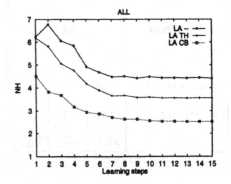

Fig. 9. Number of Hypothesis Spaces (NH) for Acquiring the *Itoh-Ci-8* Concept

Fig. 10. Number of Hypotheses (NH) for the Entire Data Set

The pure terminological reasoning machinery which does not incorporate the qualification calculus always achieves an inferior level of learning accuracy and generates more hypothesis spaces than the learner equipped with the qualification calculus. Furthermore, the inclusion of conceptual criteria (**CB**) supplementing the linguistic criteria (**TH**) helps a lot to focus on the relevant hypothesis spaces and to further discriminate the valid hypotheses (on the range of 4% of precision). Note that an already significant plateau of accuracy is usually reached after the third step (*viz.* 67%, 73%, and 76% for **LA −**, **LA TH**, and **LA CB**, respectively, in Fig. 8; the corresponding numbers of hypothesis spaces being 6.1, 5.1, and 3.7 for **NH −**, **NH TH**, and **NH CB**, respectively, in Fig. 10). This indicates that our approach finds the most relevant distinctions in a very early phase of the learning process, i.e., it requires only a *few* examples.

In a knowledge acquisition application operating on real-world texts, it should be fair to ask what level of precision one is willing to accept as a satisfactory result. We may discuss this issue in terms of degrees of learning accuracy. Under

Concept Hypotheses	LA –	LA TH	LA CB	Concept Hypotheses	LA –	LA TH	LA CB
NOTEBOOK(0)	0.43	0.43		NOTEBOOK(0)	0.43	0.43	
PORTABLE(0)	0.43	0.43		PORTABLE(0)	0.43	0.43	
PC(0)	0.43	0.43		PC(0)	0.43	0.43	
WORKSTATION(0)	0.43	0.43		WORKSTATION(0)	0.43	0.43	
DESKTOP(0)	0.43	0.43		DESKTOP(0)	0.43	0.43	
LASERPRINT(0)	1.00	1.00	1.00	LASERPRINT(0)	1.00	1.00	1.00
INKJETPRINT(0)	0.75	0.75	0.75				
NEEDLEPRINT(0)	0.75	0.75	0.75				
	ϕ:0.58	ϕ:0.58	ϕ:0.83		ϕ:0.52	ϕ:0.52	ϕ:1.00
Learning Step 5				**Learning Step 6**			
NOTEBOOK(0)	0.43	0.43		NOTEBOOK(0)	0.43	0.43	
PORTABLE(0)	0.43	0.43		PORTABLE(0)	0.43	0.43	
PC(0)	0.43	0.43		PC(0)	0.43	0.43	
WORKSTATION(0)	0.43	0.43		WORKSTATION(0)	0.43	0.43	
DESKTOP(0)	0.43	0.43		DESKTOP(0)	0.43	0.43	
LASERPRINT(0)	1.00	1.00	1.00	LASERPRINT(0)	1.00	1.00	1.00
	ϕ:0.52	ϕ:0.52	ϕ:1.00		ϕ:0.52	ϕ:0.52	ϕ:1.00
Learning Step 7				**Learning Step 8**			
LASERPRINT(0)	1.00	1.00	1.00				
	ϕ:1.00	ϕ:1.0	ϕ:1.00				
Learning Step 9							

Table 7. Learning Steps for a Text Featuring *"Itoh-Ci-8"* (continued)

ideal conditions, one might require a 100% learning accuracy. Fig. 11 gives the number of texts being processed under this constraint and the associated number of learning steps, given the three types of criteria, *viz.* **LA -**, **LA TH**, and **LA CB**. Under the rigid condition that the most specific concept specializing the unknown item is to be learned, the three criteria require almost the same number of learning steps on the average. This is simply due to the fact that the knowledge base we supply has not a full coverage of any domain segment, even in a limited domain such as information technology. (The knowledge base currently comprises 325 concept definitions and 447 conceptual relations.) The picture changes remarkably (cf. Fig. 12), if we only require a level of precision that does not fall below a learning accuracy of 80%. This also means that more general or slightly incorrect concept descriptions are accepted as a proper learning result, though more specific and entirely correct concept descriptions might have been

	# texts	steps		# texts	steps
LA –	26	4,68	LA –	58	4,69
LA TH	31	4,16	LA TH	74	4,36
LA CB	39	4,15	LA CB	85	3,71

Fig. 11. Learning Steps for LA = 1.0   Fig. 12. Learning Steps for LA = .8

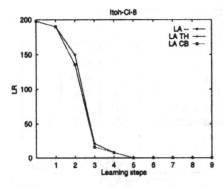
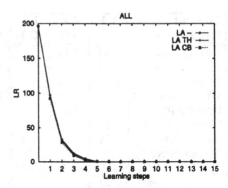

Fig. 13. Learning Rate (LR) for Acquiring the *Itoh-Ci-8* Concept

Fig. 14. Learning Rate (LR) for the Entire Data Set

worked out, at least in principle. About double the number of texts are being processed, but the number of learning steps are decreasing <u>only</u> for the full qualification calculus (*viz.* applying criterion **LA CB**). We may thus conclude that, granted an LA level of 80%, at least for the full qualification calculus only 15% of the learned concepts will be erroneous still. (Note the contrast to the LA values depicted in Fig. 8, which are derived from *averaging* single LA values.)

Summarizing this discussion, we may conclude that lowering the requirements on acceptable precision rates of learning results – within reasonable limits, of course – produces still valid learning hypotheses that are built up in less than four learning steps on the average.

3.2 Learning Rate

The learning accuracy focuses on the predictive power of the learning procedure. By considering the *learning rate*, we supply data from the step-wise reduction of alternatives of the learning process. Fig. 14 depicts the mean number of transitively included concepts for all considered hypothesis spaces per learning step (each concept hypothesis denotes a concept which transitively subsumes various subconcepts); the corresponding graph for the sample *Itoh-Ci-8* case is depicted in Fig. 13. Note that the most general concept hypothesis, in our example, denotes OBJECT which currently includes 196 concepts. In general, we observed a strong negative slope of the curve for the learning rate.

After the first step, slightly less than 50% of the included concepts are pruned (with 93, 94 and 97 remaining concepts for **LR CB**, **LR TH** and **LR –**, respectively). Again, learning step 3 is a crucial point for the reduction of the number of included concepts (ranging from 16 to 21 concepts). These data are almost exactly mirrored in the *Itoh-Ci-8* graph in Fig. 13. Summarizing this evaluation experiment, the quality-based learning system yields competitive accuracy rates (a mean of 87%), while at the same time it exhibits significant and valid reductions of the predicted concepts (up to two, on the average).

4 Related Work

Our approach bears a close relationship to the work of [13], [4], [17], [18], [25], and [10], who aim at the automated learning of word meanings from context using a knowledge-intensive approach. But our work differs from theirs in that the need to cope with *several competing* concept hypotheses and to aim at a *reason-based selection* is not an issue in these studies. Learning from real-world textual input usually provides the learner with only sparse and fragmentary evidence so that multiple hypotheses are likely to be derived requiring subsequent assessment. So, we stress the need for a hypothesis generation and evaluation component as an integral part of large-scale real-world text understanders [8] operating in tandem with concept learning devices.

The work closest to ours has been carried out by Rau *et al.* [17]. As in our approach, concept hypotheses are generated from linguistic and conceptual data. Unlike our approach, the selection of hypotheses depends only on an on-going discrimination process based on the availability of these data but does not incorporate an inferencing scheme for reasoned hypothesis selection. The difference in learning performance – in the light of our evaluation study in Section 3 – amounts to 8%, considering the difference between **LA** - (plain terminological reasoning) and **LA CB** values (terminological metareasoning based on the qualification calculus). Hence, our claim that we produce competitive results.

Note that the requirement to provide learning facilities for large-scale text knowledge engineering also distinguishes our approach from the currently active field of information extraction (IE) [3]. The IE task is defined in terms of a *fixed* set of *a priori* templates which have to be instantiated (i.e., filled with factual knowledge items) in the course of text analysis. In particular, no new templates have to be created. This step would correspond to the procedure we described in this contribution.

As far as the field of knowledge engineering from texts is concerned, i.e., text understanding and knowledge assimilation, our system represents a major achievement through the complete automatization of the text understanding and knowledge acquisition process. Previous studies mainly dealt with that problem by either hand-coding the content of the textual documents [24, 9, 19, 20, 1, 11], or providing semi-automatic, interactive devices for text knowledge acquisition [12, 26, 14], or using lexically oriented statistical approaches to text analysis [23].

5 Conclusion

We have presented a concept acquisition methodology which is based on the incremental assignment and evaluation of the quality of linguistic and conceptual evidence for emerging concept hypotheses. The principles underlying the selection and ordering of quality labels are general, as are most conceptual quality labels. The concrete definition of, e.g., linguistic quality labels, however, introduces a level of application-dependence. Nevertheless, as quality criteria are ubiquitous, one may easily envisage quality labels coming from sources other than linguistic and conceptual knowledge (e.g., a vision system may require quality labels which account for different degrees of signal distortion, 2D vs. 3D representations, etc. in order to interpret visual scenes in the course of learning new gestalts). No specialized learning algorithm is needed, since learning is a (meta)reasoning task carried out by the classifier of a terminological reasoning system. However, heuristic guidance for selecting between plausible hypotheses comes from the different quality criteria. Our experimental data indicate that given these heuristics we achieve a high degree of pruning of the search space for hypotheses in very early phases of the learning cycle.

Acknowledgements. We would like to thank our colleagues in the CLIF group for fruitful discussions and instant support, in particular Joe Bush who polished the text as a native speaker. K. Schnattinger is supported by a grant from DFG (Ha 2097/3-1).

References

1. R. Agarwal and M. Tanniru. Knowledge extraction using content analysis. *Knowledge Acquisition*, 3(4):421–441, 1991.
2. D. Aha, D. Kibler, and M. Albert. Instance-based learning algorithms. *Machine Learning*, 6:37–66, 1991.
3. D. Appelt, J. Hobbs, J. Bear, D. Israel, and M. Tyson. FASTUS: A finite-state processor for information extraction from real-world text. In *IJCAI'93 - Proc. 13th Intl. Joint Conf. on Artificial Intelligence*, pages 1172–1178, 1993.
4. F. Gomez and C. Segami. The recognition and classification of concepts in understanding scientific texts. *Journal of Experimental and Theoretical Artificial Intelligence*, 1:51–77, 1989.
5. U. Hahn, M. Klenner, and K. Schnattinger. Learning from texts: A terminological metareasoning perspective. In S. Wermter, E. Riloff, and G. Scheler, editors, *Connectionist, Statistical and Symbolic Approaches to Learning for Natural Language Processing*, pages 453–468. Berlin: Springer, 1996.
6. U. Hahn, M. Klenner, and K. Schnattinger. A quality-based terminological reasoning model for text knowledge acquisition. In N. Shadbolt, K. O'Hara, and G. Schreiber, editors, *EKAW'96 - Proc. 9th European Knowledge Acquisition Workshop*, pages 131–146. Berlin: Springer, 1996.
7. U. Hahn, S. Schacht, and N. Bröker. Concurrent, object-oriented natural language parsing: the PARSETALK model. *International Journal of Human-Computer Studies*, 41(1/2):179–222, 1994.
8. U. Hahn, K. Schnattinger, and M. Romacker. Automatic knowledge acquisition from medical texts. In J. Cimino, editor, *AMIA'96 - Proc. 1996 AMIA Annual Fall Symposium (formerly SCAMC). Beyond the Superhighway: Exploiting the Internet with Medical Informatics*, pages 383–387. Philadelphia/PA: Hanely & Belfus, 1996.
9. K. Handa and S. Ishizaki. Acquiring knowledge about a relation between concepts. In *EKAW'89 - Proc. of the European Knowledge Acquisition Workshop*, pages 380–390, 1989.
10. P. Hastings. Implications of an automatic lexical acquisition system. In S. Wermter, E. Riloff, and G. Scheler, editors, *Connectionist, Statistical and Symbolic Approaches to Learning in Natural Language Processing*, pages 261–274. Berlin: Springer, 1996.
11. R. Kaplan and G. Berry-Rogghe. Knowledge-based acquisition of causal relationships in text. *Knowledge Acquisition*, 3(3):317–337, 1991.

12. J. Möller. Knowledge acquisition from texts. In *EKAW'88 - Proc. 2nd European Knowledge Acquisition Workshop*, pages 25-1 – 25-16, 1988.
13. R. Mooney. Integrated learning of words and their underlying concepts. In *CogSci'87 - Proc. 9th Annual Conf. of the Cognitive Science Society*, pages 974–978, 1987.
14. B. Moulin and D. Rousseau. Designing deontic knowledge bases from regulation texts. *Knowledge-Based Systems*, 3(2):108–120, 1990.
15. B. Nebel. *Reasoning and Revision in Hybrid Representation Systems*. Berlin: Springer, 1990.
16. S. Nirenburg and V. Raskin. The subworld concept lexicon and the lexicon management system. *Computational Linguistics*, 13(3-4):276–289, 1987.
17. L. Rau, P. Jacobs, and U. Zernik. Information extraction and text summarization using linguistic knowledge acquisition. *Information Processing & Management*, 25(4):419–428, 1989.
18. U. Reimer. Automatic acquisition of terminological knowledge from texts. In *ECAI'90 - Proc. 9th European Conf. on Artificial Intelligence*, pages 547–549, 1990.
19. L. Ruqian and C. Cungen. Towards knowledge acquisition from domain books. In B. Wielinga, J. Boose, B. Gaines, and M. Schreiber, G. van Someren, editors, *Current Trends in Knowledge Acquisition*, pages 289–301. Amsterdam: IOS Press, 1990.
20. G. Schmidt and F. Schmalhofer. Case-oriented knowledge acquisition from texts. In B. Wielinga, J. Boose, B. Gaines, and M. Schreiber, G. van Someren, editors, *Current Trends in Knowledge Acquisition*, pages 302–312. Amsterdam: IOS Press, 1990.
21. K. Schnattinger and U. Hahn. A terminological qualification calculus for preferential reasoning under uncertainty. In *KI'96 - Proc. 20th Annual German Conf. on Artificial Intelligence*, pages 349–362. Berlin: Springer, 1996.
22. K. Schnattinger, U. Hahn, and M. Klenner. Terminological meta-reasoning by reification and multiple contexts. In *EPIA'95 - Proc. 7th Portuguese Conf. on Artificial Intelligence*, pages 1–16. Berlin: Springer, 1995.
23. M. Shaw and B. Gaines. KITTEN: Knowledge initiation and transfer tools for experts and novices. *International Journal of Human-Computer Studies*, 27:251–280, 1987.
24. D. Skuce, S. Matwin, B. Tauzovich, F. Oppacher, and S. Szpakowicz. A logic-based knowledge source system for natural language documents. *Data & Knowledge Engineering*, 1(3):201–231, 1985.
25. S. Soderland, D. Fisher, J. Aseltine, and W. Lehnert. CRYSTAL: Inducing a conceptual dictionary. In *IJCAI'95 - Proc. 14th Intl. Joint Conf. on Artificial Intelligence*, pages 1314–1319. San Mateo/CA: Morgan Kaufmann, 1995.
26. S. Szpakowicz. Semi-automatic acquisition of conceptual structure from technical texts. *International Journal on Man-Machine Studies*, 33:385–397, 1990.

Acquisition of Conceptual Structure in Scientific Theories

Dean M. Jones and Ray C. Paton
Department of Computer Science,
University of Liverpool,
Liverpool, L69 7ZF, UK
{dean,rcp}@csc.liv.ac.uk

Abstract

This paper details an approach to the acquisition of a specific kind of knowledge that found in causal scientific theories. We are especially concerned with the conceptual structure found in such theories as we assume them to be cognitive objects. The acquisition of this conceptual structure should take into account the structure of the underlying cognitive models. We have developed a software tool that assists in the early acquisition stages of the knowledge-based system (KBS) development cycle.

1. Introduction

Some of the major problems that are experienced in KBS development can be due to a lack of understanding of the type knowledge being represented. It is well known that there are many different types of knowledge, any or all of which may form part of the knowledge of a single domain. For effective KBS development, each type of knowledge should be acquired and represented using tools appropriate to it. An understanding of how an expert's knowledge of a domain is organised is necessary in order to be able to select the most appropriate representation(s). Previously, we have argued that, rather than move directly from an expert's explanation to a formal representation, an intermediate stage is necessary in which the domain is characterised semi-formally (Paton *et al.*, 1994b). This characterisation is then used as the basis for making decisions about issues such as how appropriate the development of a KBS is, the representation formalism to use, and so on.

In this paper, we outline an approach to the acquisition and representation of knowledge of a particular kind, causal knowledge. This kind of knowledge "may be relevant over a wide range of applications" (Charlet *et al.*, 1996). More specifically, we address theories of cellular and molecular biology, which we have previously suggested (Jones and Paton, 1994) are largely composed of causal, non-mathematical knowledge. We present a tool that aids knowledge acquisition in the difficult, early stages of an analysis and which produces a semi-formal representation. We illustrate the steps involved and the analysis of the output using examples from an acquisition project in a biological domain.

2. Scientific Theories

Since our aim is to represent scientific theories, the first question we must address is "What is the form of knowledge in scientific theories?". The philosophy of science gives us many different answers to this questions. Whilst a complete summary is not possible here, we will give brief outlines of two of the most influential views of the twentieth century, followed by our objections to them and an outline of a third position that we will adopt.

2.1 Theories are Syntactic Objects

From the early part of this century until around 1970, the prevailing conception of the structure of scientific theories was the syntactic, or law-statement, view, a position which is closely associated with the philosophical standpoint of logical positivism. According to this perspective, a scientific theory consists of two parts:

(i)   a formal logical system in the form of a series of logical statements that are inferred deductively from an initial set of postulates, or axioms, and

(ii)   a set of correspondence rules that interpret the symbols of the logical system in relation to the real world, in order to provide a semantic interpretation of the logic.

Some of the logical statements are to be interpreted as universal generalisations, or scientific laws, and theories are tested by comparing results predicted by these laws with empirical data. Whilst it is not usually claimed that this is the form of theories as used by scientists, it has been used in the reconstruction of theories for analytical purposes, where a theory is seen to be contained in the logical statements.

2.2 Theories are Semantic Objects

One of the earliest formulations of the successor to the syntactic view, called the semantic or model-theoretic view, was due to Suppes (1960). Suppes' main argument was based on the view that correspondence rules don't provide an adequate semantics for a logical system, therefore the concept of truth is inapplicable as a formal system has no meaning in itself. Rather, we should talk about models of a theory, which are abstract entities in which all of the statements of a formal logical system are true. The semantics of a theory can be provided directly by defining a class of models. Theories include two kinds of linguistic entities:

(i)   a class of predicates or models that act as definitions, and

(ii)   a set of statements that classify some real world system as being a kind of model

The structure corresponding to a model is not an axiomatic system but a definition. The semantics of the theory is provided directly by the definition of a class of models, which can be done in various ways, the usual method being to use complex mathematical structures such as set-theoretical predicates (Suppes, 1960) or state spaces (van Fraassen, 1980).

2.3 Theories are Cognitive Objects

Our objections to both of these views of theories can be summarised in two different, though related, points:

(i)   whilst a highly mathematical representations may be suitable for theories based on this form of knowledge (e.g. relativity theory) they are not adequate for scientific theories where mathematical formulations are rare, such as the biological theories that we aim to represent.

(ii)   both of these views are highly idealised conceptions of science that pay little heed to the fact that theories are products of the human cognitive system and rarely (if ever) used or presented in the forms suggested by either viewpoint.

While it may be true that reconstructions in the syntactic or semantic form is useful in analytical philosophy, this does not mean that they are accurate representations of scientific theories. We base our analysis on the assumption that scientists use refined versions of ordinary reasoning and representational processes (Giere, 1988; 1992). Scientific theories, as the products of these processes, are cognitive objects. They are representational systems and as such are not qualitatively different from the everyday common-sense theories that we hold about the world, although they are far more rigorously tested. Such testing may eventually lead to such a degree of refinement that a mathematical representation of a theory is possible. However, scientific theories that have not (and may never) reach this state are best studied and represented using the methods of the cognitive sciences.

One of our aims is the representation of non-mathematical theories such those found in the biological sciences. To a large extent, knowledge of these domains is in the form of *iconic models* (Harré, 1970), where an iconic model is a "thing, or process, which behaves similarly to some other thing or process, or in some other way than its behaviour is similar to it" (p. 174). It is instructive if we compare this definition with view given in Johnson-Laird (1983) that the structure of mental models is identical to the structure of the states of affairs, whether perceived or conceived, that the models represent.

We now turn to a theory of cognitive organisation that we have found useful in our analysis of scientific theories.

3. Idealised Cognitive Models

The classical theory of concepts suggests that they can be represented as a set of necessary and sufficient attributes i.e. the attributes are collectively sufficient to define the concept and individually necessary in order for some individual to be categorised as an example of that concept. While this definition is sufficient for simple concepts such as 'triangle', it will not suffice for more complex concepts where such a representation can only account for a few stereotypical examples.

According to Lakoff (1987), complex concepts are the result of the convergence of several Idealised Cognitive Models (ICMs), which are necessarily simple for the following reasons (McCauley, 1986): in reasoning about our environment, we need to use simplified models of it, as we do not easily deal with a lot of complexity. If we are unable to understand our world using models that match its complexity, we are unlikely to use such models in order to perform the simplification. Therefore, we use simplified, or idealised, models. There are two basic types of ICM:

(i)   Propositional - commonly characterised as frames or scripts.

(ii)   Image-schematic - "dynamic patterns that connect up a vast range of different experiences that manifest the structure . . . [they are] not the same as mental pictures but are abstract images that are not confined to any one sense modality." (Johnson, 1987)

Two further kinds involve mappings between these basic types:

(iii)   Metaphoric - mappings from a propositional or image-schematic ICM in one domain to a corresponding structure in another domain.

(iv)   Metonymic - metonymy is the use of one aspect of some entity to refer to, or otherwise stand for, the entity as a whole. For example, in a part-whole structure, there may be a function from a part to the whole that enables the part to stand for the whole. Metonymic ICMs therefore involve a link from one element of model to another element of the same model.

Lakoff uses 'mother' as an example of a cluster concept. Here, we restrict ourselves to the convergence of three ICMs, although more could be given. These ICMs could be represented as follows:

$$(\forall x)(\exists y)\ birth\_mother(x) \rightarrow gave\_birth\_to(x,y)$$
$$(\forall x)(\exists y)\ nurturant\_mother(x) \rightarrow raised(x,y) \wedge female(x)$$
$$(\forall x)(\exists y)\ genetic\_mother(x) \rightarrow developed\_from\_egg\_of(y,x)$$

If somebody satisfies one or more of these ICMs, they will be categorised as a mother:

$$(\forall x)\ mother(x) \rightarrow birth\_mother(x) \vee nurturant\_mother(x) \vee genetic\_mother(x)$$

The stereotypical mother satisfies all three models:

$$(\forall x)\ stereotypical\_mother(x) \rightarrow birth\_mother(x) \wedge$$
$$nurturant\_mother(x) \wedge genetic\_mother(x)$$

We can also define other types of mother in terms of these ICMs:

$$(\forall x)surrogate\_mother(x) \rightarrow birth\_mother(x) \wedge$$
$$\neg(genetic\_mother(x) \vee nurturant\_mother(x))$$
$$(\forall x)\ biological\_mother(x) \rightarrow genetic\_mother(x) \wedge \neg birth\_mother(x)$$
$$(\forall x)\ natural\_mother(x) \rightarrow genetic\_mother(x) \wedge birth\_mother(x)$$

Currently, we are not advocating that the final KBS should be represented in terms of ICMs, but are making the lesser claim that knowledge of their existence can help us develop in the development of a KBS.

3.1 Knowledge Analysis Using ICMs

Having outlined the Idealised Cognitive Model theory of cognitive organisation, we now turn to our application of this theory to KBS development and describe a knowledge analysis tool that has been developed to assist in this. We concentrate here on the image-schematic type of ICM.

     Image-schematic ICMs are similar in many respects to the representational structures known variously as *frames* (Minsky, 1981), *scripts* (Schank and Abelson, 1977) and *schemata* (Rumelhart, 1977). As with image-schemata, frames are structured objects that represent a generic level of knowledge. While we do not disagree with the utility of frames as models of some aspects of human cognition, they are too specific to play a role in the early stages of knowledge acquisition. An individual frame applies to a particular well-known situation type and is not of general applicability across different kinds of situations. As image-schemata are more generic and are found in all kinds of domains, we believe that they can exploited in the KA process.

The analysis presented here has much in common with recent common-sense ontologies of the real world. For example, Hobbs (1996) proposes "a general structure for a ... set of *core theories* of a very abstract character ... The fact that the core theories apply so widely means that they provide a great many domains of discourse with a rich vocabulary" (p. 819). Note that we are not suggesting the use of specific domain ontologies in knowledge acquisition, which has been much discussed lately (e.g. van Heijst *et al.*, 1997). One of the major problems that we envisage with this tactic is described by O'Leary (1997) as "ontology stationarity". In disciplines where knowledge changes little, reuse of ontologies is a practical option and may yet become widespread. However, in other disciplines, changes in expert knowledge can be rapid and substantial. Under such circumstances, libraries of ontologies would quickly become out of date, violating the principal of reuse which led to their introduction. In the biological domains that we are concerned with, knowledge is likely to change as quickly and fundamentally as in the area of information technology that O'Leary cites as an example of a turbulent domain. There is currently, for example, much debate concerning the fundamental model on which theories of one particular cellular signalling system are built, that of the immune system[1].

A useful comparison might be to look at another application of a theory of psychology to the knowledge development process. Kelly's Personal Construct Theory (PCT) has a well-developed, well-known application (e.g. Gaines and Boose, 1988). The fundamental axiom of PCT is that an individual's conception of a real-world event is constrained by anticipations that are formed prior to perception. These anticipations, referred to as templets, fulfill a similar role in PCT as that image-schemata in the theory of ICMs as both provide a pre-perceptual structure to the external environment. The repertory grid method developed by Kelly for eliciting personal constructs has been successfully used as the basis for a range of KA tools (e.g. Shaw and Gaines, 1983; Boose and Bradshaw, 1987). Our proposal is that the theory of ICMs may also be a useful aid in KBS development. We suggest that by identifying the individual ICMs that structure some part of an expert's knowledge, the analyst can represent a domain piece by piece and thus avoid being immediately confronted by the complexity that is inherent in scientific domains. To this end, we have developed TACKLE - a KA tool to assist us

---

[1]The debate is between (a) the received view which suggests that the immune system reacts to foreign matter, or non-self, in the body, and (b) a recent model which suggests that the immune system reacts to the Four Ds - danger, death, destruction and distress (Matzinger, 1994). In (a), there is a fundamental distinction made between "self" and "non-self" that is not made in (b). It is likely an existing ontology of the theory of the immune system would be based on (a). Using such an ontology as the starting point for a knowledge acquisition project conducted with an expert who subscribes to model (b) would cause serious problems from the outset.

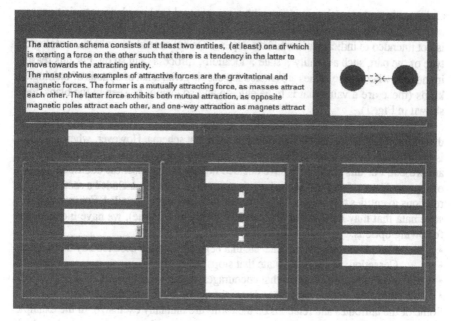

The attraction schema consists of at least two entities, (at least) one of which is exerting a force on the other such that there is a tendency in the latter to move towards the attracting entity.
The most obvious examples of attractive forces are the gravitational and magnetic forces. The former is a mutually attracting force, as masses attract each other. The latter force exhibits both mutual attraction, as opposite magnetic poles attract each other, and one-way attraction as magnets attract

Fig. 1. Example of TACKLE form

in testing this hypothesis. We now look at this and the individual image-schemata documented in it in more detail.

4. TACKLE: A Tool for Acquiring Conceptual Knowledge

TACKLE was developed using Delphi™, the Object Pascal Visual Programming environment. It consists of a set of forms, each of which corresponds to an individual image-schema. On each form, there is are sections for the parts, properties and relations that may apply to the particular image-schema. The user chooses to instantiate a particular image-schema and then fills in the form according to that instantiation. As an example, consider the attractive force schema shown in Fig. 1. The labelled slots can be given values, thus defining an instantiation of a schema.

We employ image-schemata to define anticipations in a domain. Previously, Fillmore's case frames (Fillmore, 1968) have been used in a similar way (e.g. Paton, *et al.*, 1994a) and these will serve as a useful point of reference. Woods (1975) defines a case as "the name of the role that a noun phrase or other participant takes in the state or activity expressed by the verb of a sentence." (p. 57). The case frame for a verb is the list of all possible such participants for a particular verb. Case frames have been used previously in knowledge acquisition to explicitly form expectations about the entities involved in some event. Similarly, on each form in TACKLE, we have provided slots for the various roles and attributes that may be involved in an instantiation of an image-schema. There are, of course, differences in the approaches, the most important being that image schemata are not tied to individual verb phrases but describe "recurring patterns of experience" (Johnson, 1987). Thus, they are independent of both language and domain and as such provide us with a generic tool for knowledge acquisition.

For the parts involved in a schema, we have included an entry for its kind. This is not intended to indicate an immediate super-class but should describe the ontological type of the part, such as 'entity', 'state', 'location', 'process' and so on. For this reason, in the area where these values are entered the user is given a list of options of ontological kinds (these are a value that is to be entered and so cannot be seen in the blank form shown in Fig. 1).

In Johnson (1987), the relations in each schema are internal, in the sense that they are relations between the individual parts of that schema. However, when a schema is instantiated, the internal relations that are included can be inferred from the parts that are present. For this reason, we have decided not to give the user the additional burden of separately specifying the internal relations. Instead, we have included a section where relations to entities that are not part of the core schema can be detailed. For example, for schemata that may be dynamic (i.e. involve change over time), we have included the following options:

- Initiation: some event, state, etc that begins the action described by the schema,
- Cessation: some event, state that stops the action,
- Promotion: some agent that encourages or enhances the action,
- Inhibition: some agent that deters the action from occurring.

Some of the attributes and relations on the forms are mutually exclusive. In the example shown, if the attracting entity always exhibits an attractive force (such as a mass, which always exhibits a gravitational pull), there will be no values for slots that refer to some dynamic action.

Where there is an attribute of a schema that can have one of two values (e.g. permanent or temporary), there is always an additional option of 'not-available', which covers various situations, such the information has not yet been elicited, the attribute is relevant to a particular instantiation, and so on.

The schemata are organised into the groups shown in Fig. 2. The user is initially presented with the Top Level form, selects the schemata group that is of interest. From there, an individual schema can be selected. While this categorisation is not done arbitrarily, there are many such arrangements that could be made. The classification of image-schemata is done mainly for pragmatic, rather than theoretical, reasons. If the user is presented with a list of over thirty schemas to choose from, then the selection of the correct schema may seem daunting and become too time-consuming as individual schemata are examined in turn. However, a meaningful arrangement of the image-schemas into types and sub-types hopefully alleviates this burden.

We will now describe the six different types of schema that we have included, giving a more detailed example of each. Many of these were drawn directly from, or inspired by, other sources. The major source was Johnson (1987).

4.1 Forces

Our first and most common experiences of causal effects are produced by physical forces that act on us and we bring to bear to act on parts of our environment. This experience produces an general conceptualisation of causality in terms of physical forces, the most basic example of which is the compulsive force schema (Johnson, 1987). This consists

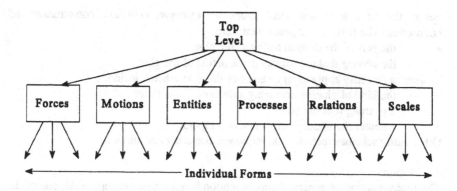

Fig. 2. Organisation of forms within TACKLE

of a single force that tends to move some body from one location to another. It is often used to conceptualise more elaborate causal forces, such as acting to move an entity from one state to another, e.g. "to go from hot to cold".

In including the compulsive force schema in TACKLE, we need to provide some expectations of different parts, attributes and relations that may be associated with it. The parts are:

- the entity that is subject to the force,
- initial location,
- final location,
- intermediate path.

Some of the available attributes are:

- one-shot/continuous: Rieger and Grinberg (1977) distinguish between these two types of causation. In one-shot, the causal force need only be present momentarily in order to produce an effect whereas in the continuous type the causal effect disappears when the causal force is no longer applied.
- threshold: when a causal effect depends on a threshold value being exceeded, the effect does not start at same time as the cause, there is some intermediate state that must be passed through.

Other force schemas included in TACKLE are attractive force, blockage, counterforce, diversion, and enablement, all of which are described in more detail in Johnson (1987). Using combinations of these schemata, complex causal interactions can be modelled using a domain-independent platform. This, we believe, facilitates communication between domain expert and knowledge engineer.

4.2 Entities

Entity schemata are formed as a result of our experience of parts of our environment as individual objects. They are often then used to conceptualise non-discrete parts of the world as individual entities. As an example, consider the glue schema. Glue is a pervasive concept that is used as a conceptualisation and explication device in a diverse set of domains (Paton, 1997). It is most commonly used to convey an adhesive capability but is also used to denote ideas about, for example, cohesion, combination and connection. The parts of the glue schema are:

- the part of the domain acting as the glue
- the objects that are subject to the action of the glue.

Properties that may apply to an instance of the glue schema include:

- the kind of glueing action e.g. adherence, coherence
- the strength of the bond
- whether the bond is permanent or temporary

Other entity schemas include link, sequence, container and surface.

4.3 Motions

The representation of generic forms of motion is not a new concept in AI, one of the more familiar treatments being given in the Conceptual Dependency Theory (CDT) of Schank and Abelson, 1977). In CDT, there are several kinds of actions that can be loosely collected together under the category "motion". These included ATRANS (abstract transfer), PTRANS (physical transfer), MTRANS (mental transfer), INGEST, EXPEL and MOVE. In TACKLE, we do not distinguish between kinds of motion on the basis of the entities involved but instead distinguish between different forms of motion. Thus, we do not distinguish between ATRANS, PTRANS and MTRANS, as they all involve movement along a path, but identify different motions such as cycle, wave, displacement, emergence and enclosure.

4.4 Processes

Although we have identified motion and processes as two different categories of schema, it could be argued that, as both are dynamic, they should be coalesced into a single grouping. While we recognise this as a valid opinion, we would defend our distinction as valid for the following reasons:

(a)   motion schemas involve a change in the *location* of an entity without any other change, whereas

(b)   process schemas relate to some change in the *form* of an entity or entities, i.e. that which was present before the process began is not the same as that which is present when the process is over.

However, this situation is complicated by the fact that processes are often conceptualised and explicated in terms of motion between states (and often represented as such in AI systems). This is convenient for our sake, as any process encountered that does not conform to one of those included can be represented using one of the motion schemas. Process image-schemas that we have represented include decomposition, formation, absorption and dissociation.

4.5 Relations

One of the most prevalent relations we use in our understanding of our world is the part-whole structure. Many KBS systems utilise partonomies (part-whole hierarchies) as means of structuring and reasoning about knowledge. The study of the part-whole relations has a rich history. Probably the most notable discussion of this subject in AI literature is Winston *et al.* (1987), who distinguish six kinds of part-whole connections, based on whether the relation is functional, homeomerous (part is of same kind as whole) and/or separable (part can be physically separated from whole):

- component/integral object - functional, not homeomerous, separable,
- member/collection - not functional, not homeomerous, separable,
- portion/mass - not functional, homeomerous, separable,
- stuff/object - not functional, not homeomerous, not separable,
- feature/activity - functional, not homeomerous, not separable,
- place/area - not functional, homeomerous, not separable.

However, as Gerstl and Pribbenow (1995) suggest, this classification is not domain-independent as it differentiates between wholes that are physical objects, spatial areas and activities. We adopt their analysis as it is a language-independent classification based on the compositional structure of the whole rather than its ontological type. Consequently, they identify three different kinds of wholes:

- complex - composed of components that are quite different from the whole and from each other, such as a car engine,
- collection - a set of elements of the same kind, for example, a sugar-lump which is a collection of sugar crystals,
- mass - an homogeneous entity where the parts are not fundamentally different from the whole, e.g. water.

They also distinguish between two different ways in which part-whole structure can be imposed that are independent of any inherent compositional structure:

- segment - imposing some external scheme, such as inside-outside, and
- portion - separation of whole into parts on basis of some property e.g. all of the red parts

These options are included as attributes of the part-whole relation in TACKLE. Other image-schematic relations include matching pairs, balance, and polar opposites.

4.6 Scale

According to Johnson (1987), the scale schema is "basic to both quantitative and qualitative aspects of our experience." Hobbs (1995) describes a scale as "a very common and very useful kind of system." As we suggested earlier, the biological systems we are concerned with involve little in the way of formal mathematics. Most measurements will be performed against qualitative scales as, in such complex physical systems, it is usually difficult to obtain accurate quantitative values (Bratko, 1988; Ironi et al., 1990). Scales are found throughout TACKLE as many attributes of instances of schemata will be assigned values e.g paths have a length, forces have strength and so on. However, where a more complex specification of a scale is required, the SCALE form is used. The parts of a scale that can be specified are:

- top and bottom of a scale
- subscale(s)
- indistinguishability relation - the means of determining that two values on the scale are different, e.g. for the number scale, this relation is equality (Hobbs, 1995).

Attributes of the SCALE form include:

- whether the scale is a total or partial ordering,
- whether the scale is linear, exponential, etc.,
- whether the scale is qualitative or quantitative.

4.7 Example of TACKLE Analysis

As an example of the kind of output produced by a TACKLE acquisition session, we have included in Fig. 3 part of the results produced from an analysis of the domain of cellular signalling. This was the result of acquisition from the relevant sections of a standard textbook on the molecular biology of the cell (Alberts *et al.*, 1989). The information shown in Fig. 3 was acquired solely from the section of text below that describes the effect of steroid hormones.

> "Being relatively small (molecular weight≈300) hydrophobic molecules, they are thought to cross the plasma membrane by simple diffusion. Once inside the target cell, each type of steroid hormone binds tightly but reversibly to a complementary receptor protein. The binding of the hormone causes the receptor protein to undergo a conformational change (a process called receptor activation) that increases its affinity for DNA an enables it to bind specific genes in the nucleus and regulate their transcription." (p. 690)

The output of this initial acquisition stage has several uses. One that has been successfully employed is that definition of an "intermediate ontology". We have described each of the image-schemata included in TACKLE as a class in an Ontolingua ontology. This ontology is domain-independent and can therefore be used in almost any analysis. Describing some piece of the knowledge of a domain in terms of an image-schema is equivalent to instantiating a class in this ontology. This intermediate ontology then provides an opportunity for the knowledge engineer to reflect on the state of analysis and can subsequently be used the basis for further acquisition.

Presently, TACKLE presents results of an acquisition session in the form of the database tables that record instances of the schemata. As the present version is only a prototype developed for the purpose of testing a hypothesis, we are not concerned with obtaining more sophisticated forms of output. However, if TACKLE proves to be a useful tool, this situation will need to be rectified. We suggest some improvements in this respect in the next section.

5. Conclusions

Scientific theories are not formal mathematical constructs, they are mental models. We have outlined a theory of cognition that provides at least a partial explanation of how these models are organised and we have described the prototype of a knowledge acquisition tool, TACKLE, based on these principles. This views the knowledge acquisition process as a modelling enterprise

One of the main objectives in developing TACKLE was to overcome the language barrier that is encountered by knowledge engineers in the initial stages of the representation process. By allowing a representation of the domain in terms that are common to both analyst and expert, it is hoped that TACKLE will aid communication and explanation of domain-specific concepts. It is not only in terms of language that TACKLE provides commonality between expert and analyst, but in structural, organisational terms also.

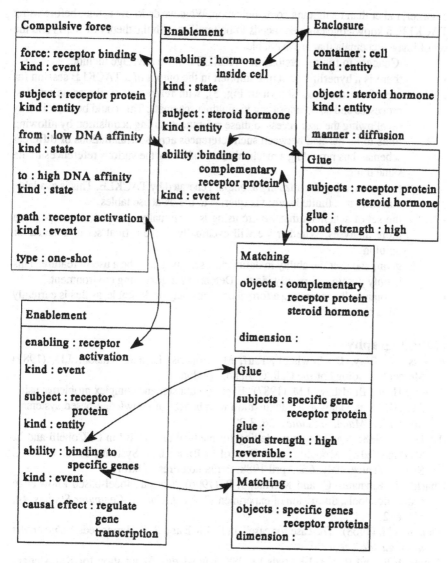

Fig. 3. Example output of TACKLE analysis

We do not mean to suggest that a domain can be completely characterised in terms of image-schemata but that they provide a knowledge engineer with a useful, pre-formalisation, means of acquiring and talking about knowledge in unfamiliar domains. Of course, it is possible that in trying to understand domain-specific concepts in image-schematic terms might lead to increased confusion between the expert and the knowledge engineer, rather than facilitating communication. What we do know is that, before using TACKLE, a knowledge engineer needs to be familiar with the theory of ICMs and the set of image-schemata that are available.

Changes to future versions of TACKLE that we envisage include:

- there is a hyperlink structure implicit in the output of a TACKLE session (as seen from the links shown in Fig. 3), with references to the same entities, processes and so on appearing in multiple schemata. This could be exploited by (a) allowing the user access to these references during acquisition by allowing links to be defined between such references across instantiations of different schema, thus providing a mechanism of following the various references to the same thing,

  (b) representing the links in the output generated by TACKLE. This is available currently in a limited form via queries to the database tables

- the set of schemata that we are using is continually changing as we perform more analyses. Whether we will eventually arrive a final set is a matter of opinion

- giving the user the ability to define new schemata may be a useful feature. This is only possible currently via the Delphi™ programming environment.

- automatically generating a formal ontology may be desirable, as this is currently done by hand.

6. Bibliography

Alberts, B., Bray, D., Lewis, J., Raff, M., Roberts, K. and Watson, J.D. (1989) Molecular Biology of the Cell, Garland, London.

Boose, J.H. and Bradshaw, J.M. (1987) "Expertise transfer and complex problems: using AQUINAS as a knowledge acquisition workbench for knowledge-based systems", *Int. J. Man-Machine Studies*, **26**, 3-28.

Bratko, I. (1988) "Qualitative modelling for medical diagnosis" in C. Cobelli and L. Mariana (eds.), Modelling and Control in Biomedical Systems, Proc. 1st IFAC Symp., Venice, Italy, 6-8 April 1988, Pergamon Press, Oxford.

Charlet, J., Reynaud, C. and Krivine, J.-P. (1996) "Causal model-based knowledge acquisition tools: discussion of experiments", *Int. J. Human-Computer Studies*, **44**, 629-652.

Fillmore, C.J. (1968) "The case for case", in E. Bach and R.T. Harms (eds.) *Universals in Linguistic Theory*.

Gaines, B.R. and Boose, J.H. (eds.) (1988) Knowledge Acquisition for Knowledge-Based Systems, Academic Press, London.

Gerstl, P. and Pribbenow S. (1995) "Midwinters, end games and bodyparts: A classification of part-whole relations", *Int. J. Human-Computer Studies*, **43**, 865-889.

Giere, R.N. (1988) Explaining Science, University of Chicago Press, Chicago, IL.

Giere, R.N. (ed.) (1992) Cognitive Models of Science, University of Minnesota Press, MI.

Harré, R. (1972) The Philosophies of Science, Oxford University Press, Oxford.

Hobbs, J.R. (1995) "Sketch of an ontology underlying the way we talk about the world", *Int. J. Human-Computer Studies*, **43**, 819-830.

Ironi, L., Stefanelli, M. and Lanzola, G. (1990) "Qualitative models in medical diagnosis", *Artificial Intelligence in Medicine*, **2**, 85-101.

Johnson-Laird, P.N. (1983) Mental Models, Cambridge University Press, Cambridge.

Jones, D.M. and Paton, R.C. (1994) "The role of verbal and visual metaphors in biological theories", presented at the *Conference on Information-Oriented Approaches to Logic, Language and Computation*, June 12-15, St. Mary's College, Moraga, California.

Lakoff, G. and Johnson, M. (1980) Metaphors We Live By, University of Chicago Press, Chicago, IL.

Matzinger P. (1994) "Tolerance, danger, and the extended family", Annual Review of Immunology, **12**, 991-1045.

McCauley, R.N. (1987) "The role of theories in a theory of concepts", in U. Neisser (ed.) *Concepts and Conceptual Development*, Cambridge University Press, Cambridge.

Minsky, M. (1981) "A framework for representing knowledge", in J. Haugeland (ed.) *Mind Design*, MIT Press, Cambridge, MA.

Paton, R.C., Nwana, H.S., Shave, M.J.R. and Bench-Capon, T.J.M. (1994a) "An examination of some metaphorical contexts for biologically motivated computing", *British Journal for the Philosophy of Science*, **45**, 505-525.

Paton, R.C., Lynch, S., Jones, D.M., Nwana, H.S., Bench-Capon, T.J.M. and Shave, M.J.R. (1994b), "Domain characterisation for knowledge-based systems", *Proceedings of A.I. 94 - Fourteenth International Avignon Conference*, 41-54.

Paton, R.C. (1997), "Glue, Verb and Text Metaphors in Biology", *Acta Biotheoretica*, **45**, 1-15

Rieger, C. and Grinberg, M. (1977) "The declarative representation and simulation of causality in physical mechanisms", Proceedings of the 5th International Joint Conference on Artificial Intelligence, **77**, pp. 250-256 Cambridge, MA.

Schank, R.C. and Abelson, R. (1977) Scripts, Plans, Goals and Understanding, Lawrence Erlbaum, Hillsdale, NJ.

Shaw, M.L.G. and Gaines, B.R. (1983) "A computer aid to knowledge engineering", *Proceedings of BCS Conference on Expert Systems*, December, Cambridge, 263-271.

Suppes, P. (1960) Axiomatic Set Theory, Van Nostrand, Princeton, NJ.

van Fraassen, B.C. (1980) The Scientific Image, Clarendon Press, Oxford.

van Heijst, G., Schreiber, A. Th. and Wielinga, B.J. (1997) "Using explicit ontologies in KBS development", *Int. J. Human-Computer Studies*, **46**, 183-292.

Winston, M.E., Chaffin, R. and Herrman, D. (1987) "A taxonomy of part-whole relations", *Cognitive Science*, **11**, 417-444.

Woods, W.A. (1975) "What's in a link: foundations for semantic networks", in D.G. Bobrow and A.M. Collins (eds.) *Representation and Understanding: Studies in Cognitive Science*, 35-82, Academic Press, NY.

Designing Operators for Constructing Domain Knowledge Ontologies

Rodrigo Martínez-Béjar[1], V. Richard Benjamins[2,4] and Fernando Martín-Rubio[3]

[1] Spanish Scientific Research Council (CSIC), Avda. La Fama, 1, C.P. 30080, Murcia, Spain, Email: rodrigo@natura.cebas.csic.es

[2] Department of Social Science Informatics, University of Amsterdam, Roetersstraat 15, 1018 WB Amsterdam, The Netherlands

[3] Department of Computing Sciences, University of Murcia, Murcia, Spain, Email: fmartin@dif.um.es

[4] Artificial Intelligence Research Institute (IIIA), Spanish Scientific Research Council (CSIC), Campus UAB, 08193 Bellaterra, Barcelona, Spain, Email: richard@iiia.csic.es, http://www.iiia.csic.es/~richard

Abstract Many researchers agree that the reuse of ontological components is an important research area in Knowledge Acquisition. However, it has been argued that there is still much to do in this field. For example, one of the topics that requires more research is that of developing methods to build ontologies. In this sense, it is important to define formal methods which provide us with operative frameworks to build ontologies. In this paper, for problems that satisfy a well-defined set of assumptions, we propose a mathematical approach that permits to build domain knowledge ontologies. We present such an operative framework based on both Sets Theory and mereological considerations. The approach comprises a set of ontological operators to extract domain knowledge. Finally, an example is put forward showing the application of these ontological operators.

1   Introduction

The reuse of knowledge components, for example that of problem-solving methods, has been addressed during the last decade by many researchers (Wielinga *et al.*, 1992; Benjamins, 1993). As a result, there are now several tools/frameworks which provide such kind of support, including the Generic Task approach (Chandrasekaran, 1987), the PROTÉGÉ framework (Musen, 1989), and the KADS methodology (Wielinga *et al.*, 1992).

Although there is no full agreement in the Knowledge Acquisition (KA) community about the ontology concept, ontologies can be basically viewed as intensional descriptions of the domain knowledge in some field that allow for obtaining reusable knowledge components (van Heijst *et al.*, 1997). In any case, most researchers think that having libraries of reusable ontological components should improve the knowledge-based systems (KBSs) development process. Building ontologies is, however, not a trivial issue for which there are currently not many available methods (van Heijst *et al.*, 1997).

The so-called Knowledge Functions-based approach is a principled, mathematical functions-based approach that permits to formally analyse the elicited knowledge independently of the elicitation technique employed (Martínez-Béjar et al., 1996; Martínez-Béjar and Martín-Rubio, 1997). The purpose of this paper is to formally derive operators to build domain knowledge ontologies. The aim is achieved by using a set of mathematical functions in combination with Mereology (Lesniewski, 1916; Simons, 1987; Borst and Akkermans, 1997) that allows for obtaining ontological vocabularies as well as a set of restrictions that must be satisfied by the structure of the domain knowledge ontology. The ideas in this paper are developed, based on, and will be illustrated with, an existing KBS project for environmental planning in Spain.

In the overall development process of a KBS, this work should be situated immediately after the knowledge elicitation phase; in the analysis phase. Therefore, the results of this work can be useful for modern knowledge acquisition methodologies, including PROTÉGÉ (Puerta et al., 1992), KADS (Wielinga et al., 1992) and VITAL (O'Hara et al., 1994), since these are concerned with conceptual modelling based on the elicited knowledge.

The structure of the paper is as follows. Section 2 offers a brief overview of the more recent ontology definitions found in the AI literature. In Section 3, we describe the main aspects of the knowledge functions-based approach together with the assumptions that were taken into account in this approach. Section 4 introduces a formal semantic that uses both knowledge functions and mereological concepts to derive ontological operators and a set of properties that restrict the ontology. Section 5 shows an example where a part of the theory introduced in the previous sections is used to analyse fragments of texts by applying the ontological operators previously built. Finally, in Section 6 we present conclusions.

2 Domain Knowledge Ontologies

Traditionally, philosophers have used the term *ontology* when they dealt with problems related to the existence or the nature of being. KA researches have made use of this term, for example, in the fields of knowledge modelling and conceptualisation, although they employ the term ontology with another meaning. Within the KA community, there is no full agreement on the meaning of the word ontology.

It has been argued that the term ontology embraces the terminology used in a particular task or domain as well as the semantic interpretation of the terms underlying such a terminology (Albert, 1993). Another ontology perspective is the one explicated by Wielinga and Schreiber (1993). These authors have dealt with the manner in which ontologies should be constructed. In particular, they propose to formulate ontologies at the knowledge level, since it is intended to apply the notion of ontology to human beings (and, in principle, to all knowledgeable agents).

More recently, Gruber (1994) has attempted to delimit the ontology definition for AI systems by shifting the ontology concerns from what "exists" to what "can be represented". Guarino and Giaretta (1995) have gone one step beyond. In particular, for these authors, an ontology is a set of predicates and functions, both kinds of elements operating on a logical language[1]. In addition to this, they have pointed out that the elements of such a set can be used as cornerstones when one attempts to design a particular representation.

Finally, van Heijst *et al.* (1997) have proposed an ontology definition based on the definitions mentioned above. They define ontology as an explicit knowledge-level specification of a conceptualisation[2]. Moreover, they assume that the particular domain and the particular task to be carried out can have an influence on the conceptualisation. In this paper, we adopt this definition, and view an ontology as the conjunction of a vocabulary describing domain elements along with the restrictions between the elements, for example ¬father(x, x). In other words, an ontology constrains the structure and contents of domain knowledge. Domain knowledge, on the other hand, provides descriptions about factual situations in a certain domain.

3 Knowledge Functions

Originally, the knowledge functions-based (KF-based) approach was conceived as a mathematical kernel, which provides a framework to derive formal parameters for comparing knowledge elicitation techniques (Martínez-Béjar *et al.*, 1996). In further work, this approach has been modified for use as a formal framework to analyse fragments of text (Martínez-Béjar and Martín-Rubio, 1997). Currently, two KBSs have been implemented based on the application of this approach in the knowledge analysis phase (Martínez-Béjar *et al.*, 1997).

In the KF-based approach, knowledge functions are applied to fragments of text in order to extract different types of domain knowledge such as concepts, relations, properties, etc. The basic idea is that knowledge engineer applies the knowledge functions to the fragments of text, and the expert validates the so-obtained domain knowledge. In order to be obtain valid results, the KF-based approach requires that the problems to which it is applied are, what we call, "knowledge engineering solvable" problems (KE-solvable). To be KE-solvable, a problem must satisfy the following assumptions.

1. The task to be realised can be decomposed in "well-known" subtasks (cf. the task classification of KADS (Wielinga *et al.*, 1992)).
2. For each of the subtasks identified, there is an expert available and the number of experts is constant during the entire knowledge elicitation process (KEP).
3. The persons who elicit the knowledge from the expert are the same during the KEP.
4. Once validated and approved by the expert, the elicited knowledge will not be invalidated in further sessions (monotonic knowledge growth).

---

[1]In the ontology literature, the *logical language* is usually referred to as the *vocabulary* of the language.
[2]In this paper, a conceptualisation is viewed as a set of informal rules that delimit the structure of a part of the reality, which an agent employs to isolate and organise relevant objects and relevant relations (Guarino, 1997).

In our application (environmental planning), these four assumptions were satisfied. We are, however, aware of the fact that the "monotonic growth of knowledge" assumptions is not always realistic. In the following, we describe the knowledge functions for extracting domain knowledge from fragments of text.

ASS function Let K_{ru} be the set of possible fragments of texts which can be elicited from human experts, and let K_c be the set of semantically different *concepts* underlying K_{ru}. The *Association* operator, written ASS, is defined as a function which maps K_{ru} to K_c in order to obtain the semantically different concepts underlying a fragment of text elicited from some expert.

ISA function Given a hierarchy of concepts elicited earlier, the *Ascendant* operator, written ISA, is defined as a function which maps K_c to itself in order to obtain the father concept of a concept obtained after applying the ASS operator to a particular fragment of text. Both concepts have been obtained by applying the ASS function.

PRO function Let K_p be the set of properties relative to K_c. The *Properties* operator, written PRO, is defined as a function which maps the Cartesian product $K_{ru} \times K_c$ to K_p in order to obtain for each concept the set of properties involved in a particular fragment of text from which that concept has been obtained (i.e., after having applied the ASS operator to that fragment). For example, by assuming that r is a fragment of text, and z is a concept belonging to ASS(r), PRO (r, z) provides the set of properties, which have to do with z, implicitly or explicitly referenced in r. In order to solve possible ambiguity problems, each of the so obtained properties can be written as *concept.property*, where *property* = PRO (r, z) and *concept* = z.

VAL function Let K_v be the set of possible values associated to the elements of K_c. The *Values* operator, written VAL, is defined as a function which maps the Cartesian product $K_{ru} \times K_c \times K_p$ to K_v. For instance, by assuming that r is a fragment of text elicited from one or more experts, that the concept $z \in$ ASS(r), and that the property $u \in$ PRO(r,z), VAL(r,z,u) provides the value corresponding to the concept z for the property u in such a way that it can explicitly be extracted from r. Possible ambiguity problems can be solved by introducing the notation *concept.property.value*, where *value* is equal to VAL(r,z,u); *property* is the property referenced by *value*, that is, *u*; *concept* is the concept to which *value* is linked, that is, *z*.

MASS function Let R be a non-empty set of fragments of texts. The *multiple association* operator, written MASS, is defined as follows:

$$\text{MASS}(R) \quad = \quad \bigcup_{j=1}^{\text{Card}(R)} \text{ASS}(r_j)$$

where r_j stands for the jth fragment belonging to R.

MISA function Let R be a non-empty set of fragments of texts, and let C be equal to MASS(R). The *multiple ascendants* operator, written MISA, is defined as

$$MISA(C) \quad = \quad \bigcup_{j=1}^{Card(C)} ISA(c_j)$$

where c_j stands for the jth concept belonging to C.

MPRO function Let r be a fragment of text, such that C = ASS(r). The *multiple properties* operator, written MPRO, is defined as follows:

$$MPRO(r, C) \quad = \quad \bigcup_{k=1}^{Card(C)} PRO(r, c_k)$$

where c_k stands for the kth element belonging to C.

EPRO function Let R be a non-empty set of fragments of texts, and C be equal to MASS(R). The *extended property* operator, written EPRO, is defined as follows:

$$EPRO(R, C) = \bigcup_{j=1}^{Card(R)} MPRO(r_j, C_j)$$

where C_j = ASS (r_j).

MPVAL function Let r be a fragment of text, and let c be a concept belonging to ASS(r) such that P = PRO(r,c). The *multiple properties value* operator, written MPVAL, is defined as follows:

$$MPVAL(r, c, P) = \bigcup_{i=1}^{Card(P)} VAL(r, c, p_i)$$

where p_i stands for the ith element belonging to P.

MCVAL function Let r be a fragment of text, and let C be equal to ASS(r) such that P = MPRO(r, C). The *multiple concepts value* operator, written MCVAL, is defined as follows:

$$MCVAL(r, C, P) = \bigcup_{i=1}^{Card(C)} MPVAL(r, c_i, P)$$

where i stands for the ith element belonging to C.

EVAL function Let R be a non-empty set of fragments of texts, let C be equal to MASS(R) and let P be equal to EPRO(R, C). The *extended assessment* operator, written EVAL, is defined as follows:

$$EVAL(R, C, P) = \bigcup_{i=1}^{Card(R)} MCVAL(r_i, C, P)$$

where r_i stands for the ith element belonging to R.

REL function Let K_r be the set of possible relationships distinct to the one underlying the ISA function (i.e., father-to-child relationships and vice versa) that can be defined between two properties belonging to one or more concepts associated to a fragment of text, written f. Notice that, from now on, "f" stands for fragment of text (instead of the "r" used until now), and "r" will denote relation.

The *relation* operator, written REL, is defined as follows:
REL: K_f x K_p x K_p → K_r, such that REL(f, p_i, p_j) permits to obtain the set of relationships referenced in r between two properties $p_i ≠ p_j ∈$ MPRO(f, C) where C = ASO(f).

Making use of the notation employed for the VAL operator, the notation *relationship(concept_i.property_i, concept_j.property_j)* can be adopted, where relationship = REL(f, p_i, p_j). Moreover, since relations are intended to be found, graphs can be said to be an adequate mechanism that can play an important role as a complementary knowledge representation system of the one provided by Sets Theory.

According to the former definition, some immediate properties can be established:

1. Commutativity
   $∀p_i ≠ p_j ∈$ MPRO(f,C), REL(f, p_i, p_j) = REL(f, p_j, p_i).

2. Transitivity
   $∀p_i ≠ p_j ≠ p_k ∈$ MPRO(f,C), [REL(f, p_i, p_j) ≠ φ] $∧$ [REL(f, p_j, p_k)] ≠ φ → [REL(f, p_i, p_k) ≠ φ]

MREL function Let f be a fragment of decision text, and let P be equal to MPRO(f,C), where C = ASO(f).
The *multiple relations* operator, written MREL, is defined as follows:

$$MREL(f, P, P) = \bigcup_{\substack{i,j=1 \\ i≠j}}^{Card(P)} REL(f, p_i, p_j)$$

where p_i stands for the ith property belonging to P.

EREL function Let F be a set of fragments of decision text, and let P be equal to EPRO(F,C), where C = MASO(F).
The *extended relations* operator, written MREL, is defined as follows:

$$EREL(F,P,P) = \bigcup_{i=1}^{Card(F)} MREL(f_i, P_i, P_i)$$

where f_i stands for the ith fragment of decision text belonging to F, P_i = MPRO(f_i, C).

With these knowledge functions we can extract various types of domain knowledge which are present in elicited knowledge.

4 Combining Knowledge Functions and Mereology to Derive Ontological Operators

Some of the knowledge functions mentioned in previous sections can directly be used to obtain explicit ontological vocabularies for a particular domain, since these functions provide us with both conceptual and relational definitions. In particular, ASS, PRO, VAL and their respective extensions (i.e., MASS, MPRO, EPRO, MVAL, MPVAL, MCVAL and EVAL) can be directly considered as ontological operators that permit to obtain ontological vocabularies across different domains. However, there are some restrictions on the relational operators of the KF-based approach. In particular, ISA and its extension MISA assume that relationships in a conceptual hierarchy are limited to taxonomic relations.

In the context of the KF-based approach, the set of ontological operators would be more robust if PART-OF relationships could also be present in conceptual hierarchies. This is the reason why, in this work, the relationships between concepts and sub-concepts are supposed to be either IS-A relationships or part-of relationships, which are the study object of the Classical Mereology (CM). This is the formal theory about the concepts *part*, *overlap* and *sum* (see also Simons, 1987; Borst and Akkermans, 1997). Although Lesniewsky (1916) gave the first CM formulation, in this paper the one given by Leonard and Goddman (1940) is employed. They asserted the following:

a) definitions

1. p is part of c iff p is discrete from everything which c is discrete from.

2. p is a proper part of c iff p is a part of c and c is not a part of p.

3. p_1 and p_2 overlap iff they have a common part.

4. p is the sum of some entities iff p is discrete from exactly those entities that are discrete from each of them.

5. p is the product of some entities iff p is the sum of all their common parts.

6. p is an atom iff it has no proper part.

b) axioms

1. p_1 is discrete form p_2 iff p_1 and p_2 do not overlap.

2. If p_1 is part of p_2 and p_2 is part of p1, then p_1 and p_2 are identical.

3. For any pair of entities, their sum exists.

Eschenbach and Heydrich (1995) have argued that using CM in analysing different domains can help to know more about these domains. They have shown that CM is applicable to three different restricted domains provided that these are embedded in a less restricted domain. In this work, a restricted domain being embedded in that of Leonard and Goddman (1940) has been defined. This domain will be referred to as a *hierarchical restricted domain* (HRD).

As it has been put forward before, the KF-based approach involves a knowledge representation schema based on both Topology and Sets Theory (Martínez-Béjar and Martín-Rubio, 1997). We can make use of the possibilities that such schemata offer in terms of the above set of previous mereological concepts. This is done in the following, where we will present new ontological operators (which are not knowledge functions).

Operator 1: PHRD(t) Let F(t) be a non-empty set of fragments of decision text analysed until the instant t; let MASS be the multiple association operator; and let HRD be a hierarchical restricted domain. The *partial hierarchical restricted domain* until the instant t, written *PHRD(t)*, is defined as the set MASS(F(t)).

Operator 2: M-father Let c_i be a concept belonging to a non-empty PHRD(t) such that c_i is a proper part of another concept c_j. The *mereological father* of c_i, written *M-father(c$_i$)*, is defined as the concept c_j.

Operator 3: children Let c_i be a concept belonging to a non-empty PHRD(t). The set of *children concepts* of c_i, written *children(c$_i$)*, is defined as $\{c_k \in$ PHRD(t) such that ISA(c_k) = c_i\}.

Operator 4: PPRO Let F(t) be a non-empty set of fragments of decision text analysed until the instant t; let PRO be the property operator; and let c_j be a concept belonging to the PHRD(t) associated to F(t). The *partial property operator* until the instant t, written *PPRO*, is defined as follows:

$$PPRO(F(t), c_j) = \bigcup_{i=1}^{Card(F(t))} PRO(f_i, c_j)$$

where f_i stands for the ith fragment of decision text belonging to F(t).

Operator 5: INH Let c_i and c_j be two different concepts belonging to a non-empty PHRD(t) such that either c_j = ISA(c_i) or c_i = PART-OF(c_j). The set of inherited attributes until the instant t, written *INH(F(t),c$_i$)*, is defined as follows

$$INH(F(t), c_i) = \begin{cases} \Phi \text{ if } c_i \text{ is the root concept of the PHRD(t) or } c_i = \text{PART-OF} (c_j) \\ PPRO(F(t), c_j) \text{ otherwise} \end{cases}$$

Operator 6: SPE Let c_i be a concept belonging to a non-empty PHRD(t). The set of specific attributes until the instant t, written *SPE(F(t),c$_i$)*, is defined as the set PPRO(F(t), c_i).

Operator 7: ATT Let c_i be a concept belonging to a non-empty PHRD(t). The set of attributes for c_i until the instant t, written ATT(F(t), c_i) is defined as the union set INH(F(t),c_i) $\cup$ SPE(F(t),c_i).

Operator 8: degree_of_overlapping Let c_i and c_j be two different concepts belonging to a PHRD(t). The degree of overlapping between c_i and c_j in the context of F(t), written *degree_of_overlapping(F(t),c_i,c_j)*, is defined as the intersection set ATT(F(t), c_i) $\cap$ ATT(F(t), c_j)

Operator 9: M-product Let C be a non-empty sub-set of concepts belonging to F(t). The *mereological product* of C with respect to F(t), written *M-product (F(t),C)*, is

defined as the intersection set $$\bigcap_{k=1}^{Card(C)} ATT(F(t),\ c_k)$$

where c_k stands for the kth concept belonging to C

Until now, we have presented a set of operators to extract domain knowledge ontologies based on a combination of the KF-based approach and Mereology. Now we will propose several formal properties useful for verifying the ontology (e.g., its consistency). A valid ontology has to satisfy all properties. These properties are especially important when the expert decides to *rename* existing knowledge entities (e.g. attributes) in taxonomic organisations. Non-fulfilment of a property means that a rename operations has (unforeseen) side effects that need to be taken care of. The following properties can be established.

PROP1 For every concept c_i in a PHRD(t), the following holds:

SPE(F(t), c_i) $\cap$ INH(F(t), c_i) = ϕ

In words, given a non-root concept, the intersection of its inherited and specific attributes is empty.

PROP2 For every pair of concepts $c_i \neq c_j \in$ PHRD(t) for which there exist two different concepts c_1, c_2 $\in$ PHRD(t) defined as c_1 = ISA(c_i) and c_2 = ISA(c_j), respectively, the following holds:

degree_of_overlapping(F(t),c_i,c_j) > 0

Thus, concepts belonging to the same taxonomic sub-tree always have attributes in common.

PROP3 For every non-root concept c_i in a PHRD(t), the following holds:

$INH(F(t), c_j) \subseteq ATT(F(t), asc(c_i))$, where

$$asc(c_i) = \begin{cases} ISA(c_i) \text{ if there exists } c_j \in PHRD(t) \text{ such that } c_j = ISA(c_i) \\ M\text{-}father(c_i) \text{ otherwise} \end{cases}$$

Thus, for every non-root concept, inherited attributes also are attributes of the father concept.

PROP4 For every concept c_i in a PHRD(t) for which $children(c_i) \neq \phi$, the following holds:

$$[Card(children(c_i)) \geq 2] \rightarrow [M\text{-}product(F(t), children(c_i)) \subseteq ATT(F(t), c_i)]$$

In words, sibling concepts have the attributes of the father in common.

PROP5 For every pair of concepts $c_i \neq c_k \in PHRD(t)$ for which $children(c_i) \neq \phi$ and $children(c_k) \neq \phi$, the following holds:

$$\exists\, c_j \in PHRD(t) \text{ such that } [c_i \in children(c_j)] \text{ and } [c_k \notin children(c_j)] \rightarrow$$
$$[degree\_of\_overlapping\,(F(t),c_i,c_j) \geq degree\_of\_overlapping\,(F(t),c_i,c_k)]$$

Thus, father and child concepts have the largest number of attributes in common (as opposed to, for example, siblings).

5 Example

In this section we will illustrate the application of the ontological operators on a sample fragment of text, and subsequently we will verify the constructed domain ontology by applying the properties. Suppose that the following information until t_j is available:

$F(t_j)$ = {"*If the vegetation is very low, there is only one stratum and the seasonal_variation is medium, then the area under study has got a low visual fragility (VF)*", "*If there exists a predominance of pine merged with stone outcrops then the area under study has got a high visual quality (VQ)*"} = $\{f_1, f_2\}$.

At this point, we can apply the ontological operators defined above to capture the implicit knowledge:

1. By applying the ASS operator to f_1 and f_2 respectively, we get:
   $ASS(f_1)$ = {natural_vegetation, vegetation_landuse}, $ASS(f_2)$={pine, vegetation_landuse}.

2. Based on this, we can calculate $PHRD(F(t_j))$ as follows:
   $PHRD(F(t_j))$ = $MASS(F(t_j))$ = {pine, natural_vegetation, vegetation_landuse}.

3. The M-father and the ISA operators are applied to the elements of $PHRD(F(t_j))$:

   $ISA(pine) = \{natural\_vegetation\}$;
   $M\text{-father}(natural\_vegetation) = \{vegetation\_landuse\}$;
   $M\text{-father}(vegetation\_landuse) = ISA(vegetation\_landuse) = \phi$.

4. By considering the above steps and the definition of the children operator, the following is obtained:

   $children(pine) = \phi$;
   $children(natural\_vegetation) = \{pine\}$;
   $children\ (vegetation\_landuse) = \phi$.
   This means that the preconditions for PROP5 do not hold and, hence, PROP5 cannot be tested.

5. Then, the PRO operator is applied to each fragment of decision text:
   $PRO(f_1,natural\_vegetation) = \{height, number\_of\_strata, seasonal\_variation\}$;
   $PRO(f_1, vegetation\_landuse) = \{VF\}$;
   $PRO(f_2,pine) = \{merging\_with\_stone\_outcrops, predominance\}$;
   $PRO(f_2,vegetation\_landuse) = \{VQ\}$;

6. By taking into account step 5, we obtain the following:

   $SPE(F(t_i), pine) = PPRO(F(t_i), pine) = PRO(f_2, pine) =$
     $\{merging\_with\_stone\_outcrops, predominance\}$;
   $SPE(F(t_i),natural\_vegetation) = PPRO(F(t_i),natural\_vegetation) =$
     $PRO(f_1,natural\_vegetation) = \{height, number\_of\_strata, seasonal\_variation\}$;
   $SPE(F(t_i), vegetation\_landuse) = PPRO(F(t_i),vegetation\_landuse) = \{VF, VQ\}$

7. By using the INH operator, the following is obtained:

   $INH(F(t_i),vegetation\_landuse) = \phi$;
   $INH(F(t_i),natural\_vegetation) = \phi$;
   $INH(F(t_i),pine) = \{height, number\_of\_strata, seasonal\_variation\}$

8. If the ATT operator is now applied to the results obtained for the moment, we get the following:

   $ATT(F(t_i),vegetation\_landuse) = \{VF, VQ\}$;
   $ATT(F(t_i),natural\_vegetation) = \{height, number\_of\_strata, seasonal\_variation\}$;
   $ATT(F(t_i),pine) = \{height, number\_of\_strata, seasonal\_variation,$
     $merging\_with\_stone\_outcrops, predominance\}$;

So far, we applied the operators to construct a partial domain ontology for environmental planning. In the following steps, we will verify the ontology against the properties.

9. By applying PROP1, we get the following:

   $SPE(F(t_i),$ vegetation_landuse$) \cap INH(F(t_i),$ vegetation_landuse$) = \phi$;
   $SPE(F(t_i),$ natural_vegetation$) \cap INH(F(t_i),$ natural_vegetation$) = \phi$;
   $SPE(F(t_i),$ pine$) \cap INH(F(t_i),$ pine$) = \phi$;
   and, hence, PROP1 holds.

10. If PROP2 is now applied, the following can be obtained:

    degree_of_overlapping$(F(t_i),$ natural_vegetation, pine$) = 3$;
    and, hence, PROP2 also holds.

11. By applying PROP3, the following can be written:

    $INH(F(t_i),$natural_vegetation$) = \phi$;
    $ATT(F(t_i),$ M-father(natural_vegetation)$) = ATT(F(t_i),$ vegetation_landuse$) = \{VF,$ VQ$\}$;
    So, $INH(F(t_i),$natural_vegetation$) \subset ATT(F(t_i),$ M-father(natural_vegetation));

    $INH(F(t_i),$pine$) = \{$height, number_of_strata, seasonal_variation$\}$;
    $ATT(F(t_i),$ ISA(pine)$) = ATT(F(t_i),$ natural_vegetation)$) = \{$height, number_of_strata, seasonal_variation$\}$.
    So, $INH(F(t_i),$ pine$) = ATT(F(t_i),$ ISA(pine)) and, hence, PROP3 holds.

12. PROP4 cannot be applied in this case, since Card(children$(c_i)) < 2$ $\forall$ $c_i \in$ PHRD(t), I = 1,..,3.

13. PROP5 cannot not be applied because its preconditions do not hold (see step 4 above).

In conclusion, we see that the domain ontology satisfies all properties for which the preconditions hold.

6   Conclusion

Reusable ontologies play an important role in the development process of knowledge-based systems. They enable the construction of domain knowledge (application ontologies) from reusable components, instead of building them from scratch. The construction of an ontology is, however, still a difficult and costly process. In this paper, we have presented a formal approach that helps in the construction of domain ontologies.

We have proposed a set of ontological operators that enable the structured extraction of domain ontology knowledge from textual fragments (under certain assumptions). These operators are based on an integration of our previous work on mathematical knowledge functions (Martínez-Béjar *et al.*, 1996) with the classical Mereology from Leonard and Goddman (1940). The knowledge engineer applies the ontological operators on the text and validates the results with the expert(s). In this sense, the role of the expert is important as abstractions of concepts and properties have to be performed in the analysis of the fragments of text. In future work we will attempt to automate the application of knowledge functions to "generate" automatically a first draft of a domain knowledge ontology.

To illustrate the usefulness of the mathematical artefacts designed in this work, we have shown an example where a simple domain knowledge ontology is constructed using the formal framework here proposed. The knowledge underlying the example stems from a real problem involving environmental planning by assessment in Spain.

The approach presented is concerned with the construction of ontologies starting from knowledge elicited from experts. The ontologies that we build are therefore application ontologies and domain ontologies (depending on the generality of the knowledge obtained). In this sense our approach is complementary to work on Ontolingua (Gruber, 1993) and the Kactus approach (Schreiber, 1995), as these provide methods and techniques to configure ontologies from already existing (base) ontologies.

Although the ontological operators are a first step forward in making ontology construction more methodological, much work remains to be done. Applying the ontological operators is a process for which the knowledge engineer is responsible. It might therefore require a considerable amount of time. Moreover, one of the underlying assumptions is that, once validated, the approach does not allow its later modification (monotonic knowledge growth). This has not been a problem in the environmental planning application we were concerned with. However, in general this might be a too strong assumption.

Acknowledgement

Rodrigo Martínez-Béjar was supported by the Spanish Scientific Research Council (CSIC) through an Institutional Research Grant (FPU). Richard Benjamins was partially supported by the Netherlands Computer Science Research Foundation with financial support from the Netherlands Organisation for Scientific Research (NWO), and by the European Commission through a Marie Curie Research Grant (TMR).

References

Alberts, L. K. (1993). *YMIR: an ontology for engineering design*, PhD Thesis, University of Twente.

Benjamins, V.R. (1993). *Problem Solving Methods for diagnosis*, PhD Thesis, University of Amsterdam.

Borst, P., and Akkermans, H. (1997). Engineering Ontologies, *International Journal of Human-Computer Studies*, 46: 365-406.

Chandrasekaran, B. (1987). Towards a functional architecture for intelligence based on generic information processing tasks, In *Proceedings of the 10th IJCAI*, 1183-1192, Milan, Italy.

Cooke, N. J. (1994).Varieties of knowledge elicitation techniques, *International Journal of Human-Computer Studies*, Vol. 41:801-849.

Cordingley, E. S. (1989). Knowledge elicitation techniques for knowledge-based systems, In D. Diaper Ed. *Knowledge Elicitation: Principles, Techniques, and Applications*, 89-175, New York: John Wiley and Sons.

Eschenbach, C., and Heydrich, W. (1995). Classical mereology and restricted domains, *International Journal of Human-Computer Studies*, 43: 723-740.

Gruber, T.R (1993). *A Translation Approach to Portable Ontology Specifications*, Knowledge Acquisition, 5 (2): 199-220

Gruber, T.R. (1994). Towards principles for the design of ontologies used for knowledge sharing, In N. Guarino and R. Poli (Eds.), *Formal Ontology in Conceptual Analysis and Knowledge Representation*, Boston, MA: Kluwer.

Guarino, N. (1997). Understanding, building and using ontologies, *International Journal of Human-Computer Studies*, 46: 293-310.

Guarino, N., and Giaretta, P. (1995). Ontologies and knowledge bases: towards a terminological clarification, In Mars, N. Ed., *Towards Very Large Knowledge Bases: Knowledge Building and Knowledge Sharing 1995*, 25-32, Amsterdam, IO Press.

Leonard, H.S., and Goddman, N. (1940). The calculus of individuals and its uses, *Journal of Symbolic Logic*, 5: 45-55.

Lesniewski, S. (1916). Foundations of a general theory of manifolds (in Czech), *Prace Polskiego Kola Naukowe w Moskwie*, Sekcya matematycznoprzyrodnicza, 2, Moscow.

Martínez-Béjar, V.R., Benjamins, R., Martín, F., and Castillo, V. (1996). Deriving formal parameters for comparing knowledge elicitation techniques based on mathematical functions, In B. R. Gaines and M. Musen (Eds.), *Proceedings of the 10th Banff Knowledge Acquisition for Knowledge-Based Systems Workshop*, Vol. 2: 59.1 - 59.20, Banff, Canada.

Martínez-Béjar, R., Cádenas, J. M., and Martín-Rubio, F.(1997). Fuzzy Logic in Landscape Assessment, In *Proceedings of the European Symposium on Intelligent Techniques*, 234-238, Bari, Italy.

Martínez-Béjar, R., and Martín-Rubio, F. (1997). A mathematical functions-based approach for analysing elicited knowledge, To appear in *Proceedings of the Ninth International Conference on Software Engineering and Knowledge Engineering*, Madrid, Spain.

Musen, M. A. (1989). Automated support for building and extending expert models, *Machine learning*, 4: 347-376.

O'Hara, K., Motta, E., and Shadbolt, N. (1994). Grounding GDMs: A Structured Case Study, *International Journal of Human-Computer Studies*, Vol. 40: 315-347.

Puerta, A. R., Egar, J., Tu, S., and Musen, M. (1992). A multiple-method shell for the automatic generation of Knowledge acquisition tools, *Knowledge Acquisition*, 4:171-196.

Schreiber, A. T. (1993). Operationalizing models of expertise, In A. T. Schreiber, B. J. Wielinga, and J. A. Breuker (Eds.), *KADS: A Principled Approach to Knowledge-Based System Development*, 119-149, London: Academic Press.

Schreiber, A. T., Wielinga, B.J, and Jansweijer, W.H.J (1995). The KACTUS View on the 'O' Word, In D. Skuce, N. Guarino and L. Bouchard (Eds.) *IJCAI Workshop on Basic Ontological Issues in Knowledge Sharing*

Simons, P. (1987). *Parts, A Study in Ontology*, 5-128, Oxford: Clarendon Press.

van Heijst, G., Schreiber, A. T., and Wielinga, B. J. (1997). Using explicit ontologies in KBS development, *International Journal of Human-Computer Studies*, **45**: 183-292.

Wielinga, B. J., Schreiber, A. T., and Breuker, J. A. (1992). KADS: a modelling approach to knowledge engineering, *Knowledge Acquisition*, Vol. 4:5-53.

Reuse of Problem-Solving Methods and Family Resemblances

Rainer Perkuhn

Institute AIFB
University of Karlsruhe (TH)
D-76128 Karlsruhe, Germany
e-mail: perkuhn@aifb.uni-karlsruhe.de

Abstract

In the last years a common notion of a Problem-Solving Method (PSM) emerged from different knowledge engineering frameworks. As a generic description of the dynamic behaviour of knowledge based systems PSMs are favored subjects of reuse. Up to now, most investigations on the reuse of PSMs focus on static features and methods as objects of reuse. By this, they ignore a lot of information of how the PSM was developed that is, in principle, entailed in the different parts of a conceptual model of a PSM.

In this paper the information of the different parts of PSMs is reconsidered from a reuse process point of view. A framework for generalized problem-solving methods is presented that describes the structure of a category of methods based on family resemblances. These generalized methods can be used to structure libraries of PSMs and - in the process of reuse - as a means to derive an incarnation, i.e. a member of its family of PSMs.

For illustrating the ideas, the approach is applied to the task rsp. problem type of parametric design.

Keywords: Problem Solving Methods, Reuse, Similarities, Categories of PSMs

1   Introduction

Most current knowledge engineering frameworks consider a notion of a Problem-Solving Method (PSM) that converged from a number of different approaches (Generic Tasks [Chandrasekaran, Johnson, and Smith, 1992], CommonKADS [Schreiber et al., 1994], Method-to-Task Approach [Eriksson et al., 1995], Components of Expertise [Steels, 1990], GDM [Terpstra et al., 1993], MIKE [Angele, Fensel, and Studer, 1996]). A PSM is a knowledge level description of a problem-oriented, but domain-independent reasoning strategy. Augmented with domain-specific knowledge a PSM can be reused across different applications. By reuse of PSMs, the development time of knowledge based systems is shortened, the quality of the system is improved, the maintenance is simplified, and the overall costs are reduced - computed against the investment cost for systematic reuse. In this context it seems to be worth while investigating systematic approaches to planned reuse.

Loosely speaking, reuse means finding an adequate component to a given task description out of a given set of reuse candidates. This leads to the following issues:

- determining what is a reuse candidate,
- organizing the set of reuse candidates (library, repository),

- describing the characteristics of tasks and components (indexing),
- supporting the lookup mechanism (retrieval),
- defining a metric for assessing the adaquacy of the found component(s).

Most current approaches take implicitly a notion of a PSM as a candidate for reuse as granted. Based upon these prerequisites they attempt to characterize the functionality of a PSM from a competence point of view. A suitable description of the competence might be used for indexing and, by matching against the goals of a given task, also for retrieval. But, instead of drawing conclusions from the competence (and further) information for the structure of the library, the approaches treat the components as totally isolated from each other.

In general, minor attention is paid to the relation between tasks, between PSMs and between tasks and PSMs. Some taxonomies for tasks rsp. problem types have been suggested (e.g. [Breuker and van de Velde, 1994]). With the assumption that a task rsp. problem type in the taxonomy can be related to a limited number of PSMs, the retrieval can be split up into two steps: First, determining the problem type, and second, selecting a PSM from the (small) set of PSMs attached to the problem type. But none of the suggested taxonomies can cope with the fact that there is no such thing as a pure analytical or generative task. Every diagnosing task involves the aspect of generating a report to present the result of the analytical step. A configuration task cannot ignore analytical knowledge to distinguish acceptable and not acceptable configurations - besides the trivial task of unconstrained configuration. A comprehensive reuse framework should be able to offer e.g. the PSM propose&revise for both tasks. Even, it might be more straightforward to relate propose&revise to a generative task since the effort spent on reusing might mirror the likeliness of the relation.

An approach that tries to capture the intertwining of tasks is that of a suite ([Breuker, 1994]). A suite relates the problem types of the above mentioned taxonomy to each other. It prescribes a standard ordering by defining a successor relation between the problem types that is assumed to be held for most applications. But, to be really useful in a reuse framework a suite contains insufficient information. It is just one meta-level structure for all tasks. The gain of information by using a suite is very small. The suite fits every task and may be instantiated accordingly. But there is no support of how this information narrows the range of applicable PSMs.

Instead of one meta-level structure it would be reasonable to suggest several structures for different task clusters or families. Each structure should handle a specific task type and contain more information than a suite.

The next section discusses the role categories can play in the reuse process and introduces the notion of family resemblances.

The following section shows how the relation between tasks can be exploited to derive a structure for a category of PSMs based on family resemblances. To assess the relevance of the features of a PSM for a family structure, this section reconsiders the motivation of the different parts of the common notion of a PSM.

Section 4 illustrates the ideas with a case study for the task rsp. problem type of parametric design; section 5 concludes and discusses related and future work.

2   Categories and Family Resemblances

Normally, only a few PSMs are really suitable to accomplish a given task. Even with an exhaustive characterization of a PSM's competence the space of all reusable PSMs has to be searched one way or the other. The retrieval process starts at one point and repeats to look for the next candidate if the previous attempt failed - until success or failure for the last candidate. Obviously, it is not reasonable to treat the space of all PSMs as an unordered flat collection because then retrieval is linear search. In an ideal reuse scenario the retrieval would start at one or possibly several entry points according to the competence of the PSMs. A mismatch would then trigger continuing search in the neighbourhood of the entry point. But for this, the notion of neighbourhoodness of PSMs has to be established on some kind of similarity measure between PSMs. The metric of similarity is based on some set of features and defined as the ratio of the weighted sum of the common features by the weighted sum of the distinctive features ([Tversky, 1977]) - given suitable sets of features and weights.

A first idea to support browsing through the space of PSMs would be to categorize the methods. Repeating this step results in a taxonomy of PSMs that can be used as a hierarchical structure of a library. Taxonomies enable hierachical instead of linear search but they are - as mentioned above - not suitable for categorizing PSMs with respect to tasks the PSMs should accomplish. But there is a way to combine most of the advantages of categories and to avoid the restrictions of strict taxonomies.

Classical theory of categorization defines categories based on necessary and sufficient conditions on a certain set of features: if (and only if) an object has all the features of a category, then it is a member, i.e. if one feature is missing, an object is definitely not member of the category. As a consequence there is a clear border and distinction between members and non-members. So, in a taxonomy it is not possible to have two different categories, e.g. one for PSMs for parametric design tasks and one for PSMs for diagnosis tasks, and an object, e.g. the PSM propose&revise, belonging to both of these categories (as shown in figure 1.a). A cognitive theory of categorization weakens the membership defini-

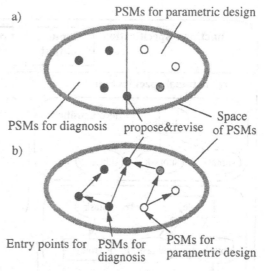

Figure 1.   Categories of PSMs based
a) on necessary and sufficient conditions and
b) on family resemblances

tion via necessary and sufficient conditions and focusses on the structure of a category according to the degree of similarity between objects ([Wittgenstein, 1953], [Rosch, 1975], [Lakoff, 1991]). In this framework a category is represented by one or several prototypes. A prototype is a possibly virtual - in the sense of not necessarily existent - object that unites all the features that are considered most prominent for this category.

E.g. the prototype of the category "birds" is a two-feet flying, egg-laying animal of certain size and shape. But of course, pinguins would be called birds although they do not fly. And there is no reason to assume that the prototype has a real counterpart of exactly the same size and shape. The prototype is just a projection of the condensed experiences with objects that are considered members of the category and a constructed means to express its structure. The membership to a category is a gradual property depending on the closeness to the prototype(s). If a category is so diverse that it cannot be expressed by one prototype solely (e.g. the category "games") the category may be also represented by several prototypes. The underlying notion of the relation between several prototypes and the closeness between a prototype and the elements of a category is termed family resemblances. In the following, some features of PSMs are discussed to derive prototypical structures. These generalized prototypical PSMs can then be used to describe a family of PSMs and as a means in the reuse process to come to an incarnation of a member of this family.

3 Families of PSMs

The notion of a PSM consists of a functional and operational specification. The functional specification describes the competence of a PSM and its interface to the environment. The operational specification comprises four main parts (s. figure 2):

- the decomposition of the task into several subtasks,

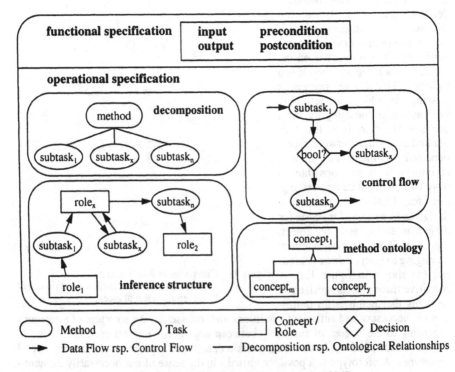

Figure 2. (Parts of the) Description of a PSM (cf. [Angele et al., 1996])

- an inference structure for this level of decomposition, i.e. the data flow between the subtasks,
- a control mechanism that constrains the order of accomplishing the subtasks in order to meet the PSM's competence with respect to the goals achievable by the subtasks, and
- a method ontology that describes the concepts used by the method (and their interrelationships).

Provided an adequate model of an application domain (domain ontology) and a suitable mapping of the domain-specific concepts to the method-specific concepts, a PSM can be reused across several domains and applications.

To be able to assess the relevance of the different features of a PSM for a notion of similarity, first, the motivation that led to the different parts respectively is reconsidered. Thereupon it is possible to elaborate their specific contribution to the conceptual model of a PSM.

3.1 Reconsidering Task Structure Analysis

Understanding a PSM as a way to break down one complex task into several subtasks is the knowledge engineering variant of the divide-and-conquer principle. In addition, the special aim of a task structure analysis is to figure out what aspect of the problem makes it a hard problem. Refining the goal of a task by several subgoals of its subtasks reveals the simple and crucial parts of the problem. The crucial parts show that, where, and what kinds of mostly heuristic, specific knowledge is necessary to make the whole process computational tractable.

Obviously, the decomposition process can be repeated for every new subtask until finally the tasks can be accomplished by elementary steps that can be written down straightforward as inference actions. These are the leaves in the resulting tree consisting of alternating levels of, on the one hand, matching alternative methods (or elementary inference actions) to tasks and, on the other hand, decomposing each method into several subtasks (s. figure 3).

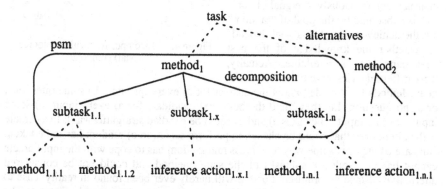

Figure 3. Embedding the notion of PSM into the method-to-task paradigm (cf. [Angele et al., 1996])

But these figures are a little bit misleading. It must be stressed that a PSM is only one

179

step of decomposition; a PSM determines new subtasks and, by this, sets up new goals. The decomposition does not constrain the way of how to achieve the new goals. So, the part of the tree beneath a PSM should be treated separately from the PSM itself. Of course, the complete specification of the dynamic part of a knowledge based system is one instantiation of the tree after deciding for one of each alternative. Nevertheless, a description of a conceptual model of a PSM as shown in figure 2 is set up on top of the notion of subtasks rsp. their goals and does not look into the task internal details. Also, from the reuse process point of view a PSM is primarily a means for one step of the top down analysis.

Corrolary 1 - Task decomposition

A PSM is a way to decompose one task into several subtasks. The goal of the overall subtask is broken down by setting up new subgoals for the subtasks. A PSM does not prescribe how these (sub-)goals have to be achieved.

The notion of a PSM does not restrict the way how the subgoals are related to each other and to the goal of the overall task. Of course, if all subtasks are successfully accomplished, the goal of the major task should have been met. But the subgoals may depend on each other and be coherent. The subgoals need not to be mutually exclusive. One goal may be subsumed by another - provided that the specific knowledge required to achieve this goal is available. So, in the following the goals of a method's subtasks should not be considered disjoint. At least for a subset of all possible inputs they may overlap.

The following example is intended to illustrate this idea. If one task is to decide for the next candidate (e.g an employee to be assigned to an office room) the method "select" sets up two subtasks (in other cases, more and different subtasks would be possible).

"Oracle" has the goal to select always the best next candidate, "random" only to present one (arbitrarily selected) candidate (e.g. due to the alphabetical order of their names). Obviously, the goal of "oracle" is subsumed by the goal of "random" but the achievability of this goal depends on whether the knowledge of the best next candidate is available. Actually, three different cases have to be distinguis-

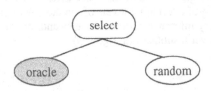

Figure 4. Decomposition with a coloured (optional) component

hed: Methods for "oracle" know the answer for a) every question, b) some questions, or c) no question. I.e. they yield the best next candidate for a) every input, b) some input, or c) no input. The cases a) and c) could be handled straightforward: In a) oracle is the alternative that could be chosen to perform select, in c) random has to be taken. But case b) requires some way to express that random has to cope with the input oracle cannot handle. Both are subtasks of the same method and could not be considered alternatives. Since an omniscient oracle will hardly ever been found in reality, case a) will be ignored in the following. The other two cases are represented in figure 4: The difference between them is described by a colour, but the similarity is captured by integrating them into one common underlying structure. In the extreme case c) that no specific oracle knowledge is available it would be reasonable to be able to wipe out these nodes from the figures of the task decomposition tree. Therefore, they should be marked as optional components. In the reuse process the optional components can be checked with respect to the necessary knowledge and be treated accordingly.

Corrolary 2 - Relations between subtasks, optional components

> The goals of the subtasks of a PSM are not necessarily mutually exclusive. Some subgoals may overlap, some subgoals may be subsumed by other subgoals. In case of subsumption the subsumed goal should be marked as optional.

The relation between the optional subtasks and the specific knowledge they require is documented best as a kind of inference structure.

3.2 Reconsidering Inference Structures

An inference structure describes the data flow between the subtasks that are the result of the decomposition. The ways of the possible data flow is represented by directed links between the subtasks; the structure of the data is specified as roles on the links (s. figure 2). Roles contain the (derived) static knowledge of the inference structure. A role may be a data interface between two subtasks or between a subtask and the domain specific knowledge. In the latter case the role the domain knowledge plays in the inference process is expressed in form of a mapping.

Inference structures can be seen in the reuse process twofold. On the one hand, as part of a complete specification they are objects for reuse, on the other hand, as interpretation models they are means for reuse. In the context of a reuse process-oriented framework the latter aspect is more attractive. As an interpretation model an inference structure is used to check whether the necessary knowledge for each subtask is available from the application domain rsp. whether any domain knowledge can be elicitated and interpreted in a way that it can fill the role in the inference structure. Elicitating and interpreting are highly creative acts but spending time and effort on them is reasonable only to a certain extent. Finally, the interpretation model is judged binary either suitable or not. But taken the motivation of the task decomposition seriously there is no reason to assume that the applicability of one subtask depends on the availability of some specific knowledge other subtasks require. A really useful interpretation structure should separate these affairs. Then, the evaluation of the interpretation structure does not yield a binary, but a gradually decision - depending on what different kinds of knowledge are available.

Of course, some kinds of knowledge are really necessary and are, as such, the crucial features for a binary decision. But, in the case that the goal of one subtask is subsumed by or overlaps with goals of other subtasks, it is sufficient that their common goal can be achieved one way or the other. If the goal of the coherent tasks can be achieved by some subset of them alone, the rest is optional. In the

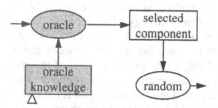

Figure 5. Inference struture with coloured (optional) components

following the relation between an optional role and the subtasks that use the knowledge of this role is defined and illustrated as a colour. The colouring of an inference structure shows what kinds of knowledge are not binary decisive for the suitability of the structure and what dependants of the role also can be wiped out if the knowledge is not available. This way, this structure can be used to derive different incarnations that are all members of the same family of PSMs.

Corrolary 3 - Coloured inference structures

> An inference structure describes the data flow between the subtasks (that are the result of the decomposition) via roles. The coherence between optional tasks and the specific knowledge they require is defined by a colour. All nodes of the same colour can be deleted from the structure if the specific knowledge role cannot be filled.

The information that was collected up to this point to characterize a family of PSMs can be condensed to a notion of a coloured inference structure including a specification of the goals of the subtasks. The information of the decomposition is an intrinsic feature of the inference structure. Most part of this information can already be specified by a new version of the language KARL ([Angele et al., 1996]). The revised version of KARL allows to describe PSMs on a formal and conceptual level, especially goals and competences can be expressed by pre- and postconditions. But, up to now there is no way to treat the different parts separately and, by this, to really support the reuse process. For illustration purposes an alternative is preferred: Another way to express the characteristics of a PSM is a graph grammar rule (s. figure 5, cf. GDM [Terpstra et al., 1993]): A method is rewritten by its inference structure. Missing optional knowledge leads to deleting all same coloured parts of the inference structure. But it should be noted that it is a misinterpretation to treat a task-decomposition tree only as the result of recursive applications of grammar rules, i.e. as a word of the language accepted by the grammar. A method can be seen as a rule, but the selection of a PSM to a given task involves some aspects that cannot be expressed if hidden in rewriting. The matching of a PSM's competence against the goal of a task may reveal (hidden) assumptions of the PSM, e.g. the single-fault-assumption or the assumption of acyclic revise rules ([Benjamins, Fensel, and Straatman, 1996]). Assumptions trigger different processes of checking properties of the domain knowledge or reformulating the task ([Fensel and Schoenegge, 1997]). Afterwards, if the method-to-task adaptation did not run into a dead end, plugging in the method enables a new rewriting step. A PSM grammar cannot separate the different aspects, it ignores the essence of a PSM. But it is a useful instrument to reconstruct the development process.

Most of the issues discussed up to this point can be easily transferred to the notion of a method ontology. The concepts and relations may be also optional and coloured according to the colours of the roles (and vice versa). Further, it would be interesting to compare the relation between method and subtask ontologies (cf. [Studer et al., 1996]) to the expressiveness of the graph grammar rules for the methods. Since this paper attempts to present a coherent view of the especially dynamic part of a PSM, the aspect of method ontologies is not elaborated any further. Instead a brief sketch of how control knowledge can be characterized is presented.

3.3 Reconsidering Control Knowledge

The last aspect of a PSM that has not been considered yet is the ordering of the subtasks. The control knowledge specifies when each subtask may be accomplished - dependent on the goals of other subtasks. Thinking in the paradigm of e.g. Structured Analysis control flow may expressed in terms of sequence, alternative, and iteration.

If there is a reason to stick to this paradigm and to the assumption of a single processor system the control can be illustrated by flow diagrams (s. figure 2). Then, the control knowledge of a generalized PSM with optional components can be described

- by enumerating all control flows for all possible incarnations or
- by using coloured flow diagrams similar to coloured inference structures.

Leaving the paradigm and relaxing the single processor assumption opens new ways to describe control knowledge.

Once again, the motivation of the task decomposition helps to introduce a wide notion of control knowledge. The initial state before task decomposition consists of a problem to be solved. Unfortunately, the solution of the problem is not obvious. The only way to solve the problem in one step would be to ask an oracle that always yields the correct solution. This is the first trivial model a knowledge engineer might have about the problem solving process. The aim of decomposition is to set up subgoals that could be achieved with less miraculous knowledge. The knowledge engineer attempts to break down the goal to be able to cope with - at least some of - the subgoals. The degree of how well understood a subtask is might affect organizational models especially how the subtasks could/should be distributed between a human expert and the system. A very critical but incomplete understood task e.g. deciding what to do next in an emergency case of a nuclear plant should rest with a human expert as long as possible.

Generalizing this szenario of two agents to a multi-agent szenario enables constellations in which each subtask has its own agent. Of course, the agents need a way to communicate with each other e.g. via a blackboard. But on top of the constellation control knowledge can be easily specified without the restrictions of structured analysis. Every agent just has to know what kinds of knowledge it expects from which (data delivering) predecessor and what conditions must hold on this input. Then, an agent can start accomplishing its task immediately when the expected input is provided and satisfies the constraints.

Corrolary 4 - Control knowledge

Control knowledge has to specify what constraints have to be satisfied by the input a subtasks expects from its (data delivering) predecessors. Subtasks can be accomplished as soon as the complete expected input is provided that satisfies the constraints.

By this, this framework also captures parallel - possibly competing - subtasks that will become even more important in the near future. Nevertheless, coming back from internet visions downto earth, if agent-oriented specifying of control is not wanted, the framework can be used at least as a means to derive a control flow specification in the mentioned terms: Starting with the "last" subtask that delivers the output of the method the control flow specification may be constructed backwards - by iteratively comparing what a subtask expects with what its predecessors can provide it with.

4 One Family of PSMs for the Task Type Parametric Design

In the following the ideas of the last two sections are illustrated with an example. A simplified version of the task type parametric design (cf. [Motta and Zdrahal, 1996]) sets up a goal for the framework. Then different subgoals and the relation to each other are discussed and result in a description of a simple family structure.

The similarity of names for the subtasks to subtask names of well-known PSMs is purely arbitrary. They are not intended to suggest a 1:1-mapping of the family structure to existing PSMs. But they may indicate a way of how a similar incarnation of the family structure can be derived.

4.1 Parametric Design

The task type of parametric design works with a system model that describes the structure of the system to be designed with a number of parameters. Designing means that a value has to be assigned to every parameter from its specific range.

SYSTEM

PARAMETER$_1$: { RANGE$_1$ }

. . .

PARAMETER$_n$: { RANGE$_n$ }

If there is no restriction of what a correct (or good) design is, then the values can be arbitrarily taken from the respective ranges. But normally designs are least distinguished between correct and incorrect assignments. Initially well-chosen values enable a straightforward search for a correct assignment. Sometimes, a subset of the parameters can be made responsible for the failure and, sometimes, the reason why a design is incorrect can be explained and named. The reason becomes particularly useful if it can be connected to a way how to improve the assignment at least locally. But this local change may effect that the assignment is still incorrect due to other reasons.

4.2 Subtasks and the Family Structure

The overall goal of a parametric design task is to find an assignment that maps each parameter to a value out of its range. If only a subset of possible assignments are valid assignments the validity must be checked, e.g. with a boolean function that yields TRUE if the assignment is valid and FALSE otherwise. So, constrained parametric design has to find a valid assignment with respect to this test. Of course, normally, a design is assessed according to a quality metric and the goal is to find the best possible design. But for simplification reasons this aspect is not considered any further.

Based on this framework, the task can at least be split up into two subtasks: One that has the goal to find a possibly partial assignment and the other one has the goal to decide whether this assignment is valid or not. The subtasks do not restrict the degree of freedom whether the first task has to generate a complete assignment or whether it starts with a subset of the parameters that is extended after a successful test. This decision can be seen as part of the control knowledge that is not discussed in detail. To briefly sketch the idea, the succeeding task has to specify whether it expects an assignment for one, several or all parameters.

This first vague approximation of a "method" is shown in figure 6 as uncoloured objects.

parametric design:

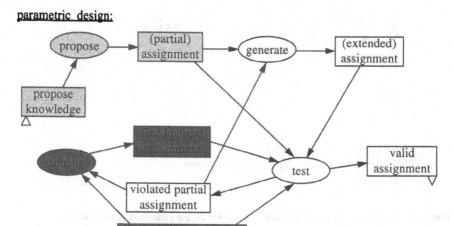

Figure 6.   Family structure of the category of PSMs for the task type parametric design

Instead of generating arbitrary assignments and searching the space of all possible assignments unsystematically, knowledge about good (initial) values for at least some of the parameters would improve the search. Of course, only an oracle could always offer valid assignments but starting with presumably good values lowers the average search time. The goal of this task of proposing "good" values is somehow subsumed by the goal of "generate". Even less efficient "generate" will deliver the same values - but after some failed iterations of generating and testing. So, it is not really necessary to have propose knowledge for every parameter because "generate" can help in that situation as a backup or default subtask. Presumably in most cases there is propose knowledge only for a subset of the parameters so that a partial assignment has to be extended by arbitrary generated values for the rest of the parameters.

The relation of this goal to propose knowledge and the optionality of this coherent area is shown by light grey colouring of the nodes in the left upper corner of figure 6.

More sophisticated test knowledge may also yield a subset of the parameters that is responsible for the violation. Then, the violation can be repaired locally, i.e. only values of some parameters of this subset have to be exchanged. This specific knowledge and the dependent nodes of the structure are marked with dark grey in figure 6.

If there is no special knowledge of how this could be done, again arbitrary partial assignments for this subset of parameters can be generated and tested until the partial assignment does not cause the violation any more (if possible). Although this local repair helps to avoid testing a lot of assignments it does not guarantee that the resulting assignment is valid. It may be invalid due to other conditions so the test has to follow once again. The same holds even if some special revise knowledge is available that tells how to fix a violated constraint. Since this goal is subsumed by the rest of this exchange:

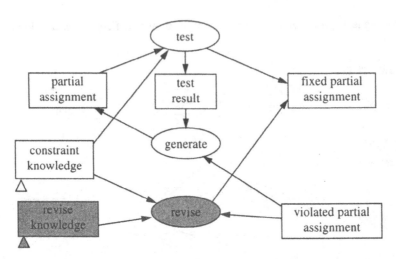

Figure 7.   Family structure of the category of PSMs for the (sub-)task type exchange

structure the subtask and the required knowledge are marked as optional and coloured middle grey (cf. figure 7).

In this family the subtask "test" mostly determines the control flow. If it expects a complete model, then possibly the two preceding subtasks "propose" and "generate" have to be repeated until all parameters have assigned values, otherwise a subset of assigned parameters from one of them once accomplished may be sufficient (Complete vs. Extend Model Then Revise, [Motta and Zdrahal, 1996]). The "generate" subtask only has to be performed if the subtask "test" demands an assignment for some parameter the "propose" task does not have the knowledge about good values for.

4.3   Using the Family Structure to Derive PSMs

The resulting structure represents one family of PSMs for parametric design tasks. As mentioned above there is no need that a counterpart PSM exists in reality. But it can be used to partially structure the library and as a means to derive different incarnations.

Retrieving a component from the library is separated into two steps. First, one or more family structures are selected from the library out of a limited number of "reference structures" according to the competence. And second, each selected structure is used to browse through the category it describes. The first step is not the subject of this paper but could be briefly sketched as matching the competence against the task goal. For the described parametric design family it is necessary that the central concept of the task is a system model that can be described by parameters. If the central activity is assigning "correct" values to the parameters, then this family is a possible candidate for the next step. Then the colouring of the family structure can be used as the underlying principle for a questionnaire. The uncoloured roles are necessary features - if they cannot be filled, the structure is excluded from further consideration. The coloured roles mirror the family structure of the category, they are useful but not necessary features. If these roles cannot be filled, all nodes of the same colour can be wiped out. Otherwise the process continues with refining the structures. But in any case, the structure is a means to navigate through the space of PSMs.

Depending on the availability of the above described roles it seems to be straightforward to derive incarnations of the family that are very close rsp. can be refined to well-known PSMs:

- if none of the optional roles is available, the structure is reduced to almost generate&test (cf. figure 8),

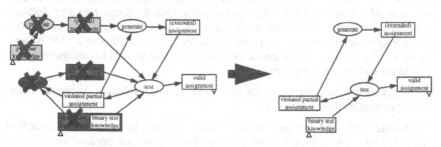

Figure 8. Instantiating the family structure to the PSM generate&test

- if all optional roles are available, the structure strongly resembles propose&revise.

The insight that the two methods are very closely related to each other (according to family resemblances) is strongly supported by the mincer metaphor that showed how one could be transformed into the other (cf. [Fensel and Straatman, 1996]).

Table 1 summarizes the scope of the family described by figure 6 and figure 7. Every (optional) role triggers a question, the dependencies between roles trigger follow-up questions. Further roles independent from the two shown in the table would spawn up further dimensions.

Is knowledge of this special kind available?	binary decision? No Yes → ↓	constraint knowledge? No Yes → ↓	revise knowledge? No ↓	Yes ↓
Yes → propose knowledge? No →	unconstrained propose (&generate)	propose (&generate) &test	propose (&generate) &exchange	propose (&generate) &revise
	unconstrained generate	generate &test	generate &exchange	generate &revise

Table 1. Underlying structure for questionnaire ("→" means follow-up question rsp. decision for row or column, shading means already documented PSM)

By representing the structure of a family of PSMs explicitly a questionnaire can easily be derived. Furthermore, by making explicitly the dependencies between the optional roles e.g. in a table similarity between two members can be expressed: Neighbours in the table are very closely related to each other, greater distances express a lower similarity measure.

5   Conclusion, Related and Future Work

The presented framework is one of the few approaches to tackle the problem of the relation between the subtasks of specific task rsp. problem types. Based on a non-classical notion of categorization a way to structure a family of PSMs is suggested. The description of this family structure is grounded on the well-established, but slightly reconsidered notion of a PSM. The paper aimed to shift the focus from a product-oriented to a process-oriented view on the reuse of PSMs. For this, generalized PSMs incorporate more information than only the binary distinction whether a PSM is suitable or not. By deriving an incarnation of the family this artefact is configured according to the specific circumstances.

Other approaches that investigate the relation between tasks discuss taxonomies, task-decomposition methods, or suites.

Taxonomies (e.g. [Breuker and van de Velde, 1994]) would be ideal for hierarchical search but they cannot cope with the fact that there are no clear borders between categories of PSMs for different task types.

Task-decomposition methods ([Benjamins, 1993]) try to cover a space of PSMs for one task but they suffer from the same disadvantages as taxonomies. They are not able to express the specific difference between the decomposition of the method and the sophisticated selection and adaptation process before plugging in a method.

The deficiencies of the notion of a suite ([Breuker, 1994]) are already discussed above. Although this idea is applied to specific task types ([Benjamins, 1995]) the benefits of a suite remain unclear. Neither the way how to use a suite, nor the way how to exploit the result is documented.

But there is some other work that already use an implicit notion of a family structure.

In the context of the CommonKADS approach a collection of questions rsp. questionnaires about task features is discussed ([Aamodt et al., 1993]) to support the selection of a method for an identified task type. GDM proposes a set of rewrite rules. The configuration of a PSM depends on the selection and application of some of the GDM rules ([Terpstra et al., 1993]). Although, at first glance, these are different issues there is a strong relation between the selection of rules in GDM and the ordering of questions about the task features: Both check some properties of the task rsp. problem type and yield a similar result, namely a PSM. The rule selection and the question ordering look also very similar to wiping out coloured nodes in this approach but GDM and CommonKADS use the common underlying structure of similar family members only implicitly. An explicit representation of the family structure enables a systematic approach to construct questionnaires and to guide the application of grammar rules.

Some new results on automated configuration of PSMs also take some kind of family structure for granted. In this framework, PSMs are derived from more common but task specific parametrized structures ([ten Teije, 1997]). One structure is examined in detail for diagnosis. With specific values for the parameters this structure is instantiated to a PSM. Some parameters may obtain the empty set as value with the consequence that they can be ignored. This resembles the optional components in the approach discussed in this paper, but the relation to the other subtasks and the embedding in an incremental reuse process is not considered.

In the future the relation of family structures to parameters (in the configuration-of-

PMSs-as-parametric-design-paradigm [ten Teije et al., 1996]) and to assumptions (cf. [Benjamins, Fensel, and Straatman, 1996]) will be investigated. Furthermore the specification of control knowledge has to be elaborated. For this, more family structures of different task types have to be developped and specified formally - currently the task types diagnosis and assessment are investigated. Most insights are then expected from using the family structures in real life reuse applications.

Acknowledgements

I would like to thank Rudi Studer, Dieter Fensel, Robert Engels, Stefan Decker, and Michael Erdmann for many interesting discussions, and the anonymous referees for valuable and stimulating comments.

References

[Aamodt et al., 1993] A. Aamodt, B. Benus, C. Duursma, Chr. Tomlinson, R. Schrooten, and W. van der Velde: *Task Features and their Use in CommonKADS*. Deliverable 1.5. Version 1.0, Consortium, University of Amsterdam, 1993.

[Angele et al., 1996] J. Angele, S. Decker, R. Perkuhn, and R. Studer: Modeling Problem Solving Methods in New KARL. In: *Proceedings of the 10th Knowledge Acquisition for Knowledge-Based Systems Workshop (KAW'96)*, Banff, Canada, November 1996, 1-1 - 1-18.

[Angele, Fensel, and Studer, 1996] J. Angele, D. Fensel, and R. Studer: Domain and Task Modeling in MIKE. In: A. Sutcliffe, D. Benyon, F. van Assche (Eds.): *Domain Knowledge for Interactive System Design*, Chapman & Hall, 1996, 149-163.

[Benjamins, 1993] R. Benjamins: *Problem Solving Methods for Diagnosis*. Ph.D. Thesis, University of Amsterdam, Amsterdam, 1993.

[Benjamins, 1995] R. Benjamins: Suite in Dm: A suite of problem types in diagnostic methods. In: *Proceedings of the Knowledge Engineering Forum '95 (KEF'95)*, St. Augustin, Germany, March 1995, 7-18.

[Benjamins, Fensel, and Straatman, 1996] R. Benjamins, D. Fensel, and R. Straatman: Assumptions of Problem-Solving Methods and their Role in Knowledge Engineering. In: *Proceedings of the 12th European Conference on Artificial Intelligence (ECAI'96)*, Budapest, August 1996, 408-412.

[Breuker, 1994] J.A. Breuker : A suite of problem types. In: [Breuker and van de Velde, 1994], 57-87.

[Breuker and van de Velde, 1994] J.A. Breuker and W. van de Velde (Eds.): *The CommonKADS Library for Expertise Modeling*. IOS Press, Amsterdam, 1994.

[Chandrasekaran, Johnson, and Smith, 1992] B. Chandrasekaran, T.R. Johnson, and J.W. Smith: Task-Structure Analysis for Knowledge Modeling. *Communications of the ACM*, 35(9), 1992, 124-137.

[Eriksson et al., 1995] H. Eriksson, Y. Shahar, S.W. Tu, A.R. Puerta, and M.A. Musen: Task Modeling with Reusable Problem-Solving Methods. *Artificial Intelligence*, 79, 2, 1995, 293-326.

[Fensel and Schoenegge, 1997] D. Fensel and A. Schoenegge: Hunting for Assumptions as Developing Method for Problem-Solving Methods. To appear in: *Workshop Proceedings Problem-solving Methods for Knowledge-based Systems in Connection with the Fifteenth International Joint Conference on Artificial Intelligence (IJCAI'97)*, Nagoya, Japan, August 1997.

[Fensel and Straatman, 1996] D. Fensel and R. Straatman: Problem-Solving Methods: Making Assumptions for Efficiency Reasons. In: *Proceedings of the 9th European Knowledge Acquisition Workshop (EKAW'96)*, Nottingham, England, May 1996, Lecture Notes in Artificial Intelligence (LNAI), vol. 1076, Springer-Verlag, Berlin, 1996, 17-32.

[Gennari et al., 1994] J.H. Gennari, S. Tu, Th.E. Rothenfluh, and M.A. Musen: Mapping Domains to Methods in Support of Reuse. *International Journal of Human-Computer Studies (IJHCS)*, 41, 1994, 399-424.

[Lakoff, 1991] G. Lakoff: *Women, fire, and dangerous things: what categories reveal about the mind.* University of Chicago Press, Chicago, 1991.

[Motta and Zdrahal, 1996] E. Motta and Z. Zdrahal: Parametric Design Problem Solving. In: *Proceedings of the 10th Banff Knowledge Acquisition for Knowledge Based Systems Workshop (KAW'96)*, Banff, Canada, November 1996, 9-1 - 9-20.

[Newell, 1982] A. Newell: The Knowledge Level. *Artificial Intelligence*, 18, 1982, 87-127.

[Puerta et al., 1992] A. R. Puerta, J. W. Egar, S. W. Tu, and M. A. Musen: A Multiple-Method Knowledge Acquisition Shell for the Automatic Generation of Knowledge Acquisition Tools. *Knowledge Acquisition*, 4, 1992, 171-196.

[Rosch, 1975] E. Rosch and C.B. Mervis: Family Resemblances: Studies in the Internal Structure of Categories. *Cognitive Psychology*, 7, 1975, 573 - 605.

[Schreiber et al., 1994] A.Th. Schreiber, B.J. Wielinga, R. de Hoog, H. Akkermans, and W. van de Velde: CommonKADS: A Comprehensive Methodology for KBS Development. *IEEE Expert*, December 1994, 28-37.

[Schreiber, Wielinga, and Breuker, 1993] G. Schreiber, B. Wielinga, and J. Breuker (Eds.): *KADS. A Principled Approach to Knowledge-Based System Development.* Knowledge-Based Systems, vol. 11, Academic Press, London, 1993.

[Steels, 1990] L. Steels: Components of Expertise. *AI Magazine*, 11(2), 1990, 29-49.

[Studer et al., 1996] R. Studer, H. Eriksson, J.H. Gennari, S. Tu, D. Fensel, and M.A. Musen: Ontologies and the Configuration of Problem Solving Methods. In: *Proceedings of the 10th Banff Knowledge Acquisition for Knowledge Based Systems Workshop (KAW'96)*, Banff, Canada, November 1996, 11-1 - 11-20.

[ten Teije, 1997] A. ten Teije: *Automated Configuration of Problem Solving Methods in Diagnosis.* Ph.D. Thesis, University of Amsterdam, Amsterdam, 1997.

[ten Teije et al., 1996] A. ten Teije, F. van Harmelen, Guus Schreiber, and Bob Wielinga: Construction of Problem Solving Methods as Parametric Design. In: *Proceedings of the 10th Banff Knowledge Acquisition for Knowledge Based Systems Workshop (KAW'96)*, Banff, Canada, November 1996, 12-1 - 12-20.

[Terpstra et al., 1993] P. Terpstra, G. van Heijst, B. Wielinga, and N. Shadbolt: Knowledge Acquisition Support Through Generalized Directive Models. In: J.-M. David, J.-P. Krivine, and R. Simmons (eds.): *Second Generation Expert Systems*, Springer, Berlin, 1993, 428-455.

[Tversky, 1977] S. Tversky: Features of similarity. *Psychological Review*, 84, 1977, 327 - 352.

[Wittgenstein, 1953] L. Wittgenstein: *Philosophical Investigations.* Macmillan, New York, 1953.

Specification of Flexible Knowledge-Based Systems

Christine Pierret-Golbreich and Xavier Talon

LRI URA CNRS 410

Université Paris Sud

91405 Orsay Cedex, France

Abstract

The paper focuses on the specification of flexible knowledge-based systems. A flexible system is capable of adapting its reasoning to the current problem. Its control is not deterministically defined but dynamically calculated. First, we present how TFL, the TASK formal language, enables to specify such a dynamic control. In TFL, a system is specified in terms of *problems*, reasoning *processes*, domain *structures*, *strategies* and *task-modules*. Strategies describe heuristics for selecting or configuring the most relevant reasoning process at runtime. All these elements are specified by algebraic data types. For processes, an adaptation of classical data types was needed. Operators inspired from preferential logics were introduced for strategies. Second, we describe how TFL enables to address the problem of verifying the dynamic knowledge base. We show how it can be formally proved that a process is correct with respect to a given problem. To summarize, TFL specifications provide both a precise description of the underlying reasoning of flexible systems and a framework for its verification.

1 Introduction

A large number of present engineering frameworks, referred as task-method frameworks, reflect Newell's knowledge level principle (Newell, 1982). Knowledge-based systems are modeled in terms of the problems (tasks) expected to be solved, e.g. diagnosis, office allocation, elevator configuration etc., the problem-solving *processes* (methods) that should be applied to solve them, e.g. heuristic-classification, propose & revise etc., the *domain structures* (models) that should be used for their application, e.g. causal, hierarchical models etc. Most approaches assume that the control of the systems is deterministically defined. They describe it by a rigid task-method decomposition tree, with a fixed procedural control flow. Different formal languages have been proposed to support a precise and unambiguous specification of knowledge-based systems. Except DESIRE, which is not task oriented, most of them, KARL, ML^2, $K_{BS}SF$, ForKADS, QIL, are based on KADS (Schreiber & al., 1993). Mainly focused on the domain or inferences, they enable to represent only a procedural control. For example P-KARL (Fensel, 1995), a variant of dynamic logic restricted to deterministic programs, is used like a procedural language to describe the control flow between the different inferences. Well adapted to specify systems with a fixed control, these formal languages are inappropriate for specifying *flexible* systems. Indeed, flexible systems involve a meta-control which dynamically calculates the next process to be applied. At each step of the resolution, either a relevant process is selected among alternative ones, or a suited process is configured from several sub-problems. For that purpose, flexible systems require an explicit representation of problems, processes and also an additional category of knowledge, *strategies*. Strategies describe heuristics used by the meta-control for the dynamic selection or configuration of the most relevant reasoning process. Not designed to specify a dynamic control, existing formal languages provide no satisfying means of specifying problems, processes, or strategies.

Recently, the TASK Formal Language TFL (Pierret-Golbreich & al., 1996), has been defined to address the specification of *flexible* knowledge-based systems. TFL is the specification language of TASK (Pierret-Golbreich, 1996), an engineering framework for the construction of flexible systems, from their specification to their implementation. TFL is an algebraic language offering two important advantages. First, it enables to precisely define all the knowledge of flexible systems, both of the object-system and of the meta-system responsible for controlling the resolution. While the domain is specified by classical algebraic data types (ADT), an adaptation of classical data types was necessary for the control. Problems, processes and strategies of the object and meta-system are thus specified by ADTs. The other advantage of TFL is to provide a framework to verify the *dynamic* knowledge base. Much effort has been spent on verifying the domain, whereas dynamic knowledge was rather neglected. However, flexible systems involve large amounts of dynamic knowledge. After been specified, this knowledge must be verified to be correct. Indeed, from the static viewpoint of knowledge acquisition, it is necessary to verify that each process (e.g. propose & revise), said to be applicable to one problem (e.g. parametric design), is really correct to solve it. Next, from the dynamic viewpoint of problem solving, it must be verified that a specific process selected at runtime to solve a problem is really suited to it.

First, the primitives of *problem, process, strategy* and *task-module* provided by TFL to specify flexible systems are described. Then, the problem of verifying the dynamic knowledge base is considered. We show that in TFL the proof of a process correctness with regards to a problem is brought back to the relevance proof.

2 Specifying control knowledge in TFL

TFL is based on the algebraic language PLUSS (Bidoit, 1989). The semantics associated with a specification in PLUSS is of the "set of models" type. ADTs were by definition developed to specify data types and their privileged use is the specification of procedural programs. Thus, a challenging issue was to investigate if it was possible to use this formal technique to specify the *dynamics* of knowledge-based systems, by definition dedicated to problems where there does *not* exist a reasonable algorithmic solution. A main contribution of the approach is to propose an adaptation of data types that enables to specify all the dynamic knowledge types of a flexible knowledge-based systems, *problems, problem-solving processes, strategies* and *task-modules*.

2.1 Problem specification

An original point of TASK is its clear distinction between *what* is expected to be achieved by the system, and *how* it should be achieved: a *problem* specifies a task to achieve, whereas a *process* describes a problem-solving method which exhibits some functionality. In TFL, primitives to specify problem and process are provided with a clear and precise semantics, opposed to existing languages, like KARL (Fensel, 1995), ML² (van Harmelen & al., 1992) where they are lacking.

Informally, a problem specification defines the output and postcondition that should be met from a given input, initial preconditions and available resources. For example, parametric design is a Problem Type characterized by a set of parameters P_i and of values v_j for the parameters as *input*, a set of internal requirements and of constraints as *resources*. Given some *precondition* corresponding to requirements usually defined as initial assignments of values or value range of parameters, the goal to be met as *output* is a design i.e. a set of assignments (v_i, P_i) of values to parameters that fulfill some *postcondition* required from each design and some constraints that must not be violated by a valid design.

Definition 1. *A Problem Abstract Specification is an abstract description of a problem type π in terms of input I_π, output O_π, preconditions pre_π, postconditions $post_\pi$, resources R_π, where input, output are sets of domain concepts, resources is a set of domain structures, and preconditions, postconditions are boolean-expressions.*

Boolean-expressions of the sort exp-bool denote dynamic conditions, the value of which depends on the current domain data. The operator - < :: > - : exp-bool * data → bool returns the boolean value of an expression in a current context (Pierret-Golbreich & al, 1996). In the specification, '&' represents the addition of an element in a set and '∅' represents the empty set. So the set $\{m_1, m_2\}$ is represented by the term m_1 & m_2 & ∅ .

Each domain concept is specified by a specific data-type which express its properties and its instances and can be designed as an instance of the abstract data type *concept*. By example, the concept *parameter* is specified by the abstract data type *parameter* and can be designed by the constant *c-parameter* of the data-type *concept*. This is needed to design concepts as inputs or outputs of methods.

Problems are specified by use of Problem modules, like for example the module below specifying parametric design problems.

Problem module Parametric-Design

    problem pd

Axioms for abstract problem specification

    input(pd) — c-parameter & c-value & ø

    output(pd) — c-design & ø

% the precondition specifies that the initial data fulfills the user's initial requirements

% so, pre(pb) is true on D if there exists at least a piece of information I in the state D

% which fulfills the initial requirements

    pre(pb) <::> D — I ∈ D[Domain-State] ∧ initial(I)

% the postcondition specifies that in a valid design

% all parameters are assigned and the final data fulfill all requirements and constraints

    post(pb) <::> D — I ∈ D[Domain-State] ∧ valid(I)

    resources(pb) — requirement-structure & constraints-structure & ø

A Problem module is a syntactic sugar used to simplify the specification. Problem modules are next included in the specification PROBLEM, which is a classical abstract data type specification in PLUSS. Modules are used in the same way for the other types of knowledge.

spec PROBLEM

    use DATA, NAMES-PROBLEM, SET-CONCEPT, SET- RESOURCE, EXP-BOOL;

    sorts problem;

    operations

        - : problem-name → problem;

        input : problem → set-concept;

        output : problem → set-concept;

        pre : problem -→ exp-bool;

        post : problem -→ exp-bool;

        resources : problem -→ set-resources;

    Axioms for each problem module

    % for each problem 'pb'

        input(pb) — ...

        output(pb) — ...

        etc.

2.2 Process specification

Processes are specified independently of problems. A *process* describes a problem-solving method which delivers a given functionality. A process has a double semantics, static and dynamic. When applied to data, a process has a dynamic role, but when the meta-system controls the resolution, it is in turn viewed as a static element that can be selected or not. The solution found to provide processes with dynamic semantics is inspired from the *process specifications* introduced by (Kaplan, 1987) to specify concurrent processes. Its principle is quite simple. Two different entities are distinguished, data and processes. Data represent the global current state. They are specified by a classical ADT *data*. Processes represent the reasoning processes (non deterministically) applied to the data. They are specified by the ADT *process*. Processes operate on data thanks to an application operator - :: - : process x data Ø data. The detailed semantics and axiomatisation of processes are given in (Pierret-Golbreich & al., 1996). A TFL-process specification consists of three parts: (i) an abstract specification defining its static semantics, (ii) an (abstract) implementation describing its dynamic semantics, and (iii) assumptions.

Process abstract specification.

The abstract specification •p of a process P defines its functionality, i.e the problem type that can be solved by P.

Definition 2. *The problem abstract specification* π_p *which specifies P functionality is called its abstract specification.*

For example, the abstract specification $\pi_{propose}$ of the primitive process *propose* is:

$\pi_{propose}$
    input(propose)=c-parameter & c-value & c-design &ø
    output(propose) = c-design & ø
% there is information In in the state related to In+1 by propose?
    pre(propose)<::>D=In ∈ D[DomainState] ∧ propose?(In,In+1)
% information In+1 is in the state after propose application
    post(propose)<::>D=In ∈ D[DomainState] ∧ propose?(In, In+1)∧
                 In+1 ∈ D[Domain-State]
    resources(propose) = propose-structure & ø

Note that the axioms of a composed process abstract specification are automatically generated from its components thanks to the axioms defining the semantics of the operators in the specification module PROCESS.

Process Implementation

The process implementation IMPp, is the dynamic part describing the reasoning process, opposed to its abstract specification which defines its functionality. For example, the implementation of *propose* is given by the axiom propose :: D = apply-inference(propose?) :: D, where 'propose?' is a domain relation used for the application of this inference. The implementation of a composed process like Propose & Revise is given by the axiom:

P&R =   *repeat* propose; check; *if* violations? *then* revise
          until all-assigned? true

In terms of software engineering, π_p is the abstract specification of P while IMPp is an abstract "implementation" of P.

Process Assumptions.

Assumptions ASSUMp specify the process specific requirements that must be fulfilled to ensure the process correct behavior when it is applied to the data. In (Benjamins & al., 1996) we have distinguished several kinds of assumptions, epistemological, teleological, pragmatic. For example, an epistemological assumption that must be satisfied to ensure the correct behavior of the process propose is that the network related to the relation propose? should be non cyclic: affected-by(P_1, P_2) → ¬affected-by (P_2, P_1)

2.3 Strategy specification

Strategies represent the heuristic knowledge required by the meta-system to dynamically control the choice of the next process to be applied at each step of the resolution. The strategy language (Talon & al., 1997) is based on the notion of preference issued from preferential logics (Ryan, 1992) (Andreka & al., 1994).

Preferences

Preferences are used in TFL to represent the dynamic ordering of processes. A preference states the current priority order governing a set of processes. Two types of preferences are defined:
• *Atomic preferences* involve a unique method. A process can be positively or negatively privileged. A positive preference for a process *m* denoted +*m* assigns *m* with a priority, whereas a negative preference denoted -*m* assigns it with a penality. Two preferences +*m* and -*m* for the same process *m*, are said to be incompatible.
• *Composed preferences.* Two operators inspired from (Andreka, 1994) are defined to compose preferences, the *but* and *on the other hand* operators. The *but* (noted '/') combines two preferences in assigning the second preference with a greater priority than the first one. Thus, *p/q* returns all the atomic preferences resulting from *q* together with all the atomic preferences from *p* which are not incompatible with *q* ones. The operator *on the other hand* (noted '‖') combines two preferences having incomparable priorities. It returns a combination from which contradictions have been

excluded. Thus, $p \| q$ returns all the non incompatible atomic preferences resulting from p and q. These two operators allow the definition of any complex preference. The semantics of preferences in TFL (Talon & al., 1997) is inspired from (Andreka, 1994) who has given an algebraic axiomatisation defining the equivalence of terms.

Strategies

In TASK, strategies describe heuristics. A strategy does not directly correspond to a preference. It is the result of its evaluation in a given context which is represented as a preference. The meta-system dynamically evaluates the strategies to obtain the preference prescribing the priority according which the processes will be considered at the current step. Atomic strategies are built from *foci*, *composed* strategies are built by means of the *'but'*, *'on the other hand'* and *'iff'* operators.

• A *focus* defines a constraint on the static semantics of the processes. It is used to focus on a particular subset of processes. For instance, the foci f_1, f_2 and f_3, respectively defined by the axioms resources(f_1) = hierarchy & ø, resources(f_2) = heuristic-network & ø, and input(f_3) = c-parameter & ø, respectively focus on the processes requiring a hierarchy, the processes requiring a heuristic association network or the processes having parameters as input. The operator *'$'* applies a focus F to a set P of processes, thus returning a subset SP of processes.

• An *atomic strategy* is a heuristics which can either favor or disfavor some processes. A *positive* strategy $+F$ (where F is a focus) expresses that the processes dynamically privileged by this focus benefit from a positive preference. A *negative* strategy $-F$ expresses that the processes dynamically privileged by this focus benefit from a negative preference. For example, the strategy $+f_1$ assigns hierarchical processes with a positive preference, while $+f_2$ favors heuristic processes.

• *Composed strategies* in TFL are built from two operators similar to those introduced to combine preferences. The *but* (noted ' / ') combines two strategies in privileging the second one. Thus, S_1 / S_2 is equivalent to S_2 complemented by the non contradictory part of S_1. *On the other hand* (noted '‖') combines two strategies considered as having incomparable priorities. It returns a combination of the two strategies in identifying and removing the contradictions. For example, the strategy $+f_2 / +f_1$ assigns a greater priority to hierarchical processes than to heuristic processes.

• *Conditional strategies*. Depending on the context of the resolution, some choices which are well suited at a particular step of the resolution can become completely irrelevant at another step. Conditional strategies S *iff cond* are introduced to capture such context dependency. S *iff cond* means that the strategy S is activated if the condition *cond* is true in the context C. Dynamic conditions *cond* are represented by terms of the sort exp-bool. For example, the strategy $(+f_2/+f_1)$ iff available?(hierarchy) favors hierarchical processes if a hierarchy is available in the domain.

The operator '#' evaluates strategies. Axioms (i) and (ii) mean that the preference resulting from the evaluation of an atomic strategy +F (resp. -F) in the context C where F, for a set of processes P, focuses on the processes $m_1, .., m_n$, is the combination of their positive (resp. negative) preferences. Axioms (iii) (iv) defines the evaluation of conditional strategies, and (v) (vi) of composed strategies:

(i) $F\$P = \{m_1, ..., m_n\} \Rightarrow +F\#C = +m_1||...||+m_n$

(ii) $F\$P = \{m_1, ..., m_n\} \Rightarrow -F\#C = -m_1 ||...||-m_n$

(iii) $j <::> C = True \Rightarrow S$ *iff* $j \# C = S \# C$

(iv) $j <::> C = False \Rightarrow S$ *iff* $j \# C = \wedge$

(v) $S_1 || S_2 \# C = (S_1 \# C) || (S_2 \# C)$

(vi) $S_1 / S_2 \# C = (S_1 \# C) / (S_2 \# C)$

This language enables to have any number of strategic levels and also to overcome the limitations of the numerical coefficients used in the operational languages to tackle the problem of conflicting strategies.

2.4 Task-module specification

TASK provides yet another original primitive which does not exist in other languages, the task-module primitive. It has been introduced to gather into a single unit the particular processes and strategies which are relevant to a given problem. Thus, a task-module describes a specialist having a particular competence. Its specification consists of three parts: (i) an abstract specification, (ii) an implementation, (iii) assumptions.

Task-module abstract specification

The abstract specification π_T of a module T defines its competence, i.e. the problem type for which T is specialized.

Task-module Implementation

The task-module implementation IMP_T, specifies the local dynamic knowledge base that fulfills the module competence. It is composed either of a base of processes together with local strategies for their selection or of a local base of sub-problems together with local strategies for their configuration. For example, let be *t-classif* a task-module specialized in *classification* and having several classification processes $m_1, m_2,$ etc. at its disposal. Its implementation is given by the next axioms defining its local processes and stating to privilege the hierarchical processes if a hierarchy is available and those having parameters as input :

processes(t-classif) = m_1 & m_2 & m_3 & m_4 & m_5 & ø

strategies(t-classif) = $(+f_2/+f_1)$ iff available?(hierarchy) // $+f3$

Thus TFL offers the different primitives required to specify the control of flexible systems precisely and unambiguously. In addition it provides a suited framework to verify the dynamic knowledge base.

3 Verifying dynamic knowledge

The different knowledge types that are specified are not independent. A problem is related to processes that must be relevant and correct to solve it; a process is also related to particular structures of domain knowledge that must be suited to its application. Therefore, such a specification introduces important questions about the overall knowledge base correctness. Two types of verification are identified to establish its correctness: intra-category and inter-category verification. Intra-category verification concerns completeness and consistency of each category (problem, process, etc.). Inter-category verification concerns the relations between two types of knowledge. This section is focused on the *dynamic* knowledge verification. It addresses both the intra-category verification of processes and the inter-category verification between problems and processes. But to tackle this problem, it was first necessary to precise the notions of process correctness and relevance. After presenting how we formalize these notions, we give two important theorems about correctness of processes, based on conditional positive calculus.

3.1 Process correctness

We first distinguish notions of correctness of a process with regards to (w.r.t) a problem and process correctness.

Correctness w.r.t. a problem

Informally, a process is considered *correct w.r.t a problem*, if its application enables to solve the problem. So we define a process P as being *partially correct w.r.t a problem* specification π iff, whenever the initial data D fulfill the precondition $pre(\pi)$, when the process P terminates, the final data obtained after P application necessarily satisfy the postcondition $post(\pi)$. In other words, if $pre(\pi)$ is true then, after P terminates, $post(\pi)$ is necessarily true. In TFL, this definition is formalized as follows.

Definition 3. *A TFL-process P is said to be partially correct w.r.t a problem specification* π, *iff in applying the axiomatization of the positive conditional calculus, it is possible to prove that when P terminates the formula* Γ *is valid in* $Alg(\Sigma_{Process}, E_{Process})$ *with* Γ :

$pre(\pi) <::> D = true \sum post(\pi) <::> (P :: D) = true.$

Process correctness

Informally, a process is considered correct if its implementation meets its (own) functional specification.

Definition 4. *Let be a process P with the abstract specification π P ($I\pi$, $O\pi$, preπ , postπ , Rπ). The process P is said to be partially correct, if it is partially correct w.r.t its own specification π P:*

$Alg(\Sigma$ *Process*, *EProcess*$)$ $\models$ *pre*(π P) <::> D = true $\Rightarrow$ post(π P) <::> (P :: D) = true

3.2 Process relevance

Informally, a process is considered *relevant w.r.t a problem*, if its functionality matches the problem. To formalize the relevance relation, we first introduce an order relation comparing the difficulty of problems.

Problem difficulty

Informally, a problem π_2 is *more difficult than* π_1 if the requirements on its input are weaker whereas the requirements on its output are stronger. In other words, if π_2 is solved then π_1 is also solved.

Definition 5. *Let be two problems π_2 = (I_2, O_2, pre$_2$, post$_2$, R_2) and π_1 = (I_1, O_1, pre$_1$, post$_1$, R_1). π_2 is said to be more difficult than π_1 (noted $\pi_1 \leq \pi_2$), if the next formulae are valid in Alg(Σ Problem, EProblem)*

$$\pi_1 \leq \pi_2 \quad iff \quad X \text{ is-a-}I_1 \Rightarrow X \text{ is-a-}I_2$$
$$pre(\pi_1) < :: > D \Rightarrow pre(\pi_2) < :: > D$$
$$post(\pi_2) < :: > D \Rightarrow post(\pi_1) < :: > D$$
$$X \text{ is-a-}O_2 \Rightarrow X \text{ is-a-}O_1$$

For example, multiple fault diagnosis is more difficult than single fault diagnosis since finding any kind of fault is more difficult than finding only single faults. We easily proved from the conditional calculus axiomatization that this relation is an order relation (Pierret-Golbreich, 1996b).

Theorem 1. *The difficulty relation is a partial order relation on problems*

Relevance relation

The relevance relation can now be defined as follows.

Definition 6. *A process P is said to be relevant to the problem* π *if the specification* π_p *of P is more difficult than* π : *P relevant to* π *iff* $\pi \le \pi_p$

3.3 Proof obligations.

The first obligation that we identified for proving the correctness of the dynamic knowledge base concerns the intra-category verification of processes: each process P should be partially correct. Other proof obligations concern the inter-category verification between processes and problems: it is necessary to verify that a process related to a problem (i) is relevant to it (relevance proof), (ii) is correct to achieve it (correctness proof). Below are two important theorems about these verifications, the demonstrations of which are given in (Pierret-Golbreich, 1996b).

Consistency of the processes specification

Each TFL process is correct by construction. The reason for this is that the abstract specification of a composed process is automatically derived from its components in respecting the PROCESS semantics.

Theorem 2. *Each TFL-process P is partially correct i.e. if a TFL-process terminates then*

$$Alg(\Sigma_{Process}, E_{Process}) \models pre(\pi_p) < :: > D = true \Rightarrow post(\pi_p) < :: > (P :: D) = true$$

This theorem has first been demonstrated for the inferences, then extended to any composed process by induction on the composition operators. In that way, to prove the partial correctness of the TFL-processes, it is only necessary to verify their syntactical correction and the consistence of the specification PROCESS.

Sufficient condition of a process correctness w.r.t a problem specification

The following theorem now exhibits a sufficient condition to prove the correctness of a process w.r.t a problem specification.

Theorem 3. *If a process P is relevant to a problem* π, *then process P is partially correct w.r.t problem* π.

Proof. Assume P is relevant to π. From Theorem 1
pre(P) < :: > D = true $\Rightarrow$ post(P) <::> (p :: D). = true (1)
By definition, from $\pi \le \pi_p$:
pre (π_p) <::> D = true $\Rightarrow$ pre(P) <::> D = true   (2)
post(P) <::> D = true $\Rightarrow$ post(π_p) <::> D = true   (2')
from (1) and (2)
pre (π_p) <::> D = true $\Rightarrow$ post(P) <::> (p :: D). = true (3)

from (2') and (3)

pre (π_p) <::> D = true $\Rightarrow$ post(π_p) <::> (p :: D)

Thus, to prove that a process P is partially correct w.r.t a problem π, it is sufficient to prove that P is relevant to π. This theorem is particularly interesting, because in that way, the proof of process correctness w.r.t a problem is brought back to its relevance proof. In other words, instead of a dynamic proof, a static proof is sufficient.

4 Related works and Conclusion

This work must be situated in the more general context of TASK, an engineering framework for the construction of flexible systems (Pierret-Golbreich, 1996). TASK provides an informal modelling language, a formal language and an implementation language.

The modeling and implementation languages were first developed. The modeling language, the first prototype of which was the task language of MAD (Analytic Method for task Description) initially developed at INRIA in 1989 (Scapin & al., 1990) is supported by a graphic tool. MAD has been used to model several applications, like supervision of air traffic, home automation, emergency situation (Sebillotte, 1995) etc. Successive operational languages, TASK (Pierret & al. 1991), LISA (Delouis, I., 1993), TASK+ (Talon & al., 1996) have then been developed to enable an efficient execution of the tasks. They all offer a dynamic control of the resolution, but LISA operationalized a reflective approach, while TASK+ provides a real strategic reasoning. LISA has already been used to realize different systems for real applications in the field of electric networks at EDF (French Electricity) like COPILOTE (Krivine & Delouis, 1991), AUSTRAL (Bredillet & al., 1994). The task languages, informal or operational, both turned out a real success. On the one hand, quite a lot of methodologies have now adopted such a task language to describe the dynamic knowledge, e.g. MACAO (Aussenac & al., 1991), MOISE (Ermine, 1993) already applied to about 30 industrial projects. On the other hand, research carried out about LISA have been an important reference in the realization of two industrial software, LIS@RT, a new version of LISA developed by EDF for its industrial use (Jacob-Delouis, & Jehl, 1996), and Control, a Power Classes library commercialized by Ilog. Faced to the increasing use of task languages, the next step was to define a formal language, in order to satisfy two important needs that arise in developing real-world flexible systems: needs of precise specification and of verification of their dynamic knowledge. TFL, which is the most recent language of the TASK framework, was developed for that purpose. TFL is presently being evaluated on a real-world application concerning crisis management of severe accidents.

The paper presented how TFL provides a precise description of the underlying reasoning of flexible systems and a framework for its verification. We first described how the different primitives required to formalize a dynamic control for flexible systems, problems, processes (Pierret-Golbreich & al., 1996), and strategies (Talon & al., 1997), are provided with a clear and precise semantics and axiomatization thanks to ADTs. Compared to KARL and ML^2, TFL is more expressive. The other languages do not provide an explicit specification of problems, processes and modules. Moreover, TFL allows to express not only an algorithmic but also a dynamic control. New KARL (Angele & al., 1996), an extension of KARL lately investigated, pursues the idea to offer primitives like TFL ones, to formalize tasks (problems) and problem-solving methods (processes). Similar to our approach, (Fensel & al., 1996) have also recently proposed a formal semantics for specifying the reasoning of knowledge-based systems, based on Modal Logic of Creation and Modification, (MLCM++). However, so far neither KARL nor MLCM++ deal with strategic reasoning. Their specification is limited to knowledge-based systems with a fixed control. They specify neither the meta-control nor the strategies necessary to dynamically control the resolution of flexible systems. TFL is thus the only formal language really appropriate to flexible systems. Then, we presented how TFL provides a suited formal framework for verifying dynamic knowledge. We established two results about the consistency: first, each TFL-process is partially correct, provided it respects the PROCESS specification syntax and semantics; second, if a process is relevant to a problem, then it is correct to solve it. Although we have not already exhibited a real example of a correctness proof, too difficult to do by hand, nevertheless this paper has brought to light important theoretical results. These results make a step towards future tools for assisting the verification of the dynamic knowledge of flexible systems. In a future work we will investigate how to drive an interactive proof, to make a diagnosis in case of an automatic proof failure, and to take assumptions into account.

5 References

Andreka, H., Ryan, M. and Schobbens P.-Y. 1994. Laws of Generalised Priority Operators, In International Workshop on Information Systems - Correctness and Reusability (ISCORE'94), R. Wieringa, R. Feenstra (Eds.), VUA IR-357, World Scientific Publishers.

Aussenac, N., Frontin, J., Soubie J.L. 1991. *Evolution d'une représentattion des connaissances pour l'acquisition.* In Knowledge Modelling and Expertise Transfert, 21-24, IOS.

Angele J., Decker, S., Perkuhn R., Studer R. 1997. Modeling Problem-solving Methods in NewKARL. In 7th workshop Knowledge Engineering Methods and Languages, KEML 97, Milton Keynes, England.

Benjamins, R. and Pierret-Golbreich, C. 1996. Assumptions of Problem-Solving Methods. *Lecture Notes in Artificial Intelligence*, 1076, 9th European Knowledge Acquisition Workshop, N. Shadboldt and K. O'Hara and G. Schreiber (Ed.), 1-16, Springer-Verlag

Bidoit, M. 1989. PLUSS, un langage pour le développement de spécifications algébriques modulaires. Thèse d'Etat, Université Paris Sud.

Bredillet, P., Delouis-Jacob, I., Eyrolles, P., Jehl, O., Krivine J.P., Thiault, P., (1994). The AUSTRAL Expert System for Power Restorationon Distribution Systems, In Fifth Symposium in Intelligent Systems Application to Power Systems (ISAP'94), Montpellier, France

Chandrasekaran, B., Johnson, T. R. and Smith, J. W. 1992. Task-structure analysis for knowledge modelling. *Communications of th ACM*, 35(9), 124-137.

Ermine, J-L. 1993. Génie logiciel et génie cognitif pour les systèmes à base de connaissances. Lavoisier Ed.

Fensel D. 1995. The Knowledge Acquisition and Representation Language KARL. Boston, Dudreccht, London: Kluwer Academic Press.

Fensel, D. and Groenbaum, R. 1996. MLPM: Defining semantics and Axiomatisation for Specifying the Reasoning Process of Knowledge-based Systems. In 12th European Conference on Artificial Intelligence, Budapest.

Krivine, J. P., & Delouis, I. (1991). Interactive Knowledge-Based System for Assistance in the Analysis and Reinforcement of Power Subtransmission Networks. In Third Symposium on Expert Systems Application to Power Systems, Tokyo, Japon.

Newell, A. (1982). The knowledge level. *Artificial Intelligence*, 18.

Pierret-Golbreich, C. and Delouis I. 1991. *TASK: task centered representation.* In 8th Conference of the Society for the Study of Artificial Intelligence and Simulation of Behavior, Steels and Smith Ed., Springer-Verlag.

Pierret-Golbreich, C. 1996. TASK, un environnement pour le développement de systèmes à base de connaissances flexibles. Thèse d'Habilitation à diriger des recherches. Université Paris Sud.

Pierret-Golbreich, C. 1996b. Correctness of Methods w.r.t Problems Specifications, Workshop on Validation Verification and Refinement of Knowledge-based systems of the 12th European Conference on Artificial Intelligence, Wahlster Ed., Wiley & Sons, Ltd.

Pierret-Golbreich, C. and Talon, X. 1996. TFL: an algebraic language to specify the dynamic behaviour of KBS. *The Knowledge Engineering Review*, Vol 11: 3 253-280, Cambridge Press.

Puerta, A., Agar, J.,Tu, S., and Musen, M. 1992. A multiple method shell for the automatic generation of knowledge acquisition tools. Knowledge Acquisition, 4, 171-196.

Ryan, M. D. 1992. *Representing defaults as sentences with reduced priority*, In B. Nebel and W. Swartout (Ed.), Third International Conference on Principles of Knowledge Representation and Reasoning (KR'92), Morgan Kaufmann.

Scapin, D.L., Pierret-Golbreich, C. 1990. *Towards a method for task description: MAD.* In Berlinguet L. and Berthelette D. (Ed.), Work with Display Units 89. 371-380, Elesevier Science Publishers.

Schreiber, Wielinga and Breuker, J. 1993. KADS. A principled Approach to Knowledge-Based Systems Development. *Knowledge-Based Systems*, vol. 11, Academic Press, London.

Steels, L. 1990. Components of expertise. *AI Magazine*, 28-40

Sebillotte, S. and Fallah, D. 1995. Task description "Resolve the emergency situation: Fire", Final Technical report Esprit Project Intuitive P6593.

Talon, X. and Pierret-Golbreich, C., 1996. TASK: from the specification to the implementation. In 8th IEEE International Conference on Tools with Artificial Intelligence, 80-88, IEEE Computer Society Press.

Talon, X. and Pierret-Golbreich, C. 1997. A language to specify strategies for flexible problem-solving . In 7th Knowledge Engineering Methods and Languages Workshop , KEML 97, Milton Keynes, England.

van Harmelen and Balder, 1992. (ML)2, a formal language for KADS conceptual models. *Knowledge Acquisition*, 4:1, 1992.

Problem Solving for Redesign*

Anita Pos[1] and Hans Akkermans[1] and Remco Straatman[2]

[1] University of Twente (UT)
Department of Computer Science
P.O. Box 217
NL-7500 AE Enschede
The Netherlands
E-mail: {pos,akkerman}@cs.utwente.nl
[2] University of Amsterdam (UvA)
Department of Social Science Informatics (SWI)
Roetersstraat 15
1081 WB Amsterdam
The Netherlands
E-mail: remco@swi.psy.uva.nl

Abstract. A knowledge-level analysis of complex tasks like diagnosis and design can give us a better understanding of these tasks in terms of the goals they aim to achieve and the different ways to achieve these goals. In this paper we present a knowledge-level analysis of *redesign*. Redesign is viewed as a family of methods based on some common principles, and a number of dimensions along which redesign problem solving methods can vary are distinguished. By examining the problem-solving behavior of a number of existing redesign systems and approaches, we came up with a collection of problem-solving methods for redesign and developed a task-method structure for redesign.

In constructing a system for redesign a large number of knowledge-related choices and decisions are made. In order to describe all relevant choices in redesign problem solving, we have to extend the current notion of possible relations between tasks and methods in a PSM architecture. The *realization* of a task by a problem-solving method, and the *decomposition* of a problem-solving method into subtasks are the most common relations in a PSM architecture. However, we suggest to extend these relations with the notions of *task refinement* and *method refinement*. These notions represent intermediate decisions in a task-method structure, in which the competence of a task or method is refined without immediately paying attention to its operationalization in terms of subtasks. Explicit representation of this kind of intermediate decisions helps to make and represent decisions in a more piecemeal fashion.

1 Introduction

The concept of reusable *problem-solving methods (PSMs)* is present in many current knowledge engineering frameworks, e.g. Generic Tasks (Chandrasekaran, 1988), Com-

---

* This work has been funded by NWO/SION within project 612-322-316, "Evolutionary design in knowledge-based systems" (the REVISE-project). Participants in the REVISE-project are: the TWIST group at the University of Amsterdam, the AI department oAmsterdam and the STEVIN group at the University

ponents of Expertise (Steels, 1990), Method-to-Task (Gennari *et al.*, 1994), role-limiting methods (McDermott, 1988), GTMD (O'Hara & Shadbolt, 1993) and COMMONKADS (Wielinga *et al.*, 1993). The interest in PSMs originates from the need to describe and explicate generic aspects of the problem solving behavior of knowledge based systems. One possible use of PSMs lies in comparing the problem solving behavior of different knowledge based approaches and systems for the same or similar tasks.

In this paper we focus on *comparing* PSMs for *redesign*, and on identifying and representing relevant choices in constructing and selecting PSMs for redesign tasks. As the notion of redesign incorporates many different methods it is best characterized as a family of problem-solving methods. We have made a knowledge-level analysis of redesign, and come up with a collection of problem-solving methods for this task. This collection was obtained in a bottom-up manner by examining the problem solving behavior of existing redesign systems and approaches, most notably those developed in the REVISE-project. Within this project the redesign of technical systems (Eldonk *et al.*, 1996), simulation models (Pos *et al.*, 1997), compositional architectures (Brazier *et al.*, 1996b) and control knowledge in knowledge based systems (Straatman, 1995) is studied.

The number of knowledge based decisions made during the design of a redesign system is large and diverse. In order to describe all relevant choices and decisions in a task-method structure, we need to extend the current notion of possible relations between tasks and methods. The general notion of a prblem-solving method as a direct link between a task goal and the decomposition of this task into subtasks, is not in itself sufficient to describe all the relevant choices and decisions. The notions of task refinement and method refinement are introduced to represent intermediate decisions in constructing and selecting PSMs. In these intermediate decisions, the competence of a task or method is refined without immediate attention being paid to the operationalization of this task or method. This corresponds to changing the exact nature of the problem with the aim of making it easier to solve. Explicit representation of these types of intermediate decisions help to represent decisions in a more piecemeal fashion.

The structure of the paper is as follows: In section 2, we present an extended architecture of a task-method structure, based on the additional notions of task refinement and method refinement. In section 3 we present our view on redesign, and distinguish a number of dimensions along which redesign approaches can differ. We also present some excerpts from a collection of problem-solving methods for redesign, and use these as examples to illustrate the additional refinement relations proposed and their role in describing and comparing tasks and problem-solving methods in a task-method structure. Section 4 concludes the paper, and points out some implications for knowledge engineering.

2 Modeling framework

A general view on tasks, methods and their mutual relations is the following: A *task* is characterized by a goal it can achieve. A task can potentially be realized by a number of problem-solving methods (PSMs). A *problem-solving method* describes a way to solve a task: it decomposes a task into subtasks, each associated with a subgoal, and/or into primitive inferences, that directly achieve goals. Recently, focus has shifted from the description of reasoning strategies per se to the description of assumptions underlying these reasoning strategies (Akkermans *et al.*, 1994; Benjamins *et al.*, 1996). The idea is that PSMs provide solutions to tasks by making *assumptions* about the precise definition of their functionality, and about the available domain knowledge. With this idea in mind,

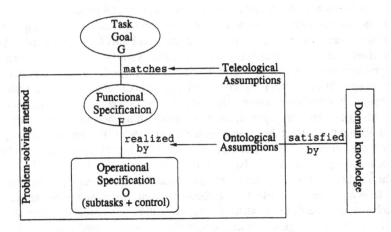

Fig. 1. The architecture of a PSM.

(Benjamins *et al.*, 1996) states that a PSM consists of three subparts (presented in figure 1):

- its *functional specification*. This is a declarative description of the input/output behavior of the PSM.
- its *operational specification*. This is an account of how to realize that behavior. The operational specification of a PSM decomposes a task into subtasks and/or primitive inferences, and defines an ordering over these operators.
- its *assumptions*. Problem-solving methods make assumptions on the precise definition of their functionality (*teleological assumptions*) and on the availability and properties of domain knowledge (*ontological assumptions*). Teleological assumptions are introduced in matching a task goal to the functional specification of a PSM if the functional specification of a PSM is more restricted than the task goal it is meant to achieve. Ontological assumptions are introduced when realizing the functional specification of a PSM by its operational specification, since operationalization often depends on the availability and properties of domain knowledge.

We tried to use this framework to establish a task-method structure for problem solving behavior of different redesign systems and approaches, similar to the task-method structure for diagnosis presented in (Benjamins, 1993). However, although the PSM architecture in (Benjamins *et al.*, 1996) is rich, it does not adequately cover all (intermediate) types of design decisions we encountered. The current framework provides a limited number of relations between tasks and methods: a task goals can be *matched* to the functional specification of a problem-solving method, and a problem-solving method can be *realized* by an operational specification which decomposes the functional specification in a number of subtasks. While trying to construct a task-method structure for redesign, we encountered two types of *intermediate* decisions that can not easily be represented in this framework; we call them *task refinement* and *method refinement*, respectively.

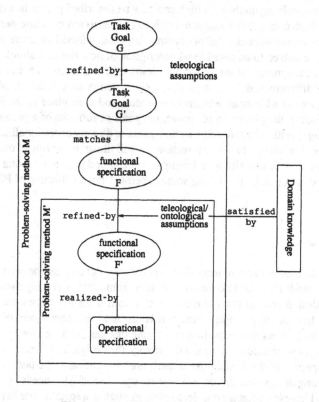

Fig. 2. An extended architecture for PSMs.

- *Task refinement* refines a task goal G into a more specific task goal G' but without directly making explicit *how* the task should be solved. Refinement of a task specializes a task goal into a weaker task goal by making additional teleological assumptions about the precise definition of the tasks functionality.
- *Method refinement* refines the functional specification F of a PSM into a more refined functional specification F' without making explicit how exactly this functional representation should be operationalized in terms of (control over) subtasks and/or primitive inferences. Competence refinement of a problem-solving method may introduce both additional teleological assumptions on the precise definition of the functional specification of a PSM as well as additional ontological assumptions on additional knowledge structures that should be available in the domain knowledge.

The *competence description* (Akkermans *et al.*, 1994) of a method or goal describes its problem space and requirements on the solution it produces. Under this definition, both decisions described above can be viewed as competence refinements, since they refine the functional specification of a task or method without directly making explicit how this competence could be achieved. This allows us to describe *families* of strongly related problem-solving methods, which can now be described purely in terms of their *competence*. Both forms of refinement are only to be used as *intermediate* steps in a task-method structure: the ultimate goal of constructing a task-method structure is still to relate a task to be solved to an operational description of how this task should be solved. However, the recognition of these two additional relations allow to better distinguish and separate different reasoning steps in the construction of a task-method structure. Figure 2 shows the additional refinement relations, and their place in the PSM architecture. Of course, the process is recursive, i.e. goals of subtasks of a problem-solving method can again either be refined to weaker goals or directly operationalized by an operational specification etc. In the next section we will illustrate the role of our additional refinement relations in describing and comparing tasks and problem-solving methods in a task-method structure by presenting some excerpts from a collection of PSMs for the task of redesign.

3 Redesign

Redesign is an inherent part of most design processes, but can also be seen as a family of design methods in itself. In contrast to design-from-scratch, redesign starts out with an existing design description and modifies this until it fits the current needs as good as possible. In order to perform redesign it is essential that some form of knowledge is available that allows the adaptation of existing designs. This knowledge is based on the following two principles: 1) minimally change the design, and 2) maximally exploit existing properties of the domain. An underlying assumption of the task of redesign is that the existing design description is "close enough" to fulfill the needs by only limited adaptations. However, what is considered close enough in a specific case depends on the nature of the adaptation knowledge, and on the way different requirements interact.

Redesign can play two different roles in the complete design process: First, redesign can be seen as a subphase of the design process. Here, design is viewed as an iterative process that uses intermediate results as a means of getting a final design description which fulfills the requirements. The task of redesign in this context produces a new temporary design description which is (hopefully) closer to the specification than the former design description. This view is the basis for the Propose-Critique-Modify family of design methods discussed in (Chandrasekaran, 1990). Secondly, redesign can be considered in the context of reuse. Here, redesign starts with a previously constructed design description, and a new set of requirements. The previously constructed design description must now be modified to fulfill the new set of requirements. This view is often considered as part of approaches such as case-based design (see e.g. (Kolodner, 1993; Maher *et al.*, 1995)), when the already retrieved case is adapted to suit the new requirements. Although there are very subtle differences between these two views, in both cases the important issue is to bridge the gap between a set of requirements and a design description. Therefore, both Iterative Redesign and Redesign for Reuse can be captured by a single spectrum of problem-solving methods for redesign.

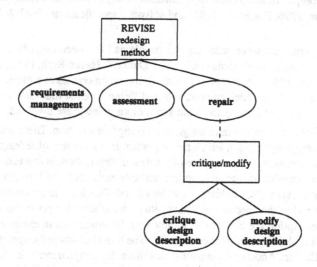

Fig. 3. A partial task-method structure for the redesign task. Rectangles represent methods and ellipses represent tasks. Dashed lines indicate that methods are alternatives for achieving the task goal. Solid lines decompose a method into its subtasks.

In the work described here, redesign is conceived as consisting of two subtasks: requirement management and management of the design description. The latter is further decomposed into assessment and repair. This decomposition of the redesign task (which we will in the remainder of this paper refer to as the "REVISE method") is motivated by work in the REVISE-project. Figure 3 presents a partial task-method structure for the REVISE method.

- *Requirement management.* This subtask is responsible for specification, management, refinement and adaptation of requirements. Some examples of PSMs for this task are discussed in section 3.1.
- *Assessment.* This subtask is responsible for determining the differences between the (properties of the) current design description and the requirements. These differences drive the repair subtask.
- *Repair.* Within this subtask, the design description is adapted such that it will better fit the requirements. Determining which part of the design description will be adapted (critique), and how it will be adapted (modify) are often tightly coupled subtasks in this task. Section 3.2 discusses some examples of PSMs for the subtask of design modification.

The main difference between the REVISE model and other models for (re)design, like Propose-Critique-Modify (Chandrasekaran, 1990), lies in the inclusion of the task of requirement management in the redesign process. In our point of view, explicit management of requirements is essential in non-routine redesign: addition, retraction and modification of the original requirements often forms a major part of any non-routine redesign task. Examples of such non-routine redesign tasks can be found in systems for redesign of compositional architectures (Brazier *et al.*, 1996b), simulation models (Pos & Akkermans, 1996; Pos *et al.*, 1997) and software specifications (Funk & Robertson, 1994).

Many systems that solve redesign-like problems have been described in literature (e.g. (Fischer *et al.*, 1987; Marcus *et al.*, 1987; Daube & Hayes-Roth, 1989; Goel, 1991; Smyth & Keane, 1996; Brazier *et al.*, 1996a)), but when one takes a closer look at the different variants of the redesign task, subtle differences exist that have an impact on how the task can be performed and what kinds of knowledge are involved.

A first source of variation in redesign is the design description. There are several aspects of the design description which are important in the context of redesign. The first of these is the *fixedness* of the structure of the design description; at one end of the spectrum, the structure of the design description can be completely fixed during redesign, and only the values assigned to parameters can be altered. This leads to parametric redesign. On the other end of the spectrum we have situations where changes to the structure of the design description are not limited in any way. Inbetween these extremes, there are cases where a skeleton structure is considered to be fixed but where the specific structure still can be filled in. Another dimension concerning the design description is the *nature of the information* presented in the design description. At one end of this spectrum the design description can purely describe the current status of the design, while at the other end the design description includes a complete plan of design steps resulting in the current design. The latter results in a form of redesign called derivational analogy (Mostow, 1989), while the former is the subject of more standard redesign approaches which directly modify the current design description (e.g. KRITIK (Goel, 1991) and 007 (Pos *et al.*, 1997)).

The requirements put on the design description provide a second source of variation in redesign. Again, there are several dimensions along which the requirements can be classified. The first of these is the *operationality* of requirements. Requirements are operational if their truth can be automatically derived from the design description by some inference method. The question to be considered is whether it is sufficient in an application domain to express needs and desires with operational requirements only, or whether there is a need to express non-operational requirements as well? The latter situation requires more extensive support for requirements management. Software design is a typical example in which the ability to express non-operational requirements is important in supporting the user in requirement specification. Another dimension with respect to the requirements posed on a design description is their *(local or global) nature*. Local requirements are applicable to a single component or parameter, while global requirements specify properties of the complete design. An example of a global requirement is the maximum weight of a device; this weight can not be attributed to a single component but is a function of the combined properties of all the components in the device.

Each redesign process requires some form of knowledge on which adaptations are possible/suitable/useful etc. The nature of the adaptation knowledge is the third source of variation in redesign. Again, there are several dimensions along which this adaptation knowledge can be characterized. The first of these is the *knowledge intensity* of the adaptation knowledge, ranging from purely search based to purely knowledge based approaches. A second dimension is the *generality* of the adaptation knowledge: how widely applicable is the adaptation knowledge. Applicatio-specific fixes are at one end of this spectrum, while very general strategies like 'divide-and-conquer' are located at the opposite end.

requirements	design description	adaptation knowledge
operational/ non-operational	structure fixed/free	search based/ plan based
local/ global	derivation/ design	specific/ generic

Table 1. Dimensions of redesign problems

Table 1 summarizes the dimensions along which redesign problems can differ. A space of redesign problems can be constructed by taking the Cartesian product of the values on each of these dimensions to form a multidimensional problem space for redesign problems. Most of the dimensions mentioned here have been described in the context of design problems other than redesign (Wielinga & Schreiber, 1997; Bernaras, 1994). This is a result of the earlier mentioned position of redesign in the spectrum of methods for design: redesign is both a part of many other design methods, like case-based design, and an umbrella for many different techniques, like parametric (re)design and configuration (re)design.

3.1 Requirement management

The subtask of requirement management is responsible for specification, management, refinement and adaptation of requirements. This task has as its input the current model, and as its output it produces an adequate set of requirements, suitable for assessment of the design description. Requirement management as a separate task is based on the observation that in general a design problem is often initiated by a statement of *needs and desires* (Bernaras, 1994). These, sometimes quite vague, needs and desires are to be interpreted and operationalized into a set of requirements suitable for automated assessment. This corresponds to the task of requirements engineering in software design (Wieringa, 1996). Figure 4 presents a partial task-method structure for the requirement management task. We identified two methods for this task: ask-user-operational-requirements or semi-automated-requirement-management. In many redesign systems, the task of requirements specification is put completely in the hands of the user, and no automated support is provided. This corresponds to the ask-user-operational-requirements PSM. On the other hand, a small number of redesign systems (e.g. (Brazier *et al.*, 1996b; Pos *et al.*, 1997; Reubenstein & Waters, 1991)) explicitly incorporate some form of semi-automated requirement management to ensure that the resulting set of requirements is adequate for further processing in the assessment task.

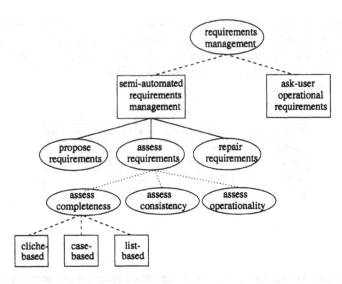

Fig. 4. A partial task-method structure for the requirement management task. Rectangles represent methods and ellipses represent tasks. Dashed lines indicate that methods are alternatives for achieving the task goal. Solid lines decompose a method into its subtasks. Dotted lines indicate competence refinement of tasks or methods. Not all methods are decomposed into subtasks and primitive inferences.

A necessary ontological assumption for including any form of semi-automated requirement specification in a (re)design system is that knowledge on how requirements relate to each other is available in the application domain. The extent and nature of this knowledge determines which form(s) of requirement management are feasible. Requirement management is primarily useful when the set of possible requirements to be posed to the (re)design system is potentially large, when the number of requirements to be simultaneously satisfied may become large or when the need for expressing non-operational requirements arises in a (re)design system due to the complexity of the domain involved. In cases where the set of possible requirements is small and requirements are not apparently interacting, requirement management is usually not necessary.

The PSM 'semi-automated-requirements-management' decomposes the task of requirement management in three subtasks: propose-requirements, assess-requirements and repair-requirements. This decomposition corresponds to the family of methods Chandrasekaran (Chandrasekaran, 1990) calls Propose-Critique-Modify. For the current example, we will focus on the assess-requirements subtask in requirement management.

Requirement assessment The assess-requirements task takes as input a set of requirements and produces a datum DA that states whether the requirements are adequate or not.

task name:	requirement assessment
goal:	KNOWN(ADEQUATE(R)) ∨ KNOWN(INADEQUATE(R))
input role:	R: set of requirements
output role:	DA: KNOWN(ADEQUATE(R)) ∨DA: KNOWN(INADEQUATE(R))

By carefully looking at requirement management in different (re)design systems we distinguish three different *competence refinements* of this requirement-assessment task to more specialized tasks. Each of these refinements requires different teleological assumptions, providing different restrictions on the *goal* of the requirement assessment task: KNOWN(ADEQUATE(R)) ∨ KNOWN(INADEQUATE(R)). The input and output roles stay the same: in each refinement the task takes as input a set of requirements R and delivers as output a statement on some aspect of the adequacy or inadequacy of R.

Assess completeness A possible way in which the competence of the assess requirement tasks can be refined is to refine the notion of 'adequacy' to the more specialized notion of 'completeness'. The goal of the thus refined assess completeness task then becomes: KNOWN(COMPLETE(R)) ∨ KNOWN(INCOMPLETE(R)). This is an example of the introduction of additional teleological assumptions: the output of the assess requirements task is restricted from a statement about the *adequacy* of the set of requirements to a more specialized statement about the *completeness* of the set of requirements.

The completeness of a set of requirements can only be assessed with respect to a specific problem or a specific set of problems. Problem-solving methods for assessing incompleteness of a requirement management in general use problem-specific knowledge to decide whether a requirement management is complete with respect to the problem(s) posed. This information can e.g. be represented the form of common forms (cliches) for different problems (Reubenstein & Waters, 1991; Pos *et al.*, 1997), in the form of cases (Maher & Balacandran, 1994) or in the form of a predefined list of requirements to be specified (Brazier *et al.*, 1996c). A necessary ontological assumption for each of these PSMs is that knowledge on when a set of requirements is supposed to be complete is present in the domain knowledge.

Other possible refinements of the requirement assessment task are checking whether the set of requirements is internally consistent (assess consistency), or checking whether each requirement is fully operationalized (assess operationality), i.e. can automatically be inferred from the design description by some inference procedure. This does not mean that these refinements are mutually exclusive: an actual redesign system can include one or more refinements.

All three tasks refinements are pure *competence refinements* of the original task goal 'assess requirements': they do not make any claims on how the task goal should be operationalized in terms of subtasks, but only on the way the task goal should be further *specified*. This allows us to view the task 'requirement assessment' as an abstract description for a family of related tasks, each of which tests a different aspect of the 'adequacy' of a set of requirements. Our purpose in constructing the notion of task refinements has been to better distinguish different steps, corresponding to different design decisions, in the construction and classification of problem-solving methods. The next step is to either refine the current task further to an even more specialized task, or to match sufficiently refined task goals to the functional description of (a family of) PSMs which might be able to achieve the goal of the refined task.

3.2 Design modification

The task of design modification modifies part of the current design description to solve one or more discrepancies between the set of requirements and the current design description. Figure 5 presents a partial task decomposition of this task. This task has as input (a part of) the design description and delivers as output a modified version of this part that is hopefully more suitable in the new situation. Three general families of problem-solving methods for this task are *substitution, transformation* and *generation* (Maher et al., 1995). *Substitution* methods substitute a part of the old design description with a new part more suitable for the new situation. *Transformation* methods are used to transform an old solution into one that will (hopefully) work in the new situation. *Generative* methods re-enact (part of) the reasoning trace to modify the design description. FIRST (Daube & Hayes-Roth, 1989), a case-based system for redesign of mechanical systems, and COBRA (Finn *et al.*, 1992), a case-based system for redesign of heat-transfer models, provide examples of the latter approach. Both systems retrieve 'redesign plans' from a case-base and transfer these plans to the new problem at hand.

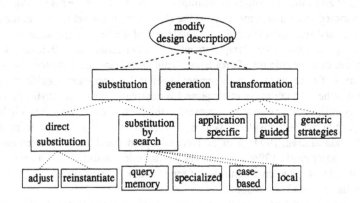

Fig. 5. A partial task decomposition of the modify-design-description task.

Several dimensions of redesign (Table 1) play a role as ontological assumptions in this choice between alternative (families of) PSMs: whether the structure of the design is supposed to be fixed, and whether the reasoning trace or the end product of design is used for redesign. Generative methods make use of a reasoning trace, while substitution and transformation methods require only the end product of design in the form of a design description. Substitution and transformation methods mainly differ in their assumptions on system structure: substitution methods assume that the system structure is fixed, while transformation methods assume that the structure of the design is adaptable.

Substitution methods can be further specialized in direct substitution methods and substitution by search. This distinction is based on the dimension of redesign concerning the *plan based versus search based* nature of adaptation knowledge. This dimension defines ontological assumptions on the type of additional knowledge necessary to make the PSMs work: substitution by search requires some sort of database in which substitution elements can be found, while direct substitution methods require procedural knowledge on how to decide on a new value for a part of the old design description. Search-based substitution methods can be further specialized by considering the *additional knowledge* necessary for searching: query memory (Hinrichs & Kolodner, 1991) requires information on *what* to look for, in the form of a partial description of the item searched for. Local search, which can e.g. be found in PLEXUS (Alterman, 1986), requires instructions on *where* to search for alternatives. Specialized search, which can e.g. be found in the SWALE system (Schank & Leake, 1989), requires instructions on *how* to find an alternative. Case based substitution, which can e.g. be found in the JULIA system (Hinrichs & Kolodner, 1991), requires instructions on how to find a *similar* case which might suggest an appropriate alternative.

Transformation methods can be further specialized by considering the *general or specific* nature of the modification knowledge used for transformation: generic strategies like 'divide-and-conquer', which can e.g. be found in JULIA (Hinrichs & Kolodner, 1991), form one end of this spectrum, while application-specific heuristics, which can e.g. be found in the VT-system for elevator design (Marcus *et al.*, 1987), form the other end of the spectrum. Systems like KRITIK (Goel, 1991) and 007 (Pos *et al.*, 1997) fall somewhere in between: the repair plans used in these systems are general enough to be applied to many different problems, but not as generic as general strategies like 'divide and conquer'.

All the method specializations discussed above are *competence refinements*: they only make claims on the functional specification of (a family of) problem-solving methods, and not on how these PSMs should be operationalized in terms of subtasks and control. Method refinements represent *intermediate* decisions in the classification of PSMs. Our purpose in constructing these intermediate relations has been to better distinguish different design decisions as separate steps in the classification of PSMs, based on the dimension underlying each design decision. They allow us to describe a *family* of related PSMs by means of an abstract functional specification common to all its members. In the original PSM framework, these intermediate, seperate design decisions would either have be compressed into direct relations between the task and the bottom-level PSMs (e.g., one way to satisfy the task 'modify design description' is to directly use the bottom-level PSM 'substitution by local search'), or an intermediate operationalization would have to be constructed for each family of PSMs in the refinement decomposition.

The task decomposition depicted in Figure 5 covers the same set of methods as the classification of adaptation methods and strategies in case-based reasoning presented in (Kolodner, 1993). This lends further support to our claim that redesign methods form a part of several more general design paradigms, of which case-based reasoning is one.

4 Conclusions & Related Work

Redesign is an inherent part of most design processes, but can also be seen as a family of design methods in itself. In the latter point of view, redesign is a family of problem-solving methods for which two questions need to be answered:"what is common to redesign?" and "which dimensions are involved in characterizing redesign?". The family of methods called redesign can be characterized by a number of common principles: redesign starts with an existing design description, and it requires some form of knowledge that allows the adaptation of designs. This knowledge is based on two underlying principles: (1) minimizing the changes being made to the design description and (2) maximizing the exploit of known properties of the design description. These characteristics can be used to differentiate this family of methods from other design methods. In order to compare different (families of) problem-solving methods for the same task we distinguished a number of *dimensions* along which redesign methods can differ: the nature of the *design description*, the nature of the *requirements* and the nature of the *adaptation knowledge* are the three main sources of variation in the family of problem-solving methods called redesign.

We also presented a general model of redesign developed in the REVISE-project. The main tasks in this general model are requirement management, artifact assessment and artifact repair. The task of requirement management has not often been modeled in other (re)design models, but is in our view essential in non-routine (re)design. Requirement management in design corresponds to the task of requirements engineering in software design (Wieringa, 1996). Each of these redesign subtasks can be achieved by one or more (families of) PSMs. In this paper we selected two subtasks, requirement management and artifact modification, and described task-structures for these subtasks in somewhat more detail. For the other redesign subtasks similar task-structures have been developed.

In developing a knowledge based system for a redesign task a large number of choices and decisions are made. In order to express all these decisions as separate reasoning steps in a task-method structure, the current notion of possible relations between tasks and methods in a PSM architecture needs to be extended. Notions of *task refinement* and *method refinement* are introduced to represent intermediate decisions in a task-method structure, in which the competence of (a family of related) tasks or methods is refined without directly paying attention to the operationalization in terms of subtasks and control. Explicit representation of this kind of abstract, intermediate reasoning steps helps to make and represent decisions in a task-method structure in a more piecemeal fashion.

The characterization of tasks and methods for redesign presented in this paper is informal. We think that this type of characterization is useful in the early stages of KBS design, where problem-solving methods are constructed and selected to construct the skeleton design model for a knowledge based system. In this early stage of KBS design, common sense descriptions of problem-solving methods and their underlying knowledge requirements (in terms of teleological and ontological assumptions made by each problem-solving method) will often be used in advance of any formal work. In a later stage, *adapters* as proposed in (Fensel, 1997), could be used to implement and formalize the additional refinement relations proposed here in an informal context.

An alternative approach to specifying and selecting PSMs is presented in (ten Teije *et al.*, 1996). Here, a family of PSMs for diagnosis tasks is represented by a skeletal functional description, with a number of subfunctions. Values for these are chosen from a fixed set to obtain a specific diagnostic function. Parametric design can then be used to construct a specific method functionality. However to construct such a skeleton and appropiate values requires a well-understood formalisation of different methods and their properties, which does not yet exist for redesign methods.

The extended PSM framework described in this paper has been used to describe relevant choices in selecting problem-solving methods for a specific redesign system in the domain of computational engineering models, called 007 (Pos *et al.*, 1997). In the near future, we plan to use this framework to describe other redesign systems, starting with the redesign systems which are at the moment being developed by the other participants in the REVISE-project. These systems focus on redesign of compositional architectures (Brazier *et al.*, 1996b) and redesign of control knowledge in knowledge based systems (Straatman, 1995), respectively.

Acknowledgments

This paper has been significantly influenced by many discussions in the REVISE-project. We would like to thank all other REVISE participants for their input. We would also like to thank Tim Menzies for his extensive comments on this paper.

References

AKKERMANS, H., WIELINGA, B., & SCHREIBER, G. (1994). Steps in constructing problem solving methods. In Gaines, B. R. & Musen, M., editors, *Proceedings of the 8th International Knowledge Acquisition Workshop (KAW'94)*, volume 2, pages 29.1–29.21, Banff, Alberta. University of Calgary, SRDG Publications.

ALTERMAN, R. (1986). An adaptive planner. In Kehler, T., Rosenschein, S., Filman, R., & Patel-Schneider, P. F., editors, *Proceedings of the 5th National Conference on Artificial Intelligence (AAAI-86)*, pages 65–69, Philadelphia, PA. Morgan Kaufman Publishers, Inc.

BENJAMINS, V. R. (1993). *Problem solving methods for diagnosis.* Ph. D. Thesis, University of Amsterdam.

BENJAMINS, V. R., FENSEL, D., & STRAATMAN, R. (1996). Assumptions of problem-solving methods and their role in knowledge engineering. In Wahlster, W., editor, *Proceedings of the 12th European Conference on Artificial Intelligence (ECAI-96)*, pages 408–412, Budapest, Hungary. John Wiley and Sons.

BERNARAS, A. (1994). Problem-oriented and task-oriented models of design in the COMMONKADS framework. In Gero, J. S. & Sudweeks, F., editors, *Artificial Intelligence in Design '94*. Dordrecht, the Netherlands, Kluwer Academic Publishers.

BRAZIER, F. M. T., TREUR, J., & WIJNGAARDS, N. J. E. (1996a). Interaction with experts: the role of a shared task model. In Wahlster, W., editor, *Proceedings of the 12th European Conference on Artificial Intelligence (ECAI-96)*, pages 241–245, Budapest, Hungary. Wiley and Sons.

BRAZIER, F. M. T., VAN LANGEN, P. H. G., TREUR, J., & WIJNGAARDS, N. J. E. (1996b). Redesign and reuse in compositional knowledge-based systems. *Knowledge Based Systems, Special Issue on Models and Techniques for Reuse of Designs*, 9(2):105–119.

BRAZIER, F. M. T., VAN LANGEN, P. H. G., TREUR, J., WIJNGAARDS, N. J. E., & WILLEMS, M. (1996c). Modelling an elevator design task in DESIRE: the VT example. *International Journal of Human-Computer Studies*, 46:469–520.

CHANDRASEKARAN, B. (1988). Generic tasks as building blocks for knowledge-based systems: the diagnosis and routine design examples. *The Knowledge Engineering Review*, 3:183–210.

CHANDRASEKARAN, B. (1990). Design problem solving: a task analysis. *AI Magazine*, 11(4):59–71.

DAUBE, F. & HAYES-ROTH, B. (1989). A case-based mechanical redesign system. In Shridharan, N. S., editor, *Proceedings of the 11th International Joint Conference on Artificial Intelligence (IJCAI-89)*, Detroit, Michigan. Morgan Kaufman Publishers, Inc.

ELDONK, S. J. M., ALBERTS, L., BAKKER, R., F.DIKKER, & WOGNUM, P. (1996). Redesign of technical systems. *Knowledge-Based Systems, Special Issue on Models and Techniques for Reuse of Designs*, 9(2):93–104.

FENSEL, D. (1997). The tower-of-adapters method for developing and reusing problem-solving methods. In *Proceedings of the European Knowledge Acquisition Workshop (EKAW-97)*. Springer-Verlag. Lecture Notes in Artificial Intelligence (LNAI).

FINN, D. P., GRIMSON, J. B., & HARTY, N. M. (1992). An intelligent modelling assistant for preliminary analysis in design. In Gero, J., editor, *Artificial intelligence in Design (AID'92)*, pages 579–596. Dordrecht, Kluwer Academic Publishers.

FISCHER, G., LEMKE, A. C., & RATHKE, C. (1987). From design to redesign. In *Proceedings of the 9th International Conference on Software Engineering*, pages 369–376, Washington, D.C. IEEE Computer Society Press.

FUNK, P. J. & ROBERTSON, D. (1994). Case-based support for the design of dynamic system requirements. In *Proceedings of the 2nd European Workshop on Advances in Case-Based Reasoning (EWCBR-94)*, pages 211–225, Chantilly, France.

GENNARI, J., TU, S., ROSENFLUH, T., & MUSEN, M. (1994). Mapping domains to methods in support of reuse. *International Journal of Human-Computer Studies*, 41:399–424.

GOEL, A. K. (1991). A model-based approach to case adaptation. In *Proceedings of the 13th Annual Conference of the Cognitive Science Society (CogSci'91)*, pages 143–148, Chicago, Illinois.

HINRICHS, T. & KOLODNER, J. (1991). The roles of adaptation in case-based design. In Dean, T. & McKeown, K., editors, *Proceedings of the 9th National Conference on Artificial Intelligence (AAAI-91)*, pages 28–33. AAAI Press / The MIT Press.

KOLODNER, J. (1993). *Case-Based Reasoning*. Morgan Kaufman Publishers, Inc.

MAHER, M. & BALACANDRAN, B. (1994). Flexible retrieval strategies for case-based design. In Gero, J. & Sudweeks, F., editors, *Artificial Intelligence in Design '94*. Dordrecht, Kluwer Academic Publishers.

MAHER, M. L., BALACHANDRAN, M. B., & ZHANG, D. M. (1995). *Case-based reasoning in design*. Hove, UK, Lawrence Erlbaum Associates.

MARCUS, S., STOUT, J., & McDERMOTT, J. (1987). VT: an expert elevator designer that uses knowledge-based backtracking. *AI Magazine*, 8(4):39–58.

McDERMOTT, J. (1988). Preliminary steps toward a taxonomy of problem-solving methods. In Marcus, S., editor, *Automating Knowledge Acquisition for Expert Systems*, pages 225–255. Boston, Kluwer.

MOSTOW, J. (1989). Design by derivational analogy: Issues in the automated replay of design plans. *Artificial Intelligence*, 40:119–184.

O'HARA, K. & SHADBOLT, N. (1993). Locating generic tasks. *Knowledge Acquisition*, 5:449–481.

POS, A. & AKKERMANS, J. M. (1996). 007: A system for automated model revision. In Javar, A., Lehmann, A., & Molnar, I., editors, *Proceedings of the 10th European Simulation Multiconference (ESM'96)*, pages 50–54, Budapest, Hungary. SCS.

POS, A., AKKERMANS, J. M., & TOP, J. L. (1997). Automated model revision. *IEEE Expert*. In Press.

REUBENSTEIN, H. B. & WATERS, R. C. (1991). The requirements apprentice: Automated assistance for requirements acquisition. *IEEE Transactions on Software Engineering*, 17(3):226–240.

SCHANK, R. C. & LEAKE, D. B. (1989). Creativity and learning in a case-based explainer. *Artificial Intelligence*, 40:353–385.

SMYTH, B. & KEANE, M. T. (1996). Using adaptation knowledge to retrieve and adapt design cases. *Knowledge-based Systems, Special Issue on Models and Techniques for Reuse of Designs*, 9(2):127–136.

STEELS, L. (1990). Components of expertise. *AI Magazine*, 11 (2):28–49.

STRAATMAN, R. (1995). Learning control knowledge in models of expertise. In Fensel, D., editor, *Proceedings of the ECML-95 Workshop on Knowledge Level Modeling and Machnine Learning*, pages I.2.1–I.2.13, Heraklion, Greece.

TEN TEIJE, A., VAN HARMELEN, F., SCHREIBER, A. T., & WIELINGA, B. J. (1996). Construction of problem-solving methods as parametric design. In Gaines, B. R. & Musen, M. A., editors, *Proceedings of the 10th Banff Knowledge Acquisition for Knowledge-Based Systems Workshop*, volume 1, pages 12.1–12.21, Alberta, Canada. SRDG Publications, University of Calgary. track: Shareable and reusable problem-solving methods.

WIELINGA, B. J. & SCHREIBER, A. T. (1997). Configuration-design problem solving. *IEEE Expert (in press)*.

WIELINGA, B. J., VELDE, W. V. D., SCHREIBER, A. T., & AKKERMANS, J. M. (1993). Towards a unification of knowledge modeling approaches. In David, J. M., Krivine, J. P., & Simmons, R., editors, *Second-generation expert systems*, chapter 14, pages 299–335. Berlin, Springer-Verlag.

WIERINGA, R. J. (1996). *Requirements Engineering: Frameworks for Understanding*. Chicester, England, John Wiley and Sons.

The Notion of Role in Conceptual Modeling

C. REYNAUD*, N. AUSSENAC-GILLES**, P. TCHOUNIKINE***, F. TRICHET***

* LRI - Univ. de Paris-Sud - Bât. 490 - 91405 Orsay Cedex - FRANCE - cr@lri.lri.fr
** IRIT - Univ. P. Sabatier - 118, rte de Narbonne - 31062 Toulouse Cedex - FRANCE - aussenac@irit.fr
*** IRIN - Univ. de Nantes - 2, rue de la Houssinière - BP 92208 - 44322 Nantes cedex 3 - FRANCE
{Francky.Trichet, Pierre.Tchounikine}@irin.univ-nantes.fr

Abstract: In this article we analyse the notion of knowledge role. First of all, we present how the relationship between problem solving methods and domain models is tackled in different approaches. We concentrate on how they cope with this issue in the knowledge engineering process. Secondly, we introduce several properties which can be used to analyse, characterise and define the notion of role. We evaluate and compare the works exposed previously following these dimensions. This analysis suggests some developments to better exploit the relationship between reasoning and domain knowledge. We present them in a last section.

Key words: Knowledge Modeling, Knowledge Roles, Objects of Reasoning, Problem Solving Methods.

1. Introduction

A knowledge based system (KBS) can be viewed as a system composed of interrelated elements. The domain model describes the knowledge specific to the domain under study, the task model characterises the goals of the application and the problems to be solved and problem solving methods describe the means and control knowledge used to perform tasks. In this article we focus on the link between the domain knowledge and how it is used during problem solving (problem solving methods). This link is often ensured by roles, i.e. a description of the role that domain knowledge plays in the problem solving process [Marcus,89]. Introduced by Mc Dermott, the notion of role appears in numerous knowledge engineering approaches, although with significantly different definitions. It may either point to the type of the domain objects that can play a role, act as a place holder for domain objects describing the role that these objects play in the problem solving process or correspond to a class which specifies an object of reasoning. These differences take their origin in the objective of the underlying modeling approach.

In this article we examine the nature of knowledge roles throughout the literature. First, we study the link between problem solving methods and domain knowledge and the benefits brought by roles during the knowledge engineering process through various representative approaches (we do not claim for an exhaustive survey): RLM, GT, KADS, OMOS, CommonKADS, TASK, EXPECT, ASTREE, VITAL-TOMAOK, MACAO-MONA, MCC and TN-PSM. Then, we introduce several properties which can be used to analyse, characterise and define the notion of role in these works. Analysing these different works in respect to these dimensions suggests developments to better exploit the relationship between problem solving and domain knowledge. We present them in a last section.

2. The Notion of Role

We have chronologically explored various research works, focusing on the role notion, its representation and use. Roles has been originally defined at a similar period in the role-limiting methods (RLM), Generic Tasks (GT) and KADS approaches. In more recent studies, this notion has become richer and more precise.

2.1. The Origins

The RLM approach has shown that acquiring knowledge to design a system is all the more efficient as the functions that knowledge plays during problem-solving are well understood [Marcus,89]. These functions, called *roles*, are specific to the problem solving method applied in the system. According to this idea, Mc Dermott's research group proposed method-oriented tools to support detailed domain knowledge acquisition. SALT, for instance, allows users to describe knowledge for design systems that apply a *propose-and-revise* strategy in terms of *parameters*, *constraints* and *revising decisions* [Marcus,89]. These *roles* represent the functional knowledge required by the *propose-and-revise* method. They specify the relevant pieces of knowledge that SALT must acquire to generate a domain-specific knowledge base. In that view, roles are method-specific but application-independent terms. In addition, they may be considered as task-independent : several tasks can be achieved by performing different methods using similar roles.

In a similar way, the GT approach emphasises on tasks and on the knowledge roles required to perform them [Bylander,88]. Roles provide a large vocabulary of task-related terms, and, additionally, tasks explicitly illustrate how domain knowledge will be used. Such a view facilitates knowledge acquisition: roles help focusing on task-relevant domain knowledge whereas the task structure guides its organisation. Note that, with GT, tasks and roles are defined in an operational shell used to design task specific knowledge bases.

The structure of *meta-class* in KADS conceptual models fulfils similar needs as roles [Wielinga,92a]. Thanks to meta-classes, the model clearly distinguishes the role of concepts during problem solving from their "meaning" in the domain. Meta-classes are defined at the inference level as the input/output parameters of inferences. They stand for domain concepts, that may play several roles, and offer a functional view on domain structures.

2.2. A Role as a Label

Roles have often been identified by a single term that is supposed to indicate a function in a reasoning. This trend is illustrated by the following works.

OMOS [Linster,92]

OMOS is a language that aims at operationalising KADS models of expertise. Building a conceptual model in OMOS includes designing a domain model (composed of classes, instances and relationships) and a method model (made of inferences and control knowledge over them). The method model is generic and domain-independent. Indeed, inferences describe actions whose input/output/control knowledge are *roles*. These two models are interrelated by specifying the mapping between domain knowledge and method roles in the inference actions. Then, solving a problem (*i.e.* running the conceptual model), dynamically builds the task model. For that purpose, the problem solver uses a *transfer* function that assigns roles to domain classes or instances, and inference actions to tuples. In OMOS, an inference action results from a two step-description:

(1) The first part defines the inference action in a generic way, by the roles it uses and the transformations it performs on domain knowledge: initialise or update a value, replace domain instances by roles or communicate with the user.

```
DEFINE-INFERENCE-ACTION Select-Ideal
WITH    INPUT-ROLE = Solution Alternative
        OUTPUT-ROLE = Possible-Solution
        CONTROL-ROLES = ((Instanciated-Criterion))
        VALUE-ASSIGNMENT = FALSE
        ROLE-ASSIGNMENT = TRANSFER
```

This inference requires the roles *Alternative Solution* as input, *Possible-Solution* as output and *Instanciated-Criterion* as control knowledge. TRANSFER indicates that the input domain knowledge (playing the role *Alternative Solution) will play the role Possible-Solution* in the following of the problem solving.

(2) The second part describes the projection of the inference onto the domain. It refers to a particular domain relation and makes explicit the mapping between this relation arguments and knowledge roles in the inference action.

```
DOMAIN-RELATION Optimal-Clamping-Tool
WITH   ARITY = 2
       TYPE-SEQUENCE = (((INSTANCE Clamping-Tool) (EXTENSION-* Turning-Requirement)))
       ARGUMENT-SEQUENCE = (Clamping-Tool Important-Turning-Requirements)
       TUPLES = (... set of domain tuples which verify the relation)
```

This relation, defined in the domain model, has two domain concepts as parameters: an instance of *Clamping-Tool* and an Extension-* of *Turning-Requirement*. Tuples represent all the pairs of related instances according to the relation. If the inference action *Select-Ideal* uses this relation for reasoning, it must be extended as follows:

```
DOMAIN-RELATION = Optimal-Clamping-Tool
  REL-ARG-TYPE =
     ((( 0. INSTANCE) ( 1. EXTENSION-*)))
  PROJ-ROLES-REL-ARGS = (((INPUT-ROLE . 0)
              (OUTPUT-ROLE . 0)
              (CONTROL-ROLES . 0) . 1))
```

Argument 0 of the relation (the first one) will play input and output roles, and argument 1 will serve as control knowledge.

To sum up, roles in OMOS are not structures. They are characterised by the way they can be assigned to domain knowledge in each inference action that uses them. This allows inferences to be described independently from the domain, and therefore enhances reusability. Furthermore, as the links between inferences and domain knowledge are made explicit, verifying the knowledge base is easier. OMOS checks that all domain concepts are associated to roles and that all domain relations required by inference actions are defined.

CommonKADS [Wielinga,92b]

At the inference and task levels, roles are names of object sets which share the same status in the problem solving (*design parameters, specification parameters*, etc.). Roles are used by inferences (tasks which cannot be decomposed) or transfer tasks (user interaction tasks). Three kinds of roles are distinguished. *Static roles* point to domain elements used in the problem solving process without being modified. *Dynamic roles* point towards elements that are modified during problem solving. *Case roles* are dynamic roles describing the problem to be solved. The designed model directly refers to the domain vocabulary after a mapping of (generic) terms used in the method (*roles*) onto the domain specific terms.

Representation of roles in CML [Schreiber,94]: CML is a structured but informal language providing a textual and graphical notation for CommonKADS expertise models. The domain knowledge description is threefold: ontologies, mapping between ontologies and domain models. An ontology reflects the structure of the domain elements at a more or less abstract level by providing several representational primitives such as concepts, relations, attributes or expressions. Domain models contain collections of domain specific statements using these primitives. In CML, roles are represented in the inference structure diagrams as the inputs or outputs of inferences or transfer tasks. In addition to their use for problem solving, they are characterised by a name and the syntactical structure of the domain items which can play them. Roles played by single domain items are distinguished from those mapped to sets of objects. Each role is locally defined in the inference where it is used.

```
inference select-parameter;
   operation-type: select;
   input-roles: parameter-set -> set of attribute-slots;
                parameter-assignments -> set of
tuples <attribute-slot, value, dependencies>;
   output-roles: parameter -> single attribute-slot;
   static-roles: formulae ∈ domain models initial-
values and calculations;
   specification: Select a parameter from the skeletal
model .........
end inference
```

In this example, parameter-set, parameter-assignments, parameter and formulae are roles which could be differently defined in another inference. On the other hand, 'attribute-slot', 'dependencies' etc. belong to the domain ontology, and 'set-of' is used to characterise the roles whose type is 'set of concepts'.

Roles in ML² [Van Harmelen,92]: ML² is a formal language based on logic for specifying and validating CommonKADS expertise models. In ML², a role is specified by a logical variable which is nameable (role name) and typed (sort). Indeed, ontological categories are represented by types organised in a hierarchy and defined in the domain ontology. The type characterises the structure of the associated domain items; it refers to the domain ontology (*instance, set-of-instances, etc.*). This syntactical characterisation is a classical one in logic where most of the naming operations are purely syntactical. Consequently, syntactically similar formulae have syntactically similar names. This also implies that, during problem solving at the inference level, rewriting rules allow role interpretation in the domain.

TASK [Pierret,96]

TASK is a coherent framework covering the whole KBS life-cycle (modeling, representation and operationalisation). The development of a KBS is viewed as an incremental process of building more and more precise and formal models. The TASK environment is composed of three languages, each of them being appropriate to one model. We only describe here tasks and methods I/O representation at the formal and operational levels. The formal specification in TASK uses Abstract Data Types (ADTs). A role is represented as a formal parameter. It can be instanciated with the application parameters if the axioms in the parameter formal specification, which represent semantic constraints, are satisfied. At the operational level, the I/O of generic tasks and methods are represented as meta-classes that implement roles. Accordingly, the I/O of the application tasks and methods are represented as classes, instances of the meta-classes defined in the generic models. Thus, in TASK, for a given application, formal specifications and operational constructs are derived by instanciating generic types or meta-classes respectively. In both cases, instanciation involves the adequacy between types or generic classes and types or application classes.

2.3. Implicit use of the role notion

Although they do not explicitly represent roles, some works, as the two examples below, exploit the relation between domain knowledge and how it is used during problem-solving.

EXPECT [Swartout,96]

As a workbench, EXPECT supports the development of KBS. In EXPECT, a method describes a particular problem-solving competence. It is characterised by its goal, its results and a body encoded with a specific language. Using reflective capabilities, EXPECT automatically analyses how methods are encoded. From the analysis of the types of the domain elements they use, it retrieves what is required to perform them. These capacities help to guide domain knowledge acquisition but also to design method-independent tools. An advantage of this approach is that the knowledge-acquisition tool is not hard-encoded. The way knowledge is used is calculated from how methods are defined, and therefore methods can be modified without modifying the tool. Moreover, new methods can be built by analogy with existing ones that share similar goals.

```
(defmethod check-capacity-constraint
  ...
  :method-body        (is-smaller-or-equal
    (obj (r-capacity (r-rented-equipment ?c)))
    (than (r-volume-to-move ?c))))
```

In the body of this method, *"is-smaller-or-equal"* operates on the property *r-capacity* of an object of *r-rented-equipment* type. Then, EXPECT can detect that there is a domain object O of that type for which the method cannot be performed because *r-capacity* has no value. It can ask for this missing knowledge and justify its request by mentioning that a domain element which "plays the role r-capacity" for O is needed.

ASTREE [Reynaud,97]

Given an application task, ASTREE tries to automatically identify a method that achieves it. The approach assumes that the domain ontology depends a lot on the way knowledge will be used in reasoning. The idea is then to acquire first the domain ontology and to exploit it so as to find appropriate methods to achieve a target task. Even though the process it runs is generic (*select, match, ...*), the identified methods always are application-specific because derived from the interpretation of a domain ontology and from the definition of an application target task. Thus, method or task I/O refer to terms in the domain ontology. More precisely, task I/O definitions contain : [1] names of domain entities or attributes the instances or values of which respectively are the task input or output, [2] a syntactical indication about their structure (*a, a set of, a list of, sets of, lists of*), [3] constraints if syntactical characterisations of domain concepts used as input or output of the task must be specified. The constraints describe states of domain concepts with domain terms (see the example below). They can be used in different ways. They can delimit the values of attributes mentioned in the input or output part. They can also restrict the instances to those with attributes of particular values and/or to those related to some specified (or not specified) instances by a given relationship. A structured language helps to define these constraints. Thus, in ASTREE, not only the nature and structure of a concept can be specified, but its status can also be characterised. Furthermore, as ASTREE is an automatic tool, the domain ontology is represented in a formal language so that it could contain structured information useful to identify methods and the definitions of the tasks and methods are written in a structured language.

Let us illustrate the constraint language with the task of allocating rooms to employees where input data = a EMPLOYEE [e], output data = a ROOM[r]. Constraints on the output data may be imagined as follows:
"[Size-R[r] = large and Pos-R[r] = central] or Size-R[r] = small"
  if we want the allocated room to have either a large size and a central position or a small size
"contains-computer [r, Sun]" if we want to allocate a room in which a computer Sun is already set up.

2.4. When roles are more than labels

More recently, roles have not been considered only as labels any longer. They are more precisely characterised by additional properties, as in the following approaches.

VITAL - TOMAOK [Leroux,95]

As part of the VITAL project, TOMAOK developed a rewrite grammar to refine an application problem-solving model. The approach is based on a tight coupling between domain and problem solving. To design a model, generic inference primitives coming from generalised directive models (GDM) are reused and adapted. Each model component progressively evolves. To refine the inference structure and the meta-view of the domain, the rules examine the roles or the domain element types which the roles stand for. This may lead to introduce new inferences and new roles, or to characterise better roles or domain elements. The notion of role is essential in TOMAOK. Domain elements have to satisfy the syntactical and semantic constraints required by roles. Moreover, role properties specify the conditions in which a generic method can be applied and decomposed to model a given application.

In GDM, the role description renders, at a meta-level, the domain knowledge organisation. It reflects the ontological commitments implied by the other categories of the model. All the descriptions form what is called the meta-domain, a component that does not exist in KADS expertise model. A role is a strongly typed structure characterised by several types: one characterises its use in the inference structure (static, dynamic, case, dynamic-control, case-control) ; a syntactical one defines constraints on domain elements (their type and their syntactical structure) ; a semantic one can be either a role of the method ontology (i.e. *class of decision, finding*) for instances, values or concepts, either "logical" or "calculated" for expressions, or the name of a relation for structures. Roles are represented with frames in the I/O part of each inference. Beside its types, each role contains the definitions of all the concepts which it can map to. These definitions are specific to each role ; each concept only contains the attributes required in the inference where the role is defined.

For example, the role SOLUTION is defined in several inferences: it is generated by INSTANCIATE and is an input of VERIFY. SOLUTION is defined the same way in all these inferences. However, the definitions of the associated concepts, which may appear in other roles, only mention the properties which are useful in the inference where the definition is given.

```
Role Name: SOLUTION
Role Type: Dynamic Role
Denoted Knowledge Syntactic Type: Set of Concepts
Denoted Knowledge Semantic Type: Correspondence
Denoted Knowledge Qualification:
Role Domain Definition:
    Concept Name: ROOM
    Concept Properties:
        Property Name: NAME
        Property Type: IDENTIFIER
            Type definition: String - Values Range:
        Property Name: SIZE
        Property Type: ROOM SIZE
            Type definition: Enumerated - Values Range:
    [Single Twin] ....
    Concept Name: EMPLOYEE
    Concept Properties: ...
```

The Role Notion in MACAO [Aussenac,94a], [Aussenac,94b]

MACAO is a general methodology for knowledge acquisition and modeling which provides techniques and guidelines to knowledge engineers. Applying MACAO results in designing a two-fold conceptual model, where domain knowledge (a conceptual network) is separated from problem solving knowledge (a task-method decomposition tree).

Roles in MONA [Matta,95]: Knowledge is represented using MONA, a conceptual formalism specific to MACAO and adapted from the LISA operational language [Delouis,95]. The MACAO workbench offers tools for detailed and schematic knowledge elicitation as well as knowledge and diagram editors to structure knowledge in a model and represent it with MONA. The MONA primitives are quite basic in conceptual modeling: concepts, typed relations and expressions for domain modelling ; tasks, methods and roles to represent problem solving knowledge. Each primitive is represented with a frame, described both in natural language and by its relations with other structures. To this extent, MONA is similar to CML. Roles have been defined to represent the method and task inputs and outputs with a domain independent vocabulary. This structure has been introduced to make possible connections between domain and problem solving knowledge explicit. By this means, generic problem solving methods can be refined to design an application problem solving model. Further-more, the problem solving model is more efficient to guide knowledge elicitation. Roles are characterised by their name and the set of domain items that can play them: concepts, concept attributes or their values. However, because MONA is a conceptual and not an operational language, the mapping of roles to domain items was not completely specified. This problem arose during the ZTM experimentation.

An operationalisation of roles: ZTM [Beaubeau,96]: The goal of the ZTM project was to define, with the ZOLA operational language [Istenes,96], operational structures corresponding to MONA primitives. However, running the model required to better define roles. In addition to their global definition, roles should convey information about which of the possible domain items is actually playing it at a step of the problem solving. So it seemed necessary to keep track of the context in which domain knowledge could play a given role, by indicating the input or output of the task or method where this role was used. Consequently, in ZTM, roles are now represented by specific objects with a name, the task or method characteristics where they are used, and, for each, the different possible domain values that can play this role. This value can be a concept or a role, depending on whether the role is played by domain knowledge or by another role.

```
Role Name: set-of-components
Possible Values:
        Value 1   Link to a domain concept: set-of-persons
                  Related characteristic: input-context, task Assign-places-to-components
        Value 2   Link to a role: [set-of-components, input-context, task Assign-places-to-components]
                  Related characteristic: parameter, method Assignment-with-criteria
        Value ...
```

In this example, *set-of-components* describes, at an abstract level, the input of task *Assign-places-to-components* [value 1] and the parameters of method *Assignment-with-criteria* [value 2]. In value 1, *set-of-components* can be assimilated to a static role which points to *set-of-persons* when used as the input of task *Assign-places-to-*

components. In value 2, *set-of-components* can be considered as a dynamic role ; there is no explicit link to domain knowledge, but a reference to another role : the parameters of method *Assignment-with-criteria* are the *set-of components* used as input of task *Assign-places-to-components*.

MCC [Causse,93]

In the MCC approach, K. Causse proposes to add a level for the description of roles, which are considered as reasoning entities manipulated by the reasoning process. This level is the heuristic level. It is at the interface of the domain level and the reasoning level. This heuristic level allows the natures of the roles to be specified and meta-information on the roles to be expressed as attributes of the reasoning entities. This way, roles are neither embedded inside the methods of problem solving nor assimilated to the domain knowledge. They have a specific status and can be studied as such. We present below an illustration of a MCC structure equivalent to the notion of role : a schema.

schema hypothesis
    com: an hypothesis holds for a system state which may cause the observed symptoms;
    refers to: state;
    rel: cause-p: hypothesis or complaint;
    rel: inv-cause-p: hypothesis;
    rel: stated-by: evidence;

In this example, the "hypothesis" structure is domain-independent, except its attribute "refers to". Indeed, usually, schemas are expressed in reference to problem solving methods. This "hypothesis" structure has been defined for the systematic diagnostic method but not in reference to the domain of car diagnosis, which was the one of the application.

The TN-PSM Approach [Beys,96]

Recently, so as to facilitate reuse of similar problem solving methods across different tasks, Beys proposes to represent methods using task independent terms. These methods are called Task Neutral Problem Solving Methods (TN-PSM). Each TN-PSM contains assumptions which specify syntactical constraints over the structure or the properties of the manipulated knowledge as illustrated below. Pursuing this approach, [Beys,96] suggests that the usability versus reusability trade-off can be tackled by automating the process of uncovering the domain structure required by the method.

```
psm cover;
     input:         leaves: Sets of leaf nodes that need to be covered;
     output:        cover: Sets of root nodes that cover the leaves;
     competence:    ...
     sub-tasks:     ...
     additional roles: ...
     control-structure: ...
     structure-assumptions:       ∃ X in the ontology such that: X: sequence(x₁, x₂, ...., xₙ),
```

$\exists$ X in the ontology such that: $X: sequence(x_1, x_2, ..., x_n)$,

$\forall i \in [1,n]$ binary-relation (x_i, A_{i-1}, A_i)

$\forall i \in [1, n-1]$, class(A_i) A_0 = set of leaves, A_n = set of roots

property-assumptions: $\forall i \in [1,n]$ if $A_{i-1} = A_i$, asymmetric (x_i), irreflexive (x_i), transitive (x_i) endif one-to-many relation (X);

end psm cover;

3. Analysis of the Notion of Role

We have identified several criteria to analyse and characterise roles in the previous works. In the following, we present the results of our analysis.

3.1. The dimensions of our analysis

The Modeling Process

The representation and the use of roles differ according to the knowledge modeling process. A priori, knowledge roles are not useful when modeling consists in designing a conceptual model from the domain interpretation such as in ASTREE. Nevertheless, this notion can be introduced to verify the model, to support the acquisition of detailed knowledge (MACAO) or to acquire and explicitly represent control knowledge (MCC). On the other hand, the notion of role is essential when a top-down modeling approach (partial or not) is adopted, i.e. when global generic models are reused (GT) or different components are reused (CML, RML), combined and refined (TOMAOK). In such approaches, the primitives of the generic components (and mainly the roles) are described in an abstract way so as to be applicable across various domains (GT, RLM, CML) or even various tasks (TN-PSM).

The Definition, Description and Localisation of a Role

The early approaches to knowledge level modeling (RLM, GT, KADS) focus on model-based reasoning. They emphasise the distinction between the knowledge level and the implementation level. The problem-solving process is described at an abstract level. The required knowledge is denoted by its role in reasoning (a brief commentary gives the meaning of each role), providing guidance in knowledge acquisition (what knowledge should be acquired and which it will play) and enabling reuse of generic constructs. In such a context, domain models are not emphasised. Thus, the choice of precise and proper names for roles, denoting precisely their place in reasoning, is essential. In these approaches the connection between domain and problem solving is defined as a projection (RLM), a mapping relation (OMOS) or an instanciation process (TASK). This way, each role is a functional label which is linked to a set of domain concepts.

Later, the interest of combining the reuse of generic components and data abstraction has been recognised. A stronger coupling between domain and problem solving is then necessary. As a consequence, the semantics of the roles must be described more precisely. This leads, for example, to add indications about the semantic type of the knowledge required by a method to play a role (TOMAOK). This also leads to the characterisation of the roles with particular attributes (MCC).

More recently, some works proposed to add syntactical properties or to substitute the semantic definition of a role by a syntactical one (TN-PSM, MCC). These properties can refer to the structure of the required knowledge or to mathematical properties (reflexive, symmetric, transitive, etc.). Syntactical properties of a role allow to partially automate mapping between domain knowledge and problem-solving. Indeed, various elements of domain knowledge can satisfy the same syntactical properties while all these elements may not be equally adequate to play a given role. In that case, when the semantics of a role is totally ignored, a domain expert has to interpret the results of the mapping process.

Finally, whatever the description of a role is, its representation can be either local (OMOS, TOMAOK) to a task or a method or global to the whole model (MCC). In most approaches it is local but sometimes, roles are viewed as independent reasoning objects. Furthermore, the connection between domain and problem solving is often a link between roles and concepts defined at the domain level. However, definitions of domain concepts can also be included in task or method definitions (OMOS, TOMAOK).

The Level of Formalisation

Whatever the nature of the role definition, whether it is represented with an independent primitive or not, it can be represented using a formal language or not. As a consequence, the range of formalisation levels goes from very weak formalisms such as frames with natural language descriptions (CML, MACAO) or frames with a formal language (TOMAOK, MCC) to operational primitives (OMOS, RLM, GT) or logical predicates (ML^2, TN-PSM).

This dimension is crucial. However, we do not intend to report here the debate concerning the interests and limitations of a formal model versus an unformal one. The same arguments apply for roles, which are part of the modeling language: unformal representations are obviously relevant in the early steps of knowledge acquisition and modeling, whereas formal representations provide more guidance either in the testing and validation steps, or to acquire detailed knowledge and refine a model.

3.2. The use of Roles in the Modeling Process

It is interesting to identify the various reasons that motivated the introduction of the role notion in each modeling approach. We have listed the main kinds of guidance that role may provide in a knowledge engineering environment :

- to acquire additional knowledge: acquire detailed domain knowledge that instanciate the problem-solving method (RLM, GT) or refine the problem-solving method itself (OMOS);

- to test and check the model: either to check if all the domain knowledge required by the problem-solving method is available (RLM, EXPECT) or to validate the model structure by running it (OMOS, ML[2]) or by showing an abstract and easy-to-understand representation of the problem-solving process (MACAO. CML);

- to reuse generic components (GT, KADS. RLM, TASK) or to make it easier to reuse specific components (MACAO. MCC).

4. Discussion

Our analysis has shown that the definition and description of roles closely depend on why they have been defined in the modeling approach. Given the guidance that we expect from a modeling environment, we promote a double characterisation of roles.

4.1. Connection Between how Roles are Represented and their use

A role can be a means to guide the acquisition of different kinds of knowledge, in particular when the modeling approaches are model-driven. The problem solving method is then viewed as a skeletal model, in which generic knowledge requirements are defined, and that has to be instanciated. The expert is asked about domain concepts, instances or control knowledge that play roles, according to their meaning denoted by their names or to their definition. Thus, roles provide strong guidance for the model instanciation process. They are the means by which knowledge acquisition tools can interact with the user in method-oriented terminology. Such tools prompt the user for method-specific knowledge types and can prevent him from entering expressions that conflict with the definitions of these types in the problem-solving method. These tools are all the more efficient as roles are well structured. Automatic matching with domain knowledge according to syntactical or semantical criteria may also be possible with a formal representation of roles. However, a good semantical characterisation is difficult to achieve.

When the modeling process enables a distinct representation of various types of knowledge (*i.e.* domain, task and inference knowledge), roles can be suitable for verification (OMOS. GT, RLM). All domain concepts must be associated to roles, all the relations required by tasks must be defined at the domain layer. In the particular case where the notion of role is not explicit (EXPECT, ASTREE), though manipulated by reflective tools, methods directly refer to domain concepts. Then we can verify that their instances are defined in the domain model and that required attributes are valued. Moreover, other kinds of verifications are possible when using formal specifications (ML[2], TASK). They help check the correspondence between the types of roles and the types of the domain concepts they stand for. Formal specifications can also be used to prove the correctness of a model as done in software engineering. Finally, the operational description allows prototyping to evaluate the behaviour of the KBS under development (ZTM, OMOS).

Roles can also be a means to support the conceptual model design. The overview shows two illustrations. First of all, roles can help to select a way to expand an initial abstract problem-solving model (TOMAOK, OMOS). Thus, they provide guidance to progressively refine a selected model that defines precise knowledge requirements or knowledge roles. Roles specify the syntactical and semantical constraints that associated domain concepts must satisfy. Properties and types of the elicited knowledge are criteria to select the applicable rule to refine the initial model. Secondly, roles can facilitate the modeling process thanks to the representation of control knowledge (MCC). In that case, roles are reasoning entities defined as such with attributes expressing meta-information. They point to domain knowledge but additional knowledge that would not exist outside the reasoning scope can also be represented. This representation allows control knowledge to be clearly defined and labelled. It is a way to facilitate the construction of problem solving methods.

Reuse being a current important issue in knowledge engineering, many works aim at enabling partial reuse of problem-solving models. The implications of this objective on roles differ according to whether the reuse scope is a task-specific context (GT, KADS) or not (TN-PSM). The inference primitives can be described at two levels: a generic one, which qualifies the I/O according to their function in the inference and in the task to be achieved, and another one which establishes a link with domain concepts. On the contrary, task-neutral approaches propose to describe roles in a merely syntactical manner: their name is very general and they are not linked to domain concepts. Such a representation is supposed to make reuse of similar methods across different tasks easier. Reuse is also an important dimension for role because of its impact on the representation language. Formal specifications facilitate a clear understanding of roles. They can be useful for specifying reusable methods. Finally, reuse also depends on the description of roles. A role is all the more reused since it is precisely defined, both with syntactical and semantical properties.

4.2. Towards a double characterisation of roles

The advantages provided by the numerous uses of the roles convinced us to consider this notion in a problem-solving model (PSM). Roles are different from domain concepts and must be clearly distinguished because they are of another epistemological type. They make sense only in the context of PSM, not in the context of application models. On the opposite domain concepts are not dependent of any reasoning. In addition, we consider that roles have to be represented as specific structures. That way, they can be more easily manipulated by the reasoning process and easily characterised with intrinsic properties.

Furthermore we consider that roles must be characterized both from a syntactical and a semantical point of view. Their syntactical characterisation may correspond to structural or property assumptions (TN-PSM). Yet, unlike the current advances that promote the syntactical characterisation of roles against their semantic labelling, we consider that their task-oriented name and semantic characterisation should not desappear. When knowledge modelling combines abstraction and reuse, the two aspects are important. In a bottom-up context, the model is interpreted by both the expert and the designer. The semantics of the roles plays a major part. Role labels would be all the more understandable as they are defined in keeping with the *task* problem-solving model. It will be also easier for the expert to guide the mapping between domain knowledge and roles. In the TN-PSM approach, the domain knowledge is automatically mapped to the methods by testing the syntactical constraints. Thereafter, a domain expert has to interpret the results of the mapping. But how can it be done without precising the semantics of the roles ?

This conclusion leads us to discuss the ways the semantics of roles can be defined. In many research works, this semantics is only denoted by a name with a brief comment on the role meaning. So the semantics has to be intuitively deduced from the name. To make this process more powerful, the role names sometimes refer to terms in method ontologies which describe them (TOMAOK). This assumes that such ontologies are available. In MCC, roles have their own attributes, which contributes to define their semantics. We could also imagine to build state models (SM) to define them. In most object-oriented analysis methodologies, SMs specify the various states of the processed objects as well as the events that make an object evolve from one state to another. In a similar way, the semantics of a role could be defined by all its possible states at the different times of the reasoning process and by the methods or inferences which make it change from one state to another. Then, a SM would be specific to a given PSM. This view is borrowed from ASTREE in which the notion of state is defined for the domain concepts in the I/O of tasks. That way, a role could be identified by the name of a reasoning object in a particular state.

Finally, the definitions of the roles must be supplemented with indications on the types of the domain concepts which can play them. Very often, the connection between domain and problem solving is a mapping relation between roles and domain concepts. Our analysis convinced us that this mapping must be more precise. It is in fact a relation between roles and domain concepts *in a certain state* (ASTREE).

5. Conclusion

In this article, we have stressed the key importance of roles at the frontier between domain and problem solving knowledge in conceptual modeling. They help make explicit some of the implicit assumptions, also called ontological commitments, that problem solving methods impose to domain knowledge. Several uses of the notion of roles can be identified. We have shown that they affect its existence, its characterisation and its representation.

An exploration of the state of the art has revealed a tendency that promotes a formal syntactical description of roles in order to broaden the reusability of the methods that use them. Moreover, these works consider roles as a sub-product of inference actions. Our position is quite different. First of all, we consider that roles should be isolated as such, in specific structures, so that they could be easily identified and that a system could reason about them. Secondly, we claim the advantages of keeping a semantics in the roles to facilitate their interpretation and to increase their interest in non-generic models. This is why we have investigated possible ways to define this semantics. Thirdly, and for this purpose, we consider that the state of roles is crucial. Furthermore, the states of the domain concepts are to be considered in the mapping relation between roles and domain concepts.

However, practically implementing such a notion raises several major issues, still at the heart of the debate [Van Heijst,97] that we have not answered yet: how to decide of a role label ? role definitions might be redundant with concept specification: how can we avoid it ? It increases the number of structures in the conceptual model: is it realistic ? We feel like experimenting our approaches with the new definitions we gave to roles. By this means, we will test our hypotheses and certainly have some answers to these questions.

References

Aussenac-Gilles N., "How to combine data abstraction and model refinement: a methodological contribution in Macao". *A future for Knowledge Acquisition*, Proc. of EKAW94. Berlin: Springer Verlag. LNAI 867, pp. 262-282. 1994.

Aussenac-Gilles N., Matta N., " Making the method of problem solving explicit with Macao: the Sisyphus case-study ". *International Journal of Human Computer Studies*. 40, pp. 193-219. 1994.

Beaubeau D., Aussenac N., Tchounikine P., "Mona au pays des roles". Rapport IRIT/96-23-R, Juil. 96.

Beys B., Benjamins V. R., Van Heijst, G., " Remedying the Reusability - Usability Trade-off for Problem Solving Methods". *Proc. of KAW'96*, Gaines & Musen ed., Banff: SRDG Publications Univ., Nov. 1996.

Bylander T., Chandrasekaran "Generic tasks in knowledge-based reasoning: the right level of abstraction for knowledge acquisition". In B.R. Gaines & J. H. Boose. Eds. *Knowledge Acquisition for Knowledge-Based Systems*. Vol. 1, pp. 65-87. London: Academic Press. 1988.

Causse K.. " Heuristic control knowledge ". *Knowledge Acquisition for Knowledge Based Systems*. Proc. of EKAW'93. Aussenac N., Boy G., Gaines B.. Linster M., Ganascia J.G., Kodratoff Y. Eds. LNAI 723. Heidelberg: Springer Verlag. pp. 183-199. 1993.

Delouis I. Krivine J.P.. " LISA, un langage réflexif pour opérationaliser les modèles d'expertise ". *Revue d'Intelligence Artificielle*. Volume 9:1. pp. 53-88. Paris: Hermès. 1995.

Istenes Z., Tchounikine P., " Zola: a language to Operationalise Conceptual Models of Reasoning". *Journal of Computing and Information* (Proc. of ICCI'96) 2:1, pp. 689-706, 1996.

Leroux B., Laublet P., " Steps towards a Unified Approach to Knowledge Modelling". *Proc. of VIth European Japanese Conf. on Information Modelling and Knowledge Bases.* Amsterdam: IOS Press. 1995.

Linster M., " Knowledge Acquisition Based on Explicit Methods of Problem Solving ". PhD Thesis, Univ. of Kaiserslautern. Feb. 1992.

Marcus S. McDermott J., " SALT: a knowledge acquisition tool for propose and revise systems". *Artificial Intelligence*, 39, pp. 1-37, 1989.

Matta N., " Méthodes de résolution de problèmes: leur explicitation et leur représentation dans Macao-II". Thèse de l'Université P. Sabatier, Toulouse. Oct. 1995.

Pierret-Golbreich C. Talon X., " TFL, an algebraic language to specify the dynamic behavior of Knowledge-Based Systems ". *The Knowledge Engineering Review*, Volume 11:3, pp. 253-280. 1996.

Reynaud C., Tort F., " Using Explicit Ontologies to Create Problem Solving Methods ". *International Journal of Human Computer Studies.* 46, pp. 339-364. 1997.

Schreiber G., Wielinga B., Akkermans H., Van de Welde W., Anjewierden A., "CML: The CommonKADS Conceptual Modeling Language ". *A future for Knowledge Acquisition.* Steels L., Schreiber G., Van de Velde W., eds. LNAI n°867, pp. 1-25. Berlin: Springer Verlag. 1994.

Swartout B., Gil Y., "Flexible knowledge acquisition through explicit representation of knowledge roles". AAAI Spring Symp. Acquisition, learning and demonstration: automating tasks for users. Stanford (USA). March 1996.

Van Harmelen F. Balder J., "(ML)^2: A Formal language for KADS models of expertise ". *Knowledge Acquisition*, 4 (1), pp. 127-161, 1992. Special issue : 'The KADS approach to knowledge engineering'.

Van Heijst G., Schreiber A., Wielinga B. " Roles are not classes: a reply to Nicola Guarino ". *International Journal of Human Computer Studies.* 46, pp. 311-318. March 1997.

Wielinga B., Schreiber G., Breuker J., " KADS: a Modeling Approach to Knowledge Engineering". *Knowledge Acquisition*, 4(1). pp. 5-54, 1992. Special issue : 'The KADS approach to knowledge engineering'.

Wielinga B.J. Van De Velde W. Schreiber G. Akkermans H., "Towards a unification of knowledge modelling approaches". In David, J.-M., Krivine, J.-P., Simmons R., eds., *Second Generation Expert Systems*, Springer-Verlag. 1992.

Knowledge Acquisition First, Modelling Later

Debbie Richards and Paul Compton

Department of Artificial Intelligence
School of Computer Science and Engineering
University of New South Wales
Sydney, Australia
Email: {debbier, compton}@cse.unsw.edu.au
Tel: +61 02 9385 3940
Fax: +61 02 9385 1814

Abstract: Current approaches to knowledge acquisition are based on the idea of modelling with the major effort being put into the initial development, hopefully resulting in models that facilitate reuse etc. There are problems with this in that the situated nature of knowledge leads to the domain model being a partial view resulting in maintenance problems. In contrast, the Ripple Down Rules (RDR) approach emphasizes incremental refinement whereby a knowledge base is built up over time by correcting errors as they occur. Such an approach reduces maintenance problems, but does not provide a model of the domain terms the expert uses, their relationships and various abstraction hierarchies which will facilitate reuse. The paper here describes an approach to discovering a conceptual structure in the domain using Formal Concept Analysis after or during incremental development of the knowledge base. We believe that not only does this assist maintenance and facilitate reuse of the knowledge for such purposes as critiquing and explanation, but it may be a more useful way of helping the experts discover and express significant concepts.

1. The Role of Models

One of the main thrusts in KBS development are: the use of problem solving methods (Chandrasekaran 1986, Schreiber, Weilinga and Breuker 1993, McDermott 1988, Steels 1993, Puerta et al 1992) and the use of ontologies (Guha and Lenat 1990, Patil et al 1991, Pirlein and Struder 1994). Both approaches rely on modelling at the knowledge level (Newell 1982). Schmalhoffer, Aitken and Bourne (1994) criticise a knowledge level approach as being unable to adequately handle changes in context and because everyone's model will differ depending on their frame of reference (Clancey 1991). Clancey defines a model as "merely an abstraction, a description and generator of behaviour patterns over time, not a mechanism equivalent to human capacity" (Clancey 1993, p. 89). An individual's model will also vary over time (Gaines and Shaw 1989). If we take a situated viewpoint of knowledge as something that is constructed to fit a particular situation then the reliance on finding a *good* model as a prerequisite for system development is risky.

In the above approaches the purpose of modelling is to allow the capture of expertise in a structured and systematic way. Certainly these methods do provide greater systematisation which provides greater security in how a project is proceding and because of this seem to have significant industrial success. However, it remains an open question of whether they actually alleviate the knowledge acquisition bottleneck (Menzies and Compton 1995). We take a more behavioral approach to building KBS that does not require the intervention of a knowledge engineer, at least once the initial data modelling has been carried out. The method, Ripple Down Rules (RDR) provides for incremental knowledge acquisition whereby errors are corrected as they occur and the knowledge base is incrementally refined. The resulting system in essence links features in the data to related conclusions, without using conceptual structures or an abstraction hierarchy. The aim of the present work is to explore techniques for retrospectively discovering such conceptual models from the simpler performance knowledge in the KBS. The benefits of doing this are to enable reuse of the knowledge for such purposes as explanation and critiquing.

To reuse knowledge it seems obvious that we need to understand the knowledge we have already. Analysis of rule bases has been generally limited to verification and validation of rule-bases for their original use, rather than for an alternative use. Previous research on analysing existing knowledge bases for the purpose of reuse has been manual and informal via approaches such as "careful analysis" (Clancey 1985 and Hemmann 1993, p.2). Thus, although we did not need to develop models for KA, inferencing or maintenance of the knowledge we wanted to find the symbolic models contained in our KBS because of their "explanatory value as psychological descriptions" Clancey 1993, p.89) and their usefulness in instruction (Schon 1987). To this end, this paper reports on work that has been done to add the ideas from Formal Concept Analysis (FCA) (Wille 1982) to multiple classification MCRDR. RDR and FCA are described in more detail in the next two sections. We then look at how the techniques have been combined and finish with a discussion of the findings and future work.

2. Ripple Down Rules

The original motivation for RDR was to attempt to deal with the situated nature of the knowledge provided by experts, particularly as observed during KBS maintenance (Compton & Jansen 1990). RDR can be seen as offering validated case based KA, although the knowledge provided is viewed as applying in the context of the case and is not considered to be necessarily generally applicable. A rule is only added to the system when an actual or hypothetical case has been given a wrong conclusion. The case that prompted a new rule to be added, known as the cornerstone case, is stored in association with the new rule to provide validated KA. The reason why RDR is described as providing validated KA is that the method does not allow the expert to add any rules which would result in any of the cornerstone cases being given a different conclusion from that stored. The validation of rules offered by RDR is not total validation, but ensures that as the system is incrementally developed, the previous performance of the system is maintained, at least with respect to the cornerstone cases.

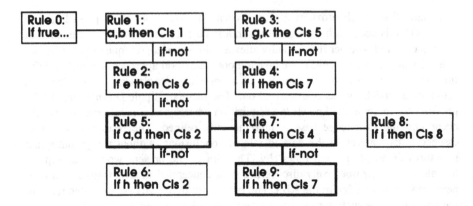

Figure 1. A single classification RDR KBS. Each rule can be seen as a pathway that leads from itself back to the top node which is rule 0. The highlighted boxes represent rules that are satisfied for the case {a,d,h}

In initial studies, where the focus was on tasks which only required a single classification per case, rules were linked in a binary tree structure and a single case was stored with each rule. When a conclusion had to be corrected a new rule was added at the end of the inference path through the tree giving the wrong conclusion. The rule had to then distinguish between the new case and the case associated with the rule that gave the wrong conclusion (Compton & Jansen 1990). We can define a single-classification RDR as a triple <rule,X,N>, where X are the exception rules and N are the if-not rules (Scheffer 1996). In Figure 1 the exception or true rules branch to the right and the if-not or false rules branch downwards. When a rule is satisfied the exception rules are evaluated and none of the lower rules are tested. The major success for this approach has been the PEIRS system, a large medical expert system for pathology laboratory report interpretation built by experts without the support of a knowledge engineer (Edwards et al 1993). It was also built whilst in routine use. Despite the fact that knowledge is added in random order, simulation studies have shown that knowledge bases produced by correcting errors as they occur are at least as compact and accurate as those produced by induction (Compton, Preston and Kang 1994 & 1995).

More recently we have developed RDR to deal with classification tasks where multiple independent classifications are required (Kang, Compton and Preston 1995, Kang 1996). Multiple Classification (MCRDR) is defined as the triple <rule,C,S>, where C are the children/exception rules and S are the siblings. All siblings at the first level are evaluated and if true the list of children are evaluated until all children from true parents have been exhausted. The last true rule on each pathway forms the conclusion for the case. Figure 2 shows an example of an MCRDR KBS. This approach allows for n-ary trees, but is most simply understood in terms of a flat rule structure, where all rules are evaluated against the data. When a new rule is added, all cases associated with the KBS could reach this rule, so that the rule must distinguish between the present case and all the stored cases.

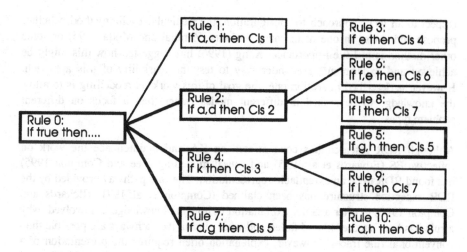

Figure 2. An MCRDR KBS. The highlighted boxes represent rules that are satisfied for the case {a,d,g,h,k}. We can see that there are three independent conclusions for this case, Class 2 (Rule 2), Class 3 (Rule 4) and Class 8 (Rule 10).

In the approach developed, the expert is required firstly to construct a rule which distinguishes between the new case and one of the stored cases. If other stored cases satisfy the rule, further conditions are required to be added to exclude a further case and so on until no stored cases satisfy the rule. Surprisingly the expert provides a sufficiently precise rule after two or three cases have been seen (Kang, Compton and Preston 1995). Rules which prevent an incorrect conclusion by providing a null conclusion are added in the same way. The MCRDR system produces somewhat more compact knowledge bases with less repetition than RDR even for single classification domains, probably because more use is made of expertise rather than depending on the KB structure (Kang 1996). MCRDR was chosen for this study since the ability to provide multiple conclusions for a given case is more appropriate for many domains and, more importantly, because the problem of how to handle the false "if-not" branches (Richards, Chellen and Compton 1996) does not exist.

Following the distinction made by Clancey (1985), RDR research to-date has involved heuristic classification, with only one exception involving heuristic construction (Mulholland et al 1993). From an RDR perspective, the important difference between construction and classification is that components of the solution may depend on each other as well as the data initially provided to the system. To avoid an explosion in knowledge this is normally handled by some sort of inference cycle so that as conclusions are reached they are added to working memory and further conclusions can be arrived at. However, the lack of an inference cycle in RDR is precisely what makes it relatively simple to ensure that the same pathways are used by the same cases during system development. The challenge for RDR for construction tasks is to deal with the apparent requirement for an inference cycle, some way of controlling this and deciding when and how it should terminate. With respect to an RDR approach to configuration, the particular cyclic method, whether propose and revise in one of its many variants (Zdrahal and Motta 1995) or some other method is of little importance. Kang (1996) has suggested how this might be achieved and experiments are under way to test the feasibility of this approach. However as described in section one, the goal of this work on modelling is to allow the knowledge to be reused in different modes rather than a focus on different problem types.

Although RDR research has concentrated on KA and maintenance the work on reflective ES (Edwards et al 1995) and causal modelling (Lee and Compton 1995) has found RDR to be an extendable representation. The rule pathway provided by the RDR exception structure has been claimed (Compton et al 1991, Richards and Compton 1996) to offer a better explanation of how the knowledge has evolved, why a rule has both succeeded and failed and what alternative pathways are possible than conventional rule traces. However, explanation often requires the presentation of a model of the concepts that a rule or collection of rules represents. For critiquing we need to determine whether the user's conclusion are the same or within acceptable limits of the system's conclusion. This requires determining the closeness of rule pathways and some measure of the extent of similarity. Thus in trying to find the underlying models in the KB rules we decided to investigate Formal Concept Analysis.

3. Formal Concept Analysis and our Implementation

Formal Concept Analysis, first developed by Wille (1982), is a mathematically based method of finding, ordering and displaying formal concepts (Wille 1992). A concept in FCA is comprised of a set of objects and the set of attributes associated with those objects. The set of objects forms the extension of the concept while the set of attributes forms the intension of the concept. Knowledge is seen as applying in a context and can be formally defined as a crosstable as in Figure 3 below. The rows are objects and the columns are attributes. An X indicates that a particular object has the corresponding attribute. This crosstable is used to find formal concepts. The following description of FCA follows Wille (1982). The screen dumps shown in Figures 4-7 are our implementation, called MCRDR/FCA, which is an enhancement of the current MCRDR for Windows system.

	Has feathers	suckles young	warm-blooded	cold-blooded	breeds in water	breeds on land	has scales
Bird	X		X			X	
Reptile				X		X	X
Amphibian				X	X		
Mammal		X	X			X	
Fish				X	X		X

Figure 3: Context of "Vertebrates of the Animal Kingdom"

A formal context (κ) has a set of objects G (for *Gegenstande* in German) and set of attributes M (for *Merkmale* in German) which are linked by a binary relation I which indicates that the object g (from the set G) has the attribute m (from the set M) and is defined as: κ = (G,M,I). Thus in figure 3 we have the context κ of animals with G = {bird, reptile, amphibian, mammal and fish} and M = {has feathers, suckles young, warm-blooded, cold-blooded, breeds in water, breeds on land, has scales}. The crosses show where the relation I exists, thus I = {(bird, has feathers), (bird, warm-blooded), (bird, breeds_on_land), (reptile, has_scales) ,..., (fish, has scales)}.

A formal concept is a pair (X,Y) where X is the *extent*, the set of objects, and Y is the *intent*, the set of attributes, for the concept. The derivation operators:

$$X \subseteq G: X \mapsto X' :=\{m \in M \mid gIm \text{ for all } g \in X \}$$
$$Y \subseteq M: Y \mapsto Y' :=\{g \in G \mid gIm \text{ for all } m \in Y\}$$

are used to construct all formal concepts of a formal context, by finding the pairs (X″,X′) and (Y′,Y″). We can obtain all extents X′ by determining all row-intents {g}′ with g ∈ G and then finding all their intersections. Alternatively Y′ can be obtained by determining all column-extents {m}′ with m ∈ M and then finding all their intersection. This is specified as:

$$X' = \bigcap_{g \in X} \{g\}' \qquad\qquad Y' = \bigcap_{m \in Y} \{m\}'$$

Less formally, we take the set of objects, G, to form the initial extent X which also represents our largest concept. We then process each attribute sequentially in the set M, finding the intersections of the extent for that attribute with all previous extents. Once the extents have been found for all attributes, the intents X′ for each extent X may be found by taking the intersection of the intents for each object within the set. Thereby we determine all formal concepts of the context κ by finding the pairs (X,X′).

Figure 4 shows the eleven formal concepts that were derived for the formal context in Figure 3 by finding the intersection of sets of attributes for each object and then finding the sets of objects that have those intents. The concepts have been ordered by intents to show the subsumption relations that exist. It can be seen that concepts two, five, eight and ten are subsets of concepts the that follow and each of these concepts start a new pattern of concepts. Alternative orderings are possible as for example concept two is a subset of concepts seven and ten but to show this would require duplication of concept rows. It is interesting to note that the larger the intent the smaller the extent and visa versa. This means that the more attributes used to describe an object reduces the number of objects that can be described in that manner. Conversely, the more objects in the extension the less attributes can be found in the intension which describe those objects.

Concept Matrix

File

| Return to Modelling | | Show Diagram | | Save Concepts | |

Attributes-Objects

Co	1	2	3	4	5	6	7	1	2	3	4	5
1								X	X	X	X	X
2		X						X	X		X	
3		X	X					X			X	
4	X	X	X					X				
5				X				X	X		X	
6				X	X			X			X	
7			X	X	X			X				
8				X		X			X		X	
9				X	X	X					X	
10		X	X				X			X		
11	X	X	X	X	X	X	X					

1	(HAS_FEATHERS=YES)	1	Rule 1	%BIRDO
2	(WARM_BLOODED=YES)	2	Rule 2	%REPTL
3	(BREEDS_ON_LAND=YES)	3	Rule 3	%AMPHN
4	(COLD_BLOODED=YES)	4	Rule 4	%MAMML
5	(HAS_SCALES=YES)	5	Rule 5	%FISHO
6	(BREEDS_IN_WATER=YES)			
7	(SUCKLES_YOUNG=YES)			

Figure 4: The concept matrix screen from MCRDR/FCA. Eleven (11) concepts have been found. Each row represents a concept. The columns show the attributes, which are listed first, followed by the objects. As was shown in the formal context in Figure 3, there are seven attributes and five objects, here labelled 1-7 and 1-5 respectively. The labels have been converted to numbers to allow the relationships between concepts and the possible patterns to be more readily seen. Full labelling can be obtained by using the pop-up windows as shown in this figure or by clicking on the attribute, object or concept number. The top and bottom concept, concepts one and eleven, show the concepts which include all objects and all attributes, respectively.

To present a visualisation of our ordered set of concepts as a line diagram it is necessary to compute the predecessors and successors of each concept. Predecessors are found by finding the largest subconcept of the intents for each concept. Successors are found by finding the smallest superconcept of the intents. A superconcept is a set that has all of the members of another set and additional members. A subconcept is a set that has fewer members than another set but all the members it has are contained in the other set. We only concentrate on finding sub or super concepts of the intents or extents because they are inversely related and using either set will give the same result. Figure 5 shows the list of successors and predecessors for the formal context in Figure 3. In MCRDR/FCA the successor list was used to identify concepts higher in the diagram, the parents, and the predecessor list identified concepts lower in the diagram, the children. The number of levels of parents and children are used to layout the line diagram and an algorithm for graph layout is given in Richards and Compton 1997b. However, just as users have different views of their knowledge, there is not one fixed way of drawing line diagrams and often a number of different layouts should be used (Wille 1992). The user may also reposition any of the nodes to their satisfaction providing a node is not moved higher than any of its parents or lower than any of its children. More formally, we use the subsumption relation $\leq$ on the set of all concepts formed such that $(X_1,Y_1) \leq (X_2,Y_2)$ iff $X_1 \subseteq X_2$. For a family (X_i,Y_i) of formal concepts of κ the greatest subconcept, the join, and the smallest superconcept, the meet, are respectively given by:

$$\bigvee_{i \in I} (X_i,B_i) := ((\bigcup_{i \in I} A_i)'', \bigcap_{i \in I} B_i) \qquad \bigwedge_{i \in I} (X_i,B_i) := (\bigcap_{i \in I} A_i, (\bigcup_{i \in I} B_i)'')$$

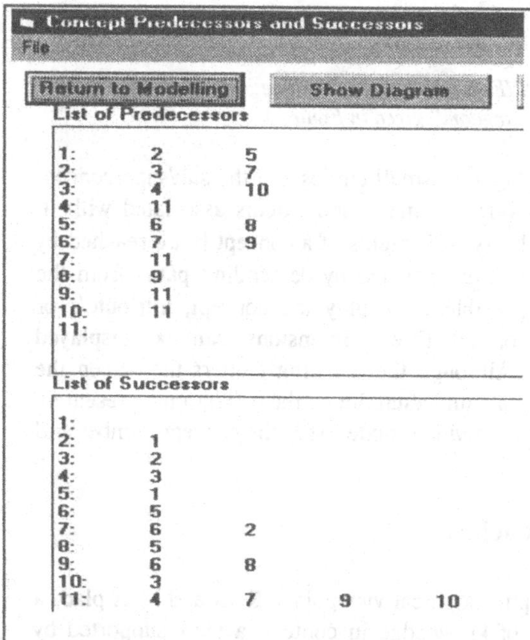

Figure 5: The MCRDR/FCA screen which shows the list of predecessors and successors for concepts generated for the vertebrate domain shown in figure 3.

From Lattice Theory, the ordered concept set can be used to form a complete lattice, called a concept lattice and denoted $B(\kappa)$. The concept lattice structure is seen as a superior representation to a semantic net because it provides "hierarchical conceptual clustering of the objects (via the extents) .... and a representation of all implications between the attributes (via its intents)" (Wille 1992, 497). As noted in section 4 there are limitations to the extensional definition of a concept and we only use the intensional definition for some of our work. However, for the development of the concept matrix, see Figure 4, and the concept lattice, see Figure 6, we do employ Wille's definition of a concept.

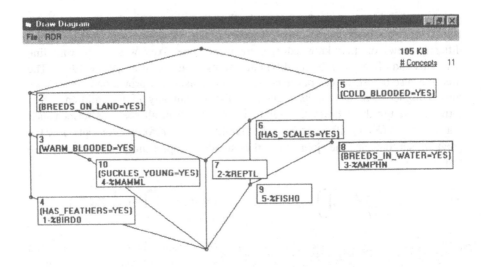

Figure 6: The diagram screen in MCRDR/FCA which shows the line diagram for the formal context of the "Vertebrates of the animal kingdom" given in Figure 3.

In Figures 6 and 7 the concepts are shown as small circles and the sub/superconcept relations as lines. Each concept has various intents and extents associated with it. The labelling has been reduced for clarity. All intents of a concept β are reached by ascending paths from β and all extents are reached by descending paths from the concept β. In MCRDR\FCA it is possible to display the concept, attribute/s or object/s belonging to each node or all three dimensions can be displayed concurrently, as in Figures 6 and 7. Although the labelling clutters the screen the extra information is important in understanding the diagram presented. Alternatively, the user can click on an individual node to see the concept number and all of its extents and intents.

4. Combining the Two Approaches

RDR and FCA are based on similar philosophical viewpoints. RDR and FCA place a strong emphasis on the importance of knowledge in context, a view supported by much of the knowledge reuse community (Guha and Lenat 1990 and Patil et al 1992). Compton and Jansen (1990) found that experts do not offer explanations of why they made a decision rather they offer a justification and that justification will depend on the situation. FCA is also "guided by the conviction that human thinking and communication always take place in *contexts* which determine the specific meaning of the concepts used" (Wille 1996, p. 23).

RDR and FCA both see that KA should be a task primarily performed by the expert and reduce modelling to the tasks of classifying objects (cases) and the identification of the salient features. However, they approach classification from alternative perspectives. FCA is concerned with identifying the similarity between objects, the conjunction of sets of attributes. RDR looks at differences between cases (objects) and is conceptually close to research based on Personal Construct Psychology (Kelly 1955) using Repertory Grids (Gaines and Shaw 1989) and the use of a discernability matrix in Rough Sets (Pawlak 1991). Another difference is the strong emphasis on incremental KA, validation and maintenance in RDR. The development of crosstables in FCA, like the use of Repertory Grids (Gaines and Shaw 1989), requires up-front consideration of the whole domain and does not consider incremental maintenance.

We wanted to use the rules in the RDR KBS as our starting point for developing a formal context rather than relying on the expert to define a crosstable because we felt that the RDR approach to KA was probably less demanding for experts than the development of crosstables and due to the incremental nature of acquisition and maintenance using RDR. To enable this, the RDR KBS was converted to a flat structure by sequentially traversing the KB for each rule picking up the conditions from the parent rule until the top node with the default rule was reached. From this flattened KBS the user chose either the whole KB or a more narrow focus of attention from which to derive a formal context. When the whole KB was chosen the rules and rule conditions formed the extents and intents, respectively. Such a global view is only feasible for small, if not very small, KBS. As with any graphical representation, as the number of rules being modeled grew, the line diagram became too cluttered to be comprehensible. Therefore, to limit the concepts to a manageable size that could be viewed in a matrix or a line diagram the user was asked to narrow their focus of attention to a particular rule or conclusion. Our approach is similar to that proposed by Ganter (1988) where the context is shortened to find subcontexts and subrelations. The decomposition of a concept lattice into smaller parts is a strategy that has previously been found useful (Wille 1989a).

It seemed probable that a user may want to carry out modelling in connection with a particular case. In this situation the user could select a case and then the rules and conclusions associated with that case were presented as the defaults from which to select. The user could also click the LIST ALL CONCLUSIONS button to see a list of all conclusion codes from which to pick. If the CONCLUSION command button was clicked, all rules using the specified conclusion were selected and added as objects to the set G, forming the extents of the context. As each extent was added the conditions of the rules were added to the set M of attributes to form the intents of the context, first checking to see if any attributes had already been added by previous rules. Where the relation I held, that is object g had attribute m, a cross was marked in the appropriate row and column. If the user chose a particular rule then that rule was added as the first object with the rule conditions as the initial intension. Every condition in each rule in the flattened RDR rule base was searched for a match on the initial set of attributes. If a match was found, that rule was added to the extension and all new attributes (conditions) found in the matching rule were also added to the intension. The result was a formal context K comprised of a set of objects G and attributes M connected by the binary relation I. An alternative selection screen has also been developed that provides the user with views based on conditions, attributes, rules or conclusions with numerous options at various levels of abstraction to assist the user in including the aspects of the knowledge base of interest to them.

Our treatment of each rule condition, which is actually an attribute-value pair, as an attribute is similar to the technique known as *conceptual scaling* (Ganter and Wille 1989) which has been used to interpret a many-valued context into a (binary) formal context. A many-valued context, such as that represented in an RDR KBS, is a quadruple (G,M,W,I) where I is a ternary relation between the set of objects G, the set of attributes M and the set of attribute values W (merkmalsWerte in German). Essentially, each attribute is treated as a separate formal context with the values as attributes associated with each of the original objects. A scale is chosen, such as a nominal scale (=) or an ordinal scale (≥), to order these attributes. From the many contexts, one for each attribute, the concepts are derived.

Once a formal context has been generated from the users selection we proceeded to find concepts, order them using the subsumption relation ≤, compute predecessors and successors and draw a line diagram according the process described in section 3. We could have ordered the formal context before derivation of the concepts to provide a possibly more visually pleasing order of concepts in the concept matrix but since this does not affect the calculation of predecessor and successors or the graph layout and the best order is unclear we chose not to order the crosstable.

5. Results-to-Date and Discussion

Our main interest was to develop tools to assist understanding of what conceptual models and possible abstractions existed in the performance knowledge being captured using RDR. Such understanding could be used for explanation or teaching, to assist KA, improve validation of the knowledge and provide a tool for the comparison of multiple conceptual models. The two main modelling tools provided by FCA are the concept matrix and the line diagram, shown in figures 4 and 6 respectively. The line diagram provides a more hierarchical understanding of the sub and super relationships in the domain. A major problem, however, with the line diagram is picking the appropriate amount or part of the knowledge base to model. If too much is chosen then the diagram is incomprehensible. As mentioned in Section 4, there are numerous options the user can choose from and the contexts from multiple views can be combined to provide a wide range of hierarchical and orthogonal perspectives. From our own investigations, if there is no particular starting point of interest it is useful to first gain a total view to initially identify interesting aspects of the knowledge. If the total view is incomprehensible then the user can print the list of concepts generated to identify interesting concepts, such as a set of attributes used by a large number of objects, as the basis for further exploration. Another option is to use the predecessor, successor or attribute order list to identify if a particular concept is the parent of a number of other concepts.

Thus far we have used our approach in three different domains. The first one was a 60-rule Blood Gases KBS which had been developed from the cornerstone cases associated with the 2000+ PEIRS rules. This knowledge is complex with many causal relationships between elements of the knowledge base. We have been able to identify which attributes are of importance for which conclusions and what conditions are likely to occur together. When we viewed the KBS at the attribute level without regard for the attribute values in the conditions we could see that the conclusion families that the expert had identified were confirmed by the model built using MCRDR/FCA. Our next plan for this domain is to look at the whole PEIRS KBS and see if we can identify which conclusions are close or the same as others and how they can be condensed to a more manageable number of conclusions.

Our second case study involved using MCRDR/FCA to compare the conceptual models of four independent advisors in an agricultural domain known as LOTUS which concerns the adaptation and management of the *Lotus Uliginosis cv* Grasslands Maku for pastures in the Australian state of New South Wales. Using the concept matrices and preordering the contexts it was possible to see the patterns between the conceptual models, to identify which concepts where the same, how they differed and to see what additional attributes or conclusions were considered important by one advisor but not others. The LOTUS and blood gases work are reported in Richards and Compton 1997a and 1997b.

We are currently looking at using the SISYPHUS III domain for testing the usefulness of MCRDR/FCA for learning the main concepts in the domain. Figure 7 shows the key differences between classifying a rock as either plutonic or volcanic. We can that when GRAIN-SIZE = COARSE a rock is plutonic (%PL000) and if GRAIN-SIZE = FINE a rock is VOLCANIC (%VC000). However, when GRAIN-SIZE = MEDIUM then if SILICA = LOWISH it is a volcanic rock otherwise if SILICA = VERY-HIGH or INTERMEDIATE it is a plutonic rock. The line diagram has shown us what attribute-value pairs are the critical ones for these conclusions.

In our latest work, we have been using the subsumption lattice to assist the user with KA by showing them how the selected conclusion or proposed rule fits in with the existing knowledge in the KBS. By comparing rule pathways we are able to critique a new rule and warn the user of possibly inconsistent conclusions. For this work we only use the intensional definition of a concept as the extensional definition is too restrictive/specific and as Zalta (1988) points out an intensional definition implies an extensional definition but the converse is possibly but not necessarily true.

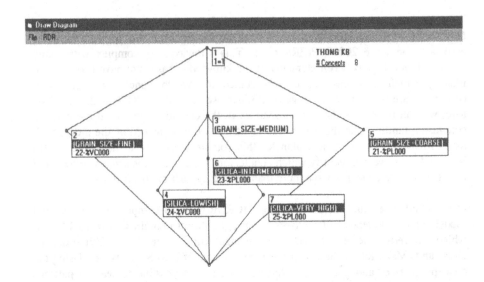

Figure 7: The line diagram for the SISYPHUS III domain using MCRDR/FCA. The foci of attention are the conclusions %VC000 - Volcanic and %PL000-Plutonic.

6. Future Directions

Our preliminary results appear promising. From the domains studied thus far we have found that the inclusion of FCA tools into RDR supports the derivation of concepts and the relationships between them without the need for prior modelling of those concepts. A major concern is picking the appropriate level of granularity at which to model and we have been investigating the ways in which contexts may be restricted while ensuring that relevant rules/pathways which do not match exactly are still included in our context. The approach described here took a simple view of a rule condition as an attribute but we are investigating the use of different *conceptual scales*, the use of a distance-weighted nearest neighbour algorithm and a fuzzy approach using borderline sets and ranges.

Other related research that will be considered includes: the use of rough sets to find relationships in KBS (Richards, Gambetta and Compton 1996); a comparison of concept lattices to concept maps (Gaines and Shaw 1995); the use of *attribute exploration* for acquisition of formal contexts (Wille 1989b) and review of work which combined the use of repertory grids and FCA (Spangenberg and Wolff 1988). A comparison of the above approaches may show whether consideration of similarities or differences between objects is more useful in a practical sense and what are the relative benefits of each. Our primary goal is to see how these techniques, combined possibly with others, can be used to provide a tool-kit of features and interaction modes that allow the user to change the mode of use to suit their particular situation and needs.

Acknowledgements

RDR research is supported by Australian Research Council grants. The authors would like to thank Phil Preston for being a sounding board for different implementation issues and for the MCRDR software on which this is based and thanks to Rudolf Wille who provided the foundations for finding concepts

References

Chandrasekaran, B. and Johnson, T. (1993) Generic Tasks and Task Structures In David, J.M., Krivine, J.-P. and Simmons, R., editors *Second Generation Expert Systems* pp: 232-272. Springer, Berlin.

Clancey, W.J., (1985) Heuristic Classification *Artificial Intelligence* 27:289-350.

Clancey, W.J., (1991) The Frame of Reference Problem in the Design of Intelligent Machines In K. VanLehn, ed. *Architectures for Intelligence*, Erlbaum, Hillsdale.

Clancey, W.J., (1993) Situated Action: A Neurological Interpretation Response to Vera and Simon *Cognitive Science*, 17: pp.87-116.

Compton, P. and Jansen, R., (1990) A Philosophical Basis for Knowledge Acquisition.. *Knowledge Acquisition* 2:2

Compton, P., Edwards, G., Kang, B., Lazarus, L., Malor, R., Menzies, T., Preston, P., Srinivasan, A. and Sammut, C. (1991) Ripple Down Rules: Possibilities and Limitations *6th Banff AAAI Knowledge Acquisition for Knowledge Based Systems Workshop*, Banff (1991) 6.1 - 6.18.

Compton, P., Preston, P. and Kang, B., (1994) Local Patching Produces Compact Knowledge Bases *A Future in Knowledge Acquisition* Eds L. Steels, G. Schreiber and W. Van de Velde, Berlin, Springer Verlag, pp:104-117.

Compton, P., Preston, P. and Kang, B. (1995) The Use of Simulated Experts in Evaluating Knowledge Acquisition, *Proceedings 9th Banff Knowledge Acquisition for Knowledge Based Systems Workshop* Banff. Feb 26 - March 3 1995, Vol 1:

Edwards, G., Compton, P., Malor, R, Srinivasan, A. and Lazarus, L. (1993) PEIRS: a Pathologist Maintained Expert System for the Interpretation of Chemical Pathology Reports *Pathology* 25: 27-34.

Edwards, G., Kang, B., Preston, P. and Compton, P. (1995) Prudent Expert Systems with Credentials: Managing the expertise of Decision Support Systems *Int. Journal Biomedical Computing* 40:125-132.

Gaines, B. R. and Shaw, M.L.G. (1989) Comparing the Conceptual Systems of Experts *The 11th International Joint Conference on Artificial Intelligence* :633-638.

Gaines, B. R. and Shaw, M.L.G. (1995) Collaboration through Concept Maps *CSCL'95 Proceedings* September 1995.

Ganter, B. (1988) Composition and Decomposition of Data *In Classification and Related Methods of Data Analysis* (Ed. H. Bock) pp:561-566, North-Holland, Amsterdam.

Ganter, B. and Wille, R. (1989) Conceptual Scaling *In Applications of Combinatorics and Graph Theory to the Biological Sciences* (Ed. F. Roberts) pp:139-167, Springer, New York.

Guha, T.V., and Lenat, D.B. (1990) CYC:A Mid-Term Report *AI Magazine* 11(3):32-59

Hemmann, Thomas (1993) Reusable Frameworks of Problem Solving In Catherine Peyralbe (ed.) *IJACI-93 Workshop on Knowledge Sharing and Information Interchange* Chamberry, France, August 29, 1993.

Kang, B., Compton, P. and Preston, P (1995) Multiple Classification Ripple Down Rules: Evaluation and Possibilities *Proceedings 9th Banff Knowledge Acquisition for Knowledge Based Systems Workshop* Banff. Feb 26 - March 3 1995, Vol 1: 17.1-17.20.

Kang, B., (1996*) Validating Knowledge Acquisition: Multiple Classification Ripple Down Rules* PhD Thesis, School of Computer Science and Engineering, University of NSW, Australia.

Kelly, G.A, (1955) *The Psychology of Personal Constructs* New York, Norton.

Langlotz, Curtis P. and Shortliffe, Edward E. (1983) Adapting a Consultation System to Critique User Plans. *International Journal of Man-Machine Studies 19*, 479-496.

Lee, M. and Compton, P. (1995) From Heuristic Knowledge to Causal *Explanations Proc. of Eighth Aust. Joint Conf. on Artificial Intelligence AI'95*, Ed X. Yao, 13-17 November 1995, Canberra, World Scientific, pp:83-90.

McDermott, J. (1988) Preliminary Steps Toward a Taxonomy of Problem-Solving Methods *Automating Knowledge Acquisition for Expert Systems* Marcus, S (ed.) Kluwer Academic Publishers, pp: 225-256.

Menzies, T.J. and Compton, P. (1995) The (Extensive) Implications of Evaluation on theDevelopment of Knowledge-Based Systems In *Proceedings 9th Banff Knowledge Acquisition for Knowledge Based Systems Workshop* Banff. Feb 26 - March 3 1995,.

Mulholland, M., Preston, P., Sammut, C., Hibbert, B. and Compton, P. (1993) An Expert System for Ion Chromatography Developed using Machine Learning and Knowledge in Context *Proceedings of the 6th Int. Conf. on Industrial and Engineering Applications of Artificial Intelligence and Expert Systems* Edinburgh.

Newell, A. (1982) The Knowledge Level *Artificial Intelligence* 18:87-127.

Patil, R. S., Fikes, R. E., Patel-Schneider, P. F., McKay, D., Finin, T., Gruber, T. R. and Neches, R., (1992) The DARPA Knowledge Sharing Effort: Progress Report In C. Rich, B. Nebel and Swartout, W., *Principles of Knowledge Representation and Reasoning: Proceedings of the Third International Conference* Cambridge, MA, Morgan Kaufman.

Pawlak, Zdzislaw (1991) *Rough Sets: Theoretical Aspects of Reasoning about Data* Kluwer Academic Publishers Dordrecht.

Pirlein, T. and Studer, R. (1994) KARO: An Integrated Environment for Reusing Ontologies *A Future for Knowledge Acquisition 8th European Knowledge Acqusition Worksop EKAW'94*, pp:220-225. Springer Verlag.

Puerta, A. R, Egar, J.W., Tu, S.W. and Musen, M.A. (1992) A Mulitple Method Knowledge Acquisition Shell for Automatic Generation of Knowledge Acquisition Tools *Knowledge Acquisition 4*(2).

Rector, A. L. (1989) Helping with a Humanly Impossible Task: Integrating KBS into clinical care" In *Proceedings of the Second Scandinavian Conference on AI*, SFCAI'89.

Richards, D ., Gambetta, W. and Compton, P (1996) Using Rough Set Theory to Verify Production Rules and Support Reuse *Proceedings of the Verification, Validation and Refinement of KBS Workshop, PRICAI'96* 26-30 August 1996, Cairns, Australia, Griffith University.

Richards, D., Chellen, V. and Compton, P (1996) The Reuse of Ripple Down Rule Knowledge Bases: Using Machine Learing ot Remove Repetition *Proceedings of Pacific Knowledge Acquisition Workshop PKAW'96*, October 23-25 1996, Coogee, Australia.

Richards, D and Compton, P (1996) Building Knowledge Based Systems that Match the Decision Situation Using Ripple Down Rules, *Intelligent Decision Support '96* 9th Sept, 1996, Monash University.

Richards, D. and Compton, P. (1997a) Combining Formal Concept Analysis and Ripple Down Rules to Support the Reuse of Knowledge *Proceedings of the 9th International*

Conference on Software Engineering Knowledge Engineering SEKE'97 Madrid June 18-20 1997.

Richards, D. and Compton, P. (1997b) Unovering the Conceptual Models in RDR in *Proceedings of the International Conference on Conceptual Structures ICCS'97* Seattle August 4-8 1997, Springer Verlag (in print).

Salle, J.M. and Hunter, J., (1990) Computer/User Cooperation Issues for Knowledge-Based Systems: A Review *Technical Report Aberdeen University* AUCS/TR9003

Scheffer, T. (1996) Algebraic Fundation and Improved Methods of Induction of Ripple Down Rules *Proceedings of Pacific Knowledge Acquisition Workshop PKAW'96*, October 23-25 1996, Coogee, Australia.

Schmalhofer, F.J., Aitken, S. and Bourne, L. E. (1994) Beyond the Knowledge Level: Descriptions of Rational Behaviour for Sharing and Reuse *A Future for Knowledge Acquisition 8th European Knowledge Acqusition Worksop EKAW'94*, pp:220-225. Springer Verlag.

Schon, D.A. (1987) *Educating the Reflective Practitioner* Jossey-Bass, San Francisco, CA.

Schreiber, G., Weilinga, B. and Breuker (eds) (1993) KADS: A Principles Approach to Knowledge-Based System Development *Knowledge-Based Systems* London, England, Academic Press.

Shadbolt, N., (1996)URL:http://www.psyc.nott.ac.uk/aigr/research/ka/SisIII

Steels, L. (1993) The Componential Framework and Its Role in Reusability In David, J.M., Krivine, J.-P. and Simmons, R., editors *Second Generation Expert Systems* pp: 273-298. Springer, Berlin.

Spangenberg, N and Wolff, K.E. (1988) Conceptual Grid Evaluation In H.H. Bock ed. *Classification and Related Methods of Data Analysis* Elsevier Science Publishers B.V. North Holland.

Wille, R. (1982) Restructuring Lattice Theory: An Approach Based on Hierarchies of Concepts In *Ordered Sets* (Ed. Rival) pp:445-470, Reidel, Dordrecht, Boston.

Wille, R. (1989a) Lattices in Data Analysis: How to Draw them with a Computer In *Algorithms and Order* (Ed. I. Rival) pp:33-58, Kluwer, Dordrecht, Boston.

Wille, R. (1989b) Knowledge Acquisition by Methods of Formal Concept Analysis In *Data Analysis, Learning Symbolic and Numeric Knowledge* (Ed. E. Diday) pp:365-380, Nova Science Pub., New York.

Wille, R. (1992) Concept Lattices and Conceptual Knowledge *Systems Computers Math. Applic. (23)*6-9:493-515.

Wille, R. (1996) Conceptual Structures of Multicontexts *Conceptual Structures: Knowledge Representation as Interlingua* (Eds. P.Eklund, G. Ellis and G. Mann) pp:23-390, Springer.

Zalta, E.N. (1988) *Intensional Logic and the Metaphysics of Intentionality*, Cambridge, Massachusetts, MIT Press.

Zdrahal, Z and Motta, E. (1995) An In-Depth Analysis of Propose and Revise Problem Solving Methods *9th Knowledge Acquisition for Knowledge Based Systems Workshop* Banff, Canada, SRDG Publications, Departments of Computer Science, University of Calgary, Calgary, Canada pp:38.1-38.20.

Knowledge Acquisition for the Onboard Planner of an Autonomous Spacecraft

Benjamin D. Smith[1]
Kanna Rajan[2]
Nicola Muscettola[2]

[1] Jet Propulsion Laboratory
California Institute of Technology
4800 Oak Grove Drive M/S 525-3660
Pasadena, CA 91109-8099
smith@aig.jpl.nasa.gov
[2] NASA Ames Research Center
Mail Stop 269-2
Moffett Field, CA 94035
{kanna,mus}@ptolemy.arc.nasa.gov

Abstract. Deep Space One (DS1) will be the first spacecraft to be controlled by an autonomous closed loop system potentially capable of carrying out a complete mission with minimal commanding from Earth. A major component of the autonomous flight software is an onboard planner/scheduler. Based on generative planning and temporal reasoning technologies, the planner/scheduler transforms abstract goals into detailed tasks to be executed within resource and time limits. This paper discusses the knowledge acquisition issues involved in transitioning this novel technology into spacecraft flight software, developing the planner in the context of a large software project and completing the work under a compressed development schedule. Our experience shows that the planning framework used is adequate to address the challenges of DS1 and future autonomous spacecraft systems, and it points to a series of open technological challenges in developing methodologies and tools for knowledge acquisition and validation.

1   Introduction

The future of the space program calls for ambitious missions of exploration and scientific discovery. Searching for life on Mars, Europa and elsewhere in the solar system and beyond will require the solution of several challenging technical and organizational problems. A central one is the implementation of increasingly capable and autonomous control systems to ensure both mission accomplishment and mission safety [17, 6, 15]. Without these systems missions will have to be run with the current, traditional approach. This relies on frequent communication with Earth and teams of human experts guiding step by step a mission through its tasks and analyzing and reacting to the occurrence of malfunctions. The cost and logistics difficulties of this approach, however, are so high that it cannot be reasonably carried over to the expected growth of missions and mission capabilities. Autonomy technology is an answer to these problems.

The Remote Agent (RA) [12, 13] will be the first artificial intelligence-based autonomy architecture to reside in the flight processor of a spacecraft and control it for 6 days without ground intervention. The mission on which RA will fly is Deep Space One (DS1), the first deep-space mission of NASA's New Millennium Project. RA achieves its high level of autonomy by using an architecture with three components: an integrated planning and scheduling system (PS) that generates sequences of actions (plans) from high-level goals, a intelligent executive (EXEC) that carries out those actions and can respond to execution time anomalies, and a Model-based Identification and Recovery system (MIR) that identifies faults and suggests repair strategies. Each module covers a different function in the architecture and uses a different computational approach. One characteristic however is common to all of them: the reliance on models of the domain that are largely independent from the task to be fulfilled. These models allow the module to rely on a much deeper understanding of the structural characteristics of the domain than possible with classical rule-based approaches, facilitating model analysis and model reuse.

This paper discusses the knowledge acquisition process used for models and heuristics of the planning and scheduling system (PS) of DS1. We started the process with an approach to planning knowledge representation [10] that had been demonstrated in a rapid-prototype effort [12]. With DS1 we had to face additional challenges due to having to develop PS in the context of the development of the full flight software, to the additional complexity of the domain, to the compressed schedule for development and to the risk-management requirements. Also, architectural solutions internal to RA had to be enhanced due both to the increase in capabilities that were needed to control a real spacecraft and to the need to provide sounder software engineering approaches. We will describe how the knowledge acquisition process was carried out and the strengths and weaknesses we found in our current approach.

Section 2 deals with the Remote Agent software architecture highlighting the details of the planner and it's plan representation. Section 3 deals with issues in knowledge acquisition including references to the spiral development process, model acquisition and interfaces to external experts. Section 4 deals with the open issues as a result of the development process including the need for validation and debugging tools. Conclusions appear in Section 5.

2 The Remote Agent and Planner Architectures

The RA architecture consists of four distinct components (Figure 1), the *Planner/Scheduler*, the *Mission Manager* [11], the *Smart Executive* (EXEC) [14] and the *Mode Identification and Recovery* (MIR) system [16, 17] .

The execution of plans by the EXEC is achieved by interaction with a Mode Identification system and a lower level real time monitoring and control component. MIR provides the EXEC with a level of abstraction to reason about the

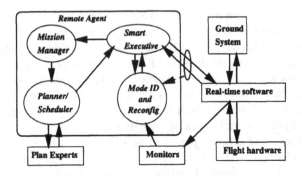

Fig. 1. RA architecture

state of the various devices it commands. The *monitoring* layer takes the raw sensor data and discretizes it to the level of abstraction needed by MIR. Finally, the *control and real-time system* layer takes commands from the executive and provides the actual control of the low level state of the spacecraft. It is responsible for providing the low level sensor data stream to the monitors. Details of the Remote Agent architecture can be found in [12, 13].

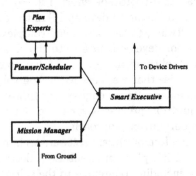

Fig. 2. Planner/Scheduler Architecture

The planner/scheduler (PS) generates a detailed plan of action from a handful of high-level goals, based on knowledge of the spacecraft contained in a domain model. The model describes the set of actions, how goals decompose into actions, the constraints among actions, and resource utilization by the actions. The planning engine searches the space of possible plans for one that satisfies the constraints and achieves the goals. The action definitions determine the space of plans. The constraints determine which of these plans are legal, and heavily prune the search space. The heuristics guide the search in order to increase the number of plans that can be found within the time allocated for planning.

Figure 2 describes the overall view of the Remote Agent Planner/Scheduler.

The Mission Manager (MM) contains the long term mission plan with goals for the entire mission. Ground operators can interact with the MM to modify the plan by adding, removing or editing goals in the mission plan. The MM also provides the EXEC with an interface to the Planner. When the EXEC requests a new plan, MM selects a new set of goals from the mission profile, based on internal way points. It combines this with the initial state provided by the EXEC and generates a partial plan for the planner. When the EXEC has completed execution of this plan the cycle is completed when it sends a new request to the MM for the next planning horizon. For the RA experiment the plan horizon will consist of two segments each three days long.

2.1 Knowledge Representation of the Planner

The knowledge representation of the planner is distributed among the domain models, the planner heuristics, the mission profile and the plan experts. The domain models encode the behavioral and operational constraints imposed on the spacecraft by the mission and the hardware. The heuristics guide the planner search to decrease the computational resources needed to find a plan and to increase plan quality. The mission profile encodes the long term goals and mission requirements as determined by the ground controllers and mission designers, and resides in the Mission Managers temporal database. Finally the plan experts are special-purpose software modules, written and maintained by other teams, with which the planner interacts to obtain knowledge that cannot be easily encoded in the plan model.

Model Representation. The PS uses a hybrid planning/scheduling representation that models continuous processes on parallel timelines to describe actions, states and resource allocations. PS provides also for temporal and parametric flexibility and uses planning experts.

Plans consist of several parallel *timelines*, each of which consists of a sequence of *tokens*. A timeline describes the evolution of a spacecraft state over time, and the tokens describe those states. For example, consider one timeline that describes the main engine. If the plan is to start in standby, fire up the engine, and return to standby, the timeline would have one token for each of those processes. Each token has a start time, and end time, and a duration. Each token can have zero or more arguments (e.g., the thrust level at which to fire the engine).

The plan model consists of definitions for all the timelines, definitions for all the tokens that can appear on those timelines, and a set of temporal constraints that must hold among the tokens in a valid plan. The planner model is described in a domain description language (DDL), and is represented as part of the planner's data base also called the Plan DB.

Temporal constraints are specified in DDL by *compatibilities*. A compatibility consists of a *master token* and a boolean expression of temporal relations that must hold between the master token and *target tokens*. An example is shown in Figure 3.

```
(Define_Compatibility
   ;; compats on SEP_Thrusting
   (SEP_Thrusting ?heading ?level ?duration)
   :compatibility_spec
   (AND (equal (DELTA MULTIPLE (Power) (+ 2416 Used)))
        (contained_by (Constant_Pointing ?heading))
        (met_by (SEP_Standby))
        (meets  (SEP_Standby))))

(Define_Compatibility
   ;; Transitional Pointing
   (Transitional_Pointing ?from ?to ?legal)
   :parameter_functions
      (?_duration_ <- APE_Slew_Duration (?from ?to ?_start_time_))
      (?_legal_    <- APE_Slew_Legality (?from ?to ?_start_time_))
   :compatibility_spec
   (AND (met_by (Constant_Pointing ?from))
        (meets  (Constant_Pointing ?to))))

(Define_Compatibility
   ;; Constant Pointing
   (Constant_Pointing ?target)
   :compatibility_spec
   (AND (met_by (Transitional_Pointing * ?target LEGAL))
        (meets  (Constant_Pointing    ?target * LEGAL))))
```

Fig. 3. An example of a compatibility constraint in the planner model.

The first compatibility says that the master token, SEP_THRUSTING (when the Solar Electric Propulsion engine is producing thrust), must be immediately preceded and followed by a standby token, temporally contained by a constant pointing token, and requires 2416 Watts of power. Constant pointing implies that the spacecraft is in a steady state aiming its camera towards a fixed target in space. Transitional pointings turn the spacecraft. The SEP standby state indicates that the engine is not thrusting but has not been completely shut off. A plan fragment based on these compatibilities is shown in Figure 4.

Heuristics. Heuristics guide every choice point of the planners search. On each iteration of the search, the planner chooses an unresolved compatibility constraint and a way to resolve it: by constraining an existing token to satisfy the constraint, adding a new token that satisfies it, or assuming that it will be satisfied by some token in the next horizon. There are other decisions as well, such as grounding under-constrained argument values.

For example, the heuristic in Figure 5 prevents backtracking due to cycling. The attitude timeline alternates between constant pointing tokens and transi-

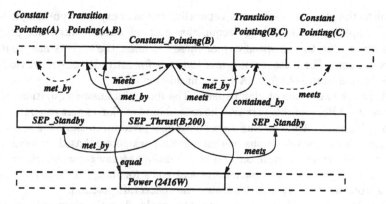

Fig. 4. Plan Fragment

```
Method Connect
  ;; connect only, defer and add are disallowed.
  master { Transitional_Pointing; }
  target { Constant_Pointing; }
```

Fig. 5. Cycle Avoidance Heuristics

tional pointing tokens. Once a constant pointing token is added, it has compatibilities that could add transitional pointing tokens, which can in turn add constant pointing tokens add infinitum. The last heuristic breaks the cycle by saying that a transitional pointing token can *connect* to an existing constant pointing token, but can never *add* one.

Mission Profile. The goals for the entire mission are stored in an on-board file called the *mission profile*, which is managed by the Mission Manager. The profile captures mission operations knowledge, such as when the communications passes are scheduled, how much fuel is allocated for each segment of the mission, when various mission phases start and stop, and so on. The profile also serves as the primary interface with the ground controllers. The ground team commands the spacecraft at a high level by changing or adding goals to the profile.

Plan Experts. A large software project like the DS1, requires the contribution of several teams with specialized knowledge. *Planning Experts* are programs developed and maintained by other teams. They coordinate with the planner but which are not strictly part of its domain representation.

A prime example is the Attitude control Planning Expert (APE), which answers queries about how long the turn will take and whether a given turn violates pointing constraints (e.g., will the turn expose the camera to a damaging bright radiation source). How violation constraints are calculated is completely opaque to the planner. As a result, separating the plan experts from the planning model simplifies the knowledge acquisition and software maintenance process. Quite often, due to the specificity of these modules, the code is also reusable across missions. For instance, much of the code for attitude constraint violation in APE came from NASA/ESA's Cassini mission [5].

There are two kinds of plan experts. The first kind answers questions about constraints. APE is of this variety. The second kind of plan expert generates goals for the planner to achieve. These on-board goal generators allow the spacecraft to make autonomous decisions, within certain parameters, based on local information. The prime example on DS1 is the on-board navigator, which provides goals on trajectory related maneuvers and goals for images of nearby celestial bodies from which NAV can determine the spacecraft position.

The planner asks the goal generators for goals when the planner is ready for them. The goal generators have no visibility into the plan, other than whatever information provided in the request. When the goals are returned, the planner decides how they will be achieved in the plan, or whether they are achieved at all. If the plan is over-constrained, goals can be rejected based on a global prioritization scheme.

3 The Knowledge Acquisition Process

Traditionally flight software for a spacecraft consists only of low level device drivers, attitude control system and simple sequence execution capabilities. Commanding done from ground allows the operational and mission constraints to be designed and implemented at a later time, sometimes even after launch. With on-board autonomy, the design process must take a more comprehensive view to the full mission life cycle including from the *very beginning* the modes, operations and expected behaviors of the spacecraft in the domain models. To accomplish this we used a spiral development model [1].

In the following sections we discuss the knowledge acquisition process and methodology for the planner and the resulting problems and issues they raised.

3.1 The Spiral Development Process

In spiral development [1], functionality is added incrementally in distinct software releases. This allows base functionality to be understood and developed before moving to more complex functionality. Processes and standards are also refined in each spiral. At the end of each development cycle, project teams meet to discuss the obstacles they encountered and the lessons they learned. The DS1 spiral process is discussed further in [8].

At the beginning of each spiral, the mission engineers created a baseline scenario that would exercise the new functionality for that spiral while still requiring the old functionality. The hardware management team (HWMT) then arranged several days of knowledge acquisition meetings with the hardware developers, who would detail the software requirements for their hardware to work correctly.

Each of the modeling and software development teams sent representatives to these meetings. The hardware developers presented the baseline behavior for the upcoming spiral, and the modelers asked questions to elicit further details. Since each component of the RA models the hardware at a different level, having representatives from each team was particularly helpful in identifying interaction issues across the different levels.

The DS1 Spiral releases were designated R1 through R3. To give the reader the scope of development that took place, we show the evolution of the planner model sizes for each revision in Tables 1, 2 and 3.

From the PS perspective each revision in the spiral development model involved successively sophisticated constraint modeling of the spacecraft. In the first revision the model only dealt with simple turns and picture taking for navigation images; more complex issues such as power, thermal modeling were ignored. In the next revision the model included the modeling the SEP engines and obtaining more detailed trajectory information from the navigation expert. The third spiral release added power management, advanced turns, and comet fly-by related activities.

In each revision of the Spiral development approximately eight weeks were needed for knowledge capture and another eight weeks for model development and tuning of the planner search.

Subsystem	R1	R2	R3
Mission events	0	1	3
Power	0	0	2
Ion Propulsion	1	5	5
Attitude control	3	4	4
Communications	0	1	2
MICAS	1	1	6
Beacon experiment	0	0	2
RCS system	1	1	3
Navigation	3	3	4
Planner/scheduler	1	1	1
Total	10	17	32

Table 1. Number of timelines changed in the model for each development release.

3.2 Model Acquisition

Model aquisition in each cycle started with the cognizant system engineer specifying the baseline functionality to be covered, layered on top of designs of subsystems already implemented. Each team then developed a specification called a *Problem Statement* which described how that functionality would be achieved.

Subsystem	R1	R2				R3			
	Tot	Add	Mod	Del	Tot	Add	Mod	Del	Tot
Mission events	0	1			1	5			6
Power	0				0	3			3
Ion Propulsion	1	11	1		12	1	3		13
Attitude control	4	4			8	6	2	1	14
Communications	0	3			3	2	2		5
MICAS	3	5			8	14			22
Beacon experiment	0				0	4			4
RCS system	1				1	4	1		5
Navigation	6		2		6	3			9
Planner/scheduler	2				2				2
Total	17				41				69

Table 2. Number of token modifications to the model for each development release.

Subsystem	R1	R2	R3
Mission events	0	2	4
Power	0	0	0
Ion Propulsion	3	11	14
Attitude control	2	11	16
Communications	0	3	7
MICAS	3	3	20
Beacon experiment	0	0	4
RCS system	0	0	2
Navigation	4	3	7
Planner/scheduler	2	2	2
Total	16	36	76

Table 3. Number of compatibilities changed in the model for each development release.

For the planner, this described changes to the planning model and engine and described changes to interfaces with the EXEC and plan experts. Teams with interfaces with the planner (especially the EXEC) would comment and propose design changes and any additional requirements. After a few iterations of this process, the modeler would update the *Token Dictionary*. The token dictionary details the syntax and semantics of each token type on all the timelines and forms the primary document for all negotiated informal interfaces with the EXEC.

We used an informal elicitation methodology to acquire the models described in the problem statements. The elicitation began with a standard list of questions about how the subsystem operated and what constraints or interactions it had with other subsystems. These would then lead to more detailed questions. The captured knowledge was compiled in a semi-formal document and approved by the engineers in a separate session. There was no formal methodology to ensure coverage other than the constraints of the baseline scenario. Nonetheless, this was adequate to build the plan models and successfully complete the scenarios for each spiral release. In retrospect, an aquisition methodology that resulted in a formal specification with guaranteed coverage would have been useful for rigorously validating the model (see Section 4.3).

Issues in Domain Modeling. In modeling for the DS1 mission, we discovered that a relatively large number of modeling tasks were easy to do, given the syntax and semantics of DDL. In a couple of cases we had to introduce auxiliary timelines to support the planner's reasoning process.

For instance it was necessary to schedule the correct amount of SEP **thrust** within a planning horizon. Simply put, this would require computing the duration of each SEP **thrust** token and performing a summation over the planning horizon. To do so however, a somewhat circular approach was needed by defining a new timeline which would use variable codesignation and propagate accumulated thrust values based on temporal durations of the SEP **thrust** tokens; something not altogether intuitive. Figure 6 illustrates this situation with the **Max Thrust** duration specifying the thrust duration *needed* in the horizon; SEP **thrust** tokens actually *performing* the thrusting action and Accumulated **thrust** tokens showing a running *count* of the thrust.

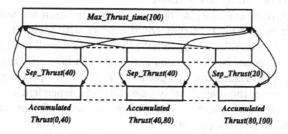

Fig. 6. A plan fragment implementing thrust accumulation within a plan horizon

As mentioned earlier, with each iteration of the development cycle the planner models were made consistently more realistic. Knowledge acquisition from each spiral cycle effectively ended up affecting the planner's domain model and it's heuristics. While syntactic modifications and its semantic interpretation were the primary drivers of model development (especially if interface requirements at the token level were to be negotiated with the EXEC (see Section 3.4)) we discovered that significant development time was spent aligning the heuristics with the model changes so that planner convergence was possible.

Heuristics. Because of the tight coupling of the domain model to the heuristics, changes to the model almost always require corresponding changes to the heuristics. This makes it difficult to introduce incremental changes to the model. Normally, a family of timelines corresponding to a new device or capability can be added with minimal impact on other timelines. Most of the constraints are among the timelines in the family, with a handful of constraints to external resources such as power or spacecraft attitude. However, the new timelines change the optimal search strategy, and this requires the heuristics to be re-tuned.

3.3 Unmodeled Activities

Sometimes the ground controllers want to execute unusual maneuvers that are not modeled the planner. For example, they may want to execute a high-speed turn (normally disallowed) in order to jar loose a stuck solar panel. The model must provide a way for the ground controllers to execute contingency maneuvers such as this without uploading a new model. Changing the model maybe fine for permanent patches, but the time and cost needed to develop and test the patch makes them impractical for one-time emergency maneuvers.

In support of this requirement the model provides a `special activity` token that can stand in for any activity the ground wants to execute but is not otherwise supported by the planning model. The ground controllers insert the token where they want it in the mission profile. It can be scheduled for a specific time, or scheduled relative to other events. The activities performed by the token are specified in a file of time-tagged low-level commands that the EXEC executes at the beginning of the token.

Since the actions executed in the special activity token are not modeled by the planner, it is possible that they could conflict with planned activities. For example, the plan could be trying to hold the spacecraft still in order to take an image while the special activity token is executing a high speed turn. To avoid such conflicts, constraints can be specified between the special activity token and other tokens in the plan. In this case, attitude dependent activities would be disallowed while the special activity token was active. These constraints can be specified in the mission profile.

3.4 Interfaces

The interfaces between the planner and other parts of the flight software impact the knowledge acquisition and representation. The planner has two main interfaces: interfaces with *plan experts*, and interfaces with the *Smart Executive* component of the RA.

Plan Expert Interfaces. Negotiating the plan expert interfaces was among the easiest of the knowledge acquisition tasks. This is largely due to the opaqueness of the plan experts to the planner and vice versa. The bulk of the knowledge acquisition was in the very first meeting, where the focus was understanding how the plan expert worked and explaining planner concepts to the plan expert developers. In the case of APE, the planning team needed to understand how to specify a turn, and what information was needed for APE to compute a turn. The details of how turns are computed were irrelevant.

Once this initial knowledge acquisition was completed, subsequent interface negotiations were completed in a matter of hours, usually by phone or email. The interfaces were formally defined as C structures that specified the information passing from the planner to the plan expert and back. These were captured in an interface control document, and in an executable interface specification language.

In some cases, the planner used assumptions about the inner workings of the plan expert to improve efficiency. For example, the legality and duration of a turn changes slowly and continuously over time. This allows a turn to be moved a couple hours ahead or back in the plan as needed without affecting its duration or legality. The planner model and heuristics exploited this knowledge to simplify the design and speed up the search. Assumptions of this sort were rare, and captured explicitly in the interface control documents.

EXEC Interfaces. The interfaces between the planner and the Smart Executive (EXEC) are embodied by the timeline and token definitions included in the planner's model.

In order for the EXEC to execute plans, it must know what tokens can appear in the plan and how to expand those tokens into detailed commands to the real-time flight software. This creates a very strong coupling between EXEC and the planner. All of the timelines, tokens, and their semantics were negotiated at the beginning of each spiral before any implementation took place. However, if the need for another token was discovered during development, or some token needed another argument, or the semantics were wrong, then the EXEC and PS had to change their implementations accordingly. Because the tokens are such a major part of the model implementation, changes of this sort occurred in every development spiral despite strong efforts to prevent them.

Several solutions to this interface issue were considered for DS1. One successful approach was to use *information hiding* to create private token arguments. Additional arguments are often needed to hold values derived from other arguments, or to propagate values from other tokens. The need for these arguments often goes unnoticed until development begins in earnest. Private arguments are seen by the planner, but are do not appear in the plan. This allowed modelers to add arguments for bookkeeping and propagation purposes without impacting the EXEC. This capability was introduced at the end of the R2 spiral, and used with great success in R3.

Interface Management Process. To ensure disconnects were kept to a minimum, another requirement added by the project during the design phase of each revision, was the development of *Problem Statements*, with details of each modules' design, interfaces and assumptions for that revision cycle. The planner in addition also had a token dictionary with the negotiated token level interfaces with the EXEC. With the EXEC with which the planner representation was tightly coupled, any agreements and assumptions in the planner's model were accurately document and easily accessible via a world wide web (WWW) interface to the dictionary and disconnects caught early on. In order to avoid disconnects with respect to the hardware specifications, especially as hardware delivery quantified the performance, the HWMT was the central point of contact for disseminating information.

The project also made sure that after the interface parties and the design phase for each cycle, but *before* the various teams started actually developing code, a *concept review* would take place. Each team would publish a short document detailing their design choices and the assumptions made, especially towards generating the scenario in the current cycle and the interface requirements. Any disconnects found would require the project to follow through with the team in question to ensure the new design actually covered the complete scenario.

3.5 Distributed Development

Because of geographically distributed teams, design documents and interface agreements were exchanged primarily via a WWW interface with auto-posting features as mentioned in [2]. The use of the Internet was decisive in successfully collaborating over remote sites especially when exchanging device level knowledge. For instance, the HWMT would be able to post power budget allocations over different devices which could be abstracted, parsed and built into a table for lookup during model generation time. This would ensure that the planner models were consistent in their power budgets with those of the system engineering and actually viable for generating robust plans.

Additionally, for short design and concept reviews, a "meet-me" telephonic system was in place with people calling into a central number while accessing the web and viewing the same document simultaneously. This greatly helped in cutting down the time, effort and expense of commuting to a central site. Note also that a revision control system [3] was in place for all the source code.

4 Open Issues

The DS1 project presented several challenges in knowledge acquisition, representation, and validation. The DS1 planner proved capable of addressing these issues, at least to the extent needed to satisfy the requirements of DS1. However, there are a number of issues that must be resolved before this technology can be used on a risk-intolerant science mission by spacecraft engineers with minimal support from the planner development team.

4.1 Acquiring Heuristics is Difficult

Good heuristics are needed to make the planner search computationally tractable. Heuristics tell the planner what decisions are most likely to be best at each choice point in the planner search algorithm, thereby reducing the search. Developing a good set of heuristics for the DS1 planner is currently very difficult, both because it requires an intimate knowledge of how the planner search algorithm interacts with the model, and because the planner requires exceptionally good heuristics to achieve computational tractability. The DS1 model developers had this experience and so were able to develop good heuristics, but these obstacles must be overcome before spacecraft engineers can be expected to develop heuristics on their own.

One solution is to provide tools that derive heuristics automatically. Such tools have been discussed in the machine learning and planning literature. Two of the more promising approaches are to derive heuristics automatically through a static analysis of the plan model [4] or to learn them by watching the behavior of the planner over several runs on a given model [9]. Unfortunately, the DS1 planner requires exceptionally good heuristics to achieve tractability, and these methods generally do not produce heuristics of that caliber. The sensitivity of the planner to the heuristic must be reduced before automatic heuristic acquisition can be feasible.

4.2   Development and Debugging Tools are Needed

Modeling could be made considerably easier with even a few simple tools. Although there was insufficient time to develop them for DS1, our experience with developing and debugging models suggested a number of desirable features. Developing tools along these lines is one of our near term goals.

Plan Visualization Tools. One problem with the current system is that it is very difficult to understand what the planner is doing, despite copious output. This makes it difficult to isolate the decisions that lead to bugs in the plan, or prevent the planner from finding any plan at all. A visualization tool would help modelers to track the planners behavior, as well as making it easier for new users to understand how the planner works.

Deactivating Timelines. When debugging, the modeler often suspects the bug is within a small family of timelines. But as the model gets more complex, it becomes difficult to focus on the behavior of those timelines. A simple way to address this problem is to disable irrelevant timelines. The planner ignores the timelines and all compatibilities associated with them. This facility is rather easy to add, though there was insufficient time to implement given the compressed DS1 schedule.

Model Visualization Tools. As the model gets larger, it becomes harder to keep in mind all the constraints among the parts of the model. A model visualization tool that displayed a graphic view of the model (or a subset) and the constraints would help the modeler view this information as a whole.

4.3 Large Scale Validation of the Remote Agent Planner

Before any spacecraft is launched, its flight software must be throughly tested and validated. The same is true for autonomous flight software. However, the validation methods used for traditional software are not generally applicable to autonomous software. New methods must be developed.

The planner can generate several thousand different plans, depending on the mission goals, the spacecraft state, goals generated on-board by plan experts and variations on the model parameters. To fully validate the planner, one must be sure that it will generate a correct plan for every one of those possible situations, and that the plan can be executed correctly by the EXEC.

An alternative to generating and testing several thousand plans is to use formal methods to validate the models and to verify that the planner produces plans that are consistent with the model. One approach is to capture the flight rules and other requirements formally as constraints, and ensure that the model is consistent with all of them, and that no constraints have been missed. A related possibility is to convert the models into a human-readable form and have them approved by cognizant system engineers (domain experts).

Tools for automatically generating and validating plans can greatly reduce this cost. One of the tools we considered for DS1 but did not have time to implement was a constraint checker that tested whether the plan satisfied certain correctness constraints. These include the constraints in the model, plus additional constraints derived from flight rules and other operational constraints.

5 Conclusion

DS1 will be the first deep-space spacecraft under autonomous control. The complexity of this domain raised a number of important knowledge acquisition and representation issues, some of which we were able to address and some of which remain open. Issues were also raised by the fast-paced spiral development cycle, the embedding of the planner within the autonomy architecture, and the risk-management requirements of the space flight domain.

These issues are not unique to DS1, and are likely to occur on other projects that require autonomous control of a complex environment. As the role of autonomy increases in space exploration and other areas, so will the importance of finding good solutions to these issues.

6 Acknowledgments

This paper describes work partially performed at the Jet Propulsion Laboratory, California Institute of Technology, under contract from the National Aeronautics and Space Administration. This work would not have been possible without the extraordinary effort and dedication of the rest of the Remote Agent Planning Team: Steve Chien, Charles Fry, Sunil Mohan, Paul Morris, Gregg Rabideau, and David Yan.

References

1. Barry Boehm. A Spiral Model of Software Development and Enhancement. *Computer*, pages 61–72, May 1988.
2. Michael Compton, Helen Stewart, Vinod Baya, Martha Del Alto, Bob Kanefsky, and Jason Vincent. Electronic collaboration for the New Millenium: Internet-based Tools and Techniques for Sharing Information. In *http://ic-www.arc.nasa.gov/ic/projects/nmp-doc/nmp-doc-pres.pdf*, 1997.
3. Per Cederqvist et.al. Concurrent Versions System. In *http://www.loria.fr/ molli/cvs-index.html*, 1996.
4. Oren Etzioni. Acquiring Search Control Knowledge via Static Analysis. *Artificial Intelligence*, 62, 1993.
5. G.M.Brown, D.Bernard, and R.Rasmussen. Attitude and Articulation Control for the Cassini Spacecraft. a fault tolerance overview. In *14th AIAA/IEEE Digital Avionics Conference*, 1995.
6. Barbara Hayes-Roth. An Architecture for Adaptive Intelligent Systems. *Artificial Intelligence*, 72, 1995.
7. IEEE. *Proceedings of the IEEE Aerospace Conference*, Snowmass, CO, 1997.
8. Sanford Krasner and Douglas E. Bernard. Integrating Autonomy Technologies into an Embedded Spacecraft System—Flight Software System Engineering for New Millennium. In *Proceedings of the IEEE Aerospace Conference* [7].
9. Steven Minton. Automatically configuring constraint satisfaction programs: A case study. *Constraints*, 1(1), 1996.
10. Nicola Muscettola. HSTS: Integrating planning and scheduling. In Mark Fox and Monte Zweben, editors, *Intelligent Scheduling*. Morgan Kaufmann, 1994.
11. Nicola Muscettola, Ben Smith, Charles Fry, Steve Chien, Kanna Rajan, Gregg Rabideau, and David Yan. On-Board Planning for New Millennium Deep Space One Autonomy. In *Proceedings of the IEEE Aerospace Conference* [7].
12. Barney Pell, Douglas E. Bernard, Steve A. Chien, Erann Gat, Nicola Muscettola, P. Pandurang Nayak, Michael D. Wagner, and Brian C. Williams. A Remote Agent Prototype for Spacecraft Autonomy. In *Proceedings of the SPIE Conference on Optical Science, Engineering, and Instrumentation*, 1996.
13. Barney Pell, Douglas E. Bernard, Steve A. Chien, Erann Gat, Nicola Muscettola, P. Pandurang Nayak, Michael D. Wagner, and Brian C. Williams. An Autonomous Spacecraft Agent Prototype. In *Proceedings of the First International Conference on Autonomous Agents*. ACM Press, 1997.
14. Barney Pell, Erann Gat, Ron Keesing, Nicola Muscettola, and Ben Smith. Plan Execution for Autonomous Spacecraft. In Louise Pryor, editor, *Procs. of the AAAI Fall Symposium on Plan Execution*. AAAI Press, 1996.
15. M. Tambe, W. Lewis Johnson, R. M. Jones, F. Koss, J. E. Laird, Paul S. Rosenbloom, and K. Schwamb. Intelligent Agents for Interactive Simulation Environments. *AI Magazine*, 16(1):15–39, Spring 1995.
16. Brian C. Williams and P. Pandurang Nayak. A model-based approach to reactive self-configuring systems. In *Procs. of AAAI-96*, pages 971–978, Cambridge, Mass., 1996. AAAI Press.
17. Brian C. Williams and P. Pandurang Nayak. Immobile Robots, AI in the New Millennium. *AI Magazine*, Fall, 1996.

Information Tuning with KARAT:
Capitalizing on Existing Documents

Bidjan Tschaitschian, Andreas Abecker, and Franz Schmalhofer

German Research Center for Artificial Intelligence (DFKI) GmbH
P.O. Box 2080, D-67608 Kaiserslautern, Germany
Phone: ++49 631 205-3484; Fax: ++49 631 205-3210; E-Mail: tschaits@dfki.uni-kl.de

Abstract: Organizations store their information in electronic or paper documents. This information is severely underutilized in the daily work of most organizations. Because there are no effective means to access the documents,
employees do not find relevant information, or are not even aware of its existence. We describe Information Tuning - a first step towards knowledge management in enterprises. Information Tuning capitalizes on existing documents and
enables better exploitation of the contained knowledge by adding the background, context, and meta information which is necessary for making possible
beneficial utilization, sharing, and reuse. We present an Information Tuning
method which evolved from model-based knowledge acquisition from texts, and
illustrate the method with application examples. Information Tuning is supported by the KARAT tool which applies techniques from text analysis and
hypertext technology.

1 Introduction

Enterprise Knowledge Management (cf. [47],[2]) and Organizational Memories (or,
better *Organizational Memory Information Systems* - OMIS) at the core of its support
([42],[39]) are emerging terms in management as well as in the information sciences.
Many successful research prototypes developed by the AI community focus on capturing and dissemination of tacit enterprise knowledge [5] which is manifested, e.g. in
sophisticated, complex design decisions. For instance, remarkable results have been
achieved in capturing design rationale in product development. Here, well-known representation and reasoning methods from knowledge-based systems, case-based reasoning, or issue-based information systems can be successfully applied (see, e.g.
[35],[21]).

On the other hand, for industrial practice, we see an enormous application potential
in somehow complementary efforts: in numerous applications, it is not necessarily the
first and most important step to make explicit and formalize highly sophisticated tacit
knowledge; on the contrary, there *are* already considerable knowledge corpora embodied in electronic and paper archives: in product and project documentation, technical
manuals, lessons-learned archives, best practice databases, personal memos, etc. But,
those existing knowledge assets are rarely used in everyday work. There are no effective means to access the documents, employees do not find relevant information, or are
not aware of its existence. Even if they know the knowledge sources, they cannot
assess their importance and validity in the current situation because they do not know
the context in which the documents have been created (cf. [29],[20],[25]).

We suggest to prepare existing sources for better exploitation and beneficial use of
the knowledge assets by *Information Tuning*. With this method a significant value-

Fig. 1. OMIS Sample Application

added can already be achieved with sparse formal knowledge. In contrast to the traditional knowledge-based approach, we do not encode the whole knowledge in a formal representation, but primarily rely on the existing sources as they are. Formal structures are used for organizing, annotating, and linking together these sources thus enabling their better utilization. This sparse formalization can be compared with parts of the ontological engineering in conventional KBS development, but without filling the concrete application knowledge bases. Furthermore, our formal models have the only purpose of structuring the domain in a way that alleviates later retrieval and reuse. Thus, they do not have to be as "deep, exhaustive, and consistent" as if they were the basis for automated problem solving.

Figure 1 sketches an application scenario we found in a large German software company in the context of building up a Call-Center (cp. [44]). The project goal was to improve dissemination and utilization of the company's product knowledge, which formerly has been documented in voluminous paper folders or depending on individual experience. The example illustrates several observations we found frequently in industrial practice: Typically, the ideal information flow involves many people, with rather different views, performing many tasks in the enterprise; significant parts of the knowledge involved is rapidly changing, e.g. due to new product features; other parts are very informal by nature, e.g. individual experiences. Building, maintaining, and sharing formal representations of such knowledge is often not possible in an economic way. However, a human operator could immediately process the original informal document if she was provided with it in the right situation and probably equipped with some meta information (e.g. about author, date, creation context of the document etc.). On the other hand, in an enterprise there often exists also knowledge which is essentially (semi-)formal by nature, e.g., business process models, software architecture diagrams, catalogues about compatibility relations, error documentation forms, error hierarchies, and so on. Such knowledge can often very easily be prepared to serve for organizing and structuring the more informal parts.

Roughly speaking, we propose to fill a *communication gap* rather than a processing gap for knowledge. The objects to be communicated are existing knowledge sources (texts, documents, ...), the prerequisite for effective communication are formal organization structures, formal annotations, and links between knowledge items. Information Tuning is a pragmatic approach to determining and providing these prerequisites.

We will discuss the task and the method in Section 2. Section 3 describes the KARAT tool for performing Information Tuning in practice. Since the main ("technical") activity is associating and linking together elements of formal models and parts of documents, it is nearby to employ hypertext technology for comfortable handling. Since the main ("semantic") effort is to map knowledge items onto the appropriate formal categories, automatic text categorization techniques are employed for generating suggestions. In Section 4, we present some examples how Information Tuning can act in practice. After some words about implementation issues in Section 5, we conclude with some remarks on related work, limitations, and future work in Section 6.

2 Information Tuning: Task and Method

We propose to accompany information units by the meta-knowledge necessary for:
- *Finding the appropriate portion of relevant knowledge for a task at hand:*
  - The given information sources (typically text documents) must be filtered for minimal autonomous information units. This requires the identification of relevant information and possibly its reformulation for comprehensibility and unambiguity. In this way, valuable information that is buried in large text documents can be extracted for later use.
  - The information units are *classified* according to (several) formal models describing, e.g. the application domain, the enterprise organization, business processes, etc. This multi-criteria organization is central for knowledge utilization because it allows accurate purposeful access. It can also serve as a prerequisite for intelligent conceptual retrieval mechanisms which exploit heuristic knowledge about the formal models structuring the repository.

- *Understanding, interpreting, and evaluating a knowledge item in varying situations:*
  - The information units are augmented by background information about their origin, validity, preconditions, explanations, implicits, importance, etc. This *context explication* can be done, e.g. by annotating with natural language comments, storing the author or modification date, classifying wrt. predefined description/evaluation schemata, ... Thus, essential know-how related to the specific information unit is unveiled and clarified by the organization's employees as users of the approach.
  - Information units can be linked together with especially interpretable hyperlinks (describing, e.g., associations, hints, logical dependencies, time relations, preferable presentation order ...). This reflects the network character of knowledge and facilitates navigation in the information space. Furthermore, it provides means to handle the effects of infomation change and maintain an information repository.

Our approach has been developed for tuning text-based information collections, i.e. setting-up a more intelligent OMIS from a corpus of available documents. However, it can also be used for inserting new information into an existing OMIS. The method can be subdivided into three major phases (see Figure 2): In the *preparation phase* a set of

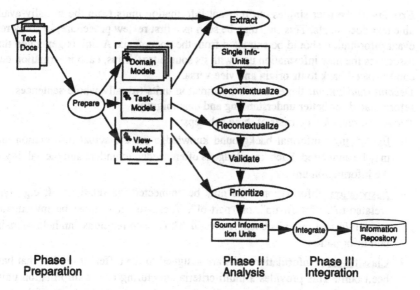

Fig. 2. Overview of the Information Tuning Method

different models is established. Together with initially available texts documents, these models form the input to the *analysis phase* which is decomposed as follows: first of all, separate information units are extracted from the initial texts. These text segments (e.g. whole sentences) are then decontextualized (reformulated) and recontextualized (explained, associated, and classified). This enables a subsequent efficient and effective validation and prioritization of information units. The information units together with the source documents and models are stored in the information repository. Please note that the method does not prescribe a fixed sequence of steps as it might be suggested by the figure. Instead, it describes actions that can be done in several cycles, maybe partly in parallel, partly building on results from prior steps, until an information repository of desired quality (in terms of the needed usefulness and usability) is reached. The *integration phase* comprises storing in the information repository and the various aspects of usage. We discuss the separate phases in some more detail:

Preparation: the set of structuring models has to be established. Basically, one can define arbitrary models which are suited for easing access and utilization of knowledge items. For instance, a view model could reflect the different roles and competencies within an organization, task models might be represented as business process models [31], and domain models could provide meaningful decompositions of different areas or departments within the organization. If surveying the OMIS literature for organizing principles for corporate knowledge competencies, the most prominent approach (by van Heijst et al. [42]) proposes to characterize knowledge items according to the dimensions task, role, and domain. Other authors (see [16]) embed these ideas into the world of business processes and product models.

Analysis: the analysis phase consists of the following five steps:

- *Extraction:* the user singles out relevant information units from the initially available text documents. This step may be seen as a first review procedure, i.e. only relevant information should be extracted from the documents. A link is generated that associates the new information unit with its source text. Thus, each information unit can be traced back to its origin and vice versa.
- *Decontextualization:* the extracted information units (usually whole sentences) are reformulated for better understanding and unambiguity.
- *Recontextualization* consists of three substeps:
  - <u>Explanation</u>: informal background knowledge for the actual information unit may be annotated. Such knowledge is often needed to understand the validity of the information unit.
  - <u>Association</u>: information units may be connected via relations of, e.g., type "related-to", "follow-up", or "part-of". These relations must be investigated when information units become invalid. Thus, such relations can help to maintain information.
  - <u>Classification</u>: information units are assigned to the different models that have been built. This provides a multi-criteria structuring of the information units, e.g. according to business processes, groups of people, departments of the organization etc. Consequently, it enables a multi-criteria retrieval of possibly relevant information.
- *Validation:* information units may be reviewed to detect inconsistencies and identify gaps. The structuring of the information units can now be utilized to retrieve small, manageable subsets of possibly related information and prove consistency and completeness (manually).
- *Prioritizing:* the relevance of an information unit may be judged as "rule", "recommendation", or "optional". Such judgements are often easier to establish when the respective information unit is compared to possibly related information. Again the multi-criteria structuring of the information units allows to retrieve related information.

  Integration: the information units together with the source documents and models are stored in an information repository. This allows for a very flexible utilization of the available information. Several criteria can be combined to retrieve relevant information. Currently, these criteria comprise searching for information units

- with a specific substring in any of their textual descriptions (decontextualized information, explanation)
- from specific (groups of) authors (creators or modifiers)
- with specific priority or a combination of priorities
- that were created or modified on, before, between, or after specific dates
- that have been classified to specific classes of specific models

  When a user needs specific information in his/her current context of work, he/she would select the respective class in his/her task model and retrieve the stored information.

3 Tool Support for Information Tuning

The KARAT tool for Information Tuning mainly builds on technologies:

- The basic technology for realizing comfortable user support, establishment, visualization and handling of complex relationships is *Hypertext*. It is the basic technology for "knowledge editing" at the "syntactic level".
- (Semi-automatic) support for establishing formal models as well as classification and retrieval of information units is given by adapting and integrating techniques and tools from *Information Retrieval* and *Document Analysis and Understanding*. This supports the more "semantic level" of Information Tuning.

3.1 Text Analysis Techniques in KARAT

Text analysis and information retrieval techniques are able to automatically index [18], classify [15] [43] [14], and search [22] natural language texts. Such techniques can be beneficially employed in several phases of the KARAT method: First of all, the user should be supported in the adaptation and enrichment of the different models during the preparation phase. Secondly, fast and sophisticated search mechanisms are needed to enable a quick and thorough exploration of the available text documents. Finally, text analysis techniques may provide suggestions for the classification of information units according to the different models. In the following, we take a closer look at the embedded text analysis techniques with respect to the phases of the KARAT method.

Preparation Phase: In the construction of the different models, information retrieval techniques automatically extract a word-list of relevant terms out of the collection of initially available text documents. Therefore, the texts are analyzed by a morphological component, i.e. the inflected word forms occurring in the text are reduced to their respective stems. Afterwards, a *stop word reduction* utilizes the part-of-speech information to delete irrelevant words. The (most frequent) remaining terms may be used as suggestions for the categories of the models. After the completion of the models, the same automatic indexing techniques are utilized to find keywords (also called *weighted index terms* or *descriptors*) for the categories of the models. Therefore, relevant text sequences are filtered out of the original text documents for each model category, i.e. only paragraphs including the respective category's name are considered. Again, a morphological analysis with stop-word reduction is performed on these text segments. Afterwards, an indexing component performs a *frequency analysis* of all remaining word stems [30] and ranks the terms according to relative or absolute frequency. Finally, the user may modify the resulting list of index terms (e.g. add or delete words) and the remaining keywords are attached to the respective model category. These keywords are employed later in the analysis phase to provide suggestions for the classification of the information units.

Analysis Phase: At present, parsing techniques for deep text understanding are too inefficient and error-prone when applied to complex real world problems. However, *shallow* text analysis techniques may very well be integrated into the *information extraction* and *recontextualization* steps for search and classification tasks.

Extraction: In identifying relevant information units in the initial texts the user needs support to browse the documents and to locate identical, similar, or related text sequences. Therefore, a search engine for single words and morphological word stems is provided. This enables the retrieval of all occurrences of different word forms and word compositions derived from *one* single word stem.

However, for the detection of typical formulations and text phrases a *pattern matcher* is required that matches all occurrences of so-called *text patterns* in the current text. Text patterns may be defined which involve arbitrary nestings of conjunction, disjunction, negation, skip (up to n words) and optionality operators [14].

In addition to these word-based techniques, we also employ a kind of similarity-based search to retrieve text segments which appear to be relevant in a user-defined context. Such a context would be defined by the selection of one or more model categories. Based on the keyword lists for the specific model categories, respective paragraphs of the available text documents can be identified and suggested.

Recontextualization: The central task of the recontextualization step is the classification of the extracted information units according to the previously established models. Here, the problem is distinct from the one of finding similar information in the extraction phase, but the solution is quite similar. In the first case, the model categories (a context) are given and appropriate text segments have to be found while in the second case the information unit is given and respective model categories have to be suggested.

To classify the information units according to the different models, we utilize two distinct text categorization approaches:

- IR-based classification: This classifier is based on ideas from information retrieval [30] and utilizes the lists of keywords gained during the preparation phase. For the classification of the given information unit, its index terms are calculated first. Afterwards, these index terms are matched against the keyword-lists and, for each model and category, weights are calculated according to a weighted-sum classification formula [15]. These weights are normalized by the number of index terms. The winning category is the one with the maximal weight.
- Rule-based classification: The rule-based classifier allows more flexible formulations of features (by going beyond the word-level) and a hierarchical modeling of the underlying class model [43]. Typically, features collected in the current document are used as *initial facts*. These may be single words, morphological word stems, or even text patterns used to capture a word's pragmatics. *Certainty factors* which represent an estimate of the feature's occurrence in the document may be attached to the input features. *Rules* conjoin these features (as rule conditions) with the classes (as rule action) or with concepts (if a hierarchical model is given) which themselves are indicators for the classes. The rules may also be attached with certainty factors, so that the final classification process consists of propagating these certainty factors through the rule network. Final output of the classification are the classes along with certainty factors. The final winning class is the one with the maximal value.

3.2 Hypertext Techniques in KARAT

A variety of different relations between documents, text segments, and models are established following our Information Tuning method. In particular, an information unit is associated with its source text, its natural language explanation, the chosen categories from the different models, and closely related information units (e.g. follow-up information). Hypertext techniques are ideally suited to organize the involved data and their relations. They are applied to construct nodes from the respective texts, model categories, and information units. These nodes are then connected with links according to the existing relations. The resulting hypernet provides means to

- access related information directly (flexible and fast browsing),
- (over-) view interrelated information units graphically,
- keep track of effects of changes (maintenance),
- trace information,
- fade in/out specific pieces of information, ...

Figure 3 illustrates some applications of hypertext taken from an application of the KARAT tool in requirements engineering (see Section 4.2):

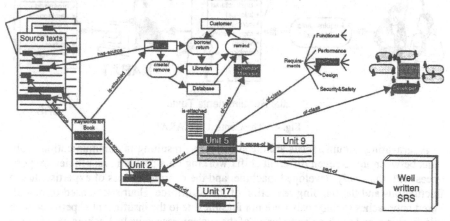

Fig. 3. Examples for the Different Applications of Hypertext in KARAT.

- In the **Preparation Phase**, the chosen category identifiers are linked to the respective occurrences in the word-list of relevant terms and the source texts. Furthermore, each keyword list is attached to the corresponding model category.
- In the **Analysis Phase**, during information extraction, information units retrieved for a certain word or text pattern are automatically linked to the respective text segments in the source text with a "has-source" link; several search results are temporarily linked to each other as a hypertrail to guide the user from one retrieved text segment to the next or previous one. Within recontextualization, the user may provide a natural language explanation, links to related information, and a classification of information units according to the different models. For related information such as follow-ups, hypertext provides means to present them graphically as a subnet with links of just one specific type. For text classification, model categories suggested by the text analysis tools may be graphically presented through highlighting the respective nodes in the models.

4 Information Tuning Sample Applications

To get a better impression of possible tasks and benefits of Information Tuning, we briefly describe two different applications currently under work in our research group. We present two examples in less detail in order to show the variety of problems tackled; if one is interested in more detailed information, he or she is referred to the respective publications.

4.1 Information Tuning for Intelligent Fault Recording

The problem. A modern coal mine employs a newly-developed, highly complex machine in order to reach the highest possible productivity in black-coal mining. It is of vital importance to maximize the technical availability of this machine as any disruption will cause a significant loss in coal production. Consequently, the diagnosis and repair of occuring faults should be performed as fast as possible. Due to the complexity of the machine and the auxiliary units this is a very demanding task (cf. [3]).

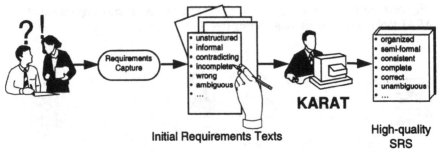

Fig. 4. The Context of KARAT.

Aggravating circumstances are the shift-work - resulting in communication problems between up to seven different shifts working on a problem, insufficient experiences with the newly-developed machine, and the continuous loss of expertise due to fluctuations and the ongoing reduction of the workforce. Heuristics-based or model-based approaches to diagnosis were not feasible due to the insufficient experience with this machine, and the high complexity of the system, respectively. Lacking experiences also led to ill-defined and incomplete cases, hindering the use of CBR technology.

Information Sources. There exist databases and paper-bound fault records documented by numerous people in ordinary text, all of them using different levels of detail and vocabulary. Since diagnosis process, repair actions, and possibly other faults are closely interwoven, the clear definition of "cases" is problematic. As an additional (up to now rather unsuffiently used) information source, there exists technical background information, e.g. wiring diagrams, data tables, assembly instructions.

The models. We found a detailed machine model comprising both the component hierarchy and the functional relations between components a good starting point for organizing observations and activities. Further structures could be put on the fault records using well-known concepts from knowledge-based diagnosis, e.g. a fault hierarchy.

The goal. The system shall provide a comfortable environment for unambiguously documenting diagnosis experiences in a well-structured manner. The recorded entries are still natural language notices; however, the embedding of formal structures allows efficient retrieval and flexible processing. The formal models also link together recorded experiences and supporting (hypertext) background knowledge. Flexible information structuring allows to take into account new tasks or a priori not known relevant context factors. Multi-criteria selection and adequate presentation of information units enables, e.g., identification of weak points in the machine, training of new personnel on old cases, or exploration of optimal diagnosis and repair strategies.

Contributions. On the one hand, KARAT could be used to support the initialization of the system's knowledge-base which is constructed by analyzing the previously used databases and paper-bound fault logs. On the other hand, the KARAT functionality and tool served as a blueprint for design and implementation of the especially tailored software. The system will be operational within 1997.

4.2 Information Tuning for Requirements Engineering

The problem. A high-quality software requirements specification (SRS) is an essential precondition for the development of a successful software system. High-quality in requirements engineering refers to criteria like consistency, completeness, correctness, clarity, structure, unambiguity, minimality, traceability, and maintainability [41].

Information Sources. In the problem analysis and requirements gathering phases, requirements are captured and stored in a number of informal natural language documents which stem from informal technical notes, notes from meetings or phone calls, statements of work, requests for proposal, interviews with customers or users, manuals etc. [46]. Often, requirements in these initial texts are poorly structured, contradicting, incomplete, wrong or unnecessary, ambiguous, hard to follow or validate, etc. In order to fulfill the needed and expected quality of a well-written SRS this information has to be carefully reviewed, revised, and organized (cf. Figure 4).

The models. In the preparation phase, one or more domain models, a requirements taxonomy, and a view model are established. These models are employed later on to organize requirements according to multiple criteria. A specific model (which here replaces the general task models in arbitrary knowledge management applications) is the *requirements taxonomy*. It describes problem-independent categories of requirements, such as performance, interface, functionality, etc. (e.g. IEEE standard 1002-1987 [17]). The *view model* comprises the different roles of all stakeholders involved in the software development process. In addition to roles, a view model may also comprise the individual stakeholders. Three examples of the different kinds of models are shown in Figure 5.

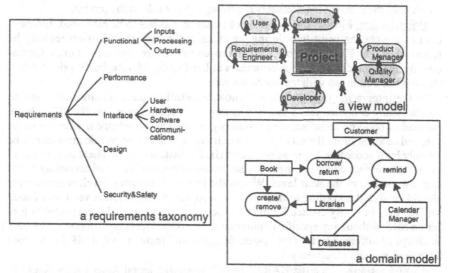

Fig. 5. Examples of a Domain Model, a Requirements Taxonomy, and a View Model.

The goal. Because the main objective of the whole SRS establishment process is to "tune the information" contained in initial requirements texts, all KARAT steps contribute in some way to this goal. We sketch some benefits by linking the respective activities and the concerned quality criteria: The extraction step implicitly includes a validation of requirements with respect to *correctness* and *minimality*. Obviously irrelevant information (e.g. design decisions or implementation details) is already filtered out at this stage. Keeping a link from the extracted text to the source is important to support requirements *traceability*.

Since extracted text segments may not be clear without the context of the source text, a reformulation (decontextualization) of the requirement units is required to improve *clarity* and *unambiguity*.

In the recontextualization step, the requirement units are further explained, associated, and classified by the requirements engineer:

- Natural language annotations may be provided to explain each requirement's need. This will further improve the *clarity* of the requirements.
- Related requirements may be linked either automatically or manually (e.g. causal links to follow-up requirements). Such links enhance the *traceability, modifiability* and *maintainability* of requirements.
- Most importantly, requirements are classified according to the previously established models by choosing respective categories from each model. The resulting requirements *structure* provides means to divide requirements into manageable sets of presumably related requirements that should be reviewed together.

Validation: The previous steps facilitate tests for *consistency* and *completeness* in the validation step. On the one hand, the requirements engineer now starts with a relevant set of requirements without major errors within single units. On the other hand, he can work on small sets of closely related requirements utilizing their model-based, multi-criteria organization. Besides this, he is able to prepare special review documents for specific persons (e.g. a collection of all "user" and "interface" requirements). Thus, the reviewers are not overburdened by the whole set of requirements but have to check only the relevant requirements according to their role in the project.

Prioritization: Finally, the *relevance* of requirements has to be estimated. Independent of the chosen priority ordering we claim that more reliable priorities may be found when (small) sets of closely related requirements are examined at once. Consequently, the structure of the requirements is utilized again. Obviously, the prioritization step may be combined with the validation step.

In the integration phase, the set of (now, hopefully) sound requirements may be automatically compiled into a standard as well as an organization specific SRS scheme (instead of building an information repository) as long as the scheme is reflected in the selected models. From the set of sound requirements, structured text documents can be flexibly built according to pre-selected criteria. For instance, a document may be structured with respect to the requirements taxonomy at the top-level and according to the domain models at the next level. Within the lowest structuring level, requirements should be sorted according to their priorities. Additionally, different versions of such an SRS may be easily created for different persons. Managers and users probably prefer an SRS without any specific requirements from developers or different developers in charge of different parts of the system design would prefer a specific SRS concerned with their specific requirements.

Contributions. Since the KARAT tool (Knowledge-based Assistant for Requirements Analysis at Telekom) was originally developed for software requirements engineering in a leading German telecommunications company, we have the most application experience in this area. The KARAT system prototype is currently used in first field tests in the software development department of our customer company.

5 Implementation

Figure 6 shows some of the KARAT user interface components, namely the document browser, the information browser, and the model editor. We use Netscape Navigator enhanced with a JAVA applet as document browser. Information browser and model editor are implemented in ParcPlace Digitalk VisualWave Smalltalk. Documents, models, and information units are stored and managed in the object-oriented GemStone database. The Hypertext Abstract Machine (HAM) is employed for hypertext management tasks, such as establishing and updating links between information units and the different models. Two text analysis tools implemented in C and C++ [9] are currently coupled to the KARAT kernel. MORPHIC-PLUS is a tool for the inflectional morphological analysis of the German language [24]. With its lexicon size of about 53 000 word stems, it reaches a good word coverage. The INFOCLAS2 system includes an automatic indexing component with different weighting functions as well as a word-based text classification component [15].

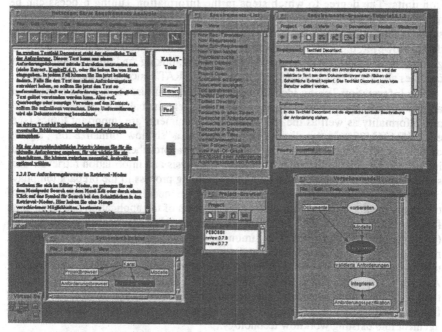

Fig. 6. Screenshot of the KARAT Tool With Document Browser, Information Browser, and Models.

6 Summary

A core component of systematically accomplished Knowledge Management in enterprises is an Organizational Memory Information System which captures, preserves, updates, disseminates, retrieves, and actively reminds of enterprise-critical information. Our experiences strongly suggest that (among others) the need for deeply interwoven handling of data, formal knowledge, and documents, a still unchanged predominance of informal knowledge representations and text-based documents, and the need for minimal up-front knowledge engineering for system development are key properties of feasible solutions in industrial practice [20]. Regarding these practical constraints, we presented a pragmatic approach to preparing existing text-based information collections for a better systematic exploitation. The approach is heavily influenced by prior work in knowledge acquisition from texts and cooperative knowledge evolution (cf., e.g., [28],[32],[33]), but its ultimate goal is not the full formalization of some corpus of knowledge, but adding that portion of formal and meta knowledge which is necessary for successful sharing and reuse.

The model-based classification of information units with respect to multiple criteria is a core issue of our approach. The underlying knowledge acquisition method takes informal documents as input and guides a user in the Information Tuning process. Active assistance in this process of extraction, structurization, and utilization of information from texts is given by the KARAT tool which employs text analysis techniques for information extraction and text categorization in combination with hypertext techniques for a flexible, user-centered handling of text documents, models, and information units. The degree to which steps in the Information Tuning process can be automated is highly application specific. At present, we do not plan to fully automate subtasks since this would not be feasible in the applications we have investigated in depth. However, the tool can provide useful suggestions, and even without such suggestions the comfortable interface with its browsing, linking, and information retrieval facilities already makes a strong contribution to KARAT's success in the applications.

The Information Tuning idea fits very well in recent discussions and research in application-oriented Knowledge Management, where the balance between formality and informality as well as the role of existing documents are important topics (see, e.g., [35],[36],[37]). In this discussion, we promote a "shallow formalization", a point of view which - compared with deep understanding approaches - showed also convincing practical results in the areas of document analysis and information retrieval. This shallow approach alleviates also the model-building process in the preparation phase of Information Tuning. Of course, the quality of the models determines the quality of the whole results. However, an ontological analysis of the application has to be done for *each* knowledge-based system, but, maybe for other approaches in more depth (what we must do has much in common with what van Heijst *et al.* call a missing methodology for ontology building at the *macro* level [42]). Our applications showed that one can already achieve good results with rather simple, straight-forward models. Another interesting point is the minimization of up-front knowledge engineering for the preparation phase through building on existing information sources. The use of business process models seems a promising approach for embedding Knowledge Management into existing workflow technology.

Our approach taps into a growing flow of interest on meta knowledge for information finding and use. So, we will clarify whether helpful advice for designing and filling the structuring models could also come from fundamental considerations about meta knowledge as e.g. done by Guha with his Meta Content Format (MCF [13]), or from areas like Digital Libraries [6].

Future work for further developing the Information Tuning method could investigate the question how much "semantics" can be given to models and links and how those can be exploited (as, e.g., done in issue-based information systems [35]). A modest form could be to allow the user to formulate constraints over models, e.g. that after Information Tuning each information unit associated to a certain concept in a certain model must be linked (with a certain link type) to some information unit associated to some other certain concept in some other model. However, we regard it an important property of our approach that we aim at reasonably good results with cheap effort instead of extremely good results at high costs. In this trade-off, it is not easy to decide how much expressive power should be provided at the cost of increased modeling effort and more complex system handling.

Another topic of our future work is the role of CSCW: In the acquisition of organization-specific information from available text documents several people may be able to beneficially contribute. The KARAT tool allows for collaboration between different people in both the acquisition and the utilization of information. All data are stored and managed by an object-oriented database. Documents, models, and information units may be read by the whole personnel of a company. Changes to a specific information unit may only be done by a project leader or the creator of that information unit. Nevertheless, other people should have the opportunity to comment each information unit. Therefore, a simple messaging and a more specific information annotation component have been integrated into the KARAT tool. With the annotation component the user can change (a copy of) each information unit and send it as suggestion to the creator or project leader. Furthermore, the KARAT tool gives the user direct access to text- and voice-based talk tools. The CSCW functionality enables an efficient and effective communication between several users of the system.

7 References

[1] A. Abecker, A. Bernardi, K. Hinkelmann, O. Kühn, and M. Sintek. Towards a Well-Founded Technology for Organizational Memories. *In: [12]*, 1997.

[2] A. Abecker, St. Decker, K. Hinkelmann, and U. Reimer. *Knowledge-Based Systems for Knowledge Management in Enterprises.* Workshop at the 21st Annual German Conf. on AI (KI-97), Freiburg, Germany, September 1997.

[3] A. Bernardi, M. Sintek, and A. Abecker. Combining Artificial Intelligence, Database Technology, and Hypermedia for Intelligent Fault Recording. *Submitted.* April 1997.

[4] G. Bruno. *Model-Based Software Engineering.* Chapman & Hall, 1995.

[5] Choo Chun Wei. Information Management for the Intelligent Organization: Roles and Implications for the Information Professions. 1995.

[6] D. Clay, S. Geffner, J. Gottsegen, B. Gritton, and T. Smith. A General Framework for Constructing Conceptual Models of Metadata in Digital Libraries. *In: First IEEE Metadata Conference, Silver Spring, Maryland, USA.* April 1996.

[7] A. M. Davis. *Software Requirements, Objects, Functions and States.* Englewood Cliffs, NJ: Prentice Hall, 1993.

[8] H. S. Delugach. Analyzing Multiple Views of Software Requirements. In Nagle, Gerholz, and Eklund (Eds.), *Conceptual Structures - Current Research and Practice*, Ellis Horwood Limited, Chichester, England, 1992.

[9] A. Dengel, R. Bleisinger, F. Fein, R. Hoch, F. Hönes, and M. Malburg. Office-MAID — A System for Office Mail Analysis, Interpretation and Delivery. *Proc. of First International Workshop on Document Analysis Systems (DAS'94)*, pages 253-275, Kaiserslautern, Germany, October 18–20 1994.

[10] M. Dorfman and R. Thayer (Eds.). *Standards, Guidelines, and Examples of System and Software Requirements Engineering.* Washington, D.C.: IEEE Computer Science Press, 1990.

[11] A. P. Gabb and D. E. Henderson. *Navy Specification Study Report 3: Requirements and Specification (DSTO-TR-0192).* Salisbury, South Australia: DSTO Electronics and Surveillance Research Laboratory, 1995.

[12] B. Gaines, M. A. Musen, et al. (eds.). *AAAI Spring Symposium Artificial Intelligence in Knowledge Management.* Stanford University, March, 1997.

[13] R.V. Guha. Towards a theory of meta-content.
http://mcf.research.apple.com/mc.html

[14] P. J. Hayes, P. M. Andersen, I. B. Nirenburg, and L. M. Schmandt. TCS: A Shell for Content-Based Text Categorization, *Proc. of 6th Conference on AI Applications*, pages 320-326, Santa Barbara, CA, 1990.

[15] R. Hoch. Using IR Techniques for Text Classification in Document Analysis. *Proc. of 17th International Conference on Research and Development in Information Retrieval (SIGIR'94)*, pages 31-40, Dublin City, Ireland, July 3-6 1994.

[16] J. Hofer-Alfeis and S. Klabunde. Approaches to Managing the Lessons Learned Cycle. *In: [47]*. 1996.

[17] IEEE Standards Collection: Software Engineering. IEEE, 1993.

[18] P. S. Jacobs. *Text-Based Intelligent Systems: Current Research and Practice in Information Retrieval*. Lawrence Erlbaum, Hillsdale, 1992.

[19] Knowledge Systems Laboratory, Institute for Information Technology, National Research Council Canada. *FuzzyCLIPS Version 6.02A User's Guide*. 1994.

[20] O. Kühn and A. Abecker. Corporate Memories for Knowledge Management in Industrial Practice: Prospects and Challenges. *Journal of Universal Computer Science*. Springer Verlag, 1997. *To appear.*

[21] O. Kühn and B. Höfling. Conserving Corporate Knowledge for Crankshaft Design. *In: Seventh International Conference on Industrial & Engineering Applications of Artifical Intelligence & Expert Systems (IEA/AIE'94)*, Gordon and Breach Science Publishers. Also as DFKI RR-94-08. 1994

[22] J. Liang and J. D. Palmer. A Pattern Matching and Clustering Based Approach for Supporting Requirements Transformation. *Proc. of the First International Conference on Requirements Engineering (ICRE '94)*, April 1994.

[23] D. Lukose. Knowledge Management Using MODEL-ECS. *In: [12]*, 1997.

[24] O. Lutzy. *Morphic-Plus: Ein morphologisches Analyseprogramm für die deutsche Flexionsmorphologie und Komposita-Analyse*. DFKI Document D-95-07 (in German).

[25] Marble Associates *Inc. Leveraging Knowledge through a Corporate Memory Infrastructure*. April 1994.

[26] J. A. McDermid. *Software Engineer's Reference Book*. Oxford: Butterworth Heinemann Ltd., 1991.

[27] J. A. McDermid, A. Vickers, and B. Whittle. Requirements Elicitation and Analysis: Goals, Problems and Approaches. *Workshop on Requirements Elicitation for Software-based Systems (RESS)*, Keele, England, July 12-14 1994.

[28] J.-U. Möller. Knowledge Acquisition from texts. *Proc. of the European Knowledge Acquisition Workshop (EKAW'88)*, Gesellschaft für Mathematik und Datenverarbeitung mbH, Sankt Augustin, Germany, 1988.

[29] K. Romhardt. Processes of Knowledge Preservation: Away from a Technology Dominated Approach. *In: [2]*. 1997. *To appear.*

[30] G. Salton and M. J. McGill. *Introduction to Modern Information Retrieval*. New York: McGraw Hill, 1983.

[31] A.-W. Scheer. *Architektur integrierter Informationssysteme, Grundlagen der Unternehmensmodellierung*. 2nd edition, Springer Verlag, 1992.

[32] F. Schmalhofer and B. Tschaitschian. Cooperative Knowledge Evolution for Complex Domains. *In: G. Tecuci and Y. Kodratoff (eds). Machine Learning and Knowledge Acquisition - Integrated Approaches*. Academic Press, 1995.

[33] G. Schmidt. *Modellbasierte, interaktive Wissensakquisition und Dokumentation von Domänenwissen (MIKADO), DISKI Vol. 90, infix Verlag*, 1995.

[34] M. L. G. Shaw and B. Gaines. Knowledge and Requirements Engineering. *Proc. of the 10th Banff Knowledge Acquisition for Knowledge-Based Systems Workshop*, Banff, Alberta, Canada, 1995.

[35] S. B. Shum. Representing Hard-to-Formalise, Contextualised, Multidisciplinary, Organisational Knowledge. *In: [12]*, 1997.

[36] S. B. Shum. Balancing Formality with Informality: User-Centred Requirements for Knowledge Management Technologies. *In: [12]*, 1997.

[37] D. Skuce. Hybrid KM: Integrating Documents, Knowledge Bases, and the Web. *In: [12]*, 1997.

[38] I. Sommerville. *Software Engineering*. Workingham, England: Addison Wesley, 1992.

[39] E. W. Stein and V. Zwass. Actualizing Organizational Memory With Information Technology. *Information Systems Research* Vol. 6, No. 2: 85-117, 1995.

[40] B. Tschaitschian, I. John, C. Wenzel. Integrating Knowledge Acquisition and Text Analysis for Requirements Engineering. *Internal Report*. DFKI, 1996.

[41] B. Tschaitschian, C. Wenzel, and I. John. Tuning the quality of informal software requirements with KARAT.. *In: E. Dubois, L. Opdahl, and K. Pohl (eds.). REFSQ'97: Third Int. Workshop on Requirements Engineering: Foundation for Software Quality*. Held at CAiSE*97, Barcelona, 1997.

[42] G. van Heijst, R. van der Spek, and E. Kruizinga. Organizing Corporate Memories. *Tenth Knowledge Acquisition for Knowledge-Based Systems Workshop KAW'96*. November 1996.

[43] C. Wenzel and R. Hoch. Text Categorization of Scanned Documents Applying a Rule-based Approach. *Proc. of the Fourth Annual Symposium on Document Analysis and Information Retrieval (SDAIR'95)*, pages 333-346, 1995.

[44] St. Wess: Intelligent Systems for Customer Support: Case-Based Reasoning in Help-Desk and Call-Center Applications. *In: [2]*. 1997. *To appear.*

[45] B. J. Wielinga, A. T. Schreiber, and J. A. Breuker. KADS: A Modelling Approach to Knowledge Engineering. Knowledge Acquisition, 4(1), 1992.

[46] D. P. Wood, M. G. Christel, and S. M. Stevens. A Multimedia Approach to Requirements Capture and Modeling. *Proc. of the First International Conference on Requirements Engineering (ICRE '94)*, pages 53-56, Colorado Springs, CO, April 18-22 1994.

[47] M. Wolf and U. Reimer (eds). *PAKM-96: First Int. Conference on Practical Aspects of Knowledge Management*. Basel, Switzerland, October 1996.

Syntactic Parsing as a Knowledge Acquisition Problem

Sean Wallis and Gerry Nelson

Department of English (Survey of English Usage),
University College London, Gower Street, London, UK.
[s.wallis, g.nelson]@ucl.ac.uk

Abstract. Corpus linguistics involves the construction and annotation of large databases of text from spoken and written language. These have applications in NLP and taught grammar. This annotation represents the problem of the KA "bottleneck" in a new application area. This paper introduces parse checking as a KA problem, and compares it to other tree-oriented KA methodologies such as laddering and clustering. It argues that corpus linguistics represents a significant application area for KA. The laddering tools discussed here have been used to process thousands of tree structures. The paper compares two tools in use on the ICE-GB corpus. One tool, ICE Tree II, exploits the structure of grammatical trees more fully than the other. Timing results show a main learning effect which dominates any difference comparison. However, the more integrated tool reduces the scope for error.

1   Introduction

In the past two or three decades, the increasing availability and sophistication of computation has given birth to a new methodology in linguistic research. *Corpus linguistics* is based on the collection, storage, analysis and retrieval of large databases of naturally occurring speech and writing. Such databases can yield insights into language which have hitherto been unavailable.

In this field, grammarians are motivated by the prospect of improving published grammars by including data from spoken English (e.g., Greenbaum, 1996a). This has traditionally received little attention compared with its written counterpart. Corpus based research provides a platform for the collection and analysis of English "as she is spoke." For natural language processing researchers, it offers possibilities for improving automatic parsers.

Several corpus-based projects are being carried out at present, especially in English linguistics. These include the International Corpus of English (ICE; Greenbaum, 1996b), the British National Corpus (BNC; Burnage and Dunlop, 1992) and the English component of the EU LE-PAROLE project[1]. Corpora do not consist of text alone. Additional structural information describing aspects of the text, broadly termed *annotation*, is essential to the context. For grammarians and NLP researchers, it is necessary to annotate text syntactically: for every sentence in the corpus, a tree analysis should be provided.

However, significant corpora are large, and their syntactic annotation is time-consuming. The necessary size for a specific application is geared to its use, but for most research purposes, the bigger the corpus is, the better. Automatic methods of annotation are required, since manual annotation alone is "slow, expensive and difficult" (EAGLES, 1996).

---

[1] LE-PAROLE can be found on "http://www2.echo.lu/langeng/en/le2/le-parole/le-parole.html".

Yet automatic methods are themselves flawed. The only plausible solution is a combination of automatic parsing and manual checking. This classic Catch-22 is the knowledge acquisition (KA) "bottleneck".

For the KA community, parse-checking represents a significant application. The primary reason is simply scale. This paper describes the construction, annotation and checking of a one million word corpus, consisting of around 84,000 trees, all of which must be manually checked. It describes an empirical comparison of times to perform a KA task using two distinct tools employing different KA assumptions.

This paper is organised along the following lines. We introduce the ICE project and summarise the annotation scheme. We then motivate parse checking as a specifically KA problem and outline the structural implications that derive from this (§3). Then we introduce two tree editing tools (ICE Tree and ICE Tree II), employing the observations from the previous section. In §5, we summarise an empirical evaluation of these two tools for the annotation process. We then discuss the results and make some salutary points on the nature of such an evaluation in the conclusions.

2 The ICE Project

The International Corpus of English (ICE) is coordinated by the Survey of English Usage, University College London (Greenbaum, 1992). ICE is a collaborative project involving teams in 18 countries where English is spoken as a first or an official second language. Each team is collecting a corpus of one million words (500 × 2,000-word text samples) of its own national or regional variety of English, both written and spoken. The aim of the project is to provide research material for comparative studies of English throughout the world. The annotation tools and representation schemes applied to the corpora have been developed at the Survey of English Usage. Their application to the British corpus (ICE-GB), as described in this paper, may be seen as a pilot project for ICE as a whole.

There are two major stages in syntactically annotating ICE corpora. The first is *grammatical tagging*, a semi-automatic process which assigns a wordclass label or *tag* to every word in the corpus (Greenbaum and Ni, 1996). Wordclass tags consist of the wordclass itself, such as *noun*, followed by additional refining features in parentheses. These indicate whether a noun, for instance, is *common* or *proper*, *singular* or *plural*. The tag for a common, singular noun is N(com, sing).

The second stage is *syntactic parsing*. Using the grammatical tags assigned during the first stage, and a complex formal grammar, the parsing algorithm analyses the syntactic structure of each sentence, determining its constituents, the relations between constituents, and their internal structure. This level of analysis considers groups of words – phrases and clauses – and the hierarchical relations between them.

The formal grammar defines the possible syntactic roles of each constituent. For example, noun phrases in English can perform a number of roles, including subject (*The man* is coming), object (*I saw the man*), and adverbial (*I saw him the day before yesterday*). Conversely, these roles may be performed by a number of constituent types. While the role of subject is most commonly performed by a noun phrase, as in *The man* is coming, it can also be performed by a clause (*Leaving home* is traumatic). In the ICE parsing scheme, the roles of subject, object, etc., are known as *functions*, and their realizations in a particular sentence are known as *categories*. So in *I saw the man*, "*I*" has the function of subject, SU, and the category of noun phrase, NP. This noun phrase is further analysed as a noun phrase head, NPHD, with the category of singular, personal pronoun, PRON(pers, sing).

We can express this as "SU:NP ——— NPHD:PRON(pers, sing) ······ *I*" where each node is labelled *<function>*:*<category>*. Syntactic structure is represented as a syntactic tree. The tree for the sentence *I saw the man* is drawn in figure 1.

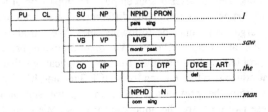

Fig. 1. ICE syntactic annotation for *I saw the man*

For each of the 84,000 sentences in the ICE-GB corpus, a single syntax tree is produced by the parsing algorithm. However, parsed output may be erroneous for a number of reasons.

- *Incorrect tagging.* The original assignment of tags may be incorrect, with consequential problems in the parse.
- *Ambiguous interpretation.* In some cases several tree structures are valid for a particular sentence.
- *Incomplete parsing.* Sometimes the parser will fail to produce a complete and correct analysis. This occurs most frequently when it attempts to parse informal spoken English, where it may encounter unfamiliar structures.

Whatever the source of an error, the only recourse is to manual intervention.

3   Syntactic parsing as a KA problem

3.1   Corpus annotation and the KA cycle

Knowledge acquisition has often been considered a combination of algorithm and human effort. Automatic approaches to knowledge generalisation, such as *machine learning* (Major and Shadbolt, 1992), *data mining* (Cupit and Shadbolt, 1996) and *textual extraction* (Bowden et al., 1996), have complemented elicitation of expertise. Knowledge acquisition, to paraphrase (Wallis and Shadbolt, 1993), is "algorithm-mediated elicitation."

Rule acquisition in KA

The integration of inductive rule learning and elicitation, for example, may be summarised by the hierarchical two space process of cyclic interactions in figure 2a. This is a hierarchical generalisation of two-space models of learning (Michalski and Stepp, 1983) and elicitation. The major interaction is, naturally, between expert and computer – the 'representation' and 'formalisation' spaces respectively. Both major spaces contain secondary processes relating 'instance' and 'generalisation' spaces.

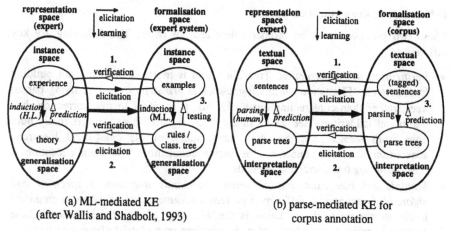

(a) ML-mediated KE
(after Wallis and Shadbolt, 1993)

(b) parse-mediated KE for
corpus annotation

Fig. 2. Two cyclic models of KA

The virtue of this figure is that it illustrates the relation between two distinct levels of elicitation. Of *instances*, whereby data elements are acquired; and of *generalisations*, whereby simple generalised structure is acquired (e.g., a set of rules or a classification tree). Induction proposes structure from patterns in the instance space. Introducing simple structure into the instance space, such as hierarchical variables (Wallis, 1997) or population probability estimates, can improve the accuracy and the meaningfulness of the inductive process.

There are therefore three subprocesses in this model that are worthy of research within the auspices of KA.

1. The elicitation of instances.
2. The elicitation of instance generalisations.
3. The biasing of learning for KA to exploit archetypal or structured instances.

Each subprocess has to be considered in the light of the overall process since successfully elicited instance structure becomes the raw material for induction.

Corpus annotation

Compare this with the process of parse-annotating corpora (figure 2b). Parsing is a non-trivial analytic method which generates a compositional tree structure containing syntactic functions and superordinate categorisation. Real parsers are imperfect and must be supported by human intervention, within (Leech and Garside, 1991) or after the process (Marcus et al., 1993). Emphasising that the parse process is cyclic underlines the point that verified trees can be used to improve future parsing.

We therefore require an integrated approach, analogous to learning-mediated KE. This implies research effort in three complementary areas:

1. The elicitation of tagged sentences.
2. The elicitation of tree structures.
3. Parsing algorithms.

The focus of this paper is point (2), mediated by this context.

Differences in the acquisition process

These two processes may be brothers: they are not twins. The following are key differences.

- *Verification not construction.* Tree elicitation is mostly correction, not building from scratch. 'Elicitation' in this framework is *primarily* one of verifying parsed trees, rather than constructing anew. (In this, it is closer to rule correction than traditional laddering – see §3.3.) In the study reported here, experts rarely built trees from scratch. On the other hand, much of the categorical hierarchy acquisition literature concerns constructive acquisition. The main exception is post-clustering tree correction methods.
- *Multiple schemes exist, but consistency demands that one is specified and enforced.* Grammarians differ over preferred schemes. One of the main empirical issues in grammatical annotation is the adequacy of the representation. These arguments relate to the choice of node labelling or preferred clause construction. They are not critical aspects for general KA or for a tree elicitation tool.
- *Representation schemes are complex and must be learned.* The corollary to the previous point is that the process of checking texts is itself highly skilled. Parse checking is labour intensive, even with computer support. Understanding any single grammatical scheme in its totality and applying it consistently is difficult.
- *Interpretation is contextual, not global.* Conflicting valid interpretations of a single sentence may exist. Here the recourse must be to context, which therefore must be available.

Other differences arise because of differing representational constraints. To clarify this argument we contrast syntax trees with their commonest KA relative, *categorical hierarchies.*

3.2   Comparing syntactic and categorical hierarchies

A successful acquisition tool should render structural constraints explicit in the interface and gainfully exploit them to simplify the elicitation process.

Syntactic hierarchies

A syntactic hierarchy is a compositional hierarchy of sentence structure. It is a hierarchy consisting entirely of 'part-of' relations, which collectively define clause structure and necessarily form a strict acyclic tree (figure 3a).

As with categorical hierarchies, a form of 'inheritance' is possible. This is *not* downward default inheritance: a component is a part of the whole, and properties of the whole are not ascribable to a particular part. Rather, this type of inheritance is from part to whole, *upwards*, mediated by specific knowledge. For example, a car engine does not formally 'inherit' the properties of its components, but by convention one may refer to the "cylinder capacity of the engine" as a property inherited from its cylinders. Likewise, some features of a main clause may be inherited by the overall parse unit. This suggests heuristic or knowledge based support for inheritance only.

Syntactic hierarchies annotate a sentence, and are therefore strongly constrained by its presence. Four key global properties of these trees are summarised by figure 3. The

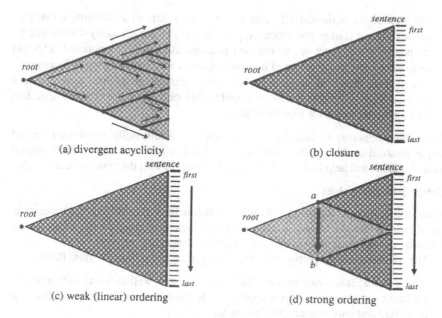

(a) divergent acyclicity   (b) closure

(c) weak (linear) ordering   (d) strong ordering

Fig. 3. Global properties of syntax trees

sentence is tagged by the leaf nodes of the tree, and it is therefore closed. This entails, not merely linear ordering over the tags – but, if crossing relations are to be avoided – strong ordering as well.

Strong ordering (figure 3d) is defined as the following property:-

> "For any parent node, *a*, preceding its immediate sibling, *b*, the last node covered by *a* precedes the first node covered by *b*."

Strong ordering should be assumed for the following reasons. Corpus-based grammar involves commentary on sentences *as they are*, not on how grammarians would idealise them. Therefore unexpected word flow should be explained within the annotation scheme, not by allowing relations to flow everywhere.

Overlapping sentences (mostly in spoken conversation) are separated into different utterances and analysed separately.

Additional constraints limit the content of each node. To summarise, the linguistic constraints on syntactic hierarchies are as follows.

1. *Acyclic tree structure.* The trees are "clean": divergent acyclic trees. No provision for assigning multiple parents to one node is necessary.
2. *Closure.* Tree structures are enclosed between a fixed root node and the set of leaf nodes. The former is the parse unit node, the latter comprises the tagged sentence. It is therefore closed before and after the sentence. Rather than 'laddering up' or 'laddering down,' one 'ladders between' the parse unit root and the sentence.
3. *Strong ordering.* The sentence imposes a strong ordering over the tree and its constituents.

4. *Intra-nodal restrictions.* Each node in the tree consists of a function, a category and a series of feature properties. Applicable features are primarily determined by the category, and function and category pairs are also similarly restricted. This can be used to provide a short set of options consistent with the category or function.

5. *Inheritance.* Since it is a form of compositional hierarchy, some upward compositional inheritance may be possible, but only on a heuristically specified basis. This is an area for future research.

These constraints may be used by an elicitation tool. Additionally, previously elicited corpus material could be used (using a form of case-based retrieval) to both support parse decisions and help linguists familiarise themselves with the grammatical scheme.

Categorical hierarchies

Much of the work on acquiring knowledge of hierarchical information has focused on *categorical hierarchies*, that is, abstracted typological hierarchies. In a categorical hierarchy the elements are related by directional subcategory relations.

The following are properties of "clean" categorical hierarchies (Wallis, 1997).

1. *Well-defined subcategorisation.* Subcategories are well-defined and mutually exclusive, not fuzzy or overlapping. It follows that multiple parenthood is prevented and only true acyclic trees result.

2. *Explicit enumeration.* The enumeration of subcategories is explicit: it is known whether any list of children exhausts the set of possibilities at any point.

3. *Meaningfulness.* Each element in a categorical hierarchy represents a real and meaningful set of instances in the world. Laddering down is therefore the introduction of *at least two* new non-empty subsets at any point: the set of instances where x is true and the set where x is false.

4. *Differentiation.* Sets implicitly have a *differentia*, a differentiating attribute (in the above case, x), the properties of which vary with the subcategory.

5. *Inheritance.* If each class value is considered as an idealised type, or *frame* (Minsky, 1975), then frame properties may be inherited downwards unless locally contradicted, using a version of *default logic* (Etherington and Reiter, 1983). Alternatively, a *monotonic* representation limits the assignment of properties to any class to properties that are true for every member of the class.

6. *Optional ordering.* Class values may be explicitly mapped to an appropriate numeric axis: discrete (such as integers) or continuous (reals). This renders a hierarchy of kind as a hierarchy of scale and imposes a similar strong ordering on the tree as the anchoring of syntax trees in sentences.

In summary, like grammatical trees, clean categorical hierarchies are *strict trees* (acyclic, directed and divergent). They may optionally be ordered onto a scale, in which case mutual exclusivity requires that they are *strongly ordered*. However they are only closed if mapped onto a closed discrete numeric range. Usually one can extend the range by introducing elements before or after the current extent; and further subdivide leaf categories.

3.3 Eliciting categorical hierarchies

A number of methods have been proposed for the elicitation of structured information, including computer implementations as *tools*. To contrast these we consider three basic questions regarding the knowledge representation.

- *Typology of relations.* What do the relations between elements mean, e.g., are they categorical or arbitrary ? Alternatively, are relations not elicited but indirectly emergent from a clustering algorithm ?
- *Typology of nodes.* Are all the elements in the structure of one type or of several ?
- *Structural properties.* Is the overall structure a tree or a graph (can it be cyclic) ?

We could consider the minimal set of techniques specifically aimed at well-defined hierarchies. This would be a mistake, however, if by doing so we ignored other possible techniques and their possible adaptation. The table below surveys a collection of possibly relevant techniques. Of these, three elicit acyclic categorical hierarchies (multiple-parent allocation is an awkward addition).

The first of these is laddering by protocols, or hierarchically-organised structured interviewing (Corbridge et al., 1994; Major and Reichgelt, 1990). Elicitation proceeds in a general-to-specific or a specific-to-general fashion, driven by automatically formulated questions. The computer generated protocols make it more restrictive than a free-form technique, rather they attempt to direct the expert.

An alternative to this is the direct-manipulation free-form approach, where the aim is to physically arrange dissociated elements in the hierarchy, establishing links. The SET workbench (Paskiewicz et al., 1991), for example, provides a laddering tool using a 'drag-and-drop' procedure. One elicits concepts and arranges them.

These two forms of laddering are complementary. Protocols are often preferred for tree construction. They are ideal for an expert working alone who is unfamiliar with the idea of laddering. They are less ideal for working with an existing hierarchy.

The "spider map" (Jonassen et al., 1993) is a radially-presented tree, constructed from the centre outwards. Although described as a pen-and-paper method, it could be implemented as simply a different laddering visualisation.

Repertory grid systems generate 'dendrogram' cluster hierarchies from strictly constrained (ordered, fixed-range) instances that are first elicited. This hierarchical

KA technique	relations	nodes	structure
laddering* spider maps	categorical	one	tree
semantic nets causal interaction maps	named	multiple	graph
pattern notes	arbitrary	multiple	graph
tree constructions	arbitrary	multiple	tree
ordered tree technique	arbitrary	either	tree
content structures	arbitrary	one	graph
repertory grid analysis*	clustered	one	tree
PathFinder Nets	clustered	one	graph

Fig. 4. Elicitation techniques for structural knowledge
(those not marked '*' are surveyed from Jonassen et al., 1993)

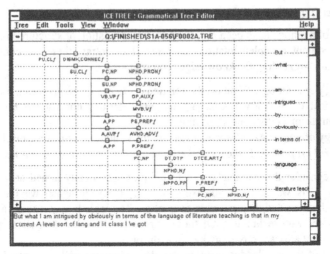

Fig. 5. ICE Tree I on an example sentence

division of elements may be used as a basis for a clean domain typology. The result must inevitably be verified, requiring an editing tool. The remaining techniques listed are difficult to limit to simple category relations (Wallis, 1997).

An important contrast is between construction and verification tools. Numerous methods can arrive at an approximate tree (with differing degrees of completeness), but the final structure can only be properly corrected by direct editing.

4   ICE Tree II – a KA tool for syntactic trees

We first introduce ICE Tree I – the predecessor of ICE Tree II. This is a 'naive' tree editor in that it involves no linguistic constraints, either to the visualisation or user interface. We then briefly summarise and discuss ICE Tree II, a tool redesigned around these constraints. Both programs were written for 80386+ PC-compatibles in Windows 3.1. Both used the same ICE annotation scheme on similar data[2].

4.1   Version 1: a naive tree editor

ICE Tree I (Quinn and Porter, 1996) uses an explicit tracing grid to place and locate nodes, which scrolls within a window. The sentence is placed on the right of the grid. The user interface is based on a Cartesian 'drawing' analogy – the grid indicates 'drafting lines' on a worksheet (see figure 5). A second window shows the sentence.

The first problem arises with deep trees. Beyond a depth of 8 nodes it is impossible to see the sentence alongside all the tree elements describing it. One reason for this is simply unscalability. But this is viewing the problem within a drawing framework. The grid dominates the tree; the sentence is tied to the grid.

This drawing analogy had other repercussions. Elements could be placed on the grid without being placed in the tree; a second operation was required to add them to the tree. The grid, rather than the tree, directed elicitation.

---

[2] ICE Tree II is available from the Survey of English Usage. A time-limited demonstration version is available across the Internet via "http://www.ucl.ac.uk/english-usage/".

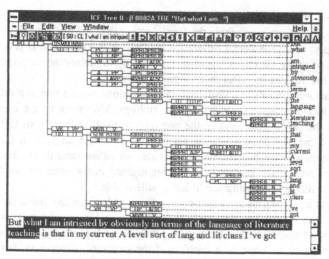

Fig. 6. ICE Tree II on the same sentence

Only one linguistic constraint is applied in ICE Tree I: function and category consistency. Problems due to the grid include:

- *Operation complexity.* A simple 'move' operation can involve a mode change, a pair of selections and a second mode change back.
- *Indirect operations.* The corollary to the first point is that some operations are filtered through the drawing perspective when they are intuitively logical (e.g., placing a node on the grid and connecting it, rather than placing it in the tree).
- *Inexplicit visualisation.* The corresponding effect on visualisation is one that does not reveal illegalities. Crossed or potentially cyclic links could be introduced and are hidden by the visualisation.

Finally, at some point an illegal tree would have to be constrained to a legal representation, typically when saved to file. A forgiving interface allows for undetected errors to be introduced. The inevitable consequence: missing data and potentially scrambled files. Users persevered but a rethink was required.

The primary lesson is to base the tool around the tree structure, rather than another layer with other properties, like a grid. If we ensure that this tree is always in a legal state then a clear visualisation is possible. A legal tree must conform to the linguistic constraints in §3.2. How can these be implemented effectively ?

4.2   Version 2: a radical redesign

The visualisation in the ICE Tree II editor is based around the *tree* itself. Initially, the tree structure spans the entire window and is scaled to fit. It is drawn as a series of connected 'cards', similar to laddering tools such as ALTO (Major and Reichgelt, 1990) or the SET laddering tool (Paskiewicz et al., 1991). The sentence is drawn separately as a 'ruler' across the leaves.

Aspects of the style of presentation can be simply altered but the visualisation integrity is maintained. For familiarity's sake, an initial setting is similar to version 1 (justified first-most, oriented left-to-right). The only major stylistic difference is the display of nodal information within the 'cards' rather than below them (figure 6).

Put simply, the fundamental difference between ICE Tree I and II is whether the tree is *implicit* in the Cartesian layout or it explicitly organises the display. Changing the view of the tree has no effect on its logical integrity.

The structure controls the visualisation. Operations on the tree are relative to a currently selected node, or set of contiguous siblings. Movement up the tree shifts the selection to the parent; sideways to the previous or next sibling; down to the closest geometric sibling. A 'focus' operation narrows the view to a single branch rather than the whole tree; a 'hide branch' operation hides an entire subordinate branch. Each branch spans part of the sentence; shown highlighted in the sentence window at the bottom of the display. The sentence 'ruler' is still visible.

Focus and hide controls are a tree-oriented way of limiting the visualisation extent. They allow the expert to consider just a clause, or ignore particular subclauses. However, as we commented in relation to protocols in laddering, relying only on the tree to direct elicitation can be a problem if the structure is incorrect. Scrolling and manual rescale functions are also provided.

4.3 Applying linguistic constraints to ICE Tree II

To recap from §3.2, constraints on the *tree* are acyclicity, strong ordering and closure; and on *nodes*, intra- and inter-nodal dependencies (inheritance).

1. *Acyclic tree structure.* Every operation stipulates that only strict trees can exist. Single parenthood is guaranteed by move commands which substitute one parent for another, and is exploited by operations on a single node or sibling group.
2. *Closure.* The structure is closed by the sentence and the root. This means that one can insert nodes between the leaves or the root, but not above the root or below the leaf nodes. Nor can one add nodes to create a branch without a sentence attached. Deletion, movement, and addition are all subject to this restriction.
3. *Strong ordering.* This prevents 'crossing lines' occurring in the tree and, with closure, strictly enforces the relationship between the (ordered) sentence and the tree. Move operations are limited both by a set of legal 'targets' for any movable node, and a strict subset of 'vulnerable' parent nodes which would have to be removed if the current node or nodes were moved away. These sets are calculated prior to, and highlighted during, each move operation. Figure 7 indicates the procedure for calculating legal candidates[3]. Figure 8 illustrates the effect of attempting to move the leaf stranded preposition (PS) "by" in figure 6.
4. *Intra-nodal constraints.* These are the set of legal co-occurring combinations of function and category. Only certain categories are meaningful with respect to particular functions and are therefore allowed to coincide. This co-occurrence relation R is clearly *symmetric* and *nonreflexive*. It is also invertable (R^{-1}). These

---

[3] The procedure is as follows. From the current node(s), trace three paths: one from the current parent to the root, and one on either side, travelling down to the sentence and back up. Mark as targets all nodes met that are not leaves or below the current node(s). Mark as vulnerable those candidate nodes above the current which have only one child until either the root or a node with more than one child is met.

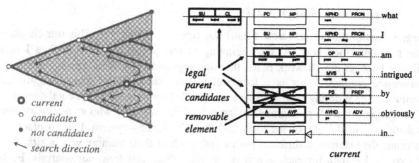

Fig. 7. Enforcing legal target
candidature for a new parent

Fig. 8. Possible legal parents
for PS : PREP *by*

relations are exploited in the interface to (a) indicate errors, and (b) provide an easily selectable 'short list' of compatible categories or functions.

Relevant features are controlled in a similar manner. They are organised into named mutually exclusive classes (by a manual post-hoc analysis of the parsing scheme). Thus *singular* and *plural* are grouped under the class *number*. Feature classes are exploited to prevent contradictory feature assignment. Features that become irrelevant (if a category changes, for example) are hidden. Similarly, as there is a set of permissible features for each category, a 'short list' is available.

5. *Inheritance.* It might be possible to use the global structure to infer higher level feature properties (as an automatic post-elicitation critique, say). There is some scope for enforcing inheritance from child to parent node with respect to certain features. For example, the transitivity feature of a main verb will typically be duplicated by the transitivity feature of the verb phrase containing it. However, the main significance of such features at the clausal level is precisely when the features are missing below it. Complications arise in many spoken or informal texts due to missing (*ellipted*) words, e.g., *Have you finished? - Yes I have.*

Inheritance can be seen as an example application of a more general knowledge-based critiquing system, which supports parse checking by detecting impossible correspondences or proposing specific changes to nodes. ICE Tree II uses a simple KBS to convert a different parsing scheme (TOSCA) to ICE. This process is performed prior to editing as well as before writing the tree to file. However, inheritance has not been implemented and remains a worthwhile research topic.

5   Empirical evaluation

This chapter describes the application of ICE Tree I and II to checking the ICE-GB corpus. Empirical data collected and the form of the data reflects an actual process of annotation, with specific peculiarities. Initially, automatic parsing was attempted with a version of the TOSCA parser (van Halteren and Oostdijk, 1993). Sentences that failed this process (typically larger or 'problematic' sentences) were reparsed by an alternative parser using the ICE scheme (Fang, 1996). Notwithstanding the evident problems in analysing this trial, we believe that there are a number of lessons.

5.1 The trial: annotating ICE-GB

A large subset of the corpus (around half) was reparsed in this way. This was checked in the trial described here. At the beginning of this process, only ICE Tree I was available; later, at the 16 week point, this was supplanted by ICE Tree II for all the experimental subjects. This is a longitudinal case study rather than a controlled experiment. The ordering represents an unavoidable bias on the experimental design.

The subjects were 9 post-graduate linguists of varying ages who were given some initial training in the use of the tools and the ICE parsing system. Due to practical constraints they started at different points and much of their training was *in situ*. The first two weeks' data for each expert is therefore discarded from our analysis. Each expert experienced a dramatic increase in performance after two or three texts (figure 9).

Text checking times were rounded to within 30 minutes and self-reported each week. This data was collected by the Survey of English Usage for audit purposes. We discarded data for twelve unreported texts and for the first two weeks of each participant. This left 422 times. Each time was 'normalised' by estimating the time to complete a 2,000-word text[4].

Normalisation assumes that the average difficulty of unchecked trees is similar to the difficulty of those checked, and therefore that the total time increases in proportion. To test this, actual and estimated completion times were correlated against the proportion of words checked (the 'coverage'). Scattergraphs were plotted (see appendix) and Pearson's correlation coefficient, r, calculated.

This gave a value of r for [actual time × coverage] of +0.35 and for estimated time of -0.30. The positive effect on actual time by increasing coverage is to be expected. The negative effect on estimated time indicates some slight overcompensation by the above formula; i.e., checked trees were more difficult than average.

This implies either a complication of the post-hoc analysis to compensate, or a different experimental design. One could attempt an analysis based on the ratios of nodes in each tree, but surface complexity is only one source of parse difficulty. This remains a source of some noise in the data. However, providing this noise does not vary significantly over time, it does not represent a major bias.

5.2 Results

Six of the nine participants reported sufficient data to be plotted independently. The average time to complete was plotted by week. This is shown in figure 9.

Each subject experienced a dominant learning effect, shown by the consistent downward trend in the data. This was true whether experts started with ICE Tree I or II (compare subjects A and F). It is therefore impossible to distinguish the learning effect from any benefit accrued from ICE Tree II – a fundamental problem in the experimental design.

On the other hand, there is no major *penalty* incurred in learning the more complex system, and the learning clearly transfers from one to the other. This suggests that the

---

[4] Estimated time to complete whole text $T_{TOTAL} = T_{+} \times (n_{-} + n_{+})/n_{+}$,
where n_{+} and n_{-} represent the number of text units, checked and unchecked, respectively.

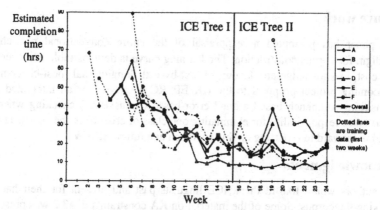

Fig. 9. Comparative graph of estimated completion time per text by week

vast majority of learning is in the domain of expertise, not in tool use. In other words, experts improved their performance by making parsing decisions more quickly rather than becoming more able with the tool. In fact, experts unanimously reported that the redesigned tool was more intuitive and *less* distracting to their decision making.

The inconclusiveness of these results in showing tool design benefits highlights a problem with the 'case study' approach. Even when the same group of experts uses two tools for the same task, the major effect, irrespective of the tool, is one of expertise learning. Even with a 'proper' within-subjects experimental design (subjects randomly assigned a tool at the start and switching over half-way), this learning effect would outweigh the more subtle advantages of one tool. The gain of one tool over another may be *significant*, but small.

6 Conclusions

Syntactic corpus annotation is an emerging field which shares much of the topology of simple KA. It brings algorithms and expertise to bear on large amounts of data. It is therefore of interest to the acquisition community as a significant application of KA.

Corpus linguists cannot afford poor tools. ICE tools will be supplied to other ICE teams from Ireland to Singapore. Tools must be robust and maintainable by non-computer literate staff to be effective in corpus linguistics. We therefore make no apology for borrowing insights from knowledge representation and acquisition.

Empirical trials determined by an external goal are often problematic in analysis. However, this trial does illustrate one clear point. Learning effects dominate any gain in completion time made by one tool over another. A barely adequate tool can be as fast or as slow as a sophisticated one if most of the time the subject is thinking.

However, the use of representational constraints, without slowing down tool use, reduces the probability of casual errors. This has been taken further by ICE Tree II, which has been extended to include an environment for composing whole corpus texts. This unifies two versions of the text (a parsed version and another containing a variety of non-syntactic annotations) using a combination of a simulated annealing algorithm and tool. The application of KA to corpus linguistics promises to be a fruitful one.

Future work

This paper has prompted a reappraisal of the entire conventional post-checking paradigm for corpus construction. The learning curve is demonstrable evidence of the high cost, in knowledge and labour, of text-by-text 'longitudinal' post-checking. In a forthcoming project proposal to the UK EPSRC we argue for an integrated corpus acquisition workbench based around error-based ('transverse') checking where each expert takes responsibility for eliminating one class of error from the corpus at a time. We look forward to reporting on this approach at a future EKAW.

Acknowledgments

The authors would like to thank ICE linguists past and present for their hard work checking the corpus. Some of the material on KA constraints in §3.2 was presented at ICAME '96. Thanks are also due to Nigel Shadbolt for comments on a draft version of this paper.

References

BOWDEN, P., HALSTEAD, P. and ROSE, T.G. (1996), Extracting Conceptual Knowledge From Text Using Explicit Relation Markers, (in Shadbolt, O'Hara and Schreiber, 1996, 147-162).

BURNAGE, G., and DUNLOP, D. (1992), Encoding the British National Corpus, in Aarts, J., de Haan, P., and Oostdijk, N. (eds.) (1992), *English Language Corpora: Design, Analysis and Exploitation*, Papers from the 13th international conference on English Language research on computerized corpora, Nijmegen 1992, Amsterdam: Rodopi.

CORBRIDGE, C., RUGG, G., MAJOR, N.P., SHADBOLT N.R., and BURTON, A.M. (1994), Laddering: technique and tool use in knowledge acquisition, *Knowledge Acquisition* (1994) 6, 315-341.

CUPIT, J., AND SHADBOLT, N.R. (1996), Knowledge Discovery in Databases: Exploiting Knowledge-Level Redescription (in Shadbolt, O'Hara and Schreiber, 1996, 245-261).

EAGLES (1996), Syntactic Annotation: Survey of Annotation practices. EAG-TCWG-SASG/2. Pisa: Consiglio Nazionale delle Ricerche. Istituto di Linguistica Computazionale.

ETHERINGTON, D.W., and REITER, R. (1983), On Inheritance Hierarchies With Exceptions, reprinted in Brachman, R.J., and Levesque, H.J. (eds.) (1985), *Readings in Knowledge Representation*, San Mateo, CA: Morgan Kaufman.

FANG, A.C. (1996), The Survey Parser: Design and Development (Chapter 11 in Greenbaum, 1996b, 142-160).

GREENBAUM, S. (1992), A New Corpus of English: ICE, in Svartvik, J. (ed.), *Directions in Corpus Linguistics: Proceedings of Nobel Symposium 82*, Stockholm 4-8 August 1991, Berlin: Mouton de Gruyter.

GREENBAUM, S. (1996a), *The Oxford English Grammar*, Oxford: Oxford University Press.

———— (ed.) (1996b), *Comparing English Worldwide: The International Corpus of English*, Oxford: Clarendon Press.

———— and NI, Y. (1996), About the ICE Tagset (Chapter 8 in Greenbaum, 1996b, 92-109).

HALTEREN, H. VAN and OOSTDIJK, N. (1993), Towards a Syntactic Database: the TOSCA Analysis System, in Aarts, J, de Haan, P. and Oostdijk, N. (eds), *English Language Corpora: Design, Analysis and Exploitation*. Amsterdam: Rodopi.

JONASSEN, D.H., BEISSENER, K., and YACCI, M. (1993), Structural Knowledge: Techniques for Representing, Conveying, and Acquiring Structural Knowledge, Hillsdale, NJ: LEA.

LEECH, G. and GARSIDE, R. (1991), Running a Grammar Factory: on the compilation of parsed corpora, or treebanks, in Johansson, S. and Stenström, A.-B. (eds), *English Computer Corpora: Selected Papers and Research Guide*. Berlin: Mouton de Gruyter, 15-32.

MAJOR, N.P., and REICHGELT, H. (1990), ALTO: An Automated Laddering Tool, in Wielinga, B., Boose, J., Gaines, B. Schreiber, G., van Someren, M. (Eds.) (1990), *Current Trends in Knowledge Acquisition*, 222-236, Amsterdam: IOS Press.

MAJOR, N.P., and SHADBOLT, N.R. (1992), CNN: Integrating Knowledge Elicitation with a Machine Learning Technique, in Proceedings of *JKAW-92*.

MARCUS, M., MARCINKIEWICZ, M.A. and SANTORINI, B. (1993), Building a Large Annotated Corpus of English: The Penn Treebank. *Computational Linguistics* 19, 2, 313-330.

MICHALSKI, R.S. and STEPP, R.E. (1983), Learning from observation: conceptual clustering, in Michalski, R.S., Carbonell J.G. and Mitchell T.M. (Eds.), *Machine Learning: an Artificial Intelligence Approach*, 331-363, Palo Alto: CA, Tioga.

MINSKY, M. (1975), A Framework for the Representation of Knowledge, in Winston, P. (Ed.), *The Psychology of Computer Vision*, New York: McGraw Hill, 211-277.

PASKIEWICZ, T., PATTEN, C., SHADBOLT, N.R., SWALLOW, S., and WALLIS, S.A. (1991), Functional specification of SET tools, *SET deliverable D006*, University of Nottingham.

QUINN, A., and PORTER, N. (1996), ICE Annotation Tools, (Chapter 6 in Greenbaum, 1996b, 65-78).

SHADBOLT, N.R., O'HARA, K. and SCHREIBER, G. (eds.) *Advances in Knowledge Acquisition*, Proceedings of EKAW '96, Berlin: Springer-Verlaag.

WALLIS, S.A. (1993), Machine Learning with Knowledge, in *Proceedings of MLnet Workshop on Scientific Discovery 1993*, MLnet.

————— (1997), *Exploiting hierarchical sets in A.I.*, PhD Thesis (submitted), University of Nottingham.

————— and SHADBOLT, N.R. (1993), Induction as Knowledge Acquisition, *Dept. of Psychology Postgraduate Conference 1993*, Department of Psychology, University of Nottingham.

Appendix

The figures below show scattergraphs of actual and estimated time to complete by coverage fraction, for expert data taken after a training period of 2 weeks. Pearson's product moment correlation coefficient, r, is a mild positive 0.35 for increasing coverage with time, whilst the product of estimated time and coverage has a mild negative -0.30, indicating some overcompensation.

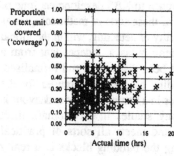
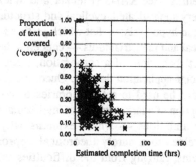

(a) coverage × time ($r = 0.35$)   (b) coverage × est. time ($r = -0.30$)

Fig. 10. Scattergraphs of actual and estimated time by size of task (coverage)

Building Up and Making Use of Corporate Knowledge Repositories

Gian Piero Zarri   and   Saliha Azzam

Centre Nat. Recherche Scientifique
EHESS - CAMS
54, boulevard Raspail
75270 PARIS Cedex 06, France
zarri@cams.msh-paris.fr

Department of Computer Science
The University of Sheffield
211 Portobello Street
SHEFFIELD, S1 4DP, UK
S.Azzam@dcs.shef.ac.uk

Abstract. In this paper, we present a methodology (and some concrete experiments) for the construction and use of corporate knowledge repositories. They can be defined as on-line, computer-based storehouses of expertise, knowledge, experience and documentation about particular aspects of a corporation. We consider here only the 'textual component' of corporate knowledge — i.e., all sorts of economically valuable, natural language documents like news stories, telex reports, internal documentation (memos, policy statements, reports and minutes), normative texts, intelligence messages, etc. In this case, the construction of effectively usable corporate knowledge repositories can be achieved with the translation of the original documents into some type of conceptual format. The 'metadocuments' obtained in this way can then be stored into a knowledge repository and, given their role of advanced document models, all the traditional functions of information retrieval, e.g., searching, retrieving and producing an answer (and other functions like intelligent navigation inside the repository) can be performed directly on them.

1   Introduction

Until now, the problem of dealing with the dispersed know-how that exists in a corporation ('corporate memory') has normally been dealt with as a problem of 'modelling', see KADS (Breuker and Wielinga 1989), EM (Bubenko 1993), etc. In this very sophisticated, cyclical and structured approach to KBS development, one of the main hypothesis — that which justifies the use of these sorts of methodologies as practical and industrial tools — concerns the possibility of detecting, within the global 'expert' behaviour of a corporation, a set of elementary tasks, independent from a particular application domain. Once the tasks have been discovered and formalised, they can be used to set up libraries of basic building blocks, to be reused for the description of a large number of intellectual processes in a company. This endeavour is really ambitious — which explains why so many studies in this domain limit themselves to a purely theoretical approach — and meets all sorts of practical problems, ranging from the difficulties in defining the building blocks in a really general way to the ambiguities concerning which aspects (the model or the code) of the blocks can really be reused.

In this paper, we suggest that a more modest, but less fuzzy and immediately useful, approach to the practical use of corporate memory (which should not be neglected), can be found in the (at least partially automated) construction and use of corporate knowledge repositories. They can be defined as on-line, computer-based storehouses of expertise, knowledge, experience and documentation about particular aspects of a given corporation. We will consider here only the 'textual component' of corporate knowledge — i.e., all sorts of economically valuable, natural language (NL) documents like news stories, telex reports, internal documentation (memos, policy statements, reports and minutes), normative texts, intelligence messages, etc. In this case, the construction of effective repositories can be achieved by the translation of the original documents into some type of advanced conceptual representation (semantic nets, frames, conceptual graphs, etc.) — this approach can also be interpreted as a sophisticated indexing or categorisation technique. The 'metadocuments' obtained in this way can then be stored in a knowledge repository and, given their role of advanced document models, all the traditional functions of information retrieval, e.g., searching, retrieving and producing an answer and other functions like intelligent navigation inside the repository, can be executed directly on them.

In the following, we describe a prototypical system designed to exploit a knowledge repository of metadocuments that we have (partially) built up thanks to the aid of the European Commission (Esprit project NOMOS, P5330 and LRE project COBALT, P61011) and of the French National Centre for Scientific Research (CNRS). A similar proposal is outlined, to some extent, in (Trigano 1994), which also concerns a system for the processing of NL documents in a corporate knowledge context. Their approach, however, seems to be more conventional. Section 2 gives the general architecture of the prototype. In Section 3., we : i) introduce NKRL (Narrative Knowledge Representation Language), the conceptual language we use for the production of metadocuments ; ii) comment quickly on the first of the two main blocks of the prototype, the acquisition sub-system. We examine the interrogation sub-system in more depth in Section 4 ; this sub-system exploits the canonical format of the metadocuments to implement some advanced search and retrieval applications.

2 A prototype for dealing with the textual component of corporate knowledge

Fig. 1 gives a very general overview of the architecture of the system we propose. All the blocks shown in this figure have been implemented, at least in a preliminary form, and tested ; however, the procedures concerning the selection and the activation of the high-level inference procedures, at the bottom, realised in a CNRS environment, are still not integrated in the existing prototype. This last, created mainly in a NOMOS/COBALT context, has been implemented in COMMON LISP. In NOMOS/COBALT, we have used as support platform an object-oriented environment : CRL (Carnegie Representation Language) in the NOMOS version, QSL (Quinary Semantic Language) in the COBALT version.

Supposing the integrated system already exists, the original NL documents, on the left, pass through the NL processing modules which constitute the core of the acquisition sub-system. This sub-system executes, essentially, a conversion of the 'meaning' of the original documents into NKRL format. The results of this translation are stored in the central knowledge repository (metadocument knowledge repository) ; in very large environments it should also be possible, of course, to think in terms of distributed communicating repositories. Some functions, not shown in Fig. 1 for simplicity's sake, allow browsing and maintenance operations on the contents of the repository. Moreover, in order to check the correctness of the translation and to supply the user with a means of being informed in real time of the main characteristics of the analysed documents, some possibilities of immediate display of the resulting NKRL code have been added in the COBALT context.

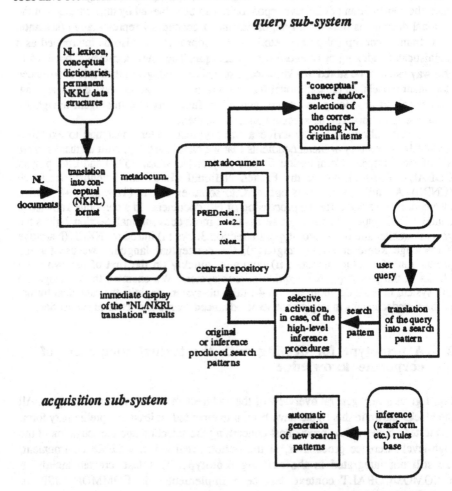

Figure 1 - Architecture of a system for dealing with the textual component of corporate knowledge.

The boxes on the right-hand side of Fig. 1 represent the query sub-system of the prototype. The user's queries are, firstly, translated into search patterns or sequences of search patterns — search patterns are NKRL data structures which represent the general framework of information to be searched for, by filtering or unification, within the metadocument repository. The metadocuments can i) directly unify the original query (search pattern) ; ii) unify some new search patterns obtained by inference from the original one (see below, Section 4). After the unification of the patterns with one or more metadocuments, these are presented to the user. The output can be shown in two different formats, which can also coexist : i) in a concise, tabular format (immediate display) ; ii) as the original NL messages, if they have been stored along with the corresponding metadocuments.

3 A quick glimpse of NKRL

NKRL (Narrative Knowledge Representation Language) supplies a language-independent description of the semantic content (the "meaning") of non-trivial NL documents, like the textual corporate documents introduced in Section 1.

3.1 The basic structures

NKRL is a two layer language. The lower layer supplies a set of general tools and consists of four integrated components

The descriptive component tools are used to set up the formal NKRL expressions ('templates') describing general classes of narrative events, like "move a generic object", "formulate a need", "be present somewhere". Templates encode, therefore, the standard features of various ordinary events and human activities. Templates are structured in a hierarchy, H_TEMP(lates), which can be equated with a taxonomy (ontology) of events — one of the most important characteristic of the NKRL formalism.

Templates' instances (called occurrences), i.e., the NKRL representations of single specific events like "Tomorrow, I will move the wardrobe", "Lucy was looking for a taxi", "Peter lives in Paris", are in the domain of the factual component. Templates and occurrences are characterised by a tripartite format :

$$(P_i \ (R1 \ a1) \ (R2 \ a2) \ ... \ (Rn \ an)) \ ,$$

where the central element is a semantic predicate P_i — like BEHAVE, EXPERIENCE, MOVE, PRODUCE etc. — which represents a named relation that exists between one or more arguments a_i introduced by means of roles R_i — like SUBJ(ect), OBJ(ect), SOURCE, etc. From a formal point of view, a metadocument consists, therefore, of the association of several templates and/or occurrences, tied up with particular binding structures, see (Zarri 1994), that represent the logico-semantic links which can exist between them (the co-ordination and subordination links, using a metaphor from the domain of natural language).

The definitional component supplies the formal representation of all the general notions, like *physical_entity*, *taxi_*, *location_*, which can be used as arguments in the two components above. Their representations in NKRL terms are called concepts (basically, their data structures can be equated to frames), and are grouped into a hierarchy, H_CLASS(es) — H_CLASS corresponds well, therefore, to the usual concept ontologies.

The instances of concepts, like lucy_, wardrobe_1, paris_ are called individuals, and pertain to the enumerative component. For more details about other important tools of NKRL — e.g., those allowing the representation of modal or temporal information — see (Zarri 1992), (Zarri 1994).

The upper layer of NKRL includes some standard conceptual structures built up making use of the descriptive and definitional tools above ; it consists of two parts :

a) The first part is a catalogue, where we can find a description of the formal characteristics and the modalities of use of the well-formed, 'basic' templates (like "moving a generic object" mentioned above) associated with the language — presently, about 150, pertaining mainly to a (very general) socio-economico-political context where the main characters are human beings or social bodies (e.g., a company). The set of legal, basic templates included in the catalogue can be considered, at least in a first approach, as fixed. This means that : i) a system-builder himself does not have to create the knowledge needed to describe the events specific to a (sufficiently) large class of NL documents ; ii) it becomes easier to secure the reproduction and the sharing of previous results.

b) The second part is made up of the general concepts which pertain to the upper levels of H_CLASS — such as *human_being, physical_entity, modality_*, etc. — and which form a sort of standard, invariable ontology.

3.2 An example

We can now supply, Fig. 2, an example of NKRL code (a metadocument consisting only of occurrences). It represents a small fragment of news in the COBALT's style : "Milan, October 15, 1993. The financial daily Il Sole 24 Ore reported Mediobanca had called a special board meeting concerning plans for capital increase".

```
c1)   MOVE    SUBJ   (SPECIF sole_24_ore financial_daily): (milan_)
              OBJ    #c2
              date-1: 15_october_93
              date-2:

c2)   PRODUCE SUBJ   mediobanca_
              OBJ    (SPECIF summoning_1 (SPECIF board_meeting_1
                            mediobanca_ special_))
              TOPIC  (SPECIF plan_1 (SPECIF cardinality_ several_)
                            capital_increase_1)
              date-1: circa_15_october_93
              date-2:
```

Figure 2 - An example of NKRL coding.

In Fig. 2, c1 and c2 are the symbolic names of two occurrences, instances of NKRL basic and derived templates. MOVE and PRODUCE are predicates ; SUBJ, OBJ, TOPIC (the theme, 'apropos', of the event(s) or situation(s) represented in the occurrence) are roles. The arguments sole_24_ore, milan_, mediobanca_ (an Italian merchant bank), summoning_1, etc. are individuals ; *financial_daily*, *special_*, *cardinality_* (which pertains to the *property_* sub-tree of H_CLASS) and *several_* (belonging, like *some_*, *all_* etc., to the *logical_quantifier* sub-tree of H_CLASS) are concepts. The attributive operator, SPECIF(ication), is one of the NKRL operators used to build up structured arguments (or 'expansions'), see also, below, Section 4 ; the SPECIF lists, with syntax (SPECIF e_1 p_1 ... p_n), are used to represent some properties which can be asserted about the first element e_1, a concept or an individual, of the list, e.g., sole_24_ore in the occurrence c1, summoning_1 and plan_1 in the occurrence c2. *several_* is used within a *cardinality_* SPECIF list as a standard way of representing the plural number mark, see c2.

The arguments, and the templates/occurrences as a whole, may be characterised by the addition of determiners (attributes). In particular, the location attributes (lists) are associated with the arguments by using the colon, ':', operator, see c1. For a complete description of the temporal determiners date-1 and date-2, see (Zarri 1992).

Note that the MOVE basic template at the origin of the occurrence c1 is used to translate any event concerning the transmission of an information ("The financial daily Il Sole 24 Ore reported ..."), see also Fig. 3 below. It makes use of what is called a 'completive construction'. Accordingly, the filler of the OBJ(ect) slot in the occurrence (here, c1) which implements the transmission template is always a symbolic label (here, #c2) which refers to another occurrence, i.e., that bearing the informational content to be communicated ("...Mediobanca had called a meeting..."). For details about the other sorts of NKRL structures (binding structures) which allow to build up second order objects from templates and occurrences, see, e.g., (Zarri 1994).

3.3 The NKRL hierarchies (ontologies), H_TEMP and H_CLASS

Given the importance of the 'ontologies' — ontology of events (H_TEMP) and ontology of concepts (H_CLASS) — in the NKRL context, we reproduce in Fig. 3 and 4 an (extremely simplified) image of the NKRL upper level. As already stated, this contains a description of the basic templates (H_TEMP upper level) and of the general concepts (H_CLASS upper level).

Fig. 3 is a schematic representation of the H_TEMP hierarchy, where only the branches BEHAVE, MOVE and PRODUCE have been developed to some, very limited extent. In this figure, the syntactic description of the templates is particularly sketchy : e.g., all the symbolic labels have been eliminated, and the templates are discriminated only through the associated natural language comments. A more realistic picture of a template can be deduced from the occurrences (template instances) of Fig. 2 above. The codes '!' and '≠' mean, respectively, 'mandatory' and 'forbidden' (e.g., in the 'transmit an information to someone' template, MOVE sub hierarchy, the presence of a DEST(ination) role is expressly required).

Fig. 4 is a schematic representation of the upper level of H_CLASS (hierarchy of concepts, definitional component).

. **H_TEMP** ('hierarchy of predicative templates')

.. **BEHAVE** templates ; predicate : BEHAVE

... 'external manifestation of the subject' ; ≠OBJ
....   'acting in a particular role' ; MODAL < *role_* [ex: *rugby_player*] >
....   'manifest a particular quality' ; MODAL < *quality_* >

... 'focus on a result' ; ≠ OBJ, DEST, TOPIC; ≠mod. 'against, for' ; !GOAL bind. struct.
....   'act explicitly to obtain the result' ; ≠modulator 'ment'
....   'wishes and intentions' ; ! modulator 'ment'

... 'concrete attitude toward someone/so.thing'; !OBJ, MODAL; ≠DEST, GOAL; ≠'ment'

.. **EXIST** templates ; predicate : EXIST ; !location of the SUBJ ; ≠DEST

.. **EXPERIENCE** templates ; predicate : EXPERIENCE ; !OBJ ; ≠DEST

.. **MOVE** templates ; predicate : MOVE

... 'moving a generic entity' ; OBJ < *entity_*>
....   'move a material thing' ; OBJ < *physical_entity* >
.....   'change the position of something' ; ≠DEST (ex: 'move the wardrobe')
.....   'transfer something to someone' ; !DEST (ex: 'send a letter to Lucy')

... 'generic person displacement' ; SUBJ = OBJ = <*human_being*> ; !loc. of SUBJ, OBJ

... 'transmit an information to someone' ; !DEST
....   'transmit a generic information' ; OBJ < *type_of_information* [ex: *message_*] >
....   'transmit a structured information' ; OBJ 'label of binding/predicat. occurrence'

.. **OWN** templates ; predicate : OWN ; !OBJ ; ≠DEST

.. **PRODUCE** templates ; predicate : PRODUCE ; !OBJ

... 'conceive a plan or idea' ; !modulator 'ment'

... 'creation of material things' ; OBJ < *physical_entity* > ; ≠modulator 'ment'

... 'perform a task or action' ; OBJ < *action_name* >
....   'acquire, buy' ; OBJ < *purchase_* >
....   'sell' ; OBJ < *sale_* >

... 'relation involvem.' ; SUBJ (COORD); OBJ *mutual_agreem.* MODAL <*relationsh._*>

... 'production of events by an active cause' ; SUBJ < *active_cause* > ; OBJ < *event_*>

.. **RECEIVE** templates ; predicate : RECEIVE ; !OBJ ; ≠DEST

Figure 3 - Schematic H_TEMP hierarchy (ontology of events).

The two high-level branches stem from two concepts that — adopting the terminology used, e.g., in (Guarino, Carrara and Giaretta 1994) — we have labelled as *sortal_concepts* and *non_sortal_concepts*. The specialisations of the former, like *chair_*, *city_* or *european_city*, can have instances (chair_27, paris_), whereas the specialisations of the latter, like *butter_* (a *substance_*), or *colour_*, can admit further specialisations (subsets), see *peanut_butter* or *red_*, but do not have instances.

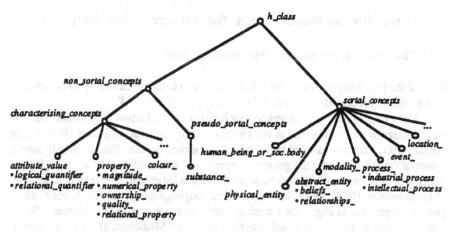

Figure 4 - A (really abridged) view of the 'upper level' of H_CLASS.

3.4 Translating into NKRL format

The NL/NKRL 'translation' operations, see the left-hand side of Fig. 1 above, have been described in depth in several papers, see, e.g., (Azzam 1995), (Zarri 1995). Their basic philosophy consists in locating, within the original texts, the syntactic and semantic indexes which evoke the conceptual structures to be used to represent these texts. The related algorithmic procedures are centred around two main principles:

a) They make use of rules — evoked by particular lexical items in the text examined and stored in proper conceptual dictionaries — which take the form of 'generalised production rules'. Their left hand side (antecedent part) is always a syntactic condition, expressed as a tree-like structure, which must be unified with the results of the general parse tree produced by the syntactic specialist of the translation system. If the unification succeeds, the right hand sides (consequent parts) are used, e.g., to generate well-formed NKRL conceptual structures ('triggering rules').

b) They employ, within the rules, proper sophisticated mechanisms to deal with the variables. For example, in the specific, 'triggering' family of NKRL rules, the 'antecedent variables' (*a*-variables) are first declared in the syntactic (antecedent) part of the rules, and then 'echoed' in the consequent part, where they appear in the form of arguments and constraints linked with the roles of the activated conceptual structures (templates). They 'capture' — during the match between the antecedents and the results of the syntactic specialist — NL or NKRL elements to be used for filling up the activated templates, and building then the final NKRL structures.

The translation procedures are, obviously, crucial for the success of the approach defended in this paper. Information on the efficiency, the effectiveness and the limitations of these procedures can be found, e.g., in (Zarri 1995).

4 Using the metadocuments for interrogation purposes

4.1 The basic querying and inferencing modalities

Each of the four components of the NKRL language is characterised by an association with a class of proper inference procedures, see, e.g., (Zarri 1994).

For example, the key inference mechanism of the factual component (and the basic inference tool of NKRL) is the Filtering and Unification Module (FUM). The primary data structures handled by FUM are the search patterns that, as already stated, represent (in NKRL terms) the general properties of information to be searched for, by filtering or unification, within a metadocument knowledge base --- a search pattern can be considered an NKRL equivalent of a natural language query, see Fig. 1. For clarity's sake, we reproduce in Fig. 5 the search pattern corresponding to the question : "What was the theme of the recent board meeting called by Mediobanca?" that, obviously, unify with occurrence c2 in Fig. 2 ; the scope of this pattern is relatively general, see the constraints on the OBJ(ect) variable x. The two dates of Fig. 5 constitute the 'search interval' linked with the pattern, to be used to limit the search for unification to the slice of time that it is considered appropriate to explore, see (Zarri 1992).

```
((?w    IS-OCCURRENCE
        :predicate    PRODUCE
        :SUBJ         mediobanca_
        :OBJ          (SPECIF ?x (SPECIF ?y mediobanca_))
        :TOPIC        ?z)
        (1_october_93, 20_october_93)
        ((?x    IS-A    (:OR assembly_ adjournment_ dissolution_))
         (?y    IS-A    board_meeting)
         (?z    IS-A    planning_activity)))
```

Figure 5 - A simple search pattern.

Note that the most interesting component of the FUM module is represented by the matching algorithm which unifies the complex structures — like (SPECIF summoning_1 (SPECIF board_meeting_1 mediobanca_ special_) in occurrence c2 of Fig. 2 — which, in the NKRL terminology, are called structured arguments (see the next sub-Sections for more details).

4.2 The AECS sub-language

In Fig. 2 above (or in Fig. 5), the arguments made up of a SPECIF(ication) list are then examples of NKRL structured arguments (or 'expansions').

In NKRL, structured arguments of templates and occurrences are built up in a principled way by making use of a specialised sublanguage, AECS, which includes four binding operators, the disjunctive operator (ALTERNative = A), the distributive operator (ENUMeration = E), the collective operator (COORDination = C), and the attributive operator (SPECIFication = S), see, e.g., (Zarri 1994), (Zarri and Gilardoni 1996). Their intuitive meaning is given in Table 1. Accordingly, structured arguments in NKRL are lists of undefined length, which may include both concepts and individuals and which are labelled using the AECS operators.

Table 1. NKRL operators for structured arguments.

Operator	Mnemonic Description
ALTERN	The 'disjunctive operator'. It introduces a set of elements, i.e., concepts, individuals, or lists labelled with other expansion operators. Only one element of the set takes part in the particular relationship with the predicate defined by the role-slot to be filled with the expansion ; however, this element is not known.
COORD	The 'collective operator' : all the elements of the set take part (necessarily together) in the relationship with the predicate defined by the role-slot.
ENUM	The 'distributive operator' : each element of the set satisfies the relationship, but they do so separately.
SPECIF	The 'attributive operator'. It is used to link a series of attributes (properties) with the concept or individual that constitutes the first element of the SPECIF list, in order to better characterise this last element. Each attribute appearing inside a SPECIF list can be recursively associated with another SPECIF list.

From a formal semantics point of view, we can note that, e.g. :

a) $(\text{SPECIF } e_1 \text{ a b}) = (\text{SPECIF } e_1 \text{ b a})$;
b) $(\text{ENUM } e_1 \text{ } e_2) = (e_1 \text{ AND } e_2 \text{ AND } \neg (\text{COORD } e_1 \text{ } e_2))$.

The first formula says that the order of the properties a, b, ... associated with en entity e_1, a concept or an individual, is not significant. The second formula enunciates in a more formal way what is already stated in Table 1 : the main characteristic of the ENUM lists is linked with the fact that the entities e_1, e_2, ... take part obligatorily in the particular relationship between the structured argument and the predicate expressed by the role that introduces the arguments, but they satisfy this relationship separately. A full description of the semantics of AECS can be found, e.g., in (Gilardoni 1993).

Because of their recursive nature, the AECS operators could give rise to very complex expressions, difficult to interpret and disentangle (unify). Therefore, to build up well-formed expansions, the definitions of Table 1 are used in association with the so-called 'priority rule', which can be visualised by using the following expression:

$$(ALTERN\ (ENUM\ (COORD\ (SPECIF)))).$$

This is to be interpreted as follows : it is forbidden to use inside the scope of a list introduced by the binding operator B, a list labelled in terms of one of the binding operators appearing on the left of B in the priority expression above — e.g., it is impossible to use a list ALTERN inside the scope of a list COORD — an example of the use of this rule can be found, e.g., in (Zarri 1994).

4.3 A query language for structured arguments

Returning now to the FUM module, we have seen that the AECS language allows us to describe complex relations among concepts and individuals. While, sometimes, a query about an AECS structure must be able to exploit completely the information carried by this structure, the situation in which only a part of this information is really useful is relatively frequent. Take as an example the AECS expression (COORD john_ paul_), that expresses the fact that both John and Paul take part in a particular event in a co-ordinated manner. While sometimes this is exactly the information looked for with a query (i.e., whether they are involved 'necessarily together' in the event, it is often the case that the information we want to obtain is simply if John (or Paul) takes part in the event.

Therefore, a query language operating on the AECS structures must be able to express a wide range of query modalities (including the two evoked before), and to obtain constantly the correct results. Keeping in mind that it is always possible to express the AECS structures (lists) in term of trees, we can state here the following basic requirements for the AECS-query language which is part of the FUM module :

1) It must be possible to specify a 'perfect match', defined as a match that succeeds if and only if the tree representations of the query and of the target (matched) AECS expression, have strictly identical structures (apart from variables). As an example, we can say that the query (ENUM ?x ?y) succeeds against the target AECS expression (ENUM credit_lyonnais mediobanca_), but fails against (COORD credit_lyonnais (SPECIF mediobanca_ merchant_bank)) or against (ENUM credit_lyonnais mediobanca_ chase_manhattan).

2) It must be possible to specify a perfect match apart from 'cardinality', i.e., a match that succeeds if and only if the query, and the target AECS expression, have identical structures — apart from variables and, chiefly, without taking into account the cardinality of the AECS lists. In this case, (ENUM ?x ?y) succeeds against (ENUM credit_lyonnais mediobanca_) and against (ENUM credit_lyonnais mediobanca_ chase_manhattan), but fails, obviously, against (COORD credit_lyonnais mediobanca_).

3) It must be possible to specify a 'subsumed' match, i.e., a match that succeeds if and only if the query, and the target AECS expression, carry information which can be considered as globally congruent from a semantic point of view. For example, we admit here the presence, in the target (matched) expression, of

additional SPECIF lists (additional lists of attributes). According to this paradigm, (COORD *?x ?y*) succeeds against (COORD credit_lyonnais mediobanca_), against (COORD credit_lyonnais (SPECIF mediobanca_ *merchant_bank*)), and (COORD credit_lyonnais mediobanca_ chase_manhattan).

4) Obviously, it must be possible to mix the above kinds of queries, in such a way that, for example, *a perfect match is required for the top level structure of the query and target trees but not for the underlying parts* (see also the examples of Fig. 6 below). In this way, e.g., (ALTERN *?x ?y*) can match against (ALTERN chase_manhattan (COORD credit_lyonnais mediobanca_)).

We can now define a query language for AECS structures. For clarity's sake, the query language is based on the logical structures of the original AECS sub-language, augmented to allow i) the use of variables, and ii) the correct specification of the kind of match required by the query. The AECS query language is therefore defined in the following way : take the AECS descriptive language as the basis, but allow :

- The use of variables (*?x*), possibly with constraints, instead of concepts or individuals.
- The use of the special construct STRICT-SUBSUMPTION, taking as an argument an NKRL entity (variable, concept or individual), or a complex AECS structure. Bearing in mind the priority rule introduced in the previous sub-Section, these complex AECS structures, expressed as trees, may consist of : a simple list COORD (coord-list) ; a coord-tree, subsuming at least two coord-lists ; an enum-tree, subsuming one or more coord-tree (or coord-list) ; an altern-tree, subsuming any of the previous tree-structures.
- The use of the special construct STRICT-CARDINALITY, taking as an argument an NKRL entity, or one of the AECS structures listed in the previous paragraph.

STRICT-CARDINALITY and STRICT-SUBSUMPTION have the following operational meaning :

- the presence of a STRICT-SUBSUMPTION operator forces the interpretation of the argument according to a 'no-subsumption' rule, thus requiring a perfect match, see point 1 before, on the type (NKRL entity, coord-branch, coord-tree, enum-tree, altern-tree)) of the argument ;
- the presence of a STRICT-CARDINALITY operator forces the interpretation of the argument according to a 'fixed-cardinality' rule, thus requiring a perfect match, see point 2 before, on the cardinality of the argument ;
- the absence of any of the two special operators implies the 'subsuming' rule, see point 3 before, thus producing a successful match if the semantics of the query construct *is subsumed* by the semantics of the matched construct.

The algorithms which exploit the AECS-query language to unify two AECS structured arguments are described, e.g., in (Zarri and Gilardoni 1996).

For illustrative purposes, we give in Fig. 6 some examples which relate to different modalities of matching the target AECS structure : (ENUM chase_manhattan (COORD credit_lyonnais (SPECIF mediobanca_ *merchant_bank*) city_bank)).

- The query : (ENUM *?x* (STRICT-SUBSUMPTION (COORD credit_lyonnais mediobanca_ city_bank))) succeeds, binding *x* to chase_manhattan. Note that the STRICT-SUBSUMPTION operator concerns only the general structure of the coord-trees, and not the structure of the single coord-branches.
- The query : (ENUM *?x* (COORD credit_lyonnais (STRICT-SUBSUMPTION mediobanca_) city_bank)) fails, because of the STRICT-SUBSUMPTION restriction which prevents mediobanca_ from matching a coord-branch.
- The query : (ENUM *?x* (STRICT-CARDINALITY (COORD credit_lyonnais mediobanca_))) fails, because of the STRICT-CARDINALITY restriction.
- The query : (STRICT-SUBSUMPTION (ENUM *?x* (COORD credit_lyonnais mediobanca_))) succeeds, binding *x* to chase_manhattan. The STRICT-SUBSUMPTION restriction only concerns the top-level structure of the enum-trees.
- The query : (ENUM *?x* credit_lyonnais) succeeds, binding *x* to chase_manhattan.
- The query : (STRICT-SUBSUMPTION (ENUM *?x* (STRICT-SUBSUMPTION credit_lyonnais))) fails, due to the (STRICT-SUBSUMPTION credit_lyonnais) restriction.
- The query : (STRICT-SUBSUMPTION (COORD credit_lyonnais mediobanca_)) fails.
- The query : (COORD credit_lyonnais mediobanca_) succeeds.

Figure 6 - Examples of AECS unifications

4.4 An example of high-level inference procedures

The querying and inference mechanisms outlined in the previous sub-Sections are used as basic building blocks for implementing all sorts of high-level inference procedures. For example, high-level procedures that have been studied in depth in a CNRS context are the 'transformation rules', see (Zarri 1986).

In database theory, the notion of 'transformation' (used for operations of semantic query optimisation) is usually linked with that of 'semantic equivalence' between two queries : two queries are considered as semantically equivalent if their answer is the same for all database states which satisfy a given set of integrity constraints. In an NKRL context, the notion of transformation acquires a wider significance. NKRL transformations deal with the problem of obtaining a plausible answer from a database of factual occurrences also in the absence of the explicitly requested information, by searching semantic affinities between what is requested and what is really present in the repository. The fundamental principle employed is that of transforming the original query into one or more different queries which are not strictly 'equivalent' but only 'semantically close' to the original one.

To give a very simple example, suppose that, working in the context of an hypothetical metadocument database about university professors, we should want to ask a question like : "Who has lived in the United States", even without an explicit representation of this fact in the repository. If the repository contains some information about the degrees obtained by the professors, we can tell the user that, although we do not explicitly know who lived in the States, we can nevertheless look for people having an American degree. This last piece of information, obtained by transformation of the original query, would indeed normally imply that some time was spent by the professors in the country, the United States, which issued their degree.

Transformation rules are made up of a left hand side — an NKRL statement (search pattern) representing the linguistic expression which is to be transformed —

and one or more right hand sides — NKRL representations of one or more linguistic expressions that must be substituted for the given one. A transformation rule can, therefore, be expressed as : A (left hand side) $\Rightarrow$ B (right hand side). The 'transformation arrow', '$\Rightarrow$', has a double meaning :

- operationally speaking, the arrow indicates the direction of the transformation : the left hand side A (the original search pattern) is removed and replaced by the right hand side B (one or more new search patterns) ;
- from a logical point of view, the arrow means that the information obtained through B implies the information we should have obtained from A.

In reality, the 'always true' implications (noted as $B \rightarrow A$, where we assume that the symbol '$\rightarrow$' represents, as usual, the implication arrow) are not very frequent. Most transformations found in real world applications represent 'modalised implications'. We will note them as $\Diamond(B \rightarrow A)$, which means 'it is possible that B implies A'. '$\Diamond$' is the usual modal operator for 'possibility', which satisfies then the relation $\Diamond p = \neg \blacklozenge \neg p$ with respect to the second modal operator, '$\blacklozenge$ = necessity'. An example of modalised transformation is given by the transformation T1 in Fig. 7, which allows us to deal with the informal example above about "university professors" ; as we can see, the antecedent and consequent of T1 are formed by search patterns, slightly simplified here for clarity's sake. Transformation T1 says : "If someone (x) receives a title from an official authority by means of an official document, then it is possible that he has been physically present at that moment in the place (k) where the authority is located". This rule, for example, is not always valid in the case of an university degree (a degree could be obtained in a correspondence school, etc.). Nevertheless, it is possible to see that, in this case, the semantic distance between an always true' implication and a 'modalised' one is not too important, as it is becomes possible, at least in principle, to change T1 into a true transformation by the addition of a few constraints on the variable p , for instance the constraint: $p \neq$ <obtainable_by_correspondence_degree>. More examples, and a complete 'theory' of transformations, can be found in, e.g., (Zarri 1986).

```
T1)    EXIST    SUBJ    x : [l]    ⇒    RECEIVE    SUBJ      x
                                                    OBJ       y
                                                    SOURCE    w : [l]
                                                    MODAL     z

                x   =   <human_being>
                y   =   <title_ >
                w   =   <authority_>
                z   =   <official_document>
                l   =   <location_>
```

Figure 7 - A simple example of 'transformation' rule.

4.5 Future developments

We can now provide some additional details about the functioning of the query sub-system of the prototype. Returning to the general architecture of the prototype in Fig.

1 above, we can see that a search pattern may be generated from outside the system when it directly represents, in a deductive retrieving style, the NKRL translation of a query issued by the user — this corresponds to the basic mode of functioning of the query sub-system of the prototype. But, in some cases, it may also be generated automatically from inside the system during the execution of the inference procedures.

Let us consider, in fact, what will happen to a search pattern corresponding directly to a user's NL query when we obtain no answer — i.e., we have failed to unify the search pattern with an NKRL item of information which is part of a metadocument — or when, having recovered some information, we want to know more. In such cases we can consider, as a first hypothesis, a situation where the NKRL image of the information which could supply a plausible answer effectively exists in the central knowledge base, but it might be difficult to retrieve and recognise. Under this hypothesis, we will ask the query system to automatically transform the initial search pattern by substituting it with another 'semantically equivalent' pattern, see above.

Unfortunately, the problems associated with the practical utilisation of this type of (implemented) approach are not only technical (construction of appropriate inference engines), but concern mainly the way of i) discovering the common sense rules which constitute the real basis of the transformation procedures, and ii) formalising the rules so that we can obtain a sufficient degree of generality. These two activities can be executed *a priori* only to some extent, because knowledge engineers find difficulties in predicting all the possible practical situations. Concretely, the transformation rules are established often *a posteriori*, by abstracting and formalising some procedures empirically found in order to solve particular 'cases'.

This is why we plan to introduce, in a more complete version of the prototype, the possibility of having recourse to Case-Based Reasoning (CBR) techniques, see, e.g., (Kolodner 1992). Given that the 'rules', where they exist, are normally considered a more economic use than 'cases', we would like to use the CBR procedures not only for providing the users with a specific, sophisticated and up-to-date problem-solving modality, but also, at the same time, for blazing a trail toward the subsequent creation of a practical set of transformation rules to be stored in the rule base, and which will subsume all the different concrete cases used empirically to set up an useful solution.

5 Conclusion

In this paper, we have suggested that a modest, but pragmatically useful modality of use of the 'textual component' of corporate knowledge could be obtained by translating this component into conceptual format (metadocuments). In this case, it becomes possible to use this knowledge taking into account the specific characteristics of its proper semantic content (its 'meaning'). For example, when the user does not know *a priori* what sort of knowledge is stored in a given repository, the query mechanism can still provide plausible answers. See, by contrast, some current proposals for describing and indexing WWW NL documents like Meta Content Framework, Semantic Header or Dublin Core (Weibel *et al.* 1995), that are unable to execute fine-grained, content-based retrieval operations because they concern only the 'external' identification framework of these documents (subject, author, title, language, creation date ...) and they neglect the representation of the 'internal' semantic content.

The different versions of the implemented components have been tested as far as possible, and their performances seem to be satisfactory — e.g., the acquisition sub-system, in the NOMOS version, takes 3 min 16s on Sun SparcStation 1 with 16Mb to process a full article of the French General Taxation Law (on average, 4 sentences and 150 wordforms) ; 1 min 06s for the longest sentence. However, it is difficult to provide a full assessment of the performance of the system, given that it has been tested, until now, on relatively small corpora of original documents. For example, in the COBALT project, we have used a corpus of about 200 candidate news items which have then been translated into NKRL format, and examined through a query system in order to i) confirm their relevance ; ii) extract their main content elements (actors, circumstances, locations, dates, amounts of shares or money, etc.). Of the candidate news, 80% have been (at least partly) successfully translated; 'at least partly' means that, sometimes, the translation was incomplete due, e.g., to the difficulty of instantiating correctly some binding structures.

References

Azzam, S.: Anaphors, PPs and Disambiguation Process for Conceptual Analysis. Proc. of the 14th Int. Joint Conference on Artificial Intelligence. San Francisco: Morgan Kaufmann, 1995.

Breuker, J.A., and Wielinga, B.J.: Model Driven Knowledge Acquisition. Topics in the Design of Expert Systems. Amsterdam: North-Holland, 1989.

Bubenko, J.A.: Extending the Scope of Information Modelling. Proc. of the Fourth Int. Workshop on the Deductive Approach to Information Systems and Databases. Lloret: Universitat Politecnica de Catalunya, 1993.

Guarino, N., Carrara, M., and Giaretta, P.: An Ontology of Meta-Level Categories. Proc. of the Fourth Int. Conference on Principles of Knowledge Representation and Reasoning (KR'94). San Francisco: Morgan Kaufmann, 1994.

Kolodner, J.L.: An Introduction to Case-Based Reasoning. Art. Int. Review 6 (1992) 3-34.

Trigano, P.: Automatic Indexation and Knowledge Storing. Proc. of the 2nd Int. Symposium on the Management of Industrial and Corporate Knowledge - ISMICK'94. Compiègne: Institut International pour l'Intelligence Artificielle (IIIA), 1994.

Weibel, S., Godby, J., Miller, E., and Daniel, R.: OCLC/NCSA Medatada Workshop Report. Dublin (Ohio): OCLC Online Computer Library Center, 1995.

Zarri, G.P.: The Use of Inference Mechanisms to Improve the Retrieval Facilities from Large Relational Databases. Proc. of the 9th Int. ACM Conference on Research and Development in Information Retrieval. New York: ACM, 1986.

Zarri, G.P.: Encoding the Temporal Characteristics of the Natural Language Descriptions of (Legal) Situations. Expert Systems in Law. Amsterdam: Elsevier, 1992.

Zarri, G.P.: A Glimpse of NKRL, the 'Narrative Knowledge Representation Language'. Knowledge Representation for Natural Language Processing in Implemented Systems - Papers from the 1994 Fall Symposium. Menlo Park (CA): AAAI Press, 1994.

Zarri, G.P.: Knowledge Acquisition from Complex Narrative Texts Using the NKRL Technology. Proc. of the 9th Banff Knowledge Acquisition for Knowledge-Based Systems Workshop. Calgary: Dept. of Computer Science of the University, 1995.

Zarri, G.P., and Gilardoni, L. Structuring and Retrieval of the Complex Predicate Arguments Proper to the NKRL Conceptual Language. Proc. of the 9th Int. Symposium on Methodologies for Intelligent Systems (ISMIS'96). Berlin: Springer-Verlag, 1996.

Modelling Competitive Co-operation of Agents in a Compositional Multi-Agent Framework

Frances Brazier, Pascal van Eck and Jan Treur

Department of Mathematics and Computer Science, Vrije Universiteit Amsterdam
De Boelelaan 1081a, NL-1081 HV Amsterdam, The Netherlands
URL: http://www.cs.vu.nl/, Email: {frances,patveck,treur}@cs.vu.nl

1 Introduction

In many multi-agent domains competitive agents need to co-operate. In this paper a generic model for competitive agents is introduced: a model which can be used to support the design of agents in diverse knowledge-intensive domains. An example of the type of multi-agent situation in which this model can be applied is one in which a number of agents wish to access a given (information) resource and explicit knowledge is available (to either the accessing agents, or the resource to be accessed, or all agents involved) on appropriate orderings or priorities between the transactions from the different agents. This model includes explicit knowledge of possible communication and co-operation strategies for individual agents, but also identifies the type of communication needed between agents and the interaction needed between agents and the material world, specified in the compositional multi-agent system modelling framework DESIRE [1,2].

DESIRE is briefly introduced in Section 2. In Section 3, the role of competitive co-operation in a competitive situation is discussed. A generic model of an arbitrary competitive agent is presented in Section 4. Section 5 describes a generic model for limited resource acquisition. In Section 6, a comparison is made with an algorithmic approach to limited resource access in the domain of operating systems (see for example [4]). Discussion and further research are presented in Section 7.

2 The Multi-Agent Modelling Framework DESIRE

The multi-agent compositional modelling framework DESIRE provides support for the design of a conceptual model of the behaviour of (interacting) agents. Compositional agent models define the structure of the architectures: components in a compositional model are directly related to agents and their tasks. Existing generic agent models can be used to design specific agent models. During analysis and design, relevant components in a generic model are refined by (1) more detailed analysis of the tasks of which such components are comprised and/or (2) inclusion of specific domain knowledge. The five types of knowledge represented in the DESIRE framework at a conceptual level, detailed level and at an operational level are:

- The compositional structure of agents and their tasks. Tasks can be composed or primitive and are characterised by their input and output knowledge structures;
- Interaction within and between agents and tasks;
- Temporal relations between tasks, represented by rules in a temporal logic;
- Delegation of tasks to agents;
- Knowledge structures.

The representation at the operational level is automatically generated from the representation at the detailed level.

3 A Generic Agent Model

To model an agent capable of competitive co-operation, a generic model of an agent, developed in other multi-agent domains, is employed [6]. This model fulfils the four characteristics required for the weak notion of agency described in [7]: agents must be capable of (1) maintaining interaction with their environment by observing and performing actions in the world: *reactivity*; (2) taking the initiative: *pro-activeness*; (3) performing social actions like communication and co-operation: *social ability*; and (4) operating without the direct intervention of other (possibly human) agents: *autonomy*.

This generic agent model has six top-level components as shown in Figure 2. Interaction with the environment is performed by the components Maintain World Information and World Interaction Management. Social actions are managed by the components Agent Interaction Management and Cooperation Management. The agent's processes are co-ordinated by the component Own Process Control, enabling the agent to act autonomously and take the initiative if this is required. Tasks specific to the agent itself are included in the component Agent Specific Tasks. In most domains of application, these six components are further refined, as illustrated for competitive co-operation in Section 5 below. In general, refinement of a generic model involves specialisation (i.e., components within components are distinguished) and instantiation (i.e., (domain) specific instances of signatures and knowledge are defined). Agent models differ in the level of refinement required depending on the relative importance of the characteristics involved. Knowledge required to refine agent models includes (1) knowledge of an agent's priorities with respect to its processes, (2) knowledge of which and how information is exchanged with other agents and the external world, (3) knowledge of how information received from the external world and other agents is to be analysed and (4) knowledge of how co-operative an agent is in given situations in relation to other agents. (In [8], other approaches to agent-based knowledge modelling can be found).

Within DESIRE, agents are modelled as components that run concurrently, equipped with information links for inter-agent information exchange. Task control at the top level of a multi-agent system is minimal: it is most often restricted to the initiation of agents, an external world and the links between agents. As components, agents have their own internal agent task control. This task control knowledge specifies (asynchronous) information exchange to other agents and the world, and (concurrent) activation or suspension of internal components.

4 Competitive Agents in Co-operative Information Systems

In many real life situations, co-operation is an effective approach for allocation of limited resources. In this paper, housing is the limited resource used to illustrate the use of a generic model for competitive co-operation. Allocation of apartments within the city to individuals (with a monthly rent between x and y) is regulated by governmental policy. Two key characteristics of the policy are the role assigned to the real estate agents, namely that of co-ordination agents, and the use of a static priority scheme (duration of an individual's subscription).

Practice shows that groups of subscribed individuals co-operate—together they determine their chances and determine individual and group strategies. In deadlock situations the real estate agent is responsible for conflict resolution. To design an agent system to support an individual in need of an apartment, a model of the interaction and knowledge required to effectuate strategies such as those discussed above, is needed. This example is used below to illustrate the generic aspects of competitive co-operation.

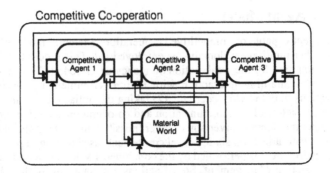

Competitive Co-operation

Fig. 1: Three agents and the material world.

5 A Generic Model of a Competitive Co-operative Agent

Competitive co-operation for resource allocation requires at least two agents and a material world. In Figure 1, three agents are depicted for the purpose of illustration. In this figure, the rounded boxes represent (composed or primitive) components, in this case agents. The small boxes attached to the components' sides, represent the agents' input and output interfaces. The links in Figure 1 between agents are defined to allow communication between agents; the links between the agents and the material world are defined to allow observations and actions to be performed. Task control is not depicted.

Figure 2 shows the composition of an individual agent and the information exchange between its components. In the following paragraphs, each of these components will be described. Due to space restrictions, it is not possible to provide more detail; instead the interested reader is referred to [5].

Maintain World Information The component Maintain World Information stores the information an agent has about the world state, namely presence of agents and resources. This information can be acquired by observation of the world (via World Interaction Management), communication with other agents, or (defeasible) reasoning.

Agent Specific Tasks In this generic agent model, only one agent specific task is modelled, namely Obtain Resource. Other agent specific tasks are not specified in the generic model (e.g. tasks in which the need to access a resource is determined).

Cooperation Management The component Cooperation Management consists of the following four components (see Figure 3):
- **Update Current Agent Information** All relevant information on other agents, often obtained by communication and/or (defeasible) reasoning, is maintained here.
- **Determine Access** Input facts about (1) the world; e.g., obtained by observation, communication, or (default or closed world) assumptions, (2) priorities between agents (received from the component Determine Priority) and (3) co-operativeness of other agents (received from the component Determine Cooperation), are used to analyse a world state (no matter how it was reached) and to draw conclusions about access to a resource.

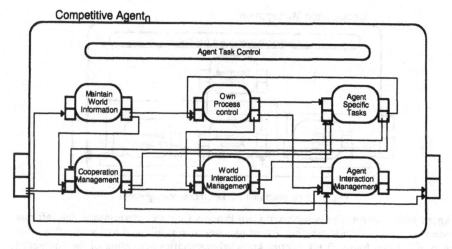

Fig. 2: Agent task composition and information exchange.

Most of the knowledge used in Determine Access specifies the conditions under which access to the resource will not be granted. The two rules shown below determine whether there is a conflict in the sense that another agent and the agent itself are both interested in accessing the resource. Note that the knowledge specified in this knowledge base does not refer directly to the application domain described in Section 4. It is generic in the sense that it can in principle be used for all domains in which limited access to resources plays a role.

If wants_resource(A) **and** wants_resource(self)   **then** conflicting_needs(A,self)

If conflicting_needs(A,self) **and** has_priority_over(A,self) **then** access_blocked_by(A)

- **Determine Priority** The task of the component Determine Priority is to determine which of two agents may access the resource first, if a conflict exists. The instantiation of Determine Priority contains domain specific knowledge, such as knowledge required for the domain outlined in Section 4. It is important to note that this knowledge may not always be sufficient to derive a unique conclusion: there may be circumstances in which no priority can be assigned.
- **Determine Cooperation** Knowledge of which agents are willing to co-operate with which other agents acquired through observation and reasoning, is used by this component to determine the level of co-operation. In the generic agent model, three options for static facts about the agent self are specified: one for a shy agent, one for a bold agent and one for a moderate agent:

If concluded(no_access_decision) **and** modest(self)   **then** to_communicate_to(A,ok)

World Interaction Management, Agent Interaction Management and **Own Process Control** The tasks of the component World Interaction Management are (1) to perform observations (including observation of the presence and relevance of other agents) and (2) to perform the action proposed by Obtain Resource in the component Agent Specific Tasks. The component Agent Interaction Management manages communication between an agent and other agents. The role of the component Own Process Control is to determine which information is needed to decide whether access to a resource is allowed, and where this information is to be found.

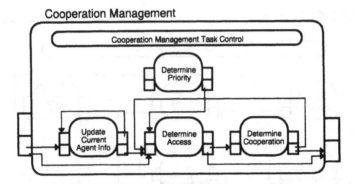

Fig. 3: Composition of Cooperation Management.

Agent task control The component Own Process Control determines which information is needed to decide whether access to a resource is allowed and where this information is to be found. Task control knowledge specifies activation of the component Own Process Control in one of the following ways: (1) The component Agent Interaction Management notices that one of the other agents requests attention, for example to access a resource, and notifies Own Process Control of the fact that new information has been received. On the basis of this new information, Own Process Control may decide that Cooperation Management is to be activated to determine whether access is to be granted. (2) The component Agent Specific Tasks expresses a need for information to the component Own Process Control, which decides which specific information is needed and where it is to be found. If Own Process Control recognises the need to access a limited resource, the component Cooperation Management is activated first to determine whether access is allowed. If access is allowed, Obtain Resource is activated.

6 Comparison with an Algorithmic Approach

The specification of the task model presented in this paper can be compared to approaches to mutual exclusion problems in more conventional environments, such as the algorithm described by Ricart and Agrawala [4]. Ricart and Agrawala's algorithm assumes the following conditions hold: (1) each agent notices each other agent's presence; (2) communication never fails; (3) each agent has the same *complete* knowledge of priorities between agents and (4) if agent A has higher priority than agent B, agent B is assumed to communicate that it grants access to the resource to agent A.

If these conditions hold, the task model described in this paper specifies the same process as the algorithm. The conditions describe a rather strictly defined domain of application, as found in, for example, the domain of operating systems. For less strictly defined real world domains, however, incompleteness of observations, defeasible communications, incomplete knowledge of priorities, inconsistencies between conclusions drawn by different agents, uncooperative agents, etc. are most common. The compositional model introduced here is particularly suitable in these domains for the following reasons: (1) by virtue of the reflective structure of the model, different strategies can be modelled with minimal effort, (2) assumptions with respect to for instance communication, priorities and co-operation appear explicitly in the model, and (3) the different types of knowledge are explicitly distinguished. The distinction between different types of knowledge and different types of behaviour results in flexibility, adaptability and transparency: essential characteristics of a knowledge-based approach.

7 Discussion and Future Research

In this paper, a generic model is presented for competitive agents in a domain that requires limited access to a given resource. Modelling the specific types of knowledge involved and the behaviour of agents in relation to each other results in a transparent compositional model. One specific domain of co-operation has been used, in which resource access is granted first on the basis of (given) priorities, and (if no decision can be taken) on the basis of dynamically observed co-operativeness of other agents. However, the modularity of the architecture, in which both static and dynamic behaviour are explicitly specified, allows for flexible adaptability to other strategies. Current research focuses among others on the further development of the semantics of the framework ([2]), on verification and validation ([3]) and on modelling beliefs, desires, intentions and commitments in multi-agent systems.

Acknowledgements This research was partly supported by ESPRIT III BRA project 6156 DRUMS II on Defeasible Reasoning and Uncertainty Management Systems.

References

1. Brazier, F.M.T., Treur, J., Wijngaards, N.J.E., and Willems, M. Formal specification of hierarchically (de)composed tasks. In: Gaines, B.R. and Musen, M. (eds.), *Proc. of the 9th Banff Knowledge Acquisition for Knowledge-Based Systems Workshop*, Vol. 2, pp. 25/1-25/20, SRDG Publications, Deptartment of Computer Science, University of Calgary, 1995.
2. Brazier, F.M.T., Treur, J., Wijngaards, N.J.E., and Willems, M. Temporal semantics of complex reasoning tasks. In: Gaines, B.R. and Musen, M. (eds.), *Proc. of the 10th Banff Knowledge Acquisition for Knowledge-Based Systems Workshop*, Vol. 1, pp. 15/1-15/17, SRDG Publications, Deptartment of Computer Science, University of Calgary, 1996. Extended version to appear in *Data and Knowledge Engineering*.
3. Cornelissen, F., Jonker, C. and Treur, J. Compositional verification of knowledge-based systems: A case study for diagnostic reasoning. In: *Proc. European Knowledge Acquisition Workshop EKAW'97*, Springer-Verlag, 1997 (this volume).
4. Ricart, G. and Agrawala, A.K. An optimal algorithm for mutual exclusion in computer networks. *Comm. ACM*, Vol. 24(1), pp. 9-17, Jan. 1981.
5. Brazier, F.M.T., Van Eck, P.A.T. and Treur, J. Modelling cooperative behaviour for resource access in a compositional multi-agent framework. In: Fiadeiro, J.L. and Schobbens, P.-Y. (eds.) Proc. 2nd Workshop of the ModelAge Project, ModelAge'96, Universidade de Lisboa, 1996.
6. Brazier, F.M.T., Dunin Keplicz, B., Jennings, N. and Treur, J. DESIRE: Modelling Multi-Agent Systems in a Compositional Formal Framework, *International Journal of Cooperative Information Systems*, Vol. 6, Huhns, M. and Singh, M. (eds.), Special Issue on Formal Methods in Cooperative Information Systems: Multi-Agent Systems, 1997.
7. Wooldridge, M.J. and Jennings, N.R. Intelligent agents: Theory and practice. *The Knowledge Engineering Review*, 10(2):115-152, 1995.
8. Dieng, R., Corby, O. and Labidi, S. Agent-based knowledge acquisition. In: Steels, L., Schreiber, G. and Van de Velde, W. (eds.) *A Future for Knowledge Acquisition. Proc. EKAW'94.* LNAI, Vol. 867, pp. 63-82, Springer-Verlag, 1994.

An Instrument for a Purpose Driven Comparison of Modelling Frameworks

Frances M.T. Brazier and Niek J.E. Wijngaards

July 9th, 1997

Artificial Intelligence Group
Department of Mathematics and Computer Science
Vrije Universiteit Amsterdam
de Boelelaan 1081a, 1081 HV Amsterdam, The Netherlands
Email: {frances, niek}@cs.vu.nl
URL: http://www.cs.vu.nl/~wai

Keywords: purpose-driven comparison, knowledge engineering, modelling frameworks.

Abstract. During the past decade a number of modelling frameworks for knowledge based systems have been developed. In this paper an approach to the comparison of modelling frameworks is proposed, based on the aims and purposes behind the frameworks. A purpose oriented comparison of the frameworks DESIRE, CommonKADS, PROTÉGÉ-II, MIKE, VITAL and KARL provides insight in their differences and similarities.

1 Introduction

During the past decade much research within the field of knowledge engineering has focussed on the development of frameworks to support the design of knowledge based systems. To understand and appreciate the differences between the different modelling frameworks a number of comparisons between languages and frameworks have been made.

Problem-oriented comparison (comparison based on the application of an approach to one given problem) to both languages (Treur & Wetter, 1993; Harmelen, Lopez de Mántaras, Malec & Treur, 1993) and modelling frameworks (Linster, 1991, 1994; Fensel, 1995; Schreiber & Birmingham, 1996) as a joint activity, has increased understanding of different modelling frameworks. An advantage of problem-oriented comparison is that a well-described problem in which specific aspects of a problem are highlighted provides a concrete basis for comparison. A disadvantage is that the problem needs to be sufficiently well-defined to allow for comparison and sufficiently broad to be able to identify strengths and weaknesses of approaches. Another disadvantage is that solutions may differ significantly making comparison difficult.

Fensel and van Harmelen (1994) compared KADS languages on the basis of *modelling primitives*. An advantage of this approach to comparison is the well defined scope of application. A disadvantage is that the approach bases comparison on syntactical ('superficial') similarities and not on the semantic background.

Another approach to the comparison of modelling frameworks is to analyse the purposes and aims behind a framework. A method for *purpose-driven comparison* of *languages* is proposed in (Revise, 1996), in which a number of goals behind the design of two formal specification languages are identified and compared. Design choices are related to the goals pursued. An advantage of purpose-driven comparison is that a list of possible purposes provides a well-defined basis for comparison. Disadvantages are that the purposes behind an approach have not always been made explicit, and that the concrete implications of differences are not always obvious.

In this paper an instrument for a purpose-driven comparison of *modelling frameworks* is proposed: purpose-driven and not problem-driven, modelling framework comparison and not language comparison. As a result, modelling frameworks are characterised on the basis of the goals they have been designed to pursue, and on the design choices made to achieve these goals within the framework.

2 An Instrument to Compare Modelling Frameworks

To design an instrument with which modelling frameworks can be compared: (a) existing comparisons of languages and frameworks were studied and analysed (Treur & Wetter, 1993; Harmelen, Lopez de Mántaras, Malec & Treur, 1993; Fensel & Harmelen, 1994; Linster, 1991, 1994; Fensel, 1995; Schreiber & Birmingham, 1996); (b) a number of frameworks and languages were analysed on the basis of available

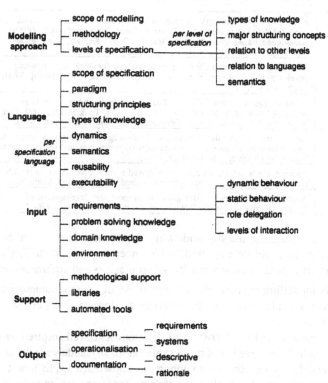

Fig. 1. Purposes of a modelling framework organised as elements per category.

literature (including Mazza, Fairclough, Melton, de Pablo, Scheffer, and Stevens, 1994; Sage & Palmer, 1990; Revise, 1996) and, in some cases on the basis of hands-on experience; and (c) research groups (from the Vrije Universiteit Amsterdam, Universiteit van Amsterdam, University of Karlsruhe, Stanford University, Open University and Université de Paris-Sud) evaluated the instrument and the specific results for their modelling framework.

The instrument distinguishes five categories of elements of modelling frameworks. As shown in Figure 1: (1) the characteristics of the methodology behind the modelling framework including levels of specification, (2) the modelling and specification languages, (3) the support provided, (4) the input required to model and specify a knowledge-intensive system, and (5) the output of modelling and specification.

3 A Purpose Driven Comparison

The instrument has been used to compare six modelling frameworks originally designed for knowledge intensive domains and still currently subject of research: DESIRE, CommonKADS, PROTÉGÉ-II, MIKE, VITAL, and TASK. These modelling frameworks are designed to support the complete development process of knowledge intensive systems from knowledge acquisition to operationalisation. The modelling frameworks are each briefly described below.

DESIRE	A modelling framework within which tasks can be modelled, specified and operationalised is presented in Brazier, Treur, Wijngaards and Willems (1995, 1996) (knowledge based systems) and Brazier, Dunin-Keplicz, Jennings and Treur (1997) (multi-agent systems).
Common-KADS	An advanced and comprehensive methodology for integrated knowledge-based system development (Wielinga, Schreiber. Breuker, 1992; Hoog, Martil, Wielinga, Taylor, Bright, Velde, 1994).
PROTÉGÉ-II	A knowledge-acquisition shell including problem solving methods as well as tools for acquiring knowledge (Musen, 1990; Puerta, Egar, Tu & Musen, 1992; Gennari, Altman, Musen, 1994, Eriksson, Puerta, Gennari. Rothenfluh, Tu & Musen, 1995).
MIKE	An approach for the development of knowledge-based systems integrates semiformal specification techniques, formal specification techniques, and prototyping into a coherent framework (Angele, Fensel, Studer, 1996).
VITAL	An approach to structured knowledge-based system development including a knowledge engineering and a project management methodology (Shadbolt, Motta, Rouge. 1993).
TASK	A modelling framework designed to support the development of knowledge-based systems (Pierret-Golbreich, 1993; Talon and Pierret-Golbreich, 1996).

Analysis of the results for the six modelling frameworks shows that although shared purposes exist (as could be expected) differences between modelling frameworks have been made explicit. Below a number of similarities and differences are listed.

- All six modelling frameworks support reuse of generic components: models / problem solving methods & ontologies, domain independent & domain dependent.
- The frameworks MIKE, VITAL, and CommonKADS (all inspired by the KADS-I "philosophy") are very similar: the same (kinds of) models are distinguished.
- PROTÉGÉ-II provides the most support for knowledge acquisition: the PROTÉGÉ-II framework generates tools for each knowledge acquisition task.

- The MIKE framework provides extensive support for the representation of the raw material obtained via knowledge elicitation (e.g. video, texts, ...).
- The VITAL framework provides extra support for the project management.
- The DESIRE framework provides support and tools for simulation of concurrent processes.
- The CommonKADS framework includes tools with which the environment of a knowledge-based system can be modelled.
- Strategic, dynamic interaction between components / systems / agents is explicitly modelled in meta-level architectures in DESIRE. TASK includes limited reflection and strategic knowledge as well. Limited reflection is included in (ML)^2 and NewKARL for other purposes.
- The KADS-like frameworks, the DESIRE framework and the TASK framework include a formal specification language with a formal semantics.
- Hybrid control is provided by both the TASK and the DESIRE frameworks.

The comparison of modelling frameworks, based on the purposes for which the frameworks have been designed, can be used to support the selection of a modelling framework. For example, to design a diagnostic reasoning system in a medical domain, for which specific knowledge needs to be acquired for large numbers of physicians, the PROTÉGÉ-II modelling framework provides the most support. If, however, a system is to be designed in which the reasoning behaviour and strategies of two co-operating agents is to be explicitly modelled, the DESIRE framework is most appropriate. If the environment of a system is of importance, the CommonKADS and MIKE modelling frameworks provide the most support. Strategical reasoning is supported by both TASK and DESIRE, reflective reasoning is most supported by DESIRE. All frameworks support prototyping to some extent, varying from automated prototype generation of the entire detailed specification language to hand-made partial prototyping of parts of the detailed specification language.

4 Conclusions

Application of the proposed instrument has made a number of distinctive characteristics of the different approaches explicit, providing a basis for comparison.

This instrument can play a useful role in structuring reuse and translation of parts of modelling frameworks, application specific models, libraries (see Motta, 1997), generic structures, etc.

The comparison of frameworks, based on the purposes for which the frameworks have been designed, can be used to support the selection of a modelling framework. The instrument provides a means to structure the comparison. The instrument can also be used as a 'shopping list': a shopping list for the knowledge engineer in search of models, tools and methodologies. The knowledge engineer should be able to combine parts of various modelling frameworks into a 'new' modelling framework which is most suited to the situation at hand. The instrument would benefit from consensus in the research community on terminology for the description of modelling frameworks - a goal that may one day be reached.

Acknowledgements

This research has been (partially) supported by the Dutch Foundation for Knowledge-based systems (SKBS), within the A3 project "An environment for modular knowledge-based systems (based on meta-knowledge) for design tasks" and NWO-SION within project 612-322-316: "Evolutionary design in knowledge-based systems" (REVISE).

Several people have contributed to this paper: Stefan Decker and Michael Erdmann (University of Karlsruhe, Mike), Frank van Harmelen (Vrije Universiteit Amsterdam & Univeristeit van Amsterdam, CommonKADS), Enrico Motta (Open University, VITAL), Christine Pierret-Golbreich (Université de Paris-Sud, TASK), Remco Straatman (University of Amsterdam, CommonKADS), Jan Treur (Vrije Universiteit Amsterdam, DESIRE), and Samson Tu (Stanford University, PROTÉGÉ-II).

References

ANGELE, J., FENSEL, D., and STUDER, D. (1996). Domain and Task Modelling in MIKE. *Proceedings of the IFIP WG 8.1/13.2 Joint Working Conference, Domain Knowledge for Interactive System Design.* Geneva, Switzerland, May 8-10th, 1996.

BRAZIER, F.M.T., DUNIN-KEPLICZ, B.M., JENNINGS, N.R. and TREUR, J. (1997), DESIRE: modelling multi-agent systems in a compositional formal framework, In: HUHNS, M. and SINGH, M. (Eds.), *International Journal of Cooperative Information Systems, IJCIS* vol. 6 (1), special issue on Formal Methods in Cooperative Information Systems: Multi-Agent Systems, pp. 67-94.

BRAZIER, F.M.T., TREUR, J., WIJNGAARDS, N.J.E., and WILLEMS, M. (1995). Formal specification of hierarchically (de)composed tasks. In B.R. Gaines and M.A. Musen (Eds.). *Proceedings of the 9th Banff Knowledge Acquisition for Knowledge-Based Systems Workshop, KAW '95,* 1995, 2, pp. 25/1-25/20. Calgary: SRDG Publications, Department of Computer Science, University of Calgary.

BRAZIER, F.M.T., TREUR, J., WIJNGAARDS, N.J.E. and WILLEMS, M. (1996). Temporal semantics and specification of complex tasks. In: GAINES, B.R., and MUSEN, M.A. (Eds.), *Proceedings of the 10th Banff Knowledge Acquisition for Knowledge-based Systems workshop (KAW'96),* Calgary: SRDG Publications, Department of Computer Science, University of Calgary, pages 15/1-15/17.

ERIKSSON, H., PUERTA, A.R., GENNARI, J.H., ROTHENFLUH, T.E., TU, S.W., and MUSEN, M.A. (1995). Custom-Tailored Development Tools for Knowledge-Based Systems. In: GAINES, B.R. and Musen, M.A. (Eds.). *Proceedings of the 9th Banff Knowledge Acquisition for Knowledge-Based Systems Workshop,* SRDG Publications, Department of Computer Science, University of Calgary, 1995, pp. 26/1-26/19.

FENSEL, D. (1995). Formal Specification Languages in Knowledge and Software Engineering, *The Knowledge Engineering Review,* Vol 10(4), pp. 361-404.

FENSEL, D. and HARMELEN, F. VAN (1994). A comparison of languages which operationalise and formalise KADS models of expertise. *The Knowledge Engineering Review,* 9, pp. 105-146.

GENNARI, J.H., ALTMAN, R.B., and MUSEN, M.A. (1994). *Reuse with PROTÉGÉ-II: From Elevators to Ribosomes.* Knowledge systems laboratory, KSL-94-71, Stanford University School of Medicine, 1994.

HARMELEN, F. VAN, LOPEZ DE MÁNTARAS, R., MALEC, J., and TREUR, J. (1993). Comparing Formal Specification Languages for Complex Reasoning Systems. In: (Treur & Wetter, 1993), pp. 257-282.

HOOG, R. DE, MARTIL, R., WIELINGA, B.J., TAYLOR, R., BRIGHT, C., AND VELDE, W. VAN DE (1994). The CommonKADS model set. Technical Report KADS-II/M1/DM1.1b/UvA/018/6.0/FINAL, SWI, University of Amsterdam, 1994.

LINSTER, M. (1991). Sisyphus'91 part 2: Models of problem solving. Statement of the sample problem. In: SMEED, D., LINSTER, M., BOOSE, J.H., and GAINES, B.R. (Eds.). *Proceedings of the EKAW'91*, Glasgow, University of Strathclyde.

LINSTER, M. (1994). Sisyphus '91/92: Models of problem solving. *International Journal of Human-Computer Studies*, 40, 1994, pp. 189-192.

MAZZA, C., FAIRCLOUGH, J., MELTON, B., PABLO, D. DE, SCHEFFER, A., and STEVENS, R. (1994). *Software Engineering Standards*. Prentice Hall.

MOTTA, E. (1997). A comparative analysis of modelling frameworks. Working paper. Knowledge Media Institute, The Open University.

MUSEN, M.A. (1990). An editor for the conceptual models of interactive knowledge-acquisition tools. In: BOOSE, J.H. and GAINES, B.R. (Eds.). *The Foundations of Knowledge Acquisition*. Knowledge-Based Systems, Academic Press Limited, 4, 1990, pp. 135-160.

PIERRET-GOLBREICH, C. (1993). Task Model Perspective of Knowledge Engineering, *7th European Knowledge Acquisition Workshop*, EKAW'93, Springer-Verlag.

PUERTA, A.R., EGAR, J.W., TU, S.W., and MUSEN, M.A. (1992). A multiple-method knowledge-acquisition shell for the automatic generation of knowledge-acquisition tools. *Knowledge Acquisition*, 1992, 4, pp. 171-196.

REVISE (project) (1996). A Purpose Driven Method for Language Comparison. In: SHADBOLT, N., O'HARA, K., and SCHREIBER, A.TH. *Advances in Knowledge Acquisition. 9th European Knowledge Acquisition Workshop, EKAW'96*. Lecture Notes in Artificial Intelligence, volume 1076, pp. 66 - 81.

SAGE, A.P. and PALMER, J.D. (1990). *Software Systems Engineering*. John Wiley and Sons.

SCHREIBER, A.TH., and BIRMINGHAM, W.P. (1996). Editorial: the Sisyphus-VT initiative. *International Journal of Human-Computer Studies*, 44, 1996, pp. 275-280.

SHADBOLT, N., MOTTA, E., and ROUGE, A. (1993). Constructing Knowledge-Based Systems. *IEEE Software*, November, pp. 34-38.

TALON, X. and PIERRET-GOLBREICH, C. (1996). TASK: from the specification to the implementation. *8th IEEE International Conference on Tools with Artificial Intelligence*, pp. 80-88, IEEE Computer Society Press.

TREUR, J. and WETTER, TH (Eds.) (1993). *Formal Specification of Complex Reasoning Systems*. Ellis Horwood.

WIELINGA, B.J., SCHREIBER, A.TH., and BREUKER, J.A. (1992). KADS: a modelling approach to knowledge engineering. *Knowledge Acquisition*, 4, 1992, pp. 5-53.

Knowledge Discovery in Rule Bases

Timo Breidenstein[1,2], Isabelle Bournaud[1] and Francis Wolinski[2]

[1] Université Pierre et Marie Curie, LIP 6, 4 place Jussieu, F-75252 Paris Cedex 5
[2] Informatique CDC, DTA/RDT, 113 rue Jean Marin Naudin, F-92220 Bagneux

Abstract. In rule based, automated management systems, knowledge is represented *explicitly* as long as it is necessary for the functioning of the system. However, some knowledge which might be quite useful for maintenance purposes, remains *implicit* and disseminated in the rule base. We present an original approach for the discovery of such implicit knowledge, based on machine learning techniques. We will illustrate the use of our approach in the book-keeping domain, where it has proven its interest within the scope of an industrial project.

1 Introduction

Management systems are subject to frequent and complicated maintenance operations. Rule-based implementation makes management systems comprehensible and usable for domain experts, and enables them to participate directly in the development process. However, some knowledge remains *implicit* and disseminated in rule bases. For example, in the portfolio book-keeping system of the Caisse des Dépôts et Consignations (CDC), the rules for "trading costs" specify that these costs have to be booked to accounts of type 63 _7 ___1; some other rules specify that "profits" and "losses" have to be booked respectively to accounts of type 73 _____1 and 63 _____1. Thus, these rules specify *explicitly* the accounts to be used in each case. But as a whole, these rules also contain *implicitly* the fact that at CDC "trading costs" and "losses" are considered as "charges" which have to be booked to accounts of type 6 _____, according to French accounting regulations.

In this article, we propose to use machine learning to extract two kinds of implicit knowledge from rule bases. On the one hand, general and pertinent rules, applying to several situations which have to be managed in analogous ways. On the other hand, taxonomies of domain concepts, represented by graphs of subsets of attribute values describing the situations to be managed. These taxonomies are deduced from the factorizations specified by general rules. By making this implicit knowledge explicit, we hope to facilitate the maintenance of management processes by domain experts.

2 An Approach to Knowledge Discovery

We proposed a rule based knowledge representation model for management processes [3] [4]. This model provides for the possibility to factorize implicit, disseminated knowledge into *general rules*.

Our approach to knowledge extraction from such rule bases is composed of two stages. During the first stage, we construct general rules from rule clusters made up from rules which represent similar knowledge. We use the machine learning system COING [1] [2] to perform the clustering task. The second stage eliminates general rules which are not pertinent to domain experts.

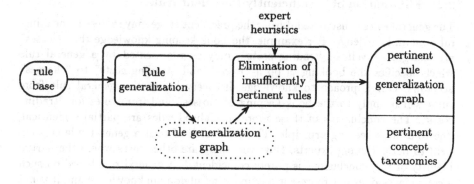

Fig. 1. Our approach to knowledge discovery in rule bases

2.1 Rule Generalization

Rule generalization is done in two steps. First, the rules are categorized into clusters and their conclusions are generalized. Then, each cluster is transformed into a general rule by associating a premise to it.

Rule Clustering with COING. In a rule base, there may be several rules with partially identical conclusions. For example, several rules of a book-keeping system may specify that an amount has to enter in the accounts with a factor of $\frac{1}{100}$: three rules respectively for the situations where the amount is in lira, in pesetas and in yen. The knowledge that amounts in "soft currencies" have to be booked with a factor of $\frac{1}{100}$, and that lira, peseta and yen are such "soft currencies" is not stated explicitly, but it is implicitly present in the rule base.

In order to discover this kind of implicit knowledge in a rule base, it is necessary to identify sets of rules (clusters) which have partially identical conclusions. To do so, we use the system COING of conceptual clustering [1], [2]. COING identifies *all* sets of rules with partially identical conclusions, builds a cluster for each of these sets, and associates the common part of these rules' conclusions to it. This construction relies on a domain independent generalization technique.

Construction of Premises. In order to transform each cluster produced by COING into a general rule, we associate a premise to each of them. This premise is build from those of the rules in the cluster.

After this first stage, a rule conclusion and a rule premise are associated to each cluster built by COING. Thus, each cluster may be considered as a general rule. The result of this stage is represented as a comprehensive rule generalization graph which materializes the set inclusion relation between the corresponding clusters.

2.2 Elimination of Insufficiently Pertinent Rules

The general rules constructed during the precedent stage may represent meaningful domain knowledge. For example, the book-keeping knowledge that "losses" are charges as well as "trading costs", may be represented by a general rule which specifies the booking of both "losses" and "trading costs" to "charges" accounts. Our approach to knowledge discovery builds this general rule from rules which apply to the book-keeping of "losses" and from rules for "trading costs". The conclusions of these more specialized rules are partially identical, due to a book-keeping principle. The conclusion of such a general rule is *pertinent* to book-keeping experts. However, there are other cases where the partial identity of rule conclusions is purely coincidental. A general rule based on such a coincidence does not represent any meaningful domain knowledge and it is not pertinent to domain experts.

Non pertinent general rules do not provide any useful domain knowledge and complicate the comprehension of the rule generalization graph by experts. In order to eliminate rules which are insufficiently pertinent we use domain-oriented heuristics to formalize the notion of *pertinence of general rules*. We specify a numeric "pertinence function" which associates a pertinence value to each general rule. Such a notion of rule "interestingness" is also used in the TRAVELERS system [6]. Thus, the rule generalization graph is reduced to a pertinent rule generalization graph, which is comprehensible to domain experts.

From a graph of pertinent generalizations one can deduce concept taxonomies which are pertinent too. The rules' premises specify subsets of possible values for attributes of the situations which have to be managed. If we consider for a given attribute the set inclusion graph of these subsets, we obtain a taxonomy of concepts for the given attribute.

3 Application to Book-keeping

We apply our method as part of an industrial project which allows to specify book-keeping systems based on unstructured rule bases [7]. We illustrate the application of our approach to the book-keeping domain with a base of 69 book-keeping rules, each of them specifying an account number for a booking [4].

First Stage. For this initial rule base, we obtained a comprehensive rule generalization graph with 50 general rules (cf. Fig. 2). Compared to the number of initial rules, the number of general rules is considerable. This is due to the fact that, whenever the conclusions of some rules have anything in common, COING builds a cluster of these rules.

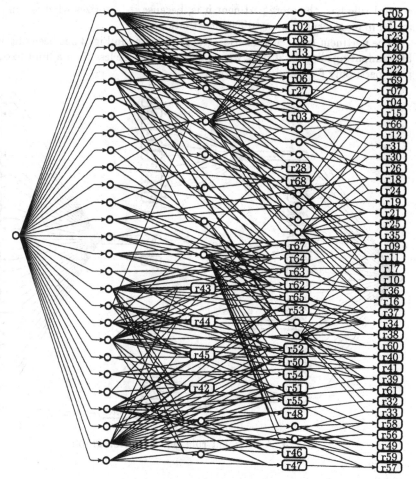

Fig. 2. The comprehensive rule generalization graph

Second Stage. We use a pertinence function which combines heuristics from the book-keeping domain (weighting and first factor) with domain-independent heuristics (second factor). The pertinence of a general rule r is calculated by:

$$\text{pertinence}(r) = \left\{ \begin{array}{c} \text{total weight of the} \\ \text{account number positions} \\ \text{specified in } r\text{'s conclusion.} \end{array} \right\} * \left\{ \begin{array}{c} \text{nb. of } r\text{'s direct} \\ \text{specialisations} \end{array} \right\}$$

The heuristics from the book-keeping domain consider that, the further an account number position is to the left, the more meaningful it is, and the more meaningful account number positions are specified in a rule's conclusion without being already specified in more general rules, the more pertinent the rule is. The domain-independent heuristic considers that, the more direct specializations a general rule has, the more pertinent it is, because it factorizes what is common to the management of many different situations.

The pertinent rule generalization graph presented in Fig. 3 has been obtained by eliminating all general rules with a pertinence value less than a limit fixed by an expert; only 6 general rules remain:

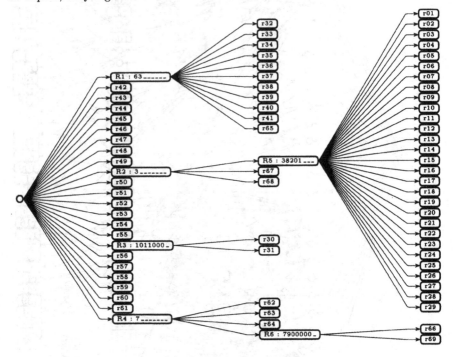

Fig. 3. A pertinent rule generalization graph

The remaining general rules in this example are pertinent from a bookkeeping point of view. For example, rule R_5 specifies that all exchange accounts, which are used for multi-currency operations, have account numbers of type "38201 _ _ _".

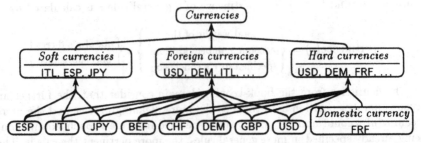

Fig. 4. A currency taxonomy deduced from the rules shown in Fig. 3

From such a graph of pertinent rule generalization we may deduce concept taxonomies. Figure 4 shows a currency taxonomy which represents the set inclusion relation between currency sets used by the premises of the book-keeping rules. The fact that ITL, ESP and JPY form a node in this taxonomy reveals that these currencies are treated similarly by one or more rules. Concept taxonomies may help experts in analyzing rule bases [4].

4 Conclusion

In this paper we present an approach to extract implicit knowledge from rule bases. Our approach uses machine learning techniques to build generalization hierarchies of rules from existing rule bases. General rules reduce redundancy by factorization and thus facilitate rule base maintenance.

The goal of the system TIERESIAS [5] is also to facilitate rule base maintenance. TIERESIAS relies on organizational meta-knowledge to guide the interactive transfer of domain knowledge from a human expert to a knowledge base. The organizational meta-knowledge has to be provided by an expert.

One interesting research direction is the use of our knowledge discovery approach in order to provide meta-knowledge which might guide the acquisition of domain knowledge.

References

1. Isabelle Bournaud and Jean-Gabriel Ganascia. Construction de hiérarchies conceptuelles pour l'organisation de connaissances. In *Langages et Modèles à Objets (LMO)*, pp 120–133, Leysin (CH), October 1996. École Polytechnique Fédérale de Lausanne.
2. Isabelle Bournaud. *Regroupement conceptuel pour l'organisation de connaissances*. PhD Thesis, Université Paris VI, Paris (F), October 1996.
3. Timo Breidenstein and Francis Wolinski. Un modèle de représentation de connaissances pour l'imputation comptable. In *Langages et Modèles à Objets (LMO)*, pp 215–227, Leysin (CH), October 1996. École Polytechnique Fédérale de Lausanne.
4. Timo Breidenstein. *MAGE : une méthode de modélisation des processus de gestion. Application à l'imputation comptable*. PhD Thesis, Université Paris VI, Paris (F), June 1997.
5. Randall Davis. Knowledge Acquisition in Rule-Based Systems – Knowledge about Representations as a Basis for System Construction and Maintenance. In Donald Arthur Waterman and Frederick Hayes-Roth, editors, *Workshop on Pattern-Directed Inference Systems*, pp 99–134, Honolulu, Hawaii, 1977. Academic Press.
6. John A. Major and John Mangano. In *Selecting among rules induced from a hurricane database*. Proc. of KDD-93 : the AAAI-93 workshop on Knowledge Discovery in Databases, pp 28–39, 1993.
7. Projet Assistant Comptable. Spécifications détaillées rétro-conception. Internal report, Informatique CDC, SOPRA, Quadrant, June 1996.

Supporting Probability Elicitation by Sensitivity Analysis*

Veerle M.H. Coupé [1] and *Linda C. van der Gaag* [2]

[1] Center for Clinical Decision Sciences,
Department of Public Health, Erasmus University Rotterdam,
P.O. Box 1738, 3000 DR Rotterdam, The Netherlands,

[2] Department of Computer Science, Utrecht University,
P.O. Box 80.089, 3508 TB Utrecht, The Netherlands,

Abstract. When building a Bayesian belief network, generally a huge number of probabilities have to be assessed. We argue that the elicitation of these probabilities can be supported by iteratively performing *sensitivity analyses* on the network, starting with rough, initial assessments. Giving insight into which probabilities require high accuracy and which do not, performing a sensitivity analysis allows for focusing elicitation efforts on the more critical probabilities of the belief network.

1 Introduction

Bayesian belief networks by now are known as intuitively appealing representations of uncertainty, useful in addressing complex problem domains [1]. A *belief network* basically is a representation of a probability distribution on a set of statistical variables [2]. It encodes, in a graphical structure, the variables of importance in a domain under study, along with their influential interrelationships. The strengths of these relationships are quantified by conditional probabilities.

Bayesian belief networks are generally developed with the help of domain experts. Although requiring considerable effort, building the graphical structure of a belief network is quite practicable. In fact, building a network's structure has parallels to designing domain models for more traditional knowledge-based systems, for which well-known knowledge-engineering techniques are available [3]. Unfortunately, quantifying the graphical structure is a far harder task. Quantification amounts to assessing various probabilities. Although for most domains of application probabilistic information is available from literature or from statistical data, experience shows that it seldom is directly amenable to encoding in a belief network. Experts, therefore, will have to assess the majority of the probabilities required, even though they are often reluctant to do so.

---

* The investigations were (partly) supported by the Netherlands Computer Science Research Foundation with financial support from the Netherlands Organization for Scientific Research (NWO).

For probability elicitation from experts, various techniques are available from the field of decision theory [4]. Unfortunately, these techniques tend to be too time-consuming to be of practical use for assessing the huge number of probabilities for a belief network. In this paper, we observe that not every assessment requires high accuracy. Some probabilities have more impact on a belief network's behaviour than others. To gain insight into the level of accuracy that is required for the various probabilities, we propose performing a *sensitivity analysis* [5]. The basic idea of sensitivity analysis of a belief network is to systematically vary initial assessments for the network's probabilities and study the effects on its behaviour. For the less influential probabilities rough estimates may suffice, whereas for the more critical ones further elicitation efforts may be worthwhile. We feel that iteratively performing sensitivity analyses and refining critical probabilities will ultimately yield a sufficiently robust belief network.

2 Bayesian Belief Networks

A *Bayesian belief network* is a representation of a joint probability distribution on a set of statistical variables. Characteristic of a belief network is its graphical structure composed of nodes and arcs. Each node represents a variable that takes its value from a set of discrete values; we will restrict the discussion to binary variables V, taking one of the values *true*, denoted v, and *false*, denoted $\neg v$. The arcs in the structure represent the influential relationships among the variables. The tail of an arc indicates the cause of the effect at the head of the arc. Absence of an arc between two variables means that these variables do not influence each other directly, and hence are conditionally independent.

We consider the following fragment of (fictitious) medical information [6]:

> "Metastatic cancer is a possible cause of a brain tumour, and is also an explanation for increased total serum calcium. In turn either of these could explain a patient falling into a coma. Severe headaches are also associated with a brain tumour."

In this fragment, five variables are identified: metastatic cancer (MC), a brain tumour (B), an increased level of serum calcium (ISC), falling into a coma (C), and severe headaches (SH). The relationships among these variables are encoded in the graphical structure shown in Figure 1. The arc $B \to SH$, for

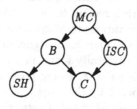

Fig. 1. An example belief network.

example, reflects that the presence of a brain tumour is a possible cause of severe headaches.

In a belief network, the strengths of the relationships among the represented variables are described by conditional probabilities. For each node, the probabilities of its values are specified, conditional on the various possible values for its parents in the graphical structure. For our example network, we assume the following probabilities:

$$p(mc) = \qquad 0.20 \qquad p(isc \mid mc) = \quad 0.80 \qquad p(c \mid b, isc) = \qquad 0.80$$
$$p(b \mid mc) = \quad 0.20 \qquad p(isc \mid \neg mc) = 0.20 \qquad p(c \mid \neg b, isc) = \quad 0.80$$
$$p(b \mid \neg mc) = 0.05 \qquad p(sh \mid b) = \qquad 0.80 \qquad p(c \mid b, \neg isc) = \quad 0.80$$
$$p(sh \mid \neg b) = \qquad 0.60 \qquad p(c \mid \neg b, \neg isc) = 0.05$$

These probabilities reflect, for example, that knowing whether or not metastatic cancer is present has a considerable influence on the probability of an increased level of serum calcium in a patient. The probabilities further reveal that in the presence of *either* a brain tumour or an increased level of serum calcium, a patient is likely to fall into a coma; otherwise, a coma is highly unlikely.

A belief network defines a unique probability distribution and can therefore be used for calculating any prior or posterior probability of interest. For this purpose, efficient algorithms are available [2, 7].

3 Building a Bayesian Belief Network

Building a Bayesian belief network for a domain of application involves various tasks. After the variables of importance and their associated values have been identified, the graphical structure of the network in the making is elicited. To this end, domain experts are interviewed. Since the experts are allowed to express their knowledge in a form they feel comfortable with, using causality for a guiding principle, their statements and, hence, the structure of the network, tend to be quite robust. The task of building a belief network's graphical structure has parallels to designing knowledge-based systems in general. Well-known knowledge-engineering techniques can therefore be used for this task.

Once the graphical structure of a belief network is built, its quantification commences. Quantifying a network's structure amounts to assessing various conditional probabilities for the represented variables. Although probabilistic information is often available from literature or from statistical data, experience shows that it seldom contributes to the entire quantification task. As a consequence, a huge number of probabilities remain to be assessed by domain experts. The field of decision theory offers various techniques for the elicitation of judgemental probabilities [4]. These techniques are designed to avert well-known problems of bias and poor calibration typically found in human probability assessment. Application of these techniques to assessing probabilities for a belief network, however, is generally hampered by the huge number of probabilities required. Supplementary techniques tailored to belief-network quantification are therefore being sought [8].

4 Sensitivity Analysis

Sensitivity analysis is a general technique from the field of decision theory for studying the effects of the uncertainties in the parameters of a model on this model's outcome [5]. For a Bayesian belief network, sensitivity analysis provides for studying the effects of the uncertainties in the network's probabilities on a probability of interest and, hence, for uncovering the critical probabilities. Elicitation efforts may then be focused on the more critical probabilities, while for the less critical ones rough estimates may suffice. We envision iteratively performing sensitivity analyses and refining critical probabilities until satisfactory behaviour of the belief network in the making is obtained or until the costs of further elicitation outweigh the benefits of higher accuracy.

For a belief network, the simplest type of sensitivity analysis is to systematically vary one of the network's probabilities, keeping all others fixed. Such a sensitivity analysis is termed a *one-way sensitivity analysis*. In a *two-way sensitivity analysis*, two probabilities are varied simultaneously. In addition to the separate effects of variation of the two probabilities, a two-way sensitivity analysis reveals the joint effect of their variation on a probability of interest. In essence, it is also possible to vary more than two probabilities at the same time. As the results of such an analysis generally are hard to interpret, we confine ourselves to presenting one-way and two-way sensitivity analyses.

We illustrate performing a *one-way sensitivity analysis* on our example belief network. We systematically vary the probability $p(mc)$ of a patient presenting with metastatic cancer and the probability $p(b \mid \neg mc)$ of a brain tumour in the absence of metastatic cancer, respectively, and study the effects of their separate variation on the prior probability $\Pr(b)$ of a patient developing a brain tumour. The results of these two analyses are shown in Figure 2. The left subfigure shows

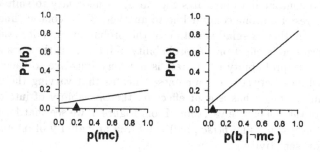

Fig. 2. Two one-way sensitivity analyses for the example belief network.

that varying the prior probability $p(mc)$ of metastatic cancer from 0 to 1 has just a minor effect on $\Pr(b)$: the probability $\Pr(b)$ of a brain tumour slowly increases from 0.05 to 0.2 approximately. Varying the probability $p(b \mid \neg mc)$ of a brain tumour in the absence of metastatic cancer in a patient, on the other hand, has a much stronger effect: $\Pr(b)$ now ranges from 0.05 to 0.8. It may be worthwhile, therefore, to focus further elicitation efforts on the probability $p(b \mid \neg mc)$.

We now illustrate performing a *two-way sensitivity analysis* on our example network. We vary the probabilities $p(b \mid mc)$ and $p(isc \mid mc)$ of a brain tumour and an increased level of serum calcium in the presence of metastatic cancer simultaneously and study their joint effect on the probability $Pr(c)$ of a patient falling into a coma. The results of the analysis are shown in Figure 3. The con-

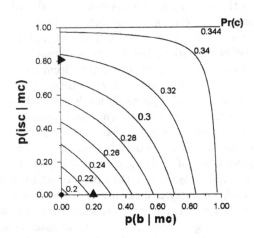

Fig. 3. A two-way sensitivity analysis for the example belief network.

tour lines connect the combinations of values for the two probabilities under study that result in the same value for the probability of interest. The distance between two contour lines indicates the variation necessary to shift the probability of interest from one contour line to another. If the contour lines are very close to one another, a small variation in the probabilities under study suffices to have considerable effect on the probability of interest; if the lines are further apart, then the probability of interest is not very sensitive to their variation. Unequal distance between contour lines indicates that varying the two probabilities simultaneously has a joint effect on the probability of interest beyond the effects of their separate variation. From Figure 3, we see that for the assessments $p(b \mid mc) = 0.2$ and $p(isc \mid mc) = 0.8$ the probability of interest shows a relatively low sensitivity.

In the sensitivity analyses described so far, we have taken for the probability of interest a *prior* probability, allowing for assessment of the overall robustness of a belief network. A sensitivity analysis can also be performed with respect to a *posterior* probability. In the presence of case-specific observations, a belief network may reveal unanticipated sensitivities. Such an analysis, therefore, allows for validating the network's robustness for specific cases or profiles (for example, of various patient populations). Further details on sensitivity analysis of belief networks are provided in a more elaborate paper [9].

5 Conclusions

When building a Bayesian belief network, a huge number of probabilities will have to be assessed. To support the elicitation of these probabilities, we have proposed iteratively performing sensitivity analyses on the network in the making, starting with rough, initial assessments. Sensitivity analysis of a belief network provides for assessing the sensitivity of a probability of interest to the various probabilities specified in the network and, hence, for assessing the network's robustness. A one-way sensitivity analysis serves to reveal the effect of varying a single probability on a probability of interest, whereas a two-way sensitivity analysis yields further insight into the joint effect of varying two probabilities simultaneously. We have argued that performing sensitivity analyses on a belief network allows for focusing elicitation efforts on the more critical probabilities. By iteratively performing sensitivity analyses and refining critical probabilities, a sufficiently robust belief network will result.

The computational complexity of performing sensitivity analysis on a belief network of realistic size is an issue of major concern. We have found, however, that the results of various types of sensitivity analysis obey simple functional relationships, that can be exploited to reduce the computational burden involved. Further research will aim at uncovering and detailing additional properties that will allow for the use of sensitivity analysis as a practical aid for probability elicitation for belief networks.

References

[1] D.E. Heckerman, E.J. Horvitz, and B.N. Nathwani. Toward normative expert systems. Part 1: The Pathfinder project. *Methods of Information in Medicine*, vol. 31, 1992, pp. 90 – 105.

[2] J. Pearl. *Probabilistic Reasoning in Intelligent Systems. Networks of Plausible Inference*. Morgan Kaufmann, Palo Alto, 1988.

[3] G. Guida and C. Tasso. *Topics in Expert System Design*, North-Holland, Amsterdam, 1989.

[4] D. von Winterfeldt and W. Edwards. *Decision Analysis and Behavioral Research*. Cambridge University Press, New York, 1986.

[5] M.G. Morgan and M. Henrion. *Uncertainty, a Guide to Dealing with Uncertainty in Quantitative Risk and Policy Analysis*. Cambridge University Press, 1990.

[6] G.F. Cooper. *NESTOR: a Computer-based Medical Diagnostic Aid that Integrates Causal and Probabilistic Knowledge*. Report HPP-84-48, Stanford University. 1984.

[7] S.L. Lauritzen and D.J. Spiegelhalter. Local computations with probabilities on graphical structures and their application to expert systems. *Journal of the Royal Statistical Society, Series B*, vol. 50, 1988, pp. 157 – 224.

[8] M.J. Druzdzel and L.C. van der Gaag. Elicitation of probabilities for belief networks: combining qualitative and quantitative information. *Eleventh Conference on Uncertainty in Artificial Intelligence*, 1995, pp. 141 – 148.

[9] V.M.H. Coupé, L.C. van der Gaag, J.D.F. Habbema. Sensitivity analysis: an aid for belief-network quantification, submitted for publication.

Towards More Collaboration Between Machine Learning Systems and their Users

Jean-Marc GABRIEL

Sherpa project (INRIA Rhône-Alpes)
ZIRST 655 Avenue de l'Europe,
38330 Montbonnot Saint Martin, FRANCE
(Jean-Marc.Gabriel@inrialpes.fr)

Abstract. This article investigates a way to deepen collaboration between Machine Learning Systems (MLS) and their users through the generation of explanations. More precisely, it focuses on the advises that may be given for helping the user during the evaluation of the MLS results and their correction. This is illustrated through the system EILP, an explanatory interface that supports the user during these tasks.

1. Introduction

Machine Learning Systems[1] (MLS) aims at supporting the user for acquiring descriptions of concept. Integrated into a Knowledge Base System (KBS), such descriptions will be used afterwards to predict the membership of a particular instance to the learned concepts. An important characteristic of MLS is the use of biases that influence the learning process by choosing one description rather than another [Mitchell, 80]. Some of them, like input knowledge, have to be managed by the user. However, since the user does not have any *a priori* knowledge about MLS biases behaviours, one shot learning are not often satisfactory and his intervention must be required several times again. In other words, the user must deal with a propose-and-revise process that involves (1) the capture of the inputs, (2) the evaluation of the results of the learning process and the elicitation of problems, and (3) the correction of the inputs according to the previous problems. Since the user is not a MLS engineer, these tasks remain problematic and their carrying out requires significant support.

This article introduces a work done for helping an end-user to deal with a MLS. This work has lead to the design of an Explanatory Interface for Learning Processes (EILP) developed over the MLS KBG [Bisson, 92]. Before describing the main aspects of this interface (§3.), a short insight of KBG will be given (§2.). To conclude (§4.), this work will be put back among current approaches.

2. A Short Insight of KBG

KBG is a MLS that provides a hierarchy of classes by means of examples and counter-examples of a concept. The hierarchy corresponds to an operational description of the concept (see Fig. 1). In order to belong to the concept, any instance must have a description that can be filtered by all the classes between the root and one leaf. Thus, each branch of the hierarchy represents one description of the concept.

---

[1] The scope of this paper is narrowed to Similarity Based Learning system of which characteristic is the extraction of common features from examples (of the concept to learn) regrouped according to their similarity.

The user have to gives the set of concept example or counter-example ; each one is described by a set of features[2]. Each feature holds at least one entity (i.e. a distinct identifiable element in the domain) and possibly some values (that assess the entities accordingly to the feature). For instance, the example *Truck-1*, described by the set of features *carries(truck-of-suzie,billet-wood)*, *is-marchandise(billet-wood)*, *number(billet-wood,50)*, *horsepower(truck-of-suzie,high)*, is composed of the entities *truck-of-suzie* and *billet-wood*.

The hierarchy is built by means of two successive tasks. The first one is a categorisation process that groups iteratively the most similar examples together. Example similarity is computed through the similarities of their common description (entities and features). The second task consists in pruning the hierarchy with the set of counter-examples. Each class is tested with the counter-example set. Classes and features that reject a counter-examples are kept whereas the other are removed. The most general classes that instanciate no counter-examples become leafs.

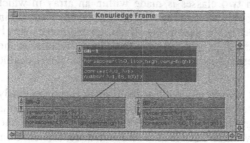

Fig. 1. Instance of KB generated by KBG.

3. Explanations and Advises

First of all, EILP gives explanations[3] that support the user to understand what are the goals of the MLS, how it achieves learning, what kinds of evaluation are expected, what are the correction operators that are available and their general effects on the results. Then, as the explanation remains relatively prosaic, EILP also proposes opportunistic advises that fit the currently focused knowledge. Such dynamic advises aims to help the user (1) in determining more deeply the problems related to the results according to his own domain knowledge and (2) in identifying the most adequate corrections for solving the problems.

The general statements ground this collaboration are more detailed now through the presentation of the three main modes that capture the steps of the propose-and-revise process : the exploration mode, the evaluation mode and the correction mode.

3.1. Exploration Mode

The exploration mode provides a set of information, questions and explanations useful to understand the results as well as the way they were computed. Information includes the display of :

---

[2] The representation language is derived from the First Order Logic and does not deal with negation and function symbols but allows types.
[3] They are obtained by the selection of both a knowledge item (e.g. a class) and a question related to it (e.g. "How did you build it ?").

• the hierarchy with facilities to get examples set and rejected counter-examples set of each classes[4] (within subviews),

• the way classes and entities description were compared, i.e. their matching,

• the similarity values between classes, entities and features.

3.2. Evaluation Mode

The evaluation advocated by EILP consists of three embedded strategies : an evaluation of the learning process, an evaluation of the appropriateness of the model and an evaluation of its accuracy.

Evaluation of the Learning Process. In order to evaluate the decision made at each learning step, each display is designed for the comparison of the knowledge generated by the system (e.g. examples regrouping, similarities, ...) within the whole set of the knowledge currently considered. For instance, the presentation of the similarity between two classes is made within an array in which all of the class similarities[5] present at this learning step are displayed. Thus, during the exploration of the learning process, the user meets all chosen and non-chosen hypotheses treated by the system. The comparison between the chosen hypothesis and the whole set of possible hypotheses enables and incites the user to have a critical look on the system decisions.

However, it is not always obvious for the user to be continuously aware of such a strategy. In order to help him, EILP proposes him to look at non chosen hypotheses (e.g. examples regrouping) that could have been be selected (the examples of the regrouping are very similar) and lead to results that are different from the actual results (i.e. this regrouping and the actually chosen one are not very similar). Such hypotheses are called *Missed Learning Points (MLP)* (see Fig. 2).

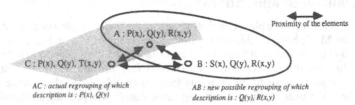

Fig. 2. Elements A and C have been regrouped together though A could have been regrouped with B. The new regrouping [AB] leads to a new description that is not very similar to the actually chosen [AC]. However, [AB] will be proposed by EILP.

If the new hypothesis seems interesting to the user, EILP helps him to correct the learning process according to it. Otherwise, he may take a look at other hypotheses. By this way, EILP takes advantage of the user exploration by proposing opportune MLP (which challenge the learning process) when, for instance, class regrouping are subjected to his attention.

Evaluation of the Appropriateness of the Model. In order to support the user in evaluating the appropriateness of the model with respect to the user domain knowledge, EILP advocates him to interpret the KB. It means to assign the name of a

---

[4] As for the classes, the user can get the actual domain entities that correspond to each entity appearing within the class descriptions.
[5] It is also done for entity and feature similarities.

domain concept to each class. If the class is a leaf, the concept has to be related to the concept to learn, otherwise it is an intermediate concept. For instance, the class *GR-3* (Fig. 1.) could be interpreted as the concept "heavyweight".

EILP supports the user by providing methods for interpretation. For instance, it focuses the user's attention on both the intention and the extension of the class (i.e. respectively the description of the class and the set of examples covered by the class). In addition, EILP emphasises several cases that may infirm the interpretation. For instance, it asks the user about the membership of examples to the concept (i.e. the class interpreted) that are (1) similar to the related class but (2) not covered by the class[6]. If this is the case (some examples are covered by the class), the interpretation is incoherent with the class extension and a particular output problem is detected. Either the user must refine his interpretation of the class or he has to search into the learning process for the reasons that have lead to such a flaw (why the examples do not belong to the class). This brings the user to correct the learning process within the correction mode (§3.3.).

Evaluation of the Accuracy of the Results. For most of MLS and revision systems, KB accuracy is evaluated through a set of testing examples and counter-examples[7]. Testing examples and counter-examples can lead to two kinds of problems. The first one is an over-generalization that is detected when a leaf-class covers test counter-examples (it may imply the addiction of new discriminating features). The second one is an over-specialization that is detected when a test example is not covered by any leaf (it may imply the removing of non discriminating features).

In most standard approaches (e.g. FORTE [Richards & al., 95], A3 [Wogulis, 93]), blames are expressed through the most guilty features ; i.e. features that appear for most problems. However some problems should be considered distinctly according to several different features that do not minimise the number of corrections. In order to take into account the disparity of the cause of flaws, the strategy of EILP consists in focusing the user on the set of test examples (resp. counter-examples) that were rejected (resp. recognised) for roughly the same reasons. In order to identify such examples and counter-examples, EILP first selects the features that are involved in most flaws (features that reject examples and features that recognise counter-examples) and then choose the most similar test examples (resp. test counter-examples) according to the previous features. The advantage of this approach is that the set of examples (from which prototype are extracted) that share the same behaviour and that can be treated by the user as chunk of knowledge, is generated.

Obviously, the user can let the system work in a stand alone way. In this case, EILP searches the hierarchy path for guilty features by using the strategy of FORTE (i.e. annotating as revision point features responsible of the greatest part of failures).

---

[6] EILP looks also at counter-examples not rejected by the class. If one of them does not belong to the concept, this means that the concept has an incoherent generality binding with the subclass that actually rejects the counter-example. The interpretation must change or counter-examples must be rejected by the current class according to the way they are rejected by the subclass.

[7] In fact, sets of examples and counter-examples are generally split into a learning set which is used to build the results and a test set which is used to test the accuracy of the results.

3.3. Correction Mode

Once the user has identified a specific problem, he must determine the set of corrections that will lead to its solving. More precisely, he has to elaborate a path from an output problem to input corrections, that is made up of correction operators and that will produce the output correction. A correction operator holds (among other things) the goal of the operator, the set of methods available for the resolving of the goal (they point on other correction operators) and the knowledge on which the operator is applied.

Due to the inherent lack of domain knowledge of the MLS, the user has to choose the set of operator by himself. For that, he must forecast the effect of each of them on the expected result. In order to support him for this task, EILP gives him several kinds of advises and warnings that aim at preventing potential side effects that may spoil interpreted classes or accurate items. On the one hand, interpreted classes correspond to knowledge which is meaningful for the user. On the other hand, accurate knowledge have an operational significance for the system.

Side effects are detected through the comparison of the knowledge involved by the chosen correction and *Correction Instability Points* (CIP). Whenever CIP are related with an interpreted classes or with some accurate items, EILP warns the user about it. EILP distinguishes two kinds of CIP.

The first kind of CIP, *Accuracy Instability Points* (AIP), concerns accurate item knowledge. An AIP is any kind of relevant item identified during the pruning of the hierarchy. The purpose is to avoid the deletion of accurate information without to be sure that the user is aware of the accuracy of information. The accuracy criterion remains the one used to evaluate the accuracy of the KB, but its scope is no more narrowed to classes and features. The accuracy is also computed for predicate, entity and value. In some cases, a deletion can be avoided by the change of feature representation. For instance, if the user wants to delete the feature *horsepower(x, [low,high])* while *horsepower(x,[high,very-high])* is accurate, EILP urges the user on to express the value difference through the predicate name (this may give *powerful(x)* and *not-powerful(x)*).

The second kind of CIP, *Matching Instability Point* (MIP) concerns object (i.e. entity, feature or example) matching. The key idea is to let the user looking at case where the modification changes the relation between the corrected object and other objects :

• that must not be concerned by the modification,

• that belong to interesting classes (interpreted or accurate ones),

• whose classes are not parents (i.e. more or less general) with the class concerned by the correction.

The underlying idea of MIP is closed to the one of MLP (cf. §3.2.). It relies on the detection of non chosen hypotheses that could be selected according to a relative slight modification, but which may lead to significant changes of the KB. The main difference here is that CIP are triggered by the correction operator applied on the current corrected knowledge. If the correction leads to achieve CIP, EILP warns the user about it in order to help him to possibly reconsider the correction operator.

4. Related Works and Conclusion

Some investigations related to the problematic of user/system interaction have be done through *the interactive approach* (in which the user must answer to the questions of the system : CLINT [De Raedt & *al.*, 92], APT [Nédellec & *al.*, 92]), *the balanced approach* (in which the user may intervene freely at each of the different steps of the learning process : MOBAL [Morik, 93]), and *the configuring approach* (in which the user may parametrize the system according to the encountered specific learning problem : NINA [Adé & al., 95], HAIKU [Nédellec & *al.*, 1994]). However most of these works have given greater place to the improvement of the system accuracy and have less carried on the study of the user requirements.

The collaborative approach proposed in this article combines the advantages of (1) the interactive approach by providing hypotheses for helping the KB revision (without narrowing the user to the specific hypothesis provided by the system) and (2) the balanced approach by enabling the user to use the hypothesis he wishes including his own ones (but also provides support for the choice of the hypotheses). Furthermore, it follows the configuring approach by presenting the roles of the biases (e.g. the way objects are compared) but extends its scope by urging the user to challenge the biases behaviours.

For that, it provides support to the user during :
- the elicitation of problems trough :
  - the interpretation of the KB
  - the study of KB accuracy according to test set
  - the analysis of the learning process
- the correction of problems through the anticipation of altering side-effects of input modifications.

References

[Adé & al., 95] H. Adé, L. De Raedt & M. Bruynooghe. Declarative Bias for Specific-to-General ILP Systems. *Machine Learning*, 20. pp. 119-154. 1995.

[Bisson, 92] G. Bisson. Learning in FOL with a similarity measure. In *Proceedings of 10th National Conference on Artificial Intelligence (AAAI)*. San-Jose. pp. 82-87. 1992.

[De Raedt & *al.*, 92] L. De Raedt & M. Bruynooghe. An Overview of the Interactive Concept-Learner and Theory Revisor CLINT. In *Inductive Logic Programming*. S. Muggleton (eds.). Academic Press. pp 163-191. 1992.

[Gabriel, 97] J.M. Gabriel. When Explanations enable Cooperation between a Machine Learning System and its User. To appears in the Proceedings of the 6th International Conference on Intelligent Systems (ICIS'97), Boston. 1997.

[Mitchell, 80] T.M. Mitchell. The Need for Biases in Learning Generalizations. Technical Report, Rutgers University, New Brunswick. 1980.

[Morik, 93] K. Morik. Balanced Cooperative Modeling. *Machine Learning*, 11. pp. 275-235. 1993.

[Nédellec & *al.*, 1994] C. Nédellec & C. Rouveirol. Specifications of the HAIKU system. Research Report n°928, Université de PARIS Sud. 1994.

[Nedellec, 92] C. Nedellec & K. Causse. Knowedge Refinement using Knowledge Acquisition and Machine Learning Methods. In *Proceedings of the 6th European Knowledge Acquisition Workshop, EKAW'92*. pp 171-190. 1992.

[Richards & *al.*, 1995] B.L. Richards & R.J. Mooney. Automated Refinement of Firts-Order Horn-Clause Domain Theories. *Machine Learnings, 19*. 1995.

[Wogulis,93] J. Wogulis. Handling Negation in First-Order Theory Revision. In *Proceedings of IJCAI'93 workshop on Inductive Logic Programming*, Chambéry, France. Morgan Kaufmann. 1993.

COATIS, an NLP System to Locate Expressions of Actions Connected by Causality Links

Daniela Garcia

Université de Paris-Sorbonne, Cams-Lalic
96, boulevard Raspail, 75006 Paris, France
and
EDF-DER, IMA-TIEM
1, avenue du General-De-Gaulle, 92141 Clamart Cedex, France

Abstract. COATIS is an automatic tool designed to locate certain actions expressed in texts. Rules of contextual exploration, activated by the presence of linguistic indicators of causality in sentences, enable COATIS to locate expressions that denote field actions and that are linked by causal relations. COATIS processes technical texts of any domain, in the French language. It is therefore particularly suitable for use in causal knowledge acquisition from texts.

1 Introduction

The notions of *transfer*, *entity* and *movement*, expressed by natural languages, have been extensively studied for instance by Talmy [18, 19], Langacker [14], Jackendoff [11] and Pustejovski [16], but the systematic study of the encoding of causality by natural languages is still in its early stages. Several research studies of systematic description of vocabulary (*verbs of movement* are analyzed by means of schemas by M. Abraham in [1], *semantic transitivity, aspectuality schema* and *diathesis schema* had been studied by J.-P. Desclés in [5], while particular semantic domains such as relations of *localisation* and *whole-part* relations were also recently studied and presented in [13] and [12]) have been conducted with the aim to get knowledge from texts without any information about the field described in the processed text.

In this paper, we set out the results concerning the notions of action and causal relations between actions as expressed by verbs of the French language. The model we built is coupled with the *Strategy of the Contextual Exploration* to obtain the COATIS computer system. This system aims to index the processed text by the actions expressed within it and that are organized by causal links. We start by explaining (Section 2) how we organized the French verbs that express causal links between actions. We then describe (Section 3) the COATIS system.

2 Semantic Organization of Causality as it is Expressed in French

A classic distinction between the efficient causality and the causality that is able to be described by formal representations, has long been established and we take it into account. We distinguish between the efficient causality where one action provokes a different action that comes later in time ("*Massive deforestation of the planet leads to global cooling*"), and the causality that substitutes the notions of cause and effect by regularities encountered between actions ("*Energy is proportional to mass*"). We extend this distinction with an original work on the organization of the efficient causal relations.

2.1 Efficient Causality as Expressed by French Verbs

The idea of efficient causality as an oriented relation between actions, can be expressed by French verbs. French verbs such as *provoquer* (to provoke), *gêner* (to disturb), *résulter* (to result), or *conduire à* (to lead to), are called *indicator verbs of causality* (or *indicators* for short). The indicators that express efficient causality relations can (i) clarify the nature of the produced effect (-disturbing-[1], -letting-, -modification-, -creation-, etc.), or (ii) clarify the intervention of the causal action (-contribution-, -collaboration-). Figure 1 presents an extract of the model comprising twenty-three specific relations of causality (nineteen relations of efficient causality and four relations of formal causality).

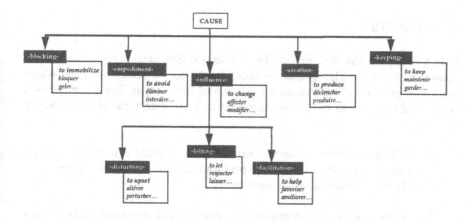

Fig. 1. *Semantic organization of the relations of efficient causality (extract).*

The model presented below comes primarily from the manual classification of indicator verbs found in technical texts. Some of the classes we describe were first brought forward by the American linguist Leonard Talmy [20].

2.2 Efficient Causalities Clarifying the Produced Effect

One causal action can *block*, *impede*, *influence*, *create* or *keep* another action. The two relations -blocking and -keeping- respectively extend the relations -impediment-

---

[1] We note each specific causal relation between two hyphens.

and -creation- that render an account of two extreme notions. Between the two notions, -creation- and -impediment-, non categoric influences from one action to another one are possible.

One causal action can *facilitate, let* or *disturb* another action. These three relations can be ordered according to a qualitative feature which is associated with the relation of -influence-: the relation of -facilitation- is a modification that is *more or less positive*; the relation of -letting- is a *nil* modification; the relation of -disturbing- is a modification that is *more or less negative*.

As described above, the organization of efficient causalities clarifying the nature of the produced effect justifies the existence of a continuum between -blocking- and -keeping-. Indeed, the -facilitation- relation, taken to extremes, becomes a -creation-. And the relation of -disturbing-, varying in its intensity, merges into the relation of -impediment- when it goes beyond the extrem limit.

Other authors are currently engaged in research on verb classification. Note in particular the work of Patrick Saint-Dizier described in [17], as well as the results exposed by Beth Levin in [15]. Jacques François in [8] is interested in the notion of causality as a criteria for classifying the *causation verbs of change*.

Our model is based on an analysis of texts with frequent occurrences of 253 verbs carrying the notion of efficient causality.

3 COATIS

COATIS applies the Strategy of the Contextual Exploration [7] to detect expressions of action. The method is applied sentence by sentence to the whole text. The presence of an indicator (e.g., one of the verbs in Fig. 1) activates a contextual exploration of the sentence that seeks to detect the clues necessary to:

– decide if the indicator is likely to express a causal relation in the text or, on the contrary, to show that an interpretation of causality is impossible;
– identify the arguments of the relation.

This is the general organization of a system that processes texts by the Strategy of the Contextual Exploration. This method is still implemented and used to resolve problems such as knowledge modelling from texts (SEEK system is presented in [13], automatic abstracting [2], as well as tense and aspect analysis [6]). These systems are implemented as Knowledge Base Systems where the knowledge used is only a linguistic one. Figure 2 illustrates an example of a sentence processed by COATIS.

COATIS is implemented in SMECI[2]. The system applies to texts that have first been processed by LEXTER [3], a terminology extraction software that performs a morpho-syntactic analysis of a corpus of French texts on any technical domain and yields a network of noun phrases.

---

[2] SMECI[TM] - from ILOG[TM] - is a Knowledge-Based System generator.

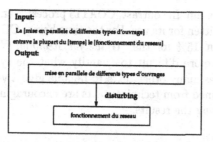

Fig. 2. *An example of a sentence processed by COATIS. The noun phrases between brackets are the noun phrases detected by LEXTER.* The sentence processed is "Putting different kinds of equipment in parallel generally hinders the operation of the network". *The result of the process is that the two expressions of action* "Putting different kinds of equipment in parallel" *and* "operation of the network" *are in causal relation of -disturbing-.*

Linguistic indicators are not sufficient to detect the presence of a causal relation in a sentence. Account must be taken of their occurrence. In order to keep only those utterances that express causality, it is necessary to examine the context of the indicators detected, in order to locate relevant clues. The rules of contextual exploration analyze different kind of information, e.g. morpho-syntactic (detecting for exemple the occurrence of an infinitive verb preceding or following the occurrence of the indicator); or morphologic (for example, the presence in part of the indicator context, to be determined by the system, of a French linguistic unit ending in *-ment, -ion, -ure, -ise, -age, -aison, -yse*, etc.).

COATIS criteria for selecting LEXTER units are essentially connected to the relative position of different units in the sentence: LEXTER units, chosen prepositions depending on indicators, verbs with a morphology feature (infinitive, past or present participle, conjugated) and punctuation. The noun phrase selected (one LEXTER unit) is then explored to search for additional clues that would confirm the first causal interpretation of the indicator (e.g. the presence of a French noun ending in *-ment, -ure, -age*, etc.). This second exploration is necessary because the morphological information is only relevant when it is present in a certain part of the sentence.

The organization of indicator verbs also makes it possible to specify the causal value concerned (-creation-, -disturbing-, -collaboration-, etc.).

One of the main features of COATIS is its independence with regard to the subject field processed. Indicators and clues are independent of any specific field. COATIS does not need a particular domain dictionary to operate. It is therefore a useful tool for causal knowledge acquisition from texts, since no preliminary domain knowledge is required.

At present, there are few computerized systems with the same operational designs, and it seems difficult to compare COATIS with other systems. Quote from the work of Gary C. Borchardt [4]: it is about a system which locates the causal relations in written texts according to the directives provided by the constructor of the system. In contrast, COATIS processes any technical text that is not specifically written for its use. For the time being, COATIS does not make a lot of noise (about 15% for the *"Guide for Regional Networks Planning"*); however it is much more difficult to quantify what the system does not find, so we have to process many other texts to be able give a verdict. However, the results already obtained from technical texts are encouraging, as is the feedback from cogniticians using the results.

4 Using Results of COATIS

COATIS can be used for different applications. COATIS results are helpful in constituting action terminology for a given domain. They can also be helpful in building a causal model of a domain: COATIS provides (i) a number of expressions of action and (ii) a basic organizational structure based on causal relations. Moreover, we have listed a number of additional contributions to the modelling process:

- When resolving problems of inference, if we have detected that "A -letting- B" and if we moreover know that A is carried out, then B becomes possible ; if we have detected that "A -cause- B" and that A is carried out, then B is carried out or going to be carried out at a certain point.
- When building a causal network, if "A -cause- B" and "B -cause- C", we should ask the expert if we can add the relation "A -cause- C".
- When testing the coherence of the knowledge gathered, if "A -cause- B" and "B -hinder- C", and if the relation "A -cause- C" exists in the network, we have to argue this apparent paradox by considering it as a particular case or an exception, or even by leaving it out altogether.

The results provided by COATIS are being used in the HYPERPLAN [10] project which concerns the building of a Technical Documentation Consulting System (TDCS) for the *"Guide for Regional Networks Planning"* (150.000 words): part of the text indexing takes into account the causal information identified by COATIS [9].

5 Conclusion

The approach adopted to building COATIS aims to find an operational method for constructing representations from a text, taking into account the causality notion. While our university research team is engaged in theoretical research, we are implementing a number of automatic tools to process texts. The independence of these systems with regard to a particular field and their ability to adapt to many different texts was made possible by the support of a strong theoretical base : a linguistic model under construction that explores and seeks to model the general notions expressed by natural languages, e.g. *membership, localisation, whole-part* relation, *movement, transfer* and... *causality*.

References

1. Abraham, M.: Analyse sémantico-cognitive des verbes de mouvement et d'activité : Contribution méthodologique à la constitution d'un dictionnaire informatique des verbes. PhD EHESS Paris (1995)
2. Berri, J., Le Roux, D., Malrieu, D, Minel, J.-L.: SERAPHIN main sentences automatic extraction system. Proceedings of the Second Language Engineering Convention Londres October (1995)
3. Bourigault, D.: LEXTER, a Natural Language Processing Tool for Terminology Extraction. Proceedings of the 7th EURALEX International Congress Goteborg (1996)
4. Borchardt, G.-C.: Thinking between the Lines, Computers and Comprehension of Causal Descriptions. MIT Press Cambridge Massachusetts (1994)
5. Desclés, J.-P.: Langages applicatifs, Langues naturelles et Cognition. Hermés Paris (1990)
6. Desclés, J.-P., Jouis, C., Oh, H.-G., Reppert, D.: Exploration contextuelle et sémantique: Un système expert qui trouve les valeurs sémantiques des temps de l'indicatif dans un texte. Knowledge Modelling and expertise transfer. D.Herin-Aime, R. Dieng, J.-P. Regourd, J.-P. Angoujard (eds) IOS Press Amsterdam Washington DC Tokyo (1991) 371–400
7. Desclés, J.-P., Minel, J.-L.: L'exploration contextuelle. In Le résumé par exploration contextuelle. Communications to the Cogniscience-Est Meeting, Nancy, November 1994. Technical Report CAMS 95(1) (1995) 3–17
8. François, F.: Changement, causation, action. Librairie Droz Genève-Paris (1989)
9. Garcia, D., Aussenac-Gilles, N., Courcelle, A.: Exploitation, pour la modélisation, des connaissances causales détectées par COATIS dans les textes. Proceedings of 7th Journées d'Acquisition des Connaissances. Sète France (1996)
10. Gros, C., Assadi, H., Aussenac-Gilles, N., Courcelle, A.: Task Models for Technical Documentation Accessing. Proceedings of the 10th European Knowledge Acquisition Workshop. Nottingham (UK) (1996)
11. Jackendoff, R.: Semantics and Cognition. Cambridge (Mass.) MIT Press (1983)
12. Jackiewicz, A.: Expression lexicale de la relation d'ingrédience. Faits de Langue 7 (1996)
13. Jouis, C., Mustafa-Elhadi, W.: Conceptual Modeling of Database-Schema using linguistic knowledge. Application to Terminological databases. Proceedings of the First Workshop on Application of Natural Language to Databases (NLDB:9295). AFCET Versailles France (1995) 103–118
14. Langacker, L.: Foundation of Cognitive Grammar. Standford Univ. Press 1 (1987)
15. Levin, B.: English Verb classes and Alternations, Preliminary investigations. University of Chicago Press (1993)
16. Pustejovski, J.: Generative Lexicon. MIT Press (1995)
17. Saint-Dizier, P.: Verb semantic Classes for French: Construction and Semantic Representation. Proceedings of IFIP, Conference on verb semantic classes. Univ. of Pennsylvania (1995)
18. Talmy, L.: Semantics and Syntax of Motion. Syntax and Semantics 4 NY Academic Press (1975) 181–238.
19. Talmy, L.: How Language Structures Space, Spatial Orientation: Theory, Research and Application. H. Pick, L. Acredolo (eds.) Prenum Press (1983)
20. Talmy, L.: Force dynamics in language and cognition. Cognitive Science 12 (1988) 49–100

Using Knowledge Acquisition
to Build Spoken Language Systems

Stefan Kaspar and Achim Hoffmann
School of Computer Science and Engineering
University of New South Wales
Sydney, NSW 2052, Australia
Email: {chebe,achim}@cse.unsw.edu.au

Abstract. The development of spoken language interfaces is of increasing importance due to the progress in speech recognition technology. Unfortunately, the development of comprehensive dialog system is still too labour-intensive to allow their widespread dissemination. This paper presents a new approach to the design of spoken language dialog systems. We view the design task as a knowledge acquisition and knowledge maintenance task. We developed a workbench, PIA, which allows continuous knowledge acquisition and maintenance without a knowledge engineer. It uses also the available data to produce suggestions of how to amend the current knowledge base to accommodate new cases of recorded dialog interactions. First experimental results with our workbench are promising.

1 Introduction

A spoken language system engages the user in a dialog to achieve some goal. A spoken language system combines speech recognition, natural language processing and human interface technology. The system has to recognise words to obtain a meaning in terms of the application and has to give an appropriate response. Spoken languages systems have been built for various tasks, like air and train travel information [10], urban exploration [5], etc. The process of designing a spoken dialog system is not only very labour intensive but still requires a lot of expertise. Most of the current applications are heavily domain dependent. Currently, the high cost of porting such systems to new applications represents a major obstacle to widespread deployment. One of the most labour and expertise-intensive tasks is the construction of a domain model, which provides semantic and syntactic constraints for understanding speech with respect to a certain application [2]. These constraints define how users refer to things, how they ask questions or provide information.

We have developed a framework for rapid prototyping of spontaneous speech dialog systems, employing keyword-based spontaneous speech understanding. Our goal was to provide a development tool that allows to design a spoken dialog system of any size in reasonable time.

The rest of the paper is organised as follows: In section 2, we give an overview of our spoken dialog prototyping system PIA. In section 3, we show how the problem can be effectively addressed by our knowledge acquisition approach. Section 4 contains the conclusions.

2 System Overview of PIA

2.1 Architecture

PIA consists of five components: the dialog controller, the knowledge acquisition workbench, the dialog design tool, the speech recognition engine, and the audio output engine. The dialog design tool is a graphical programming interface to define the structure of a spoken dialog. A dialog is designed by filling a number of identical data objects called dialog units. These data objects will be interpreted by the dialog controller, the central element of our system. The dialog controller's task is it to guide a user through the dialog. One of the main tasks of the dialog controller is to make assumptions about the possible user input at a certain time. It does this by extracting the information in the dialog units and taking the history of the previous interactions into account.

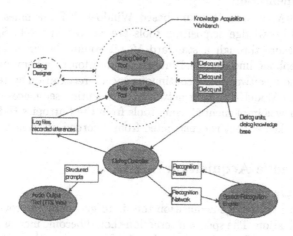

Fig. 1. System architecture of PIA.

2.2 Dialog Design Language (Knowledge Representation Language)

We developed our dialog design language (DDL) that is used as knowledge representation language for our system PIA. Our dialog description language should accomplish two things. Firstly, it should provide the dialog designer with tools for rapid prototyping of spoken dialogs. The underlying complicated algorithmic structure that is common to most of the spoken user machine interactions should be hidden from the designer. Secondly, a DDL should have a structure which as much as possible separates what is fixed in a dialog from what is cyclically upgraded in the process of knowledge acquisition. The information that is sought by the system, (the slots that have to be filled), and in what order, is usually known from the beginning and will be fixed. However, the way people fill these slots might not be clear a priori.

The basic element in our DDL (dialog description language) is the so called dialog unit (DU). For example a dialog unit DATE is concerned with a specific date of the year. A dialog unit might be built from subunits. Our DU DATE might have three subunits: DAY MONTH YEAR. The design of a spoken dialog interface consists of the filling of the frames of the dialog units. A dialog unit has the following frames: rules frames, the subunit frame, and the prompts frame. The rules frame lists the words or phrases with which people refer to that dialog unit. A rule is a sequence of words together with wild-cards, something like *what time ** , * what movies *. The subunits that make up the dialog unit, and their logical relationship with other subunits is defined in the subunit frame. All dialog units are listed in some subunit frame except for the master dialog unit. A dialog unit without subunits is called terminal DU. The prompts frame lists texts from which the dialog controller chooses the appropriate system output.

2.3 Implementation

Our system PIA runs on Pentium based Windows NT machines. The dialog controller and knowledge acquisition tools are written in C++. Spoken input and output occurs through a standard 16 bit sound-blaster or an analog or digital T1 telephone line using a Dialogic corporation telephony board. At the moment we use a software-only continuous speech recognition system based on Hidden Markov Model matching networks representing sequences of triphones. The recogniser was implemented using tools from the Entropics Hidden Markov Toolkit [1]. Spoken output is constructed from recorded utterances.

3 Knowledge Acquisition in PIA

3.1 Principle

The goal of our knowledge acquisition tool is to gradually improve our spoken language application. The speech interaction should become increasingly natural and less error prone. The information flow from the user to the system and back should become smoother. We believe that not even the best dialog designer will be able to predict the rich variety with which people ask for things and respond to questions. Our approach suggests that experimentation with real users be performed in several steps, starting with a basic bootstrap system and cyclically upgrading it. That is, we design an initial dialog using our DDL as described above. One or several users then test this bootstrap system. The whole interaction is recorded. In a next step the dialog designer making use of the knowledge acquisition tool, modifies the dialog using the recorded interaction. Once all the possible modifications have been made, the improved system is applied to new users, and new interactions are recorded. This process may be repeated as often as necessary. In every cycle the system adds, removes, or modifies rules. The task is to produce rules that are as general as possible without being difficult to recognise or easily confused with a rule from another DU.

3.2 The knowledge acquisition process in PIA

The nature of the knowledge acquisition process in PIA contrasts many approaches to Knowledge Acquisition, such as KADS [8, 9]. It is more in line with incremental approaches to Knowledge Acquisition and maintenance, such as Ripple-Down Rules [3, 4], which essentially avoid a time-consuming initial problem analysis phase. In PIA our approach seems to work, because it is possible to gradually improve the dialog structure and to describe it at the knowledge level [7]. This works due to the fact that in PIA local amendments to particular rules can be made without risking adverse effects due to complex interactions of multiple rules. This is possible, because, firstly, the interaction between rules is fairly limited. Secondly, we developed a mechanism as sketched in 3.3, which can control most of the potentially adverse interactions while it searches for suitable amendments which do not cause conflicts.

The definition of dialogs can be split into two parts: The interaction of the various dialog units with each other on the one hand. On the other hand, the collection of all allowed utterances to trigger a particular system action associated with a dialog unit.

The first part is defined initially: For each piece of information which should be extracted from the user a dialog unit is set up. Depending on the possible outcomes further dialog units may be called. The initial structure of the complete set of dialog units is given by a tree like dependency graph as represented in our dialog design language. Usually, this does not cause significant problems. This is often a simple task, since the purpose of the system is clear.

The second part is normally a continuous knowledge acquisition process which aims at gradually covering the most commonly used utterances. The incremental acquisition of dialog models in PIA proceeds through cycles consisting of two stages:

1. Listening to dialog speech data, the expert first inputs a sequence of keywords that are included in the user's utterance. Out-of-vocabulary words and pauses are replaced by wild-cards. This process is repeated for every utterance recorded in one knowledge acquisition cycle.

2. In the second stage, our system tries to modify the existing rules for all the DUs that have new utterances assigned. For this process for every DU we organise all the existing keyword strings and rules into a special data structure. Basically we have five main string arrays called NEW, OLD, RULES, CRITICAL and OTHERS. NEW stores all the keyword strings that have been assigned to this DU in the first step described above. OLD contains the keyword lists from previous knowledge acquisition cycles. RULES is identical to the content of the rules frame. CRITICAL list words or word sequences that are known to be difficult for recognition. OTHERS contains the rules belonging to all the other DUs. The program now tries to divide the strings in NEW into three groups; If in the actual dialog the DU has correctly been called by the utterance it is added to MATCHED. If the DU should have been called because there is a matching rule but the speech recogniser gave the wrong output it is added to WRONG SR. NO MATCHING will contain the keyword sequences for which there is no matching rule.

The modification algorithm used for the second stage consists of five steps:

1. Add all the strings in MATCHED to OLD.
2. Generalise (see below) all the utterances in NO MATCHING and add the produced rules to RULES
3. For every utterance in WRONG SR pick the rule in RULES that should have been matched and add it to CRITICAL
4. For all the rules that are newly added to CRITICAL pick all the strings in OLD that are matched by this rule only.
5. Generalise these strings and replace the critical rule with the rules produced in the generalisation process.

3.3 Generalise rules

The critical task of our knowledge acquisition process is generalisation. Let us assume a list of rules and a long list of typed utterances (keyword sequences) is given. The goal is to find a new list of shorter rules and the list itself should contain less rules as well. The new rules must ensure that all given utterance strings are still matched, but none of the utterance strings from other DUs is matched. Furthermore the generalisation algorithm has to make sure that the rules do not match a rule listed in CRITICAL, i.e. to avoid rules which are difficult to recognise or to discriminate against other rules. Our heuristic algorithm for generalisation is based on the AQ learning algorithm [6] for generating disjunctions of conjunctive terms. Our generalisation algorithm works as follows:

For every rule do:

1. Rank the words in the rule according to how often they occur in OTHERS.
2. Define the word with the lowest ranking (the one with smallest number of occurrences in OTHERS) as the new rule.
3. Repeat until the new rule does not match any string in OTHERS or CRITICAL.
   (a) From the original rule pick the words that are immediately before or immediately after the substring that makes the new rule.
   (b) If there is no word to the left (right) of the substring, prepend (append) the one to the right (left).
   (c) If the word to the left (right) has a higher occurrence ranking choose the one to the right (left) and prepend (append) it.
4. Take all the new rules and remove identical copies.

4 Conclusions

Our initial results are very encouraging. So far, we had several dialog designers with no prior experience with our system or a speech recognition tool. After a brief introduction, they were able to design their basic customised dialogs for the domain of movie information system and ticket ordering.

The strengths of our approach are twofold: Firstly, since it is difficult to determine a comprehensive coverage of the possible user utterances, our approach is well-suited to handle that in an incremental way. The dialog designer can amend the current dialog structure at any time and does not need a highly skilled specialist - as is usually the case. Secondly, it is easily possible for a dialog designer to react on weak recognition rates of the speech recognition module by changing the key phrases in the dialog model which activate certain system functions. I.e. poor recognition results are due to phonetically too similar key utterances in different dialog units. This can be alleviated by either changing the key phrases which trigger a dialog unit and/or by adapting the prompts in order to guide the user input to easier recognisable utterances. The description of the dialog structures takes place at the knowledge level. The knowledge acquisition for the dialog structure does not require an extensive prior problem analysis - instead a given structure can always be amended to cover an encountered dialog which was not properly handled. A general revision of early design decisions seemed not necessary so far. Reason being that the most difficult part in the knowledge acquisition process is to cover all relevant utterances and to be able to distinguish between them where needed. Due to our dialog design language, this can largely be handled on a local basis, i.e. amendments to a dialog box and their potential interference with other dialog boxes can be easily controlled. Further research will include the characterisations of problem classes which can be handled with our or a similar approach where a substantial problem analysis beforehand is not needed. Another issue is, how to assist a designer in a complete restructuring of the sequential organisation of a dialog; this was not needed so far, however.

References

1. Large vocabulary continuous speech recognition using HTK. In *Proceedings of ICASSP*, pages 125–128, 1994.
2. R. Cole et al. The challenge of spoken language systems:research directions for the ninties. *IEEE Transactions on Speech and Audio Processing*, 3:1–19, 1995.
3. P. Compton and R. Jansen. A philosophical basis for knowledge acquisition. *Knowledge Acquisition*, 2:241–257, 1990.
4. P. Compton, B. Kang, P. Preston, and M. Mulholland. Knowledge acquisition without knowledge analysis. In *Proceedings of the European Knowledge Acquisition Workshop*, pages 277–299. Springer-Verlag, 1993.
5. J. Glass, G. Flammia, D. Goodine, M. Phillips, J. Polifroni, S. Sakai, S. Seneff, and V. Zue. Spoken-language understanding in the mit voyager system. *Speech Communication*, 17:1–18, 1995.
6. R. S. Michalski. A theory and methodology of machine learning. *Artificial Intelligence*, 20:111–161, 1983.
7. A. Newell. The knowledge level. *Artificial Intelligence*, 18:87–127, 1982.
8. G. Schreiber, B. Wielinga, and J. Breuker. *KADS A Principled Approach to Knowledge-Based System Development*. Academic Press, 1993.
9. T. Schreiber, B. Wielinga, J. Akkermans, W. van de Velde, and R. de Hoog. CommonKADS: A comprehensive methodology for KBS. *IEEE Expert*, 9(6):28–37, 1994.
10. S. Seneff, V. Zue, J. Polifroni, C. Pao, L. Hetherington, D. Goddeau, and J. Glass. PEGASUS: A spoken language interface for on-line air travel planning. *Speech Communication*, 15:331–340, 1994.

An Assistant for a Design Project: Application to the Design of a Mixed Hardware/Software Architecture

Laurent Maillet-Contoz and Jean Sallantin

maillet_contoz@lirmm.fr, sallantin@lirmm.fr
LIRMM, UMR 5506 Université Montpellier II - CNRS
161, Rue Ada 34392 Montpellier Cedex 5 - FRANCE

Abstract. In this paper, we propose a supervision scheme for incremental design processes, applied to the supervision of hardware/software systems design. Such a frame provides to a design team a common representation for the design objects and the actions to be performed. More over, it proposes a set of primitive operations to manage knowledge in the design process. So, the designers have the opportunity to criticize the configuration of the system, by annotating the experimental results. Due to the complexity and the number of the design parameters, the supervision scheme has shown its significance, even on relatively small systems. This provides an assistant for the design and the retrieval of design objects.

1 Introduction

In the field of user-controlled processes, a working frame is often useful in order to structure the actions of the operator. Therefore, we are interested in a general frame of supervision, that provides a set of primitive actions. In this paper, we focus on the operations required to express the supervision of an incremental design process.

The supervision is obtained by the analysis of the system through the properties, that provides an evaluation of the realized system and the difference with the expected one. That may generate a new version of the system, which properties will have different values, or modify the choice of the properties used for its analysis. Globally, the interpretation of experimental results is: *i*) Analyze to draw up a choice, *ii*) Organize to exhibit a design, *iii*) Experiment a choice to measure properties.

The goal is to achieve the supervision of a process, by finding a satisfactory state by chaining analysis and generation operations. The operations are composed, while the properties are not relevant, or while the system does not correspond to the specifications.

We present in this paper a supervision mechanism, applied to the design of hardware/software systems. also called CoDesign. The design methodology is an incremental process, under the control of the designer. The principle of a CoDesign methodology is the concurrent development of the Hardware and the software parts of the system. The Software part runs on a processor, while the hardware part runs simultaneously on a dedicated hardware platform. The CoDesign involves different designer teams, according to the speciality of the tasks to perform. Therefore, it is a relevant application domain for the supervision mechanism, since it provides a uniform frame for the design process analysis. This frame is intended to answer to questions like : "Is it possible to CoDesign this system?, What kind of variability in this design?, Are there several ways to design (depending on the designers, the applications) ?"

AI technics have been proposed for design verification [4] in well-defined problems, based on functional and behavioral verifications. Constraint-based approaches have also been proposed and it has been shown that some of the artificial intelligence formalisms which support constraint-based systems are relevant to the characteristics of psychological behavior [3] and may express the user behavior. Conflict management in concurrent design has also been studied [7]. Design is much easier when the design problem can be decomposed into small pieces that can be solved independently and then easily combined to form a solution. However, when the design goals include limiting overall usage of some resources, (e.g. on computation time or silicon area), interactions often arise which make it difficult to determine what effect some decision about a small piece of an artifact will have on the overall quality of the solution. Thus decomposition becomes impossible and, if the problem is too large to handle by exhaustive search, finding a good solution is very hard. [5]. So, classical development cycles [9] are not relevant to such a design, and a spiral model will be prefered [1]. We have proposed an incremental user-guided methodology, that catches the previous knowledge of the designer, and helps to design a new application [6].

The configurations are composed of hardware and software components. In that way, this work is naturally close to an object-oriented approach. Particularly, the system has to manage the experimental results produced by the design system, and store them into a database. Then, an issue is to structure the system, to extract relevant knowledge about the design process. This provides constraints on the relation between the human operator and the machine. This has for consequences the reduction of the language used for the supervision of the system.

First, we present the supervision frame, based on a set of terms, that characterize the different actions to be performed in order to analyse the process and generate a new version of the system. Then, we will show how this frame is applied to the supervision of a CoDesign process. Some experimentations will be presented before conclusion.

2 A frame for the supervision

2.1 Definitions

The principle of such an approach is to propose a minimal set of operations, required to supervise a design process. It is based on two major steps: analysis and generation. First, the analysis of the system provides the properties that are relevant in the process. Then, if the supervision shows some lacks in the current configuration, a new version of the system is generated. it aims to provide a formulation frame to the user. It guaranties that the design will always be supervisable, even if the process does not lead to a relevant configuration. The structuration of the observed system aims at limitating the vocabulary used for the supervision and provides a better structuration of the knowledge.

Analysis The analysis of the process is decomposed in two complex operations:

Identify: It consists in identifying all the terms of the design process. This identification, achieved by denominating (definition of all the properties used in the experimentation domain) and structuring (creation of a hierarchy) all the terms used, may be interactively developed during the supervision process. This is a prerequisite to the ontology of the domain. The work on the ontology should also be applied to the task and the methods, in order to share problem-solving methods [2]. In the CoDesign frame, the physical components are defined, like memory, bus, processor core, and so on. As well, the properties are identified as hardware area, power consumption. Properties may be defined later in the process, according to the needs of the user.

Organize: The organization is achieved by the decomposition (in order to find basic properties) and the gathering (to build concepts in the experimentation domain) of the identified notions. In a CoDesign point of view, this will merge classes of design that share properties, since the basic components are organized in an inclusion hierarchy.

Generation

Establishing a choice: This is composed of two basic operations: highlighting (exploiting the valued variables) and blocking a choice (the application domain for a choice is restricted). These operations aim to help the argumentation of a designer for a design choice. As well, it gives support for drawing up a new choice, that is, suggests a new hypothesis that will be experimented.

Experimenting an hypothesis: The experimentation of an hypothesis provides measures of properties. There are two ways for experimentation: first, by propagating an hypothesis (generation of a new configuration), and studying the consequences on the system; second, the refutation of an hypothesis may occur if it is not relevant (e.g., no more choice in the design process). In the CoDesign project, the experimentation corresponds to the selection of synthesis parameters, or design rules.

2.2 Supervision scheme:

Let us now have a look at the global organization of the supervision scheme. It aims at finding a stability between the previous actions (Fig. 1).

Starting from an initial organization, the identification step provides the definition of the notions needed in the supervision process. The relevant properties that describe the system are either identified by the variables and their associated domain. Then, experimentation provides some measures of the properties.

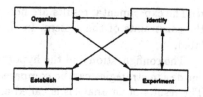

Fig. 1. The supervision scheme is based on a stability between the operations

It may propagate or neutralize a choice, that has consequences on the organization of the terms. The goal of the supervision scheme is to provide formulation features on the design process, even if it does not lead to a relevant configuration. It succeeds if the designer is able to annotate the experimental results.

The actions are chained according to the arrows. Nevertheless, the diagonal lines express the refutation of an action. For example, let us consider the system composed of Identify, Establish and Experiment. If the identification step does not extract relevant information, the user or the system must prepare a new choice. Its experimentation will provide new properties to be evaluated in the Identify step.

In this section, we have presented a frame for the supervision that help the designer for structuring the knowledge during design. Let us now have a look at the application of the supervision scheme for the design of a Hardware/Software architecture.

3 Supervision in a CoDesign environment

We use the supervision scheme for the CoDesign. Therefore, we should define the terms used in this domain, and explain what are the mechanisms of supervision, as well as how the supervision cycle works.

3.1 Application to CoDesign

Analyse to prepare a choice
The current configuration is evaluated during the analysis step. According to the properties defined on the system, an hypothesis may be built to improve its implementation. The hypothesis is composed of new choices in the design parameters, or by the modification of the partition between software and hardware. The consequences of such an analysis may be the refutation of an hypothesis that lead to the current configuration. The refutation occurs in two cases:
i) the design can not be built under the suggested hypothesis. In this case, the designer should not be able to formulate it. So the structuration of the terms is to be revised, that is the language should be restricted or adapted. The modification of this structuration eventually implies the definition of new properties of the system, that are more relevant for the design activity.

ii) The experimental results are not satisfactory. For instance, they do not meet the constraints of the system. In this case, a new hypothesis should be formulated.

The configuration and the hypothesis are stored in a database. So, the different design strategies can be compared, and modules can be retrieved as wanted. The results of an analysis is called annotation.

Experiment a choice to measure properties

The propagation of an hypothesis produces a new configuration. So, the experimentation will provide some measures of the current properties. They will be used to evaluate this configuration. The measures are provided by the design tools, at different levels of abstraction. So, the designer may choose the measure considered as the best one. Typically, usual metrics for hardware estimation is the number of blocks used for the design, that provides also the hardware area. Another one is the electric consumption.

Organize to exhibit a design

The principle of this step is to exhibit the qualities of a design through the organization of its properties. Classes of design may be suggested to the designer, so that he verifies that the configuration effectively corresponds to the current class of design. The organization of the designs provides a hierarchy, that gives inclusion relationship between basic blocks and more complex objects. This is a way to identify some subsystems. that may facilitate component reuse.

4   State of the work

We benefit now from an environment that supports the supervision scheme. All the front-end is implemented as HTML documents, with interactive objects to select synthesis parameters, and to run programs. HTML has been choosen for interoperability reasons. Future work is to provide a dynamic interface with a language like Java.

The features of this environment are: *i*) generation of the configurations, *ii*) presentation of the experimental results to the designer, *iii*) selection of the relevant measures on the configurations, *iv*) extraction of properties to be criticized. A support for annotation is also provided. The designer fills the HTML interface of the MATISSE database to store the configurations and their annotations. A useful extension is the automatic extraction of information in experimental results thanks to a loader.

The experimentations made on the Codesign have pointed out the need of an assistant for the dynamic revision. This is related to the complexity of the design tools. For instance, the architecture compiler [8] has roughly hundred parameters. The variation of these parameters causes an great extension of the solution space. Obviously, the choice of the parameters for synthesis and technology mapping tools, as well as the modification of the partition between hardware and software increases also the size of the solution space. The experimentations on very simple systems, as the gradient edge detection or the highest common factor have already shown the significance of the supervision. It better structures the construction of the solution space, and assists the designer in configuration retrieval.

5 Conclusions

We have presented in this paper a supervision scheme applied to the CoDesign. We have shown that the frame is based on a set of operations, that characterize the supervision activity. To supervise an iterative process, we have placed the user as an active supervisor, who is assisted by the frame. Then, we have presented the supervision environment. It has shown its significance to assist the designer in the design process. Thanks to the frame, the designer is able to formulate a design strategy and exhibit the reasons of a failure. The result is the production of an architecture that meets the constraints on the system, with a better structuration of design objects, as well as the propagation of the hypothesis. Future work is to dynamically adapt the interface to the user habits, and to apply learning tools in order to extract regularities in the design process, to suggest the designer a design strategy.

References

1. B.W Boehm. A spiral model of software development and enhancement. *IEEE Computer*, 1988.
2. B. Chandrasekaran and J.R. Josephson. The ontology of tasks and methods. In *Symposium on Ontological engineering, AAAI Spring Symposium Series*, 1997.
3. Francoise Darses. The constraint satisfaction approach to design: A psychological investigation. In Gerrit C. van der Veer, Sebastiano Bagnara, and Gerard A. M. Kempen, editors, *Cognitive Ergonomics: Contributions from Experimental Psychology*, Graphics Design, pages 307–325. North-Holland, Elsevier Science Publishers, Amsterdam, 1992.
4. Y. Iwasaki and B. Chandrasekaran. Design verification through function- and behavior-oriented representations. Technical Report 92-63, Knowledge Systems Laboratory, Stanford University, 1992.
5. C. W. Liew and L. Steinberg. The fad project. Technical Report CAP-TR-10, Department of Computer Science, Rutgers University, 1992.
6. L. Maillet-Contoz, S. Pillement, and J. Sallantin. A unified workbench for designing hardware/software systems. *International Workshop on Logic and Architecture Synthesis*, pages 363–370, 1996.
7. B Ramesh and K. Sengupta. Managing cognitive and mixed-motive conflicts in concurrent engineering. *Concurrent Engineering; Research and Applications*, 2(3):223–236, 1994.
8. B. Rouzeyre, D. Dupont, and G. Sagnes. Component selection, scheduling and control schemes for high level synthesis. *European Design & Test Conference '94*, pages 482–489, 1994.
9. I. Sommerville. *Le génie logiciel et ses applications*. Addison Wesley Europe/InterEditions, 1988.

REVINOS : An Interactive Revision Tool Based on the Concept of Situation

Luc Poittevin

Equipe Inférence & Apprentissage
Laboratoire de Recherche en Informatique
Bât 490, Université Paris-Sud
91405 Orsay Cedex, France
E-mail: Luc.Poittevin@lri.fr

Abstract. This paper presents REVINOS, an incremental modeling and cooperative revision tool for Knowledge Bases (KB) expressed with situation nodules. Situation nodules are simple and understandable objects which allow to specify step by step interactions between the knowledge-based system and its environment. Knowledge representation by situation nodules appears to be useful when the KB designer wants to elicit knowledge incrementally because he assumes that the knowledge expressed is temporary and can be erroneous or incomplete.

1 Introduction

We propose a knowledge representation formalism based on the *concept of situation*, designed to facilitate the understanding and revision of Knowledge Bases (KB). This work was initiated by a problem of building and maintaining French Minitel dialogues for the SNCF Company (French Railways). An incremental knowledge elicitation tool, called REVINOS, has been designed for this purpose. Revision is performed by a cooperative revision module based on machine learning methods. These machine learning methods automate "low level" tasks so that the designer of the dialogue (the user of the revision tool) can focus on the modeling and revision process, i.e. understanding, handling and creating situations in the Knowledge Base.

2 Context of this Work

The goal of the SNCF project is to provide customized information by the means of Minitel to its employees in the domains of health insurance and old-age insurance. One of the specificity of the project is the fact that the data needed to drive the dialogue are not known at the beginning of the dialogue. These data are acquired in the course of the dialogue, either in the form of questions directly asked to the minitelist or by retrieving information about the minitelist in databases. The need to get information progressively, and to ask for information only when it is necessary, leads to the idea of explicitly representing *situations*, together with the actions to do in these situations (for example ask question Q, display text T,...). This idea will be explained in the next section.

3 Knowledge Representation by Situation Nodules

3.1 The Concept of Situation

In every day's life, the word "situation" means an interpretation of the world state by a person or a group. Situation is not an objective notion, since it is relative to a person, and depends on the information about the world that this person has, as well as it depends on the purposes of the person. This subjective view of the notion of situation leads to the following key idea: a situation has a meaning only as related to a project. Thus the situation as we define it is more than knowledge about the environment ("objective" knowledge on the state of the world): it is an interpretation of the environment during the achievement of a task, i.e. a knowledge of the environment *linked to a plan in progress*.

A situation becomes more and more precise as the task progresses and as data about the environment are known. We propose therefore to represent the achievement of a task as a *chaining of situations*. The model of reasoning is schematized as follows: "In a given situation, it is suitable to execute some actions on the environment. These actions can possibly return data that take part in the redefinition or shaping of the situation."

This view of the concept of situation leads to the following approach to model knowledge: the building of KB consists in precisely and progressively eliciting the situations. The designer has to define actions related to the situations, to connect situations together and to define their chaining. In our model, a task is not only the activities that contributes to the achievement of a goal, but the goal itself [WIE 92]. A task is defined as an initial situation and a set of situations that can be derived from the initial one during the examination of the environment.

The problem solving goal is to derive a final situation, that fits to the interpretation of the environment suitable to the given task. In our case, the final situation sets the whole information to be displayed to the minitelist.

Consequently, there are two kinds of knowledge attached to each situation:

1) actions to execute: seeking for information in the environment, or simply launching the execution of an action on the environment,

2) rules for choosing the next situation from the known data.

In order to represent a situation in KB, an object called *situation nodule* (nodule meaning "little node") has been designed.

3.2 Situation Nodule

A situation nodule contains two fields: *actions* and *choosing rules*. Nodules form graphs which represent tasks. Graphs are identified by the name of their initial nodule. The initial nodule expresses a goal. This representation enables to launch the execution of another graph from nodules. The execution of the subtask (subgraph) is viewed as an action that returns information which is useful in the calling task. The algorithm of the engine is very simple:

When a nodule is activated, each of its actions is executed. These actions can return more or less structured facts which are stored in a Working Memory (WM). From this WM, choosing rules trigger the next nodule to execute. There may be no next nodule in the case the KB is incomplete, that is to say, the "situation" has not been foreseen. If the next nodule is found, it is activated in turn. The algorithm stops when a terminating nodule is encountered.

For each action the designer defines a description of the returned facts, called *declaration* of the action. This description is useful for knowing what kind of facts the action is able to return and can be stored in the WM. An action can return objects, can set relations between objects, and can set values to properties of objects.

4 Understanding the Situation

REVINOS allows the user to construct nodules graphs as well as to simulate Minitel dialogues. The user can stop a simulation at any time to "examine the situation". At that moment he may want to "understand the situation", i.e. to understand the reason of the execution of the current action. The "object to understand" will be referred to as *observation* in the following because it can be viewed as an observed example. It is the conjunction of a nodule, the current state of the WM and a nodule *path* (the set of nodules which have been activated since the initial nodule). This "observation" object is a kind of "Situation Specific Model" (SSM) as Clancey defined it ([CLA 92]). A SSM contains the description of the process which led to the current solution (a nodule path in our framework) together with the "Case Model" in the sense of CommonKADS [WIE 92] (the current nodule plus the state of the WM in our framework) ([CAU 94]).

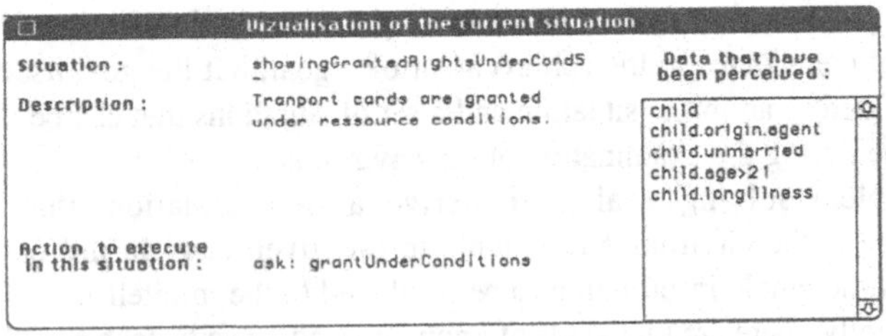

Vizualisation of the current situation		
Situation :	showingGrantedRightsUnderCondS	Data that have been perceived :
Description :	Transport cards are granted under ressource conditions.	child child.origin.agent child.unmarried child.age>21 child.longIllness
Action to execute in this situation :	ask: grantUnderConditions	

Fig. 1. *Visualization of the current situation*

To understand the observation, the user has to understand several objects (an example is given at figure 1), the action suggested for the current situation, then the set of facts that characterizes the situation. It represents the state of the WM: the set of data that have been perceived at that time. In order to understand each fact, REVINOS allows the user to explore *the* action that has returned the fact, and the nodule of the path that has executed the action.

When the user has finally understood these objects, he is able to decide if he agrees with the action selected by the system. Checking the meaning of each object in the questionable situation is a prerequisite to revision. In case the disagreement is confirmed, the user can start the cooperative revision process. During this process, the user does not need to thoroughly understand the graph, nor to handily tune choosing rules. REVINOS uses machine learning methods to avoid the user handling and correcting choosing rules. Thus the user can focus on the modeling process: he has only to handle situations, actions, facts, and links between these three kinds of objects.

5 The Revision Session

5.1 Process of the Revision

In the same way as interactive machine learning and revision tools such as in MIS ([SHA 83]), APT ([NED 92a]) or KRT ([MOR 93]), REVINOS and the user cooperate to correct and/or complete the KB. Revision session starts with a given observation (see above) that is called current example.

The revision loop consists of three steps :

While there is an example to correct

    Step 1: identification of the origin of the error.

    Step 2: execution of a revision operator, if the graph needs a revision.

    Step 3: validation by submitting to the user the repercussions of the correction.

End while

    Step 4: possibly generalization of the revision.

During each of these steps, the system asks the user to perform some tasks such as creating or modifying KB objects. During the validation stage (step 3), the system submits to the user examples which fit with the different repercussions of the correction. If an example is not validated, the system goes back to step 1 with this example. Once all examples have been validated, revision session can possibly be continued if the system detects that the corrections performed can be generalized (this step 4 is not described here, but is detailed in [POI 97]).

5.2 Identification of the Origin of the Error (Step 1)

During the dialogue, the system identifies the cause of the disagreement and the associated repair. Four causes of error are distinguished: never encountered situation, action to change, missing information, erroneous information.

Step 1 leads to the identification of an *objective* of correction, that is to say a conjunction of the name of a current nodule and of the name of a target nodule, which must be chosen from the current nodule. The alteration of the choosing rules of the current nodule must be done in such a way that the target nodule will be activated at least for the current example.

5.3 Application of a Revision Operator (Step 2)

During this stage, the system has to choose and to apply an operator relevant to the objective defined before. In some cases the system submits examples to the user in order to choose between two revision operators.

The submitted examples can be compared to "crucial objects" in MARVIN ([SAM 86]) and discriminating examples in APT ([NED 92a]). Their roles are similar since they are shown to the user in order to determine the right "generalization level" for the revision. The *modifyRule* operator suggests to spread the current correction to the set of examples using the current rule. The *replaceRule* operator is more specific and applies the current correction only to the right subset of the examples. Similarly to APT, REVINOS uses the submitted examples to compute the discriminating facts that direct either on the old nodule or on the target nodule by differentiation [NED 92b]. These discriminating facts allow to appropriately modify the choosing rules .

5.4 Validation of the Revision (Step 3)

Once the correction is performed the system computes all its repercussions and submits them to the user as examples to validate. To calculate the repercussions of the correction, REVINOS build the *cover* of the graph. The cover of a graph is the set of all possible paths of the graph, computed from the declarations of the actions and the choosing rules of the nodules. Each path is an example, expressed by the list of abstracts facts returned by the actions executed along the path. When the graph is explored the domains of possible values are updated in accordance with the choosing rules activated. Facts being values properties are computed consequently.

The repercussions are computed by stating the difference between the cover of the graph before and after the correction of the graph. Two sets are built. E+ is the set of the new examples which were not covered before the correction. E- is the set of the no longer covered examples. E+ is useful to enrich the list L of the examples to validate. E- is used to update L and to remove examples that would be now obsolete.

The examples can be generated for validation because the returned facts of actions are all declared. The submitted examples are few and expressed at a right level of abstraction (more general than observations).

6 Discussion

The situation nodules graphs have common points with decision trees, in the way ID3 ([QUI 86]) builds them. Decision trees can be seen as simplified nodules graphs, in which actions are simple attribute evaluation. Representation with nodules allows to define more complex actions and also to build more powerful rules to choose next nodule. Nodules graphs are also interesting in comparison with equivalent decision trees because of their legibility and conciseness.

Nodules graphs have also similarities with Augmented Transition Networks (ATN) ([BOB 69]): the Working Memory in nodules graphs play the same role as buffers in ATN, and subgraphs call is similar to subnetworks call. But, as decision trees, nodules do not backtrack, unlike ATN. ATN are used in grammatical parsing and natural language processing, and therefore intensively backtrack. On the other hand, by requiring to represent actions and situations explicitly, nodules set a meaning to states (or decision tree nodes), and then allow to model knowledge at the "conceptual level". Moreover ATN requires to know beforehand all the information that can be needed during their execution.

With knowledge representation by situation nodules every knowledge is bound to a context. The descriptions of situations and actions relevant to these situations are extended when new concrete situations are encountered. Therefore, our model is placed in an incremental knowledge acquisition perspective as systems like TEREISIAS [DAV 79]. This approach is opposed to a knowledge acquisition approach by modeling before operationalisation.

Incremental design of the KB with situation nodules is possible because the operationalisation is closed to the reasoning model. The concept of situation seems to be more interesting for the incremental and rapid prototyping approach than the concept of universally worthwhile rule. The notion of situation is useful when the resolution states of KBS fit to concrete situations that are understandable and to which the user can directly refer during the revision process. This makes easier the location of the correction since the tracks are explicitly represented and well-documented.

7 Conclusions

This work is based on the notion of situation and propose a new simple way to incrementally elicit knowledge . The model described above allows to concretely and progressively design KB. The machine learning techniques avoid the user to handle low level information such as viewing and tuning choosing rules.

Knowledge representation by situation nodules seem to be relevant when:
- the environment is incompletely known and the information capture in the environment can be only incrementally done,
- the order of the information acquisition is important: the "cost" of the execution of an action is significant and one wants actions to be executed only when necessary. Hence, a simple and clear representation of this order is required.
- the knowledge is strongly "contextualized", in the sense that the context has an important role in the determination of the system behavior. This entails a strong dependence between knowledge involved and the tasks in which this knowledge is useful.
- the KB designer wants to elicit knowledge incrementally because he assumes that the knowledge expressed is temporary and can be erroneous or incomplete.

Acknowledgments

This work benefits from the financial support of the ANRT. The author thanks Yves Kodratoff and Claire Nédellec, his Ph.D. advisor, for her helpful comments on this paper.

References

[BOB 69] Bobrow D.G., Fraser B. "An Augmented State Transition Network Analysis Procedure", IJCAI'69.
[CAU 94] Causse K., "A Model for Control Knowledge", in *Proceedings of Banff Knowledge Acquisition For Knowledge-Based Systems Workshop*, 1994.
[CLA 92] Clancey W.J., "Model construction operators", *Artificial Intelligence 53*, 1992.
[DAV 79] Davis R., "Interactive Transfer of Expertise: Acquisition of New Inference Rules", Artificial Intelligence 12, pp. 121-157, 1979.
[MOR 93] Morik K., Wrobel S., Kietz J.U., Emde W., "Knowledge Acquisition and Machine Learning", Academic Press, London, 1993.
[NED 92a] Nédellec C., Causse K. "Knowledge Refinement using Knowledge Acquisition and Machine Learning Methods", in *Proceedings of EKAW-92*, LNAI 599, Springer, 1992.
[NED 92b] Nédellec C., "How to specialize by Theory Refinement", in *Proceedings of the 10th European Conference on Artificial Intelligence (ECAI-92)*, pp. 474-478, 1992.
[POI 97] Poittevin L. "REVINOS : un outil de révision interactive s'appuyant sur la notion de situation", in *Proceedings of JICAA*, INRIA (Eds), Roscoff, 1997.
[QUI 86] Quinlan J.R., "Induction of Decision Trees", in *Machine Learning 1,1*, 1986.
[SAM 86] Sammut C., Banerji R.B., "Learning Concepts By Asking Questions", in *Machine Learning II: An Artificial Approach*, p. 167-192, Morgan Kaufman, 1986.
[SHA 83] Shapiro E.Y., "Algorithmic Program Debugging", The MIT Press, 1983.
[WIE 92] Wielenga B.J., Van de Velde W., Schreiber G., Akkermans H., "The CommonKADS Framework for Knowledge Modelling", in *Proceedings of the AAAI Knowledge Acquisition Workshop*, Banff, 1992.

KIDS for KADS

Remco Straatman*

SWI, University of Amsterdam, Roetersstraat 15, 1018 WB Amsterdam, NL
E-mail: remco@swi.psy.uva.nl

Abstract. In order to give more support in the construction, adaptation, and use of problem-solving methods (PSM) an explicit representation of the relevant aspects of a PSM is necessary. In [4] we propose such a framework, based on the KADS [5] methodology. KIDS [7], a transformational software development system, is based on a representation similar to our proposed framework. In this paper we investigate to what extent KIDS can be used as a basis for representations and tools for PSM development.

1 Introduction

The development and use of problem-solving methods has been extensively studied in the field of knowledge engineering. In [4] we proposed a formal framework for representing PSMs. We described how this framework could support verification, construction and use of PSMs. One of the things missing in this work is a representation of all the aspects of the framework and their relations. Current attempts at describing these concepts and/or parts of the construction process, such as [10, 1, 9] are either too informal or describe only a subset of the concepts needed.

In this paper we focus on KIDS, a transformational programming system based on a formalism that incorporates a number of the concepts (specifically goals and assumptions) missing in the representations mentioned above. The KIDS systems aids in the construction process of software, starting with a description of the task at hand and resulting in a correct and efficient program for this task. Both the formalism and techniques used in KIDS can serve as a a starting point for our own research.

In the rest of this paper we state our aims regarding the support for automated construction of PSMs, and the framework we envision for this tasks. Next, we describe the KIDS system. We describe how KIDS relates to our framework and how it could be used for constructing PSMs. We then report an example of this usage, and discuss the problems that arose. Due to space constraints, our description will be brief, see [8] for more details.

---

* The investigations were supported by the Netherlands Computer Science Research Foundation with financial support from the Netherlands Organization for Scientific Research (NWO).

2 Automatic construction and adaptation of PSMs

Our current research interest is automatic support for construction and adaptation of PSMs. According to us, these processes can be greatly improved by making explicit the relevant parts of a PSM.

Fensel and Straatman [4] present a representation framework for this purpose. Our framework does not drastically deviate from earlier work on PSMs, but rather clarifies the relations that hold between the ingredients of a PSM and presents some required extensions. In particular we extend the description of PSMs with a description of their costs, and describe the relations between function, operationalization, assumptions, and costs of a PSM.

A PSM describes how to achieve a *goal* in terms of problem-solving behavior. For this reason a PSM consists of four parts: a *functional specification* and an *operational specification* together with its *assumptions* and a *cost description*: (1) The functional specification is a declarative description of the input-output behavior the PSM was designed for. In this way, the functional description can be seen as a description of the competence of the PSM. (2) The operational specification describes how to realize the functional specification in a reasoning system. The operational specification is a high-level description of the reasoning process, not dependent on implementation details. The operational specification consists of inferences, roles, the data flow between these, and the control over the inferences. (3) The assumptions describe conditions under which the structure described in the operational description will achieve the functional specification. The assumptions put restrictions on the input and the domain knowledge. (4) The cost description describes the costs that are associated with using this PSM to achieve the functionality. The cost of a PSM denotes the amount of resources (computing space and time, user interaction, etc.) needed by the method. The relation between functional, cost, operational specification, and assumptions is essential for understanding PSMs. In our framework, given that the requirements hold, the reasoning system defined by the operational specification must exhibit the input-output behavior specified in the functional specification, at the described cost. The relation of these parts to the environment of the PSM is the following: the functional specification should match the goal description of a task and the assumptions should hold for the domain knowledge. Furthermore, the cost described in the cost description should be acceptable for this task.

The four parts of a PSM and their relationships provide strong handles for the automation of the development and adaptation of PSMs, however currently no complete formalization nor tools based on the framework are available.

3 KIDS

KIDS [7] is a tool for the semi-automatic construction of correct and efficient programs from formal problem specifications. KIDS has been used to generate efficient programs for complex, real-world tasks. We focus on KIDS because we see similarities in the underlying formalization and our framework, and the system and our intended tools.

KIDS manipulates a representation that consists of a formal specification of the problem and a specification of its realization. The problem specification consist of the desired input-output relation and the input restriction. The realization takes the form of a program specified in a high-level programming language. KIDS starts with a problem statement without realization. From this an efficient program is derived in a number of steps. KIDS contains a library of steps, each of which is proven to be function preserving. The different types of steps in this derivation are:

- *design tactics* A design tactic describes the steps necessary to instantiate an algorithm for a specific problem. The library contains tactics for global search, local search, divide-and-conquer algorithms and other "weak" methods.
- *optimizations* Transformations are available that further improve the program's performance, such as simplification of expressions, partial evaluation and finite differencing.
- *compilation* The program can be transformed into executable (LISP) code.

The development process starts by picking a tactic to apply to the functional specification, resulting in an initial program, followed by a number of simplification steps of the program. When the user is satisfied with the resulting program, it can be automatically translated to, for instance, LISP. The main use of the design tactics and transformations lies in improving efficiency. In this derivation process, the user is responsible for picking the right tactic, optimization and the focus it is applied to. The KIDS system is responsible for the actual application of the step to the focus.

Central to KIDS is the notion of *problem statement*. A problem statement can be used to specify both a problem to be solved and the input-output relation of a library algorithm. Problem statements in KIDS are formalized as theories, consisting of sorts, operations over sorts, and axioms that constrain the meaning of the operations. The elementary problem statement has the following form:

Sorts D,R
Operations
    I:D $\rightarrow$ *Boolean*
    O:D x R $\rightarrow$ *Boolean*

The *input condition* $I(x)$ constrains the input domain, D, and the *output condition* $O(x,z)$ describes the conditions under which output domain value $z \in R$ is a feasible solution with respect to input $x \in D$. Extensions of the elementary problem statement theory can then be used to specify the functionality of methods. In the library this theory describing the method's functionality is coupled to a realization (in a high-level programming language) that is described using the terms of the method theory. The user's problem is also described as a problem statement. After the user chooses a method, KIDS tries to prove that the problem statement of the method is more general than the user's problem. More general means that for every input possible in the more specific theory, the solutions in the more general theory are a superset of those in the more specific theory. Proving this provides a substitution for parts of the methods theory that were *parameterized.* With this substitution KIDS can construct a version of the method specific to the user's problem.

In [7] the application of the *global search* tactic to the N-Queens problem is described. For this example, [7] states that the original N-Queens specification cannot be compiled, the unoptimized global search program results in an implementation that spends $O(k^2)$ time per node, and takes 60 minutes to generate all 92 solutions to the 8-Queens problem. The transformations mentioned before were used to further improve the program. The final optimized version spends $O(1)$ time per node and finds all solutions in less than 1 second.

4 Using KIDS for KADS

We see two activities in the development process of KADS knowledge-based systems where KIDS can be helpful: constructing a program for a given expertise model (the "design phase" in KADS methodology), and constructing a method for a given task description. We concentrate on the second activity here. There are some obvious correspondences between KIDS and the framework we propose:

- The *input-output relation* in KIDS, O, corresponds to the functional specification of a PSM.
- The *input condition*, I, corresponds to the assumptions related to the input. *Axioms* in the theory describing the method are similar to assumptions on domain knowledge.
- The *problem statements* can be seen as formalizations of task goals and task features.
- The *body* of a specification in KIDS corresponds to our PSM_operational, the operational specification.
- A part of the *design tactics* library in KIDS can be seen as counterparts of a PSM library. The method-theory and the corresponding program of a design tactic together form, as explained above, a PSM description. The actual tactic is a procedure that prescribes how to match the theory the problem statement and how to make the corresponding program, and has no counterpart in PSM libraries.
- The second library of KIDS contains *optimizing transformations*, that can be applied to improve the efficiency of programs. There is no existing counterpart for this in work on the application of PSM's.

One of the main differences is that KIDS does not make a distinction between tasks and domains. In KIDS, a functional specification of a problem is stated directly in domain-specific terms (e.g. diagnosis of heart diseases), whereas in KADS the task (in this case: diagnosis) is separated from the domain in which the task is applied (in this case: heart diseases). What is necessary here is to devise a way to maintain this conceptual separation, without limiting the possibility for optimizations in the operationalization.

Another difference concerns the way method-specific knowledge is represented. In KIDS domain-specific knowledge needed to perform a task *is* represented (in the functional specification), but method-specific knowledge does not have a place in the specification. To apply KIDS to KADS we must also be able to explicitly describe method-specific knowledge, once again maintaining optimization opportunities.

5 An example: N-Queens in KADS

In order to test the applicability of KIDS to KADS we described a domain and a task, and tried to apply KIDS to produce a method for the task, that is suitable for the domain. We used the N-Queens problem given in [7] as the domain for this specification. Due to a lack of space we cannot give examples of the specifications here, see [8] for details. To make KIDS applicable on this we did the following:

- Identify the task the queens problem is an instance of. The N-queens problem can be classified as an assignment task, as described in [3], chapter 5. We formalized the assignment task in the KIDS language, REGROUP.
- Describe the Queens domain. The domain knowledge is equivalent to the description given in [7]. However now the domain knowledge is more clearly separated from the task definition, whereas in the original formulation the domain formulation was strongly influenced by the task definition.
- Link the task and domain. The definition of the assignment task and the definition of the queens domain have to be linked together to describe the problem we want to solve. In this case, we chose to specify the mapping of domain terms to task terms as functions in a mapping theory.

We then used KIDS to construct the method (normally we would select the appropriate problem solving method for this task from a library (e.g. [3], [2])). At first we tried to apply the KIDS tactics to the function representing the top level task, assignment. However, none of the KIDS tactics were able to successfully derive a program for the assignment task. In order to investigate whether the generic nature of this function and/or the mappings were the problem, we unfolded its definition and also unfolded all mapping functions. After simplifying the resulting function definition, we once again tried all tactics. Even for this much more specific function none of the tactics succeeded.

Unfortunately, the KIDS system is not supported by its authors, so, apart from the documentation, we had no sources to point us into any direction. Therefore, we cannot give a conclusive cause for this failure. Since we based the example on the example described in [7] it should lie within the range of what can be solved by KIDS. Our specification could contain one or more errors, or the distance between the specification of the problem and the method theory was too big for the matching component of KIDS (example specifications in the KIDS distribution also suggest this is a problem).

6 Discussion

In this paper we compared the KIDS formalism and system to our own proposed framework for adapting and constructing PSMs. KIDS captures most aspects and relations of our framework (apart from costs). The KIDS system presents a working system for the construction of efficient (high level) programs from functional specifications. We proposed how to use the techniques from KIDS to derive a PSM for a given task.

Based on this we performed an experiment by re-specifying an existing KIDS problem specification as a KADS task specification. The KIDS formalism does not make the distinction between domain specific and task knowledge that has become a standard practice in knowledge modeling. If we want to use a system based on KIDS for our purpose, this distinction should be maintainable. We then tried to derive a method for this task, using the KIDS system. Unfortunately, this experiment failed. We were unable to derive any method for the given task definition. Due to the lack of support from the developers of the KIDS system, we were unable to identify what the cause of this failure was. Our experience suggests that the problem lies in the lack of power and interactivity of the matching process between problems and methods. Before we can realize "KIDS for KADS" these questions have to be answered first.

References

1. M. Aben. *Formal Methods in Knowledge Engineering.* PhD thesis, University of Amsterdam, februari 1995.
2. V. R. Benjamins. *Problem Solving Methods for Diagnosis.* PhD thesis, University of Amsterdam, Amsterdam, June 1993.
3. J. A. Breuker and W. Van de Velde, editors. *The CommonKADS Library for Expertise Modelling.* IOS Press, Amsterdam, The Netherlands, 1994.
4. D. Fensel and R. Straatman. The essence of problem-solving methods: Making assumptions for efficiency reasons. In Nigel Shadbolt, Kieron O'Hara, and Guus Schreiber, editors, *proceedings of the 9th European Knowledge Acquisition Workshop, EKAW-96* Springer-Verlag, 1996.
5. A. Th. Schreiber, B. J. Wielinga, and J. A. Breuker, editors. *KADS: A Principled Approach to Knowledge-Based System Development* Academic Press, London, 1993.
6. D. R. Smith. Structure and design of global search algorithms. Technical Report KES.U.87.12, Kestrel Institute, Palo Alto, California, November 1987.
7. D. R. Smith. Kids: A semi-automatic program development system. *IEEE Transactions on Software Engineering,* September 1990.
8. R. Straatman. KIDS for KADS. Technical report, SWI, UvA, Amsterdam, 1996. http://www.swi.psy.uva.nl/usr/remco/postscripts/Straatman:96a.ps.gz
9. F. van Harmelen and M. Aben. Structure preserving specification languages for knowledge-based systems. *International Journal of Human Computer Studies,* 1996.
10. B. J. Wielinga, J. M. Akkermans, and A. Th. Schreiber. A formal analysis of parametric design problem solving. In B. R. Gaines and M. A. Musen, editors, *Proceedings of the 8th Banff KAW,* Alberta, Canada, 1995.

Exploiting Inductive Bias Shift in Knowledge Acquisition from Ill-Structured Domains

Luis Talavera and Ulises Cortés

Universitat Politècnica de Catalunya
Departament de Llenguatges i Sistemes Informàtics
Campus Nord, Mòdul C6, Jordi Girona 3
08034 Barcelona, Catalonia, Spain
{talavera,ia}@lsi.upc.es

Abstract. Machine Learning (ML) methods are very powerful tools to automate the knowledge acquisition (KA) task. Particularly, in *ill-structured* domains where there is no clear idea about which concepts exist, inductive unsupervised learning systems appear to be a promising approach to help experts in the early stages of the acquisition process. In this paper we examine the concept of *inductive bias*, which have received great attention from the ML community, and discuss the importance of bias shift when using ML algorithms to help experts in constructing a knowledge base (KB) A simple framework for the interaction of the expert with the inductive system exploiting bias shift is shown. Also, it is suggested that under some assumptions, bias selection in unsupervised learning may be performed via parameter setting, thus allowing the user to shift the system bias externally.

1 Introduction

One of the original goals in developing Machine Learning (ML) programs was to overcome the well-known problem of the *knowledge acquisition bottleneck* [4]. ML algorithms promised an effective way of automating the knowledge acquisition (KA) process thus reducing the interaction with experts. Furthermore, sometimes, the domain under study is *ill-structured*, that is, there is no clear idea about which concepts exist and their relationships [1]. In such a case, it is often easier for an expert to provide a set of relevant cases than to give a set of rules to describe the domain. For this reason, inductive learning appears as one of the most powerful ML methods as regards to KA.

Inductive learning systems have been traditionally split into two different approaches, namely, supervised and unsupervised learning. In *supervised* learning, every example is marked with an identifying concept label and the task of the system is to induce correct concept descriptions from the examples. On the contrary, *unsupervised* learning systems assume that there is no concept class information available. So, the system must decide which concepts exist in the domain under study and induce their descriptions. When facing an ill-structured domain, it is likely that concept labels will not be available from the expert, so unsupervised learning may be a helpful tool for the expert by providing some idea about the domain structure.

Despite all of this, great part of ML research has focused in general purpose methods, not designed for any specific application. Although this approach may seem adequate from the ML research point of view, a number of problems may arise when ML systems are applied to certain areas. KA is not an exception and we can see how successful and well known ML methods fail in some way when applied to this task. In this paper we address one aspect which we consider of great interest in the application of inductive learning methods to KA, namely the capability of performing a *bias shift*.

2   Inductive bias

Inductive learning can be characterized as a search in a hypotheses space [6]. For any given dataset, a potentially infinite number of hypotheses may be formulated and the problem of exploring all of them becomes intractable. To address this problem, inductive learning methods have to determine which hypotheses are better and discard the rest. The factors that influence the definition and selection of inductive hypotheses are called a *bias* [3]. It is easy to see that every inductive learning algorithm must include some form of bias, that is, it will always prefer some hypothesis over another. This fact explains the great attention that the idea of bias has always received from the ML community.

Early ML algorithms used only the so called *static* bias, a kind of bias which is established when learning begins and remains the same for the rest of the process. Sometimes this bias is encoded in the algorithm and it is impossible for the user to alter it, while other times some set of parameters exists which allow the user to choose the desired bias. An example of the first approach is ID3 [7] which builds a decision tree from a set of labeled instances. ID3 can build only one tree for every dataset, so it cannot alter its biases to search for different hypotheses. A completely different approach is CLUSTER/2 [5], an unsupervised system which provides the user with a set of parameters about his preferences on the concepts to be created. Therefore, the user may obtain different clusterings from the same dataset via parameter tuning. Another possibility is to have a *dynamic* bias, or a bias which may be shifted during learning, using knowledge obtained during the learning process.

From another point of view, biases may be classified into representational and procedural biases. A *representational* bias constraints the hypothesis that can be defined in the search space. This sort of bias specify a description language (e.g. first order calculus) and its primitives (e.g. the set of features allowed) thereby defining the set of representable states. A *procedural* bias determines how the system traverses the hypothesis space (for example, a preference for simpler concepts).

The ability of performing a bias shift allows inductive systems to adapt their results to different learning goals. From the ML standpoint, the most used performance goal is accuracy. Accuracy is defined in a somewhat different manner in supervised and unsupervised learning. In supervised learning, accuracy is measured as the proportion of correctly predicted labels in a set of test (unseen) instances. In unsupervised learning there are no labels available, but the former definition has been extended so that accuracy is measured not only as regards the prediction of a single class attribute, but of every attribute present in data. But high accuracies do not have to be the only goal for a learning system. The size of induced knowledge may be another important factor too. Other tasks may be concerned with comprehensibility, so that the results of the inductive system are required to be readable. In general, a proper bias selection can achieve any of these goals and improve the performance of the induced KB.

3 Bias shift and knowledge acquisition in ill-structured domains

So far, we have introduced general concepts about biases from the ML standpoint. But biases may be an important issue when unsupervised learning algorithms are applied to the KA task in ill-structured domains. The KA task is concerned with modeling KBs for specific domains in a form suitable for using in a computer program. The active participation of a human expert is needed in order to perform this task, so several tools have been developed to help human experts in different stages of the process. Nevertheless, experts still can find difficult to describe a domain if they have little experience in this domain.

An alternative approach is to use ML programs to automate the task of constructing a KB. Inductive learning seems to be the most suitable method for this task in knowledge poor environments, since it only requires a set of relevant examples from which learning is performed. If we consider a situation when an expert faces a domain without a clear structure, the KA task becomes even more laborious and slow. This is the situation in which unsupervised inductive learning systems can be more useful because they are able to find regularities among observations suggesting a conceptual structure without external advice.

Although it may appear that any unsupervised learning system can be used for the KA task, not every system is equally suited for this work. Most of the ML systems have been designed as general purpose systems, without concrete tasks in mind. But within a KA environment, one can demand some specific features to ML programs in order to work properly. When facing an ill-structured domain, one of the most important factors is to provide some sort of *user interaction*. When an expert tries to model a domain using a ML program, he may find very useful to have the chance of exploring different possibilities. This means that the learning program should provide some way of constructing different structures from a set of examples. Hence, the learning system may be able to alter its behaviour to cope with different needs or, in other words, it may be capable of performing a bias shift[1].

---

[1] For some authors, bias shift refers to the special case of selecting the bias during the learning process. We use the term in a more general sense.

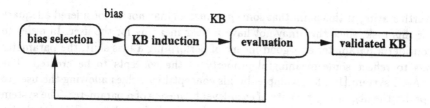

Fig. 1. A framework for KB induction using bias selection

As mentioned in Sect. 2, we can assume that every ML system has a bias. Nevertheless, not every ML system can alter its bias because it is sometimes embedded in the code of the algorithm. This sort of systems can provide only one structure for a given domain, the one which better satisfy their preferences. Thus, the expert must be strongly confident in that the system will find the right domain structure because he has no way to influence in the inductive process. When learning is supervised, the expert has knowledge about the examples he provides to the system and this situation may be acceptable. But when the expert is working with an ill-structured domain, it is likely that he would want to interact with the inductive system to see different perspectives of this domain.

From all this, we can conclude that bias shift is an important feature for inductive systems in order to be used for a KA task, particularly, in ill-structured domains. Figure 1 shows a simple framework that reflects these ideas and the interaction between the expert, the inductive biases and the inductive system. In this framework the inductive system can alter its biases and and provides the expert the chance to decide how to do it. With the selected bias the KB induction is performed and the results passed back to the expert, who evaluates these results and decides whether they are satisfactory or not. In the later case, the expert can choose another bias. We will not specify the nature of the bias which may vary from system to system and between different tasks, but suffice to say that it has to provide flexibility enough to cope with the expert goals.

4 Bias selection as parameter setting

Relevant work in bias shift has been done within the *declarative bias* approach [8] which proposes an explicit specification of biases. To allow such an specification, logical representations of the hypothesis space are used. But the discovery nature of unsupervised learning implies that, in many cases, uncertainty will be present in the studied domains. So, many unsupervised learning approaches use *probabilistic* representations of concepts instead of logical ones. This fact makes the use a declarative bias in these approaches very difficult.

However, if a bias can be characterized in some formal way, in a manner that the system behaviour can be changed by tuning some parameter, we can consider bias selection as equivalent to the parameter setting problem. Therefore, a good interaction with users in unsupervised learning algorithms, should be more easily modeled in systems capable of performing some sort of parameter tuning. It is worth stating at this point that some parameters may not be considered adequate for this task, since they may not have a clear meaning for the user. In order to consider a parameter as a good means of performing a bias shift, the parameter has to reflect some meaningful property of the concepts to be created. The ISAAC system [10], for example, builds concept hierarchies allowing the user to specify the degree o generality of each level by means of a parameter. The system assumes that more general concepts can be discriminated using less attributes than specific ones. Therefore, the induction process not only creates partitions with several degrees of generality, but also uses different sets of attributes for different parameter settings. This constitutes an example of a representational bias, as defined in Sect. 2.

Finally, we have to point out that, when interacting with the user, the number of parameters becomes an important issue too. If there are many parameters, the system may become too complex to use, while having no parameters implies a lack of flexibility. In sum, in KA environments, a high degree of autonomy is not as important as it can be from the ML point of view, rather these environments require a trade-off between autonomy and flexibility.

5 Conclusions and related work

In this paper, we have suggested the idea that inductive bias shift, can be very useful when using ML programs for the KA task, particularly when facing ill-structured domains. Although inductive bias has received great attention from ML researchers, little attention has been paid to the benefits that bias selection can provide in some tasks such as KA. Also, the KA community should consider the important role of biases when using inductive learning systems.

We have argued that in domains without a clear structure, KA demands flexibility to ML methods in order to ease the expert work. We claim that this flexibility can be achieved by means of providing the user with tunable parameters which can alter the system behaviour. This claim contrasts with some traditional idea that non-parameterized programs are better than parameterized ones. From the KA perspective, a non-parameterized system is only useful if the expert its fully confident in that the system will provide the adequate results. We think that our approach is better if the number of parameters is reasonable and they have sense for the expert. Some results using the ISAAC system seem to suggest that this idea is correct [9].

An alternative approach, but still in line with the one proposed here, is to provide the expert some way to express partial knowledge about the domain under study. We can find examples in KA [12] or also in Knowledge Discovery [2]. Although some of these approaches do not mention the concept of declarative bias, they are a very promising way of integrating such biases within systems employing probabilistic representations of concepts. This is a research area in which the KA community can provide an important contribution since prior knowledge is present in many KA environments.

Finally we have to point out that the framework proposed in this paper can be automated and performed without human intervention when a measurable performance goal for the induced KB is known [11]. In terms of the framework proposed in section 3, an automatic procedure would substitute the expert in the bias selection and validation stages. The procedure would try to maximize the evaluation function by shifting the system bias and by evaluating the performance of the induced KB until an acceptable bias is found.

Acknowledgements. We thank one anonymous referee for helpful comments on the preliminary version of this paper. This work was partially supported by the CICyT project TIC96-0878.

References

1. J. Béjar. *Adquisición automática de conocimiento en dominios poco estructurados.* PhD thesis, Facultat d'Informàtica de Barcelona, UPC, 1995.
2. J. Béjar, U. Cortés, R. Sanguesa, and M. Poch. Experiments with domain knowledge in knowledge discovery. In *Proceedings of the 1st. International Conference on the Practical Application of Knowledge Discovery and Data Mining*, London,UK, 1997.
3. D. F. Gordon and M. Desjardins. Evaluation and selection of biases in machine learning. *Machine Learning*, 20(1-2):5–22, 1995.
4. R. S. Michalski. Understanding the nature of learning: issues and research directions. In R. S. Michalski, J. G. Carbonell, and T. M. Mitchell, editors, *Machine Learning: An Artificial intelligence approach, vol.II*. Morgan Kauffmann, Los Altos, CA, 1986.
5. R. S. Michalski and R. E. Stepp. Learning from observation: Conceptual clustering. In R. S. Michalski, J. G. Carbonell, and T. M. Mitchell, editors, *Machine Learning: An Artificial intelligence approach*, pages 331–363. Morgan Kauffmann, Los Altos, CA, 1983.
6. T. M. Mitchell. Generalization as search. *Artificial Intelligence*, (18):203–226, 1982.
7. J. R. Quinlan. Induction of decision trees. *Machine Learning*, 1(1):81–106, 1986.
8. S. Russell and B. Grosof. Declarative bias: An overview. In P. Benjamin, editor, *Representation and Inductive Bias*. Kluwer Academic Publishers, Dordrecht, 1989.
9. L. Talavera. Bias selection and knowledge acquisition in ill-structured domains. Technical report, Departament de Lleguatges i Sistemes Informàtics, UPC, 1997.
10. L. Talavera and U. Cortés. Generalización y atención selectiva para la formación de conceptos. In *V Congreso Iberoamericano de Inteligencia Artificial, IBERAMIA96*, pages 320–330, Cholula, Puebla, Mexico, 1996. Limusa, Mexico.
11. L. Talavera and U. Cortés. Inductive hypothesis validation and bias selection in unsupervised learning. In Jan Vanthienen and Frank van Harmelen, editors, *Proceedings of the 4th. European Symposium on the Validation and Verification of Knowledge Based Systems, EUROVAV-97*, pages 169–179, Leuven,Belgium, 1997.
12. J. J. F. Vasco, C. Faucher, and Eugene Chouraqui. A knowledge acquisition tool for multi-perspective concept formation. In *9th European Knowledge Acquisition Workshop, EKAW'96*, pages 227–244. Springer Verlag, 1996.

The DARPA High Performance Knowledge Bases Programme

John Kingston*

AIAI
University of Edinburgh

Abstract. The HPKB programme aims to enable the development of very large knowledge bases which are comprehensive, reusable, maintainable, and address areas of interest to DARPA. These knowledge bases are expected to require foundation knowledge, knowledge acquisition facilities, and efficient problem solving techniques. The programme encourages development of multiple applications which will be tested against "challenge problems" at the end of each year of the programme.

1   Introduction

The goal of the DARPA-funded High Performance Knowledge Base programme is to produce the technology needed to enable system developers to construct rapidly (i.e. within months) knowledge bases of hundreds of thousands of axioms, rules or frames that provide comprehensive coverage of topics of interest, are reusable by multiple applications with diverse problem-solving strategies, and are maintainable in rapidly changing environments. It is envisioned that the process for constructing these knowledge bases will involve three major steps:

- **Building foundation knowledge:** creating the foundation knowledge (e.g. selecting the knowledge representation scheme, assembling theories of common knowledge, or defining domain-specific terms and concepts) to enable the construction and population of large, comprehensive knowledge bases for particular domains of interest – by selecting, composing, extending, specialising, and modifying components from a library of reusable ontologies, common domain theories, and generic problem-solving strategies.
- **Acquiring domain knowledge:** constructing and populating a complete knowledge base by using the foundation knowledge to generate domain-specific knowledge acquisition, data mining and information extraction tools. This will enable collaborating teams of domain (non-computer) experts to easily extend the foundation theories, define additional domain theories and

* John Kingston and Professor Austin Tate are the co-Principal Investigators on AIAI's "Knowledge Engineering Window on Europe" project, which is part of the HPKB programme. Thanks are due to Dr. Dave Gunning, the HPKB Program manager for DARPA, for giving his permission to describe the programme to EKAW-97 participants.

problem solving strategies, and acquire domain facts to populate a comprehensive knowledge base covering the domains of interest

- **Efficient problem solving:** enabling efficient problem solving, either by providing efficient reusable inference and reasoning procedures to operate on a knowledge base, or by providing tools and techniques to select and transform knowledge from a knowledge base into optimised problem solving modules tailored to the unique requirements of an application.

The objective of HPKB is to develop, integrate and test the technology needed to enable this process, beginning in 1997 and ending in 2000. The intention is to produce knowledge base development environments which combine the necessary foundation building, knowledge acquisition and problem solving technologies into an integrated development environment, and to use these environments to build reusable knowledge base components for multiple DARPA application projects.

The candidate applications are a set of new and on-going DARPA initiatives, all of which are building advanced information systems to improve some aspect of military operations, and all of which need knowledge-rich components. These projects include:

- **Dynamic Multi-user Information Fusion (DMIF)**, which is providing the joint warfighter with a clear and actionable picture of the battlespace through development of advanced technology to support active fusion management and generation of information products tailored to specific and evolving needs;
- **Joint Task Force (JTF) Advanced Technology Demonstration (ATD)** which is developing a portable and supportable technology base to provide command, control, communications and computer information (C4I) to a deployed Joint Task Force Commander for JTF crisis management, planning and execution.
- **Technology Development for the Joint Force Air Component Commander (JFACC)** which is developing information technologies to revolutionise the air operations planning processes, in order to enhance significantly the JFACC's ability to plan and execute and air operation at any level of crisis – major regional conflicts, coalition warfare, and operations other than war.
- **Advanced Logistics Program (ALP)** which is developing advanced information technology to support planning, execution, monitoring and replanning throughout the logistics pipeline, enabling the warfighter to project and sustain overwhelming combat power sooner and with less reliance on large DoD inventories.
- **Battlefield Awareness Data Dissemination (BADD)** which is providing warfighters at echelons from the Task Force Commander down to Battalion or lower, and especially mobile warfighters, with advanced battlefield awareness applications that are driven by near-real time data that is delivered by advanced data dissemination methods.

- Information Gathering, Processing and Analyses in support of Crisis management (Project Genoa) which is developing information tools to assist crisis managers at the highest decision levels of Government in discovering, organising, visualising and understanding information about nascent and emerging crises.

2 Development approach

The HPKB program is building multiple knowledge base development environments which will be exercised against two *challenge problems*. At the end of each year of the project, the knowledge base developers will be presented with a hypothetical situation which describes the domain to be covered, defines (using a formal ontology) the terms to be used in specifying input requests or test questions, and includes appropriate sample questions and training data. The developers will then be asked to build a knowledge based system to the problem specifications, recording how long it takes; answer a set of test questions, and record the percentage of correct answers, then modify their system to deal with a changed requirement and re-evaluate it.

3 Challenge problems

The two challenge problems will be in the following areas:

1. Crisis understanding. The aim will be to build a broad but shallow knowledge base of general geo-political knowledge to support information retrieval for crisis detection and understanding. The knowledge of the crisis understanding process will probably be drawn from sources within the CIA, either directly or via knowledge acquired for Project Genoa; the hypothetical scenario will provide some data, and further data can be gathered from open source environments such as the CIA World Factbook and the Internet. In addition, it is expected that the systems will draw on a "corporate memory" of previous crises; the form of this is yet to be determined.
2. Battlefield awareness. The aim will be to build an in-depth knowledge base of battlefield situations, operations, and logistics to support multiple military applications. The sources of knowledge for this challenge problem are yet to be defined, but are likely to include the DMIF, ALP and JFACC programs.

4 Program organisation

The organisation of the program is shown in Figure 1.

The challenge problems are being developed by two organisations, Alphatech and IET. The remaining participants are being directed towards two integration environments, in order to ensure that the multiple applications which are produced are capable of interoperability. In addition, at the HPKB kick-off meeting

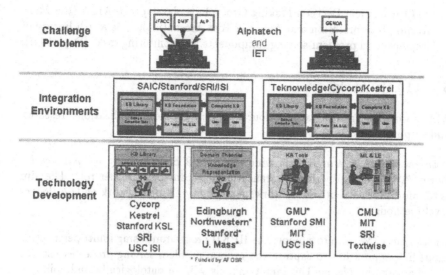

Fig. 1. HPKB Program Organisation

in June 1997, it was agreed that the Generic Frame Protocol (GFP) from SRI [SRI1997] would be used as a common basis for interoperability.

The work of some of the participants – those with whom AIAI will collaborate closely in its own work programme under HPKB – is outlined below. For more details of these and other projects, see [DARPA1997].

- **Cycorp** [Cycorp1997] is a company formed to exploit the CYC knowledge base. CYC can be considered as a very large ontology, with nearly 200 microtheories, 18,000 concepts, and 175,000 axioms; the aim within HPKB is to allow technology developers to represent knowledge quickly and faithfully.
- **ISI** from the University of Southern California aim to integrate problem-solving methods and ontologies into applications. Their work is based around EXPECT [Gil & Melz1996], which is a framework for developing KBS applications; EXPECT checks the domain information it has been given, and prompts the user to fill in information which it needs to know but does not have. This knowledge acquisition is guided by a pre-defined Interdependency Model.
- **Stanford University** (specifically, Mark Musen's group in Medical Informatics) aim to extend their existing work on Protege [Gennari1997], which supports the construction of KBS systems and knowledge maintenance tools. Protege-II has been dissembled into a collection of problem-solving components which can be mixed and matched for a particular application; the aim is to make these components more widely available by integrating with others in the HPKB program, and by making the code more widely available (e.g. by adding CORBA-compliant features).

- **MIT's** Clinical Decision Making Group have developed MAITA (the Monitoring, Interpretation and Analysis Tool Arsenal) which is a rich library of implemented problem-solving components for monitoring tasks [Doyle1997].

5 AIAI's work

AIAI's work is organised around four themes: awareness, applications, research and responsiveness.

Awareness: AIAI's aim is to provide the HPKB program with a "Window on Europe", in order to perform a transatlantic technology transfer role. The aim is to inform the U.S. of related work, particularly European work on knowledge-level methods.

Applications: We aim to support the HPKB programme using multi-perspective modelling approaches to capture the generic problem solving processes used in the challenge problems. The target models will be ontologically underpinned, probably using the ontology of CommonKADS models, but possibly making use of other modelling techniques such as IDEF3 (see [Kingston, Griffith, & Lydiard1997] for some of our previous work in this area). Outstanding modelling issues will be captured to drive the modelling process itself, thus providing a top-down approach to model development.

Research: The major focus of our awareness work will be to collect problem solving methods from around the world and to make them available to HPKB participants in a single library. The appropriate format, content, and level of abstraction of the library are all issues which need careful consideration if the library is to be both accurate and usable.

We also plan to move ahead on the representation of generic problem solving *processes*, perhaps using ontologies of processes, activities, roles, agents, or process products.

Responsiveness: We aim to tailor our plans to the needs of the initiative. We have already responded to interest in some of our previous work; further work may include organisational modelling for the battlefield awareness challenge problem, a "deep slice" demonstrator of expertise modelling for crisis understanding, a broad view on knowledge asset management within the relevant military organisations, a survey of knowledge acquisition tools, or reports and briefings on European knowledge representation techniques (such as CommonKADS) and standards (such as those emerging from the EuroKnowledge initiative).

Acknowledgements

This work is sponsored by the Defense Advanced Research Projects Agency (DARPA) and Rome Laboratory, Air Force Materiel Command, USAF, under grant number F-30602-97-1-0203. The project is monitored by the USAF Rome Laboratory. The U.S. Government is authorised to reproduce and distribute reprints for Governmental purposes notwithstanding any copyright annotation hereon. The views and conclusions contained herein are those of the authors and should not be interpreted as necessarily representing official policies or endorsements, either express or implied, of DARPA, Rome Laboratory or the U.S. Government.

References

[Cycorp1997] Cycorp. 1997. Cycorp, Inc. http://www.cyc.com/.

[DARPA1997] DARPA. 1997. High Performance Knowledge Bases. http://www.teknowledge.com/HPKB/.

[Doyle1997] Doyle, J. 1997. The MAITA project. http://medg.lcs.mit.edu/projects/maita/.

[Gennari1997] Gennari, J. 1997. HPKB Project at the Section on Medical Informatics. http://www-smi.stanford.edu/projects/protege/Hpkb-web/.

[Gil & Melz1996] Gil, Y., and Melz, E. 1996. Explicit Representation of Problem-Solving Strategies to Support Knowledge Acquisition. In *Proceedings of AAAI-96*. AAAI.

[Kingston, Griffith, & Lydiard1997] Kingston, J. K.; Griffith, A.; and Lydiard, T. 1997. Multi-Perspective Modelling of the Air Campaign Planning process. In *Proceedings of IJCAI-97*. AAAI Press.

[SRI1997] SRI. 1997. Generic Frame Protocol (GFP). http://www.ai.sri.com/~gfp.

Index

Lecture Notes in Artificial Intelligence (LNAI)

Lecture Notes in Computer Science